Craft Beer Guide to All 50 States

A Comprehensive Travel Guide to Over 1000 Breweries, Taprooms, Beer Gardens & Brewpubs in the U.S.A

By

Mark Donovan

Cover & Book Design

By

Rose Stevenson

First Edition

Contents

5

9

Introduction

To put things in simple terms, beer is a beverage made from malted cereal grains, hops, and water that is fermented through the addition of yeast. Beer can range in alcohol levels from 2% to 15%. However, this is an oversimplification of beer. While the main focus of this guide is to give you trip ideas for visiting breweries, we'll also give you a bit of background. To start, we'll give you a little bit of a primer on the types of beer and how to sample it before we get into the main focus of breweries in the United States.

History of Beer in America

Beer has gone through several periods of change in the United States, and we'll highlight the main areas and how they have impacted the art of brewing.

The first commercial brewery in the United States was in New Amsterdam (later New York City) in 1632. It was opened by the Dutch West India Company. Commercial brewing wasn't common at the time and was typically an individual endeavor. The first brewery was built as a way to keep settlers focused on developing the land rather than making beer.

Breweries become more popular through the new country as settlers advanced inland. The first breweries served several functions. A separate brewery took the dangerous tasks of home brewing out of the home. It also increased the economy of the area. Breweries and taverns became the first buildings in settlement to encourage people to stop. Commercial brewing played a large part in growing the colonies further inland.

After the Revolution, in the mid-19th century, Germans began migrating to the US and most settled in St. Louis. This influx led to an explosion in brewing, most of the focus being on lagers. Until this time, most lagers weren't brewed in the US since the yeast needed didn't travel well across the ocean. Faster ocean travel made it possible for immigrants to bring yeast strains to the US. It was around this time that Anheuser-Busch started the first large scale commercial brewing option that distributed throughout the US and no longer stuck with local breweries.

In 1920, the Prohibition had a major impact on the beer industry. Spirits and wine had a few loopholes that helped keep production going, but the beer industry has too few loopholes to keep production at its peak. Only 40% of breweries survived during the Prohibition through innovative techniques. The beer industry didn't start to recover until the late 1970s, and at this time, there were only about 100 breweries in the United States, most owned by a handful of large companies.

In the 1970s, not much other than lagers were found in the US. Two main brewers in California: Anchor Brewing Company and New Albion Brewing were starting to offer other options. This inspired other independent breweries to revive other beer styles. However, most of these recipes still couldn't be tried at home since homebrewing was illegal until 1978.

At the start of the 1990s, the number of brewers in the US nearly tripled. The new boom in craft beer was focused on ales since people were ready for a new flavor. Ales were also easy to brew and monitor, so they were a great option for new craft brewers to make quick capital. It wasn't until more recently that breweries have started making old school lagers again.

From 2010 on, craft brewing has continued to expand. Not only has the industry returned, but they are often responsible for revitalizing areas of cities. Many breweries focus on the community as they build their business. Craft brewing continues to grow and looks to keep expanding. Currently, the variety of beers available is at a peak, and we are almost at the level we were in the 17th century.

How to Serve Beer

When it comes to beer, you likely think of people sitting at a bar and drinking from a glass. However, properly serving and tasting beer is so much more than this. First, we're going to look at how to properly serve and store beer. Then we'll consider how best to drink beer. In order to properly serve and taste beer, you first need to make sure you have the right glassware.

Having and choosing the right glass can enhance your beer tasting experience. There are nearly as many glassware options as there are beer styles. Right now we are just going to look at and describe the types of beer glassware, later in the beer style guide, we'll show which glassware is best for each beer style.

Straight Stein

This is your typical beer glass and works best for lighter tasting beers. It has a narrow mouth to concentrate the aromas at the top and a handle to avoid warming the beer.

Stemmed Lager

Lagers often have fewer aromas than ales and need to be consumed at a colder temperature. This is when a stemmed glass is best. Tall and narrow, these glasses focus the aromas at the top, and the stem keeps your hand away from the beer.

Snifter

These are best for specialty beers. A short stem allows the drinker to envelop the glass and increase the temperature of the beer. This creates a fuller taste and allows the body to be appreciated. A sloped lip on the top of the glass will keep the foam intact and focus the aromas.

Pub Glass

This option is great for a variety of ales. Like red wine, ales need a glass with a wide-open mouth. The aromas rise to the top while the narrow bottom allows the glass to warm slightly. These glasses are great for stouts.

Pilsner Glasses

These glasses are great for typical Canadian ales; these have a floral, fruity aroma of an ale but are refreshing and smooth like a lager. The aromas aren't overly abundant, and the narrow glass helps focus the aromas for the drinker.

Pilsners are similar to lagers, but with a little more bitterness and aroma; this means they need a glass similar to the style. A tall glass with a flared opening helps concentrate the aromas at the top of the glass.

Pouring and Storing Beer

Another important part of beer tasting is how to properly store your beer before drinking and then how to properly pour it into your selected glass. Beer should be treated just like any other perishable food.

Beer should be stored upright in a cool place with a temperature of about thirteen degrees Celsius. You should store beer away from light since the quality of the beer is affected by both light and temperature. The shelf life of beer is about three months.

Draught beer should always be refrigerated in order to maintain freshness. You should consume beer within two to three weeks. Opened beers should be drunk completely and shouldn't be stored. Carbonation will evaporate once opened, and you'll even up with a flat beer as soon as the next day.

Beer should ideally be stored between four and five degrees Celsius. Beer tastes best served in the right glass that is dedicated completely to beer. Any residue in a glass will diminish the head of the beer. This is why you also want to be careful with how you clean your beer glasses. The glass should be dipped in clear water and then turned upside-down to drain. The beer should be served in a wet glass that was washed in mild, soap-free detergent and rinsed several times in warm water. In order to prime a glass for a rich head, you should rinse it in pure, cold water just before pouring.

The perfect beer is one with a rich head of foam. It both looks good and also provides a natural cap for the carbonation, so you have a smoother, cleaner taste. Pouring beer is an art and requires the following steps:

1. Place the neck of the bottle over the edge of a cool, wet glass while tilting the bottle to a high angle.

2. Pour the beer into the glass until there is a fine, dense-textured head.

3. Lower the bottom of the bottle to reduce flow until the foam nears the top of the glass.

22

4. Leave just enough space for the foam to rise to the lip of the glass.

How to Drink Beer

This might seem simple, but just as you would with wine, there is a right way to properly taste your beer. Consider the following tips to help you get the most out of your beer tasting experience.

1. Always drink beer from a glass or mug that is made from natural materials.

2. Pour beer into the center of a glass from 2-3 cms. Allow the foam to settle and then top off the last ¾ of the glass.

3. Drink beer in small sips in order to fully appreciate the flavor.

4. You should always drink your beer when just above room temperature.

5. Ensure you drink your beer with the right food pairings.

6. Beer bottles should be stored standing up rather than laying on their side.

Now that you know how to properly drink beer, let's consider how you can rate what you taste.

Beer Taste Ratings

There are five categories and five steps to take when it comes to rating your beer tasting:

1. Smell

2. Look

3. Taste

4. Feel

5. Savor

The first step is to smell your beer and study the bouquet/aroma. You should do this right after the beer is poured. Note the dominant aromas of the beer. These could range from sweet, sour, roasted, earthy, herbal, flowery, citrus, or anything else. Sweetness is a strong malt presence. Sour and tart can sometimes be from infected beer. Roasted flavors come from roasted grains, such as an Irish stout. Different types of hops will impart different scents; ales are often fruity, while wheat beers can be yeasty and spicy.

The second step is to look at your beer. Is it clear? Most filtered beers will be clear. Is it cloudy? Unfiltered wheat beers need to be poured, so that yeast at the bottom of the bottle is roused and poured into the drinking glass. Also, note the color of the beer; each style of beer has its own color parameters. Pilsners are golden, pale ales are often amber, and stouts are black or near-black. Is the foamy head good with retention, or is it weak? Does the lace cling to the sides of the glass, or does the beer just wash down the inside of the glass?

Now you move on the best part, the taste. This is where you'll want to note a number of different characteristics, and some will be similar to when you smelled the beer. First, you want to note the main flavor: is it malty (sweet or roasted) or hoppy (earthy, herbal, flowery, citrus, etc.)? Is there a flavor addition such as a fruit that takes over the flavor? Is there tartness or a sourness? Wheat beers and most Belgian beers taste tart, yeasty, or spicy. Does the flavor change from the first impression into a middle and finish taste? Does the final taste end suddenly or linger for a bit?

You'll also want to note how all the flavors play off each other, something referred to as "balance." Is the balance good, or does one flavor overpower all others? Also, note how well the beer is "conditioned;" this refers to the age of the beer and how all the flavors work together. Lastly, note if the level of carbon dioxide is pleasant or overpowering.

The fourth step is to notice the feel or body of the beer. What is the mouthfeel you get from the beer? Does it come across as thin and watery like an American lager, or is it full and chewy like an Imperial Stout? Does the beer "sparkle" on your tongue, or does it come across as more flat and dull?

Lastly, savor your beer to get an overall impression and drinkability for the beer. This is where you can give your feedback and overall thoughts on the beer. One thing you will definitely need to know in order to properly review beers is all 26 main categories of beer.

Beer Style Guide - Know Your Beer

American Lager	Little hop and malt character. It is a crisp, clean, and highly carbonated lager.	Color: Straw to gold	Glass : Flute	Serving Temperature: 40-45 (all serving temperatures in degrees Fahrenheit unless otherwise noted)	Food Pairings: American cuisine, spicy food, smear-ripened cheeses.
German Helles	Maltier than traditional Pilsners. They offer a touch of sweet with a full-bodied feel.	Color: Pale to gold	Glass : Flute	Serving Temperature: 45-50	Food Pairings: German cuisine, pork, brie, and Colby cheeses.
German Pilsner	Medium hop flavor with a slight note of maltiness.	Color: Straw to pale	Glass : Flute	Serving Temperature: 40-45	Food Pairings: German cuisine, poultry, fish, white cheddar cheese.
Bohemian	A noticeable	Color:	Glass	Serving	Food

Pilsner	bitter hop flavor with a floral aroma.	Straw to light amber	: Flute	Temperature: 40-45	Pairings: Spicy food, Asian cuisine, mild white cheddar cheese.
American Amber Lager	Prevalent malt flavors with varying levels of hoppiness. It has a caramel aroma and smooth taste.	Color: Gold to copper	Glass : Tulip	Serving Temperature: 45-50	Food Pairings: American cuisine, poultry, beef, white cheddar cheese.
Oktoberfest	A full-bodied beer offering a rich, toasted flavor.	Color: Pale to reddish-brown	Glass : Flute	Serving Temperature: 45-50	Food Pairings: German cuisine, meat, and vegetables, Jalapeno jack cheese.
German Schwarzbier	Less malty than expected and light in flavor with a slight sweetness.	Color: Very dark brown to black	Glass : Flute	Serving Temperature: 45-50	Food Pairings: German cuisine, spicy food, Munster cheese.
Vienna Lager	Offering a sweet, malty flavor. A subtle and crisp hop	Color: Copper to reddish-brown	Glass : Flute	Serving Temperature: 45-50	Food Pairings: German cuisine, Mexican

	drinkability.				cuisine, pork, mild cheeses.
German Dunkel	A malt-forward, chocolate flavor profile. Not overly sweet.	Color: Light brown to dark brown	Glass : Vase	Serving Temperature: 45-50	Food Pairings: Sausages, roasted vegetables, Munster cheese.
Traditional Bock	A malty, sweet beer with a toasty flavor profile.	Color: Dark brown to very dark	Glass : Tulip	Serving Temperature: 45-50	Food Pairings: German cuisine, meat, and vegetables, chocolate, aged swiss cheese.
Doppelbock	Stronger than the traditional style in terms of alcohol content with a fuller body.	Color: Copper to dark brown	Glass : Tulip	Serving Temperature: 45-50	Food Pairings: Heavy foods like red meat, pork or ham, strong cheeses.
Weizenbock	A wheat bock with a fruity, malty flavor profile.	Color: Gold to very dark	Glass : Tulip	Serving Temperature: 45-55	Food Pairings: German cuisine, meat, poultry, chocolate, Manchego cheese.

Maibock	More hoppy than a traditional bock, but still has a present malt flavor.	Color: Pale to light amber	Glass : Goblet	Serving Temperature: 45-55	Food Pairings: Italian and German cuisine, fish and shellfish, swiss cheese.
American Brown Ale	A dark beer without the bitterness of porters and stouts. Offering a medium to full-bodied profile.	Color: Deep copper to very dark brown	Glass : Nonic Pint	Serving Temperature: 50-55	Food Pairings: American cuisine, heavy foods like beef stew and red meat, aged gouda cheese.
English Brown Ale	Often having a caramel aroma and a nutty malt flavor profile.	Color: Copper to very dark	Glass : Nonic Pint	Serving Temperature: 50-55	Food Pairings: American cuisine, heavy foods like red meat, poultry, aged gouda cheese.
American Amber Ale	A malty, medium-bodied beer with a caramel flavor profile.	Color: Copper to reddish-brown	Glass : Tulip	Serving Temperature: 45-55	Food Pairings: American cuisine, meat, fish, medium cheddar

				cheese.
American Pale Ale	A medium-bodied beer with a noticeable hop flavor profile.	Color: Deep golden to copper	Glass : Tulip	Serving Temperatur e: 45-55	Food Pairings: Fish and seafood, poultry, mild or medium cheddar cheese.
Blonde Ale	A nice balance of malt and hops with an often fruity aroma.	Color: Straw to light amber	Glass : Tulip	Serving Temperatur e: 45-50	Food Pairings: Italian cuisine, spicy food, fish, pepper jack cheese.
English Bitter	The hops present a bitter flavor to this beer with an often fruity flavor.	Color: Gold to copper	Glass : Nonic Pint	Serving Temperatur e: 50-55	Food Pairings: Fried food, fish, firm English cheeses.
English Pale Ale	Also referred to as Extra Special Bitters. They feature a strong hop flavor balanced with sweet malt.	Color: Gold to copper	Glass : Nonic Pint	Serving Temperatur e: 50-55	Food Pairings: American and English cuisines, meat, English style cheeses.
American IPA	More hops lead to big herbal and	Color: Gold to copper	Glass : Tulip	Serving Temperatur e: 50-55	Food Pairings: American

	citrus flavor profiles with a higher bitterness compared to other pale ales.				and Indian cuisines, meat, poultry, fish, blue cheeses.
Imperial or Double IPA	A stronger flavor than American IPAs along with a higher bitterness.	Color: Gold to light brown	Glass : Tulip	Serving Temperature: 50-55	Food Pairings: American cuisine, meat, fish, rich cheeses.
English IPA	Similar to American IPAs, but with a weaker hop flavor.	Color: Gold to copper	Glass : Nonic Pint	Serving Temperature: 45-50	Food Pairings: American and Indian cuisines, fish, aged cheddar cheeses.
New England IPA	An enhanced hop aroma and flavor profile without the strong bitterness.	Color: Hazy golden	Glass : Nonic Pint	Serving Temperature: 45-55	Food Pairings: Pork, goat cheeses.
American Imperial Porter	Boating a malty sweetness while lacking the burnt malt taste.	Color: Black	Glass : Tulip	Serving Temperature: 50-55	Food Pairings: American cuisine, barbeque, meat, smoked gouda.
English	Similar to	Color:	Glass	Serving	Food

Brown Porter	the American style, but with less malt sweetness.	Dark brown to very dark	: Nonic Pint	Temperature: 50-55	Pairings: American and English cuisines, meat, chocolate, gruyere cheese.
Robust Porter	Stronger and more bitter with a caramel flavor profile.	Color: Very dark to black	Glass : Nonic Pint	Serving Temperature: 50-55	Food Pairings: American and English cuisines, heavy foods like stew, gruyere cheese.
American Stout	A malt flavor profile with strong chocolate and coffee notes, but with no overpowering hop bitterness.	Color: Black	Glass : Nonic Pint	Serving Temperature: 50-55	Food Pairings: Heavy food, meats, oysters, chocolate, sharp cheddar cheese.
American Imperial Stout	Strong dark beers with a malty flavor profile.	Color: Black	Glass : Snifter	Serving Temperature: 50-55	Food Pairings: Heavy foods, poultry, aged cheeses.
Oatmeal Stout	Featuring oatmeal in	Color: Dark	Glass :	Serving Temperature	Food Pairings:

	the malt blend, these beers are smooth and sweet.	brown to black	Nonic Pint	e: 50-55	Meat, shellfish, chocolate, aged cheddar cheeses.
Milk Stout	Lactose sugar added to the malt blend offers a sweet caramel and chocolate flavor profile.	Color: Black	Glass : Nonic Pint	Serving Temperatur e: 50-55	Food Pairings: Mexican cuisine, beef, chocolate, ice cream, buttery cheddar cheeses.
Irish Dry Stout	Roasted barley adds a bitterness to these dark and robust beers.	Color: Black	Glass : Nonic Pint	Serving Temperatur e: 50-55	Food Pairings: Heavy food like beef and stew, barbeque, burgers, Irish cheddar cheese.
Belgian Pale Ale	Featuring a toast malt flavor profile that doesn't overpower the flavor of the hops.	Color: Gold to copper	Glass : Tulip	Serving Temperatur e: 40-50	Food Pairings: American cuisine, fried food, fish, salad, tangy cheeses.
Belgian Triple	A lighter-bodied beer with a slight hoppy	Color: Pale to light amber	Glass : Tulip	Serving Temperatur e: 40-45	Food Pairings: Pasta dishes,

	bitterness.				meat, poultry, gouda cheese.
Belgian Quadruple	A full-bodied beer that exhibits the flavor of brown sugar and fruit.	Color: Amber to dark brown	Glass : Tulip	Serving Temperatur e: 50-55	Food Pairings: Smoked meat, goose, aged gouda.
Belgian Saison	Also known as a Farmhouse Ale. Known for earthy notes and medium hop flavor.	Color: Pale to light brown	Glass : Tulip	Serving Temperatur e: 45-55	Food Pairings: Indian and Asian cuisine, poultry, seafood, Brie cheese.
Belgian Double	Featuring a rich and malty flavor profile with spicy and fruity notes.	Color: Brown to very dark	Glass : Tulip	Temperatur e: 50-55	Food Pairings: American cuisines, barbeque, meat, washed-rind cheeses.
American Wheat	Featuring a light bready flavor profile.	Color: Straw to light amber	Glass : Flute	Serving Temperatur e: 40-45	Food Pairings: Mexican cuisine, spicy foods, poultry, mozzarella cheese.
Belgian	A light, fruity	Color:	Glass	Serving	Food

Witbier	flavor profile matches the nearly white color of this beer.	Straw to pale	: Tulip	Temperature: 40-45	Pairings: Seafood, poultry, pork, salad, soft cheeses.
Berliner Weisse	A tart and sour beer. Sometimes flavor syrups are added to dull the sour taste.	Color: Straw to pale	Glass : Goblet	Serving Temperature: 45-50	Food Pairings: German cuisine, ham, salad, Havarti cheese.
Dunkelweizen	A malty flavor profile with hints of banana flavor.	Color: Copper brown to very dark	Glass : Vase	Serving Temperature: 45-50	Food Pairings: German and Indian cuisines, fish, gouda cheese.
Hefeweizen	Offering a crisp taste with hints of apples or cloves.	Color: Straw to amber	Glass : Vase	Serving Temperature: 40-45	Food Pairings: German cuisine, fish, seafood, brick cheeses.
American Sour	These strong beers come from certain bacteria introduced during the fermentation process.	Color: Varied based on ingredients	Glass : Goblet	Serving Temperature: 40-50	Food Pairings: Fruit and strong-flavored cheeses.

Belgian Fruit Lambic	Brewed with fruit to offer a sweet and sour flavor profile.	Color: Colored based on fruit used	Glass : Tulip	Serving Temperatur e: 45-50	Food Pairings: Fruit, salad, chocolate, soft cheeses.
Flanders Red Ale	Featuring a strong sour flavor with underlying notes of malt and fruit.	Color: Copper to very dark	Glass : Tulip	Serving Temperatur e: 45-50	Food Pairings: Meat, blue, and cheddar cheeses.
Belgian Gueuze	Aged beers with a very strong sour flavor.	Color: Gold to medium amber	Glass : Tulip	Serving Temperatur e: 40-50	Food Pairings: Strong cheeses.
American Black Ale	A malty, roasted flavor profile with medium to high hop bitterness. Sometimes also called a black IPA.	Color: Very dark to black	Glass : Tulip	Serving Temperatur e: 50-55	Food Pairings: Seafood, chocolate, blue cheeses, aged gouda.
Barrel-Aged Beer	Beer aged in a wooden barrel. Sometimes wine and spirits were previously in the barrel to add to the flavor of the beer.	Color: Varies	Glass : Tulip	Serving Temperatur e: 50-55	Food Pairings: Varies depending on the beer flavor profile.
Chocolate	Chocolate	Color:	Glass	Serving	Food

Beer	can be added to any beer to offer chocolate notes.	Light brown to black	: Snifter	Temperature: 50-55	Pairings: Varies based on the beer flavor profile.
Coffee Beer	Typically added to a porter or stout.	Color: Pale to black	Glass : Nonic Pint	Serving Temperature: 50-55	Food Pairings: Meaty stew and hard cheeses.
Fruit and Vegetable Beer	Any type of beer infused with various fruit or vegetable flavors.	Color: Pale to very dark	Glass : Tulip	Serving Temperature: Varies depending on the beer style	Food Pairings: Salad and creamy cheeses.
Gluten-Free Beer	Beer made with fermented sugar and grains that don't contain gluten. The alcohol content will vary.	Color: Varies based on ingredients used	Glass : Flute	Serving Temperature: Varies depending on the beer style	Food Pairings: Varies depending on the beer style
Herb and Spice Beer	Any beer that has an added flavor from roots, herbs, or spices.	Color: Varies based on the beer style	Glass : Tulip	Serving Temperature: 45-55	Food Pairings: Varies depending on beer style.
Honey Beer	Honey added to beer provides a unique	Color: Varies based on the beer style	Glass : Tulip	Serving Temperature: 50-55	Food Pairings: Salad and Ricotta cheese.

	sweetness and flavor.			
Rye Beer	Often featuring a malty, roasted flavor profile with lower hop bitterness. Based on the underlying beer style, they can have sweet or spicy flavors.	Color: Varies based on the beer style	Glass: Vase	Serving Temperature: 45-55	Food Pairings: Spicy meat and creamy cheeses
Session Beer	Any style of beer can be in this category. Beers in this category are less strong and more drinkable. They are often popular in the summer months.	Color: Varies by beer style	Glass: Varies by beer style	Serving Temperature: Varies by beer style	Food Pairings: Varies by beer style.

Now that the basics are out of the way, we'll get into the bulk of why you're here. In the following pages, we'll list all the breweries in each state. They will be grouped by convenient trips within sections of a state. You don't have to follow the itinerary specifically, but you can research and plan your trip based on the breweries you would like to visit. Some must-visit breweries are listed to help you make a good choice.

Brewery Etiquette

When it comes to enjoying a beer at a brewery, there are some basic etiquette rules that you should follow.

First, respect everyone's opinion about beers. If you are with others, don't order for them because you feel you know what they'll like. Rather let them order based on their own preferences.

Second, if you're in a group, don't feel you need to drink at the pace of others. Everyone drinks at their own pace, and you can easily order before or after others. So savor your beer as fast or slow as you would like.

If you haven't tried a beer before, be sure to ask your server questions about it. Even if your server doesn't know, this can be a good thing since it means the brewery often has a number of new and interesting beers.

When it comes to ordering a beer, it is best to order based on flavor and not alcohol content. This shows a better understanding of rating and tasting beers. Also, make sure you are specific when ordering; order based on style or variety.

If you aren't sure what you want, then make sure to ask your bartender. They may be able to recommend something. Also, make sure you appropriately tip your bartender since they live off tips and are providing you a service.

Most breweries will expect you to consume your beer. Unlike a wine tasting, where it is expected that you won't want to swallow the wine, a beer tasting does not necessarily follow this rule. It may be seen as a faux pas for you to spit out your drink. You can and should ask to taste any beer before ordering it to be sure that you'll like it first.

State Breweries

Alabama

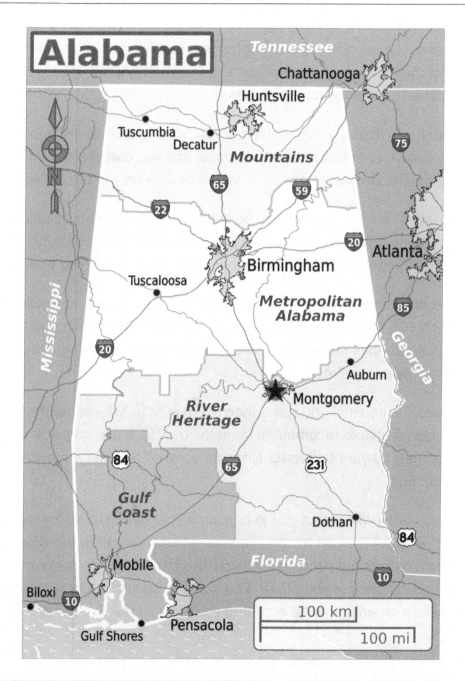

North to South

Travel the state on a north to south trip in two to three days.

Start out in Jasper at:

Tallulah Brewing Company 1804 4th Avenue South 35501 (205) 530-8555 https://www.tallulahbrewing.com/

Next head to Trussville where there are two breweries:

Ferus Artisan Ales 101 Beech Street 35173 (205) 508-3001 https://www.ferusales.com/

Slag Heap Brewing 227 Main Street 35173 (205) 537-1015 http://www.slagheapbrewing.com/

From there you can head to Birmingham, where you'll have a lot of breweries to choose from.

Birmingham District Brewing Company 2201 2nd Avenue South 35233 (205) 202-5779 https://www.birminghamdistrictbrewing.com/

Cahaba Brewing Company 4500 5th Avenue South Ste C 35222 (205) 966-9444 http://www.cahababrewing.com/

Ghost Train Brewing Company 2616 3rd Avenue South 35233 (205) 370-2487 http://www.ghosttrainbrewing.com/

TrimTab Brewing 2721 5th Avenue South 35233 (205) 703-0536 https://www.trimtabbrewing.com/

Good People Brewing Company 114 14th Street South 35233 (615) 498-4165 https://www.goodpeoplebrewing.com/

Avondale Brewing Company 201 41st Street South 35222 (205) 777-5456 https://avondalebrewing.com/

Make a stop in Alabaster and visit:

Siluria Brewing 145 1st Avenue West 35007 (205) 624-3037 http://www.siluriabrewing.com/

Then you'll come to Montgomery with two breweries:

Common Bond Brewers 424 Bibb Street 36104 (334) 676-2287
https://www.commonbondbrewers.com/

Railyard Brewing Company 12 West Jefferson Street 36104 (334) 262-0080 http://www.tavernandporterroom.com/

Take a side drive to Opelika and visit their brewery:

Red Clay Brewing Company 704 North Railroad Avenue 36801 (334) 737-5409 http://redclaybrewingcompany.com/

Stop in Phenix City at:

Chattahoochee Brewing Company 505 13th Street Ste A 36867 (334) 559-0663 https://www.beerontheriver.com/

When you're ready, head down to Dothan with a must-visit brewery:

Folklore Brewery and Meadery 153 Mary Lou Lane 36301 (334) 702-2337 https://www.folklorebrewingandmeadery.com/

Head to the coast with your first stop in Mobile at:

Haint Blue Brewing Company 806 Monroe Street 36602 (251) 888-1277 https://www.haintbluebrew.com/

From there you have two must-stops, the first in Fairhope:

Fairhope Brewing Company 914 Nichols Avenue 36532 (251) 279-7517 https://www.fairhopebrewing.com/

End your trip in Gulf Shores at:

Big Beach Brewing Company 300 East 24th Avenue 36542 (251) 948-2337 https://www.bigbeachbrewing.com/

West to East

The other way to travel Alabama is west to east and can be done in two to three days.

Start your trip in Florence and visit a must-stop brewery at:

Singin' River Brewing Company 526 East College Street 35630 (256) 760-0000 https://www.singinriverbrewing.com/

After Florence, head to Decatur with another must-visit brewery:

Cross-Eyed Owl Brewing Company 105 1st Avenue NE 35601 (256) 431-0931 http://www.xeobrewing.com/

Next, head to Madison where you'll have a couple brewery options including a must-visit:

Old Black Bear Brewing Company 212 Main Street 35758 (256) 850-4639 https://obbmadison.com/

Rocket Republic Brewing Company 289 Production Avenue 35758 (256) 325-4677 http://www.rocketrepublicbrewing.com/

It is then a short drive to Huntsville where there are multiple breweries to visit, including two must-visits:

Fractal Brewing Project 3200 Leeman Ferry Road 35801 (256) 489-5520 https://fractalbrewing.com/

InnerSpace Brewing Company 2414 Clinton Avenue W 35805 (256) 489-5599 https://innerspacebrewing.com/

Mad Malts Brewing 109 Maple Avenue NW 35801 (256) 424-3543 http://www.madmaltsbrewing.com/

Yellowhammer Brewery 2600 Clinton Avenue W 35805 (256) 975-5950 https://www.yellowhammerbrewery.com/

Straight to Ale 2610 Clinton Avenue W 35805 (256) 603-9096 https://straighttoale.com/

The next leg of your trip takes you to Cullman and a must-visit brewery:

Goat Island Craft Brewing 1646 A John H Cooper Drive 35055 (256) 590-9081 http://www.goatislandbrewing.com/

From here you can end your trip at a must-visit brewery in Gadsden:

Back Forty Beer Company 200 North 6th Street 35901 (256) 467-4912 https://www.backfortybeer.com/

Alaska

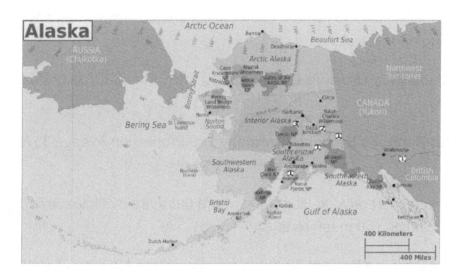

North to South

The best way to tour the majority of the brewery scene in Alaska is from North to South, from the inland area to the coast. It will take you about four to five days.

Start your trip in Fox. It is a bit out of the way, but the brewery here is a must:

Silver Gulch Brewery 2195 Old Steese Highway 99712 (907) 452-2739 https://www.silvergulch.com/

Next stopover in Fairbanks with two breweries:

Black Spruce Brewing Company 3290 Peger Road Ste B 99709 (509) 209-6621 https://www.blacksprucebeer.com/

HooDoo Brewing 1951 Fox Avenue 99701 (907) 459-2337
https://hoodoobrew.com/

Continue your trip south to a must-visit brewery in the town of Healy:

49th State Brewing Company Mile 248.4 Parks Highway 99743 (907) 683-2739 https://www.49statebrewing.com/

The next must-visit brewery on your list is in the town of Talkeetna:

Denali Brewing Company 37083 Talkeetna Spur Road 99676 (907) 733-2536 https://denalibrewing.com/

As you continue your way south you can stop at a brewery in Wasilla:

Bearpaw River Brewing Company 4605 E Palmer Wasilla Highway 99654 (907) 373-2537 http://bearpawriverbrewing.com/

And you can also stop in at a brewery in Palmer:

Arkose Brewery 650 E Steel Loop 99645 (907) 746-2337
https://arkosebrewery.com/

Your next stop is in the large city of Anchorage where you'll have plenty of breweries to choose from based on your interest with one must-visit:

Anchorage Brewing Company 148 West 91st Avenue 99515 (907) 360-5104 https://anchoragebrewing.company/

King Street Brewing Company 9050 King Street 99515 (907) 336-5464 http://www.kingstreetbrewing.com/

Midnight Sun Brewing Company 8111 Dimond Hook Drive 99507 (907) 344-1179 https://midnightsunbrewing.com/

Turnagain Brewing 7924 King Street 99518 (907) 301-1657
https://www.turnagainbrewing.com/

Glacier Brewhouse 737 West 5th Avenue Ste 110 99501 (907) 274-2739
https://www.glacierbrewhouse.com/

Then head to Eagle River:

Odd Man Rush Brewing 10930 Mausel Street Ste A1 99577 (907) 696-2337 http://oddmanrushbrewing.com/

And Girdwood:

Girdwood Brewing Company 2700 Alyeska Highway 99587 (907) 783-2739 https://girdwoodbrewing.com/

Continuing south you'll next come to Kenai:

Kassik's Brewery 47160 Spruce Haven Street 99611 (907) 776-4055 http://83e.b44.myftpupload.com/

The next town along is Soldotna with two excellent brewery choices:

St. Elias Brewing Company 434 Sharkathmi Avenue 99669 (907) 260-7837 http://steliasbrewingco.com/

Kenai River Brewing Company 308 Homestead Lane 99669 (907) 262-2337 http://www.kenairiverbrewing.com/kenairiverbrewing/Welcome.html

Stop in at the small town of Seward and their great brewery:

Seward Brewing Company139 4th Avenue 99664 (907) 422-0337 https://www.sewardbrewery.com/

Your next stop should be in the larger town of Homer, where you have two breweries to choose from:

Grace Ridge Brewing 3388 B Street 99603 (907) 399-5222 https://www.graceridgebrewing.com/

Homer Brewing 1411 Lake Shore Drive 99603 (907) 235-3626 http://www.homerbrew.com/

End your trip in the town of Kodiak that features a great brewery:

Kodiak Island Brewing Company 117 Lower Mill Bay Road 99615 (907) 486-2537 http://www.kodiakbrewery.com/new/home.htm

Southern Alaska

A shorter trip is in the Southern area of Alaska, where you can visit a few towns in one to two days.

Start your trip in the town of Haines:

Haines Brewing Company 327 Main Street 99827 (907) 766-3823 https://www.hainesbrewing.com/

Next, take a short trip to Skagway where there are two great breweries to check out:

Klondike Brewing Company 365 2nd Avenue 99840 (907) 983-2778 https://www.klondikebeer.com/

Skagway Brewing Company 250 4th Avenue 99840 (907) 983-2759 https://skagwaybrewing.com/

From here, head to the largest city on the trip with the most breweries, Juneau, including a must-visit:

Barnaby Brewing Company 165 Shattuck Way 99801 (907) 419-0916 https://www.barnabybrew.com/

Devil's Club Brewing Company 100 North Franklin Street 99801 (907) 523-2739 https://www.devilsclubbrewing.com/

Forbidden Peak Brewery 11798 Glacier Highway 99801 (907) 523-7787 https://forbiddenpeak.com/

Alaskan Brewing Company 5429 Shaune Drive 99801 (907) 780-5866 https://alaskanbeer.com/

End your trip in Ketchikan at their wonderful brewery:

47

Baleen Brewing 884 Mizzen Lane 99901 (907) 220-7492
https://www.baleenbrewing.com/

Arizona

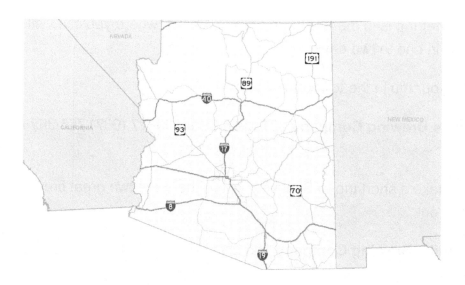

Grand Canyon Beer Trail

If you're in the area to visit the Grand Canyon and want to take a break from your outdoor activities, then consider the Grand Canyon Beer Trail. It takes you to three cities and offers many great breweries. This trip will take you up to a full day, depending on how many breweries you choose to visit.

Start your trip out in the city of Flagstaff. There are lots of breweries to choose from here, including two must-visits:

Historic Brewing Company 4366 E Huntington Drive Bldg 2 86004 (855) 484-4677 https://www.historicbrewingcompany.com/

Flagstaff Brewing Company 16 E Route 66 86001 (928) 773-1442 http://flagbrew.com/

Lumberyard Brewing Company 5 S San Francisco Street 86001 (928) 779-2739 https://lumberyardbrewingcompany.com/

Wanderlust Brewing Company 1519 N Main Street Ste 102 86004 (928) 351-7952 http://www.wanderlustbrewing.com/

Dark Sky Brewing Company 117 N Beaver Street 86001 (928) 235-4525 https://www.darkskybrewing.com/

Mother Road Brewing Company 7 S Mikes Pike Street 86001 (928) 774-9139 https://www.motherroadbeer.com/

Your next stop is in the town of Williams where there is a must-visit brewery:

Grand Canyon Brewing and Distillery 301 N 7th Street 86046 (928) 635-1911 https://www.grandcanyonbrewery.com/

The final stop in your trip is in the city of Sedona where you have a couple options to choose from, including a must-visit:

Sedona Beer Company 465 Jordan Road Ste 1 86336 (928) 862-4148 https://www.sedonabeerco.com/

Oak Creek Brewing Company 2050 Yavapai Drive Ste 2C 86336 (928) 203-9441 https://oakcreekbrew.com/

Central Arizona Breweries

If you're visiting the Grand Canyon and have a few extra days to explore the surrounding area, then the majority of breweries in Arizona can be found in the central area. There are a lot of breweries on this trip, and you likely won't have time to visit them all unless you are going to be there for several days, so visit the must-stop breweries or choose ones that offer the types of beer you're interested in. The total driving time to all these breweries is only a little over 8 hours, but you need to give yourself time to visit any brewery you are interested in visiting. If you're staying in the area, you can easily break the trip up into a few days.

Start your trip in Avondale with a must-visit brewery:

8-Bit Aleworks 1050 N Fairway Drive Bldg F Ste 10 85323 (623) 925-1650 https://www.8-bitaleworks.com/

Right next door to Avondale is Goodyear; which also has a must-visit brewery:

Saddle Mountain Brewing Company 15651 W Roosevelt Street 85338 (623) 980-9524 http://saddlemountainbrewing.com/

It is then a short seven-minute drive north to Litchfield Park and their brewery:

Transplant City Beer Company 107 W Honeysuckle Avenue 85340 (623) 535-3911 https://tcbcbeer.com/

About a half-hour drive north will bring you to Surprise and their brewery:

State 48 Brewery 13823 W Bell Road 85374 (623) 584-1095 https://www.state48brewery.com/

A twelve-minute drive southeast will take you to the small town of Peoria with three great breweries to try:

Freak'N Brewing Company 9299 W Olive Avenue Ste 513 85345 (602) 345-0589 https://freaknbrew.com/

Peoria Artisan Brewery 10144 W Lake Pleasant Parkway Ste 1130 85382 (623) 572-2816 https://peoriaartisanbrewing.com/

Richter Aleworks 8279 W Lake Pleasant Parkway Ste 110 85382 (602) 908-6553 https://richteraleworks.com/

A little further southeast will bring you to the city of Glendale and their brewery:

Throne Brewing Company 17035 N 67th Avenue Ste 6 85308 (623) 412-7770 http://www.dubinabrewing.com/

Another sixteen minutes southeast brings you to the main city of Phoenix, which can be a great place to stay a night and try out a few of their many breweries:

PHX Beer Company 3002 E Washington Street #3002 85034 (602) 275-5049 https://www.phxbeerco.com/

Walter Station Brewery 4056 E Washington Street 85034 (267) 421-6316 http://walterstation.beer/

Helio Basin Brewing Company 3935 E Thomas Road 85018 (602) 354-3525 https://www.heliobasinbrewing.com/

Helton Brewing Company 2144 E Indian School Road 85016 (602) 730-2739 https://heltonbrewing.com/

North Mountain Brewing Company 522 E Dunlap Avenue 85020 (602) 861-5999 https://www.northmountainbrewing.com/

Simple Machine Brewing Company 701 W Deer Valley Road 85027 (623) 469-9199 https://simplemachinebrewing.com/

Sun Up Brewing Company 322 E Camelback Road 85012 (602) 279-8909 https://sunup.beer/

O.H.S.O. Eatery and Nano-Brewery 4900 E Indian School Road 85018 (602) 955-0358 http://ohsobrewery.com/

Wren House Brewing Company 2125 N 24th Street 85008 (602) 244-9184 https://www.wrenhousebrewing.com/

About another half-hour will take you to the most southern city on this trip, Chandler:

SanTan Brewing Company 495 E Warner Road 85225 (480) 917-8700 https://santanbrewing.com/

The Perch Pub and Brewery 232 S Wall Street 85225 (480) 773-7688 http://perchpubbrewery.com/

Start heading northeast a short way to Gilbert, with a couple of options:

12 West Brewing Company 3000 E Ray Road Bldg 6 85296 (480) 204-6495 http://12westbrewing.com/

Flying Basset Brewing 720 W Ray Road 85233 (480) 426-1373 https://flyingbassetbrewing.com/

Arizona Wilderness Brewing Company 721 N Arizona Avenue 85233 (480) 497-2739 https://azwbeer.com/

Continue north to the larger city of Mesa where you'll find several brewery options:

Oro Brewing Company 210 W Main Street 85201 (480) 398-8247 http://www.orobrewing.com/

Desert Eagle Brewing Company 150 W Main Street 85201 (480) 656-2662 https://www.deserteaglebrewing.com/

The Beer Research Institute 1641 S Stapley Drive Ste 104 85204 (480) 892-2020 http://www.thebeerresearchinstitute.com/

Lochiel Brewing 7143 E Southern Avenue Ste 131 85209 (480) 666-0915 https://lochielbrewing.com/

Continue northeast for about a half-hour to the small town of Fountain Hills with a single brewery option:

Bone Haus Brewing 14825 E Shea Blvd Ste 101 85268 (480) 292-9541 https://www.bonehausbrewing.com/

Next, settle in for a beautiful hour and a half drive north to the small town of Pine:

THAT Brewery 3270 N Arizona HIghway 87 85544 (928) 476-3349 http://thatbrewery.com/

Continue through the Tonto National Forest about an hour west to the small community of Camp Verde:

Verde Brewing Company 724 N Industrial Drive Ste 7A 86322 (703) 969-5047 https://www.verdebrewing.com/

Continue west, and after leaving the national forest, you'll have a little bit of a drive to the larger city of Prescott with two must-visit breweries:

Prescott Brewing Company 130 W Gurley Street Ste A 86301 (928) 771-2795 https://www.prescottbrewingcompany.com/

Granite Mountain Brewing 123 N Cortez Street 86302 (928) 778-5535 http://www.granitemountainbrewing.com/

Take a half-hour drive west to the furthest west town on your trip, Skull Valley and it is a must-visit:

Barnstar Brewing Company 4050 North Tonto Road 86338 (928) 442-2337 http://www.barnstarbrew.com/

Return back the way you came, but before you start heading south again, you can stop in at Prescott Valley and their wonderful brewery:

Lonesome Valley Brewing 3040 N Windsong Drive Ste 101 86314 (928) 515-3541 http://www.lonesomevalleybrewing.com/

Then head about an hour south on Interstate 17 before heading a little east off the Interstate to Cave Creek and visit a great brewery:

Cave Creek Beer Company 7100 E Cave Creek Road 85331 (480) 488-2187 https://cavecreekbeercompany.com/

Head about an hour more south to the larger city of Scottsdale where you'll find a couple of options as well as a must-visit brewery:

Goldwater Brewing Company 3608 N Scottsdale Road 85251 (480) 350-7305 https://www.goldwaterbrewing.com/

Scottsdale Beer Company 8608 E Shea Blvd 85260 (480) 219-1844 https://scottsdalebeercompany.com/

Casa Arriba Brewing Company 15025 N 74th Street 85260 (480) 948-9969 http://www.arribamexicangrill.com/

End your trip with a short drive south to the large city of Tempe with several brewery options as well as a couple of must-visit options:

Four Peaks Brewing Company 1340 E 8th Street Ste 104 85281 (480) 303-9967 https://www.fourpeaks.com/

Huss Brewing Company 1520 W Mineral Road Ste 102 85283 (480) 264-7611 https://www.hussbrewing.com/

The Shop Beer Company 922 W 1st Street 85281 (602) 717-4237 http://www.theshop.beer/

Fate Brewing Company 201 E Southern Avenue 85282 (480) 656-9100 https://fatebrewing.com/

Pedal Haus Brewery 730 S Mill Avenue Suite 102 85281 (480) 314-2337 https://www.pedalhausbrewery.com/

Sleepy Dog Brewery 1920 E University Drive 85281 (480) 967-5476 http://sleepydogbrewing.com/

Tucson Area Beer Trail

The second-largest concentration of breweries in Arizona is in the three southern counties around the Tucson area. You can stay a few nights in Tucson and travel to surrounding cities within a two-hour drive in order to try all the options in the area. Start out in Tucson where you'll have quite a number of breweries to choose from with a few must-visit options if you don't have time visit them all:

1912 Brewing Company 2045 N Forbes Blvd Ste 105 85745 (520) 256-4851 https://1912brewing.com/

Gentle Ben's Brewing Company 865 E University Blvd 85719 (520) 624-4177 http://www.gentlebens.com/

Thunder Canyon Brewery 220 E Broadway Blvd Ste 2 85701 (520) 396-3480 http://thundercanyonbrewery.com/

Pueblo Vida Brewing Company 115 E Broadway Blvd 85701 (520) 623-7168 https://www.pueblovidabrewing.com/

Public Brewhouse 209 N Hoff Avenue 85705 (520) 775-2337 http://publicbrewhouse.com/

Copper Mine Brewing Company 3455 S Palo Verde Road Ste 135 85713 (520) 333-6140 https://www.copperminebrewing.com/

Sentinel Peak Brewing Company 4746 E Grand Road 85712 (520) 777-9456 https://sentinelpeakbrewing.com/

Iron John's Brewing Company 245 S Plumer Avenue Ste 27 85719 (520) 775-1727 https://www.ironjohnsbrewing.com/

Harbottle Brewing Company 3820 S Palo Verde Road Ste 102 85714 (520) 499-2518 http://www.harbottlebrewing.com/index.html

Dragoon Brewing Company 1859 W Grant Road Ste 111 85745 (520) 329-3606 https://dragoonbrewing.com/

Button Brew House 6800 North Camino Martin 85741 (520) 268-8543 https://buttonbrewhouse.com/

Ten 55 Brewing 110 E Congress Street 85701 (520) 461-8073 https://www.1055brewing.com/

Dillinger Brewing Company 3895 N Oracle Road 85705 (520) 207-2312 https://www.dillingerbrewing.com/

Borderlands Brewing Company 119 E Toole Avenue 85701 (520) 261-8773 https://www.borderlandsbrewing.com/

Barrio Brewing Company 800 E 16th Street 85719 (520) 791-2739 https://barriobrewing.com/

If you head south about an hour you'll come to Sonoita:

Copper Brothel Brewery 3112 Highway 83 85637 (520) 405-6721 https://www.copperbrothelbrewery.com/

From there you can drive another hour for the most southern brewery at Bisbee:

Old Bisbee Brewing Company 200 Review Alley 85603 (520) 432-2739 http://www.oldbisbeebrewingcompany.com/

Then you can head back north about a half-hour to Tombstone:

Tombstone Brewing Company 107 E Toughnut Street 85638 (520) 222-6781 https://tombstone.beer/

Stand Alone Arizona Breweries

Colorado City **Edge of the World Brewery and Pub** 70 N Central Street 86021 (928) 875-8710 https://www.edgeoftheworld.bar/

Kingman **Black Bridge Brewery** 421 E Beale Street 86401 (928) 377-3618 http://www.blackbridgebrewery.com/

Rickety Cricket Brewing 312 E Beale Street 86401 (928) 263-8444 https://www.ricketycricketbrewing.com/

Lake Havasu City **College Street Brewhouse and Pub** 1940 College Drive 86403 (928) 854-2739 http://www.collegestreetbrewhouseandpub.com/

Mudshark Brewing Company 210 Swanson Avenue 86403 (928) 453-2981 https://www.mudsharkbrewingcompany.com/

Barley Brothers Brewery 1425 McCulloch Blvd N 86403 (928) 505-7837 https://www.barleybrothers.com/

Yuma **Prison Hill Brewing Company** 278 S Main Street 85364 (928) 276-4001 https://www.prisonhill.com/

Lakeside **Pinetop Brewing Company** 159 W White Mountain Road 85929 (928) 358-1971 http://pinetopbeer.com/

Arkansas

Take a ride from north to south in Arkansas, and within a day or two, you'll be able to sample nearly all of the craft breweries in the state. Start out your trip in Bentonville with two breweries to visit:

Bike Rack Brewing Company 410 SW A Street Ste 6 72712 (479) 268-6648 http://bikerackbrewing.com/

Bentonville Brewing Company 901 SW 14th Street Ste 100 72712 (479) 903-7330 https://www.bentonvillebrewing.com/

From there head south to the town of Rogers where you have multiple brewery options as well as one must-visit brewery:

Hawk Moth Brewery 710 N 2nd Street 72756 (479) 877-1011 https://hawkmothbrewing.com/

Rendezvous Junction Brewing Company 9556 Preservation Drive 72758 (479) 381-4046 https://www.rendezvousjunction.com/

New Province Brewing Company 1310 W Hudson Road 72756 (479) 531-3233 http://www.newprovincebrewing.com/

Ozark Beer Company 109 N Arkansas Street 72756 (479) 636-2337 https://www.ozarkbeercompany.com/

Continue south to Springdale where there are two must-visit breweries:

Core Brewing and Distilling Company 2470 N Lowell Road Ste A3 72764 (479) 306-8898 https://coreofarkansas.com/

Saddlebock Brewery 16600 Saddlebock Lane 72764 (479) 422-1797 https://saddlebock.com/

Head west a little way to Siloam Springs:

Ivory Bill Brewing Company 516 E Main Street 72761 (479) 599-9606 https://www.theivorybill.com/

In Fayetteville, there are several breweries to choose from including a couple of must-visits:

JJ's Beer Garden 3615 N Steele Blvd 72703 (479) 263-2562 http://www.thejbgb.com/

Crisis Brewing 210 S Archibald Yell Blvd 72701 (479) 582-2337 https://crisisbrew.com/

Apple Blossom Brewing Company 1550 E Zion Road 72703 (479) 287-4344 http://appleblossombrewing.com/

Fossil Cove Brewing Company 1946 N Birch Avenue 72703 (479) 644-4601 https://www.fossilcovebrewing.com/

The next leg of your trip is a longer drive. You'll head about an hour south to the town of Fort Smith and a must-visit brewery:

Fort Smith Brewing Company 7500 Fort Chaffee Blvd 72916 (479) 242-3722 https://www.fsbrewco.com/

From here your trip takes you inland with about an hour drive east to the town of Paris with a must-visit brewery:

Prestonrose Farm and Brewing Company 201 Saint Louis Valley Road 72855 (707) 502-5544 http://prestonrose.squarespace.com/

The next stage is about a two-hour drive east and slightly south to the main town of Little Rock and several must-visit breweries:

Lost Forty Brewing 501 Byrd Street 72202 (501) 319-7275 https://www.facebook.com/lost40beer

Rebel Kettle Brewing Company 822 E 6th Street 72202 (501) 374-2791 https://www.rebelkettle.com/

Stone Throw's Brewing 402 E 9th Street 72202 (501) 244-9154 http://www.stonesthrowbeer.com/

Vino's Brewpub 923 W 7th Street 72201 (501) 375-8466 http://www.vinosbrewpub.com/

End your trip about an hour southwest in the beautiful and quaint town of Hot Springs with two breweries, one of them a must-visit:

SQZBX Brewery 236 Ouachita Avenue 71901 (501) 609-0609 https://sqzbx.com/

Superior Bathhouse Brewery 329 Central Avenue 71901 (501) 624-2337 https://www.superiorbathhouse.com/

California features the most breweries of any state in America. There are almost a thousand craft breweries to experience in California. You could spend months in the state and probably still not visit them all. So we're going to break them down by region. It is best to choose an area you want to visit and then check out the brewery websites to choose which ones you want to visit on your brewery tours.

Shasta Cascade Brewery Trail

The northwestern corner of California is full of rugged beauty and wilderness. Among this outdoor activity wonderland, you'll also find plenty of wonderful craft breweries to enjoy. Start your trip in Chico, where you have a few breweries to choose from.

Secret Trail Brewing Company 132 Meyers Street Suite 115 95928 (916) 709-4820 https://www.secrettrailbrewing.com/

Sierra Nevada Brewing Company 1075 E 20th Street 95928 (530) 893-3520 https://sierranevada.com/

British Bulldog Brewery 14540 Camaren Park Drive 95973 (530) 892-8759 http://www.britishbulldogbrewery.com/

Take a drive about a half-hour southeast to the little town of Oroville with two brewery options:

Feather Falls Casino Brewing Company 3 Alverda Drive 95966 (530) 533-3885 https://featherfallscasino.com/

Miner's Alley Brewing Company 2053 Montgomery Street 95965 (530) 693-4388 http://www.minersalleybrewingco.com/

Circle back north about a half-hour to the small town of Magalia with a must-visit brewery:

Feather River Brewing Company 14665 Forest Ridge Road 95954 (530) 873-0734 http://www.featherriverbrewing.com/

Next, take about a two-hour drive north to the larger town of Redding where there are three great breweries to enjoy:

Final Draft Brewing Company 1600 California Street 96002 (530) 338-1198 https://www.finaldraftbrewingcompany.com/

Fall River Brewing 1030 E Cypress Avenue Ste D 96002 (530) 605-0230 https://www.fallriverbrewing.com/

Woody's Brewing Company 1257 Oregon Street 96001 (530) 768-1034 https://woodysbrewing.com/

From here it is about another hour drive north to the quaint town of Dunsmuir with a must-visit brewery:

Dunsmuir Brewery Works 5701 Dunsmuir Avenue 96025 (530) 235-1900 https://www.dunsmuirbreweryworks.com/

The last two breweries offer you a choice of which direction to go. You can continue north to the small town of Etna with a must-visit brewery:

Etna Brewing Company 131 Callahan 96027 (530) 467-5277
http://etnabrew.com/

From Etna, you can take a three and a half-hour drive southeast to the city of Susanville. It is a long drive, but the must-visit brewery here makes the trip worth it:

Lassen Ale Works 724 Main Street 96130 (530) 257-7666
https://www.lassenaleworks.com/

North Coast Beer Trail

If the coast is more of your preferred environment, then take a drive up or down the coast. You'll not only get to enjoy wonderful ocean views, but you'll also find a number of small craft breweries to try as well.

Start your trip in the small town of Crescent City where there is a must-visit brewery:

SeaQuake Brewing 400 Front Street 95531 (707) 465-4444
https://seaquakebrewing.com/

Next, take a beautiful drive a little over an hour south to the little town of McKinleyville and two great breweries to try while enjoying the local scenery and culture:

Humboldt Regeneration Brewery and Farm 2320 Central Avenue Unit F 95519 (707) 738-8225 http://www.humboldtregeneration.com/

Six Rivers Brewery 1300 Central Avenue 95519 (707) 839-7580
https://sixriversbrewery.com/

Take an 11-minute drive a little inland to your next stop of Blue Lake and their must-visit brewery that is worth a small side trip:

Mad River Brewery 195 Taylor Way 95525 (707) 668-4151
https://www.madriverbrewing.com/

Take a ten-minute drive back to the coast and the small town of Arcata:

Redwood Curtain Brewing Company 550 S G Street #6 95521 (707) 826-7222 https://redwoodcurtainbrewing.com/

Continue 13 minutes down the coast to the city of Eureka with a must-visit brewery:

Lost Coast Brewery 617 Fourth Street 95501 (707) 445-4480 https://www.lostcoast.com/

Another 21 minutes down the coast brings you to the quaint coastal town of Fortuna and another must-visit brewery:

Eel River Brewing Company 1777 Alamar Way 95540 (707) 725-2739 http://eelriverbrewing.com/

Continue down the coast for another hour and a half to the small town of Shelter Cove:

Gyppo Ale Mill 1661 Upper Pacific Drive 95589 (707) 986-7700 https://gyppo.com/

From here it is a long two and half-hours drive through redwoods and coast to the town of Fort Bragg and a must-visit brewery:

North Coast Brewing Company 455 N Main Street 94357 (707) 964-2739 https://northcoastbrewing.com/

Take a drive further south down the coast before moving slightly inland to the small town of Boonville, home to another must-visit brewery:

Anderson Valley Brewing Company 17700 Highway 253 95415 (707) 895-2337 https://avbc.com/

Continue heading about a half-hour inland to the town of Ukiah:

Ukiah Brewing Company 102 S State Street 95482 (707) 468-5898 https://ukiahbrewing.com/

A little less than an hour drive south on the 101 freeway takes you to the small town of Healdsburg with a must-visit brewery:

Bear Republic Brewery 345 Healdsburg Avenue 95448 (707) 433-2337
https://bearrepublic.com/

Another half-hour south and a little west towards the coast takes you to the small town of Guerneville:

Stumptown Brewery and Smokehouse 15045 River Road 95446 (707) 869-0705 http://www.stumptown.com/

A twenty-minute drive south takes you to Sebastopol with two brewery options.

3 Disciples Brewing 5511 Volkerts Road 95472 (707) 228-7309
https://www.3dbrews.com/

Crooked Goat Brewing 120 Morris Street #120 95472 (707) 835-4256
http://www.crookedgoatbrewing.com/

Just nine minutes east takes you to Santa Rosa with a wide selection of breweries to choose from along with a must-visit brewery:

Russian River Brewing Company 725 4th Street 95404 (707) 545-2337
https://russianriverbrewing.com/

Seismic Brewing Company 2870 Duke Court 95407 (707) 544-5996
http://seismicbrewingco.com/

Third Street Aleworks 610 3rd Street 95404 (707) 523-3060
https://thirdstreetaleworks.com/

Cooperage Brewing Company 981 Airway Court 95403 (707) 293-9787
https://cooperagebrewing.com/

HenHouse Brewing 322 Bellevue Avenue 95407 (707) 978-4577
https://www.henhousebrewing.com/

Moonlight Brewing Company 3350 Coffey Lane 95403 (707) 528-2537
https://moonlightbrewing.com/

Old Possum Brewing Company 357 Sutton Place 95405 (707) 303-7177
http://www.oldpossumbrewing.com/

A short nine minute drive south brings you to the small town of Cotati:

Grav South Brew Company 7950 Redwood Drive #15 94931 (707) 753-4198 https://www.facebook.com/GravSouth/

Once you're ready head twelve minutes south to a well known, must-visit brewery in Petaluma:

Lagunitas Brewing Company 1280 N McDowell Blvd 94954 (707) 769-4495 https://www.lagunitas.com/

Head east about twenty-minutes to the town of Sonoma for the next leg of your trip:

Sonoma Springs Brewing Company 19449 Riverside Drive Ste 101 95476 (707) 938-7422 https://www.sonomaspringsbrewing.com/

About a half-hour drive southwest will circle you back towards the coast and your next stop in the city of Novato:

Moylan's Brewery 15 Rowland Way 94945 (415) 898-4677
http://moylans.com/

Indian Valley Brewing 1016 Railroad Avenue 94945 (415) 301-4983
https://www.indianvalleybrewing.com/

Head about fifteen minutes south on the freeway where the last grouping of towns are close together. The first stop is in San Rafael:

Pond Farm Brewing Company 1848 4th Street 94901 (415) 524-8709
https://www.pondfarmbrewing.com/

Seven minutes east takes you to Fairfax:

Iron Springs Pub and Brewery 765 Center Blvd Ste A 94930 (415) 485-1005 https://ironspringspub.com/

Another twelve minutes south takes you to Larkspur and a must-visit brewery:

Marin Brewing Company 1809 Larkspur Landing Circle 94939 (415) 461-4677 http://www.marinbrewing.com/

End your trip another ten minutes south in Mill Valley:

Headlands Brewing Company 16 Forrest Street 94941 (415) 890-4226 https://headlandsbrewing.com/

Inland Empire Beer Trail

The two large counties of San Bernardino and Riverside make up the Inland Empire in southern California. While many feel this is nothing but desert; there are actually some great breweries and can be an excellent place to spend a few days enjoying some great craft brews. Start your trip high in the mountains at Big Bear Lake with a must-visit brewery:

Big Bear Lake Brewing Company 40827 Stone Road 92315 (909) 878-0283 http://www.bblbc.com/

After you leave the mountain, drive about an hour north to Apple Valley for a brewery that lives up to its name:

Off the Grid Brewery 13615 John Glenn Road, Suite A 92507 (760) 247-5600 http://www.otgbrew.com/

Next head back south about twenty-minutes to the city of Hesperia:

Oak Hills Brewing Company 12221 Poplar Street Unit #3 92344 (760) 244-8278 https://www.oakhillsbrewing.com/

From here you'll take about a half-hour drive over the mountains to the other side and the town of Rancho Cucamonga where there are several great breweries to try:

No Clue Craft Brewery 9037 Arrow Rte Ste 170 91730 (909) 989-2394 https://nocluebrew.com/

Kings Brewing Company 8560 Vineyard Avenue Ste 301 91730 (909) 727-3333 https://www.kingsbrewingco.com/

Hamilton Family Brewery 9757 Seventh Street Ste 802 91730 (909) 261-2870 https://www.hamiltonfamilybrewery.com/

Rowdy's Brew Company 10002 6th Street Ste A 91730 (909) 929-2722 https://rowdysbrewco.com/

Sour Cellars 9495 9th Street Unit B 91730 (909) 294-5183 http://sourcellars.com/

Just seven minutes west you come to the town of Upland with a few breweries and two must-visit destinations:

Rok House Brewing Company 1939 W 11th Street Suite A 91786 (909) 981-0020 https://www.rokhousebrewing.com/

Last Name Brewing 1495 W 9th Street #603 91786 (909) 579-0032 https://www.lastnamebrewing.com/

Rescue Brewing Company 167 N 2nd Avenue 91786 (909) 266-9696 https://rescuebrewingco.com/

Another five minutes west takes you to the town of Montclair with a couple options and a must-visit destination:

Sandbox Brewing Company 4650 Arrow Highway a9 91763 (909) 929-0108 http://www.sandboxbrewingcompany.com/

Dragon's Tale Brewing 8920 Vernon Avenue Ste 122 91763 (909) 529-2688 https://dragonstalebrewery.com/

Next head about a half-hour south to Corona:

Skyland Ale Works 109 N Maple Street Suite C 92880 (951) 817-3037 http://skylandaleworks.com/index.html

Main Street Brewery 300 N Main Street 92880 (951) 371-1471 http://www.mainstreetbrewery.com/

Stone Church Brewing 2785 Cabot Drive Ste 160 92883 (951) 433-0121
https://www.stonechurchbrewing.com/

A further half-hour south brings you to Lake Elsinore:

Craft Brewing Company 530 Crane Street Suite C 92530 (951) 226-0149 https://craftbrewingcompany.com/

Even more options along with a must-visit brewery are just twelve more minutes south at Murrieta:

8 Bit Brewing Company 26755 Jefferson Avenue Ste F 92562 (951) 677-2322 https://www.8bitbrewingcompany.com/

Inland Wharf Brewing Company 26440 Jefferson Avenue Ste A 92562 (951) 795-5260 https://inlandwharfbrewing.com/

Electric Brewing Company 41537 Cherry Street 92562 (951) 696-2266 http://electricbrewingcompany.com/

You'll then reach your southernmost destination after a short nine minute drive and you'll have plenty of breweries to choose from. But there are two you must-visit if you don't have time for any more in Temecula:

Garage Brewing Company 29095 Old Town Front Street 92590 (951) 676-1339 http://www.garagebrewpizza.com/

Refuge Brewery 43040 Rancho Way Ste 200 92590 (951) 506-0609 https://www.refuge.beer/

Wiens Brewing Company 27941 Diaz Road Ste A 92590 (951) 553-7111 https://www.wiens.beer/

Aftershock Brewing Company 28822 Old Town Front Street 92590 (951) 972-2256 https://aftershockbrewing.com/

Relentless Brewing Company 42030 Avenida Alvarado Ste F 92509 (951) 296-9400 https://www.relentlessbrewing.com/

Ironfire Brewing Company 42095 Zevo Drive Ste #1 92590 (951) 296-1397 http://ironfirebrewing.com/

Black Market Brewing Company 41740 Enterprise Circle North Ste 109 92590 (951) 296-5039 https://blackmarketbrew.com/

Next take about a forty minute drive back up north to Riverside with lots of brewery options to try:

Route 30 Brewing Company 9860 Indiana Avenue Ste 19 92503 (951) 776-7083 http://www.route30brewing.com/

Wicks Brewing Company 11620 Sterling Avenue 92503 (951) 351-1880 https://www.wicksbrewing.com/

Thompson Brewing Company 9900 Indiana Avenue Suite #7 92503 (951) 956-0480 http://thompsonbrewing.com/

Heroes Restaurant and Brewery 3397 Mission Inn Avenue 92501 (951) 248-0722 https://www.heroesrestaurantandbrewery.com/

Euryale Brewing Company 2060 Chicago Avenue #A17 92507 (951) 530-8865 https://euryalebrewing.com/

Just ten more minutes north is the small town of Colton with a great brewery option:

3 Iron Brewing Company 898 Via Lata Drive 92324 (909) 533-4892 http://www.3ironbrewingco.com/

Head east about ten minutes to Redlands with a couple of options along with a must-visit brewery:

Ritual Brewing Company 1315 Research Road 92374 (951) 314-8057 https://ritualbrewing.com/

Escape Craft Brewery 721 Nevada Street Ste 401 92374 (909) 713-3727 https://escapecraftbrewery.com/

Hanger 24 Brewing 1710 Sessums Drive 92374 (909) 389-1400
https://hangar24brewing.com/

Another fourteen minutes east takes you to the city of Yucaipa:

Brewcaipa Brewery 35058 Yucaipa Blvd 92399 (909) 797-2337
http://www.brewcaipa.com/

About a forty minute drive east into the desert area will bring you to
Thousand Palms:

Coachella Valley Brewing Company 30640 Gunther Street 92276 (760)
343-5973 https://cvbco.com/

From here a short eighteen minute drive brings you to a must-visit brewery
and the end of your trip in La Quinta:

La Quinta Brewing Company 77917 Wildcat Drive 92211 (760) 200-
2597 http://www.laquintabrewing.com/

Los Angeles and Surrounding Area

If you're more of a city person, then find a great place to stay in Los
Angeles and take your time exploring the breweries in the greater Los
Angeles area while taking a few short trips into the surrounding area for
other great breweries. In between, you can enjoy a number of tourist sites
and attractions in the area as well. First, let's look at all of the breweries in
the greater Los Angeles area:

Highland Park Brewery 5127 York Blvd 90042 (323) 739-6459
https://hpb.la/

Dry River Brewing 671 S Anderson Street 90023 (213) 375-5235
https://www.dryriverbrewing.com/#home-section

Golden Road Brewing 5410 W San Fernando Road 90039 (213) 373-
4677 http://www.goldenroad.la/

Tirebiter Brewery 2502 South Figueroa Street 90007 (323) 781-6283
https://tirebiterbrewery.com/

Indie Brewing Company 2301 E 7th Street C-100 90023 (323) 354-4285
https://indiebrewco.com/

Mumford Brewing 416 Boyd Street 90013 (213) 346-9970
http://www.mumfordbrewing.com/

Arts District Brewing Company 828 Traction Avenue 90013 (213) 519-5887 http://artsdistrictbrewing.com/

Imperial Western Beer Company 800 North Alameda Street 90012 (213) 270-0035 https://www.imperialwestern.com/

Iron Triangle Brewing Company 1581 Industrial Street 90021 (323) 364-4415 http://www.irontrianglebrewing.com/

Eagle Rock Brewery 3056 Roswell Street 90065 (323) 257-7866
http://www.eaglerockbrewery.com/

Boomtown Brewery 700 Jackson Street 90012 (213) 617-8497
https://www.boomtownbrew.com/?v=7516fd43adaa

Angel City Brewing Company 216 S Alameda Street 90013 (310) 329-8881 https://angelcitybrewery.com/

Bonaventure Brewing 404 S Figueroa Street #418a 90071 (213) 236-0802 http://www.bonaventurebrewing.com/

The Stalking Horse Brewery 10543 W Pico Blvd 90064 (424) 832-7511
https://www.thestalkinghorsepub.com/

Ohana Brewing Company 1756 E 23rd Street 90058 (213) 748-2337
https://ohanabrew.com/

Frogtown Brewery 2931 Gilroy Street 90039 (323) 452-2739
https://www.frogtownbrewery.com/

Venice Duck Brewery 4238 Coolidge Avenue 90055 (310) 383-4927
https://www.veniceduckbrewery.com/

From your home base in Los Angeles you can make trips into the surrounding area to enjoy a number of other breweries in the surrounding area:

Agoura Hills **Ladyface Ale Company** 29281 Agoura Road 91301 (818) 477-4566 https://www.ladyfaceale.com/

Anaheim

Bottle Logic Brewing 1072 N Armando Street 92806 (714) 660-2537
https://bottlelogic.com/

Brewery X 3191 East La Palma Avenue 92806 (657) 999-1500
https://www.brewery-x.com/

Anaheim Brewery 336 S Anaheim Blvd 92805 (714) 780-1888
https://www.anaheimbrew.com/

JT Schmid's Restaurant and Brewery 2610 East Katella Avenue 92806
(714) 634-9200 https://www.jtschmidsrestaurants.com/

Brewheim 1931 E Wright Circle 92806 (714) 453-4346
https://www.brewheim.com/

Noble Ale Works 1621 S Sinclair Street 92806 (714) 634-2739
https://www.noblealeworks.com/

Phantom Ales 1211 N Las Brisas Street 92806 (714) 630-9463
http://phantomales.com/

Backstreet Brewery 1884 S Santa Cruz Street 92805 (657) 236-4050
https://www.backstreetbrew.com/

Bruery Terreux 1174 N Grove Street 92806 (714) 996-6258
https://www.thebruery.com/

Arcadia **Mt. Lowe Brewing Company** 150 E St Joseph Street 91006
(626) 244-7593 http://www.mtlowebrewing.com/

Burbank

Simmzy's 3000 W Olive Avenue 91505 (818) 962-2500
https://www.simmzys.com/

Trustworthy Brewing Company 156 W Verdugo Avenue 91502 (818)
841-5040 http://trustworthybrewingco.com/

Lincoln Beer Company 3083 N Lima Street 91504 (818) 687-4206
https://www.lincolnbeercompany.com/

Carson **Phantom Carriage** 18525 S Main Street 90248 (310) 538-5834
https://phantomcarriage.com/

Chatsworth

Hand Brewed Beer 9771 Variel Avenue 91311 (818) 920-8422
https://www.handbrewedbeer.com/

The Great Beer Company 21119 Superior Street 91311 (818) 718-2739
http://greatbeerco.com/

Claremont **Claremont Craft Ales** 1420 N Claremont Blvd Ste 204-C
91711 (909) 625-5350 http://claremontcraftales.com/

Covina

Alosta Brewing Company 692 Arrow Grand Circle 91722 (626) 470-
7897 https://www.alostabrewing.com/

Arrow Lodge Brewing 720 E Arrow Highway Unit C 91722 (626) 498-
0557 https://www.arrowlodgebrew.com/

El Segundo

Surfridge Brewing Company 137 Nevada Street 90245 (424) 277-1102
https://www.surfridgebrewery.com/

Upshift Brewing 339 Indiana Street 90245 (310) 648-8246
https://upshiftbrewing.com/

El Segundo Brewing Company 140 Main Street 90245 (310) 529-3882
https://www.elsegundobrewing.com/

Gardena

Two Coast Brewing Company 1866 W 169th Street Unit H 90247 (310) 730-0055 https://www.twocoastbrewing.com/

State Brewing Company 1237 W 134 Street 90247 (310) 819-8179
https://statebrewingco.com/

Ximix Craft Exploration 13723 ½ Harvard Place 90249 (424) 292-3475
http://ximixcraft.com/

Glendale

Brewyard Beer Company 906 Western Avenue 91201 (818) 409-9448
https://www.brewyardbeercompany.com/

Pacific Plate Brewing Company 1302 S Brand Blvd B 91204 (818) 839-1765 https://www.pacificplatebrewing.com/

Hawthorne

Los Angeles Ale Works 12918 Cerise Avenue 90250 (424) 456-4191
https://www.laaleworks.com/

Common Space Brewery 3411 W El Segundo Blvd 90250 (424) 456-4355 https://www.commonspace.la/

Huntington Beach

Four Sons Brewing 18421 Gothard Street Unit 100 92648 (714) 421-0137 https://www.foursonsbrewing.com/

Riip Beer Company 17214 Pacific Coast Highway 92649 (714) 248-6710 https://riipbeer.com/

Long Beach

Ambitious Ales 4019 Atlantic Avenue 90807 (562) 285-7199 https://www.ambitiousales.com/welcome

Beachwood BBQ and Brewing 210 E 3rd Street 90802 (562) 436-4020 http://www.beachwoodbbq.com/

Steady Brew Beer Company 2936 Clark Avenue 90815 (562) 982-4046 https://www.steadybrewing.com/

Belmont Brewing Company 25-39th Place 90803 (562) 433-3891 https://www.belmontbrewing.com/

Long Beach Beer Lab 518 W Willow Street 90806 (562) 341-3659 https://lbbeer.com/

Liberation Brewing 3630 Atlantic Avenue 90807 (562) 349-0133 https://www.liberationbrewing.com/

Monrovia

Hop Secret Brewing Company 162 W Pomona Avenue 91016 (626) 386-5960 https://www.hopsecretbrewing.com/

Over Town Brewing Company 227 W Maple Avenue 91016 (626) 408-5814 https://www.overtownbrew.com/

Wingwalker Brewing 235 W Maple Avenue 91016 (626) 720-1983 https://www.wingwalkerbrewing.com/

Palmdale

Transplants Brewing Company 40242 La Quinta Lane #101 93551 (661) 266-7911 https://transplantsbrewing.square.site/

Lucky Luke Brewing 610 W Avenue O Suite 104 93551 (661) 270-5588 https://www.luckylukebrewing.com/

Pomona

Homage Brewing 281 S Thomas Street #101 91766 (909) 461-6962 https://www.homagebrewing.com/vlx0qsyy06re7geov1sv2leuup161w

Innovation Brew Works 3650 W Temple Avenue 91768 (909) 979-6197 http://www.ibrewworks.com/

Old Stump Brewing Company 2896 Metropolitan Place 91767 (909) 860-9052 http://www.oldstumpbrewery.com/

Sanctum Brewing Company 560 E Commercial Street Unit 21 91767 (909) 345-0253 https://www.sanctumbrewing.com/

King Harbor Brewing Company 2907 182nd Street 90278 (310) 542-8657 https://www.kingharborbrewing.com/

San Fernando Brewing Company 425 Park Avenue 91340 (818) 745-6175 http://www.sanfernandobrewingcompany.com/#latest-buzz

San Pedro

Brouwerij West 110 E 22nd Street Warehouse No. 9 90731 (310) 833-9330 https://www.brouwerijwest.com/

San Pedro Brewing Company 331 W 6th Street 90731 (310) 831-5663 https://sanpedrobrewing.com/

Pocock Brewing Company 24907 Avenue Tibbitts Suite B 91355 (661) 775-4899 https://www.pocockbrewing.com/

Santa Monica Brew Works 1920 Colorado Avenue Suite C 90404 (310) 828-7629 https://santamonicabrewworks.com/

Ten Mile Brewing 1136 E Willow Street 90755 (562) 612-1255 https://tenmilebrewing.com/

Progress Brewing 1822 Chico Avenue 91733 (626) 552-9603 http://www.progress-brewing.com/

Tarantula Hill Brewing Company 244 Thousand Oaks Blvd 91360 (805) 538-1191 https://tarantulahillbrewingco.com/

Torrance

Smog City Brewing 1901 Del Amo Blvd 90501 (310) 320-7664 https://smogcitybrewing.com/

HopSaint Brewing Company 5160 W 190th Street 90503 (310) 214-4677 https://www.hopsaint.com/

Strand Brewing Company 2201 Dominguez Street 90501 (310) 517-0999 https://strandbrewing.com/store/

The Dudes' Brewing Company 1840 W 208th Street 90501 (424) 271-2915 http://www.thedudesbrew.com/

Absolution Brewing Company 2878 Columbia Street 90503 (310) 490-4860 https://www.absolutionbrewingcompany.com/

Scholb Premium Ales 2964 Columbia Street 90503 (424) 731-3470 https://www.drinkscholb.com/

Monkish Brewing Company 20311 S Western Avenue 90501 (310) 295-2157 https://www.monkishbrewing.com/

Yorkshire Square Brewery 1109 Van Ness Avenue 90501 (424) 376-5115 http://yorkshiresquarebrewery.com/

Red Car Brewery and Restaurant 1266 Sartori Avenue 90501 (310) 782-0222 http://redcarbrewery.com/

Cosmic Brewery 20316 Gramercy Place 90501 (424) 259-2337 https://cosmicbrewery.com/

Wolf Creek Brewing 27746 McBean Parkway 91354 (661) 263-9653 https://www.wolfcreekbrewingco.com/

Van Nuys

Reel Brewery 14933 Calvert Street 91411 (818) 555-5555 https://www.reelbrewery.com/

MacLeod Ale Brewing Company 14741 Calvert Street 91411 (818) 631-1963 https://www.macleodale.com/

Ventura

Surf Brewery 4561 Market Street Suite A 93003 (805) 644-2739 http://surfbrewery.com/

Poseidon Brewing Company 5777 Olivas Park Drive Unit Q 93003 (805) 477-0239 https://www.poseidonbrewingco.com/

Concrete Jungle Brewing Project 4561 Market Street 93003 (805) 650-4816 http://concretejunglebrew.com/

Ventura Coast Brewing Company 76 South Oak Street 93001 (805) 667-8640 https://www.vcbc.beer/

Leashless Brewing 585 East Thompson Blvd 93001 (805) 628-9474 https://www.leashlessbrewing.com/

MadeWest Brewing Company 1744 Donlon Street 93003 (805) 947-5002 https://madewest.com/

Anacapa Brewing Company 472 E Main Street 93001 (805) 643-2337 https://www.anacapabrewing.com/

Westlake Village

14 Cannons 31125 Via Colinas Suite 907 91362 (818) 699-6165
https://www.14cannons.com/

Five Threads Brewing Company 31133 Via Colinas Suite 109 91362
(805) 457-5990 http://www.fivethreadsbrewing.com/

San Diego and Surrounding Area

At the Southern end of California, you can take a tour of the many
breweries in San Diego and take a few days to travel the surrounding area
to see what other great breweries are found along the ocean area. Start
your trip in the small town of Alpine with a must-visit brewery:

Alpine Beer Company 1347 Tavern Road 91901 (619) 445-2337
https://alpinebeerco.com/

Take a forty minute drive through the mountains to the town of Julian with
a couple options, including a must-visit brewery:

Julian Beer Company 2307 Main Street 92036 (760) 765-3757
https://julianbeercompany.com/

Nickel Beer Company 1485 Hollow Glen Road 92036 (760) 765-2337
https://nickelbeerco.com/

Next head west about a half-hour to Ramona with a must-visit brewery:

Smoking Cannon Brewery 780 Main Street Suite I 92065 (760) 407-
7557 https://smokingcannonbrewery.com/

Head southwest about another half-hour to El Cajon:

Burning Beard Brewing Company 785 Vernon Way 92020 (619) 456-
9185 https://burningbeardbrewing.com/

Creative Creature Brewing 110 North Magnolia Avenue 92020 (619)
201-8180 http://www.creativecreaturebrewing.com/

Just seven more minutes west brings you to the small town of La Mesa with a couple other options:

Helix Brewing Company 8101 Commercial Street 91942 (619) 741-8447 https://drinkhelix.com/

Bolt Brewery 8179 Center Street 91942 (619) 303-7837 https://boltbrewery.com/

Another half-hour southwest brings you to the coast and the city of Chula Vista with several options. But if you can only visit one then there is a must-visit brewery while you're here:

Bay Bridge Brewing 688 Marsat Court 91911 (619) 934-7371 https://baybridgebrewing.com/

Chula Vista Brewery 294 3rd Avenue 91910 (619) 616-8806 https://www.chulavistabrewery.com/

Thr3e Punk Ales Brewing Company 259 3rd Avenue 91910 (619) 271-4853 http://3punkales.com/red/

NOVO Brazil Brewing Company 2015 Birch Road Suite 1017 91915 (619) 869-4274 https://novootay.com/

Head north up the coast about sixteen minutes to Coronado with a great brewery:

Coronado Brewing Company 170 Orange Avenue 92118 (619) 437-4452 https://coronadobrewing.com/

Just twelve minutes away you come to the biggest concentration of breweries on this tour in the major city of San Diego. You likely won't be able to visit them all, but there are a couple of must-visit options:

Bay City Brewing Company 3760 Hancock Street 92110 (619) 727-4926 https://baycitybrewingco.com/

Protector Brewery 8680 Miralani Drive #128 92126 (858) 757-9160
https://www.protectorbrewery.com/

Mission Brewery 1441 L Street 92101 (619) 544-0555
http://missionbrewery.com/

Thorn Brewing Company 3176 Thorn Street 92104 (619) 501-2739
http://thorn.beer/

Second Chance Beer Company 15378 Avenue of Science #222 92128
(858) 705-6250 https://www.secondchancebeer.com/

32 North Brewing Company 8655 Production Avenue Ste A 92121 (619)
363-2622 https://www.32northbrew.com/

Karl Strauss Brewing Company 5985 Santa Fe Street 92109 (858) 273-
2739 https://www.karlstrauss.com/

Half Door Brewing Company 903 Island Avenue 92101 (619) 232-9845
http://www.halfdoorbrewing.com/

Automatic Brewing Company 3416 Adams Avenue 92116 (619) 255-
2491 https://www.automaticbrewingco.com/

Kairoa Brewing Company 4601 Park Blvd 92116 (619) 295-1355
https://www.kairoa.com/

Pariah Brewing Company 3052 El Cajon Blvd Suite B 92104 (619) 642-
0545 https://www.pariahbrewing.com/

Societe Brewing Company 8262 Clairemont Mesa Blvd 92111 (858)
598-5409 https://societebrewing.com/

Helm's Brewing Company 4896 Newport Avenue 92107 (619) 795-1991
http://helmsbrewingco.com/

Bitter Brothers Brewing Company 4170 Morena Blvd 92117 (619) 961-
6690 http://bitterbrothers.com/

Fall Brewing Company 4542 30th Street 92116 (619) 501-0903
http://www.fallbrewingcompany.com/

North Park Beer Company 3038 University Avenue 92104 (619) 255-2946 https://www.northparkbeerco.com/

Hillcrest Brewing Company 1458 University Avenue 92103 (619) 269-4323 https://hillcrestbrewingcompany.com/

Groundswell Brewing Company 6304 Riverdale Street 92120 (619) 820-0961 http://groundswellbrew.com/

Abnormal Beer Company 16990 Via Tazon 92127 (858) 618-2463 https://abnormalbeer.co/

AleSmith Brewing Company 9990 AleSmith Court 92126 (858) 549-9888 http://alesmith.com/

Kilowatt Brewing 7576 Clairemont Mesa Blvd 92111 (858) 715-3998 https://kilowatt.beer/

Attitude Brewing Company 1985 National Avenue 92113 (619) 795-4269 https://attitudebrewing.com/

Knotty Brewing Company 842 Market Street 92101 (619) 269-4337 http://knottybrewing.com/

Deft Brewing 5328 Banks Street Suite A 92110 (858) 799-1228 https://www.deftbrewing.com/

Amplified Ale Works 4150 Mission Blvd #208 92109 (858) 270-5222 https://amplifiedales.com/

Saint Archer Brewing Company 9550 Distribution Avenue 92121 (858) 225-2337 https://www.saintarcherbrewery.com/

Resident Brewing Company 1065 Fourth Avenue 92101 (619) 717-6622 http://www.residentbrewing.com/home.php

Green Flash Brewing Company 6550 Mira Mesa Blvd 92121 (858) 622-0085 https://www.greenflashbrew.com/

Division 23 Brewing 7408 Trade Street 92121 (858) 752-1924 https://www.division23brewing.com/

Harland Brewing Company 10115 Carroll Canyon Road 92131 (858) 800-4566 https://harlandbeer.com/

Hodad's Brewing Company 5010 Newport Avenue 92107 (619) 224-4623 https://hodadies.com/about-us/hodads-brewing/

Savagewood Brewing Company 9879 Hibert Street Suite F 92131 (858) 577-0350 https://savagewoodbrewing.com/

Pacific Beach Ale House 721 Grand Avenue 92109 (858) 581-2337 https://pbalehouse.com/

Pure Project 9030 Kenamar Drive #308 92121 (858) 252-6143 https://www.purebrewing.org/

Original 40 Brewing Company 3117 University Avenue 92104 (619) 255-7380 https://original40brewing.com/

New English Brewing Company 11545 Sorrento Valley Road Suite 305 92121 (619) 857-8023 https://www.newenglishbrewing.com/

Latchkey Brewing Company 1795 Hancock Street 92110 (858) 284-7076 https://latchkeybrew.com/

Border X Brewing 2181 Logan Avenue 92113 (619) 787-6176 https://borderxbrewing.com/

Circle 9 Brewing 7292 Opportunity Road Ste C 92111 (858) 634-2537 http://circle9brewingco.com/

Duck Foot Brewing Company 8920 Kenamar Drive Suite #210 92121 (858) 433-7916 https://duckfootbeer.com/

San Diego Brewing Company 10450 Friars Road 92120 (619) 284-2739
https://www.sandiegobrewing.com/

Longship Brewery 10320 Camino Santa Fe C 92121 (858) 246-7875
https://www.longshipbrewery.com/

California Wild Ales 4202 Sorrento Valley Blvd Suite L&M 92121 (855)
953-2537 https://www.californiawildales.com/

When you're finished exploring all the breweries you can in San Diego,
then head about a half-hour up the coast to the town of Del Mar with a
single brewery option:

Viewpoint Brewing Company 2201 San Dieguito Drive 92014 (858) 356-
9346 https://www.viewpointbrewing.com/

Five minutes north is the small community of Solana Beach with another
brewery option:

Culture Brewing Company 111 S Cedros Avenue Suite 200 92075 (858)
345-1144 https://www.culturebrewingco.com/

Then another eighteen minutes north will give you a few more options and
a couple must-visit breweries in the town of Carlsbad:

Arcana Brewing Company 5621 Palmer Way Suite C 92010 (909) 529-
2337 http://www.arcanabrewing.com/

Burgeon Beer Company 6350 Yarrow Drive Suite C 92011 (760) 814-
2548 https://burgeonbeer.com/

Culver Beer Company 2719 West Loker Avenue Suite D 92010 (760)
814-2355 http://www.culverbeer.com/

Offering a range of unique, local beers to try. The tasting room is kid and
dog friendly so you can bring everyone.

Rouleur Brewing Company 5840 El Camino Real Suite 101 92008 (442)
244-5111 https://rouleurbrewing.com/

Just five minutes north you'll reach the top part of your trip and the town of Oceanside with several brewery options including a must-visit brewery:

Black Plague Brewing 2550 Jason Court 92056 (760) 631-8110
https://blackplaguebrewing.com/

Northern Pine Brewery 326 N Horne Street 92054 (760) 754-1434
https://northernpinebrewing.com/

Bagby Beer Company 601 South Coast Highway 92054 (760) 270-9075
https://www.bagbybeer.com/

Belching Beaver Brewery 1334 Rocky Point Drive 92056 (760) 732-1415
https://belchingbeaver.com/

Now head about eighteen minutes inland to the town of Vista with quite a few breweries including a must-visit destination:

Booze Brothers Brewing Company 2545 Progress Street 92081 (760) 295-0217 http://www.boozebros.com/

BattleMage Brewing Company 2870 Scott Street Suite 102 92081 (760) 216-6425 https://battlemagebrewing.com/

Mother Earth Brew Company 2055 Thibodo Road Suite D 92081 (760) 295-3074 https://www.motherearthbrewco.com/

Indian Joe Brewing 2123 Industrial Court 92081 (760) 295-3945
https://www.indianjoebrewing.com/

Wavelength Brewing Company 236 Main Street 92084 (760) 820-9283
https://www.wavelengthbrewco.com/

Eppig Brewing Company 1347 Keystone Way Suite C 92081 (760) 295-2009 http://www.eppigbrewing.com/#eppig

Ebullition Brew Works 2449 Cades Way Suite D 92081 (760) 842-1046
https://www.ebullitionbrew.com/#visit

Latitude 33 Brewing Company 1430 Vantage Court #104 92081 (760) 410-6333 http://latitude33brewing.com/

Helia Brewing Company 1250 Keystone Way 92081 (760) 216-6023 https://heliabeer.com/

Aztec Brewing Company 2330 La Mirada Drive Suite 300 92081 (800) 706-6324 http://www.aztecbrewery.com/home.html

Beach Grease Beer Company 1280 Activity Drive 92081 (760) 296-7984 https://www.beachgreasebeerco.com/home

Bear Roots Brewing Company 1213 S Santa Fe Avenue 92083 (760) 726-4204 http://bearrootsbrewing.com/

Nine minutes further inland takes you to the town of San Marcos and another wide selection of breweries to consider:

Stumblefoot Brewing Company 1784 La Costa Meadows Drive #103 92078 (760) 566-3668 https://www.stumblefoot.com/

Dos Desperados Brewery 1241 Linda Vista Drive 92078 (760) 566-6209 http://www.dosdesperadosbrew.com/

Wild Barrel Brewing Company 692 Rancheros Drive 92069 (760) 230-9205 https://wildbarrelbrewing.com/

San Marcos Brewery and Grill 1080 W San Marcos Blvd Suite #180 92078 http://www.sanmarcosbrewery.com/

Mason Ale Works 255 Redel Road 92078 (760) 798-8822 https://www.masonaleworks.com/

End your trip another seven minutes east in the town of Escondido with a few brewery options:

Jacked Up Brewery 800 W Grand Avenue 92025 (760) 300-0633 https://jackedupbrewery.com/?age-verified=6f6b25df34

Stone Brewing 1999 W Citracado Parkway 92029 (760) 294-7899
https://www.stonebrewing.com/

Plan 9 Alehouse 155 E Grand Avenue 92025 (760) 489-8817
https://www.plan9alehouse.com/

Orange County Breweries

Orange County is a great place in California with a lot of coastal towns.
There are several great breweries within this county that you can visit with
a simple one to two-day trip. Start your trip out in San Clemente with a few
options as well as a must-visit brewery:

Artifex Brewing Company 919 Calle Amanecer 92673 (949) 429-7805
http://artifexbrewing.com/

Lost Winds Brewing Company 924 C Calle Negocio 92673 (949) 361-
5922 http://lostwindsbrewing.com/

Left Coast Brewing Company 1245 Puerta Del Sol 92673 (949) 276-
2699 http://leftcoastbrewing.com/

Just nine minutes up the coast and slightly inland you'll get to the town of
San Juan Capistrano:

Docent Brewing 33049 Calle Aviador Suite C 92675 (949) 767-8170
https://docentbrewing.com/

Heading seventeen minutes inland brings you to Rancho Santa Margarita:

Laguna Beach Beer Company 29851 Aventura, D (949) 264-6821
https://www.lagunabeer.com/

Take a twelve-minute drive back towards the coast and the town of
Laguna Hills:

GameCraft Brewing 23301 Avenida De La Carlota Suite C 92653 (949)
734-0910 https://www.gamecraftbrewing.com/

Head northwest to the city of Costa Mesa where you have a few options include two must-visit breweries:

Brewing Reserve of California 2930 College Avenue Suite D 92626 (714) 884-4704 https://www.brcbeer.com/

Gunwhale Ales 2960 Randolph Avenue Unit A 92626 (949) 239-9074 https://www.gunwhaleales.com/

Salty Bear Brewing Company 2948 Randolph Avenue Unit C 92626 (714) 486-2165 https://www.saltybearbrewing.com/

Six minutes west brings you to the coastal town of Newport Beach and a must-visit brewery:

Chihuahua Cerveza 3107 Newport Blvd 92663 (949) 771-8226 https://www.chihuahuacerveza.com/

Head back inland about fourteen minutes to the city of Tustin where you have two options, including a must-visit brewery:

Archaic Craft Brewery 140 East Main Street 92780 (714) 258-8817 https://www.centrotustin.com/brewery

Tustin Brewing Company 13011 Newport Avenue Suite 100 92780 (714) 665-2337 http://tustinbrewery.com/

Six minutes north takes you to Santa Ana where there is a must-visit brewery and a second option if you have the time:

Network Brewery 1824 Carnegie Avenue 92705 (657) 859-8004 https://www.networkbrewery.com/

Cismontane Brewing Company 1409 E Warner Suite C 92705 (949) 888-2739 https://www.cismontanebrewing.com/

Another eight minutes north brings you to Orange with another two options including a must-visit brewery:

Chapman Crafted Beer 123 N Cypress Street 92866 (844) 855-2337
https://www.chapmancrafted.beer/

Green Cheek Beer Company 2294 N Batavia Street Ste C 92865 (714) 998-8172 https://greencheekbeer.com/

Ten minutes north brings you to Placentia and the end of your Orange County trip:

Stereo Brewing 950 South Via Rodeo 92870 (714) 993-3390
https://www.stereobrewing.com/

The Bruery 717 Dunn Way 92870 (714) 996-6258
https://www.thebruery.com/

California Central Coast

If you want to enjoy your coastal breweries with a little more driving distance in between and a little more time to experience the coast, then consider taking this trip. You'll cover the area between Los Angeles and the San Francisco bay area while staying along the coast. You'll enjoy great beers and wonderful views along the way. Start out in Camarillo just north of Los Angeles with a couple options and a must-visit brewery:

Institution Ale Company 3841 Mission Oaks Blvd 93012 (805) 482-3777
https://www.institutionales.com/

Flat Fish Brewing Company 126 N Wood Road 93010 (805) 484-9600
https://flatfishbrewing.com/

Next head north up the 101 by about a half-hour to Carpinteria for a few more options:

Rincon Brewery 5065 Carpinteria Avenue 93013 (805) 684-6044
https://www.rinconbrewery.com/

Island Brewing Company 5049 6th Street 93013 (805) 745-8272
http://www.islandbrewingcompany.com/#drink-together

Just a little further up the coast, you come to the main city of Santa Barbara with a few options as well as a must-visit destination:

Brass Bear Brewing 28 Anacapa Street #E 93101 (805) 770-7651
http://www.brassbearbrewing.com/

Night Lizard Brewing Company 607 State Street 93101 (805) 770-2956
https://nightlizardbrewingcompany.com/our-brews/

Third Window Brewing Company 406 E Haley Street 93101 (805) 979-5090 https://www.thirdwindowbrewing.com/

Pure Order Brewing Company 410 N Quarantina Street 93103 (805) 966-2881 http://pureorderbrewing.com/

The next stop is thirteen minutes north in the small town of Goleta which actually has a decent selection of breweries:

M. Special Brew Company 6860 Cortona Drive Ste C 93117 (805) 968-6500 https://www.mspecialbrewco.com/

Captain Fatty's 6483 Calle Real 93117 (805) 364-2968
http://www.captainfattys.com/

Draughtsmen Aleworks 53 Santa Felicia Drive 93117 (805) 387-2577
https://www.draughtsmenaleworks.com/

Hollister Brewing Company 6980 Marketplace Drive 93117 (805) 968-2810 https://www.hollisterbrewco.com/

After following the coast for a little bit, you'll go inland and end up in the quaint town of Solvang with a must-visit brewery:

Solvang Brewing Company 1547 Mission Street 93463 (805) 688-2337
https://solvangbrewing.com/

The town of Buellton is just next door and only a six-minute drive with another must-visit brewery:

Figueroa Mountain Brewing Company 45 Industrial Way 93427 (805) 350-9435 http://www.figmtnbrew.com/

Continue up the 101 north about a half-hour to Santa Maria:

Santa Maria Brewing Company 1451 Fairway Drive 93455 (805) 922-2225 https://www.santamariabrewing.co/

The freeway then curves you back towards the ocean, and you will come to Grover Beach:

ManRock Brewing Company 1750 El Camino Real 93433 (805) 270-3089 https://www.manrockbrewing.com/

A quick sixteen-minute drive brings you to San Luis Obispo with three great brewery options to enjoy:

SLO Brew 855 Aerovista Place 93401 (805) 543-1843 http://www.slobrew.com/

Bang the Drum Brewery 1150 Laurel Lane St. 160 (805) 242-8372 https://bangthedrumbrewery.com/

Central Coast Brewing 6 Higuera Street 93401 (805) 783-BREW http://www.centralcoastbrewing.com/

Head back to the coast to the quaint town of Morro Bay with a must-visit brewery:

Three Stacks and a Rock Brewing 3118 Main Street Suite D 93442 (805) 771-9286 http://threestacksandarockbrewing.com/

Head inland about a half-hour to Paso Robles, it is a popular winery destination and is also home to several great breweries:

Silva Brewing 525 Pine Street Suite B 93446 (805) 369-2337 https://www.silvabrewing.com/

Firestone Walker Brewing Company 1400 Ramada Drive 93446 (805) 225-5911 https://www.firestonebeer.com/

BarrelHouse Brewing Company 3055 Limestone Way 93446 (805) 296-1128 https://www.barrelhousebrewing.com/

From here the trip takes the longest drive of an hour and a half north to the city of Salinas and a must-visit brewery:

Monterey Coast Brewing 165 Main Street 93901 (831) 758-2337 http://montereycoastbrewing.com/

Now you go back to the coast to the town of Marina:

English Ales Brewery 223a Reindollar Avenue 93933 (831) 384-1253 https://englishalesbrewery.com/

Travel south along the coast to the town of Monterey with a must-visit brewery:

Alvarado Street Brewery 426 Alvarado Street 93940 (831) 655-BEER http://www.alvaradostreetbrewery.com/

The next-door sister city to the south Carmel-by-the-Sea also features a great brewery:

Yeast of Eden Mission Street & 7th Avenue Carmel Plaza Suite 112 93923 (831) 293-8621 https://yoebeer.com/

Then head back north about a half-hour to the city of Watsonville with a couple options, including a must-visit brewery:

Corralitos Brewing Company 2536 Freedom Blvd 95076 (831) 728-2311 http://www.corralitosbrewingco.com/

Elkhorn Slough Brewing Company 65 Hangar Way D 95076 (831) 288-3152 http://elkhornsloughbrew.com/blog/

Specializing in small-batch specialty beers. Mostly offering barrel-aged wild ales. Enjoy a one of a kind beer tasting experience when you stop here. Your next stop is sixteen minutes west to Capitola:

Sante Adairius Rustic Ales 103 Kennedy Drive 95010 (831) 462-1227
http://rusticales.com/

Next door is a three-minute drive to the small town of Soquel:

Discretion Brewing 2703 41st Avenue Ste A 95073 (831) 316-0662
https://www.discretionbrewing.com/

Drive about twenty-minutes to Scotts Valley in the north:

Steel Bonnet Brewing Company 20 Victor Square 95066 (831) 454-8429 https://www.steelbon.net/

From there end your trip about eight minutes south in Santa Cruz where there are plenty of options to choose from:

Humble Sea Brewing Company 820 Swift Street 95060 (831) 621-2890
https://humblesea.com/

Uncommon Brewers 303 Potrero Street Suite 40-H (831) 621-6270
https://www.uncommonbrewers.com/

Santa Cruz Mountain Brewing 402 Ingalls Street 95060 (831) 425-4900
https://scmbrew.com/

Seabright Brewery 519 Seabright Avenue (831) 426-2739
https://seabrightbrewery.com/

Shanty Shack Brewing 138 Fern Street 95060 (831) 316-0800
http://www.shantyshackbrewing.com/

New Bohemia Brewing Company 1030 41st Avenue 95062 (831) 350-0253 https://www.nubobrew.com/

Santa Cruz Ale Works 150 Dubois Street 95060 (831) 425-1182
http://www.santacruzaleworks.com/

Offering four different and unique beer styles on tap for you to taste and find a new favorite.

Desert to Mountain Trail

If you want to enjoy all the climates and brewery styles that California has to offer, then this trail is for you. It may be a bit further spread apart than other trails, but it gives you a chance to experience a little of everything. For a longer trip and a great experience, you can start in Holtville at the southern border of California:

Humble Farmer Brewing Company 116 N Imperial Avenue #C 92251 (760) 545-0037 https://www.humblefarmerbrewing.com/

From there it is a five and a half-hour drive north to the eastern border of California and a great brewery experience in the small town of Tecopa:

Death Valley Brewing 102 Old Spanish Trail Highway 92389 (760) 852-4273 http://www.deathvalleybrewing.com/

From here it is about three hours back inland to the small town of Inyokern:

Indian Wells Brewing Company 2565 N Highway 14 93527 (760) 377-5989 http://mojavered.com/

The next stage takes you about an hour drive west to a must-visit brewery in the town of Kernville:

Kern River Brewing Company 13415 Sierra Way 93238 (760) 376-2337 https://www.kernriverbrewing.com/

Take a three-hour drive north to the great small town of Bishop with a lot of outdoor activities and a must-visit brewery:

Mountain Rambler Brewery 186 South Main Street 93514 (760) 258-1348 https://www.mountainramblerbrewery.com/

A little less than an hour drive takes you to the end of your trip in the mountains at June Lake:

June Lake Brewing 131 S Crawford Avenue 93529 (760) 616-4399
https://www.junelakebrewing.com/

Gold Country Brewery Trail

Taking a brewery tour of the Gold Country is a great way to experience history, the beautiful outdoors, and wonderful beers all at the same time. You can easily complete the trip in a day or two, but with so much to see and do, you might want to plan a longer trip.

Start your trip in the north at the small town of Blairsden with a must-visit brewery:

The Brewing Lair 67007 CA Highway 70 96103 (530) 394-0940
http://www.thebrewinglair.com/

Take about a two-hour drive over the mountains among beautiful scenery to find yourself in the quaint little town of Nevada City:

Three Forks Bakery and Brewing Company 211 Commercial Street 95959 (530) 470-8333 https://www.threeforksnc.com/

Just five minutes south is the next town of Grass Valley with a must-visit brewery:

Grass Valley Brewing Company 141 E Main Street 95945 (530) 271-2739 https://www.gvbrew.com/

Continue almost another half-hour south to the town of Auburn with a few brewery options as well as a must-visit brewery:

Moonraker Brewing Company 12970 Earhart Avenue 95602 (530) 745-6816 https://www.moonrakerbrewing.com/

Crooked Lane Brewing Company 536 Grass Valley Highway 95603 (530) 878-5232 https://crookedlanebrewing.com/

Knee Deep Brewing Company 13395 New Airport Road Ste. H 95602 (530) 797-HOPS https://kneedeepbrewing.com/

Auburn Alehouse Brewery 289 Washington Street 95603 (530) 885-2537 https://auburnalehouse.com/

Take a seventeen-minute drive west to the small town of Lincoln with a couple of brewery options:

Slice Beer Company 665 6th Street 95648 (916) 408-6889 https://www.slicebeer.com/home

GoatHouse Brewing 600 Wise Road 95648 (916) 740-9100 https://www.goathousebrewing.com/

Just fourteen minutes more brings you to the small town of Loomis:

Loomis Basin Brewing Company 3277 Swetzer Road 95650 (916) 259-2739 https://loomisbasinbrewing.com/

The next stop south is Rocklin with a couple great options:

Out of Bounds Brewing Company 4480 Yankee Hill Road #100 95677 (916) 259-1511 https://www.outofboundsbrewing.com/

Moksa Brewing Company 5860 Pacific Street 95677 (916) 824-1366 https://moksabrewing.com/

From there you come to Roseville:

Monk's Cellar 240 Vernon Street 95678 (916) 786-6665 http://monkscellar.com/

Next, it is about a half-hour drive to the community of El Dorado Hills:

Mraz Brewing Company 2222 Francisco Drive Suite 510 95762 (916) 934-0744 http://mrazbrewingcompany.com/

Head east about a half-hour to a must-visit brewery in the small town of Camino:

Jack Russell Brewing Company 2380 Larsen Drive 95709 (530) 647-6222 http://jackrussellbrewery.com/

Then come back west and slightly south to the small town of Diamond Springs and another must-visit brewery:

Solid Ground 552 Pleasant Valley Road 95619 (530) 344-7442
https://www.solidgroundbrewing.com/

Then head south twenty-minutes to end your trip in Plymouth with a must-visit brewery:

Amador Brewing Company 9659 Main Street 95669 (209) 507-1900
https://www.amadorbrewing.com/

Central Valley Brewery Trail

Take a trip through the Central Valley. In the southern part of the trail, the breweries are a little more spread out and may take a little bit of driving in between. Once you get to the northern portion of the trail, you can easily find a place to stay and drive to the breweries of your choice for a few days while exploring other sites in the nearby area. Start your trip at the southern end of the Central Valley in the city of Bakersfield:

Great Change Brewing 4200 Resnik Court 93313 (661) 735-5016
http://www.greatchangebrewing.com/

Temblor Brewing Company 3200 Buck Owens Blvd 93308 (661) 489-4855 https://temblorbrewing.com/

Dionysus Brewing Company 6201 Schirra Court Suite 13 93313 (661) 833-6000 https://www.dionysusbrewing.com/

Lengthwise Brewing Company 7700 District Blvd 93313 (661) 836-ALES http://lengthwise.com/

About an hour drive north on the freeway brings you to the city of Tulare:

Kaweah Brewing Company 1054 E Walnut Avenue 93274 (559) 623-9093 https://www.kaweahbrewing.com/

Another forty minutes north on the freeway is the small city of Sanger with a must-visit brewery:

House of Pendragon Brewing Company 1849 Industrial Way 93657 (559) 875-2508 http://hopbeer.com/

From here, a quick eighteen-minute drive west brings you to the city of Fresno with several options include quite a few must-visit breweries:

The Mad Duck Craft Brewing 7050 N Marks Avenue 93711 (559) 840-3825 https://www.madduckcraft.com/

Sequoia Brewing Company 777 East Olive Avenue 93728 (559) 264-5521 http://sequoiabrewing.com/

Full Circle Brewing Company 620 F Street 93706 (559) 264-6323 https://fullcirclebrewing.com/

Tioga-Sequoia Brewing Company 745 Fulton Street 93721 (559) 487-2337 http://tiogasequoia.com/

Amalgamation Brewing Company 6585 North Santa Fe Avenue 93722 (559) 375-1771 https://www.amalgamationbrewing.com/

Twelve minutes northeast of Fresno is the town of Clovis:

Tactical Ops Brewing 1131 Railroad Avenue 93612 (559) 765-4930 http://www.tacticalopsbrewing.com/

About an hour drive east to the foothills of the mountains is well worth your time to stop at a must-visit brewery in Oakhurst:

South Gate Brewing Company 40233 Enterprise Drive 93644 (559) 692-2739

From there head about fifty minutes back west to the town of Madera and another must-visit brewery:

Riley's Brewing Company 28777 Avenue 15 ½ 93638 (559) 577-3445 https://www.rileysbrewing.com/

When you're ready to take the hour drive north to the town of Turlock with another must-visit brewery:

Dust Bowl Brewing Company 3000 Fulkerth Road 95380 (209) 250-2043 https://dustbowlbrewing.com/

Just eleven minutes north is the town of Ceres with another option:

Blaker Brewing 1063 Montclaire Drive 95307 (209) 585-4040 https://www.blakerbrewing.com/

Another quick six-minute drive north brings you to the city of Modesto:

St Stans Brewing 1028 11th Street 95354 (209) 284-0170 https://www.ststans.com/

About a half-hour more northwest brings you to Tracy:

Morgan Territory Brewing 1885 N MacArthur Drive 95376 (209) 834-8664 https://morganterritorybrewing.com/

Thirty minutes north brings you to the city of Lodi with a few brewery options as well as a must-visit brewery:

The Dancing Fox 203 School Street 95240 (209) 366-2634 https://www.dancingfoxlodi.com/

Lodi Beer Company 105 South School Street 95240 (209) 368-9931 https://www.lodibeercompany.com/

Idol Beer Works 100 South Sacramento Street 95240 https://www.idolbeerworks.com/

Another twenty-five minutes north brings you to the town of Elk Grove just south of Sacramento:

Tilted Mash 9175 Union Park Way 95624 (916) 714-MASH https://tiltedmash.com/

About twenty-six minutes will take you through Sacramento and to the northeast with the town of Carmichael:

River City Brewing Company 6241 Fair Oaks Blvd Suite G 95608 (916) 550-5093 https://www.rivercitybrewing.net/

Continue east about eighteen more minutes to Folsom:

Red Bus Brewing 802A Reading Street 95630 (916) 467-7790 https://www.redbusbrew.com/

Circle back southwest to the southern suburb of Sacramento, Rancho Cordova where you have several options along with a must-visit brewery:

Fort Rock Brewing 12401 Folsom Blvd Suite 110 95742 (916) 936-4616 http://fortrockbeer.wpengine.com/

Claimstake Brewing Company 11366 Monier Park Place 95742 (916) 661-5249 http://claimstakebrewing.com/index.html

Burning Barrel Brewing Company 11210 Sun Center Drive Suite B 95672 (916) 382-4846 https://www.burningbarrelbrewco.com/

Head about fifteen minutes west to the main city of Sacramento where you have many options to choose from and two must-visit breweries if you don't have time for anymore:

New Glory Craft Brewery 8251 Alpine Avenue 95826 (916) 451-9355 https://www.newglorybeer.com/

Tower Brewing Company 1210 66th Street 95819 (916) 272-4472 https://www.towerbrewingcompany.com/

New Helvetia Brewing Company 1730 Broadway 95818 (916) 469-9889 https://www.newhelvetiabrew.com/

Sacrament Brewing 1616 J Street 95814 (916) 492-2850 https://sacrament-brewing.business.site/

Urban Roots Brewing and Smokehouse 1322 V Street 95818 (916) 706-3741 https://www.urbanrootsbrewing.com/

Device Brewing Company 8166 14th Avenue Suite A 95826 (916) 737-2739 http://devicebrewing.com/

At Ease Brewing Company 1825 I Street 95811 (916) 431-7940 https://www.ateasebrewing.com/

Hoppy Brewing Company 2425 24th Street Suite B 95818 (916) 451-4677 http://hoppy.com/home-hoppy/

King Cong Brewing Company 1709 Del Paso Blvd 95815 (916) 514-8041 https://kingcongbrewing.com/

Alaro Craft Brewery 2004 Capitol Avenue 95811 (916) 436-7711 https://alarobrewing.com/

Fountainhead Brewing Company 4621 24th Street 95822 (916) 228-4610 https://www.fountainheadbrewingco.com/

Big Sexy Brewing Company 5861 88th Street Ste 800 95828 (833) 310-4777 https://www.bigsexybrewing.com/

Porchlight Brewing Company 866 57th Street 95819 (916) 476-5384 https://porchlightbrewingcompany.com/

Track 7 Brewing Company 3747 West Pacific Avenue Suite F 95820 (916) 520-4677 https://track7brewing.com/

Big Stump Brewing Company 1716 L Street 95811 (916) 668-7433 https://www.bigstumpbrewco.com/

Just next door by about four minutes is the suburb of West Sacramento:

Yolo Brewing Company 1520 Terminal Street 95691 (916) 379-7585 https://www.yolobrew.com/

Bike Dog Brewing Company 2534 Industrial Blvd Suite 110 95691 (916) 572-0788 https://bikedogbrewing.com/

Head east another eighteen minutes to the city of Davis with a few different options along with two must-visit breweries:

Dunloe Brewing 1606 Olive Drive 95616 (530) 231-3502
https://www.dunloebrewing.com/

Three Mile Brewing Company 231 G Street #3 95616 (530) 564-4351
https://www.threemilebrewing.com/

Super Owl Brewing 1260 Lake Blvd Ste 121 95616 (530) 746-5992
http://www.superowlbrewing.com/

The goal here is to provide something for everyone. There are activities and free drinks for the kids, as well as a welcoming atmosphere for pets. There are wonderful craft beers on tap with a rotating selection, so you'll always find something you like.

Sudwerk Brewing Company 2001 2nd Street 95618 (530) 756-2739
https://www.sudwerkbrew.com/

Started in 1989 with the focus on producing high-quality, authentic German lagers. Using traditional brewing methods along with modern-craft techniques, you'll experience a great lager when you stop in here for a tasting.

About a half-hour southwest will bring you to the city of Fairfield with two options, including a must-visit brewery:

DNA Brewing Company 1740 Travis Blvd 94523 (925) 233-5384
https://www.dnabrewingco.com/

Heretic Brewing Company 1052 Horizon Drive 94533 (707) 389-4573
http://www.hereticbrewing.com/

At this brewery, they push the boundaries of beer making. Stop in here if you want to try something different from ordinary beer.

Just four minutes east is the sister city of Suisun City:

True Symmetry Brewing Company 315 Marina Center 94585 (707) 202-6000 https://www.truesymmetry.beer/

Head back north about twenty-minutes to the town of Winters with two options including a must-visit brewery:

Hooby's Brewing 7 E Main Street Suite D 95694 (530) 794-6118 https://www.hoobysbrew.com/

Berryessa Brewing Company 27260 Highway 128 95694 (530) 795-3526 https://www.berryessabrewingco.com/

All beers are unfiltered and naturally carbonated. The beers are rotated on a regular basis, so if you are looking for a specific style, you should call first to see if they have it on tap; otherwise, just come to sample whatever great beers are on tap at the moment.

From here head north and east by about twenty-minutes to the town of Woodland with a must-visit brewery:

Blue Note Brewing Company 750 Dead Cat Alley 95695 (530) 358-4677 https://bluenotebrewingcompany.com/

All the beers here are made with the finest ingredients for the freshest and best-tasting beers. There are twelve beers on tap, so you are sure to find something you'll enjoy.

About forty minutes will bring you to the northern end of the Central Valley and the town of Yuba City:

Sutter Buttes Brewing 421 Center Street 95991 (530) 790-7999 https://www.sutterbuttesbrewing.com/

High Sierra Breweries

Take a trip along the beautiful mountains of the Sierras. There are only three stops on this trip, but there are plenty of wonderful breweries to try, including quite a few must-visit breweries. Start at the southern end with

Mammoth Lakes where you have a couple options including a must-visit brewery:

Distant Brewing 568 Old Mammoth Road 93546 (760) 525-0462 http://blackdoubtbrewing.com/

Mammoth Brewing Company 18 Lake Mary Road 93546 (760) 934-7141 https://mammothbrewingco.com/

Brewing award-winning beers since 1995. Offering six year-round beers of varied styles as well as a rotating selection of seasonal beers. From here it is about a three-hour scenic drive among the mountains to the town of South Lake Tahoe with multiple options including three must-visit breweries:

South of North Brewing Company 932 Stateline Avenue Suite B 96150 (530) 494-9805 https://www.southofnorthbeer.com/

Stateline Brewery 4118 Lake Tahoe Blvd 96150 (530) 542-9000 https://www.statelinebrewery.com/

The Brewery at Lake Tahoe 3542 Lake Tahoe Blvd 96150 (530) 544-2739 http://www.brewerylaketahoe.com/

The main focus is on handcrafted ales. You can have a range of options to choose from as well as seasonal ales.

South Lake Brewing Company 1920 Lake Tahoe Blvd 96150 (530) 578-0087 https://www.southlakebeer.com/

The largest craft brewery and indoor tasting room on the South Shore of Lake Tahoe. All beers are made on-site, and you can enjoy them in a great relaxing atmosphere.

Cold Water Brewery and Grill 2544 Highway 50 96150 (530) 544-4677 http://www.tahoecoldwaterbrewery.com/

An all-grain brewery offering handcrafted beers made on-site. Enjoy their full range of beers along with great food in their wonderful tasting room.

Another hour and a half north brings you to the southern destination of Truckee:

FiftyFifty Brewing Company 11197 Brockway Road Suite 1 96161
https://www.fiftyfiftybrewing.com/

San Francisco Bay Area

Start your trip out in San Francisco where you'll find plenty of breweries, but if you don't have time to visit them all then at least head to the must-visit breweries:

Pine Street Brewery 1270 Pine Street #1 94109 (415) 744-4062
https://www.pinestreetbrewery.com/

Seven Still Brewery and Distillery 1439 Egbert Street 94124 (415) 914-0936 https://www.sevenstillsofsf.com/

San Francisco Brewing Company 3150 Polk Street 94109 (415) 484-BEER https://sfbrewingco.com/

Laughing Monk Brewing 1439A Egbert Avenue 94124 (415) 678-5157
https://www.laughingmonkbrewing.com/

Speakeasy Ales and Lagers 1195 Evans Avenue 94124 (415) 642-3371
https://goodbeer.com/

Standard Deviant Brewing 280 14th Street 94103 (415) 590-2550
https://standarddeviantbrewing.square.site/

Barrel Head Brewhouse 1785 Fulton Street 94117 (415) 416-6989
http://www.barrelheadsf.com/#about

Bartlett Hall 242 O'Farrell Street 94102 (415) 433-4332
http://bartletthall.com/

Beach Chalet Brewery and Restaurant 1000 Great Highway 94121
(415) 386-8439 https://www.beachchalet.com/#new-page

Sufferfest Beer Company 1075 E 20th Street 95928
http://sufferfestbeer.com/

Cellarmaker Brewing Company 1150 Howard Street 94103 (415) 863-3940 https://cellarmakerbrewing.com/

Triple Voodoo Brewing 2245 3rd Street 94107 (415) 598-8811 https://www.triplevoodoo.com/

Barebottle Brewing Company 1525 Cortland Avenue 94110 (415) 291-2404 https://www.barebottle.com/

Fort Point Beer Company 644 Mason Street 94129 (415) 906-4021 http://fortpointbeer.com/

Sunset Reservoir Brewing Company 1735 Noriega Street 94122 (415) 571-8452 http://sunsetbeersf.com/

Anchor Brewing Company 1705 Mariposa Street 94107 (415) 863-8350 https://www.anchorbrewing.com/

The first and oldest craft brewery in the United States. The beers are made from an all-malt mash in traditional copper, using the methods that have been in place since the Gold Rush days. Stop in today to see what makes the beers so great.

Southern Pacific Brewing 620 Treat Avenue 94110 (415) 341-0152 https://www.southernpacificbrewing.com/

Producing clean, dry, true-to-style beers. There is plenty of wonderful core beers to enjoy, but you can also find a number of special brews to enjoy as well.

Local Brewing Company 69 Bluxome Street 94107 (415) 932-6702 https://localbrewingco.com/

The focus is on creating interesting and approachable beers. There are over a dozen rotating beers on tap and some excellent hot sandwiches to enjoy.

Harmonic Brewing 1050 26th Street 94107 (415) 872-6817
http://harmonicbrewing.com/

An independent craft brewery that celebrates the culture of San Francisco. They brew a rotating selection of lagers and ales with a focus on balance and drinkability. Be sure to try their flagship Kolsch, crisp lagers, and bright IPAs.

Black Hammer Brewing 544 Bryant Street 94107 (628) 222-4664
https://blackhammerbrewing.com/

Crafting small-batch ales and lagers through traditional techniques and modern innovations. Stop here to try something new and wonderful. When you're ready to head just thirteen minutes south to the suburb of South San Francisco with a few more options as well as a must-visit brewery:

Armstrong Brewing Company 415 Grand Avenue 94080 (650) 989-8447 https://www.armstrongbrewing.com/

47 Hills Brewing Company 137 South Linden Avenue 94080 (650) 867-8476 http://47hillsbrewingcompany.com/

Creating balanced and interesting beers through innovative brewing techniques and environmentally sensible practices. Eight more minutes south brings you to Burlingame:

Steelhead Brewing Company 333 California Drive 94010 (650) 344-6050 https://steelheadbrewery.com/brewery-restaurant-burlingame/

Take a seventeen-minute drive west to the coast and the town of Pacifica:

Pedro Point Brewing 55A Bill Drake Way 94044 (650) 735-5813
https://www.pedropointbrewing.com/

Follow the coast about twenty-minutes south to the town of Half Moon Bay with a couple options including a must-visit brewery:

Sacrilege Brewery 730 Main Street 94019 (650) 276-7029
https://sacrilegebrewing.com/

Hop Dogma Brewing Company 270 Capistrano Road #22 94019 (650) 560-8729 http://hopdogma.com/

Half Moon Bay Brewing Company 390 Capistrano Road 94019 (650) 728-2739 https://www.hmbbrewingco.com/

Crafting beers from the finest in-house ingredients. There is a constantly changing list of specialty and seasonal beers to try. Head back east about twenty-minutes to the town of Belmont with a must-visit brewery:

Alpha Acid Brewing Company 121 Industrial Road Unit #11 94002 (650) 394-4728 https://www.alphaacidbrewing.com/

Experimenting with ingredients to offer you a range of unique beers. The primary focus is on IPAs, but you're sure to find something that pleases your palate. Just four minutes south is the city of San Carlos:

Devil's Canyon Brewing Company 935 Washington Street 94070 (650) 592-BREW https://www.devilscanyon.com/

Blue Oak Brewing Company 815 Cherry Lane 94070 (415) 273-9676 https://www.blueoakbrewing.com/

Another six minutes south is Redwood City with a couple options, including a must-visit brewery:

Ghostwood Beer Company 965 Brewster Avenue 94063 https://www.ghostwoodbeer.com/

FreeWheel Brewing Company 3736 Florence Street 94063 (650) 365-2337 http://freewheelbrewing.com/

Combining English tradition with American ambition to offer beers that are full-flavored and balanced. About twenty-minutes further south is the city of Sunnyvale with a few options including a must-visit brewery:

Off the Rails Brewing Company 111 South Murphy Avenue 94086 (408) 773-9500 https://offtherailsbrewing.com/

Faultline Brewing Company 1235 Oakmead Parkway 94085 (408) 736-2739 https://template.citycheers.com/851

Rabbit's Foot Meadery 1246 Birchwood Drive 94089 (408) 747-0770 https://www.rabbitsfootmeadery.com/

Stop by for something different by trying their award-winning meads. Combining the latest in fermentation technology with historical recipes to offer you unique alcoholic beverages. The city of Santa Clara is just eleven minutes south with a couple of options including a must-visit brewery:

Taplands 1171 Homestead Road 95050 (408) 709-2990 http://www.taplands.com/#taplands

Golden State Brewery 1252 Memorex Drive 95050 (408) 727-2337 http://www.goldenstate.beer/

The first brewery in Santa Clara since Prohibition. Enjoy wonderful beers from a state-of-the-art taproom that is kid and dog friendly. Nine minutes south is San Jose with nearly as many brewery options as San Francisco:

Clandestine Brewing Company 980 S 1st Street Ste B 95110 (408) 520-0220 http://www.clandestinebrewing.com/

Tilt Brewing Company 357 E Taylor Street 95112 (408) 278-1008 http://tiltbeer.com/

Camino Brewing 718 S 1st Street 95113 (408) 352-5331 https://caminobrewing.com/

Lazy Duck Brewing 1723 Rogers Avenue Suite E 95112 http://www.lazyduckbrewing.com/

Hapa's Brewing Company 460 Lincoln Avenue Ste 90 95126 (408) 982-3299 https://hapasbrewing.com/

Strike Brewing Company 2099 S 10th Street Unit 30 95112 (669) 342-6480 https://www.strikebrewingco.com/

Uproar Brewing Company 439 S First Street 95113 (408) 673-2266
https://www.uproarbrewing.com/

Hermitage Brewing 1627 S 7th Street 95112 (408) 291-0966
https://hermitagebrewing.com/

Floodcraft Brewery and Taproom 777 The Alameda 95126 (408) 207-1126 http://floodcraftbrewing.com/

Campbell is ten minutes southwest and has a must-visit brewery:

Campbell Brewing Company 200 East Campbell Avenue 95008 (408) 796-7584 https://www.campbellbrewing.com/

Dedicated to brewing full-flavored beers with a focus on quality. Come try their exciting beers today. Another nine minutes southwest brings you to the end of the trail in Los Gatos:

Loma Brewing Company 130 North Santa Cruz Avenue 95030 (408) 560-9626 https://www.lomabrew.com/

Napa and Lake Counties

These two counties are at the heart of wine country in California. They don't have nearly as many breweries, but what they do have are excellent choices. Take a day or two to travel these two counties and enjoy the wonderful brews you can sample. Start your trip out in Napa with a couple of options and a must-visit brewery:

Tannery Bend Beerworks 101 S Coombs Street Suite X 94559 (707) 681-5774 https://tannerybendbeerworks.com/

Downtown Joe's American Bar and Grill 902 Main Street 94559 (707) 258-2337 https://www.downtownjoes.com/

Trade Brewing 731 1st Street 94559 (707) 492-8223
http://tradebrewing.com/

Focused on providing unique and delicious beers for craft beer drinkers. Using new methods and ingredients to offer a full range of unique and great tasting beers. About twenty-minutes north brings you to a must-visit brewery in the town of Saint Helena:

Mad Fritz 393 La Fata 94574 (707) 968-5058 http://www.madfritz.com/

Offering unique brewed beer in Napa Valley. Try their lagers and IPAs for a unique tasting experience. Next is the town of Calistoga another eleven minutes north:

Calistoga Inn Restaurant and Brewery 1250 Lincoln Avenue 94515 (707) 942-4101 https://www.calistogainn.com/

About a half-hour north brings you into Lake County and a must-visit brewery at Middletown:

Mount Saint Helena Brewing Company 21167 Calistoga Street 95461 (707) 987-3361 http://sainthelenabrewery.com/

Offering six styles of beer, including an award-winning pale ale and a stout. A half-hour drive brings you to Kelseyville and another must-visit brewery:

Kelsey Creek Brewing 3945 Main Street 95451 (707) 279-2311 http://www.kelseycreekbrewing.com/

Hidden among the high altitude wineries in Lake County is this gem of a brewery. Offering a full range of beers for the new drinker to the aficionado: try everything from a light blonde ale to a robust bourbon barrel stout. The last leg of your trip brings you to the town of Lakeport:

O'Meara Bros. Brewing Company 901 Bevins Street 95453 (707) 262-1234 https://www.omearabros.com/

East Bay Breweries

The East Bay of California is known for a lot of blue-collar and hardworking towns. They also feature a number of great breweries where you can enjoy an excellent beer in a relaxing atmosphere at the end of a long, hard day. Let's consider what you can do in a couple day trip around the East Bay and the breweries they have to offer. Start your trip out in the northern part of the East Bay at Vallejo at:

Mare Island Brewing Company 851 Waterfront Avenue 94592 (707) 556-3000 https://www.mareislandbrewingco.com/

Fifteen minutes south is the city of Martinez with two breweries, one of them is a must-visit:

Del Cielo Brewing 701 Escobar Street #A 94553 (925) 293-4286 https://www.delcielobrewing.com/

Five Suns Brewing 701 Escobar Street Suite C 94553 (925) 957-6706 http://www.fivesunsbrewing.com/

Taste unique and refreshing beers in a laid back atmosphere. The beers here are classic, off-centered, or new because variety is key to enjoying a great beer. Another twelve minutes south brings you to the city of Concord:

Epidemic Ales 150 Mason Circle Suite J 94520 (925) 566-8850 https://www.epidemicales.com/

Next is Walnut Creek, just another nine minutes south:

Calicraft Brewing Company 2700 Mitchell Drive 94598 (925) 478-8103 https://www.calicraft.com/

Fourteen minutes southwest is the city of Moraga:

Canyon Club Brewery 1558 Canyon Road 94556 (925) 376-2337 https://www.canyonclub.works/

Then Danville is about twenty-minutes back in an eastern direction:

Danville Brewery 200 Railroad Avenue 94526 (925) 217-4172 http://www.danvillebrewing.com/

Dublin is twelve more minutes south:

INC 82 Brewing 7370 San Ramon Road 94568 (925) 719-5961
https://www.inc82.com/

Heading east fifteen minutes brings you to Livermore with several options including a must-visit brewery:

Eight Bridges Brewing Company 332 Earhart Way 94551 (925) 961-9160 http://eightbridgesbrewing.com/

Altamont Beer Works Brewery 2402 Research Drive 94550 (925) 443-BEER http://www.altamontbeerworks.com/

Working Man Brewing Company 5542 Brisa Street Ste F 94550 (925) 269-9622 http://workingmanbrewing.com/

Shadow Puppet Brewing Company 4771 Arroyo Vista Suite B 94551 (925) 453-6498 https://shadowpuppetbrewing.com/

Specializing in producing unique beer flavor profiles through traditional brewing techniques and uncommon ingredients. Offering 22 beers to sample. The southernmost destination in the East Bay is Fremont, about a half-hour southwest:

JP DasBrew 44356 South Grimmer Blvd 94538 (510) 270-5345
https://www.dasbrewinc.com/

Consistently brewing world-class German-style beers. A great neighborhood hangout to enjoy a wonderful tasting beer. From here circle back north on the bay side of the East Bay and take about a twenty-minute drive to Hayward with a must-visit brewery:

Buffalo Bill's Brewery 1082 B Street 94541 (510) 886-9823
https://www.buffalobillsbrewery.com/

Started in 1983, this is the first brewpub in the United States. When you stop in here, you'll not only enjoy great beer, but you are enjoying a part of history that played a role in shaping the craft beer scene in the United

States. San Leandro has a couple more options and is just eleven more minutes north:

21st Amendment Brewery 2010 Williams Street 94577 (510) 595-2111 https://www.21st-amendment.com/

Drake's Brewing Company 1933 Davis Street Suite 177 94577 (510) 568-2739 https://drinkdrakes.com/

Ten more minutes north brings you to Alameda with a few options including a must-visit brewery:

Faction Brewing 2501 Monarch Street 94501 (510) 523-BREW https://www.factionbrewing.com/

Alameda Island Brewing Company 1716 Park Street 94501 (510) 217-8885 https://www.alamedaislandbrewing.com/

Almanac Beer Company 651 W Tower Avenue 94501 (415) 992-3438 https://almanacbeer.com/

Brewing a bold and delicious range of beers for you to try. Ranging from fresh ales to barrel-aged stouts. A short seven-minute drive brings you to Oakland with the most breweries in the East Bay trip and at least one must-visit brewery:

Ale Industries 3096 E 10th Street 94601 (510) 479-3185 https://www.aleindustries.com/

Original Pattern Brewing Company 292 4th Street 94607 (510) 844-4833 https://www.originalpatternbeer.com/

Federation Brewing Company 420 3rd Street 94607 (510) 496-4228 https://www.federationbrewing.com/

Temescal Brewing 4115 Telegraph Avenue 94609 (510) 899-5628 https://www.temescalbrewing.com/

Roses' Taproom 4930 Telegraph Avenue 94609 (510) 858-3969
https://www.rosestaproom.com/

Oakland United Beerworks 262 2nd Street 94607 (510) 251-8898
https://oaklandunitedbeerworks.com/

Ghost Town Brewing 1960 Adeline Street 94607 (510) 926-6728
https://www.ghosttownbrewing.com/

Novel Brewing Company 6510 San Pablo Avenue 94608 (510) 922-9974 https://www.novelbrewing.com/

Old Kan Beer and Company 95 Linden Street 94607 (510) 338-3965
http://old-kan.com/

This brewery reflects the long and rich history of brewing in Oakland. Offering light to dark and mild to full-bodied beers. When you're ready another ten-minute drive north brings you to Berkeley with another wide range of brewery options:

Jupiter 2181 Shattuck Avenue 94704 (510) 843-8277
http://www.jupiterbeer.com/#pizza/beer

The Rare Barrel 940 Parker Street 94710 (510) 984-6585
https://www.therarebarrel.com/

Fieldwork Brewing Company 1160 Sixth Street 94710 (510) 898-1203
https://fieldworkbrewing.com/

Triple Rock Brewery and Alehouse 1920 Shattuck Avenue 94704 (510) 843-2739 http://triplerock.com/

Gilman Brewing Company 912 Gilman Street 94710 (510) 556-8701
https://gilmanbrew.com/

Offering trustworthy and dependable beers. Stop in today to try their award-winning beers. El Cerrito is another ten minutes north:

Elevation 66 Brewing 10082 San Pablo Avenue 94530 (510) 525-4800
https://www.elevation66.com/home

Seven minutes north brings you to the end of the trail at Richmond with a few options including two must-visit breweries:

Armistice Brewing Company 845 Marina Bay Parkway Ste 1 94804 (510) 230-4966 https://www.armisticebrewing.com/

Benoit-Casper Brewing Company 1201 Pennsylvania Avenue 94801 (408) 695-3449 https://www.bcbrewing.com/

The first brewery in Richmond. The beers here are inspired by Belgian, Hoppy-American, and traditional German styles. The beers aren't filtered and are cold conditioned naturally.

East Brother Beer Company 1001 Canal Blvd 94804 (510) 230-4081 http://www.eastbrotherbeer.com/

Focused on tradition and brewing classic style beers. Offering several options on tap so you will find something you like.

Denver is home to a lot of breweries, and there are also plenty of other activities to do in the city. So hang out as many days as you want and take the time to enjoy some breweries. If you can't make it to all of them, then at least try to get to the must-visit breweries on this list.

Denver

Woods Boss Brewing 2210 California Street 80205 (303) 727-9203
https://www.woodsbossbrewing.com/

The Grateful Gnome Sandwich Shoppe and Brewery 4369 Stuart Street 80212 (720) 598-6893 https://www.thegratefulgnome.com/

Comrade Brewing Company 7667 E Iliff Avenue Unit F 80231 (720) 748-0700 https://comradebrewing.com/

Briar Common Brewery 2298 Clay Street 80211 (720) 470-3731
http://www.briarcommon.com/

Platt Park Brewing Company 1875 S Pearl Street 80210 (303) 968-6674
https://www.plattparkbrewing.com/

FlyteCo Brewing 4499 W 38th Avenue Ste 101 80212 (720) 772-7319
https://flyteco.beer/

The Empourium Brewing Company 4385 W 42nd Avenue 80212 (720)
361-2973 https://theempourium.com/

Strange Craft Beer Company 1330 Zuni Street Unit M 80204 (720) 985-
2337 http://strangecraft.com/

Good River Beer 918 W 1st Avenue 80223 (303) 362-0767
https://goodriverbeer.com/home

LowDown Brewery 800 Lincoln Street 80203 (720) 524-8065
http://www.lowdownbrewery.com/

Dos Luces Brewery 1236 South Broadway 80210 (720) 379-7763
https://dosluces.com/

Burns Family Artisan Ales 2505 W 2nd Avenue Unit 13 80219 (720)
693-9099 https://burnsalesdenver.com/

Little Machine 2924 W 20th Avenue 80211 (303) 284-7893
https://www.littlemachinebeer.com/

Long Table Brewhouse 2895 Fairfax Street 80207 (720) 486-0927
https://www.lngtbl.com/

Copper Kettle Brewing Company 1338 S Valentia Street #100 80247
(720) 443-2522 https://www.copperkettledenver.com/

Wit's End Brewing Company 1330 Zuni Street Unit M 80204 (720) 985-
2337 https://www.witsendbrewing.com/

Cerveceria Colorado 1635 Platte Street 80202 (720) 279-8248
https://www.cerveceriacolorado.com/

Blue Tile Brewing 1609 58th Street 80216 (720) 242-8384
https://www.coloradobrewerylist.com/brewery/blue-tile-brewing/

Banded Oak Brewing Company 470 Broadway 80203 (720) 479-8033
http://bandedoakbrewing.com/

Tivoli Brewing Company 900 Auraria Parkway 80204 (303) 582-6039
http://tivolibrewingco.com/

River North Brewery 6021 Washington Street Unit A 80216 (303) 296-2617 https://www.rivernorthbrewery.com/

Counter Culture Brewery and Grill 205 E 7th Avenue 80203 (720) 638-8786 https://www.counterculturebrewery.com/

Station 26 Brewing Company 7045 E 38th Avenue 80207 (303) 333-1825 http://www.station26brewing.co/

Chain Reaction Brewing Company 902 S Lipan Street 80223 (303) 922-0960 https://www.chainreactionbrewingco.com/

14er Brewing Company 3120 Blake Street Unit C 80205 (720) 773-1437
https://www.14erbrewing.com/

Black Shirt Brewing Company 3719 Walnut Street 80205 (303) 993-2799 https://www.blackshirtbrewingco.com/

Our Mutual Friend Malt and Brew 2810 Larimer Street 80205 (720) 722-2810 https://www.buyomfbeer.com/

Pints Pub 221 W 13th Avenue 80204 (303) 534-7543
http://www.pintspub.com/

Grandma's House 1710 South Broadway 80210 (303) 578-6754
https://www.grandmasbeer.co/

Bierstadt Lagerhause 2875 Blake Street 80205 (720) 372-3791
https://bierstadtlager.com/

Goldspot Brewing 4970 Lowell Blvd 80221 (303) 350-0287
https://www.goldspotbrewing.com/

Black Project Spontaneous and Wild Ales 1290 S Broadway A51
80210 (720) 900-5551 http://www.blackprojectbeer.com/

Crazy Mountain Brewery 471 Kalamath Street 80204 (720) 536-6800
https://crazymountainbrewery.com/

Raices Brewing Company 2060 W Colfax Avenue 80204 (720) 295-2437
https://www.raicesbrewing.com/

Bruz Beers 1675 W 67th Avenue 80221 (303) 650-2337
https://www.bruzbeers.com/

Alpine Dog Brewing Company 1505 Ogden Street 80218 (720) 214-
5170 https://alpinedogbrewery.com/

Call To Arms Brewing Company 4526 Tennyson Street 80212 (720)
328-8258 https://calltoarmsbrewing.com/

Zuni Street Brewing 2355 W 29th Avenue 80211 (303) 515-0942
https://www.zunistreet.com/

Diebolt Brewing Company 3855 Mariposa Street 80211 (918) 625-9038
https://dieboltbrewing.com/

Cerebral Brewing 1477 Monroe Street 80206 (303) 927-7365
https://cerebralbrewing.com/

Seedstock Brewery 3610 W Colfax Avenue 80204 (720) 476-7831
https://seedstockbrewery.com/

Baere Brewing Company 320 Broadway Unit E 80203 (970) 910-4810
http://www.baerebrewing.com/

Black Sky Brewery 490 Santa Fe Drive 80204 (720) 708-5816
https://blackskybrewing.com/index.html

Denver Chophouse and Brewery 1735 19th Street #100 80202 (303) 296-0800 https://www.chophouse.com/

Factotum Brewhouse 3845 Lipan Street 80211 (720) 441-4735 https://factotumbrewhouse.com/

Great Divide Brewing Company 2201 Arapahoe Street 80205 (303) 296-9460 https://greatdivide.com/

Ratio Beerworks 2920 Larimer Street 80205 (303) 997-8288 http://ratiobeerworks.com/

Spangalang Brewery 2736 Welton Street 80205 (303) 297-1276 https://spangalangbrewery.com/

TRVE Brewing Company 227 Broadway #101 80203 (303) 351-1021 https://www.trvebrewing.com/

Wynkoop Brewing Company 1634 18th Street 80202 (303) 297-2700 https://wynkoop.com/

Breckenridge Brewery 471 Kalamath Street 80204 (303) 573-0431 https://www.breckbrew.com/

The third oldest craft brewery in Colorado. Stop in to enjoy their wonderful beers while taking in beautiful mountain views.

Crooked Stave Artisan Beer Project 3350 Brighton Blvd 80216 (720) 550-8860 http://www.crookedstave.com/

A modern, artisan brewery. All the beers here are brewed with an attention to detail. Come try the flavor difference.

Denver Beer Company 1695 Platte Street 80202 (303) 433-2739 https://denverbeerco.com/

Serving premium artisan ales and lagers made from fresh ingredients. The beer selections change with the seasons, but you're sure to find something you'll enjoy.

Fiction Beer Company 7101 East Colfax Avenue 80220 (303) 931-6112
http://www.fictionbeer.com/

Each of the beers here has a unique flavor, aroma, and texture. Try an emerging beer style or an interpretation of a classic beer style.

Renegade Brewing Company 925 W 9th Avenue 80204 (720) 401-4089
https://renegadebrewing.com/

Offering creative beers that are packed with flavor. Try some of their year-round beers and make sure to try one of their specialty or seasonal beers.

Boulder

Aside from Denver, Boulder has the second most breweries. Again you can spend as many days as you need in the city visiting the breweries and taking in the sites. If you don't have enough time to visit them all, then at least make sure you visit the must-visit breweries.

Adamant Brewing and Blending 1001 Lee Hill Drive Unit 10 80302 (303) 396-0788 http://adamant.beer/

Avery Brewing Company 4910 Nautilus Court 80301 (303) 440-4324
https://www.averybrewing.com/

Vision Quest Brewery 2510 47th Street Unit A2 80301 (303) 578-0041
http://www.visionquestbrewing.com/

Gunbarrel Brewing Company 7088 Winchester Circle 80301 (800) 803-5732 https://gunbarrelbrewing.com/

Finkel and Garf Brewing Company 5455 Spine Road 80301 (720) 379-6042 http://www.finkelandgarf.com/

Mountain Sun Pub and Brewery 1535 Pearl Street 80302 (303) 546-0886 http://www.mountainsunpub.com/

Upslope Brewing Company 1898 S Flatiron Court 80304 (303) 396-1898
https://www.upslopebrewing.com/

BRU Handbuilt Ales 5290 Arapahoe Avenue 80303 (720) 638-5193
https://bruboulder.com/

Never filtered, naturally carbonated ales. Pair it with sustainably made, award-winning food options.

Sanitas Brewing Company 3550 Frontier Avenue Unit A 80301 (303) 332-2439 https://www.sanitasbrewing.com/

No matter what beer style you enjoy, be sure to try their famous lagers. You can also enjoy a crisp ale or a full-bodied stout.

Beyond the Mountain Brewing Company 6035 Longbow Drive Unit 109 80301 (303) 530-6981 https://www.beyondthemountainbrewing.com/

This award-winning brewery features 12 taps of year-round, seasonal, and small-batch beers. Everything is made from the finest ingredients to offer you exceptional beers.

Boulder Beer 2880 Wilderness Place 80301 (303) 444-8448
https://boulderbeer.com/

The first craft brewery in Colorado. Try their award-winning porters, stouts, and bitters. There are also plenty of other styles available if you prefer something else.

Asher Brewing Company 4699 Nautilus Court S 80301 (303) 530-1381
https://www.asherbrewing.com/

The first all-organic brewery in Colorado. Making excellent ales that are better for you and the environment. Come try some today.

287 Brewery Trail

If you want to get away from the big cities of Boulder and Denver, but still want to enjoy beautiful mountain views, then you should consider taking the 287 Brewery Trail. This trail can take several days to complete depending on how many breweries you choose to visit, but it will take you to a number of quaint towns along the Rocky Mountain area of Colorado.

Start your trip in the city of Fort Collins where you have many breweries to choose from as well as several must-visit breweries:

Funkwerks 1900 E Lincoln Avenue Unit B 80524 (970) 482-3865
https://funkwerks.com/

Maxline Brewing 2701 S College Avenue Unit 190 80525 (970) 286-2855
https://maxlinebrewing.com/

Coopersmith's Pub and Brewing 5 Old Time Square 80524 (970) 498-0483 https://coopersmithspub.com/

Equinox Brewing Company 133 Remington Street 80521 (970) 430-6489 https://equinoxbrewing.com/

DC Oakes Brewhouse and Eatery 3581 Harmony Road #110 80528 (970) 286-2076 https://www.dcoakesbrewhouse.com/

Purpose Brewing and Cellars 4025 S Mason Street 80525 (970) 377-4107 https://purposebrewing.com/

Envy Brewing 3027 E Harmony Road Suite 2 80528 (970) 698-6975
https://www.envybrewing.com/

Gilded Goat Brewing Company 3500 S College Avenue 80525 (970) 825-7192 https://gildedgoatbrewing.com/

Intersect Brewing 2160 W Drake Road Ste A-1 80526 (970) 682-2041
https://www.intersectbrewing.com/

Zwei Bruder Brewing 4612 S Mason Street 80525 (970) 223-2482
https://www.zweibrewing.com/default.aspx

Odell Brewing Company 800 East Lincoln Avenue 80524 (970) 498-9070 https://www.odellbrewing.com/

Developing innovative beer styles with new brewing techniques. Stop by their taproom to try the latest innovative beer.

Snowbank Brewing 225 N Lemay Avenue Ste 1 80524 (970) 999-5658 http://www.snowbank.beer/

When you come here, you get to try a wide range of beers. Be sure to try their Cranknbrew, Colorado Red, and Sourado.

Black Bottle Brewery 1611 S College Avenue Ste 1609 80525 (970) 493-2337 https://blackbottlebrewery.com/

Offering the widest selection of craft beer in Fort Collins. You can also enjoy a full wine bar in case you want to try something else.

Jessup Farm Barrel House 1921 Jessup Drive 80525 (970) 568-8345 https://www.jessupfarmbarrelhouse.com/

Brewing approachable and complex barrel-aged craft beer. Stop in to try something different and wonderful.

Rally King Brewing 1624 S Lemay Avenue Unit #4 80525 (970) 568-8936 https://rallykingbrewing.com/

Up to 18 beers on tap ranging from ales to lagers to sours. There is an option for every palate.

McClellan's Brewing Company 1035 S Taft Hill Road 80521 (970) 568-8473 http://www.mcclellansbrewingcompany.com/

A brewer of fine handcrafted cask ales that are brewed in traditional Celtic style. Enjoy your beer in a wonderful setting. Next, head a little north to Wellington:

Sparge Brewing 3999 GW Bush Avenue #101 80549 (970) 372-2780 https://www.spargebrew.com/

Old Colorado Brewing Company 8121 S 1st Street 80549 (970) 217-2129 http://oldcoloradobrewing.com/

Take a trip to Timnath in the East along 25:

Timnath Beerwerks 4138 Main Street 80547 (970) 999-5751
https://www.timnathbeerwerks.com/

Continue further east to the town of Windsor:

Mighty River Brewing Company 6383 Fairgrounds Avenue 80550 (970) 966-7955 https://mightyriverbrewing.com/

High Hops Brewery 6461 Highway 392 80550 (970) 674-2841
https://highhopsbrewery.com/

Mash Lab Brewing 4395 Highland Meadows Parkway 80550 (970) 685-0334 https://mashlabbrewing.com/mashlab/

A little further East is the small town of Severence:

G5 Brewpub 1018 Mahogany Way 80550 (970) 686-7065
https://www.g5brewpub.com/

The farthest East you can head is the city Greeley with several brewery options including two must-visit breweries:

Green Earth Brewing Company 725 10th Street 80631 (970) 702-2332
https://greenearthbrewingco.com/

Broken Plow Brewery 4731 W 10th Street Unit G 80634 (970) 301-4575
https://www.brokenplowbrewery.com/

Lonesome Buck 819 9th Street 80631 (970) 473-2825
https://www.lonesomebuck.com/

Crabtree Brewing Company 2961 29th Street 80631 (970) 356-0516
https://www.crabtreebrewing.com/

Wiley Roots Brewing Company 625 3rd Street Unit D 80631 (970) 515-7315 http://www.wileyroots.com/

A small and independently owned brewery. They have a unique focus on mixed-culture, barrel-aged, and spontaneous beers.

WeldWerks Brewing Company 508 8th Avenue 80631 (970) 460-6345
https://weldwerksbrewing.com/

Innovation and experimentation are key, as evidenced by the over 100 unique beers they have brewed. Covering a wide range of styles from classic lagers to imperial stouts and hazy IPAs. Once back on the 287, the next main city is Loveland where you have multiple brewery options as well as a must-visit brewery:

Rock Coast Brewery 414 E 6th Street 80537 (970) 617-2325
https://rockcoastbrewery.com/

Loveland Aleworks 118 West 4th Street 80537 (970) 619-8726
http://www.lovelandaleworks.com/

Verboten Brewing and Barrel Project 127 E 5th Street 80537 (970) 775-7371 https://verbotenbrewing.com/

Tilted Barrel Brew Pub 110 E 29th Street 80538 (970) 619-8950
http://tiltedbarrelbrewpub.com/

Grimm Brothers Brewhouse 623 N Denver Avenue 80537 (970) 624-6045 http://grimmbrosbrewhouse.com/

Crow Hop Brewing Company 217 East 3rd Street 80537 (970) 633-0643
https://www.crowhopbrewing.com/

Big Thompson Brewery 114 15th Street 80538 (970) 619-8138
https://www.lovelandbrewery.com/

Big Beaver Brewing Company 2707 W Eisenhower Blvd Unit 9 80537 (970) 818-6064 https://bigbeaverbrew.com/

All beers are brewed in the traditional German style with only the best ingredients. When you try their beers, you'll be able to taste the difference. Take another trip to the West this time and the city of Estes Park that has a few options including a must-visit brewery:

Rock Cut Brewing Company 390 W Riverside Avenue 80517 (970) 586-7300 https://www.rockcutbrewing.com/

Avant Garde Aleworks 920 Dunraven Street 80517 (970) 443-1117 https://avantgardealeworks.com/

Lumpy Ridge Brewing Company 513 S Saint Vrain Avenue 80517 (812) 201-3836 https://www.lumpyridgebrewing.com/

Estes Park Brewery 470 Prospect Village Drive 80517 (970) 586-5421 http://www.epbrewery.com/

Offering 12 fresh, handcrafted brews. In addition to beers, they also offer a range of excellent food for pairing. Back on the 287, stop in the town of Berthoud for a couple breweries:

Berthoud Brewing Company 450 8th Street 80513 (970) 670-0774 https://www.berthoudbrewing.com/

City Star Brewing Company 321 Mountain Avenue 80513 (970) 532-7827 https://citystarbrewing.com/

The next main city along 287 is Longmont with multiple brewery options including three must-visit breweries:

Shoes and Brews 63 South Pratt Parkway Unit B 80501 (720) 340-4290 https://www.shoesbrews.com/

Left Hand Brewing Company 1265 Boston Avenue 80501 (303) 772-0258 https://www.lefthandbrewing.com/

Collision Brewing Company 1436 Skyway Drive 80504 (720) 996-1850 https://collisionbrewco.com/

300 Suns Brewing 335 1st Avenue Unit C 80501 (303) 257-6032 https://www.300sunsbrewing.com/

Oskar Blues Brewery 1800 Pike Road 80501 (303) 823-6685 https://www.oskarblues.com/

Pumphouse Brewery 540 Main Street 80501 (303) 702-0881

http://pumphousebrewery.com/

The year-round offerings are popular and straight-forward beer styles. The seasonal beers are more creative and rotate regularly so be sure to try one when you're here.

Primitive Beer 2025 Ionosphere Street Unit 101 80504

https://primitive.beer/

The first entirely spontaneous, barrel-fermented beer "blendery" in Colorado. Using Belgian brewing techniques, the beers here are funky, yet balanced with the flavor profile.

Wibby Brewing 209 Emery Street 80501 (303) 776-4594

https://www.wibbybrewing.com/

Crafting American-influenced, German-style lagers. Here you'll be able to taste lagers that often aren't found in the craft beer community. A short trip to the West brings you to the small town of Niwot:

Bootstrap Brewing 6778 N 79th Street 80503 (720) 438-8488

https://bootstrapbrewing.com/

Cross back over the 287 and take a trip to the East and the town of Erie:

Echo Brewpub 600 Briggs Street 80516 (720) 445-5969

http://echobrewing.com/

Continue East to the town of Brighton with a must-visit brewery:

Something Brewery 117 N Main Street Unit A 80501 (720) 639-7505

https://www.somethingbrewery.com/

An uncommon and creative brewery that is focused on brewing creative and inspiring beers. Mostly offering ales, there are plenty of unique styles that are sure to please any palate. Head back to the 287 and the city of Lafayette with several options as well as a must-visit brewery:

Front Range Brewing Company 400 W South Boulder Road Suite 1650 80026 (720) 201-7481 https://www.frontrangebrewingcompany.com/

Endo Brewing Company 2755 Dagny Way 80026 (720) 442-8052 https://endobrewing.com/

Cellar West Artisan Ales 778 W Baseline Road 80302 (720) 465-9346 https://www.cellarwest.com/

Liquid Mechanics Brewing Company 297 N US Highway 287 Ste 100 80026 (720) 550-7813 http://www.liquidmechanicsbrewing.com/

Odd13 Brewing 301 E Simpson Street 80026 (303) 997-4164 http://www.odd13brewing.com/

The Post Brewing Company 105 W Emma Street 80026 (303) 593-2066 https://www.postbrewing.com/

The beers here are delicious and memorable, you'll want to drink them again and again. Enjoy excellent food as well that is designed to be paired with the various beers they offer. Head a short distance West to the city of Louisville with several options as well as a must-visit brewery:

Redgarden Restaurant and Brewery 1700 Dogwood Street 80027 (303) 927-6361 https://redgardenbrewery.com/

12Degree Brewing 820 Main Street 80027 (720) 638-1623 http://www.12degree.com/

Gravity Brewing 1150 Pine Street Unit B 80027 (303) 544-0746 http://thegravitybrewing.com/

Crystal Springs Brewing Company 657 S Taylor Avenue Unit E 80027 (303) 665-8888 https://www.crystalspringsbrewing.com/

Offering some of the best craft beer in the area made from malt and hops from around the world. Sample from 13 rotating taps. Further West is the town of Nederland with a couple options as well as a must-visit brewery:

The Very Nice Brewing Company #112 20 Lakeview Drive 80466 (303) 258-3770 http://www.verynicebrewing.com/index.html

Knotted Root Brewing Company 250 N Caribou Street 80466 (303) 258-3771 https://www.knottedrootbrewing.com/

Using elements of traditional Belgian brewing along with American experimentation to produce a wide range of beers. The focus is on unfiltered hoppy ales, smooth-style sours, and rustic farmhouse ales. Back at the end of the 287 is the city of Broomfield with a few options including a must-visit brewery:

4 Noses Brewing Company 8855 W 116th Circle Ste 4 80021 (720) 460-2797 https://www.4nosesbrewing.com/

Wonderland Brewing Company 5450 W 120th Avenue 80020 (303) 953-0400 https://wonderlandbrewing.com/

Big Choice Brewing 7270 W 118th Place 80020 (303) 469-2616 http://www.bigchoicebrewing.com/

Rails End Beer Company 11625 Reed Court Unit B 80020 (303) 353-8121 https://railsendbeerco.com/

Offering a range of options for all tastes. There are light and refreshing beers to dark, malty, and smooth beers. Cut over to the 25 and continue South to the city of Thornton:

Mother Trucker Brewery 2360 E 120th Avenue 80241 (303) 565-9459 https://www.mothertuckerbrewery.com/

Satire Brewing Company 12136 Grant Circle Suite C 80241 (720) 275-0667 https://www.coloradobrewerylist.com/brewery/satire-brewing-company/

A little further South is the town of Westminster with a couple options, including a must-visit brewery:

Frolic Brewing 12910 Zuni Street #1300 80234 (303) 993-7443
https://www.frolicbrewing.com/

Kokopelli Beer Company 8931 Harlan Street 80031 (720) 840-6835
http://kokopellibeerco.com/

A completely women-owned and operated brewpub. Featuring 30 unique taps covering the entire style spectrum of beer. From here you can head East to the city of Aurora with several options including three must-visit breweries:

Ursula Brewery 2101 N Ursula Court 80045 (720) 324-8529
http://ursulabrewery.com/

Cheluna Brewing Company 2501 Dallas Street 80010 (720) 600-0020
https://www.cheluna.com/

Peak to Peak Tap Room 16701 E Iliff Avenue 80013 (720) 446-8714
https://peakbrews.com/

Dry Dock Brewing Company 15120 E Hampden Avenue 80014 (303) 400-5606 https://drydockbrewing.com/

The first brewery in Aurora. Be sure to try their Vanilla Porter. Other options are ales and a number of fruit-flavored beer options.

Launch Pad Brewery 884 S Buckley Road 80017 (303) 745-4599
https://launchpadbrewery.com/

Using the highest quality ingredients to fuel beers with the utmost integrity. Offering a wide range of over 30 beers.

Bent Barley Brewing Company 6200 S Main Street Suite 110 80016 (303) 627-5799 http://www.bentbarley.com/index.html

Brewing classic styles of ales and lagers while also creating unique beers to challenge all who enjoy a great beer. Head back east and visit the town of Lakewood with a few options:

Old 121 Brewhouse 1057 S Wadsworth Blvd Suite 60 80226 (303) 986-0311 https://old121brewhouse.com/

Great Frontier Brewing Company 2010 S Oak Street 80227 (303) 257-5959 http://www.greatfrontierbeer.com/

Green Mountain Beer Company 2585 S Lewis Way Suite 110 80227 (303) 986-2990 https://www.greenmountainbeercompany.com/

LandLocked Ales Brewery and Taproom 3225 S Wadsworth Blvd 80277 (303) 284-8748 https://www.landlockedales.com/

Just a little north is the town of Edgewater with a couple options, including a must-visit brewery:

Joyride Brewing Company 2501 Sheridan Blvd 80214 (720) 432-7560 https://joyridebrewing.com/

Barquentine Brewing Company 5505 W 20th Avenue Suite 178 80214 (303) 955-1238 https://www.barquentinebrewing.com/

A brewer of authentic Belgian style beers. Using traditional beer recipes, but modernized for the discerning palate to enjoy. The next town to the north is Wheat Ridge:

Brewery Rickoli 4335 Wadsworth Blvd 80033 (303) 344-8988 https://www.breweryrickoli.com/

Colorado Plus Brewpub 6995 W 38th Avenue 80033 (720) 353-4853 https://www.coloradoplus.net/

The last stop north is Arvada with several options including a must-visit brewery:

Odyssey Beerwerks 5535 West 56th Avenue Suite 107 80002 (512) 633-1884 https://www.odysseybeerwerks.com/

New Image Brewing Company 5622 Yukon Street 80002 (770) 881-1010 https://www.nibrewing.com/

Some Place Else Brewery 6425 W 52nd Avenue Unit 6/6B 80002 (720) 512-4162 https://www.someplaceelse.beer/

Spice Trade Brewing 7803 Ralston Road 80002 (303) 431-9000 https://spicetradebrewing.com/

Brewing unique beer styles inspired by culinary ingredients and traditions from around the world. Come try their delicious beers today. Head further west to the city of Golden with multiple options as well as a must-visit brewery:

Barrels and Bottles Brewery 600 12th Street 80401 (720) 328-3643 https://www.barrelsbottles.com/

Holidaily Brewing Company 801 Brickyard Circle Unit B 80403 (303) 530-3593 https://holidailybrewing.com/

Over Yonder Brewing Company 18455 W Colfax Avenue Suite 103 80401 (303) 278-0399 https://www.overyonderbrewing.com/

Golden City Brewery 920 12th Street 80401 (303) 279-8092 https://www.goldencity.beer/

Ohm Brewing 1921 Youngfield Street #210 80401 (720) 535-4279 https://www.ohmbrewingcompany.com/

Cannonball Creek Brewing Company 393 N Washington Avenue 80403 (303) 278-0111 https://www.cannonballcreekbrewing.com/

New Terrain Brewing Company 16401 Table Mountain Parkway 80403 (720) 771-6997 https://newterrainbrewing.com/

Focusing on crafting exploratory beers. The beers here are constantly evolving, so you'll always have something new to enjoy. The farthest west is the town of Idaho Springs:

Tommyknocker Brewery 1401 Miner Street 80452 (303) 567-2688 https://tommyknocker.com/

As you head back to the east, stop by the town of Evergreen:

El Rancho Brewing Company 29260 US Highway 40 80439 (303) 670-2739 https://www.elranchobrewing.com/

Lariat Lodge Brewing Company 27618 Fireweed Drive 80439 (303) 807-4305 https://www.lariatlodgebrewing.com/

Head back to the 25 and take the branch off to the 85 where you come to the city of Littleton:

Coal Mine Ave Brewing 9719 W Coal Mine Avenue Unit A 80123 (720) 504-4866 https://coalmineavebrewing.com/

Jackass Hill Brewery 2409 W Main Street 80120 (720) 242-7492 https://www.jackasshillbrewery.com/

Living the Dream Brewing Company 12305 Dumont Way Unit A 80125 (303) 284-9585 https://livingthedreambrewing.com/

Locavore Beer Works 5950 S Platte Canyon Road 80123 (720) 476-4419 https://www.locavorebeerworks.com/

To the East you can find the town of Greenwood Village:

Peak View Brewing 9672 E Arapahoe Road 80112 (303) 353-4309 https://www.peakviewbrewing.com/

A little further south is Highlands Ranch with a couple options:

Grist Brewing Company 9150 Commerce Center Circle Suite 300 80129 (720) 360-4782 https://www.gristbrewingcompany.com/

3 Freaks Brewery 7140 E County Line Road 80126 (720) 299-0994 https://3freaksbrewery.com/

From here, head east to the city of Centennial with a few options including a must-visit brewery:

Resolute Brewing Company 7286 S Yosemite Street Suite 110 80112 (720) 722-1238 https://resolutebrewingco.com/

Blue Spruce Brewing Company 4151 E County Line Road Unit G 80122 (303) 771-0590 https://www.bluesprucebrewing.com/

Two22 Brew 4550 South Reservoir Road 80015 (720) 328-9038 http://www.two22brew.com/

Halfpenny Brewing Company 5150 E Arapahoe Road Unit D-1B 80122 (720) 583-0580 https://www.halfpennybrewing.com/

A family-friendly, neighborhood craft brewery. Specializing in handcrafted beers of German and English styles. To the south there is a must-visit brewery in Lone Tree:

Lone Tree Brewing Company 8200 Park Meadows Drive Ste 8222 80124 (303) 792-5822 https://www.lonetreebrewingco.com/

The lineup of beers here contains something for everyone, from classic IPAs to a Mexican lager. There are also 10 rotating seasonal taps, so you'll always have something new to try. To the east is the town of Parker:

Welcome Home Brewery 19523 Hess Road #103 80134 (303) 362-1213 https://www.ontapcu.org/business/welcome-home-brewery

Back to the west slightly is Castle Rock with a few options including a must-visit brewery:

105 West Brewing Company 1043 Park Street 80109 (303) 325-7321 https:/eric9956.wixsite.com/105westbrewing

BURLY Brewing Company 680 Atchison Way Suite 800 80109 (720) 486-0541 https://www.burlybrewing.com/

Wild Blue Yonder Brewing 519 Wilcox Street 80104 (303) 957-7689 https://wildblueyonderbrewing.com/

Rockyard Brewing 880 Castleton Road 80104 (303) 814-9273
https://www.rockyard.com/

The longest-running brewpub in Douglas County. The beers have won many awards, but none more than their German-style Pilsner. Take a drive back West to end your trip in the town of Bailey with a must-visit brewery:

Mad Jack's Mountain Brewery 23 Main Street 80421 (303) 816-2337
https://www.madjacksmountainbrewery.com/

Providing a unique product only found in this area of Colorado. Come enjoy the community atmosphere and enjoy some great, unique beers.

Pikes Peak Breweries

When visiting the breweries in this area, you can make a circle trip that can be done in a day or two, depending on how many breweries you choose to visit. Start your trip in Buena Vista:

Eddyline Brewery 102 Linderman Avenue 81211 (719) 966-6018
https://eddylinebrewing.com/

From here head about an hour east to the town of Divide where there is a must-visit brewery:

Paradox Beer Company 10 Buffalo Court 80814 (719) 686-8081
http://paradoxbeercompany.com/index.php

Focused on barrel-aged sour beers. Each beer offers a unique taste and perspective, so you'll find something pleasing to your palate. Another half-hour east brings you to the town of Manitou Springs and another must-visit brewery:

Manitou Brewing Company725 Manitou Avenue 80829 (719) 282-7709
https://www.manitoubrewing.com/

The closest brewery to Pikes Peak. Offering a variety of beers brewed on-site so you will find something your palate enjoys. A short ten minutes east brings you to Colorado Springs with many brewery options including several must-visit breweries:

Storybook Brewing 3121 N El Paso Street Ste A 80907 (719) 633-6266
https://www.storybookbrewing.com/

Smiling Toad Brewery 2028 Sheldon Avenue 80904 (719) 418-2936
https://smilingtoadbrewery.com/

Peaks N Pines Brewing Company 4005 Tutt Blvd 80922 (719) 358-6758
https://peaksnpinesbrewery.com/

Colorado Mountain Brewery 1110 Interquest Parkway 80921 (719) 963-5645 https://www.cmbrew.com/

Cogstone Brewing Company 3858 Village Seven Road 80917 (719) 418-6596 http://cogstonebrewing.com/

Atrevida Beer Company 204 Mount View Lane #3 80907 (719) 266-4200
https://www.atrevidabeerco.com/

Nano 108 Brewing Company 2402 Waynoka Road 80915 (719) 596-2337 http://www.nano108brewing.com/

Black Forest Brewing Company 11590 Black Forest Road #50 80908 (719) 396-2011 http://blackforestbrewingco.com/

FH Beerworks 521 S Tejon Street 80903 (719) 640-6814
http://www.fieldhousebrew.com/

Brass Brewing Company 318 E Colorado Avenue 80903 (719) 308-2161
https://www.brassbrewing.com/

Cerberus Brewing Company 702 W Colorado Avenue 80905 (719) 494-7977 http://cerberusbrewingco.com/

Phantom Canyon Brewing Company 2 E Pikes Peak Avenue 80903 (719) 635-2800 https://phantomcanyon.com/

Goat Patch Brewing 2727 N Cascade Avenue #123 80907 (719) 471-4628 https://www.goatpatchbrewing.com/

Red Leg Brewing Company 4630 Forge Road 80907 (719) 598-3776 https://redlegbrewing.com/

Bristol Brewing Company 1604 S Cascade Avenue 80906 (719) 633-2555 https://www.bristolbrewing.com/

Lost Friend Brewing Company 2458 Montebello Square Drive 80920 (719) 694-8501 https://www.lostfriendbrewing.com/

Deuces Wild Brewery 660 Peterson Road 80915 (719) 394-4811 https://dwbbrewery.com/

Offering a well-balanced selection of beers for any taste. Be sure to try their award-winning Scottish ale.

Trinity Brewing Company 1466 Garden of the Gods Road 80907 (719) 634-0029 http://www.trinitybrew.com/

Offering beers that challenge your palate. Everything here is done to help reduce ecological impact.

Metric Brewing 1213 North Circle Drive 80909 (719) 418-5560 https://www.metricbrews.com/

Serving award-winning beers from an ever-changing tap. Producing new styles and infinite combinations so you'll always have something new to try. When you're ready, head about a half-hour north to Monument:

Pikes Peak Brewing Company 1756 Lake Woodmoor Drive 80132 (719) 208-4098 https://www.pikespeakbrewing.com/

Another half-hour east brings you to Peyton and the halfway point of the circle:

Jaks Brewing Company 7654 McLaughlin Road 80831 (719) 375-1116 http://jaksbrewing.com/

Head south about an hour to Pueblo with a couple of breweries:

Shamrock Brewing Company 108 West 3rd Street 81003 (719) 542-9974 https://shamrockbrewing.com/

Brues Alehouse Brewing Company 120 Riverwalk Place 81003 (719) 924-9670 http://bruesalehouse.com/

Head back west a half-hour to Florence:

Florence Brewing Company 200 S Pikes Peak Avenue 81226 (719) 784-7441 https://www.florencebrewing.com/

Another hour and a half west brings you to Salida with a couple of brewery options:

Soulcraft Brewing 248 W Rainbow Blvd 81201 (719) 539-5428 https://soulcraftbeer.com/

Moonlight Pizza and BrewPub 242 F Street 81201 (719) 539-4277 https://moonlightpizza.biz/

A short eight-minute drive brings you to the last city on the trail at Poncha Springs with a must-visit brewery:

Elevation Beer Company 115 Pahlone Parkway 81242 (719) 539-5258 https://elevationbeerco.com/

Offering a handful of easy-drinking classics for everyone to enjoy. Also available are unique seasonal, specialty, and barrel-aged beers.

Mountain Range Breweries

If you want to explore the higher elevations or you enjoy the great outdoors in the mountains, there are still breweries to enjoy. This tour will take you high into the mountains to quaint ski towns where you can enjoy breweries year-round. Start your trip in Aspen:

Aspen Brewing Company 304 E Hopkins Avenue 81611 (970) 920-2739
http://aspenbrewingcompany.com/

Next head about twenty-minutes northwest to the town of Basalt:

Capitol Creek Brewery 371 Market Street 81621 (970) 279-5723
http://capitolcreekbrewery.com/

Another twenty-minutes northwest brings you to the town of Carbondale
with a must-visit brewery:

Roaring Fork Beer Company 1942 Dolores Way 81623 (970) 963-5870
http://roaringforkbeerco.com/

Here they brew beers that change with the season. They roll out about two
to three new beers each season. When you stop by, you'll always be able
to try something different. Head north about fifteen minutes to the town of
Glenwood Springs with two breweries including a must-visit brewery:

Glenwood Canyon Brewing 402 7th Street 81601 (970) 945-1276
https://www.glenwoodcanyon.com/

Casey Brewing and Blending 3421 Grand Avenue 81601 (970) 230-
9691 https://caseybrewing.com/

Focused on the idea of bringing back old-world brewing techniques to the
modern-day consumer. The beers are made with local Colorado
ingredients and entirely bottle conditioned. Now head east about a half-
hour to the town of Eagle:

7 Hermits Brewing Company 717 Sylvan Lake Road 81631 (970) 328-
6220 https://7hermitsbrewing.com/

Another sixteen minutes east brings you to a must-visit brewery in the
town of Edwards:

Gore Range Brewery 105 Edwards Village Blvd 81632 (970) 926-2739
http://www.gorerangebrewery.com/

A casual atmosphere with great microbrews makes this an excellent place to hang out. Offering well-brewed beers with the desired flavor palates. Fifteen minutes east brings you to the ski town of Vail:

Vail Brewing Company 41290 B-2 & B-3 US Highway 6 81657 (970) 470-4351 http://www.vailbrewingco.com/

Then head south about forty minutes to the historic town of Leadville:

Periodic Brewing Company 115 E 7th Street 80461 (720) 864-1012 https://www.periodicbrewing.com/

Take about an hour and a half drive through the mountains to the town of Fairplay:

South Park Brewing 285 ½ US Highway 285 80440 (719) 836-1932 https://www.southparkbrewingcolorado.com/

A half-hour north brings you to the town of Breckenridge:

Broken Compass Brewing 68 Continental Court Unit B12 80424 (970) 368-2772 http://www.brokencompassbrewing.com/

A short sixteen-minute drive brings you to Frisco with two breweries:

HighSide Brewing 720 Main Street 80443 (970) 668-2337 https://www.highsidebrewing.com/

Outer Range Brewing Company 182 Lusher Court 80498 (970) 455-8709 https://www.outerrange.com/

Five minutes away is Silverthorne with another two breweries:

The Bakers' Brewery 531 Silverthorne Lane 80498 (970) 468-0170 https://thebakersbrewery.com/

Angry James Brewery 421 Adams Avenue 80498 (970) 455-8800 https://angryjamesbrewing.com/

Next door at four minutes is the town of Dillon with two options including a must-visit brewery:

Pug Ryan's Brewery 104 Village Place 80435 (970) 468-2145
https://www.pugryans.com/

Dillon Dam Brewery 754 Anemone Terrace 80435 (970) 262-7777
http://www.dambrewery.com/

From light to bold, the selection of craft beers here provides you with a wide range of flavors. The staff will help you find something you'll enjoy based on your taste preferences. About twenty-minutes east brings you to the end of the trail in Georgetown:

Guanella Pass Brewing Company 501 Rose Street 80444 (303) 569-5167 https://www.guanellapass.com/

Mountain and Mesas Trail

The Southwest corner of Colorado is home to rugged wilderness. Whether it is mountains or mesas, there is lots to see and do in this area. There are plenty of breweries to keep you busy on a tour of this area, and you can take as many days as you need to see and do all there is in the area. Start your trip in the city of Grand Junction:

Kannah Creek Brewing Company 1960 N 12th Street 81501 (970) 263-0111 https://www.kannahcreekbrewingco.com/

Rockslide Brewery and Pub 405 Main Street 81501 (970) 245-2111
https://www.rockslidebrewpub.com/

Head slightly southeast to the town of Montrose:

Horsefly Brewery 846 East Main Street 81401 (970) 249-6889
https://www.horseflybrewing.com/

Take about an hour drive through the mountain pass to the city of Gunnison with a must-visit brewery:

High Alpine Brewing Company 111 N Main Street 81230 (970) 642-4500 http://highalpinebrewing.com/

Handcrafted beers made for taste and quality. Stop in today to try one of the many beers on tap and taste the difference. Next, you'll drive an hour south in the mountains to the town of Lake City with another must-visit brewery:

Lake City Brewing Company 130A Bluff Street 81235 (970) 944-5222 https://lcbrewco.com/

The first new brewery in Lake City in over 130 years. Mostly offering ales, but also a few stouts and porters for those who like a richer beer. About a two and a half-hour drive through the mountains brings you to the town of Pagosa Springs with two brewery options:

Pagosa Brewing Company 118 N Pagosa Blvd 81147 (970) 731-2739 https://pagosabrewing.com/

Riff Raff Brewing Company 274 Pagosa Street 81147 (970) 264-4677 https://riffraffbrewing.com/

Circle back west to the town of Bayfield about forty minutes away with a must-visit brewery:

Bottom Shelf Brewery 118 E Mill Street 81122 (970) 884-2442 http://bottomshelfbrewery.com/

The handcrafted beers here come in a variety of styles and flavors to meet the most discerning beer palate. Hand-selected hops and barley go into all the beers brewed. Drive about an hour to the town of Dolores:

Dolores River Brewery 100 S 4th Street 81323 (970) 882-4677 http://doloresriverbrewery.com/

A short fourteen minutes south brings you to the town of Cortez with two brewery options:

J. Fargo's Family Dining and Microbrewery 1209 East Main Street 81321 (970) 564-0242 http://jfargos.com/index.html

WildEdge Brewing Collective 111 North Market Street 81321 (970) 565-9445 https://www.wildedgebrewing.com/

Head back east about twenty-minutes to the town of Mancos with a must-visit brewery:

Mancos Brewing Company 550 West Railroad Avenue 81328 (970) 533-9761 https://mancosbrewingcompany.com/

Enjoy a great beer in a relaxed setting. Offering a rotating selection of bottled beers. The beers are crafted in two to seven-barrel batches while covering a broad range of beer styles. Another half-hour east brings you to the city of Durango with several options including a must-visit brewery:

Ska Brewing Company 225 Girard Drive 81303 (970) 247-5792 https://skabrewing.com/

Steamworks Brewing Company 801 E 2nd Avenue 81301 (970) 259-9200 https://steamworksbrewing.com/

Carver Brewing Company 1022 Main Avenue 81301 (970) 259-2545 https://carverbrewing.com/

Animas Brewing Company 1560 E 2nd Avenue 81301 (970) 403-8850 https://www.animasbrewing.com/

A family-friendly brewpub offering house-made beers along with Colorado wine and spirits. The flavorful craft beer can be paired with their spin on comfort food. Head about an hour north to Silverton with two brewery options:

Golden Block Brewery 1227 Greene Street 81433 (970) 387-5962 http://goldenblockbrewery.com/

Avalanche Brewing Company 1067 Notorious Blair Street 81433 (970) 387-5282 https://www.avalanchebrewing.com/

Another forty minutes north brings you to the town of Ouray with two options, including a must-visit brewery:

Red Mountain Brewing 400 Main Street 81427 (970) 325-9858
https://www.redmountainbrewingouray.com/

Ouray Brewery 607 Main Street 81427 (970) 325-7388
https://www.ouraybrewery.com/

A family-owned and operated brewery in the heart of a mountain community surrounded by outdoor activities. Enjoy award-winning beers and pub-style food. End the trip with an hour drive around the mountain peak to the town of Telluride:

Telluride Brewing Company 156 Society Drive 81435 (970) 728-5094
https://www.telluridebrewingco.com/

The Great West Trail

If you only have a day and want to experience the beauty of the Colorado mountains with excellent beer, then this trail is for you. It takes you across the Rocky Mountains and offers you the chance to sample some excellent brews. Start your trip in Hayden with a must-visit brewery:

Yampa Valley Brewing Company 106 E Jefferson Avenue Unit B 81639 (970) 276-8014 https://yampavalleybrew.com/

Brewing complex, approachable and diverse craft beers for the surrounding area. The beers here are unique, so no matter what you decide to try, you'll get a tasting experience you won't have anywhere else. Head east about a half-hour to the city of Steamboat Springs with a few brewery options:

Storm Peak Brewing Company 1885 Elk River Plaza 80487 (970) 879-1999 https://stormpeakbrewing.com/

Mountain Tap Brewery 910 Yampa Street 80487 (970) 879-6646
https://www.mountaintapbrewery.com/

Butcherknife Brewing Company 2875 Elk River Road 80487 (970) 879-2337 https://www.butcherknifebrewing.com/

About an hour drive southeast over the mountains brings you to the town of Kremmling with a must-visit brewery:

Grand Adventure Brewing Company 276 Central Avenue 80459 (970) 724-9219 https://grandadventure.us/

A unique craft brewery featuring beers made from locally sourced ingredients. Offering a large selection of beers from light American Pilsners to full-bodied Imperial Stouts. Head east about another fifty minutes Fraser with two brewery options:

Fraser River Beer Company 218 Eisenhower Drive 80442 (720) 352-1874 https://www.fraserriverbeerco.com/

Camber Brewing Company 365 Zerex Street 80442 (720) 646-5300 https://camberbrewing.com/

Just another six minutes south you'll end your trip in Winter Park:

Hideaway Park Brewery 78927 US Highway 40 80482 (970) 363-7312 https://www.hideawayparkbrewery.com/

The Peak Bistro and Brewery 78491 US Highway 40 80482 (970) 726-7951 https://www.thepeakwp.com/

Colorado Valley Trail

This short trail is perfect if you only have a day or two to spend in the area and want to taste some excellent brews. Start your trip in the town of Crestone:

Crestone Brewing Company 187 Silver Avenue 81131 (719) 256-6400 https://crestonebrewing.co/

From there head about an hour west to the town of Del Norte with a must-visit brewery:

Three Barrel Brewing Company 475 Grand Avenue 81132 (719) 657-0681 https://www.threebarrelbrew.com/

Creating handcrafted beers from San Luis Valley grown hops and malt in fresh mountain water. After a day of enjoying outdoor activities, stop by to taste some refreshing brews. Next, head southeast about a half-hour to the town of Alamosa where you have a few options and two must-visit breweries:

Square Peg Brewerks 625 Main Street 81101 (719) 580-7472 https://www.squarepegbrewerks.com/

The Colorado Farm Brewery 2070 CR 12 South 81101 (720) 739-1168 https://www.cofarmbeer.com/

Enjoy unique ales and lagers. Come experience the next evolution in craft brewing in Colorado.

San Luis Valley Brewing Company 631 Main Street 81101 (719) 587-2337 https://www.slvbrewco.com/

Offering full flavor, authentic, and excellent handcrafted beers. They are a great small-craft brewery that you need to sample. Continue east about another hour to the town of Walsenburg:

Crafty Canary Brewery 107 East 5th Street 81089 (719) 890-1112 https://craftycanarybrewery.com/

Then if you have the time, take a drive about two hours north to the town of Elizabeth and end your trail at their brewery:

The Elizabeth Brewing Company 239 Main Street 80107 (720) 335-6011 https://brewelizabeth.com/

Central Connecticut Trail

For a longer beer trail in Connecticut, take the central trail. It will take you from the northern part of Connecticut down to the coast. Depending on how many breweries you choose to visit and what other things you choose to do this trip can easily take several days, or you can complete it in a couple days. Start your trip in New Hartford:

Brewery Legitimus 283 Main Street 06057 (860) 238-7870
http://www.brewerylegitimus.com/home

From here take about a half-hour drive east to the town of Bloomfield with a couple of options:

Back East Brewing Company 1296A Blue Hills Avenue 06002 (888) 923-2739 https://www.backeastbrewing.com/

Thomas Hooker Brewing Company 16 Tobey Road 06002 (860) 242-3111 https://hookerbeer.com/

Next head north about twenty-minutes to a must-visit brewery in the town of Enfield:

Powder Hollow Brewery 504 Hazard Avenue 06082 (860) 205-0942
http://powderhollowbrewery.com/

Using the finest ingredients to offer you a fine tasting brew. In addition to a few staples of beers, they are constantly offering new flavors for you to try. Head back south about ten minutes to the town of East Windsor:

Problem Solved Brewing Company 2 North Road Unit 4 06088 (860) 623-1511 http://problemsolvedbrewing.com/

Eleven minutes brings you to South Windsor with another brewery option:

Connecticut Valley Brewing 765 Sullivan Avenue 06074 (860) 644-2707
https://www.ctvalleybrewing.com/

Manchester is just another ten minutes south and offers a couple options including a must-visit brewery:

Labyrinth Brewing Company 148 Forest Street 06040 (860) 791-2295
https://labyrinthbrewingcompany.com/

2nd Bridge Brewing Company 642 Hilliard Street Suite 2003 06042 (860) 783-8580 https://2ndbridgebrewing.com/

Focused on hop-forward ales, porters, and stouts. Bring a snack or lunch and enjoy some fresh beer. Head west for ten minutes to the main city of Hartford:

Hog River Brewing Company 1429 Park Street 06106 (860) 206-2119
https://www.hogriverbrewing.com/

Turn south again and take a ten-minute drive to Rocky Hill:

Still Hill Brewery 1275 Cromwell Avenue Building C Unit 8/9 06067 (860) 436-6368 https://www.stillhillbrewery.com/

New Britain is fifteen minutes southwest:

Alvarium Beer Company 365 John Downey Drive Suite B 06051 (860) 357-2039 https://alvariumbeer.com/

A short seven minutes west brings you to the town of Plainville:

Relic Brewing Company 95 Whiting Street Unit B 06062 (860) 255-4252 http://www.relicbeer.com/

Ten minutes further west brings you to the city of Bristol:

Firefly Hollow Brewing Company 139 Center Street 06010 (860) 845-8977 http://fireflyhollowbrewing.com/

Head south again by about fifteen minutes to the town of Southington where you have a couple options along with a must-visit brewery:

Witchdoctor Brewing Company 168 Center Street 06489 (860) 426-1924 https://witchdoctorbrewing.com/

Skygazer Brewing Company 36 Triano Drive 06489 (860) 385-4749 https://skygazerbrewingco.com/

Offering handcrafted, small-batch beers focused on the New England craft beer style. Stop in today to enjoy a fresh and unique tasting beer. Milldale also has a must-visit brewery and is just a short five minutes south:

Kinsmen Brewing Company 409 Canal Street 06479 (860) 578-4778 https://www.kinsmenbrewing.com/shop/

Come to enjoy a wide variety of craft stouts, ales, and IPAs. There is also excellent pizza to pair with your new favorite beer. Next head east about a half-hour to a must-visit brewery in the town of Middletown:

Stubborn Beauty Brewing Company 180 Johnson Street 06457 https://www.stubbornbeauty.com/

Brewing unique and full-flavored beers that give you a positive experience. Stop in to taste a quality and fresh beer that you won't find anywhere else. Another fifteen minutes farther east brings you to a must-visit brewery in the town of East Hampton:

Fat Orange Cat Brew Company 47 Tartia Road 06424 (860) 881-8045
https://fatorangecatbrewco.com/

A small, seasonal homestead brewery that specializes in high-quality small batch recipes. A twenty-minute drive southeast brings you to Salem:

Fox Farm Brewery 62 Music Vale Road 06420
http://www.foxfarmbeer.com/

Norwich is another twenty-minutes east and offers two brewery options:

These Guys Brewing Company 78 Franklin Street 06360 (860) 949-8550 https://www.theseguysbrewing.com/

Epicure Brewing 40 Franklin Street 06360 (860) 213-5706
https://www.epicurebrewing.com/

Curve southwest to the coastal town of Old Saybrook with another must-visit brewery:

30 Mile Brewing Company 39 Ragged Rock Road Unit #5 06475 (860) 339-5238 http://30milebrewingco.com/

A family-friendly micro-brewery. Offering a variety from stouts to double IPAs, there is something for everyone here. If you have a hard time making a decision, the bartenders can help you find the right beer style for you. Travel up the coast about a half-hour to the town of Groton:

Outer Light Brewing Company 266 Bridge Street 06340 (475) 201-9972
http://www.outerlightbrewing.com/

Another twenty-minutes up the coast brings you to a must-visit brewery at Stonington:

Beer'd Brewing Company 22 Bayview Avenue Unit #15 06378 (860) 857-1014 https://beerdbrewing.com/

Producing a wide variety of beers ranging from traditional year-round brews to experimental small-batch brews. The focus here is on innovative and creative beers. End your trip a short eight minutes away in the town of Pawcatuck:

Cottrell Brewing Company 100 Mechanic Street 06379 (860) 599-8213
https://www.cottrellbrewing.com/

Fairfield County Beer Trail

This is a short and simple beer trail with some great breweries. You can easily accomplish this trip in a day or two depending on how many breweries you plan to visit and what other things you plan to do while in the area. Start your trip in Newtown.

Reverie Brewing Company 57B Church Hill Road 06470 (203) 872-2124
https://reveriebrewing.com/

Head seventeen minutes southeast to Monroe:

Veracious Brewing Company 246 Main Street 06468 (203) 880-5670
http://www.veraciousbrewing.com/

Another twenty-minutes south brings you to the coastal town of Stratford with the largest number of breweries, all of them must-visits:

Fairfield Craft Ales 724 Honeyspot Road 06615 (203) 296-2530
https://fairfieldcraftales.com/

Beers inspired by songs and music. Brewing a variety from IPA to Kolsch. They have brewed over 40 different beers since they opened, so you'll have no trouble finding something you'll enjoy when you stop in here.

Athletic Brewing Company 350 Long Beach Blvd 06615 (843) 507-4783
https://athleticbrewing.com/

The first brewery in the United States completely focused on the production of non-alcoholic craft beer. Brewing small batches from innovative recipes. Be sure to give them a try on your way through the area.

Area Two Experimental Brewing 1526 Stratford Avenue 06614 (203) 335-2010 https://tworoadsbrewing.com/areatwo

A sour, barrel-aging, and experimental brewery. Here you can try beers that are wild and spontaneous. The beers are unique and highly complex.

Two Roads Brewing Company 1700 Stratford Avenue 06615 (203) 335-2010 https://www.tworoadsbrewing.com/

An extensive lineup of beers that offer a unique twist on the classic beer styles. Named as one of the top ten breweries in the United States. When you're ready, head southwest to the main city of Bridgeport:

Brewport Brewing Company 225 South Frontage Road 06604 (203) 612-4438 https://brewportct.com/

Continue down the coast about twenty-minutes to the town of Norwalk with a must-visit brewery:

Iron Brewing Company 136 Washington Street 06854 (203) 354-4010 https://ironbrewing.com/

Beers with the perfect balance of flavor and aroma. The same passion that goes into making their excellent beers is also reflected in the food you can pair your beer with. End your trip another twelve minutes down the coast in Stamford with two breweries:

Half Full Brewery 43 Homestead Avenue 06902 (203) 658-3631 https://halffullbrewery.com/

Lock City Brewing Company 54 Research Drive 06902 (203) 313-6454 https://www.lockcitybrewing.com/

Greater New Haven Beer Trail

This shorter, circular trail can take you from the coast to the inland areas of Connecticut and back again. Home to a number of must-visit breweries, this trip can take you a day or two to complete. Start your trip in the coastal town of Branford with a few options including two must-visit breweries:

Thimble Island Brewing Company 53 East Industrial Road Suite B5 06405 (203) 208-2827 https://www.thimbleislandbrewery.com/

DuVig Brewing Company 59 School Ground Road Unit 10 06405 (203) 208-2213 https://www.duvig.com/

Fresh, local, and brewed to style. Creating full-flavored, easy-drinking beers. Producing quality 'true to style' session beers that are light on alcohol content.

Stony Creek Brewery 5 Indian Neck Avenue 06405 (203) 433-4545 https://stonycreekbeer.com/

Here you will find a distinct style found nowhere else. A fusion of the clean, bold, aggressive West Coast flavors with the balance and drinkability of East Coast beers. Come try what makes these beers so unique. Just six minutes west along the coast brings you to East Haven with a few brewery options including a must-visit brewery:

Pottertown Brewing Company 250 Bradley Street 06512 (203) 909-6224 https://www.pottertownbrew.com/

Armada Brewing 250 Bradley Street 06512 (475) 441-3759 https://armadabeer.com/

Overshores Brewing Company 250 Bradley Street 06512 (203) 909-6224 http://www.overshores.com/

The first dedicated Belgian-style brewery in Connecticut and the first true brewing collective in the northeast. If you like strong beers, you'll enjoy a tasting here. Circle along the waterfront for eight minutes to New Haven with two must-visit breweries:

Rhythm Brewing Company 32 Barnett Street 06515 (203) 809-2431 https://rhythmbrewingco.com/

The flagship beer here is a modern American-style lager brewed from South African hops. This gives you an unfiltered, flavorful beer with a slight bite. Try some when you stop in today.

East Rock Brewing Company 285 Nicoll Street 06511 (475) 234-6176 https://eastrockbeer.com/

Brewing fresh and crisp German-inspired beer. Stop in today to try one of their 12 beers and wonderfully paired foods. Head inland fourteen minutes to the town of Woodbridge with a must-visit brewery:

New England Brewing Company 175 Amity Road 06525 (203) 387-2222 https://newenglandbrewing.com/

Offering a large selection of 30 eclectic and delicious beers. There is a flavor for everyone to be found here. Continue north to Hamden about twelve minutes away with two breweries, including a must-visit:

No Worries Brewing Company 2520 State Street 06517 (203) 691-6662 https://noworriesbeer.com/

Counter Weight Brewing Company 23 Raccio Park Road 06514 (203) 821-7333 https://www.counterweightbrewing.com/

Evolving the definition of big, flavorful, and hoppy beers. Offering everything from rustic Belgian ales to sturdy German lagers, come explore a full range of beers. An eleven-minute drive northeast brings you to Wallingford:

Front Porch Brewing 226 N Plains Industrial Road 06492 (203) 679-1096 https://www.frontporchbrewing.org/

Take a half-hour drive to the most northern point on your trip and a must-visit brewery at Wolcott:

Shebeen Brewing Company 1 Wolcott Road 06716 (203) 514-2336 https://shebeenbrewing.com/

The only Irish brewery in Connecticut. A must-try is their "dessert" beer known as the Cannoli Beer. This is an excellent and unique brew you won't find anywhere else. Start heading back south ten minutes to the town of Waterbury:

Brass Works Brewing Company 2066 Thomaston Avenue 06704 (203) 527-6223 https://www.brassworksbrewing.com/

Another seventeen minutes south brings you to Oxford:

Black Hog Brewing Company 115 Hurley Road Building 9A 06478 (203) 262-6057 https://blackhogbrewing.com/

Derby is another thirteen minutes south and has a must-visit brewery:

Bad Sons Beer Company 251 Roosevelt Drive 06418 (203) 308-2654 https://www.badsons.com/

Brewing with a strong focus on East Coast and New England style ales. The beers here are constantly evolving to offer you the best tasting experience possible. End your trip sixteen minutes south at the coastal town Milford:

Milford Point Brewing 230 Woodmont Road 29B 06460 (203) 701-9077 https://milfordpointbrewing.com/

Litchfield Hills

This short trail will take you to three towns in a day that showcase some great brewery options. Start your trip in the town of Colebrook in the northwestern corner of Connecticut:

Norbrook Farm Brewery 204 Stillman Hill Road 06021 (860) 909-1016 https://www.norbrookfarm.com/

Specializing in farmhouse-style beers, ales, and lagers. Stop in to try your favorite or something new today. Head south about an hour to Kent:

Kent Falls Brewing Company 33 Camps Road 06757 (860) 398-9645
https://kentfallsbrewing.com/

End your trip about a half-hour south in New Milford:

Housatonic River Brewing Company 30 Kent Road 06776 (860) 946-0266 https://www.housatonicriverbrewing.com/

Standalone Connecticut Breweries

Danielson **Black Pond Brews** 21A Furnace Street 06239 (860) 207-5295
https://www.blackpondbrews.com/

Mystic **Barley Head Brewery** 12 Water Street 06355
https://www.barleyheadbrewery.com/

Always offering four to six beers on tap that show the versatility and range of flavors. There is always something for everyone here.

Delaware

Take a drive from north or south and cover the entire state while enjoying some excellent breweries. The drive can be done in a day, but if you want to take your time visiting all the breweries and seeing other sites, then you may want to spend a couple days or more. Start your trip in the northern area of Delaware at the town of Yorklyn with a must-visit brewery:

Dew Point Brewing Company 2878 Creek Road 19736 (302) 235-8429
https://www.dewpointbrewing.com/

The only family-owned and operated microbrewery in Delaware. Offering Belgian-inspired beers in a family-friendly setting. Head southeast about twenty-minutes to the largest town in Delaware, Wilmington with several breweries including a must-visit:

Bellefonte Brewing Company 3605 Old Capitol Trail Ste C8 19808 (302) 757-4971 https://www.bellefontebrewingco.com/

Stitch House Brewery 829 North Market Street 19801 (302) 250-4280
http://girardfaire.com/takeout

Wilmington Brew Works 3129 Miller Road 19802 (302) 722-4828
https://wilmingtonbrewworks.com/

The first brewery in the largest city in Delaware since 1955. Offering new and innovative ales, lagers, and sours. Family-friendly and relaxing atmosphere. Another twenty-minutes to the southwest brings you to the town of Newark with several options including a must-visit brewery:

Midnight Oil Brewing Company 674 Pencader Drive 19702 (302) 286-7641 https://www.midnightoilbrewing.com/

Argilla Brewing Company 2667 Kirkwood Highway 19711 (302) 731-8200 https://www.argillabrewing.com/

Autumn Arch Beer Project810 Pencader Drive Suite C 19702 (302) 294-1126 https://www.autumnarch.com/

A local, small-batch, experimental brewery. Specializing in beers with a deep flavor profile with bitterness and a respect for traditional styles.

Fifteen minutes south brings you to a must-visit brewery in the town of Bear:

Stewart's Brewing Company 219 Governor's Square Shopping Center 19563 (302) 836-2739 https://www.stewartsbrewingcompany.com/

Offering six full-time ales and 40 rotating seasonal beers. Brewing a variety of ales and lagers. Enjoy them in a casual and relaxing atmosphere. Another must-visit brewery is twenty-minutes south in the town of Middletown:

Volunteer Brewing Company 120 W Main Street 19709 (302) 464-0822 https://www.volunteerbrewing.com/

The smallest brewery in Delaware and the first in Middletown. Brewing small-batch, superior ales with a small 2 barrel system. Next is the town of Smyrna another twenty-minutes south with two options, including a must-visit brewery:

Brick Works Brewing 230 S Dupont Blvd 19977 (302) 508-2523 https://www.brickworksde.com/

Blue Earl Brewing Company 210 Artisan Drive 19977 (302) 653-2337 https://blueearlbrewing.com/

Producing hoppy American ales, Belgian Specialties, German ales, and lagers. They also have a variety of seasonal offerings. Dover is another twenty-minute drive with another must-visit brewery:

Fordham and Dominion Brewing Company 1284 McD Drive 19901 (302) 678-4810 https://www.fordhamanddominion.com/

Featuring a wide variety of year-round and seasonal brews, from IPAs to stouts and everything in between. No matter what you enjoy, you'll find it here. Continue about twenty-five minutes south to the town of Milford:

Mispillion River Brewing 255 Mullet Run Street 19963 (302) 233-2844 https://www.mispillionriverbrewing.com/

Next comes Milton, twenty more minutes south:

Dogfish Head Craft Brewery 6 Cannery Village Center 19968 (888) 836-3474 https://www.dogfish.com/front

Head about twenty-minutes to the coastal town of Rehoboth Beach with a couple options including a must-visit brewery:

Big Oyster Brewery 19269 Coastal Highway 19971 (302) 227-3467 http://www.bigoysterbrewery.com/

Revelation Craft Brewing Company 19841 Central Avenue 19971 (302) 212-5674 https://revbeer.com/

Offering high-quality brews with a one of a kind experience. Stop in today to try one of their brews while enjoying the relaxing atmosphere. A short three-minute drive is the coastal town of Dewey Beach with another couple of brewery options:

38-75 Brewing 2000 Coastal Highway STE 105 19971 (302) 227-8519 https://3875brewing.com/

Dewey Beer Company 2100 Coastal Highway 19971 (302) 227-1182 https://deweybeerco.com/

Lewes is a thirteen-minute drive and has a must-visit brewery:

Crooked Hammock Brewery 16989 Kings Highway 19958 (302) 644-7837 https://crookedhammockbrewery.com/

Unique brews that are made from scratch. Offering easy drinking and approachable beers that you can sip and enjoy while relaxing. End your trip with about an hour drive to the southwest corner of Delaware and the town of Delmar with a must-visit brewery:

3rd Wave Brewing Company 501 N Bi-State Blvd 19940 (302) 907-0423 http://www.3rdwavebrewingco.com/

Producing five house beers year-round as well as a variety of seasonal beers. The taproom here has a beach theme so you can relax and enjoy your favorite beer.

Florida

Central Florida Trail

This brewery trail will take you several days or more to complete depending on how much you plan to see and do along the way. It covers quite a few breweries and takes you to many cities throughout the inland and coastal parts of Central Florida. Start your trip in the coastal town of Palm Coast:

Moonrise Brewing Company 101 Palm Harbor Parkway #123 32137 (386) 627-8614 https://www.moonrisebrewingcompany.com/

Drive 25 minutes south along the coast to the town of Ormond Beach with a few brewery options:

Ormond Brewing Company 301 Division Avenue #15 32174 (386) 795-2739 http://ormondbrewing.com/

Beachside Brewpub 1368 Ocean Shore Blvd 32176 (386) 947-7873
http://www.beachsidebrewpub.com/

Ormond Garage Brewing and Grille 48 W Granada Blvd 32174 (386) 492-7981 https://www.ormondgarage.beer/

Holly Hill is the next coastal town just twelve minutes further south:

Red Pig Brewery 101 2nd Street Unit 401 32117 (386) 238-9149
https://www.theredpigbrewery.com/

Just six minutes away is the popular tourist destination of Daytona Beach with another brewery option:

Daytona Beach Brewing Company 482 Fentress Blvd Suite N 32114 (844) 352-2337 https://www.daytonabeachbrewingcompany.com/

The next coastal town you'll come to is twenty-minutes away at New Smyrna Beach:

New Smyrna Beach Brewing Company 112 Sams Avenue 32618 (386) 957-3802 https://newsmyrnabeachbrewery.com/

Next head a half-hour inland to the town of DeLand:

Persimmon Hollow Brewing Company 111 W Georgia Avenue 32720 (386) 873-7350 https://www.persimmonhollowbrewing.com/

Head south again for fifteen minutes to the town of DeBary with a must-visit brewery:

Central 28 Beer Company 290 Springview Commerce Drive #1 32713 (386) 668-2811 https://central28beer.com/

Crafting a unique array of ales with a focus on the Belgian style. There are several year-round beer options as well as seasonal selections. Another eleven minutes south brings you to Sanford with two breweries, including a must-visit brewery:

Inner Compass Brewing 300 E 2nd Street 32771 (407) 407-1792
https://www.innercompassbrewing.com/

Sanford Brewing Company 400 S Sanford Avenue 32771 (407) 732-6419 https://www.sanfordbrewing.com/

Offering handcrafted beers, meads, ciders, and specialty sodas. Family-friendly and offering sodas for those who can't enjoy the beers. Head about another half-hour inland to Mount Dora:

Mount Dora Brewing 405 Highland Street 32757 (352) 406-2924
http://www.mountdorabrewing.com/

Next head southwest about forty minutes to Clermont with two options, including a must-visit brewery:

Suncreek Brewery 790 W Minneola Avenue 34711 (407) 850-8810
https://www.suncreekbrewery.com/

Clermont Brewing Company 750 W Desoto 34711 (321) 430-2337
https://clermontbrewingcompany.com/

The place to go for craft beer, artisanal food, and live music. Offering everything from ales to lagers, light to dark, hoppy to malty, and everything in between. Head back towards the coast to the town of Winter Garden with a must-visit brewery:

Crooked Can Brewing Company 426 West Plant Street 34787 (407) 496-6102 https://crookedcan.com/

Try amazing local beers with an enjoyable drinking experience. Using old-world techniques to create full-bodied, tastefully crisp beer. A short five minutes east is the town of Ocoee:

Tollroad Brewing 101 W McKey Street 34761 (407) 395-2742
https://www.tollroadbrewing.com/

Another twenty-minutes east brings you to the major city of Orlando with plenty of brewery options, but at least three are must-visits:

Redlight Redlight 2810 Corrine Drive 32803 (407) 893-9832
https://redlightredlightbeerparlour.com/

Half Barrel Beer Project 9650 Universal Blvd Suite #143 32819 (407) 203-3946 http://halfbarrelproject.com/

Sideward Brewing 210 N Bumby Avenue Suite C 32803 (407) 866-2195 https://sidewardbrewing.com/

Castle Church Brewing Community 6820 Hoffner Avenue 32822 (407) 635-9410 https://www.castlechurchbrewing.com/

Rockpit Brewing 2230 Curry Ford Road 32806 (407) 826-1773 https://rockpitbrewing.com/

Broken Strings Brewery 1012 W Church Street 32805 (407) 679-7519 https://www.brokenstringsbrewery.com/

Ellipsis Brewing 7500 TPC Blvd #8 32822 (407) 250-5848 https://www.ellipsisbrewing.com/

Ivanhoe Park Brewing 1300 Alden Road 32803 (407) 270-6749 https://ivanhoeparkbrewing.com/

Orlando Brewing 1301 Atlanta Avenue 32806 (407) 872-1117 http://www.orlandobrewing.com/

A certified organic brewery, the only one east of Colorado. The beers here are brewed with only four ingredients to offer you the purest form of beer possible.

Tactical Brewing 4882 New Broad Street 32814 (407) 203-2033 https://www.tacticalbeer.com/

Creating many different beer styles with a unique twist. Come try their unique beer in a fun atmosphere.

Orange Blossom Brewing Company 4410 Flagg Street 32812 (407) 540-1100 https://orangeblossombrewing.com/

Making approachable beers with a high drinkability that everyone can enjoy. Come try one of their four beers today. Just thirteen minutes northeast is the town of Winter Park with a couple other brewery options:

Bear and Peacock Brewery 1288 North Orange Avenue 32789 (407) 801-2714 https://wpdistilling.com/

Something's Brewing 750 Jackson Avenue 32789 (407) 900-8726 https://www.sibrewing.beer/

Casselberry is twelve minutes northeast and has a must-visit brewery:

Bowigens Beer Company 1014 SR 436 32707 (407) 960-7816 https://www.bowigens.com/

Brewing that focuses on taste and not style. They brew beers with a balance between art and science to bring you excellent tasting beers. Nearby is Longwood with another must-visit brewery:

Hourglass Brewing 480 S Ronald Reagan Blvd 32750 (407) 262-0056 https://hourglassbrewing.com/

Brewing mixed culture beers with every aspect of the process being done in house. Sample a wide selection of beers in a fun and inviting atmosphere. Head east again another twenty-minutes to the town of Oviedo:

Oviedo Brewing 1280 Oviedo Mall Drive 32765 (407) 542-8248 https://www.oviedobrewingco.com/

Take a forty-minute drive back to the coast and the town of Titusville:

Playalinda Brewing Company 305 South Washington Avenue 32796 (321) 225-8978 https://www.playalindabrewingcompany.com/

Head about a half-hour down the coast to the town of Cocoa:

Dirty Oar Beer Company 329 King Street 32922 (321) 301-4306 http://dirtyoarbeercompany.com/

Go fifteen minutes a little further east to Cape Canaveral with a must-visit brewery:

Florida Beer Company 200 Imperial Blvd 32920 (321) 728-4114
https://www.floridabeer.com/

The original Florida brewery offers 20 selections on tap. Currently producing 28 different types of ales, lagers, and ciders. Just eight minutes south is a must-visit brewery at the coastal town of Cocoa Beach:

Cocoa Beach Brewing Company 150 N Atlantic Avenue 32391 (321) 613-2941 http://www.cocoabeachbrewingcompany.com/

Offering a variety of traditional craft brews along with seasonal and unique beers. Everything is brewed in small, handcrafted batches. Sticking to the coast, another half-hour south brings you to Melbourne with a couple of brewery options:

Hell 'n Blazes Brewing 1002 E New Haven Avenue 32904 (321) 821-4052 https://www.hellnblazesbrewing.com/

Intracoastal Brewing Company 652 W Eau Gallie Blvd 32935 (321) 872-7395 https://intracoastalbrewingcompany.com/

Sebastian is another half-hour south with another couple of breweries:

Mash Monkeys Brewing Company 920 US Highway 1 32958 (772) 571-6283 http://www.mashmonkeysbrewing.com/

Pareidolia Brewing Company 712 Cleveland Street 32958 (772) 584-0331 https://www.pareidoliabrewing.com/

Vero Beach is about twenty-minutes south with a few options, including a must-visit brewery:

Orchid Island Brewing 2855 Ocean Drive 32963 (772) 321-1244
https://orchidislandbrewery.com/

Walking Tree Brewery 3209 Dodger Road 32960 (772) 217-3502
https://www.walkingtreebrewery.com/

American Icon Brewery 1133 19th Place 32960 (772) 934-4266
https://www.americaniconbrewery.com/

Brewing balanced, approachable, and interesting handcrafted beers. Offering everything from a classic like Pilsner to newer styles like a Milk Stout. End your trip with a twenty-minute drive to a must-visit brewery in Fort Pierce:

Sailfish Brewing Company 130 N 2nd Street 34950 (772) 577-4278
https://sailfishbrewingco.com/

When you come here, you'll be able to enjoy an authentic coastal Florida experience. Brewing beers with a bright and refreshing flavor.

Palm Beach Coast Trail

If you want to enjoy the Florida coast and take in some sunshine while tasting beers, then consider the Palm Beach Coast Trail. This short and simple trail will allow you to taste some great beers in a short one to two-day trip. Start your trip in the town of Jupiter with two brewery options, including a must-visit brewery:

Civil Society Brewing 1200 Town Center Drive Unit 101 33458 (561) 855-6680 https://civilsocietybrewing.com/

Inlet Brewing Company (561) 339-0004 https://www.inletbrewing.com/

Brewing complex beers from simple and wholesome ingredients. Stop in to try their beers, including their flagship beer Monk in the Trunk. Head south fifteen minutes to Palm Beach Gardens:

Twisted Trunk Brewing Company 2000 PGA Blvd 33408 (561) 671-2337 https://www.twistedtrunkbrewing.com/

Go about twenty-minutes south and a little inland to a must-visit brewery at Royal Palm Beach:

Royal Palm Brewing Company 543 North State Road 7 Suite 103 33411 (561) 792-5822 https://www.royalpalmbrewing.com/

Specializing in a wide variety of beer styles from American lagers to Russian Imperial stouts. There is also an ever-changing food menu to pair with your beers. Drive twenty-minutes east to the coastal town of West Palm Beach with a couple breweries including a must-visit:

West Palm Brewery 332 Evernia Street 33401 (561) 619-8813 https://www.westpalmbeer.com/

Steam Horse Brewing 1500 Elizabeth Avenue 33401 (561) 623-0091 https://www.steamhorsebrewing.com/

Brewing quality craft beers in a variety of styles, both traditional and experimental. Stop in today to try your favorite and something new. Follow the coast twelve minutes south to Lake Worth:

Mathews Brewing Company 130 South H Street 33460 (561) 812-3738 https://mathewsbrewingcompany.com/

A short eight-minute trip brings you to three breweries, two of them are must-visits in the town of Boynton Beach:

NOBO Brewing Company 2901 Commerce Park Drive 33426 (561) 320-1522 https://www.nobobrewing.com/

Due South Brewing Company 2900 High Ridge Road #3 33426 (561) 463-BEER https://www.duesouthbrewing.com/

Focusing on producing ales and lagers. In addition to year-round beers, there are also specialty and seasonal beers as well.

Copperpoint Brewing Company 151 Commerce Drive 33426 (561) 508-7676 https://copperpointbrewingcompany.com/

Offering world-class beers. To get these beers, the water is ultra-purified to offer a crisp and clean beer you won't find anywhere else. Another eight minutes south is Delray Beach:

SaltWater Brewery 1701 W Atlantic Avenue 33444 (561) 450-9519
https://saltwaterbrewery.com/

Travel thirteen minutes south to the main city of Boca Raton with three must-visit breweries:

Robot Brewing Company 2021 N Federal Highway 33431 (561) 368-4643 https://madrobotbrewing.com/

Brewing extremely small batches of flavor-forward beer. The beers include unique culinary-inspired ingredients.

Prosperity Brewers 4160 NW 1st Avenue #21 33067 (561) 325-8495
https://www.prosperitybrewers.com/

Specializing in creating classic beer styles with small-batch uniqueness. They are always pushing the barrier to provide you with unique beer flavors.

Barrel of Monks Brewing 1141 S Rogers Circle #5 33487 (561) 510-1253 https://barrelofmonks.com/

Using old world recipes with modern techniques to produce unique and delicious beers. Try their Belgian beers with a twist and find something new and unique. End your trip with a thirteen-minute drive to Pompano Beach with multiple brewery options:

Bangin' Banjo Brewing Company 3200 NW 23rd Avenue #500 33069 (954) 978-3113 https://www.banginbanjobrewing.com/

Holy Mackerel Small Batch Beers 3260 NW 23rd Avenue Suite 400 33069 (954) 261-0668 https://www.holymackerelbeers.com/

Dangerous Minds Brewing 1901 North Federal Highway Suite E115 33062 (954) 918-1698 https://dangerousmindsbrewing.com/

Odd Breed Wild Ales 50 NE 1st Street 33060 (754) 220-6099
https://www.oddbreed.com/

A small brewery focused on wild ales and farmhouse ales. All beers are aged in oak barrels to offer a unique craft brew that you must try.

Tampa Bay Area Trail

Travel from the inland area to the Gulf Coast and back again while taking this trail. You'll visit larger cities and quaint small towns. There are lots of breweries to see here, and you may not have time to visit them all. Depending on what you want to see and do this trail can be a couple days or more. Start your trip in the coastal town of Sarasota with multiple breweries and a must-visit one:

Calusa Brewing 5701 Derek Avenue 34233 (941) 922-8150 https://www.calusabrewing.com/

JDub's Brewing Company 1215 Mango Road 34237 (941) 955-2739 https://www.jdubsbrewing.com/

Big Top Brewing Company 6111 Porter Way B 34232 (941) 371-2939 https://www.bigtopbrewing.com/

Brew Life Brewing 5767 S Beneva Road 34233 (941) 952-3831 https://brewlifebrewing.com/

Sarasota Brewing Company 6607 Gateway Avenue 34231 (941) 925-2337 http://www.sarasotabrewing.com/

Four signature beers on draft year-round and 20 rotating seasonal beers. The first and only micro brewpub in Sarasota. You'll always find something new to try here. Head north up the coast by about twenty-minutes to the next coastal city of Bradenton which also has plenty of breweries and two must-visit ones:

Naughty Monk Brewery 2507 Lakewood Ranch Blvd 34211 (941) 708-2966 http://www.naughtymonkbrewery.com/

3 Keys Brewing and Eatery 2505 Manatee Avenue E 34208 (941) 218-0396 https://www.3keysbrewing.com/

Good Liquid Brewing Company 4824 14th Street W 34207 (941) 896-6381 https://thegoodliquidbrewing.com/

Motorworks Brewing 1014 9th Street West 34205 (941) 896-9892 https://motorworksbrewing.com/

Enjoy your beer in the beer garden under a beautiful 150-year-old oak tree. Offering award-winning craft beers to please any palate.

Darwin Brewing Company 803 17th Avenue West 34205 (941) 747-1970 http://www.darwinbrewingco.com/

Brewing culinary-inspired ales and lagers. Everything is based on the native flavors of Florida and America. Continue following the coast for a half-hour to the town of Apollo Beach:

Four Stacks Brewing Company 5469 N US Highway 41 33572 (813) 641-2036 https://fourstacksbrewing.com/

Heading about fifteen minutes inland you come to the town of Riverview:

Leaven Brewing 11238 Boyette Road 33569 (813) 677-7023 https://www.leavenbrewing.com/

Valrico is another fourteen minutes inland and offers another brewery:

Bullfrog Creek Brewing Company 3632 Lithia Pinecrest Road 33596 (813) 703-8835 https://bullfrogcreekbrewing.com/

Drive about forty minutes to your furthest inland point at Winter Haven with a must-visit brewery:

Grove Roots Brewing Company 302 3rd Street SW 33880 (863) 291-0700 http://groveroots.com/

Brewing inventive, artisanal beers inspired by the traditions and taste of Central Florida's citrus history. Offering four year-round beers along with rotating seasonal and specialty beers. Head back west about twenty-minutes to the brewery at Lakeland:

Swan Brewing 115 W Pine Street 33815 (863) 703-0472
https://www.swanbrewing.com/

Head north a half-hour to a must-visit brewery at Zephyrhills:

Zephyrhills Brewing Company 38530 5th Avenue 33542 (813) 363-5085
http://zbcbeer.com/

Over 20 beers are brewed in house here. There are also plenty of non-beer options for any drinking preference. Stop in to try a delicious beer or other drink. Now head southwest back to the coast and the main city of Tampa with many brewery options, but at least four that you should get to if you don't make it to all of them:

Southern Brewing and Winemaking 4500 N Nebraska Avenue 33603 (813) 238-7800 https://www.southernbrewingwinemaking.com/

Bay Cannon Beer Company 2106 W Main Street 33607 (813) 251-4553
https://www.baycannon.com/

Ulele 1810 North Highland Avenue 33602 (813) 999-4952
https://www.ulele.com/

Rock Brothers Brewing 1901 N 15th Street 33605 (813) 241-0110
https://rockbrothersbrewing.com/

81Bay Brewing 4465 W Gandy Blvd Ste 600 33611 (813) 837-2739
https://www.81baybrewco.com/

Brew Bus Brewing 4101 N Florida Avenue 33603 (813) 990-7310
https://brewbususa.com/

King State 520 E Floribraska Avenue 33603 (813) 221-2100 https://king-state.com/

Hidden Springs Ale Works 1631 N Franklin Street 33602 (813) 226-2739 http://hiddenspringsaleworks.com/

Coppertail Brewing Company 2601 E 2nd Avenue 33605 (813) 247-1500 https://coppertailbrewing.com/

Cigar City Brewing 3924 W Spruce Street 33607 (813) 348-6363 https://www.cigarcitybrewing.com/

Six Ten Brewing 7052 Benjamin Road 33634 (813) 886-0610 https://www.sixtenbrewing.com/

Late Start Brewing 1208 E Kennedy Blvd Ste 112 33602 (813) 402-2923 https://www.latestartbrewing.com/

Tampa Beer Works 333 North Falkenburg Road Unit D-407 33619 (813) 990-0700 http://tampabeerworks.com/

When you stop here, you can try three excellent beers: a juicy IPA, a smooth stout, and a refreshing Florida Weiss.

BarrieHaus Beer Company 1403 E 5th Avenue 33605 (813) 242-2739 https://www.barriehaus.com/

Serving unique craft lagers and ales. Enjoy a historic, warm, and rustic atmosphere. You'll enjoy your time and your beer.

Angry Chair Brewing 6401 N Florida Avenue 33604 (813) 892-1651 https://angrychairbrewing.com/

Most known for their stouts. However, this isn't their only focus; they also offer stouts, IPAs, sours, and porters. Come here and find the perfect beer for your taste.

Tampa Bay Brewing Company 13937 Monroe's Business Park 33635 (813) 247-1422 https://www.tbbc.beer/

Brewing flavorful and hop centered IPAs, APAs, sours, and fruit-forward Florida Weisse. In addition to year-round beers that is also a constant rotation of seasonal releases Cross the bay with about a twenty-minute drive to the other major city of St. Petersburg with a few brewery options including a must-visit:

Cycle Brewing 534 Central Avenue 33701 (727) 320-7954
https://cyclebrewing.com/

Flying Boat Brewing Company 1776 11th Avenue N 33713 (727) 800-2999 https://flyingboatbrewing.com/

Pinellas Ale Works 1962 1st Avenue S 33712 (727) 235-0970
https://www.pawbeer.com/

Green Bench Brewing 1133 Baum Avenue North 33705 (727) 214-4863
https://www.greenbenchbrewing.com/

The first microbrewery in St. Petersburg. Crafting unique beers from fresh, local, and traditional ingredients. A fourteen-minute drive takes you to a must-visit brewery at St. Pete Beach on the Gulf Coast:

Mastry's Brewing Company 7701 Blind Pass Road 33706 (727) 202-8045 http://mastrysbrewingco.com/

Using traditional brewing styles and combining them with influences from exotic locations. Here you can have the perfect beach beer experience. Continue up the coast about thirteen minutes to a brewery at Maderia Beach:

Mad Beach Craft Brewing Company 12945 Village Blvd 33708 (727) 362-0008 http://madbeachbrewing.com/

Next is a must-visit brewery at Seminole just seven minutes north:

Rapp Brewing Company 10930 Endeavor Way Suite C 33777 (727) 544-1752 http://rappbrewing.com/

Small batch, handcrafted, award-winning ales, and lagers. Occasionally they will brew beer recipes that once were thought lost. The next brewery is in Largo, ten minutes north:

Arkane Aleworks 2480 East Bay Drive #23 33771 (727) 270-7117
https://www.arkanebeer.com/

Just nine minutes more north brings you to two breweries in the town of Clearwater:

Big Storm Brewing Company 12707 49th Street N 33762 (727) 201-4186 https://www.bigstormbrewery.com/

Grindhaus Brew Lab 1650 N Hercules Avenue Unit I 33765 (727) 240-0804 https://grindhausbrewlab.com/

About twenty-minutes takes you back to the bay side and the town of Safety Harbor with two breweries to visit:

Crooked Thumb Brewery 555 10th Avenue South 34698 (727) 724-5953 https://crookedthumbbrew.com/

Troubled Waters Brewing 670 Main Street 34695 (630) 335-7890 https://troubledwatersbeer.com/

Head back to the Gulf Coast with an eleven-minute drive to the town of Dunedin which has quite a few breweries including a couple must-visit ones:

Caledonia Brewing 587 Main Street 34698 (727) 351-5105 https://www.caledoniabrewing.com/

Dunedin House of Beer 927 Broadway 34698 (727) 216-6318 https://www.dunedinhob.com/

7venth Sun Brewery 1012 Broadway 34698 (727) 773-3013 https://7venthsun.com/

Dunedin Brewery 937 Douglas Avenue 34698 (727) 736-0606 https://dunedinbrewery.com/

The oldest brewery in Florida. Stop in to try a well-crafted and satisfying brew that has been perfected after years of tasting.

Cueni Brewing Company 945 Huntley Avenue 34698 (727) 266-4102 http://www.cuenibrewing.com/

Handcrafted beers with a focus on English Ales and Belgians. Try their quality and unique craft beers today. The next two breweries, including a must-visit, are just eight minutes north in the town of Palm Harbor:

LagerHaus Grill and Brewery 3438 East Lake Business 34685 (813) 343-2449 http://www.lagerhausbrewery.com/

Stilt House Brewery 625 US 19 Alt 34683 (727) 270-7373 https://www.stilthousebrewery.com/

Offering over 30 unique flavors of beer. If you want something different, they also offer wine and cider. Nine minutes brings you to the coastal town of Tarpon Springs:

Silverking Brewing Company 325 E Lemon Street 34689 (727) 422-7598 http://www.silverkingbrewing.com/

Head inland again about ten minutes to Trinity with a must-visit brewery:

Escape Brewing Company 9945 Trinity Blvd Suite 108 34655 (727) 807-6092 https://www.escapebrewingcompany.com/

Brewing full-flavored, well-balanced ales and lagers. Enjoy a beer that is both creative and high quality. Continue about twenty-minutes inland to a brewery at Land O' Lakes:

In the Loop Brewing 3338 Land O Lakes Blvd 34639 (813) 997-9189 https://intheloopbrewingcompany.com/

Then head north about a half-hour to a brewery at Spring Hill:

Tidal Brewing Company 14311 Spring Hill Drive 34609 (352) 701-1602 https://www.tidalbrewingfl.com/

Eight minutes away is the town of Weeki Wachee with another brewery:

Marker 48 Brewing 12147 Cortez Blvd 34613 (352) 606-2509 https://curbside.marker48.com/

Another half-hour north is the coastal city of Crystal River with a must-visit brewery:

Copp Winery and Brewery 11 NE 4th Avenue 34429 (352) 564-9463
https://www.coppbrewery.com/

The only brewery and winery in Florida. The beers are produced in small quantities so they can offer a wide range of rotating beer styles. End your trip to a brewery about a fifty-minute drive inland in the city of Ocala:

Infinite Ale Works 304 South Magnolia Avenue 34471 (352) 512-0212
http://www.infinitealeworks.com/

North Florida Trail

Take this circular trail through the breweries in the northeastern corner of Florida. It can take a day or two to complete. Start your trip in the coastal town of Atlantic Beach at:

Reve Brewing 1237 Mayport Road 32233 (904) 472-1985
https://revebrewing.square.site/

Just seven minutes south is the coastal town of Jacksonville Beach with three brewery options:

Green Room Brewing 228 Third Street North 32250 (904) 254-2700
https://www.greenroombrewing.com/

Engine 15 Brewing Company 1500 Beach Blvd 32250 (904) 249-2337
http://www.engine15.com/verify.php

Ruby Beach Brewing 131 1st Avenue N 32250 (904) 372-0727
https://www.rubybeachbrewing.com/

Take a forty-minute drive down the coast to the oldest city of St Augustine with several brewery options and the first must-visit brewery on this trip:

A1A Aleworks 1 King Street 32084 (904) 829-2977
https://www.a1aaleworks.com/

Ancient City Brewing 3420 Agricultural Center Drive Suite 8 32092 (904) 429-9654 https://www.ancientcitybrewing.com/

Dog Rose Brewing Company 77 Bridge Street 32084 (904) 217-3355 https://www.dogrosebrewing.com/

Old Coast Ales 300 Anastasia Blvd 32080 (904) 484-7705 https://www.oldcoastales.com/

Bog Brewing Company 218 W King Street 32084 (904) 679-3146 http://www.bogbrewery.com/

Serving a variety of classic beer styles, Belgian-inspired ales, barrel-aged farmhouse beers, and lagers. You can also try a unique selection of seasonal beers. Next,, you'll want to take about a two-hour drive southwest and head inland to a must-visit brewery in the town of Wildwood:

Backyard Barn Winery and Microbrewery 1945 E County Road 462 34785 (352) 418-7887 http://backyardbarnwinery.com/

Offering farm-based, small-batch, handcrafted beer in a peaceful country setting. There is a wide variety to choose from, so there is something for everyone. When you're ready, head back north about an hour to the city of Gainesville with two must-visit breweries:

First Magnitude Brewing Company 1220 SE Veitch Street 32601 (352) 727-4677 https://fmbrewing.com/

Swamp Head Brewery 3140 SW 42nd Way 32608 (352) 505-3035 https://swamphead.com/

This brewery is focused on all things Florida. From the ingredients they put into their beer to the artwork on their cans, everything is focused on the great state of Florida.

Blackadder Brewing Company 618 - A NW 60th Street 32607 (352) 339-0324 https://www.blackadderbrewing.com/

Crafting Belgian-style ales and serving them in an old-world atmosphere. Stop in to try a beer and an experience. Continue about another fifty minutes north to the town of Lake City:

Halpatter Brewing Company 264 NE Hernando Avenue 32055 (386) 438-8788 https://halpatterbrewing.com/

Drive an hour east back towards the coast to a brewery in the town of Orange Park:

Pinglehead Brewing Company 14B Blanding Blvd 32073 (904) 276-5160 https://www.pinglehead.com/

About a twenty-minute drive north brings you to Jacksonville with many brewery options including three must-visit breweries:

Veterans United Craft Brewery 8999 Western Way #104 32256 (904) 253-3326 https://www.vubrew.com/

Bottlenose Brewing 9700 Deer Lake Court #1 32246 (904) 551-7570 https://bottlenosebrewing.com/

River City Brewing Company 835 Museum Circle 32207 (904) 398-2299 https://www.rivercitybrew.com/

Fishweir Brewing Company 1183 Edgewood Avenue S 32205 (904) 551-9469 https://fishweirbrewing.com/

Bold City Brewery 2670 Rosselle Street 32204 (904) 379-6551 https://www.boldcitybrewery.com/

Intuition Ale Works 720 King Street 32204 (904) 683-7720 https://intuitionaleworks.com/

Aardwolf Brewing Company 1461 Hendricks Avenue 32207 (904) 301-0755 https://www.aardwolfbrewing.com/

Wicked Barley Brewing Company 4100 Baymeadows Road 32217 (904) 379-7077 https://www.wickedbarley.com/

Known for their unique, boundary-pushing beer styles. In addition to an extensive beer list, they also have a gastro style pub to enjoy as well.

Southern Swells Brewing Company 1312 Beach Blvd 32250 (904) 372-9289 https://www.southernswells.com/

Focused on brewing New England IPAs, heavily fruited sours, Imperial Stouts, and mixed fermentation. Enjoy your beer in an inviting and friendly setting.

Hyperion Brewing Company 1740 Main Street N 32206 (904) 518-5131 https://www.hyperionbrewing.com/

Serving an endless rotating lineup of beers with a unique and refreshing experience. Offering beers from the classic and forgotten styles to those that push the boundaries of modern craft beer making. End your trip with about a 25-minute drive to the state border and the town of Yulee:

SJ Brewing Company 463646 State Road 200 Suite 13 32097 (904) 849-1654 https://sjbrewingco.com/

Florida Panhandle

Take a drive from west to east and enjoy the coastal views that is the Florida panhandle. There are a few great breweries and some wonderful historic towns to visit. You can take this tour in one or two days. Start yourself out in Milton with a must-visit brewery:

Beardless Brewhaus 6820 Caroline Street 32570 (850) 665-0663 https://beardlessbrewhaus.com/

Handcrafting small-batch beer with a focus on keeping things interesting. Offering a wide range of flagship beers along with limited releases, sours, and barrel-aged ales Take about a half-hour drive south to the coast and the popular destination of Pensacola with several brewery options along with a must-visit brewery:

Gulf Coast Brewery 500 Heinberg Street 32502 (850) 696-2335
https://www.gulfcoastbrewery.net/

Perfect Plain Brewing Company 50 E Garden Street 32502 (850) 471-8998 https://www.perfectplain.com/

Spahr Brewing Company 3541 W Fairfield Drive 32505 (850) 439-5362
http://spahrbrewingcompany.com/

Coastal County Brewing 3041 East Olive Road 32514 (850) 741-2973
https://coastalcountybrewing.com/

Goat Lips Chew and Brewhouse 2811 Copter Road 32514 (850) 474-1919 https://www.goatlips.com/

Pensacola Bay Brewery 225 Zaragoza Street 32501 (850) 434-3353
https://pbbrew.com/

Producing flavorful and authentic craft beer. Brewing without preservatives or chemicals to give you the highest quality beers. Follow the coast about a half-hour to the town of Navarre:

Ye Olde Brothers Brewery 4458 Highway 87 N 32566 (850) 684-1495
https://www.yeoldebrothersbrewery.com/

Another twenty-minutes down the coast is the town of Fort Walton Beach with another brewery:

Props Brewery and Tap Room 255 Miracle Strip Parkway SE B-19 32548 (850) 586-7117 http://www.propsbrewery.com/

Head inland about twenty-minutes to Niceville and their brewery:

3rd Planet Brewing 120 Partin Drive North 32578 (850) 502-9952
https://www.3rdplanetbrewing.com/

Drive about another twenty-minutes back to the coast and the town of Destin with a must-visit brewery:

Destin Brewery 505 Mountain Drive Unit N 32541 (850) 842-4757
https://destinbrewery.com/

Brewing a line of beers that reflect the style, flavor, and fun of Destin. They offer a core selection of beers as well as a rotating selection of their current experimentations. Follow the coast about another half-hour to Santa Rosa Beach and a couple breweries:

Grayton Beer Company 217 Serenoa Road 32459 (850) 231-4786
https://www.graytonbeer.com/

Idyll Hounds Brewing Company 845 Serenoa Road 32459 (850) 231-1138 https://www.idyllhoundsbrewingcompany.com/

Another forty minutes down the coast brings you to the popular tourist destination of Panama City:

Uncle Ernie's Bayfront Grill and Brew House 151 Bayview Avenue 32401 (850) 763-8427 http://uncleerniesbayfrontgrill.com/

Head inland on about a two-hour drive to the main city of Tallahassee and several brewery options including two must-visits:

Proof Brewing Company 1320 S Monroe Street 32301 (850) 577-0517
https://www.proofbrewingco.com/

Ology Brewing Company 118 E 6th Avenue 32303 (850) 296-2809
https://ologybrewing.com/

Lake Tribe Brewing 3357 Garber Drive 32303
https://www.laketribebrewing.com/

Brewing robust beers with diverse tastes, aromas, and pairings. All the beers have a smooth complexity that makes them easy to drink and enjoyed by all.

DEEP Brewing Company 2524 Cathay Court 32308 (850) 570-1478
http://deepbrewing.com/

Artfully crafting the finest small-batch ales and lagers. A focus on European and American styles. Offering 15 core beers on tap along with 10 seasonal and rotating offerings.

Southern Florida

Take a one or two day trip around the beautiful coastal towns of southern Florida while enjoying some excellent breweries. Start on the eastern coast of southern Florida in Port Saint Lucie with a couple breweries, including a must-visit:

Side Door Brewing Company 1419 SE Village Green Drive 34952 (772) 249-0065 https://www.sidedoorbrewingcompany.com/

Hop Life Brewing Company 679 NW Enterprise Drive Suite 101 34986 (772) 249-5055 https://www.hoplife.com/

Focused on fresh, flavorful, innovative, and high-quality craft beers. Enjoy a beer in their environmentally focused taproom. Drive about two and half-hours across Florida to the western coast and the town of Punta Gorda which also has two breweries including a must-visit:

Peace River Beer Company 1732 Steadley Avenue 33950 (941) 655-8352 https://www.peaceriver.beer/

Fat Point Brewing 611 Charlotte Street 33950 (800) 380-7405 https://fatpoint.com/

Offering flavorful and original beers inspired by the location. Their most acclaimed brew is Belgian Trippel. From here head about a half-hour south to the coastal town of Cape Coral and a must-visit brewery:

Big Blue Brewing Company 4721 SE 10th Place 33904 (239) 471-2777 https://bigbluebrewing.com/

Creating easy drinking and balanced beers for all levels of beer drinkers. The beers are made with local ingredients. Just fifteen minutes east is the city of Fort Myers with a few options including a must-visit brewery:

Millennial Brewing Company 1811 Royal Palm Avenue 33901 (239) 271-2255 https://www.millennialbrewing.com/

Fort Myers Brewing Company 12811 Commerce Lake Drive Suite 27-28 33913 (239) 313-6576 https://www.fmbrew.com/

Old Soul Brewing 10970 S Cleveland Avenue Ste 402 33907 (239) 334-4334 https://www.oldsoulbrewing.com/

Point Ybel Brewing Company 16120 San Carlos Blvd Ste 4 33908 (239) 980-2764 https://pointybelbrew.com/

Known for their East Coast Style IPAs, traditional beers, and sour ales. In five years, the beer here has won numerous awards. Head south again for twenty-five minutes to a brewery at Bonita Springs:

Momentum Brewhouse 9786 Bonita Beach Road SE Unit 1-2 34135 (239) 949-9945 http://www.momentumbrewhouse.com/

Twenty-minutes south is the main city of Naples with four breweries:

Naples Beach Brewery 4110 Enterprise Avenue Ste 217 34104 (239) 304-8795 https://www.naplesbeachbrewery.com/

Ankrolab Brewing Company 3555 Bayshore Drive 34112 (239) 330-7899 https://www.ankrolab.com/

Bone Hook Brewing Company 1514 Immokalee Road #106 34110 (239) 631-8522 https://bonehookbrewing.com/

Riptide Brewing Company 987 3rd Avenue N 34102 (239) 228-6533 https://riptidebrewingcompany.com/

Take a half-hour trip to the brewery on Marco Island:

Marco Island Brewery 1089 N Collier Blvd 34145 (239) 970-0461 https://www.marcoislandbrewery.com/

Drive about two hours back to the east coast and the town of Coral Springs:

Big Bear Brewing Company 1800 N University Drive 33071 (954) 341-5545 https://bigbearbrewingco.com/

End your trip with a two-hour drive to Islamorada along the island chains:

Islamorada Beer Company 82770 Old Highway 33036 (305) 508-9093 https://www.islamoradabeerco.com/

Florida Keys Brewing Company 200 Morada Way 33036 (305) 916-5206 https://floridakeysbrewingco.com/

The first microbrewery in the Upper Keys. Offering a great selection of year-round beers along with rotating seasonal and barrel-aged beers.

Miami-Fort Lauderdale Area

If you want a simple one or two day trip, then this is the option for you. You can stay in a local area like Miami and then travel to the breweries. Start your trip at the brewery in the coastal town of Coral Gables:

Titanic Brewing Company 5813 Ponce De Leon Blvd 33146 (305) 667-2537 https://www.titanicbrewery.com/

Follow the coast thirteen minutes north to the main city of Miami with several brewery options including several must-visit breweries:

The Tank Brewing Company 5100 NW 72nd Avenue Bay A1 33166 (305) 468-8265 https://thetankbrewing.com/

NightLife Brewing Company 1588 NW 7th Street 33125 (786) 787-2337 http://www.nightlifebrewingco.com/

Veza Sur Brewing Company 55 NW 25th Street 33127 (786) 362-6300 https://vezasur.com/

Beat Culture Brewing Company 7250 NW 11th Street 33126 (786) 431-5413 https://beatculture.com/

Lincoln's Beard Brewing Company 7360 SW 41 Street 33155 (305) 912-7390 http://lincolnsbeardbrewing.com/

J. Wakefield Brewing 120 NW 24th Street 33127 (786) 254-7779 https://jwakefieldbrewing.com/

Well known for their sours as well as a coconut-infused Hefeweizen. Some of their beers have a unique twist and depth of character, while others are traditional styles.

Concrete Beach Brewery 325 NW 24th Street 33127 (305) 796-2727 https://concretebeachbrewery.com/

Offering an artistic array of classically brewed ales and lagers. You'll find an excellent selection of different styles on tap.

Wynwood Brewing Company 565 NW 24th Street 33127 (305) 434-0323 https://www.wynwoodbrewing.com/

The first craft production brewery in Miami. They have won awards for their flagship ales and porter.

Unseen Creatures Brewing and Blending 4178 SW 74th Court 33155 (786) 332-2903 https://unseencreatures.com/

Crafting refreshing, sessional, and hop-forward beers. Focusing on balance and drinkability rather than actual beer styles. Take a twenty-minute drive inland to the brewery at Doral:

Tripping Animals Brewing 2685 NW 105th Avenue 33172 (305) 646-1339 https://www.trippinganimals.com/

Head back east to a must-visit brewery in the town of Hialeah:

Unbranded Brewing Company 1395 E 11th Avenue 33010 (786) 332-3097 https://unbrandedbrewing.com/

Using non-traditional styles, ingredients, and methods ensure you get something completely unique and different. Offering three unique beers on tap to sample. Opa-Locka is eleven minutes north with another brewery option:

Legacy Caribbean Craft Brewery 13416 NW 38th Court 33054 (786) 681-6572 http://www.legacyccb.com/

Another twenty-minute drive north brings you to the coastal town of Hollywood:

Hollywood Brewing Company 290 N Boardwalk 33019 (305) 414-4757 https://hollywood.beer/

Six minutes away is the coastal town of Dania Beach with a must-visit brewery:

3 Sons Brewing Company 236 N Federal Highway 33004 (954) 601-3833 https://www.3sonsbrewingco.com/

Brewing flavorful and unique beers. You'll find flavors here you don't find anywhere else. Stop in to try something new today. Another eight minutes north brings you to the next major city of Fort Lauderdale with several brewery options as well as a couple must-visit options:

Invasive Species Brewing 726 NE 2nd Avenue 33304 (754) 666-2687 https://invasivespeciesbrewing.bigcartel.com/

Tarpon River Brewing 280 SW 6th Street 33301 (954) 353-3193 http://tarponriverbrewing.com/

LauderAle 3305 SE 14 Avenue Building 4 33316 (954) 653-9711 https://lauderale.co/

A small-batch, electric-fired brewery that cultivates authentic ales with a local influence. The beers include a wide variety of ranging styles from blondes to imperial stouts.

Gulf Stream Brewing Company 1105 NE 13th Street 33304 (954) 766-4842 https://www.gulfstreambeer.com/

A gold medal brewery that offers an immersive experience. Offering creative, balanced beers that range across multiple styles. Head inland eleven minutes to a must-visit brewery at Lauderhill:

Yeasty Brews 3944 NW 19th Street 33311 (305) 710-7794
https://www.yeastybrews.com/

All beers are handcrafted in small batches with fresh, natural ingredients. The beers here are made with a combination of fruits, spices, and herbs for a unique tasting experience. End your trip with a twelve-minute drive back east to the town of Oakland Park:

Funky Buddha Brewery 1201 NE 38th Street 33334 (954) 440-0046
https://funkybuddhabrewery.com/

Georgia

Southern Georgia

Take a trip from the Gulf Coast into the heartland of Georgia. This trip will take you a day or two and brings you to some excellent breweries. Start your trip out in the main coastal town of Savannah with multiple brewery options include two must-visit breweries:

Southbound Brewing Company 107 East Lathrop 31415 (912) 618-0010 https://southboundbrewingco.com/

Moon River Brewing Company 21 West Bay Street 31401 (912) 447-0943 https://moonriverbrewing.com/

Coastal Empire Beer Company 79 Ross Road 31405 (912) 335-2804 http://coastalempirebeer.com/

Two Tides Brewing Company 12 W 41 Street 31401 (912) 667-0706 https://www.twotidesbrewing.com/

Small-batch, handcrafted beers that focus on modern styles and modern-takes on the classics. The beers are approachable and easy to drink.

Service Brewing Company 574 Indian Street 31401 (912) 358-1002 https://servicebrewing.com/

Crafting authentic American-made beers. Focusing on high quality, local ingredients. Producing year-round beers on a large scale while producing small batches of experimental beers. Head inland about a half-hour to Statesboro and their must-visit brewery:

Eagle Creek Brewing Company 106 Savannah Avenue Suite B 30458 (912) 486-5893 http://www.eaglecreekbrewingco.com/

The first craft brewery in Statesboro. Focused on producing delicious, interesting, and highly drinkable beers made from the best ingredients possible. About a three-hour drive southwest brings you close to the southern boundary of the state and the town of Valdosta with a must-visit brewery:

Georgia Beer Company 109 South Briggs Street 31601 (992) 399-5883 https://georgiabeerco.com/

The southernmost brewery in Georgia. Specializing in seasonal ales, stouts, and IPAs made from local ingredients. Now head northwest about an hour and a half to Albany:

Pretoria Fields Collective 120 Pine Avenue 31701 (229) 518-1770 http://pretoriafields.com/

Continue northwest another hour and a half to the town of Omaha on the western boundary of the state:

Omaha Brewing Company 1 Brew Street 31821 (229) 838-4779 http://www.omahabrewingcompany.com/

End by heading about two hours northeast to Macon and the inland heart of Georgia:

Ocmulgee Brewpub 484 2nd Street 31201 (478) 254-2848 https://ocmulgeebrewpub.com/

Piedmont Brewery and Kitchen 450 Third Street 31202 (478) 254-2337 https://www.piedmontbrewery.com/

Focusing on classic styles as well as unique and trendy styles. Offering over 20 unique varieties of beer a year.

Northeast Georgia

Take a day or two to drive this route and visit some great breweries in the north and northwest region of Georgia. You can also combine it with the Atlanta area tour if you want to spend a little extra time in the area and see even more breweries. Start your trip out at the brewery in Woodstock:

Reformation Brewery 500 Arnold Mill Way 30188 (678) 341-0828 https://reformationbrewery.com/

Head to Kennesaw, about fifteen minutes south:

Dry County Brewing Company 1500 Lockhart Drive 30144 (770) 250-0345 https://www.drycountybrewco.com/

Another twelve-minute southeast to Marietta with several brewery options including a must-visit:

Glover Park Brewery 65 Atlanta Street 30060 (404) 555-1212
https://gloverparkbrewery.com/

Ironmonger Brewing 2129 Northwest Parkway Suite 105 30067 (678) 742-8551 https://www.ironmongerbrewing.com/

Schoolhouse Brewing 840 Franklin Court Suite A 30067 (770) 361-5247 https://www.schoolhousebeer.com/

Red Hare Brewing Company 1998 Delk Industrial Blvd 30067 (770) 331-8763 https://www.redharebrewing.com/

Crafting beers that can be enjoyed anywhere for any occasion. There are six year-round beers in addition to seasonal offerings. Now head east about a half-hour to Peachtree Corners:

Anderby Brewing 110 Technology Parkway #200 30092 (770) 559-7550 https://anderbybrewing.com/

Continue about twenty-minutes east to a brewery at Lawrenceville:

Slow Pour Brewing Company 407 N Clayton Street 30046 https://slowpourbrewing.com/

Next head north about fifteen minutes to Suwanee with two must-visit breweries:

StillFire Brewing 343 US 23 30024 (770) 927-8989 https://stillfirebrewing.com/

Developing the world's most innovative beers. When you come here, you'll find your favorite beer.

Monkey Wrench Brewing 3425 Martin Farm Road 30024 https://www.monkeywrenchbrewing.com/

Using innovative brewing techniques and age-old traditions. Offering everything from the classics to off-the-wall styles. Keep heading another twenty-minutes north to Cumming with another must-visit brewery:

Cherry Street Brewing Co-op 5810 Bond Street E-2 30040 (770) 205-5512 http://www.cherrystreetbrewing.com/

Offering a mix of traditional and one-off brews. You'll always find something new, fresh and exciting on tap here. Head northeast about a half-hour to a must-visit brewery at Gainesville:

Left Nut Brewing Company 2100 Atlanta Highway 30504 (678) 827-6678 https://www.leftnutbrewing.com/

Producing craft beers and ciders of all types and flavors. Stop in to try some of their wonderful beers. Head southeast about fifty minutes to Athens with several brewery options:

Terrapin Beer Company 265 Newton Bridge Road 30607 (706) 202-4467 https://www.terrapinbeer.com/

Creature Comforts Brewing Company 271 W Hancock Avenue 30601 (706) 410-1043 http://www.creaturecomfortsbeer.com/

Akademia Brewing Company 150 Crane Drive 30622 (678) 726-2288 https://akademiabc.com/

The Southern Brewing Company 231 Collins Industrial Blvd 30601 (706) 255-2444 https://www.sobrewco.com/

Another forty minutes south brings you to Greensboro:

Oconee Brewing Company 202 North West Street 30642 (706) 920-1177 https://www.oconeebrewingco.com/

End in Augusta, about an hour east, with two must-visit breweries:

River Watch Brewery 1150 5th Street Bldg. 61 30901 (706) 421-7177 https://www.riverwatchbrewery.com/

Offering three core brews along with limited releases and experimental beers. Come here to find your next favorite beer.

Savannah River Brewing Company 813 5th Street 30901 (706) 426-8212 https://www.savannahriverbrew.com/

Brewing the finest ales, lagers, and other unique styles. Stop in today to try an old favorite or experiment and find something new.

Great Atlanta Area

If you want to experience the Atlanta area in depth and want to enjoy some great brews while there, then consider taking a tour of the surrounding area. You can easily complete this trip in a day or two if you're driving through it. Or you can get a hotel in Atlanta and take several day trips to the surrounding area breweries while enjoying other activities in the surrounding area. Start your visit your south of Atlanta in the town of Hapeville at:

Arches Brewing 3361 Dogwood Drive 30354 (678) 653-2739 https://www.archesbrewing.com/

Atlanta is just nine minutes north with many brewery options, but at least three must-visits if you don't have time to visit them all:

Second Self Beer Company 1311 Logan Circle NW 30318 (678) 916-8035 https://secondselfbeer.com/

Fire Maker Brewing Company 975 Chattahoochee Avenue NW 30318 (678) 705-8777 https://www.firemakerbeer.com/

Torched Hop Brewing Company 249 Ponce De Leon Avenue NE 30308 (404) 835-2040 http://www.torchedhopbrewing.com/

Max Lager's Wood Fired Grill and Brewery 320 Peachtree Street 30308 (404) 525-4400 https://maxlagers.com/

Eventide Brewing 1015 Grant Street SE 30315 (404) 907-4543 https://www.eventidebrewing.com/

Halfway Crooks Beer 60 Georgia Avenue SE 30312
https://halfwaycrooks.beer/

Steady Hand Beer Company 1611 Ellsworth Industrial Blvd Suite F
30318 (404) 458-5981 http://www.steadyhandbeer.com/

Scofflaw Brewing Company 1738 MacArthur Blvd NW 30318
https://scofflawbeer.com/

New Realm Brewing Company 550 Somerset Terrace NE Suite 101
30306 (404) 968-2777 https://newrealmbrewing.com/

SweetWater Brewing Company 195 Ottley Drive 30324 (404) 691-2537
https://www.sweetwaterbrew.com/

Atlanta Brewing Company 2323 Defoor Hills Road NW 30318 (404) 892-
4436 https://atlantabrewing.com/

The first craft brewery in Georgia. Focused on brewing quality, innovative
beers. Regional ingredients are used to make the beers.

Orpheus Brewing 1440 Dutch Valley Place Suite 2001 30327 (404) 347-
1777 https://www.orpheusbrewing.com/

An early focus on sour beers and wild barrels led to the first sour beer in
Georgia. Now you can try a wide range of beer styles in their taproom.

Monday Night Brewing 670 Trabert Avenue NW 30318 (404) 352-7703
https://mondaynightbrewing.com/

Brewing balanced, flavorful ales that pair well with food. They are starting
to experiment with sour beers and barrel-aged fermentation. Head east
about twelve minutes to the town of Decatur where there is a few options
including two must-visit breweries:

Three Taverns Craft Brewery 121 New Street 30030 (404) 660-3355
https://www.threetavernsbrewery.com/

Sceptre Brewing Arts 630 East Lake Drive Suite E 30030 (470) 428-4359 https://www.sceptrebrewingarts.com/

Twain's Billiards and Tap 211 East Trinity Place 30030 (404) 373-0063 https://twains.net/

Brewing bold and consistently pleasing ales. Stop in today to try some of their freshly brewed beers.

Wild Heaven Beer 135 Maple Street 30030 (404) 997-8589 https://wildheavenbeer.com/

All beers are made using the European brewing tradition but have an American creative flair. The beers have bold flavor without excess alcohol. Just four more minutes east is another brewery at Avondale Estates:

The Lost Druid 2866 Washington Street 30002 (404) 998-5679 https://thelostdruid.com/

Head northeast about ten minutes to the town of Tucker with two more options:

High Card Brewing 2316 Main Street Suite K 30084 (678) 561-2337 http://www.highcardbrewing.com/home.html

Tucker Brewing Company 2003 S Bibb Drive 30084 (833) 752-2400 https://tuckerbrewing.com/

Offering you consistently delicious lagers. The only brewery in Georgia specifically dedicated to brewing easy-to-drink and flavorful lagers. Now go northwest slightly for about ten minutes to the town of Chamblee:

Hopstix 3404 Pierce Drive 30341 (678) 888-2306 https://hopstix.com/#home

Another twelve minutes northwest brings you to another brewery in Sandy Springs:

Pontoon Brewing Company 8601 Dunwoody Place Building 500 Suite 500 30350 (813) 817-8047 https://www.pontoonbrewing.com/

Head north to Roswell another twelve minutes away and three more brewery options:

Gate City Brewing Company 43 Magnolia Street 30075 (678) 404-0961 https://www.gatecitybrewingcompany.com/

Variant Brewing Company 66 Norcross Street 30075 (678) 242-8189 https://www.variantbrewing.com/

From the Earth 1570 Holcomb Bridge Road 30076 (770) 910-9799 https://www.ftebrewing.com/

A ten-minute drive slightly northeast brings you to Alpharetta:

Jekyll Brewing Company 2855 Marconi Drive Ste 350 3005 (844) 453-5955 https://www.jekyllbrewing.com/

End your trip with a thirteen-minute drive east to a must-visit brewery in Johns Creek:

Six Bridges Brewing 11455 Lakefield Drive #300 30097 (470) 545-4199 https://www.sixbridgesbrewing.com/

A dog and kid-friendly taproom. Just a few of their many offerings include lagers, NEIPAs, pastry stouts, suasions, and fruited sours.

Northeastern Georgia

If you want to experience the rugged beauty of the mountains in Georgia, then this is the perfect trip for you. It'll probably take at least two days since mountain travel can be a little slower. But you'll want to take a leisurely trip through this area to enjoy the wonderful views. Start your trip in the eastern town of LaGrange with two breweries including a must-visit:

Wild Leap Brew Company 308 Main Street 30240 (706) 298-6400 https://www.wildleap.com/

Beacon Brewing Company 700 Lincoln Street 30240 (706) 298-6500 https://www.beacon.beer/

Brewing unique and contemporary beers in both a traditional and technical fashion. Try their beers and be amazed at the blending of local flavors. Take a forty-minute drive north to Carrollton:

Printer's Ale Manufacturing Company 940 Columbia Drive 30117 (770) 836-4253 https://printers-ale.com/

Another forty-minute drive east brings you to the town of Peachtree City with another brewery:

Line Creek Brewing Company 150 Huddleston Road 30269 (678) 545-6024 https://linecreekbrewing.com/

Then take a two-hour drive north into the mountains and stop in the mountain town of Blue Ridge with two breweries including a must-visit:

Grumpy Old Men Brewing 1315 East Main Street 30513 (404) 966-2665 https://grumpyoldmenbrewing.com/

Fannin Brewing Company 3758 East First Street 30513 (706) 675-5497 https://www.fanninbrewingcompany.com/

Beers made in the German tradition. Come for the excellent fresh beers and end up staying to enjoy the wonderful fresh air and beauty around you. When you're ready, take a drive about an hour west through the mountains to a brewery in the town of Dalton:

Cherokee Brewing 207-B W Cuyler Street 30720 (706) 529-9478 https://www.cherokeebrewingandpizzaco.com/

End your trip with a half-hour drive west to Rock Spring and a must-visit brewery:

Phantom Horse Brewing Company 56 Fieldstone Village Drive #A 30739 (706) 375-9182 https://www.phantomhorsebrewing.com/

Offering a variety of unique styles for all beer drinkers. There are light beers with subtle notes and other beers that are full and bold.

Hawaii

Hawaii is a wonderful place to have a vacation, and it is a great place to try some excellent beers. On your next trip to Hawaii, consider taking a few days to do some island hopping and experience all the breweries Hawaii has to offer. Start your trip at the main city of Honolulu with several options including three must-visit breweries:

Waikiki Brewing Company 1945 Kalakaua Avenue 96815 (808) 941-2400 https://waikikibrewing.com/

Bent Tail Brewing Company 506 Keawe Street 96813 (808) 200-2739 http://www.realgastropub.com/

Providing the largest and finest selection of craft beers in Hawaii. Come enjoy a glass of your favorite beer with 38 taps and pair it with some award-winning food.

Aloha Beer Company 700 Queen Street 96813 (808) 544-1605
https://www.alohabeer.com/

Looking towards the future of craft brewing in Hawaii, but also rooting themselves in the tradition of the past. Enjoy a variety of beer styles when you come here.

Honolulu Beerworks 328 Cooke Street 96813 (808) 589-2337
https://www.honolulubeerworks.com/

Focused on brewing delicious craft beer from unique and locally sourced ingredients. Featuring a robust barrel-aging program. Head north to the other side of the island at Kaneohe:

Stewbum and Stonewall Brewing Company 46-174 Kahuhipa Street 96815 (412) 716-7162 https://www.stewbumandstonewall.com/

Just a little east is the town of Kailua and a must-visit brewery:

Lanikai Brewing Company 175 C Hamakua Drive 96734
https://www.lanikaibrewing.com/

Brewing beers premium, local ingredients for rare and exotic beers. The result is bold and flavorful beers you won't taste anywhere else. From here head over to the island of Maui and the city of Lahaina and another must-visit brewery:

Kohola Brewery 910 Honoapiilani Highway #55 96761 (808) 868-3198
https://www.koholabrewery.com/

Known for producing clean, easy-drinking, and balanced ales and lagers. Stop in today to try one of their award-winning beers. Stay on the same island and head south to another must-visit brewery at Kihei:

Maui Brewing Company 605 Lipoa Parkway 96753 (808) 213-3002
https://mauibrewingco.com/

Brewing authentic ales and lagers. Try one of their seven year-round brews or taste a limited release. Head to the last island and the town of Kamuela:

Big Island Brewhaus 64-1066 Mamalahoa Highway 96743 (808) 887-1717 https://bigislandbrewhaus.com/

End your trip slightly southwest in Kailua-Kona:

Kona Brewing Company 75-5629 Kuakini Highway 96740 (808) 334-BREW https://konabrewingco.com/

Idaho

Northern Idaho

Take a few days to enjoy the beauty of Northern Idaho, along with the beautiful scenery and nature around you. There is plenty to see and do, so depending on how much you want to enjoy, this can be a several day-long trip. Start your trip at a must-visit brewery in Elk River:

Shattuck Brewery 52106 Highway 8 83827 (208) 596-9579 https://www.shattuckbrewery.com/

Brewing beer from locally sourced flavors for a bold taste. Their line of rotating and seasonal beers is constantly growing. From there head about an hour west to the town of Moscow with two brewery options:

Moscow Brewing Company 630 N Almon Street 83843 (208) 874-7340 http://moscowbrewing.com/index.html

Hunga Dunga Brewing 333 N Jackson Street 83843 (208) 596-4855 http://www.hungadungabrewing.com/a9gmsjvj7qc5kwxmadnkw7kouemuzp

From here it is about an hour and a half drive north to the main city of Coeur d'Alene with two more breweries:

Tricksters Brewing Company 3850 N Schrieber Way 83815 (970) 764-7128 https://www.trickstersbrewing.com/

Paragon Brewing 5785 N Government Way 83815 (208) 772-9292 https://www.paragonbrewing.com/

Head east to a brewery in Kellogg about a half-hour away:

Radio Brewing Company 319 Main Street 83837 (208) 786-6633 http://www.radiobrewingcompany.com/

Another eleven minutes east offer two more breweries in the town of Wallace:

Wallace Brewing Company 610 Bank Street 83873 (208) 752-8381 http://wallacebrewing.com/

City Limits Pub and Grill/North Idaho Mountain Brew 108 Nine Mile Road 83873 (208) 556-1120 https://northidahomountainbrew.com/

From here head about an hour back west to Post Falls with a couple options including a must-visit brewery:

Post Falls Brewing Company 112 N Spokane Street 83854 (208) 773-7301 http://postfallsbrewing.com/

Selkirk Abbey Brewing Company 6180 E Seltice Way 83854 (208) 292-4901 https://www.selkirkabbey.com/

Offering Belgian beer for every palate. Try a refreshing, spicy Saison to rich, malty Trappist and everything else in between. Just fourteen minutes northeast is another must-visit brewery in the town of Hayden:

Bombastic Brewing 11100 N Airport Road 83835 https://www.bombasticbrewing.com/

Making beers from recipes that offer unique beer styles you've likely never tried before. Come try a variety of flavors, including everything from dark beers to barrel-aged options. Head about forty minutes north to the town of Sandpoint with a few breweries including two must-visit breweries:

Matchwood Brewing Company 513 Oak Street 83864 (208) 718-2739 https://www.matchwoodbrewing.com/

MickDuff's Brewing Company 312 N First Avenue 83888 (208) 255-4351 https://www.mickduffs.com/

Offering a full lineup of handcrafted beers through a year-round selection as well as seasonal and specialty brews.

Utara Brewing Company 214 Pine Street 83864 (208) 255-2453 https://www.utaraidaho.com/

A British style brewpub serving small-batch beer along with Anglo-Indian cuisine. Come for a flavorful and cultural experience. End your trip just four minutes away at a must-visit brewery in the town of Ponderay:

Laughing Dog Brewery 1109 Fontaine Drive 83852 (208) 263-9222 https://www.laughingdogbrewing.com/

Home of many award-winning beers, including their Huckleberry Cream Ale. There are plenty of year-round beers to choose from or limited release options.

Boise Area

If you don't have a lot of time to spend or you don't want to travel too far, then consider staying in Boise. There are plenty of breweries in town and a few in the nearby areas. This will give you plenty of options to visit while enjoying other activities in the area. Within the city of Boise there are plenty of options, including multiple must-visit breweries in case you don't have time to visit them all:

Bear Island Brewing Company 1620 N Liberty Street 83704 (208) 908-2496 https://www.bearislandbrewing.com/

Highlands Hollow Brewhouse 2455 Harrison Hollow Street 83702 (208) 343-6820 https://www.highlandshollow.com/

Edge Brewing Company 525 N Steelhead Way 83704 (208) 995-2980 https://www.edgebrew.com/

Sockeye Brewing 12542 W Fairview Avenue 83713 (208) 322-5200 https://www.sockeyebrew.com/

Lost Grove Brewing 1026 S La Pointe Street 83706 (208) 286-2258 https://www.lostgrovebrewing.com/

Payette Brewing Company 733 S Pioneer Street 83702 (208) 344-0011 https://www.payettebrewing.com/

Boise Brewing 521 W Broad Street 83702 (208) 342-7655 https://www.boisebrewing.com/

Clairvoyant Brewing Company 2800 W Idaho Street 83702 (208) 890-1247 https://www.clairvoyantbrewing.com/

Cloud 9 Brewery 1750 W State Street 83702 (208) 794-0985 https://www.cloud9brewery.com/

Offering nine year-round beers, but with many more taps, you have a wide range of beers to choose from. You can also enjoy unique culinary creations along with your beer.

White Dog Brewing 705 W Fulton Street 83702 (208) 906-0609
https://www.whitedogbrewing.com/

Offering award-winning classic beers and an excellent selection of rotating beers. You'll find a number of beers here to please any palate.

Woodland Empire Ale Craft 1114 W Front Street 83702 (208) 602-9318
https://woodlandempire.com/

Focused on brewing solid, delicious, and authentic beer. Everything is made from real ingredients, not extracts or flavorings.

Mad Swede Brewing Company 2772 S Cole Road Suite 140 83709 (208) 922-6883 https://madswedebrewing.com/

Possibly some of the finest beers you'll ever try. Offering an impressive array of beers for all levels of beer drinkers. An eight-minute drive to the north brings you to Garden City with several options as well as two must-visit breweries:

Loose Screw Beer Company 4340 W Chinden Blvd 83714 (208) 629-5623 https://www.loosescrew.beer/

County Line Brewing 9115 W Chinden Blvd #107 83714 (208) 830-2456
https://www.countylinebrewing.com/

Powderhaus Brewing 9719 W Chinden Blvd 83714 (208) 473-5801
https://www.powderhausbrewing.com/

Brewing outstanding varieties of craft beer that offer the best in taste. Stop in today to try a true taste of alpine brewing.

Crooked Fence Brewing 5242 Chinden Blvd 83714 (208) 901-2090
http://www.crookedfencebrewing.com/

Offering a wide variety of styles and types. Try your favorite type from the year-round selection and then try something new with their rotating offers. About a half-hour to the west is the town of Nampa with two breweries, including a must-visit:

Crescent Brewery 1521 Front Street 83687 (208) 968-1034
https://www.crescentbeer.com/

2C Family Brewing Company 1215 First Street South 83651 (208) 995-4802 https://2cfamilybrewing.com/

Expertly brewed beers from the highest quality ingredients. Some options to try to include German lagers, Belgian ales, fruit sours, and barrel-aged beers.

Central Idaho

Take a one to two day trip from the north-central part of Idaho to the south-central corner of Idaho. You'll have plenty to see and do along the way along with several great breweries. Start your trip in Kendrick at:

Hardware Brewing Company 701 E Main Street 83537 (208) 289-5000
https://www.hardwarebrewingco.com/

Take about a three-hour drive south through the mountains to McCall with a couple of brewery options:

Broken Horn Brewing Company 201 S Mission Street 83638 (208) 315-5772 http://www.brokenhornbrewing.com/index.html

McCall Brewing Company 807 N 3rd Street 83638 (208) 634-3309
https://mccallbrew.com/

Next is about a four-hour drive over the mountains to a must-visit brewery in the town of Ketchum:

Warfield Distillery and Brewery 280 Main Street 83340 (208) 726-2739
https://drinkwarfield.com/

Craft beer made from only organic malt and whole leaf hops. Offering a full range of beer styles for all palates. Just another fifteen minutes south brings you to Hailey with a couple options including a must-visit brewery:

Sawtooth Brewery 110 N River Street 83333 (208) 806-1368
https://www.sawtoothbrewery.com/

Sun Valley Brewing Company 202 N Main Street 83333 (208) 788-0805
http://www.sunvalleybrewery.com/The_Sun_Valley_Brewery/Welcome.ht
ml

Offering twelve tap beers, many of them award winners. Pair the beers
with some excellent food options as well. End your trip with about a two
and a half-hour drive east to a must-visit brewery at Idaho Falls:

Snow Eagle Brewing and Grill 455 River Parkway 83402 (208) 557-
0455 http://snoweaglebrewing.com/

There are plenty of great beers to choose from here. Four of the best
options to try are the cream ale, IPA, brown ale, and milk stout.

Teton Valley

The Teton area of Idaho is home to some of the finest hop fields in the
world. The water sourced here comes from glacier runoff. If you want to
taste some of the finest and purest beers, then take this short day trip to
three towns and some excellent breweries. Start your trip in the town of
Pocatello with two options including a must-visit brewery:

Jim Dandy Brewing 305 E Lander Street 83201 (208) 240-0470
https://www.jimdandybrewing.com/

Portneuf Valley Brewing 615 S 1st Avenue 83201 (208) 232-1644
https://www.portneufvalleybrewing.com/

There are plenty of great beers to try here, but their most award-winning
option that you must try is the Oatmeal Stout. From here take about a two-
hour drive north to the city of Victor with another two breweries including a
must-visit:

Wildlife Brewing 145 S Main Street 83455 (208) 787-2623
http://wildlifebrewing.com/

Grand Teton Brewing 430 Old Jackson Highway 83455 (888) 899-1656
http://grandtetonbrewing.com/

Crafting high-quality ales and lagers. Made from hops grown at some of the finest hop farms in the world. Come taste the difference for yourself. End your trip ten minutes north in the town of Driggs at:

Citizen 33 Brewery 364 N Main Street 83422 (208) 357-9099
https://www.citizen33.com/

Illinois

Greater Chicago Area

When it comes to breweries and enjoying a beer after a long, hard day, no place does it better than Chicago. The city itself is home to many wonderful breweries that could easily take you weeks to visit. We'll list all the options, but give you some must-visits so you can limit yourself to what you are able to see during your trip. Then in the surrounding area, there are also some great day trips you can make if you want to get a little out of the city to enjoy your beer tasting. First, let's consider the many brewery options within the city of Chicago and the must-visit destinations if you are limited on how much time you can spend in the area:

Corridor Brewery and Provisions 3446 North Southport 60657 (773) 270-4272 https://www.corridorchicago.com/

Aleman Brewing Company 3304 N Knox Avenue 60641 (812) 340-4198 https://www.alemanchicago.com/

Band of Bohemia 4710 North Ravenswood Avenue 60640 (773) 271-4710 http://www.bandofbohemia.com/

Maplewood Brewery and Distillery 2717 North Maplewood Avenue 60647 (773) 270-1061 https://maplewoodbrew.com/

Old Irving Brewing Company 4419 West Montrose Avenue 60641 (773) 916-6421 https://www.oldirvingbrewing.com/

Moody Tongue Brewing Company 2136 South Peoria Street 60608 (312) 600-5111 https://www.moodytongue.com/

Burning Bush Brewery 4014 North Rockwell Street 60618 (847) 858-0641 https://www.burningbushbrewery.com/

Half Acre Beer Company 4257 N Lincoln Avenue 60618 (773) 248-4038 https://www.halfacrebeer.com/

Lake Effect Brewing Company 4727 Montrose 60641 (312) 919-4473 http://www.lakeeffectbrewing.com/

Bold Dog Beer Company 4727 W Montrose Avenue Suite 3 60641 (309) 883-0973 http://www.bolddogbeerco.com/

Goose Island Beer Company 1800 West Fulton Street 60612 (312) 226-1119 https://www.gooseisland.com/

Open Outcry Brewing Company 10934 S Western Avenue 60643 (773) 629-6055 http://www.openoutcrybrewing.com/

DryHop Brewers 3155 N Broadway 60657 (773) 857-3155
https://dryhopchicago.com/

Local Option 1102 West Webster Avenue 60614 (773) 348-2008
https://localoptionbier.com/

On Tour Brewing Company 1725 W Hubbard Street 60622 (312) 796-3119 https://ontourbrewing.com/

Burnt City Brewing 2747 N Lincoln Avenue 60614 (773) 295-1270
https://burntcitybrewing.com/

Twisted Hippo 2925 W Montrose 60618 (708) 844-7768
https://www.twistedhippo.com/

BiXi Beer 2515 North Milwaukee Avenue 60647 (773) 904-7361
https://www.bixi.beer/

Begyle Brewing Company 1800 West Cuyler 60613 (773) 661-6963
http://www.begylebrewing.com/home

Metropolitan Brewing 3057 N Rockwell Street 60618 (773) 754-0494
http://metrobrewing.com/

Alarmist Brewing 4055 West Peterson Avenue Rear Suite 60646 (773) 681-0877 https://alarmistbrewing.com/

Off Color Brewing 3925 West Dickens Street 60647 (312) 929-2916
http://www.offcolorbrewing.com/

Horse Thief Hollow 10426 South Western Avenue 60643 (773) 779-2739
https://horsethiefbrewing.com/

Hopothesis Beer Company 730 W Randolph Street 60661 (312) 217-0419 https://hopothesis.com/

All Rise Brewing Company 235 N Ashland Avenue 60607 (312) 226-6300 https://www.allrisebrewing.com/

Around the Bend Beer Company 2601 West Diversey Avenue 60647
http://atbbeerco.com/

Lo Rez Brewing 2101 S Carpenter 60608 (888) 404-2262
https://lorezbrewing.com/

Adams Street Brewery 17 West Adams Street 60603 (312) 427-5820
https://www.adamsstreetbrewery.com/

Midwest Coast Brewing Company 2137 West Walnut Street 60612
(312) 361-1176 https://www.midwestcoastbrewing.com/

Dovetail Brewery 1800 West Belle Plaine Avenue 60613 (773) 683-1414
http://dovetailbrewery.com/

Great Central Brewing Company 221 North Wood Street 60612 (855)
464-4222 http://www.greatcentralbrewing.com/

Eris Brewery and Cider House 4240 West Irving Park Road 60641 (773)
943-6200 https://www.erischicago.com/

Spiteful Brewing 2024 W Balmoral Avenue 60625 (773) 293-6600
https://www.spitefulbrewing.com/

Motor Row Brewing 2337 S Michigan Avenue 60616 (312) 624-8149
https://www.motorrowbrewing.com/

Pipeworks Brewing Company 3912 W Mclean Avenue 60647 (773) 698-
6154 https://pdubs.net/

Focused on brewing distinctive and creative beers. Try something different
and exciting when you're in the area.

Alulu Brewpub 2011 South Laflin Street 60608 (312) 600-9865
http://www.alulubrew.com/

Brewing you unique versions of your favorite beer styles. Pair it with
wonderful Eastern European/American pub food.

Whiner Beer Company 1400 West 46th Street 60609 (312) 810-2271
https://www.whinerbeer.com/

Focused on barrel-aged beers and using the Belgian tradition of alternative yeast fermentations. Offering four styles of ales to enjoy.

Forbidden Root Restaurant and Brewery 1746 West Chicago Avenue 60622 (312) 929-2202 http://www.forbiddenroot.com/

The first botanic brewery in Chicago. Enjoy craft beers brewed by nature. The beers here have a deep flavor that you won't find anywhere else.

Hopewell Brewing Company 2760 North Milwaukee Avenue 60647 (773) 698-6178 https://www.hopewellbrewing.com/

A progressive brewery focused on bright, clean, and accessible beer styles. Offering everything from lagers to oak-aged wild suasions, the beers are balanced and focused.

Urban Renewal Brewery 5121 N Ravenswood Avenue 60640 (774) 487-4619 https://urbanrenewbrew.com/

Offering a wide variety of styles from Kolsch to a Milk Stout and everything in between. Their beer lineup is ever-changing, so you'll always have something great to sample. Once you've explored all you want in Chicago, you can head to the outlying area. The breweries are listed in a circle of Chicago from the north to the south:

Evanston

Temperance Beer Company 2000 Dempster Street 60202 (847) 864-1000 http://temperancebeer.com/

Sketchbook Brewing Company 825 Chicago Avenue 60202 (847) 859-9051 http://www.sketchbookbrewing.com/

This small brewery is able to offer you a wide range of classic, modern and experimental style beers. There are sixteen taps offering year-round, seasonal, and limited release beers.

Smylie Brothers Brewing Company 1615 Oak Avenue 60201 (224) 999-7320 http://www.smyliebros.com/

The beers here take the best from all the classic styles to offer you something great. They focus on beers with simplicity, delicacy, and balance.

Waukegan

ZumBier 3232 Monroe 60085 (847) 420-7313 http://zumbier.com/

Black Lung Brewing Company 3233 West Monroe Avenue 60085 (847) 340-3320 https://blacklungbrewing.com/

Gurnee

Only Child Brewing Company 1350 Tri State Parkway 60031 (224) 656-5241 http://onlychildbrewing.com/

Highland Park

Ravinia Brewing Company 582 Roger Williams Avenue 60035 (847) 780-8127 https://www.raviniabrewing.com/

Lake Bluff

Lake Bluff Brewing Company 16 E Scranton Avenue 60044 (224) 544-5179 https://www.lbbrew.com/

Libertyville

Mickey Finn's Brewery 412 N Milwaukee Avenue 60048 (847) 362-6688 https://mickeyfinnsbrewery.com/

Lincolnshire

Half Day Brewing Company 200 Village Green 60069 (847) 821-6933 https://www.halfdaybrewing.com/

Glenview

Macushla Brewing Company 1516 East Lake Avenue 60025 (847) 730-5199 https://www.macushlabeer.com/

Mundelein

Tighthead Brewing Company 165 N Archer Avenue 60060 (847) 219-5470 http://www.tightheadbrewing.com/

Bosacki's Home Brewn610 E Hawley Street 60060 (224) 778-5400 https://www.bosackishomebrew.com/

Producing traditional and historic style beers. Stop by the family-friendly taproom to enjoy a fresh beer.

Niles

Une Annee 9082 W Golf Road 60714 (847) 635-0655 https://www.uneannee.com/

They started with making Belgian style ales. Over the years, the focus has expanded to fruited and unfruited American wild ales along with barrel-aged stouts.

Buffalo Grove

Prairie Krafts Brewing Company 1310 Busch Parkway 60089 (847) 913-2828 https://prairiekrafts.com/

Wauconda

Side Lot Brewery 110 Slocum Lake Road 60084 (847) 865-0281 https://www.sidelotbrewing.com/

Lake Zurich

Roaring Table Brewing Company 739 IL-22 60047 (224) 662-4562
https://roaringtable.com/

Making beer in small batches by hand. Using fermentation to use limited ingredients for a wide range of unique beer flavors.

Lake Barrington

Wild Onion Brewing Company 22221 N Pepper Road 60010 (847) 381-7308 https://onionpub.com/

Mount Prospect

The Red Barn Restaurant and Brewery 303 East Kensington Road 60056 (847) 749-0064 https://theredbarn-mp.com/

Barrington

Flesk Brewing Company 200 Applebee Street Suite E 60010 (224) 655-7291 https://www.fleskbrewing.com/

Cary Ale House and Brewing Company 208 West Main Street 60013 (847) 649-7244 https://caryalehousebrewing.com/

Crystal Lake

Crystal Lake Brewing 150 North Main Street 60014 (779) 220-9288 http://www.crystallakebrew.com/

The beers here are easy to drink and hard to forget. You'll easily want to take some home after trying a little of what they have to offer.

Woodstock

Holzlager Brewing Company 150 South Eastwood Drive 60098 (815) 308-5901 https://holzlagerbrewing.com/

ShadowView Brewing 2400 Lake Shore Drive 60098 (815) 308-5600
https://shadowviewbrewing.com/

Algonquin

Scorched Earth Brewing Company 203 Berg Street 60102 (224) 209-8472 http://scorchedearthbrewing.com/

Village Vintner Winery and Brewery 2380 Esplanade Drive 60102 (847) 658-4900 https://thevillagevintner.com/

The only winery, brewery, and restaurant in the Chicago area. Offering twelve handcrafted beers on tap at all times ranging from core styles or limited creative releases.

South Beloit

Off-Kilter Brewing 15810 Carbrey Avenue 61080 (815) 222-3138
http://www.offkilterbrewing.com/

Brewing quality handcrafted beers of the finest styles not found in commercial breweries. Focusing on the way beers used to be made and enjoyed.

Elk Grove Village

Mikerphone Brewing 121 Garlisch Drive 6007 (847) 264-8904
http://www.mikerphonebrewing.com/

Huntley

Sew Hop'd Brewery and Taproom 1 Union Special Plaza Suite 113 60142 (815) 701-8819 https://www.sewhopd.com/

Machesney Park

Pig Minds Brewing Company 4080 Steele Drive 61115 (779) 423-2147
https://pigmindsbrewing.com/

Schiller Park

Short Fuse Brewing Company 5000 N River Road 60176 (847) 260-5044 https://www.shortfusebrewing.com/

Offering crisp, bold, and original beers. Specializing in aged sour/wild beers that can be aged between 12 and 18 months.

Rockford

Prairie Street Brewing Company 200 Prairie Street 61107 (815) 277-9427 https://psbrewingco.com/

Carlyle Brewing Company 215 East State Street 61104 (815) 963-2739 http://www.carlylebrewing.com/index.html

Offering a unique place to gather with fresh-brewed beer styles to sample. Pair it with a variety of pub-style foods.

Itasca

Itasca Brewing Company 400 East Orchard Street Suite B 60143 (773) 320-7268 https://www.itascabrewingcompany.com/

Church Street Brewing Company 1480 Industrial Drive Unit C 60143 (630) 438-5725 https://www.churchstreetbrew.com/home/

Brewing traditional and unpretentious lagers and ales with a European influence. Come try one of their award-winning beers today.

Bloomingdale

Wolfden Brewing Company 112 W Lake Street 60108 (847) 610-5117 http://www.wolfdenbrewing.com/

DeKalb

Forge Brewhouse 216 N 6th Street 60115 (815) 517-0237 https://forgebrewhouse.com/

Elmhurst

Elmhurst Brewing Company 171 North Addison Avenue 60126 (630) 834-2739 https://elmhurstbrewingcompany.com/

Offering constantly changing styles and types of beer offerings based on community interest.

Saint Charles

93 Octane Brewery 1825 Lincoln Highway 60174 (630) 549-0332 http://93octanebrewery.com/

Riverlands Brewing Company 1860 Dean Street Unit A 60174 (630) 549-6293 https://www.riverlandsbrewing.com/

Offering a range of options. Some of the best to try are the New England Style IPA, thick flavored stouts, and tart sours.

Oak Park

One Lake Brewing 1 Lake Street 60302 (708) 434-5232 https://www.onelakebrewing.com/

Kinslahger Brewing Company 6806 Roosevelt Road 60304 (844) 552-4437 https://kinslahger.com/

The main focus is on creating the best lager beers you've ever tried. This isn't to say there aren't other beer types to try here, but you should definitely try their lager.

Elburn

Obscurity Brewing and Craft Mead 113 West North Street 60119 (630) 320-2255 https://www.drinkobscurity.com/

Geneva

Penrose Brewing 509 Stevens Street 60134 (630) 232-2115
http://penrosebrewing.com/

Focused on Belgian inspired session ales. Made from oak-barrel aging for fresh hop flavors. Come for a unique tasting experience.

Stockholm's 306 W State Street 60134 (630) 208-7070
http://www.stockholmsbrewpub.com/

Brewing beers in old-world tradition, meaning they are unfiltered and naturally conditioned for a full, balanced flavor. Come try their wonderful craft beers.

Lombard

Noon Whistle Brewing 800 E Roosevelt Road 60148 (708) 906-3625
https://www.noonwhistlebrewing.com/

Afterthought Brewing Company 844 N Ridge 60148
https://afterthoughtbrewing.com/

Old World tradition with a new world twist. A small, family-run brewery focused on seasonal beers. They place an emphasis on oak fermentation.

Glen Ellyn

Two Hound Red 486 Pennsylvania Avenue 60137 (630) 547-2912
https://2houndred.com/

Creating classic, innovative beers paired with classic, inventive American food. Stop in today for a unique tasting experience.

Forest Park

Exit Strategy Brewing Company 7700 West Madison Avenue 60130 (708) 689-8771 http://www.exitstrategybrewing.com/

Wheaton

Dry City Brew Works 120B N Main Street 60187 (630) 456-4787
https://www.drycitybrewworks.com/

Batavia

Energy City Brewing 2 ½ W Wilson Street Suite A-1 60510 (630) 597-5581 https://www.energycitybrewing.com/

Warrenville

Two Brothers Brewing Company 30W315 Calumet Avenue 60555 (630) 393-4800 http://twobrothersbrewing.com/

Rock Island

Wake Brewing 2529 5th Avenue 61201 (309) 558-0878
http://www.wakebrewing.com/

Radicle Effect Brewerks 1340 31st Street 61201 (309) 283-7605
https://rebrewerks.com/

Providing quality ales and lagers in a friendly and relaxing environment for those who are tired of common beers.

Berwyn

Flapjack Brewery 6833 Stanley Avenue 60402 (708) 637-4030
http://www.flapjackbrewery.com/

Downers Grove

Alter Brewing Company 2300 Wisconsin Avenue Ste 213 60515 (630) 541-9558 https://www.alterbrewing.com/

Making creative, delicious, and drinkable beers. Offering year-round, seasonal, and barrel-aged beers, so there's something for everyone here.

Westmont

Whiskey Hill Brewing Company 1115 Zygmunt Circle 60559 (630) 442-7864 https://www.whiskeyhillbrewing.com/

Employing traditional brewing methods to produce beers that emphasize flavor and quality. Come enjoy a beer in a relaxing atmosphere.

Naperville

Solemn Oath Brewery 1661 Quincy Avenue 60540 (630) 995-3062 https://www.solemnoathbrewery.com/

Oswego

Oswego Brewing Company 61 Main Street 60543 (331) 999-1991 https://oswegobrewing.com/

Woodridge

Skeleton Key Brewery 8102 Lemont Road Unit 300 60517 (630) 395-9033 https://www.skeletonkeybrewery.com/

Lyons

BuckleDown Brewing 8700 West 47th Street 60534 (708) 777-1842 https://buckledownbrewing.com/

Always offering fresh beers on their taps. Offering a range of beers in different styles. Come see what makes the beer here so great.

Willowbrook

Black Horizon Brewing Company 7560 S Quincy Street 60527 (630) 413-4964 https://www.blackhorizonbrewing.com/

A small microbrewery that produces award-winning barrel-aged beer of rotating styles and varieties. Come try their sampler to get a good taste of everything they have to offer.

Darien

Miskatonic Brewing Company 1000 N Frontage Road Unit C 60561 (630) 541-9414 https://www.miskatonicbrewing.com/

Offering everything from the traditional ales and lagers to new and wild beer styles. Come here to try an old favorite or something new and exciting.

Plainfield

Werk Force Brewing Company 14903 South Center Street 60544 (815) 531-5557 https://www.werkforcebrewing.com/

Garage Band Brewing 15025 South Des Plaines Street 60544 (815) 782-6367 https://www.garagebandbrewing.com/

Hodgkins

Blue Nose Brewery 6119 East Avenue 60525 (708) 905-5198 https://bluenosebrewery.com/

Romeoville

Metal Monkey Brewing 515 Anderson Drive Suite 900 60446 (815) 524-3139 https://www.metalmonkeybrewing.com/

Lemont

Pollyanna Brewing Company 431 Talcott Avenue 60439 (630) 914-5834 https://pollyannabrewing.com/

Shorewood

Mad Hatchet Brewing 913 Brookforest Avenue 60404 (815) 733-5380
https://www.madhatchetbrewing.com/

Willow Springs

Imperial Oak Brewing 501 Willow Blvd 60480 (708) 559-7311
http://imperialoakbrewing.com/

A small brewery that focuses on the beer first. Offering an ever-changing variety of styles with a focus on strong and barrel-aged beers.

Bedford Park

5 Rabbit Cerveceria 6398 W 74th Street 60638 (312) 895-9591
http://www.5rabbitbrewery.com/

The first US-based Latin American-inspired brewery. Stop in here to try a fresh, delicious, and unique beer you won't get anywhere else.

Channahon

River Hawk Brewery 24735 West Eames Street 60410 (815) 255-2202
https://riverhawkbrewing.com/

Joliet

Elder Brewing Company 218 East Cass Street 60432 (815) 651-4200
https://www.elderbrewingco.com/

MyGrain Brewing Company 50 East Jefferson Street Suite 106 60432 (815) 345-3339 http://www.mygrainbrewing.com/

Brewing craft beers that are intense, flavorful, and smooth. Come here to try bold beer styles that you won't easily forget.

New Lenox

Hickory Creek Brewing Company 1005 W Laraway Road Unit 260 60451 (779) 803-3974 https://www.hickorycreekbrewingil.com/

Currently offering four brews on tap with plans to expand. Mostly ale varieties are rotated regularly, so you'll always have something new to try.

Arrowhead Ales Brewing Company 2101 Calistoga Drive 60451 (815) 717-6068 https://arrowheadales.com/

Brewing to push the limits of traditional styles. Come in today to try a few of their wide range of ales, both traditional and unique.

Mokena

Tribes Beer Company 11220 West Lincoln Highway 60448 (815) 464-0248 https://www.tribesbeerco.com/

Brothership Brewing 18781 South 90th Avenue 60448 (708) 995-7014 https://www.brothershipbrewing.com/

Enjoy a quality beer in a comfortable and relaxing atmosphere. Stop in to try one of their year-round beer offerings.

Frankfort

Trail's Edge Brewing Company 20 Kansas Street 60423 (815) 277-2502 http://trailsedgebrewing.com/

Tinley Park

Hailstorm Brewing Company 8060 W 186th Street 60478 (708) 872-5377 https://www.hailstormbrewing.com/

Soundgrowler Brewing Company 8201 183rd Street 60487 (708) 263-0083 https://www.soundgrowler.com/

350 Brewing Company 7144 W 183rd Street 60477 (708) 468-8991
https://350brewing.com/

Bourbonnais

BrickStone Restaurant and Brewery 557 William R. Latham Sr. Drive
60914 (815) 936-9277 https://brickstonebrewery.com/

Enjoy handcrafted beers in an inviting atmosphere. Offering four year-
round beers to enjoy as well as seasonal releases.

Blue Island

Blue Island Beer Company 13357 Old Western Avenue 60406 (708)
954-8085 https://blueislandbeerco.com/

Brewing an inspiring take on the classic styles. Also offering specialty
beers that offer a different take on flavors and styles. So stick within your
normal or branch out and try something new and exciting.

Flossmoor

Flossmoor Station Restaurant and Brewery 1035 Sterling Avenue
60422 (708) 957-BREW http://www.flossmoorstation.com/

Rabid Brewing 17759 Bretz Drive 60430 (708) 960-3193
https://www.rabidbrewing.com/

Eastern Illinois

The eastern side of Illinois is known as the Great River region. Here you'll
be able to enjoy beautiful river valleys while sampling some excellent
breweries. It can be a one to two-day trip depending on your itinerary.
Start your trip in the Northeastern portion of Illinois at a must-visit brewery
in Freeport:

Generations Brewing 1400 S Adams Avenue 61032 (815) 616-5941
http://www.generationsbrewing.com/

Bringing clean, traditional styles of beer back to life. Offering artisan ales and lagers in all shapes and sizes. Eighteen minutes west is the town of Lena with two breweries including a must-visit:

Lena Brewing Company 9416 W Wagner Road 61048 (815) 369-5330 https://www.lenabrewing.com/

Wishful Acres Farm and Brewery 4679 N Flansburg Road 61048 (815) 990-2380 https://www.wishfulacresfarm.com/

Brewing unique and always-changing beers. The beers are made with hops grown right on the farm. Continue west about fifty minutes to a brewery in the town of Galena:

Galena Brewing Company 227 North Main Street 61036 (815) 776-9917 https://galenabrewery.com/

Now head south about an hour and a half to the town of Moline with a must-visit brewery:

Rebellion Brew Haus 1529 3rd Avenue A 61265 (309) 517-1684 http://www.rebellionbrewhaus.com/

Producing beer in small batches and the popular beers will reappear. Some good ones to try include Night Monkey Stout, Rebellion Red, Gonzo IPA, and Felon Hefe. The next stop is O'Fallon, about a four-hour drive south:

Peel Brewing Company 104 S Cherry Street 62269 (618) 726-2244 https://www.peelpizza.com/

Another forty minutes south brings you to two breweries including a must-visit in Waterloo:

Hopskeller Brewing Company 116 E 3rd Street 62298 (618) 939-2337 https://www.hopskeller.com/

Stubborn German Brewing 119 S Main Street 62298 (618) 504-2444 http://stubborngermanbrewing.com/

Specializing in the highest quality German and American beers along with bourbon barrel-aged beers. Stop in for a fun atmosphere and a great drink. A half-hour southeast brings you to a must-visit brewery at Sparta:

White Rooster Farmhouse Brewery 113 W Jackson Street 62286 (618) 449-2077 https://www.whiteroosterfarmhousebrewery.com/

An award-winning small-batch, farmhouse-style craft brewery. Focused on preserving traditional methods of brewing and fermentation with a barrel aging process. End your trip about another hour southeast to the town of Murphysboro with two options including a must-visit:

Big Muddy Brewing 1430 North 7th Street 62966 (618) 684-8833 http://bigmuddybrewing.com/

Molly's Pint Brewpub 12 N 13th Street 62966 (618) 967-6267 https://mollyspint.com/

An Irish brewpub focused on an ever-evolving selection of traditional styled beer and a rotation of specialty batches.

Central Illinois

Also known as the Land of Lincoln, the towns in this area are full of history as well as excellent breweries. This circular trip takes you through much of Illinois and will take several days to a week or more, depending on what you want to see and do. Start your trip at a must-visit brewery in Effingham in South Central Illinois:

Effing Brew Company 221 West Jefferson 62401 (217) 347-2337 https://www.effingbrewcompany.com/

Serving flavorful beers made from the freshest ingredients. You can also pair your beer with a full food menu. Head north about an hour and a half to another must-visit brewery at Decatur:

Decatur Brew Works 101 Main Street 62523 (217) 330-8683 http://www.decaturbrewworks.com/

The first brewery in Decatur and offering a number of selections. Focusing on newer, trending styles like sours and New England ales. Next head west about a half-hour to the town of Springfield with a few options including a must-visit brewery:

Anvil and Forge Brewing and Distilling 619 E Washington Street 62701 (217) 679-1195 https://anvilandforge.com/

Engrained Brewing Company 1120 West Lincolnshire Blvd 62711 (217) 546-3054 https://www.engrainedbrewery.com/

Obed and Isaac's Microbrewery 500 South 6th Street 62701 (217) 670-0627 https://www.connshg.com/obed-and-isaacs

Buzz Bomb Brewing Company 406 E Adams Street 62701 (217) 679-4157 https://buzzbombbrewingco.com/

Making sophisticated beer available to all. Visit their taproom to relax and enjoy world-class beers. About twenty-minutes north there is another brewery in Cantrall:

Rolling Meadows Farm Brewery 3954 Central Point Road 62625 (217) 725-2492 https://rollingmeadowsfarmbrewery.com/

Head northwest another twenty-minutes to a brewery in Petersburg:

Hand of Fate Brewing Company 105 E Douglas Street 62675 (217) 691-1098 https://handoffatebrewing.beer/

Now take a drive about two hours north to the town of Galesburg with another brewery:

Iron Spike Brewing Company 150 E Simmons Street 61401 (309) 297-4718 https://www.ironspikebrewpub.com/

Drive about forty minutes southeast to Peoria with a few options including a must-visit brewery:

Industry Brewing Company 8012 N Hale Avenue 61615 (309) 839-2930
http://www.industrybrew.com/

John S. Rhodell Brewery 100 Walnut Street Suite 111 61602 (309) 966-1047 http://www.rhodellsbrewery.com/wp/

Producing a wide variety of handcrafted beers, including British, American, and Belgian style beers, ales, and lagers. All with small-batch flavor. Another half-hour east brings you to a brewery in Normal:

White Oak Brewing 1801 Industrial Park Drive 61761 (309) 828-7077
http://www.whiteoak.beer/

Now head north about an hour to a must-visit brewery in Ottawa:

Tangled Roots Brewing Company 812 La Salle Street 61350 (815) 324-9549 https://tangledrootsbrewingco.com/

Following old, traditional brewing methods for a variety of beers from dark and heavy beers to crisp and delicious lagers. Head east an hour and a half to a brewery in Crete:

Evil Horse Brewing Company 1338 Main Street 60417 (708) 304-2907
http://evilhorsebrewing.com/home.html

Another brewery is about a half-hour southwest in Manteno:

Steam Hollow Brewing 450 South Spruce Street Unit C 60950
http://steamhollowbrewing.com/

Your next brewery is in Savoy about an hour and a half south:

Triptych Brewing 1703 Woodfield Drive 61874 (779) 232-3376
http://triptychbrewing.com/

Just ten minutes south is another brewery in Urbana:

Riggs Beer Company 1901 S High Cross Road 61802 (217) 718-5345
http://www.riggsbeer.com/

End your trip with a drive about forty minutes east to Georgetown and a must-visit brewery:

Big Thorn Farm and Brewery 14274 E 600 North Road 61846 (217) 550-3433 https://www.bigthornfarm.com/

Brewing cellar-fermented, real ales, and lagers at an off-grid farm. The process takes a while, but the result is a great tasting beer you won't find anywhere else.

Southwestern Illinois

Also known as the Trail to Adventure, this area offers some great breweries in a circular route that takes you from the southern area of Illinois up to the St. Louis area and back down again. You can easily do the trip in a day, or you can spend a couple days exploring other things in the area. Start your trip out at a must-visit brewery in the southern Illinois town of Alto Pass:

Von Jakob Brewery 230 Highway 127 62975 (618) 893-4500 http://www.vonjakobvineyard.com/

Enjoy your beer with incredible views of the Southern Illinois countryside. With a wide selection, you'll find a beer you like. Be sure to try their Chocolate Milk Stout. Head north about a half-hour to the town of Ava with another must-visit brewery:

Scratch Brewing Company 264 Thompson Road 62907 (618) 426-1415 https://www.scratchbeer.com/

After enjoying the outdoors at Shawnee National Forest, this is a great close brewery to unwind and enjoy a great beverage. The next brewery is in Belleville about an hour north:

4204 Main Street Brewing Company 4204 W Main Street 62220 (618) 416-7261 https://www.mainstreetbrewingco.com/

Another eighteen minutes north is Collinsville:

Old Herald Brewery and Distillery 115 E Clay Street 62234 (618) 855-8027 https://www.oldheraldbrewing.com/

Then Edwardsville is another seventeen minutes north:

Recess Brewing 307 N Main Street 62025 (618) 692-5101
http://recessbrewing.com/

Now start heading southeast about forty minutes to a must-visit brewery in Breese:

Excel Brewing Company 488 S Broadway 62230 (618) 526-7159
http://excelbottling.com/

The beer line here includes hoppy, West Coast-style beers, and traditional German-style lagers. Du Quoin is about an hour south and has another must-visit brewery:

St. Nicholas Brewing Company 12 South Oak Street 62832 (618) 790-9212 https://www.stnicholasbrewco.com/

Using the finest ingredients, the brewers here use precision and technique in order to bring you beers developed with the perfect flavor. End your trip just six minutes south in Elkville:

Route 51 Brewing Company 18967 N US 51 62932 (618) 568-2739
http://www.route51brewery.com/

Northern Indiana

The upper northeast corner of Indiana is home to some great breweries. With proper planning, you can easily visit these breweries in just a day trip. Or you can take a more leisurely pace and do it in two days. It all depends on what other activities you have planned. Start your trip out in South Bend where there are two must-visit breweries:

Crooked Ewe Brewery and Ale House 1047 Lincoln Way E 46601 (574) 217-0881 https://crookedewe.com/

South Bend Brew Werks 216 S Michigan Street 26601 (574) 334-0356 https://www.southbendbrewwerks.com/

The only family-owned and operated brewpub in South Bend. Twenty taps offer a variety of seasonal and staple beers. Pair this with some of the great food they offer.

Drewrys Brewing Company 701 S Main Street #201 60050 http://www.drewrysbrewing.com/index.html

An American beer with a German accent that brings the lager back to its roots. The brand has been around since the 1800s. Come try a beer and see why this brand has stuck around for so long. Take a seventeen-minute drive northeast to the border town of Granger with two breweries including a must-visit:

Heavenly Goat Brewing Company 7321 Heritage Square Drive 46530 (574) 217-8428 https://www.heavenlygoatbrew.com/

Bare Hands Brewery 12801 Sandy Court 46530 (574) 277-2258 https://www.barehandsbrewery.com/

Handcrafting small batches in beers from the highest quality ingredients. Offering clean, well balanced, and potent ales in a wide range of ever-changing styles. Head about seventeen minutes back southeast to a must-visit brewery in the town of Elkhart:

Iechyd Da Brewing Company 317 N Main 46516 (574) 293-0506 http://www.iechyddabrewingcompany.com/

The beers here tend to be sessional and vary from easy-drinking English mild to hoppy American IPAs. There is always something for someone here. Continue southeast about another twenty-minutes to Goshen:

Goshen Brewing Company 315 W Washington Street 46526 (574) 971-5324 https://goshenbrewing.com/

Sample twelve great beers you won't find anywhere else. Brewing a variety of traditional styles blended with unique ingredients, including barrel-aged and sour beers. The next brewery is about twenty-minute south in Syracuse:

Man Cave Brewing Company 10201 N SR 13 46567 (574) 529-1679 http://mancavebrewing.com/

Head east twenty-minutes to Wawaka:

Harry Stuff Brewing Company 4319 W US Highway 6 46794 (260) 350-9137 https://harrystuffbrewing.com/

Take a drive east and then north to a must-visit brewery in Angola about forty minutes:

Chapman's Brewing Company 300 Industrial Drive 46703 (866) 221-4005 http://www.chapmansbrewing.com/

Brewing beers of exceptional quality. Using authentic ingredients from around the world to make European-style and American ales. Now head back south about a half-hour to LaOtto:

LaOtto Brewing 202 S Main 46763 (260) 897-3360
https://laottobrewing.com/

End your trip with about a twenty-minute drive south to the city of Fort Wayne with several brewery options including a few must-visits:

GnomeTown Brewing Company 203 E Berry Street #104 46804 (260) 422-0070 https://www.gnometownbrewing.com/

Summit City Brewerks 1501 E Berry Street 46803 (260) 420-0222
http://summitcitybrewerks.com/index.html

Trubble Brewing 2725 Broadway Street 46807 (260) 750-2993
https://www.trubblebrewing.com/

Birdboy Brewing Company 210 E Collins Road 46825 (260) 579-5508
https://www.birdboybrewing.com/

Junk Ditch Brewing Company 1909 W Main Street 46808 (260) 203-4045 http://junkditchbrewingco.com/

2 Toms Brewing Company 3676 N Wells Street 46808 (260) 402-7644
https://2tomsbrewing.com/

Offering bold beers made from the highest quality ingredients. If you like craft beer, you'll enjoy the imaginative flavors and big aromas of these beers.

Hop River Brewing Company 1515 N Harrison Street 46808 (260) 739-3931 https://www.hopriverbrewing.com/

Using four basic ingredients to create unique varieties of local craft beer. Enjoy your drink in a traditional German-style taproom.

Mad Anthony Brewing Company 2002 Broadway Avenue 46802 (260) 426-2537 https://www.madbrew.com/

Stop in to try their award-winning handcrafted ales or lagers. The list of beers is always changing, so you're sure to find your new favorite beer.

Fortlandia Brewing Company 1010 Spring Street 46808 (260) 494-2337 https://www.fortlandia.com/

The first nano-brewery in Fort Wayne. Offering a diverse style of crafted lagers to barrel-aged barley wine.

Indiana Shoreline

Take a trip slightly inland and circle along the waterfront area of Indiana. There are some great breweries in this area, and with proper planning, you can easily complete this tour within a day. Or spend an extra day enjoying the beautiful waterfront area. Start your trip at a must-visit brewery in the waterfront town of Whiting:

Bulldog Brewing Company 1409 119th Street 46394 (219) 655-5284 http://bulldogbrewingco.com/

Maintaining a higher standard for ales. The oldest microbrewery in Indiana. This means you can enjoy a perfected ale that is rich in flavor. Head south ten minutes to a brewery at Hammond:

Byway Brewing 2825 Carlson Drive 46323 (219) 844-5468 https://www.bywaybrewing.beer/

Another fourteen minutes south is Dyer with a must-visit brewery:

Windmill Brewing 2121 Gettler Street 46311 (219) 440-2189
https://www.windmillbrew.com/

A brewery dedicated to creating some of the best lagers and ales. Brewing traditional styles, but there is always something for every palate. An eleven-minute drive east brings you to two must-visit breweries in the town of Griffith:

Wildrose Brewing Company 1104 E Main Street 46319 (219) 595-5054
https://www.wildrosebrewing.com/

Come here to enjoy the best American craft-style beers. Pair your beer with great sandwiches.

New Oberpfalz Brewing 121 E Main Street 46319 (219) 237-6130
https://www.newoberpfalz.com/

Producing a variety of beer styles, but specializing in classic German beer. Visit their taproom to pair your beer with fresh-made food as well. Merrillville is another nine minutes east:

Cognito Brewery 8622 Louisiana Place 46410 (219) 985-5099
https://www.cognitobrewery.com/

Nine minutes south is Crown Point with two breweries:

Crown Brewing 211 S East Street 46307 (219) 663-4545
https://www.crownbrewing.com/

Off Square Brewing 11000 Delaware Parkway 46307 (219) 310-8898
http://offsquarebrewing.com/

Head east about a half-hour to Valparaiso and a must-visit brewery:

Four Fathers Brewing 1555 West Lincolnway Ste #105 46385 (219) 464-9712 http://www.fourfathersbrewing.com/

A small family-run craft brewery focused on beers that are exciting and approachable. The taproom offers a constantly revolving selection of unique beers. Curve northeast another half-hour to the town of La Porte with their must-visit brewery:

Back Road Brewery 308 Perry Street 46350 (219) 362-7623
http://www.backroadbrewery.com/

This brewery is unique because it rotates about 40 beer recipes per year. They produce mostly ales but will do lagers in the cooler months. Then curve northwest and drive for eighteen minutes to the waterfront town of Michigan City with three must-visit breweries:

Burn 'Em Brewing 718 Freyer Road 46360 (219) 210-3784
http://burnembrewing.com/

Brewing the finest and most unique beers in the region. Stop in today to see what's on tap and try something great.

Shoreline Brewery and Restaurant 208 Wabash Street 46360 (219) 879-4677 https://www.shorelinebrewery.com/

There are always twelve beers on tap to choose from, whether it be the award-winning Beltaine Scottish Ale to the seasonal Blueberry Ale.

Zorn Brew Works 605 E 9th Street 46360 (219) 243-7157
http://zornbrewworks.com/

Enjoy a smooth and satisfying experience in every glass. Whether you want a rich, bold dark stout or mellow, pale amber ale, they have the right beer for you. Follow the shore southwest to Chesterton and a must-visit brewery:

Hunter's Brewing 1535 S Calumet Avenue 46304 (219) 728-6729
http://huntersbrewing.com/

Making boutique house brews. Handmade small-batch beers that are flavor-forward and range from traditional to creative. End your trip about another twenty-minutes down the shore in Gary:

18th Street Brewery 5725 Miller Avenue 47403 (219) 939-8802
https://www.18thstreetbrewery.com/

The second-largest brewery in Northwest Indiana. Beers range from suasions to double Indian Pale Ales. There are also double milk stouts, pilsners, and lagers.

Central Indiana

There are a lot of breweries to visit on this list, and in order to see them all, you'll definitely need to take a several day trip. If you want to limit it to a shorter trip, then you can pick and choose the breweries you want to visit, but we've listed some must-visit destinations for you. Start your trip in south central Indiana with a must-visit brewery in the town of Bargersville:

Taxman Brewing Company 13 S Baldwin Street 46106 (317) 458-0210
https://www.taxmanbrewing.com/

Brewing a wide range of Belgian inspired ales, American farmhouse ales, and Midwest seasonal beer. They also have an extensive cellaring program for wine and spirit aged beers along with sour, wild, and funky ales. Then head north about a half-hour to the main city of Indianapolis with multiple brewery options and a few must-visits:

Triton Brewing Company 5764 Wheeler Road 46216 (317) 735-2705
https://tritonbrewing.com/

Broad Ripple Brew Pub 840 E 65th Street 46220 (317) 253-2739
https://www.broadripplebrewpub.com/

Chilly Water Brewing Company 719 Virginia Avenue Suite 105 46203
(317) 964-0518 https://www.chillywaterbrewing.com/

Black Circle Brewing Company 2201 E 46th Street 46205 (317) 426-0143 http://www.blackcirclebrewing.com/

Centerpoint Brewing Company 1125 E Brookside Avenue Suite B2
46202 (317) 525-1716 https://www.centerpointbrewing.com/

Sun King Brewing Company 135 N College Avenue 46202 (317) 602-3702 https://www.sunkingbrewing.com/

Twenty Below Brewing 5408 N College Avenue 46205 (317) 602-8840 http://www.twentytap.com/

Deviate Brewing 4004 W 96th Street 46268 (317) 374-8249 http://deviatebrewing.com/

The Bier Brewery 5133 E 65th Street 46220 (317) 253-2437 https://www.bierbrewery.com/

Blind Owl Brewery 5014 E 62nd Street 46220 (317) 924-1000 https://blindowlbrewery.com/

St. Joseph Brewery 540 N College Avenue 46202 (317) 602-5670 https://www.saintjoseph.beer/

Wabash Brewing Taproom and Brewery 5328 W 79th Street 46268 (317) 938-4458 http://www.wabashbrew.com/

Round Town Brewery 950 S White River Parkway West Drive #100 46221 (317) 493-1375 http://roundtownbrewery.com/

Garfield Brewery 2310 Shelby Street 46203 (317) 602-7270 http://garfieldbrewery.com/

Metazoa Brewing Company 140 S College Avenue 46202 (317) 522-0251 https://www.metazoabrewing.com/

Creating a wide range of true-to-style traditional ales along with quirky experimental styles. Everything is always easy drinking, but big on flavor.

TwoDEEP Brewing Company 714 N Capitol Avenue 46204 (317) 653-1884 https://www.twodeepbrewing.com/

A malt-forward brewery that produces beer with color, strength, and character. Try the Brickhouse Roasted Amber Ale and the Red Sunday Irish Red Ale.

Indiana City Brewing Company 24 Shelby Street 46202 (317) 643-1103 https://indianacitybeer.com/

All beers are unfiltered for full flavor and aroma. Stop in today to try a few of their full line of beers.

Guggman Haus Brewing Company 1701 Gent Avenue 46202 (317) 602-6131 https://www.guggmanhausbrewing.com/

A small microbrewery that is constantly delivering bold versions of modern and experimental beer styles. When you're ready another half-hour north is a brewery at Whitestown:

Moontown Brewing 345 S Bowers Street 46075 (317) 769-3880 https://www.moontownbeer.com/

Another two breweries are about a half-hour east in Carmel:

Union Brewing Company 622 S Rangeline Road Ste Q 46032 (317) 564-4466 https://www.unionbrewingco.com/

Danny Boy Beer Works 12702 Meeting House Road 46032 (317) 564-0622 http://www.dannyboybeerworks.com/

Westfield is a short eight minutes north and has two options including a must-visit brewery:

Field Brewing 303 E Main Street 46074 (317) 804-9780 https://www.fieldbrewing.com/

Grand Junction Brewing Company 110 South Union Street 46074 (317) 804-5168 https://grandjunctionbrewing.com/

Brewing traditional and true-to-style beers with a heavy European influence. Come for a unique craft beer tasting experience. Head east again to Noblesville with a must-visit brewery:

Primeval Brewing 960 Logan Street 46060 (317) 678-8193 http://primevalbrewco.com/

Offering a diverse beer menu with a range of styles for all palate tastes. Try one of their year-round beers or taste a seasonal beer. Ten minutes south brings you to a brewery in Fishers:

Four Day Ray Brewing 11671 Lantern Road 46038 (317) 343-0220 https://www.fourdayray.com/

Continue another sixteen minutes south to a must-visit brewery at McCordsville:

Scarlet Lane Brewing Company 7724 Depot Street 46055 (317) 336-1590 https://www.scarletlanebrew.com/

Focusing on three main areas of beer development: stouts, Northwest IPAs/Pales, and Australian Ales. They also offer unique specialty beers throughout the seasons. A twenty-minute drive south and east brings you to Greenfield with a must-visit brewery:

Wooden Bear Brewing Company 21 W North Street 46140 (317) 318-1221 http://woodenbearbrewing.com/

The first brewery in Greenfield offering a laid-back atmosphere. Come try their wide range of beers and seasonal specials. Circle back north about an hour to the city of Muncie with three brewery options:

The Guardian Brewing Company 514 E Jackson Street 47305 (765) 273-8918 https://www.theguardianbrewingco.com/

Elm Street Brewing Company 519 N Elm Street 47305 (765) 273-2054 http://elmstbrewing.com/

New Corner Brewing Company 1900 W Mt Pleasant Blvd Suite G 47302 (765) 730-4376 http://www.newcornerbrewing.com/

Continue another half-hour north to Fairmount:

Bad Dad Brewing Company 407 W Washington Street 46928 (765) 380-0137 https://baddadbrewery.com/

Then head west to Kokomo about a half-hour away:

Half Moon Restaurant and Brewery 4051 South Lafountain 46902 (765) 455-BREW http://halfmoonbrewery.com/

Continue west about an hour to Lafayette:

Teays River Brewing 3000 S 9th Street Ste A 47909 (765) 746-6614 https://www.teaysriverbrewing.com/

People's Brewing Company 2006 N 9th Street 47902 (765) 714-2777 https://peoplesbrew.com/

Brewing classic American ales, German lagers, and more. The focus is on crafting full-flavored beers. West Lafayette is just eight minutes north:

Brokerage Brewing Company 2516 Covington Street 47906 (765) 233-2767 https://www.brokeragebrewing.com/

Another seventeen minutes north is Brookston:

Crasian Brewing Company 207 S Railroad Street Suite B 47923 (765) 563-8339 http://www.crasianbrewing.com/

Monticello is another twenty-minutes north:

Kopacetic Beer Factory 12195 US Highway 421 47960 (574) 808-3378 http://kopaceticbeer.com/

End your trip with a forty-minute drive west and north to Rensselaer:

Fenwick Farms Brewing Company 219 W Washington Street 47978 (219) 866-3773 https://fenwickfarmsbrewingcompany.com/

Southern Indiana

Take a winding trip through many towns and great breweries in the Southern portion of the state. It will take you several days to complete the tour if you visit all the breweries. Start your trip in the town of Liberty at:

Norris English Pub and Brewery 202 E Seminary Street 47353 (765) 223-2337 http://www.norrisenglishpub.com/

Take about an hour drive south to another brewery in Batesville:

Lil' Charlie's Restaurant and Brewery 504 East Pearl Street 47006 (812) 934-6392 https://www.lilcharlies.com/

Aurora is the next town about a half-hour south with another brewery:

Great Crescent Brewery 315 Importing Street 47001 (812) 655-2435 http://www.gcbeer.com/

Continue southwest about another hour to Madison:

Mad Paddle Brewery 301 West Street 47250 (812) 500-4385 http://www.norrisenglishpub.com/

Next is New Albany with two breweries about an hour further southwest:

New Albanian Brewing Company 3312 Plaza Drive 47150 (812) 949-2804 https://newalbanian.com/

Our Lady of Perpetual Hops 300 Foundation Court 47150 (812) 989-5505 https://olphbrewery.com/

Head back north an hour to Columbus with a couple options including a must-visit brewery:

Powerhouse Brewing Company's Columbus Bar 322 4th Street 47201 (812) 375-8800 http://www.powerhousebrewingco.com/

450 North Brewing Company8111 E 450 N 47203 (812) 546-0091 https://www.450northbrewing.com/

The beer menu is vast and changes often. The specialties are Hazy IPAs and Fruited Berliners, but there are plenty of traditional beer choices as well. Another half-hour north is a brewery at Greenwood:

Oaken Barrel Brewing Company 50 North Airport Parkway Suite L 46143 (317) 887-2287 https://www.oakenbarrel.com/

Continue northwest about a half-hour to Plainfield with a must-visit brewery:

Brew Link Brewing Company 770 Andico Road Suite B 46168 (317) 203-7788 https://www.brewlinkbrewing.com/

The signature beer here is the Ivory White Stout. It has a dark flavor, light color, and is, in fact, a white stout. There are also plenty of other excellent beers to enjoy when you're here. Another half-hour west is a must-visit brewery in Greencastle:

Wasser Brewing Company 102 East Franklin Street 46135 (844) 937-7371 https://www.wasserbrewing.com/home

Focusing on beers that abide by traditional styles and freestyle beers that have artistic innovations. All the beers have a distinguished flavor profile. Head south about fifty minutes to Martinsville:

Cedar Creek Winery and Brew Company 3820 Leonard Road 46151 (765) 342-9000 https://drinkatthecreek.com/

Next is Bloomington about twenty-minutes south with several breweries including three must-visit breweries:

Switchyard Brewing Company 419 N Walnut Street 47401 (812) 606-9312 http://www.switchyardbrewing.com/

Bloomington Brewing Company 514 E Kirkwood Avenue 47408 (812) 339-2256 https://www.bloomingtonbrew.com/

One of the first craft breweries in Indiana. Brewing fine ales and specialty beers for everyone to enjoy.

Function Brewing 108 E 6th Street 47408 (812) 676-1000 http://functionbrewing.com/

A rotation of twelve in-house made beers are available to choose from. There is no focus on styles, rather just varieties.

Upland Brewing Company 4060 Profile Parkway 47404 (812) 336-2337 https://www.uplandbeer.com/

The brewers here are always experimenting with traditional recipes. Using local ingredients to make wood-aged sour ales to traditional ales and lagers. The beers are complex, interesting, and approachable. Another half-hour south is a brewery in Bedford:

Salt Creek Brewery 466 Old State Route 37 47421 (812) 277-8277 https://saltcreekbrewery.beer/

Jasper has two breweries and is about another hour south:

Basketcase Brewing Company 1340 Mill Street 47546 (812) 482-4345 https://basketcasebeer.com/#!/

Schnitz Brewery and Pub 2031 Newton Street 47546 (812) 848-2739 https://www.schnitzpub.com/

Another brewery is in Ferdinand just seventeen more minutes south:

Saint Benedict's Brew Works 860 E 10th Street 47532 (812) 998-2337 https://www.saintbenedictsbrewworks.com/

Head west about a half-hour to two breweries in Evansville:

Carson's Brewery 2404 Lynch Road 47711 (812) 305-1436 https://carsonsbrewery.com/

Damsel Brew Pub 209 North Wabash Avenue of Flags 47712 (812) 909-1956 https://www.damselbrewpub.com/

End your trip with an hour drive north to Vincennes:

Vincennes Brewing Company 124 Main Street 47591 (812) 316-0485 http://www.vincennesbrewing.com/

This quick and simple trip will take you to some excellent breweries in Western Iowa. It can be an excellent day trip. Start your trip near the northwestern border in the town of West Okoboji with a must-visit brewery:

West O Beer 503 Terrace Park Blvd 51351 (712) 260-3715
https://westobeer.com/

Brewing exceptional, award-winning beers. The lineup of beers offered here rotates with the seasons. Here you'll have the best tasting experience possible. Head fourteen minutes north closer to the border to another must-visit brewery at Spirit Lake:

Okoboji Brewing Company 3705 Highway 71 51360 (712) 336-8406
http://www.brewokoboji.com/

The nine beers on tap here will constantly change with the seasons. There are always new flavors and styles to try and enjoy. Then head south about two hours to the border city of Sioux City:

Jackson Street Brewing 607 5th Street 51101 (712) 574-8403
https://jacksonstreet.beer/

Follow the border about two hours south to another brewery in Glenwood:

Keg Creek Brewing Company 111 Sharp Street 51534 (712) 520-9029
https://kegcreekbrewing.com/

End your trip with a two-hour drive northeast to a must-visit brewery in Carroll:

Carroll Brewing Company 226 E 5th Street 51401 (712) 792-2337
https://carrollbrewing.com/

Come here to enjoy a selection of high quality, easy-drinking ales, and lagers. With 30 tap lines, there is always something for every taste here.

Des Moines Area

The main city in Iowa is Des Moines, and there is a lot to see and do in the area. If breweries are your thing or if you simply want to visit a brewery after a day of exploring, then there are several great options. This tour can easily be done in a day, so you'll have extra time to explore other things. Start your trip north of Des Moines in Ankeny with two breweries, including a must-visit:

Mistress Brewing Company 1802 N Ankeny Blvd Suite 108 50023 (515) 777-2133 https://mistressbrewing.com/

Firetrucker Brewery 716 SW 3rd Street 50023 (515) 964-1284
http://www.firetrucker.com/

Brewing flavorful beers with a clean finish. While they offer a range of beers, they are best known for their dark beers like porters and stouts. Head southeast thirteen minutes to Bondurant with a must-visit brewery:

Reclaimed Rails Brewing Company 101 Main Street SE 50035 (515) 777-1443 http://www.reclaimedrailsbrewing.com/

From light, crisp pilsners to an imperial stout and everything in between, there is something for any palate here. Next, go to Des Moines fifteen minutes south:

Confluence Brewing Company 1235 Thomas Beck Road Ste A 50315 (515) 285-9005 https://www.confluencebrewing.com/

Exile Brewing Company 1514 Walnut Street 50309 (515) 883-2337 https://exilebrewing.com/

Court Avenue Brewing Company 309 Court Avenue 50309 (515) 282-2739 http://www.courtavebrew.com/

Each beer here is fresh, distinctive, and has a character all its own. This was the first brewery in Des Moines. West Des Moines is just nine minutes away with another two breweries, including a must-visit:

Fox Brewing Company 103 S 11th Street 50265 (515) 635-0323 https://www.foxbrewco.com/

Barn Town Brewing 9500 University Avenue #1110 50266 (515) 978-6767 http://barntownbrewing.com/

Brewing full-flavored, artisanal ales. Pair it with American pub-style food. Everything here is fresh and high quality. End your trip eight minutes northwest in Clive:

515 Brewing Company 7700 University Avenue 50325 (515) 661-4615 http://www.515brewing.com/

Central Iowa

This short trip takes you to a handful of cities and some great breweries. An excellent day trip if you don't have a lot of time. Start your trip in Clear Lake at:

Lake Time Brewery 801 Main Avenue Ste C 50428 (641) 357-2040 https://www.laketimebrewery.com/

Head south an hour to Ames with a couple brewery options including a must-visit:

Torrent Brewing Company 504 Burnett Avenue 50010 (515) 291-9916
http://torrentbrewingco.com/

Alluvial Brewing Company 3715 W 190th Street 50014 (515) 337-1182
http://www.alluvialbrewing.com/

Offering a limited variety of craft brews focused on quality and taste. Enjoy your beer in a dog-friendly tasting setting. Then head west about twenty-minutes to Boone:

Boone Valley Brewing 816 7th Street 50036 (515) 432-1232
http://boonevalleybrewing.com/

Another half-hour south brings you to a must-visit brewery in Polk City:

Fenders Brewing 212 W Van Dorn Street 50226 (515) 984-0011
https://www.fendersbrewing.com/

Offering a great variety of quality beers. No matter what your taste, there is something that will appeal to you. End your trip about fifty minutes more south in Winterset:

Big Rack Brew Haus 2475 Hiatt Apple Trail 50273 (515) 468-0012
http://www.bigrackbrewhaus.com/index.html

Northeast Iowa

Northeast Iowa is packed with breweries in a number of small towns. Take a circular tour of the breweries in this region and taste some unique beers you won't find anywhere else. The tour will take you at least two days, or you can extend the trip for a more leisurely journey through the area. Start your trip in Newton at:

Gezellig Brewing Company 403 W 4th Street N Maytag Building 17 50208 (641) 792-9218 https://www.gezelligbrewing.com/

Head north about a half-hour to a must-visit brewery at Marshalltown:

Iowa River Brewing Company 107 N 1st Street 50158 (641) 751-2848
https://iowariverbrewing.com/

Handcrafted beers made on the side from hops that come from around the world. There are regular beers along with seasonal beers to try. Head east a little over an hour to Amana with another must-visit brewery:

Millstream Brewing Company 835 48th Avenue 52203 (319) 622-3672
https://millstreambrewing.com/

The oldest operational brewery in Iowa and one of the oldest in the United States, in operation since 1985. Serving German-style beers and food. Head north about twenty-minutes to Cedar Rapids with several brewery options including a must-visit:

Clock House Brewing 600 1st Street SE 52401 (319) 200-4099
https://www.clockhousebrewing.com/

Iowa Brewing Company 708 3rd Street SE 52401 (319) 366-2337
https://iowabrewing.beer/

Thew Brewing Company 301 2nd Avenue SW 52404 (319) 343-8439
http://www.thewbrew.com/

Lion Bridge Brewing Company 59 16th Avenue 52404 (319) 200-4460
http://www.lionbridgebrewing.com/

Offering artisan beer produced in small batches. Producing delicious, complex, and approachable beers. Head southeast to Solon about twenty-minutes away:

Big Grove Brewery 101 W Main Street 52333 (319) 624-2337
https://biggrovebrewery.com/

Next is a must-visit brewery in Coralville about eighteen minutes south:

Backpocket Brewing 903 Quarry Road 52241 (319) 466-4444
https://backpocketbrewing.com/

You can try anything from seasonal favorites like classic lagers and sours to more experimental brews like brits and sessions. Now head east an hour to the border town of Bettendorf with two must-visit breweries:

Five Cities Brewing 2255 Falcon Avenue 52722 (563) 232-6105
http://www.fivecitiesbrewing.com/

Specializing in meticulously crafted aromatic beer. Enjoy your beer in a fun and inviting environment.

Crawford Brew Works 3659 Devils Glen Road 52722 (563) 332-0243
https://crawfordbrewworks.com/

Offering your favorite traditional beers, seasonal beers, and some things you might not even expect to taste. Follow the border north fourteen minutes to the brewery at Le Claire:

Green Tree Brewery 309 N Cody Road 52753 (563) 505-3716
https://greentreebrewery.com/

Another brewery is about another hour north at the border town of Bellevue:

River Ridge Brewing 118 N Riverview 52031
https://www.riverridgebrewing.com/

Dubuque is an hour north on the border and features a few breweries including a must-visit:

Dimensional Brewing Company 67 Main Street 52001
https://dimensionalbrewing.com/

Catfish Creek Brew Pub 1630 E 16th Street 52001 (563) 582-8600
https://catfishcharliesdubuque.com/

Jubeck New World Brewing 115 W 11th Street 52001 (775) 375-5692
http://www.jubeckbrewing.com/

Using pure, simple, and high-quality ingredients to make excellent beers. Offering a full spectrum of flavors and experimenting with new and seasonal beers. Head west to Manchester about forty minutes with a must-visit brewery:

Franklin Street Brewing Company 116 S Franklin Street 52057 (563) 927-2722 http://franklinstreetbrewing.com/

A small-batch craft brewery that provides a variety of exceptional handcrafted ales and lagers. Enjoy them in a relaxing and comfortable environment. About a half-hour north is the town of Elkader with a must-visit brewery:

Deb's Brewtopia 106 Cedar Street NW 52043 (563) 880-5666 http://www.debsbrewtopia.com/

Growing their own 18 variety of hops that are used to brew all of the beers. The first licensed brewery in Elkader in 127 years. Now head northwest to Calmar with another brewery:

PIVO Brewery 101 Huber Drive 52132 (563) 562-1053 https://www.pivoblepta.com/

Just fourteen more minutes north is Decorah with two breweries including a must-visit:

Toppling Goliath Brewing Company 1600 Prosperity Road 52101 (563) 382-6198 https://www.tgbrews.com/

Pulpit Rock Brewing Company 207 College Drive 52101 (563) 380-3610 https://www.pulpitrockbrewing.net/

A rotating tap list that balances classic styles, hop-forward beers, and unique flavor-infusions. You'll be able to experience the full spectrum of taste. Now head west about an hour to a brewery at Osage:

Limestone Brewers 518 Main Street 50461 (641) 832-3100 https://www.limestonebrewers.com/

Head a half-hour northwest to the border town of Northwood with a must-visit brewery:

Worth Brewing Company 835 Central Avenue 50459 (641) 324-9899
https://www.worthbrewing.com/

Serving handcrafted, high quality, and distinctive beers. Stop in for a classic or specialty beer that is locally made. About a half-hour south is another must-visit brewery at Mason City:

Fat Hill Brewing 17 N Federal Avenue 50401 (641) 423-0737
http://www.fathillbrewing.com/

Brewing classic old-world styles with unique local ingredients whenever possible such as wildflower honey and Aronia berries. Continue south another half-hour to a brewery at Hampton:

Rustic Brew 117 1st Street NW 50441 (641) 220-2055
https://www.rusticbrew.com/

Head back east about another hour to two breweries at Cedar Falls:

SingleSpeed Brewing 128 Main Street 50613 (319) 266-3581
http://www.singlespeedbrewing.com/

Second State Brewing 203 State Street 50613 (319) 240-0692
http://www.secondstatebrewing.com/

End your trip just eight minutes southeast at a must-visit brewery at Waterloo:

Lark Brewing 3295 University Avenue 50701 (319) 238-5275
http://larkbrewing.com/

One of Iowa's premier breweries featuring uniquely crafted beers. Offering over 200 unique and distinct beers that you won't be able to taste anywhere else.

Southeast Iowa

This short trip will only take you a day or two if you want to see more sites. It has several great breweries to enjoy. Start your trip at a must-visit brewery in Burlington:

Parkside Brewing Company 2601 Madison Avenue 52601 (319) 209-2739 http://parksidebrewing.com/

Offering unique and flavorful handcrafted beers. The award-winning beer recipes are made using premium ingredients for a great glass of beer. Head south about twenty-minutes to Fort Madison:

Lost Duck Brewing Company 723-725 Avenue H 52627 (319) 372-8255 http://www.duckbrewing.com/

The next brewery is in Kalona about an hour and a half north:

Kalona Brewing Company 405 B Avenue 52247 (319) 656-3335 http://www.kalonabrewing.com/

Then head about an hour west to another must-visit brewery in Oskaloosa:

NoCoast Beer Company 1407 17th Avenue East 52577 https://www.nocoastbeer.co/

Offering simple beer, without any additives. Come in to try their excellent beers and see how beers are supposed to be made. Another half-hour west will bring you to Knoxville and another must-visit brewery:

Peace Tree Brewing Company 107 W Main Street 50138 (641) 842-2739 http://www.peacetreebrewing.com/

Brewing handcrafted, full-flavored beers. Known for developing their unique recipes that you're sure to enjoy and not find anywhere else. End your trip with about a half-hour drive south to Albia:

Albia Brewing Company 11 Benton Avenue 52531 (641) 932-4085
http://albiabrewingcompany.blogspot.com/

Kansas

Kansas is home to a number of great breweries, and you can easily take a tour of the state and visit all of them. You can easily complete the trip in just two days, but if you want to visit all that Kansas has to offer, then plan to spend some extra time. Start your trip at a must-visit brewery in Dodge City:

Dodge City Brewing 701 3rd Avenue 67801 (620) 371-3999
https://www.dodgecitybrewing.com/

The first craft brewery in southwest Kansas. You'll find six to eight of their handcrafted beers on tap as well as delicious pizza to pair with your beer. Take a drive about two hours northeast to two breweries at Hays:

Defiance Brewing Company 2050 US Highway 40 67601 (785) 301-BEER http://www.defiancebeer.com/

Gella's Diner and Lb. Brewing Company 117 East 11th Street 67601 (785) 621-BREW https://www.lbbrewing.com/

Continue about two hours east and then slightly south to the town of McPherson and a must-visit brewery:

Three Rings Brewery 536 S 81 ByPass 67460 (620) 504-5022
https://threeringsbrewery.com/

Making the highest quality of beers from 500-year-old family recipes that are both unique and flavorful. Stop in to try a year-round or seasonal beer today. Just a half-hour further south is two must-visit breweries in the town of Hutchinson:

Salt City Brewing Company 514 N Main Street 67501 (620) 960-6210
https://saltcitybrewing.com/home

Brewing that focuses on superior ingredients and rigorous science. Their versions of the classic beers offer straightforward flavor.

Sandhills Brewing 111 West 2nd Avenue 67501 (620) 200-2876
https://sandhillsbrewing.com/

Focused primarily on oak-fermented and specialty beers. Many of the beers here take 9 to 18 months to reach a point where you can enjoy them. So be sure to try their year-round selections, but also try a specialty beer or two. Then start heading east about an hour to the main city of Wichita with several brewery options, including three must-visits:

Nortons Brewing Company 125 N St. Francis 67202 (316) 425-9009
https://nortonsbrewing.com/

Hopping Gnome Brewing 1710 E Douglas Avenue 67214 (316) 771-2110 https://www.hoppinggnome.com/

Central Standard Brewing 156 S Greenwood 67211 (316) 260-8515
https://www.centralstandardbrewing.com/

Wichita Brewing Company 8815 W 13th Street 67212 (316) 440-2885
https://wichitabrew.com/

Creating handcrafted and unforgettable ales, stouts, and IPAs. They are full of flavorful hops and character. The selection is always expanding, so you'll have plenty to choose from.

Augustino Brewing 756 N Tyler Road 67212 (316) 721-5554 https://augustinobrew.com/

Specializing in brewing great classic styles with as minimal ingredients as possible. Come try one of these excellent brews today.

River City Brewing Company 150 N Mosley Street 67202 (316) 263-BREW https://rivercitybrewingco.com/

Enjoy refreshing handcrafted ales made from palate-pleasing recipes. Continually offering several different styles of craft beer, including ever-changing seasonal beers. Continue another half-hour northeast to a brewery at El Dorado:

Walnut River Brewing Company 111 West Locust Street 67042 (316) 351-8086 https://www.walnutriverbrewing.com/

Another hour northeast will get you to the town of Emporia and a brewery:

Radius Brewing Company 610 Merchant Street 66801 (620) 208-4677 https://radiusbrewing.com/

An hour east is a must-visit brewery at Ottawa:

Not Lost Brewing Company 229 S Main 66067 (785) 214-4259 http://notlostbrewing.com/

Featuring small batches of handcrafted brews that include traditional beer styles, as well as experimental beers. Stop in to try them today. About a half-hour brings you close to the border at the town of Olathe:

Red Crow Brewing Company 15430 S Rogers Road 66062 (913) 247-3641 https://redcrowbrew.com/

Just ten minutes northeast is another brewery at Lenexa:

Limitless Brewing 9765 Widmer 66215 (913) 526-3483
http://www.limitlessbrewing.com/index.html

Six minutes closer to the border is Overland Park and another brewery:

Brew Lab 7925 Marty Street 66204 (913) 400-2343
https://www.brewlabkc.com/

Nine minutes gets you to Shawnee outside Kansas City with two breweries, including a must-visit:

Transport Brewery 11113 Johnson Drive 66203 (913) 766-6673
https://transportbrewery.com/

Servaes Brewing Company 10921 Johnson Drive 66203 (913) 608-5220
https://www.servaesbrewco.com/

Brewing high-quality beer that is ever-evolving. They are always trying new things and inventing new flavors of beer. Head about a half-hour back west away from the border to the city of Lawrence with the largest number of must-visit breweries:

Lawrence Beer Company 826 Pennsylvania Street 66044 (785) 856-0453 https://www.lawrencebeerco.com/

Black Stag Brewery and Pub 623 Massachusetts Street 66044 (785) 764-1628 https://www.blackstagbrew.com/

Offering the finest standard and most unique beer recipes. No matter what your beer taste, there will be something to enjoy here.

Free State Brewing Company 636 Massachusetts Street 66044 (785) 843-4555 http://www.freestatebrewing.com/

The first legal brewery in the state of Kansas in over 100 years. They don't focus on strict beer styles, but rather what the local crowd enjoys.

23rd Street Brewery 3512 Clinton Parkway 66047 (785) 856-2337
https://www.brew23.com/

Creating ales and lagers of exceptional quality. To ensure freshness, the beers are brewed in small batches. Try a flagship and specialty beer today.

Yankee Tank Brewing Company 3520 W 6th Street 66049 (785) 749-2999 http://www.yankeetankbrewing.com/

Offering interesting and delicious ales that have bold flavor profiles. Stop in to try their unique twist on the ale. The next largest city is about twenty-minutes further west, Topeka, with a few must-visit breweries:

Norsemen Brewing Company 830 N Kansas Avenue 66608 (785) 783-3999 http://norsemenbrewingco.com/

Iron Rail Brewing 705 S Kansas Avenue 66603 (785) 215-8123 https://www.ironrailbrewing.com/

Happy Basset Brewing Company 6044 SW 29th Street 66614 (785) 640-3151 https://www.happybassetbrewingco.com/

Using the finest ingredients to offer you an extensive beer list to choose from. The focus is on a range of ales and lagers, but there are some seasonal and specialty brews as well.

Blind Tiger Brewery and Restaurant 417 SW 37th Street 66611 (785) 267-BREW https://www.blindtiger.com/

Offering a wide variety of handcrafted ales. There are usually six flagship brews on tap along with a wide selection of seasonal and specialty beers. Continue west about another hour to a must-visit brewery at Manhattan:

Little Apple Brewing Company 1100 Westloop 66502 (785) 539-5500 https://www.littleapplebrewery.com/

The place to enjoy fine, handcrafted ales. It is also the ideal place to enjoy a great steak with your beer. End your trip with about a forty-minute drive west to a brewery in Clay Center:

15-24 Brew House 420 Lincoln Avenue 67432 (785) 777-1524
https://1524brewhouse.com/

Kentucky

Nearly all of the breweries in Kentucky can be visited in a single trip. The route can take you a day or two, depending on how many breweries you visit and how many other sites you visit. You can also choose to visit a stand-alone brewery if you want to take a little drive out of your way. Start your trip out in the main city of Louisville where there are many breweries to choose from, but if you are limited on time, there are three must-visit breweries:

Falls City Brewing Company 901 E Liberty Street 40204 (502) 540-5650
https://fallscitybeer.com/

Bluegrass Brewing Company 300 West Main Street 40202 (502) 562-0007 https://www.bbcbrew.com/

Akasha Brewing Company 909 East Market Street Suite 700 40206 (502) 742-7770 https://www.akashabrewing.com/

Great Flood Brewing Company 2120 Bardstown Road 40205 (502) 457-7711 https://www.greatfloodbrewing.com/

Against the Grain Brewery and Smokehouse 401 East Main Street 40202 (502) 515-0174 https://atgbrewery.com/

Old Louisville Brewery 625 W Magnolia Avenue 40208 (502) 333-8594 http://www.oldlouisvillebrewery.com/

False Idol Independent Brewers 1025 Barret Avenue 40204 (502) 742-1714 https://www.vgrits.com/

Holsopple Brewing 8023 Catherine Lane 40223 (502) 708-1902 http://www.holsopplebrewing.com/

3rd Turn Brewing 10408 Watterson Trail 40299 (502) 482-3373 http://3rdturnbrewing.com/

Monnik Beer Company 1036 E Burnett Avenue 40217 (502) 742-6564 https://monnikbeer.com/

Gravely Brewing Company 514 Baxter Avenue 40204 (502) 822-3202 https://gravelybrewing.com/

The world's first music brewery. Enjoy beer and Mayan street food in a unique tasting and listening experience.

Goodwood Brewing Company 636 East Main Street 40202 (502) 584-2739 https://www.goodwood.beer/

Offering fresh stouts, lagers, and ales. Using special limestone water to make an excellent beer, you won't find anywhere else.

Mile Wide Beer Company 636 Barret Avenue 40204 (502) 409-8139 https://www.milewidebeer.com/

Carefully handcrafted interesting and flavorful beer. Everything is brewed to the highest quality standards, so you'll be sure to have an excellent beer. When you're ready to head south about forty minutes to the brewery at Elizabethtown:

Flywheel Brewing 218 S Mulberry Street Suite 103 42701
https://flywheelbrewing.com/

If you want to take a side trip to Hopkinsville for another brewery:

Hopkinsville Brewing Company 102 E 5th Street 42240 (228) 209-4561
https://hopkinsvillebrewingcompany.com/

Otherwise, circle southeast about two hours to two breweries in the town of Somerset:

Jarfly Brewing Company 103 W Mount Vernon Street 42501 (606) 425-4962 http://www.jarflybrewing.com/#inline-auto126

Tap on Main 601A N Main Street 42501 (606) 451-1525
https://taponmainst.com/

Then head north about an hour to Harrodsburg with another brewery:

Lemons Mill Brewery 166 Marimon Avenue 40330 (859) 265-0872
http://lemonsmillbrewery.com/

Another forty minutes north brings you to Frankfort with a must-visit brewery:

Sig Luscher Brewery 221 Mero Street 40601 (502) 209-9138
https://sigluscherbrewery.com/

Offering their flagship Pilsner that has been brewed since the 1800s. There are also occasional specialty taproom beers to enjoy as well. A half-hour southeast brings you to the other main city of Lexington with many breweries, but three must-visits if you don't have too much time:

Fusion Brewing 1170 Manchester Street #150 40508 (859) 554-8037
https://fusion-brewing.com/

Mirror Twin Brewing 725 National Avenue 40502 (618) 406-3598
https://www.mirrortwinbrewing.com/

West Sixth Brewery 501 West Sixth Street 40508 (859) 951-6006
https://www.westsixth.com/

Alltech Lexington Brewing and Distilling 401 Cross Street 40508 (859) 225-8095 https://www.lexingtonbrewingco.com/

Pivot Brewing 1400 Delaware Avenue 40505 (859) 285-6778
https://www.pivotbrewingcompany.com/

Country Boy Brewing 436 Chair Avenue 40508 (859) 554-6200
http://countryboybrewing.com/

Making minimally processed beers that are high quality with real ingredients. Their core beers are Cougar Bait American Blonde Ale and Shotgun Wedding Vanilla Brown Ale.

Ethereal Brewing 1224 Manchester Street 40504 (859) 309-1254
http://www.etherealbrew.com/

Handcrafted microbrews designed for taste, smoothness, and quality. Their offerings are quite broad, but their focus is on Belgian farmhouse and American craft beers.

Blue Stallion Brewing Company 610 West Third Street 40508 (877) 928-2337 http://bluestallionbrewing.com/

Focusing on authentic German lagers and British ales brewed with pure, traditional ingredients. Approachable beers with character and flavor for everyone to enjoy. Cynthiana is about forty minutes north:

Maiden City Brewing 123 E Pike Street 41031 (859) 954-5151
https://www.maidencitybrewing.com/

Another brewery is about forty more minutes north in Alexandria:

Alexandria Brewing Company 7926 Alexandria Pike Ste 1 41001 (859) 694-6999 https://www.alexandriabrewingcompany.com/

A short twenty-minute drive north is Covington:

Braxton Brewing Company 25 West 7th Street 41011 (859) 462-0627 https://www.braxtonbrewing.com/

End your trip a short seven minutes west at a must-visit brewery in Ludlow:

Bircus Brewing Company 326 Elm Street 41016 (859) 360-7757 https://bircus.com/

Come sample amazing beer while enjoying an amazing circus performance. This is a tasting experience unlike anything else you'll ever experience.

Louisiana

Louisiana doesn't have many breweries, but what they do have are unique and wonderful. Take a tour of the state and visit all the breweries. Take about three days to complete the whole tour or stay longer to enjoy this wonderful state. Start your trip out in northern Louisiana at Monroe:

Flying Tiger Brewery 506 N 2nd Street 71201 (318) 547-1738

https://www.flyingtigerbeer.com/#/

Then head about an hour and a half west to a must-visit brewery in Bossier City:

Flying Heart Brewing 700 Barksdale Blvd 71111 (318) 344-8775

https://www.flyingheartbrewing.com/

Focused on enjoyable and easy to drink beers that everyone can enjoy. There are six year-round beers as well as a rotation of seasonal beers. Just four minutes southwest is the town of Shreveport with another brewery:

Great Raft Brewing 1251 Dalzell Street 71104 (318) 734-9881

https://greatraftbrewing.com/

Then head south about an hour to Natchitoches:

Cane River Brewing 108 Mill Street 71457 (318) 471-9115

http://caneriverbrewing.com/

Continue about two and a half-hour south until you get to the Gulf Coast town of Lake Charles:

Crying Eagle 1165 E McNeese Street 70607 (337) 990-4871

http://www.cryingeagle.com/

Head east to a must-visit brewery in Broussard about an hour away:

Parish Brewing Company 613 E 2nd Street Ste B 70518 (337) 315-3351

https://parishbeer.com/

Offering a range of beers for any taste. However, the best seller here is Canebrake; an easy-drinking wheat ale with honey notes that has been a bestseller since 2010. About a half-hour north is the town of Arnaudville with another must-visit brewery:

Bayou Teche Brewery 1106 Bushville Highway 70512 (337) 303-8000 https://bayoutechebrewing.com/

Crafting beers that compliment the cuisine and lifestyle of the Cajuns and Creoles. Come try a beer in this family and pet-friendly environment. Head east again by about an hour to the main city of Baton Rouge where you have a couple options, including a must-visit:

Southern Craft Brewing Company 14141 Airline Highway Ste 4J 70817 (225) 663-8119 http://socraftbeer.com/

Tin Roof Brewing Company 1624 McClung Street 70802 (601) 597-1732 https://www.tinroofbeer.com/

The largest craft brewery in Baton Rouge. Offering a variety of delicious beers served in a comfortable setting. When you're ready, head another forty minutes east to a must-visit brewery at Hammond:

Gnarly Barley Brewing Company 1709 Corbin Road 70403 (985) 318-0723 https://gnarlybeer.com/

Offering a diverse and unique selection of craft beers by borrowing techniques and recipes from around the world. The beers aren't crafted along with specific style guidelines, but rather allow the ingredients to speak for themselves. A further half-hour east brings you to the Gulf Coast town of Abita Springs with a must-visit brewery:

Abita Brewery 21084 Highway 36 70433 (800) 737-2311 https://abita.com/

Sample from over 30 brews on tap, including some you won't find anywhere else. Focusing on lagers and ales brewed in small batches, but offering a wide variety. Just fifteen minutes south is another brewery at Mandeville:

Chafunkta Brewing Company 21449-2 Marion Lane 70471 (985) 869-2349 http://www.chafunktabrew.com/

Another forty minutes south brings you to the main city of New Orleans with many breweries to choose from, but two must-visit breweries if you are limited on time:

Second Line Brewing 433 N Bernadotte Street 70119 (504) 248-8979 https://www.secondlinebrewing.com/

Miel Brewery and Taproom 405 Sixth Street 70115 (504) 372-4260 https://www.mielbrewery.com/

Port Orleans Brewing Company 4124 Tchoupitoulas Street 70115 (504) 266-2332 https://portorleansbrewingco.com/

The Courtyard Brewery 1020 Erato Street 70130 http://www.courtyardbrewing.com/

All Relation Brewing 1401 Baronne Street 70113 (504) 345-8933 https://www.allrelation.com/

Urban South Brewing 1645 Tchoupitoulas Street 70130 (504) 517-4766 https://urbansouthbrewery.com/

NOLA Brewing Company 3001 Tchoupitoulas Street 70130 (504) 613-7727 https://nola-brewing.square.site/

Brieux Carre Brewing Company 2115 Decatur Street 70116 (504) 304-4242 https://www.brieuxcarre.com/

Beers as weird and interesting as the city they are brewed in, stop by to see what's on tap and try something different.

Parleaux Beer Lab 634 Lesseps Street 70117 (504) 702-8433 https://www.parleauxbeerlab.com/

Crafting high quality, small-batch, local beers that are inspired by unexpected and imaginative interpretations on classic beer styles. End your trip with about an hour drive to a must-visit brewery in Thibodaux:

Mudbug Brewery 1878 Highway 3185 70301 (985) 492-1610
http://mudbugbrewery.com/

Offering five flagship beers along with a host of unique specialty beers that are aimed at reflecting the Cajun culture.

Maine

Southern Maine and Beaches

The Southern area of Maine and its beaches are home to some excellent breweries as well as lots of scenic views to enjoy. You can visit all of the breweries in this area within a day easily, or you can take a couple days to relax and enjoy the beautiful ocean views. Start your trip at the southern end of main in the town of Kittery with two breweries, one of them a must-visit:

Woodland Farms Brewery 306 Route 1 Suite C 03904 (207) 994-3911
https://www.wfbrewery.com/

Tributary Brewing Company 10 Shapleigh Road 03904 (207) 703-0093
https://www.tributarybrewingcompany.com/

Bringing you exceptional, true-to-style beers. Try their traditional, well-balanced, and full-bodied beers. The next brewery is in the town of York just nine minutes north up the coast:

SoMe Brewing Company 1 York Road Unit #3 03909 (207) 351-8162 http://www.somebrewingco.com/

Continue up the coast another twenty-minutes to a brewery in Wells:

Hidden Cove Brewing Company 73 Mile Road 04090 (207) 646-0228 https://www.hiddencovebrewingcompany.com/

Kennebunk is another nine minutes up the coast and has two breweries, one of them a must-visit:

Federal Jack's Restaurant and Brew Pub 8 Western Avenue 04043 (207) 967-4322 https://federaljacks.com/

Batson River Brewing and Distilling 12 Western Avenue 04043 (207) 967-8821 https://batsonriver.com/

Beers that capture the joys of New England summers. The hops are grown on a centuries-old farm and used to brew some excellent beers. Continue twenty-minutes up the coast to the oceanfront town of Old Orchard Beach:

GFB Scottish Pub 32 Old Orchard Street 04064 (207) 934-8432 http://gfbscottishpub.com/

Then head back south and inland about nine minutes to Saco with a couple options including a must-visit brewery:

Barreled Souls Brewing Company 743 Portland Road 04072 (207) 602-6439 http://barreledsouls.com/

The Run of the Mill Public House and Brewery 100 Main Street 04072 (207) 571-9648 https://www.therunofthemill.net/

Brewing 30 varieties of ales and lagers throughout the year. There is also a great selection of pub-style food to pair with your beers. Another four minutes south is a brewery at Biddeford:

Banded Brewing Company 32 Main Street Bldg 13-w Ste 102 04005 (207) 602-1561 https://bandedbrewing.com/

Head twenty-minutes west further inland to a must-visit brewery at Lyman:

The Funky Bow Brewery and Beer Company 21 Ledgewood Lane 04002 https://www.funkybowbeercompany.com/

One of the most sought after breweries in Maine. Here you'll find some of the tastiest beers you'll ever find. They are always developing new single batch flavor combos for you to try when you stop by. End your trip about a half-hour further northwest to Limerick with a must-visit brewery:

Gneiss Brewing Company 94 Patterson Road 04048 (207) 793-0046 https://www.gneissbeer.com/

German-style beers brewed in the woods of Maine. Try one of their balanced and unique beers when you stop in today.

Greater Portland Area

Portland is home to quite a few breweries in Maine. There are also some great breweries in the surrounding area. Whether you choose to stay in Portland and head out to these areas or want to spend a day driving through the area and visiting the must-visit breweries, either will offer you a great experience. Start your trip north of Portland at two breweries in Freeport:

Gritty McDuff's Brew Pub and Restaurant 396 Fore Street 04101 (207) 772-BREW https://grittys.com/

Maine Beer Company 525 US Route One 04032 (207) 776-4832 https://www.mainebeercompany.com/

Then head south along the coast just nine minutes to a brewery at Yarmouth:

Brickyard Hollow Brewing Company 236 Main Street 04096 (207) 847-0411 https://www.brickyardhollow.com/

From there drive to the main city of Portland, another thirteen minutes south with numerous breweries and a few must-visits if you don't have a lot of time:

Foundation Brewing Company 1 Industrial Way 04103 (207) 370-8187 http://foundationbrew.com/

Brewery Extrava 66 Cove Street 04101 (207) 956-7583 https://breweryextrava.com/

Bissell Brothers Brewing Company 1 Industrial Way Suite 1 & 3 04101 (207) 423-3622 https://bissellbrothers.com/

Austin Street Brewery 1 Industrial Way #8 04103 (207) 831-6387 https://www.austinstreetbrewery.com/

Goodfire Brewing Company 219 Anderson Street Unit 6 04101 (207) 808-8910 https://www.goodfirebrewing.com/

Bunker Brewing Company 122 Anderson Street 04101 (207) 450-5014 http://bunkerbrewingco.com/

Lone Pine Brewing Company 219 Anderson Street 04101 (207) 468-4554 http://lonepinebrewery.com/

Liquid Riot Bottling Company 250 Commercial Street 04101 (207) 221-8889 https://liquidriot.com/

Battery Steele Brewing 1 Industrial Way 04103 https://www.batterysteele.com/

Peak Organic Brewing Company 110 Marginal Way #802 04101 (207) 586-5586 https://www.peakbrewing.com/

Definitive Brewing Company 35 Industrial Way 04103 (207) 446-4746
https://www.definitivebrewing.com/

Allagash Brewing Company 50 Industrial Way 04103 (800) 330-5385
https://www.allagash.com/

Striving to make the best Belgian-inspired beers in the world since 1995.
Be sure to try their signature, Allagash White.

D.I. Geary Brewing Company 38 Evergreen Drive 04103 (207) 878-2337
https://www.gearybrewing.com/

The first craft brewery in New England. Their flagship ale was first poured
in 1986, and today they offer an extensive line of true-to-style
contemporary beers.

Rising Tide Brewing Company 103 Fox Street 04101 (207) 370-2337
https://risingtidebrewing.com/

Guided by creative flavors, quality, consistency, and a love of the
outdoors. An independent and family-owned brewery.

Shipyard Brewing Company 86 Newbury Street 04101 (207) 761-9665
https://shipyard.com/

Quality, handcrafted beer from Maine. The award-winning beers here are
rooted in tradition and brewed with innovation. Just seven minutes further
south is South Portland with a few more options including a must-visit
brewery:

Fore River Brewing Company 45 Huntress Avenue 04106 (207) 370-
0629 https://www.foreriverbrewing.com/

Foulmouthed Brewing 15 Ocean Street 04106 (207) 618-6977
https://foulmouthedbrewing.com/

Island Dog Brewing Company 125 John Roberts 04016 (207) 747-5258
http://islanddogbrewing.com/

Primarily producing Belgian and German-inspired ales, herb and spice ales, and seasonal ales. Come try their high-quality beers. Five more minutes south along the coast brings you to Scarborough and a must-visit brewery:

Nonesuch River Brewing 201 Gorham Road 04074 (207) 219-8148 https://nonesuchriverbrewing.com/

Combining well-crafted, approachable beers with local and natural resources to give you an excellent tasting experience in a warm and inviting location. Then head inland to Westbrook about thirteen minutes with two breweries including a must-visit brewery:

Mast Landing Brewing Company 920 Main Street 04092 (207) 887-9147 https://mastlandingbrewing.com/

Yes Brewing 609 Main Street 04092 (207) 591-0633 https://yesbrewing.com/

Focusing on sours, barrel aging, and wide-ranging collaborations. You'll always have something new and interesting to try here. End your trip another ten minutes inland at Gorham:

Sebago Brewing Company 48 Sanford Drive 04038 (207) 856-2537 http://www.sebagobrewing.com/

Maine Lakes and Mountains

Another great day trip is to take a drive through the mountains and lake valleys in Northwest Maine. There are a handful of great breweries to enjoy while taking in the breathtaking views. Start your trip out in Fryeburg at:

Saco River Brewing 10 Jockey Cap Lane Rt 302 04037 (207) 256-3028 https://sacoriverbrewing.com/

Travel about fifty minutes northeast to another brewery at Norway:

Norway Brewing Company 237 Main Street 04268 (207) 739-2126
https://www.norwaybrewing.com/

Then head north a half-hour to your first must-visit brewery at Bethel:

Steam Mill Brewing 7 Mechanic Street 04217 (207) 824-1264
https://steammillbrew.com/

Beer made from local malt and hops. The names of the beer are inspired by local landmarks. Come try any of their year-round beers today. Head northeast again to Farmington about an hour away:

Tumbledown Brewing 805 Farmington Falls Road Suite 7 04938 (207) 944-0697 https://www.tumbledownbrewing.com/

Beer brewed in small batches in the mountains of Maine. Stop in to taste the difference in a beer made in the pristine mountains. Carrabassett Valley is a half-hour north and has another must-visit brewery:

The Bag and Kettle 9004 Main Street 04947 (207) 237-2451
https://www.thebagandkettle.com/

50 years of brewing at the highest elevation of eastern breweries. The sparkling and clear mountain waters elevate the beers to a level you have to taste to believe. End your trip with an hour and a half drive to The Forks and your final must-visit brewery:

Kennebec River Brewery 1771 US Route 201 04985 (207) 663-4466
https://www.northernoutdoors.com/kennebec-river-brewery/

Crafting ales and lagers in the Northwoods. The malted barley comes from local farms. The flavorful beers have been brewed here since 1996.

Kennebec Valley

This short day trip will take you to the best of the Kennebec Valley. Start out in Lewiston with two breweries, including a must-visit:

Bear Bones Beer 43 Lisbon Street 04240 (207) 200-1324
http://bearbonesbeer.com/

Baxter Brewing Company 130 Mill Street 04240 (207) 333-6769
https://www.baxterbrewing.com/

Honest, quality, and easy-drinking beer that is for everyone. Come try these delicious beers today. Head about twenty-minutes north to another must-visit brewery at Monmouth:

Grateful Grain Brewing Company 26 Route 126 04259 (207) 933-8213
https://gratefulgrainbrewing.com/

The first, oldest, and largest brewery in Maine. They offer a flagship New England IPA, but they have a style and flavor for all beer interests. Another twenty-minutes north is a brewery in Augusta:

Cushnoc Brewing Company 243-249 Water Street 04330 (207) 213-6332 https://www.cushnocbrewing.com/

End your trip with about a fifty-minute drive north to Skowhegan with two breweries including a must-visit:

Bigelow Brewing Company 473 Bigelow Hill Road 04976 (207) 431-7265 https://bigelowbrewing.com/home.html

Oak Pond Brewing Company 101 Oak Pond Road 04976 (207) 474-3233 https://oakpondbrewery.com/

Using the finest hops and malts to create the perfect flavor and blend for lagers, ales, and seasonal brews. The beers are classic, old-world styles.

Maine Highlands

This short afternoon trip will take you to three cities and some excellent breweries. A great little afternoon to get out and get a break. Start out in the main city of Bangor with two must-visit breweries:

Bangor Beer Company 330 Bangor Mall Blvd 04401 (207) 947-6960
https://www.bangorbeerco.com/

Never settle for ordinary; the brewers here focus on experimenting with new styles, hops, and ingredients. There is something for everyone here.

2 Feet Brewing 80 Columbia Street 04401 (207) 573-1979
https://www.2feetbrewing.com/

The beer made here is always in rotation. So if you try something you like, be sure to take some home. Just across the river is another option in Brewer:

Mason's Brewing Company 15 Hardy Street 04412 (207) 659-2300
https://masonsbrewingcompany.com/

You can also head north about fourteen minutes to Orono:

Marsh Island Brewing 2 Main Street 04473 (207) 942-7678
https://www.marshislandbrewing.com/

Orono Brewing Company 20 Main Street 04473 (207) 866-4677
https://oronobrewing.com/

Black Bear Brewery 19 Mill Street Suite 4 04473 (207) 889-9123
https://www.blackbearmicrobrew.com/

Producing high-quality, handcrafted brews since 2004. There is a variety of beers made from locally grown hops and used within hours of picking.

Eastern Maine

This is another great afternoon trip you can take if you are staying in the Bangor area. There are only four towns and a handful of breweries, so you're sure to have a great day while enjoying coastal views. Start your trip in Amherst at:

Airline Brewing Company 22 Mill Lane 04605 (207) 584-2337
https://www.abcmaine.beer/

Then head south about a half-hour to Ellsworth with a must-visit brewery:

Fogtown Brewing Company 25 Pine Street 04605 (207) 370-0845
https://www.fogtownbrewing.com/

Offering a dynamic and diverse beer list that is ever-changing as they experiment with different styles and methods. No matter what you like, you'll find it here. Continue south eighteen minutes to the coastal town of Blue Hill with another must-visit brewery:

Deepwater Brewing Company 33 Tenney Hill 04614 (207) 374-2441
https://www.arborvine.com/deepwater-brew-pub

Personally handcrafted beers from the best ingredients possible. Offering a number of styles that rotate throughout the year. End your trip with about an hour drive to the other coastal town of Bar Harbor:

Atlantic Brewing Company 30 Rodick Street 04609 (207) 288-9513
http://www.atlanticbrewing.com/

Maine South to North

Take a great drive from southern Maine to northern Maine. Take the trip in one to two days, or take a little longer to enjoy the beautiful Maine sites around you. Either way, you'll get to visit many quaint towns and excellent breweries. Start your trip in Southern Maine at the city of Brunswick with a couple options including a must-visit brewery:

Flight Deck Brewing 11 Atlantic Avenue 04011 (207) 504-5133
https://www.flightdeckbrewing.com/

Moderation Brewing Company 103 Maine Street 04011 (207) 406-2112
https://www.moderationbrewery.com/

Brewing beers that showcase local ingredients, such as the elderberry beer or the lemon balm ale. Also, be sure to try their stout made with a unique British strain. Head just nine minutes east to a must-visit brewery in Bath:

Bath Brewing Company 141 Front Street 04530 (207) 560-3389
https://www.bathbrewing.com/

Focusing on traditional brewing methods for American, English, and German-style beers. However, they aren't restricted to a specific style or technique. Continue another half-hour east to the town of Westport with another must-visit brewery:

Sasanoa Brewing 61 Tarbox Road 04578 (207) 522-0840
https://www.sasanoabrewing.com/

A rustic, coastal brewery at the end of an island. Offering three year-round beers as well as three rotating seasonal beers. About forty minutes southeast is the coastal town of Boothbay Harbor with another must-visit brewery:

Footbridge Brewery 25 Granary Way 04538 (207) 352-3007
https://www.footbridgebrewery.com/

Focused on making craft beer with as many Maine ingredients as possible. Offering a broad array of styles, there is something for every palate here. Just three minutes northeast is the sister city of Boothbay with another brewery:

Boothbay Craft Brewery 301 Adams Pond Road 04537 (207) 633-3411
https://www.boothbaycraftbrewery.com/

Now head north about twenty-minutes to Newcastle and another must-visit brewery:

Oxbow Brewing Company 274 Jones Woods Road 04553 (207) 315-5962 https://oxbowbeer.com/

All the beers here are made from soft spring water that comes from the artesian well next door. Stop by to try their brews today. Waldoboro is another thirteen minutes northeast:

Odd Alewives Farm Brewery 99 Old Route One 04572 (207) 790-8406
https://oddalewives.com/

About a half-hour east is a must-visit brewery at Rockland:

Rock Harbor Brewing Company 416 Main Street 04841 (207) 593-7488
https://rockharborbrewing.com/

Try a flight of their regular beers or grab a seasonal special. Also, enjoy some delicious food in a great setting. Twenty-minutes northwest is another brewery at Union:

The Pour Farm 56 Crawfordsburn Lane 04862 (207) 785-0028
https://www.thepourfarm.com/brewery

Liberty is about a half-hour north and offers two brewery options:

Liberty Craft Brewing 7 Coon Mountain Lane 04949 (207) 322-7663
https://www.libertycraftbrewing.com/

Lake St. George Brewing 4 Marshall Shore Road 04949 (207) 589-3031
https://www.lakestgeorgebrewing.com/

Just ten minutes southeast is Searsmont with a must-visit brewery:

Threshers Brewing Company 22 Main Street Building #3 04973 (207) 975-3225 https://www.threshersbrewingco.com/

An off the beaten path destination brewery is well worth your effort to find. Here you'll find some of the best beer in New England. End your trip with about a fifty-minute drive northeast to a must-visit brewery in Winterport:

Penobscot Bay Brewery 279 S Main Street 04496 (207) 223-4500
https://www.winterportwinery.com/Default.asp

A small-batch brewery that focuses on offering fresh and flavorful handcrafted brews. Come by to try something unique like their Smoked Ale.

Monhegan

Monhegan Brewing Company 1 Boody Lane 04852 (207) 975-3958
https://monheganbrewing.com/

Fort Kent

First Mile Brewing Company 28 Market Street Suite 103 04743 (207)
316-2640 https://www.firstmilebrewing.com/

Maryland

Capital Region

Visiting the Capital Region in the Western part of Maryland offers you the
chance to visit many cities and great breweries. This trip can be
completed in about two days, or you can spend longer to visit many of the
wonderful sites in the area. Start your trip in the Northwestern portion of
Maryland in Thurmont at:

Springfield Manor 11836 Auburn Road 21788 (301) 271-0099
https://www.springfieldmanor.com/

Head about a half-hour south to the main city of Frederick with multiple breweries including three must-visit breweries:

Brewer's Alley Restaurant and Brewery 124 N Market Street 21701 (301) 631-0089 https://brewers-alley.com/

Monocacy Brewing Company 1781 N Market Street 21701 (240) 457-4232 http://monocacybrewing.com/

Rockwell Brewery 880 North East Street Suite 201 21701 (301) 732-4880 https://www.rockwellbrewery.com/

Flying Dog Brewery 4607 Wedgewood Blvd 21703 (301) 694-7899 https://www.flyingdog.com/

Idiom Brewing Company 340 E Patrick Street Suite 104 21701 (240) 578-4152 https://www.idiombrewing.com/

Brewing beer with new and experimental hops and local ingredients in order to create unique flavor profiles. Treat your palate to something excellent.

Attaboy Beer 400 Sagner Avenue Ste 400 21701 (301) 338-8229 https://www.attaboybeer.com/

Experimenting with mixed fermentation and barrel aging, to offer you a variety of beers, including IPAs, Belgians, and seasonal beers with fruits.

Midnight Run Brewing 912 N East Street 21701 (240) 651-1424 https://www.midnightrunbrewing.com/

Brewers of non-conformist ales. Try their full line of dynamic and full-flavored beers. The beers don't fit into a specific style and are sure to please any palate. Head southwest about twenty-minutes to a brewery at Brunswick:

Smoketown Brewing Station 223 West Potomac Street 21716 (301) 834-4828 http://www.smoketownbrewing.com/

Head back east to a must-visit brewery at Adamstown:

Mad Science Brewing Company at Thanksgiving Farm 1619 Buckeystown Pike 21710 (240) 409-8723 https://www.madsciencebrewing.com/

The majority of the beers on taps are a take on American and English ales. Every beer contains at least one ingredient grown on their farm. Take about a half-hour drive to Gaithersburg with two must-visit breweries:

Elder Pine Brewing and Blending Company 4200 Sundown Road 20882 https://www.elderpine.com/

Focusing on classic styles with a modern twist. Using blending as a way to combine flavors, textures, and aromas. Be sure to try their barrel-aged sour beers that are well balanced during the blending process.

Brawling Bear Brewing 15 Fulks Corner Avenue 20877 (240) 842-3272 https://www.brawlingbear.com/

Offering accessible and drinkable beers that everyone can enjoy. Most known for their IPA, but offering a wide range of beer options. The next brewery is fourteen minutes away to Laytonsville:

Waredaca Brewing Company 4017 Damascus Road 20882 (301) 774-2337 https://www.waredacabrewing.com/

Another brewery is in Brookeville ten minutes away:

Brookeville Beer Farm 20315 Georgia Avenue 20833 (301) 260-1000 https://www.brookevillebeerfarm.com/

Rockville is seventeen minutes south and has two breweries:

7 Locks Brewing 12227 Wilkins Avenue 20852 (301) 841-7123 https://www.7locksbrewing.com/

True Respite Brewing Company 7301 Calhoun Place Suite 600 20855 (301) 284-8447 https://truerespite.com/

Continue about twenty-minutes southeast to Silver Spring with a few options including a must-visit:

Denizens Brewing Company 1115 East-West Highway 20910 (301) 557-9818 https://www.denizensbrewingco.com/

Astro Lab Brewing 8216 Georgia Avenue 20910 (301) 273-9684 https://www.astrolabbrewing.com/

Silver Branch Brewing Company 8401 Colesville Road #150 20910 (301) 264-7111 https://www.silverbranchbrewing.com/

Brewing excellent beers based on European and American traditions for four flagship beers. Also, try their rotating selection of Real Ale. Fourteen minutes more south brings you to two breweries including a must-visit in Hyattsville:

Streetcar 82 Brewery 4824 Rhode Island Avenue 20781 (240) 782-0152 https://www.streetcar82brewing.com/

Franklin's Restaurant, Brewery, and General Store 5123 Baltimore Avenue 20781 (301) 927-2740 http://www.franklinsbrewery.com/

Brewing over 30 styles of beer with 11 on tap at a time. Since 2007 the beers here have won over 74 awards. Come see why when you taste their wide range of beer styles. End your trip with a half-hour drive to a brewery in Upper Marlboro:

Calvert Brewing Company 15850 Commerce Court 20774 (410) 414-8486 http://www.calvertbrewingcompany.com/

Central Maryland

This is a great tour that takes you through the Maryland countryside as well as large cities like Baltimore. You can take a couple days to tour the must-visit breweries, or you can take a longer trip to try all the breweries while experiencing the sites around you. Start your trip out in a must-visit brewery south of Baltimore in Crofton:

Chesepiooc Real Ale Brewery 2408 Crofton Blvd 21114 (410) 630-1579 https://www.brewcrab.com/

Focused on traditional cask-conditioned real ales and draught beers, but offering a range of experimental beers as well. Stop in today to try something interesting. Head eleven minutes north to Odenton with another must-visit brewery:

Crooked Crab Brewing Company 8251 Telegraph Road 21113 (443) 569-9187 https://www.crookedcrabbrewing.com/

Offering a wide variety of styles ranging in color, aroma, and flavor. Try everything from a crisp, refreshing cream ale to a rich and hearty stout. Head west about fourteen minutes to the brewery at Laurel:

Jailbreak Brewing Company 9445 Washington Blvd N Ste F 20723 (443) 345-9699 https://jailbreakbrewing.com/

Columbia is fifteen minutes north with three brewery options:

Sapwood Cellars 8980 MD-108 Suite MNO 21045 (443) 542-9304 https://sapwoodcellars.com/

Hysteria Brewing Company 9570 Berger Road 21046 (410) 630-8319 https://www.hysteriabrewing.com/

Black Flag Brewing Company 9315 Snowden River Parkway Suite C 21046 (443) 864-5139 https://www.blackflagbrewingco.com/

Another fourteen minutes northeast is Ellicott City with a must-visit brewery:

Manor Hill Brewing 4411 Manor Lane 21042 (410) 977-9758 https://manorhillbrewing.com/

The first brewery in Howard County and the largest farm brewery in all of Maryland. Using original and unique recipes to craft beers that you're sure to enjoy. About a half-hour west is Mount Airy with a few brewery options including a must-visit:

Frey's Brewing Company 8601 Mapleville Road 21771 (301) 639-7146 http://freysbrewing.com/

Red Shedman Farm Bakery 13601 Glissans Mill Road 21771 (301) 831-5889 https://redshedman.com/

Milkhouse Brewery 8253 Dollyhyde Road 21771 (301) 829-6950 http://www.milkhousebrewery.com/

Brewing traditional style ales that are seasonable and pleasing to the palate. Many of the ingredients for the beer are grown right on the farm. The next brewery is in Eldersburg about a half-hour northeast:

1623 Brewing Company 5975 Exchange Drive 21784 https://www.1623brewing.com/

Next head to Hampstead about a half-hour north:

Ruhlman Brewery 2300 Harvey Gummel Road 21074 (410) 259-4166 http://www.ourales.com/

The next brewery is in Hunt Valley about a half-hour southeast:

B.C. Brewery 10950 Gilroy Road Suite F 21031 (443) 318-4867 https://www.bcbrewerymd.com/

Then head south about a half-hour to the main city of Baltimore where there are multiple breweries and three must-visits:

Union Craft Brewing Company 1700 Union Avenue Unit D 21211 (410) 467-0290 https://www.unioncraftbrewing.com/

Nepenthe Brewing Company 3626 Falls Road 21211 (443) 438-4846 https://www.nepenthebrewingco.com/

The Brewer's Art 1106 N Charles Street 21201 (410) 547-6925
https://www.thebrewersart.com/

Wet City 223 W Chase Street 21201 (443) 873-6699
http://wetcitybrewing.com/

Monument City Brewing Company 1 North Haven Street 21224 (443) 529-8131 http://www.monumentcitybrewing.com/

Red Brick Station 8149 Honeygo Blvd 21236 (410) 931-7827
http://redbrickstation.com/

Checkerspot Brewing Company 1399 S Sharp Street 21230 (443) 388-8912 https://checkerspotbrewing.com/

DuClaw Brewing Company 8901 Yellow Brick Road 21237 (443) 559-9900 https://duclaw.com/

Suspended Brewing Company 912 Washington Blvd 21230 (410) 926-8847 https://www.suspendedbrewing.com/

Mobtown Brewing Company 4015 Foster Avenue #400 21224 (667) 309-3653 https://www.mobtownbrewing.com/

Producing fresh, innovative, and adventurous beers. You'll always find something different on tap here as they are always experimenting with ways to make great craft beer.

Peabody Heights Brewery 401 E 30th Street 21218 (410) 467-7837
http://www.peabodyheightsbrewery.com/

The first brewery to open in Baltimore City. The first batch was produced in 2012, and it has continued to expand since.

Ministry of Brewing 1900 E Lombard Street 21231 (410) 624-5623
https://ministryofbrewing.com/

There are 32 rotating beers on tap, so you're sure to find something. The beers are unique, delightful, and complex. Head east fifteen minutes to the waterfront town of Dundalk with a must-visit brewery:

Key Brewing Company 2500 Grays Road 21222 (410) 477-2337 https://www.keybrewing.com/

Offering high-quality craft ales and lagers. The beers here are traditional and true-to-style. Bel Air is a half-hour north with another must-visit brewery:

AleCraft Brewery 319 South Main Street Suite #100 21014 (410) 420-5012 https://www.alecraft.beer/

Serving small-batch ales made with creativity and distinction. Offering a rotating selection of ten artisanal ales. Continue twenty-minutes north to Street with another must-visit brewery:

Falling Branch Brewery 825 Highland Road 21154 (443) 939-4605 https://fallingbranchbeer.com/

Dedicated to creating Belgian and American style ales with an eccentric character. Using ingredients grown on-site or from other local farms. End your trip in Whiteford on the border just seven minutes north:

Slate Farm Brewery 2128 Whiteford Road 21160 (443) 528-7443 https://www.slatefarmbrewery.com/

Eastern Shore

Travel down the eastern shore of Maryland for some great breweries as well as some wonderful views and sites to see. Take a day or two to visit all the breweries or spend additional time exploring the area. Start your trip in the Northeast corner of Maryland at the brewery in Elkton:

Elk River Brewing 112 E Main Street 21921 (443) 207-8454 http://www.elkriverbrewing.com/

Just nine minutes south is a must-visit brewery in Chesapeake City:

Bayheads Brewing 2525 Augustine Herman Highway Suite D 21915
https://www.bayheadsbrewing.com/

Experimenting with a variety of styles to give guests plenty of options. However, they lean towards American style beers. The next brewery is in Stevensville a little over an hour south:

Cult Classic Brewing Company 1169 Shopping Center Road 21666 (410) 980-8097 https://www.cultclassicbrewing.com/

Saint Michaels is the next coastal town with a must-visit brewery about fifty minutes south:

Eastern Shore Brewing 605 S Talbot Street 21663 (410) 745-8010 https://easternshorebrewing.com/

The oldest brewery on the Eastern Shore of Maryland. Come in today to taste the perfect pint. Then head about a half-hour south to Cambridge to visit:

RAR Brewing 504 Poplar Street 21613 (443) 225-5664 https://rarbrewing.com/

From there head about forty minutes east to Salisbury:

Evolution Craft Brewing Company 201 E Vine Street 21801 (443) 260-2337 https://www.evolutioncraftbrewing.com/

Parsonsburg is about twenty-minutes east and has a must-visit brewery:

Tall Tales Brewing Company 6929 Heron Grove Court 21849 (410) 543-2739 https://www.talltalesbrew.com/home

Producing a quality selection of approachable beer styles. In addition to their year-round beers, there are also new and rotational beers to try. Another twenty-minutes east brings you closer to the ocean and a must-visit brewery at Berlin:

Burley Oak Brewing Company 10016 Old Ocean City Blvd 21811 (443) 513-4647 http://burleyoak.com/

Using new and traditional brewing methods to produce distinctive beers, you won't find anywhere else. End your trip at two breweries in the ocean side town of Ocean City just eleven minutes east:

Backshore Brewing Company 913 Atlantic Avenue 21842 (443) 373-1224 http://backshorebrew.com/

The Fin City Brewing Company 12913 Ocean Gateway 21842 (410) 213-1771 https://fincitybrewing.com/

Hagerstown

Antietam Brewery and Restaurant 49 Eastern Blvd 21740 (301) 791-5915 https://antietambrewery.com/index.html

Williamsport

Cushwa Brewing Company 10212 Governor Lane Blvd Suite 1012 21795 http://cushwabrewing.com/

Chesapeake Beach

Greenspring Brewing Company 2309 Greenspring Court 20732 (410) 206-3918 http://greenspringbrewingcompany.com/

Owings

Scorpion Brewing 929 Skinners Turn Road 20736 (410) 279-9700 http://scorpionbrewing.com/

Producing beer from local ingredients with an emphasis on quality, flavor, and brewing technique. Come try their rotating selection of beers.

Central Massachusetts

Central Massachusetts is home to a number of breweries. You can easily visit them within a couple days. You can also take the time to visit a number of sites and explore the great history of the area. Start your trip out at the brewery in Fiskdale:

Rapscallion 195 Arnold Road 01518 (617) 869-5702
http://drinkrapscallion.com/

Just three minutes south is a must-visit brewery at Sturbridge:

Altruist Brewing Company 559 Main Street Unit 105 (774) 241-8022
https://www.altruistbrewing.com/

Producing well-balanced and delicious beer. Stop in to try their beer that is made from quality ingredients. Twelve minutes northeast brings you to a brewery at Charlton:

Tree House Brewing Company 129 Sturbridge Road 01507 (413) 949-1891 https://www.treehousebrew.com/

Head north about twenty-minutes to Spencer with a must-visit brewery:

The Spencer Brewery 167 North Spencer Road 01562 (508) 885-8700
https://www.spencerbrewery.com/

The first and only certified Trappist beer in the United States. Made with sustainable practices, the beers here have constantly won awards. Four minutes Southwest brings you to another must-visit brewery in East Brookfield:

Timberyard Brewing Company 555 East Main Street 01515 (774) 745-8192 https://timberyardbrewing.com/

Striving to make the best beer in the world by producing beers that highlight the ingredients without being overpowering to the palate. Take a half-hour drive north to Barre for the next brewery:

Stone Cow Brewery 500 West Street 01005
https://www.stonecowbrewery.com/

The next brewery is in Gardner about a half-hour north and then slightly east:

Moon Hill Brewing Company 74 Parker Street 01440 (978) 669-0122
https://www.gardnerale.com/

Continue to the next brewery nine minutes east in Westminster:

Wachusett Brewing Company 175 State Road E Rt 2A 01473 (508) 874-9965 http://www.wachusettbrewingcompany.com/

Another fourteen minutes east brings you to Fitchburg:

River Styx Brewing Company 166 Boulder Drive Suite 112 01420
https://riverstyxbrewing.com/

Then head about twenty-minutes Southeast to another brewery at Lancaster:

Bull Spit Brewing Company 339 Seven Bridge Road 01523 (978) 706-1479 http://bullspitbrewing.com/

Seven minutes brings you to Bolton and another brewery:

Nashoba Valley Brewery 100 Wattaquadock Hill Road 01740 (978) 779-5521 https://nashobawinery.com/

Next is a must-visit brewery in Hudson just eight minutes away:

Medusa Brewing Company 111 Main Street 01749 (978) 310-1933 https://www.medusabrewing.com/

Taste the ultimate variety with offering from handcrafted American lagers to English recipe beers. You're sure to find something you'll enjoy. Next head southwest to the main city of Worcester with a few options including two must-visit breweries:

Redemption Rock Brewing 333 Shrewsbury Street 01604 (774) 530-6958 https://www.redemptionrock.beer/

Wormtown Brewery 72 Shrewsbury Street 01604 (774) 239-1555 https://wormtownbrewery.com/

Greater Good Imperial Brewing Company 55 Millbrook Street 01606 (508) 926-8736 https://greatergoodimperials.com/

Featuring the Passport Series that highlights styles of beer from around the world. Try everything from a Belgian IPA to a Russian Imperial Stout.

Flying Dreams 455 Park Avenue 01610 (508) 926-8251 https://www.flyingdreamsbrewing.com/

Offering robust, unfiltered, and full-flavored beers. No matter what you taste here, it will have a distinctive flavor all its own. Head back east about twenty-minutes to two breweries in Westborough:

Owen O'Leary's Brewpub 17 Connector Road 01581 (508) 366-9262 https://www.owenolearys.com/

Cold Harbor Brewing 108 Milk Street Suite 601581

http://www.coldharborbrewing.com/

Then head south to a must-visit brewery in Milford about a half-hour away:

CraftRoots Brewing 4 Industrial Road 01757 (508) 662-4871

https://www.craftrootsbrewing.com/

Brewing with what they grow on the land. This is the place to go for a down to earth tasting experience. End your trip about twenty-minutes west in Whitinsville at:

Purgatory Beer Company 670 Linwood Avenue 01588 (508) 596-2194

https://www.purgatorybeer.com/

Western Massachusetts

Take a circular trip of mountainous Western Massachusetts. You'll visit many towns on a trip that will take at least three to four days to visit the many breweries along the way. Start your trip in Hampden at a must-visit brewery:

Scantic River Brewery 25 Mill Road 01036 (413) 537-3427

https://www.scanticriverbrewery.com/

Known for their signature Hampden Pale Ale and North Trail IPA. They also offer a rotation of seasonal beers. Head eleven minutes north to Wilbraham:

Fieldcrest Brewing Company 2343 Boston Road 01095 (413) 596-3632

http://fieldcrestbrewing.com/

Continue north another ten minutes to Ludlow with two breweries:

Vanished Valley Brewing 782 Center Street 01056 (413) 610-1572

https://vanishedvalley.com/

Iron Duke Brewing 100 State Street Stockhouse 122 01056 (413) 624-6258 https://irondukebrewing.com/

Westfield is twenty-minutes to the west and offers two breweries:

Westfield River Brewing Company 79 Mainline Drive 01085 (413) 374-8425 https://www.westfieldriverbrewing.com/

Tin Bridge Brewing Company 487 E Main Street 01085 (413) 642-6418 https://www.tinbridgebrewing.com/

Nine minutes south gets you to a must-visit brewery in Southwick:

Black Rabbit Farm Wild Ales and Provisions 358 North Loomis Street 01077 (413) 562-2683 https://www.blackrabbitprovisions.com/

The wild ales here are light, crisp beers with a tart finish. They pair great with a variety of foods. Stop by to try these unique ales today. Circle twenty-minutes back north to a brewery at West Springfield:

Two Weeks Notice Brewing 110 Bosworth Street 01089 (413) 707-1413 https://www.twoweeksnoticebrewing.com/

Continue twelve minutes north to Holyoke at:

Holyoke Craft Beer 208 Race Street 01040 https://www.holyokecraftbeer.com/

South Hadley is a further ten minutes north with another brewery:

Drunken Rabbit Brewing Company 749A New Ludlow Road 01075 (413) 728-2739 https://www.rabbit.beer/home

Fifteen minutes north is a brewery at Amherst:

Amherst Brewing 10 University Drive 01002 (413) 253-4400 https://amherstbrewing.com/

Head southwest sixteen minutes to Florence and a must-visit brewery:

Brew Practitioners 36 Main Street 01062 (413) 584-2444 http://www.brewpractitioners.com/

Focused on brewing drinkable beers with regionally sourced ingredients. Enjoy a well balanced, classic American beer. Continue about twenty-minutes southwest to Westhampton:

Outlook Farm 136 Main Road 01027 (413) 529-9388
http://www.outlookfarm.com/index.php

Then head to Easthampton about twenty-minutes southeast:

Abandoned Building Brewery 142 Pleasant Street Unit 103A 01027 (413) 282-7062 http://abandonedbuildingbrewery.com/

New City Brewery 180 Pleasant Street 01027 (413) 529-2000
https://www.newcitybrewery.com/

Focused on reviving pre-prohibition style alcoholic ginger beer. The beers have a delicate flavor with just the right amount of heat.

Fort Hill Brewery 30 Fort Hill Road 01027 (413) 203-5754
http://www.forthillbrewery.com/

Crafting quality lagers and ales with a focus on traditional German brewing techniques. Stop in to try a tap beer or a rotating seasonal offering. Northampton is nine minutes north with two breweries including a must-visit:

Progression Brewing Company 9 Pearl Street 01060 (413) 341-3517
https://progbrew.com/

Northampton Brewery 11 Brewster Court 01060 (413) 584-9903
http://northamptonbrewery.com/

Brewing fine ales and lagers paired with outstanding food. Come enjoy a comfortable atmosphere for your tasting experience. Continue twelve minutes north to the brewery at Whately:

Hitchcock Brewing Company 129 Christian Lane 01093 (413) 695-2400
https://www.hitchcockbrewing.com/

Just four minutes north in South Deerfield is a must-visit brewery:

Berkshire Brewing Company Inc. 12 Railroad Street 01373 (413) 665-6600 https://www.berkshire-brewing.com/

The premier regional craft brewery in New England. Brewing ales and lagers in fresh, small batches. All of the beers are real, with no additives or preservatives. About twenty-minutes northeast brings you to a brewery in Millers Falls:

Element Brewing Company 30 West Main Street 01349 (413) 835-6340 http://elementbeer.com/

Then head east about twenty-minutes to Orange:

Honest Weight Artisan Beer 131 West Main Street Unit 104 01364 (413) 313-4412 http://www.honestweightbeer.com/

Head back west about a half-hour to Greenfield:

The People's Pint 24 Federal Street 01301 (413) 773-0333 https://thepeoplespint.com/

Continue west another hour to North Adams:

Bright Ideas Brewing 111 MASS MoCA Way 01247 (413) 346-6640 https://brightideasbrewing.com/

Head south about a half-hour to Dalton:

Shire Breu-Haus 63 Flansburg Avenue 01226 (413) 842-8313 https://www.shire.beer/

Great Barrington is about another fifty minutes south:

Barrington Brewery and Restaurant/Berkshire Mountain Brewery 420 Stockbridge Road 01203 (413) 528-8282 https://www.barringtonbrewery.net/

End your trip in Sheffield just eight minutes further south:

Big Elm Brewing 65 Silver Street 01257 (413) 229-2348
https://www.bigelmbeer.com/

North of Boston

The northeast corner of Massachusetts, just above the main city of Boston offers several great brewery options. You can tour them all with a couple days, or you can take a quick one day trip with stops at the must-visit breweries. Start your trip out in the northeast corner of the state with two must-visit breweries in Amesbury:

BareWolf Brewing 12 Oakland Street 01913 (617) 755-7067
https://www.barewolfbrewing.com/

Here they never brew the same beer twice. So if you like something when you come for a tasting, be sure to get some to go.

Brewery Silvaticus 9 Water Street 01913 (978) 504-2337
https://www.silvaticusbeers.com/

The main inspirations for the beers here are Belgian farmhouse ales and German-style lagers. Using these inspirations, they keep pushing forward to offer you great brews. Eleven minutes south is Newburyport with two options, including a must-visit:

Newburyport Brewing Company 4 New Pasture Road 01950 (978) 463-8700 https://nbptbrewing.com/shop/

Riverwalk Brewing 3 Graf Road Unit 15 01950 (978) 499-2337
https://riverwalkbrewing.com/

The bulk of the production is for lager beers while the rest is focused on a rotation of small, batch specialty brews. Continue about another twenty-minutes south to Ipswich with two breweries:

True North Ale Company 116 Country Road 01938 (978) 312-6948
https://www.truenorthales.com/

Ipswich Ale Brewery 2 Brewery Place 01938 (978) 356-3329
http://www.ipswichalebrewery.com/

Head southeast twenty-minutes to the coastal town of Gloucester:

Cape Ann Brewing Company 11 Rogers Street 01930 (978) 281-4782
https://www.capeannbrewing.com/

Head back southwest to the town of Beverly with two breweries including
a must-visit:

Old Planters Brewing Company 100 Corning Street 01915 (978) 522-
6446 https://www.oldplanters.com/

Gentile Brewing Company 59 Park Street Unit 1 01915 (978) 969-6496
https://gentilebrewing.com/

Beers made using traditional English-style methods and ingredients.
There are four year-round beers as well as small-batch releases to try.
Just five minutes away is Salem with another must-visit brewery:

Notch Brewing 283R Derby Street 01970 (978) 238-9060
https://www.notchbrewing.com/

The first brewing company in the United States to focus entirely on
session beers. Offering the full spectrum of session beers, so you have a
variety to choose from. Peabody has another brewery and is only five
minutes away:

Essex County Brewing Company 58 Pulaski Street Building A 01960
(978) 587-2254 https://www.essexcountybrewing.com/

Continue southwest about a half-hour to Everett with two breweries,
including a must-visit:

Night Shift Brewing 87 Santilli Highway 02149 (617) 294-4233
https://nightshiftbrewing.com/

Bone Up Brewing Company 38 Norman Street 02149 (781) 691-9092
https://www.boneup.beer/

Beers inspired by Belgian farmhouse brewing techniques while also celebrating American styles and local ingredients. Taste both of these beer cultures in a single glass. Five minutes away is another brewery at Malden:

Idle Hands Craft Ales 89 Commercial Street 02148 (781) 333-6070
http://www.idlehandscraftales.com/site/

Somerville is ten minutes away and offers four breweries:

Aeronaut Brewing Company 14 Tyler Street 02143 (617) 987-4236
https://www.aeronautbrewing.com/

Winter Hill Brewing Company 328 Broadway 02145
https://winterhillbrewing.com/

Somerville Brewing Company 15 Ward Street 02143 (800) 428-1150
https://www.slumbrew.com/

Remnant Brewing 2 Bow Market Way 02143 (617) 764-0641
https://www.remnantsomerville.com/

Continue about a half-hour southwest to Waltham:

Mighty Squirrel Brewing Company 411 Waverly Oaks Road 02452 (760) 212-0802 http://www.mightysquirrel.com/

Another brewery is nine minutes away in Newton:

Hopsters Brewing Company 292 Centre Street 02458 (617) 916-0752
https://www.hopstersbrew.com/

About twenty-minutes further south is South Natick with another brewery:

Lookout Farm Brewing Company 89 Pleasant Street South 01760 (508) 653-1178 https://www.lookoutfarm.com/

Eleven minutes west is Framingham with two breweries, including a must-visit:

Exhibit 'A' Brewing Company 81 Morton Street 01702 (508) 202-9297
https://www.exhibit-a-brewing.com/

Jack's Abby Brewing 100 Clinton Street 01702 (508) 872-0900
https://jacksabby.com/

Only brewing lagers. The lagers here have a distinctive smoothness and fullness that you won't find in any other beer. About twenty-minutes south is Hopkinton and the southernmost stop of your trip:

Start Line Brewing Company 151R Hayden Rowe Street 01748 (508) 761-2044 http://www.startlinebrewing.com/

Head north about twenty-minutes to a must-visit brewery in Hudson:

Medusa Brewing Company 111 Main Street 01749 (978) 310-1933
https://www.medusabrewing.com/

From American-style ales and lagers to traditional European-inspired recipes, you'll find a full variety in the beer selection here. Fifteen minutes northeast brings you to Maynard:

Amory's Tomb Brewing Company 76 Main Street 01754 (978) 243-0875 https://www.amorystomb.com/

About a forty-minute drive northeast to the border brings you to two breweries in Lowell:

Navigation Brewing Company 122 Western Avenue 01851
https://www.navigationbrewing.com/

Merrimack Ales 92 Bolt Street 01852 (978) 701-7225
https://merrimackales.com/

End your trip with a half-hour drive south to Woburn:

Lord Hobo Brewing Company 5 Draper Street 01801 (781) 281-0809
https://lordhobobrewing.com/

South of Boston

South of Boston has just as many breweries as the north of Boston tour. You can accomplish this trip in a day or two, depending on how in-depth you plan your trip. Start your trip in Attleboro at:

Skyroc Brewery 11 Riverbank Road 02703 (774) 331-2336
https://www.skyrocbrewery.com/

Head east about ten minutes to a must-visit brewery at Norton:

Bog Iron Brewing 33 West Main Street Unit F 02677 (508) 952-0555
https://www.bogironbrewing.com/

Brewing high-quality, boundary-pushing beers that are also accessible. Brewing a wide variety of beers so a wide audience can enjoy what they offer. Easton is ten minutes north with another brewery:

Shovel Town Brewery 50 Oliver Street 02356 (508) 205-7151
https://www.shoveltownbrewery.com/

Another half-hour north brings you to Medfield with two breweries, including a must-visit:

7th Wave Brewing 120 N Meadows Road 02052 (508) 906-6007
https://7thwavebrewing.com/

ZeLUS Beer Company 1 Green Street 02052 (774) 469-3961
https://www.zelusbeer.com/

A unique kind of beer you won't find anywhere else. A hydro-friendly beer that focuses on water profiles and low alcohol content. Be sure to stop in to try this unique beer. Then head twelve minutes east to Norwood with two breweries:

Castle Island Brewing Company 31 Astor Avenue 02062 (781) 951-2029 https://castleislandbeer.com/

Percival Beer Company 83 Morse Street 02062 (781) 352-3043 https://www.percivalbrewing.com/

Continue east to Braintree about twenty-minutes away with another brewery:

Widowmaker Brewing 220 Wood Road 02184 (781) 849-0205 https://www.widowmakerbrewing.com/

Just ten minutes away is Weymouth with two more breweries, including a must-visit:

Vitamin Sea Brewing 30 Moore Road 02189 (781) 803-2104 https://vitaminseabrewing.com/

Barrel House Z 95 Woodrock Road 02189 (331) 201-7888 https://www.barrelhousez.net/

Producing small-batch, barrel-aged beers. There are ten to twelve beers on tap, and they are constantly changing, so you'll always have something new to try. Then head south about twenty-minutes to another must-visit brewery at Hanover:

Burke's Alewerks 200 Webster Street 02339 (781) 312-8207 http://burkesalewerks.com/

Focused on traditional European and American style ales. The heart of the brewery is the community-style taproom where you can gather with friends and enjoy excellent beer. Marshfield is ten minutes east with another must-visit brewery:

Stellwagen Beer Company 10p Enterprise Drive 02050 (781) 536-8472 https://www.stellwagenbeer.com/

Small batch, handcrafted beers focused on New England roots. Continually offering a rotating selection of new beer styles. Head south to the coastal town of Plymouth twenty-minutes away with three must-visit breweries:

Second Wind Brewing Company 7 Howland Street 02360 (508) 591-5915 https://www.secondwindbrewing.com/

There is plenty to try here, including hoppy IPAs, decadent stouts, fruited sours, refreshing lagers, wheat beers, and traditional ales. No matter what you like, you'll find it here.

Independent Fermentations Brewing 127 Camelot Drive 02360 (508) 789-9940 https://independentfermentations.weebly.com/

Most brews here are inspired by the Belgian farmhouse brewing tradition, but there are also other options available. The beers are made with local ingredients.

Mayflower Brewing Company 12 Resnik Road Suite 3 02360 (508) 746-2674 https://www.mayflowerbrewing.com/

Using traditional brewing methods, you can try year-round beers that honor traditional styles or try a seasonal beer. There are also rotating specials that allow you to try different styles. Circle about an hour northwest to New Bedford with a must-visit brewery:

Moby Dick Brewing Company 16 South Water Street 02740 (774) 202-6964 https://www.mobydickbrewing.com/

Serving fine ales and lagers along with the freshest seafood and other New England dishes. Come try a beer and stroll along the historic waterfront. Another fourteen minutes west brings you to a must-visit brewery at Westport:

Buzzards Bay Brewing 98 Horseneck Road 02790 (508) 636-2288 http://buzzardsbrew.com/

Unfiltered, small-batch beer made from locally grown ingredients. When you try a beer here, you'll be tasting what beer is really supposed to taste like; the ingredients will speak for themselves. Seventeen minutes northwest brings you to a brewery at Fall River:

Canned Heat Craft Beer Company 52 Ferry Street 02721 (774) 955-0791 https://www.cannedheatbeer.com/

Bridgewater is about a half-hour north with another brewery:

Black Hat Brew Works 25 Scotland Blvd 02324 (508) 807-5172 https://www.blackhatbrewworks.com/

End your trip twelve minutes further north at Whitman with a final brewery:

Old Colony Brewing 571 Temple Street 02382 (781) 523-7105 https://www.oldcolonybrewing.com/

Greater Boston

Whether you are passing through the area or staying in Boston for a little bit and want to experience the local flavor and culture, there are some great breweries to keep you busy in the greater Boston area. Start your trip out in Boston with a few brewery options including two must-visit breweries:

Cheeky Monkey Brewing Company 3 Lansdowne Street 02215 (617) 859-0030 http://cheekymonkeyboston.com/

Harpoon Brewery and Beer Hall 306 Northern Avenue 02210 (617) 574-9551 https://www.harpoonbrewery.com/

Trillium Brewing Company 50 Thompson Place 02210 (617) 453-8745 https://www.trilliumbrewing.com/

A New England farmhouse-inspired brewery focused on brewing great beer and building a community. Brewing a diversity of beers to choose from.

Democracy Brewing 35 Temple Place 02111 (857) 263-8604 https://www.democracybrewing.com/

Enjoy a traditional public house while tasting the best beer in Boston. Stop in for great beer and stay for a great experience. Eight minutes west is Cambridge with two must-visit breweries:

Cambridge Brewing Company 1 Kendall Square 02139 (617) 494-1994 https://www.cambridgebrewingcompany.com/

Brewing handcrafted beers of many origins and influences. By brewing a broad spectrum of beer, they are able to appeal to a variety of beer drinkers.

Lamplighter Brewing Company 284 Broadway 02139 (617) 945-0450 https://lamplighterbrewing.com/

Focusing on aroma-packed and flavor-driven beers. The emphasis is on New England IPAs, barrel-aged sours, and special seasonal brews. Then seventeen minutes south brings you to Dorchester and another brewery:

Dorchester Brewing Company 1250 Massachusetts Avenue 02125 (617) 514-0900 https://www.dorchesterbrewing.com/

About a half-hour drive east towards the coast brings you to Hingham with two breweries including a must-visit:

Entitled Brewing Company 21 North Street 02043 (781) 740-1035 http://www.entitledbrewing.com/

Shakesbeer 160 Old Derby Street Suite 264 02043 (781) 269-2690 https://www.drinkshakesbeer.com/

Combining traditional brewing techniques with new American flavor profiles. Try their sophisticated and easy-drinking beers.

The Islands

There are only a handful of breweries on the island chains of Massachusetts. However, these breweries offer a great view of the ocean and a wonderfully relaxing atmosphere. You can easily visit the breweries in a day, but you may enjoy the beauty of the area so much that you decide to slow down and take your time. Start out in Oak Bluffs with a must-visit brewery:

Offshore Ale Company 30 Kennebec Avenue 02557 (508) 693-2626 https://www.offshoreale.com/

The premier brewery in Martha's Vineyard. Come for fine craft beer and excellent food within a beautiful environment. Staying on the same island, just fourteen minutes away is another brewery at Edgartown:

Bad Martha Brewing Company 270 Upper Main Street 02539 (508) 939-4415 https://www.badmarthabeer.com/

Head to your next island with about a two hour trip to the must-visit brewery in Nantucket:

Cisco Brewers Inc. 5 and 7 Bartlett Farm Road 02584 (508) 325-5929 http://ciscobrewers.com/

In addition to enjoying world-class varieties of beer, you can also enjoy wine and spirits. Come try your favorite and find a new favorite. Take another two hour trip back to the mainland coastal area of Massachusetts to two breweries in Hyannis:

Cape Cod Beer 1336 Phinney's Lane 02601 (508) 790-4200 https://capecodbeer.com/

Barnstable Brewing 485 W Main Street 02601 (774) 470-6989 https://www.barnstablebrewing.com/

Eighteen minutes west is another brewery at Mashpee:

Naukabout Brewery 13 Lake Avenue 02649 (508) 444-9822 https://www.naukabout.com/

Head back east about a half-hour to the town of South Dennis and another brewery:

Devil's Purse Brewing Company 120 Great Western Road 02660
https://www.devilspurse.com/home/

End your trip with a twenty-minute drive east to a must-visit brewery in Orleans:

Hog Island Beer Company 28 West Road 02653 (508) 255-2337
http://www.hogislandbeerco.com/

The outermost brewery on Cape Cod. Enjoy a beer on one of the most picturesque coastal areas in the United States. This is an experience you won't soon forget.

Michigan

Kalamazoo County

No trip to Michigan is complete without a tour of the excellent breweries in Kalamazoo County. You can easily complete this trip in a day, but you may want to take a little longer to enjoy the beauty and sites in the surrounding area. Start your trip out in Springfield at their must-visit brewery:

Territorial Brewing Company 256 Helmer Road N 49037 (269) 282-1694 http://territorialbrewing.com/

Offering great German-inspired beer and food. Offering two year-round beers: An American Light Lager and a Michigan Pilsner. There are also seasonal and rotating offers. Head west about twenty-minutes to your next brewery in Comstock:

Bell's Brewery 8690 Krum Avenue 49053 (269) 382-2338 http://www.bellsbeer.com/

Another seven minutes west brings you to the main city of Kalamazoo with a few options, including two must-visit breweries:

One Well Brewing 4213 Portage Street 49001 (269) 459-9240 https://www.onewellbrewing.com/

Brite Eyes Brewing Company 1156 S Burdick Street 49001 (269) 220-5001 https://briteeyesbrewingco.com/

The smallest brewery in Kalamazoo that offers you the finest in small-batch beers. There are also excellent food options to pair with your beers.

Olde Peninsula Brewpub 200 E Michigan Avenue 49007 (269) 343-2739 https://template.citycheers.com/97084

The first brewpub in Kalamazoo. Offering fresh beers that are brewed on-site. Come relax and enjoy a great tasting experience. From here head twelve minutes south to your next brewery in Portage:

Latitude 42 Brewing Company 7842 Portage Road 49002 (269) 459-4242 https://latitude42brewingco.com/

Lawton is about twenty-minutes west and has another must-visit brewery:

Barn Brewers 114 N Main Street 49065 (269) 299-0482 http://www.barnbrewersbrewery.com/

One of the first microbreweries in Michigan. Come enjoy a range of beers and ciders, plus for the underaged crowd, there are craft sodas to enjoy as well. End your trip about ten minutes northwest in the town of Paw Paw with a must-visit brewery:

Paw Paw Brewing Company 929 East Michigan Avenue 49079 (269) 415-0145 http://www.pawpawbrewing.com/

This brewery surrounds you with beautiful wilderness. Offering four beers on tap year-round along with seasonal and rotating specials.

Grand Rapids Area

Grand Rapids is known as the brewing capital of America, and it is easy to see why with all the breweries packed into this small area. You could easily drive to all the breweries within a day, but in order to enjoy a sampling of what each has to offer, you may want to reserve at least a couple days or more depending on how many breweries you plan to visit. Start your trip out in Whitehall at:

Fetch Brewing Company 100 W Colby Street 49461 (231) 292-1048 https://www.fetchbrewing.com/

Then head south about twenty-minutes to two breweries in Muskegon:

Pigeon Hill Brewing Company 500 W Western Avenue Suite 1 49440 (231) 375-5184 https://pigeonhillbrew.com/

Unruly Brewing Company 360 W Western Avenue 49440 (231) 288-1068 https://unrulybrewing.com/

Continue twenty-minutes south to two must-visit breweries in the waterfront town of Grand Haven:

Odd Side Ales 41 Washington Avenue 49417 (616) 935-7326 https://www.oddsideales.com/

While maintaining a large core of year-round and seasonal beers, they also work to stay on the leading edge of craft beers. There are always new recipes that push the boundaries of flavor combinations and craft beer categories.

Grand Armory Brewing 17 S 2nd Street 49417 (616) 414-7822
http://www.grandarmorybrewing.com/

Focusing on making a diverse range of high-quality beers. 20 taps offer you a range of beers in addition to ciders, wine, and old-fashioned sodas. Head east about a half-hour to Allendale with another must-visit brewery:

Trail Point Brewing Company 6035 Lake Michigan Drive 49401 (616) 895-2793 https://www.trailpointbrewing.com/

Handcrafted beers with a focus on quality and taste. Enjoy well-balanced beers in a place that makes you feel at home. About twenty-minutes further east is the main city of Grand Rapids with multiple brewery options and several must-visits:

Greyline Brewing Company 1727 Alpine Avenue NW 49504
https://www.greylinebrewing.com/

City Built Brewing Company 820 Monroe Avenue NW #155 49503 (616) 805-5755 https://citybuiltbrewing.com/

Founders Brewing Company 235 Grandville Avenue SW 49503 (616) 776-1195 https://foundersbrewing.com/

Harmony Brewing Company 1551 Lake Drive SE 49506 (616) 233-0063
https://harmonybeer.com/

Jaden James Brewery 4665 Broadmoor SE 49512 (616) 656-4665
https://www.cascadecellars.com/jaden-james-brewery

Brewery Vivant 925 Cherry Street 49506 (616) 719-1604
https://www.breweryvivant.com/

HopCat 25 Ionia Avenue SW 49503 (616) 451-4677
http://www.hopcatgr.com/

Creston Brewery 1504 Plainfield Avenue NE 49505 (616) 805-4523
https://www.crestonbrewery.com/

Crafting beers that will awaken your senses. Rather than focusing on styles, the beers here are based on a scale of flavors and aromas to help you find the right beer for you.

The Mitten Brewing Company 527 Leonard Street NW 49504 (616) 608-5612 https://www.mittenbrewing.com/

A vintage baseball-themed microbrewery offering handcrafted beers paired with gourmet pizzas.

Schmohz Brewing Company 2600 Patterson Avenue SE 49546 (616) 949-0860 https://schmohz.com/

One of the oldest breweries in Grand Rapids. Sixteen taps offer you a range of styles, flavors, and colors.

East West Brewing Company 1400 Lake Drive SE 49506 (616) 288-5250 http://www.eastwestbrewingcompany.com/

Artisan craft beer with a fresh local flavor. In addition to their signature, flagship beers they offer rotating seasonal selections made from all-natural ingredients.

B.O.B.'s Brewery 20 Monroe Avenue NW 49503 (616) 356-2000
http://www.thebob.com/

The first microbrewery in downtown Grand Rapids. Focusing on traditional German-style beers with the occasional one-offs. When you're ready there is another must-visit brewery six minutes south in Wyoming:

Kitzingen Brewery 1760 44th Street SW Ste 8 49509 (616) 301-1811
http://www.kitzingen-brewery.com/

Offering nine to fifteen beers on tap, including an IPA, a stout, and an authentic seasonal Hefeweizen. The focus is on German styles, and you can also enjoy wines and ciders. Head back seven minutes west to a brewery in Grandville:

Osgood Brewing 4051 Chicago Drive SW 49418 (616) 432-3881
http://www.osgoodbrewing.com/

Southwest about ten minutes brings you to your next brewery at Hudsonville:

White Flame Brewing Company 5234 36th Avenue 49426 (616) 209-5098 https://whiteflamebrewing.com/

Continue about twenty-minutes southwest to Holland with a few brewery options including a must-visit:

Brewery 4 Two 4 321 Douglas Avenue 49424 (616) 377-7773
http://www.brewery424.com/

New Holland Brewing Company 66 E 8th Street 49423 (616) 355-6422
https://www.newhollandbrew.com/

Big Lake Brewing 13 W 7th Street 49423 (616) 796-8888
https://biglakebrewing.com/

Our Brewing Company 76 E 8th Street 49423 (616) 994-8417
https://ourbrewingcompany.com/

Crafting small batches of complex beers with local ingredients. All of the beers here have names as unusual as their taste. Head another seventeen minutes south to Fennville with a must-visit brewery:

Waypost Brewing 1630 Blue Star Highway 49408 (269) 496-5096
https://www.waypostbeer.com/home

A small, independent, farm brewery. The beers are inspired by what is grown on the farm. The main beers are the classic styles with a rotating selection of what the season offers. Take about a forty-minute drive northeast to Wayland:

OpenRoad Brewery 128 S Main Street 49348 (616) 293-7855
https://www.openroadbrewing.com/

Nine minutes north is Dorr with another brewery:

5 Lakes Brewing Company 1638 142nd Avenue 49323 (616) 359-9555
https://5lakesbrewing.com/

Continue another seven minutes north to a brewery at Byron Center:

Alebird Taphouse and Brewery 2619 84th Street SW 49315 (616) 422-9007 https://www.alebird.com/

Then head east about twenty-minutes to a brewery at Caledonia:

Essential Bean Coffee and Pub 8980 N Rodgers Court Suite D 49316
(616) 891-7700 https://eb-coffee-pub.square.site/

Head north twelve minutes to Kentwood and another brewery:

Broad Leaf Local Beer 2885 Lake Eastbrook Blvd 49512 (616) 803-0602
https://broadleafbeer.com/

Ada is another fifteen minutes north:

Gravel Bottom Craft Brewery and Supply 418 Ada Drive 49301 (206) 403-8563 https://gravelbottom.com/

Comstock Park has two breweries including a must-visit and is about twenty-minutes northwest:

Speciation Artisan Ales 3720 West River Drive NE 49321
https://speciationartisanales.com/

Perrin Brewing Company 5910 Comstock Park Drive 49231 (616) 551-1957 https://www.perrinbrewing.com/

Crafting high quality and consistent beer with a leading-edge taste. With 18 to 25 beers on tap, there is always something for all palate tastes. End your trip with a seventeen-minute drive north to a must-visit brewery at Cedar Springs:

Cedar Springs Brewing Company 95 N Main Street 49319 (616) 696-2337 https://csbrew.com/

Using traditional German techniques to create excellent beers to enjoy with their traditional German Bavarian menu.

Lake Michigan Shore

Take several days to travel the Lake Michigan shoreline of Michigan. Start out in the northern tip of the state and head south along the shore to the border. You'll get to visit some beautiful waterfront towns along with tasting some wonderful beers. Start out at the northern tip of Michigan in Mackinaw City at:

Biere de Mac 14277 N Mackinaw Highway 49701 (231) 427-7007 http://bieredemac.com/

Petoskey is about forty minutes south and offers two more breweries:

Beards Brewery 207A Howard Street 49770 (231) 753-2221 https://www.beardsbrewery.com/

Petoskey Brewing Company 1844 M-119 49770 (231) 753-2057 https://www.petoskeybrewing.com/

About another twenty-minutes south is a must-visit brewery at Charlevoix:

Bier's Inwood Brewery 17959 Ferry Road 49720 (231) 675-7632 http://biersinwoodbrewery.com/

Using traditional brewing methods with new ingredients for innovative flavors. There are 12 tap lines offering a rotation of beer styles and hard cider. Boyne City is a half-hour further south and offers another must-visit brewery:

Stiggs Brewing Company 112 S Park Street 49712 (231) 497-6100
http://www.stiggsbrewingcompany.com/

The cities only producer of locally and handcrafted beer, offering a line of signature beers along with seasonal offerings. Another brewery is about forty minutes south in Bellaire:

Short's Brewing Company 121 N Bridge Street 49615 (231) 498-2300
https://www.shortsbrewing.com/

About fifty minutes away is the city of Traverse City with many brewery options and two must-visits:

Mackinaw Brewing Company 161 East Front Street 49684 (231) 933-1100 https://www.mackinawbrewing.com/

The Workshop Brewing Company 221 Garland Street Suite A 49684 (231) 421-8977 https://traversecityworkshop.com/

Rare Bird Brewpub 229 Lake Avenue 49684 (231) 943-2053
https://rarebirdbrewpub.com/

MiddleCoast Brewing Company 329 East State Street 49684 (231) 943-2739 https://www.middlecoastbrewingco.com/

The Filling Station Microbrewery 642 Railroad Place 49686 (231) 946-8168 http://thefillingstationmicrobrewery.com/

Kilkenny's Irish Public House 400 ½ W Front Street 49684 (231) 941-7527 http://www.kilkennyspub.com/kk/kilkennys-irish-pub

Right Brain Brewery 225 E 16th Street 49684 (231) 944-1239
https://www.rightbrainbrewery.com/

Brewery Terra Firma 2959 Hartman Road 49685 (231) 929-1600
http://breweryterrafirma.com/

Offering delicious, culinary-inspired beers made through sustainable methods. Come sample the many beers offered here.

North Peak Brewing Company 400 West Front Street 49684 (231) 941-PEAK https://www.northpeakbeer.com/

Known for classic styles, they have been brewing since 1997 with Up North roots. The clean beers here will resonate with all beer drinkers. Suttons Bay is about twenty-minutes more south with a single brewery:

Hop Lot Brewing Company 658 S West Bay Shore Drive 49682 (231) 866-4445 https://hoplotbrewing.com/

About a half-hour brings you to Glen Arbor:

Cherry Public House 6026-C S Lake Street 49636 (231) 226-3033 https://www.stormcloudbrewing.com/

Another half-hour brings you to a brewery in Lake Ann:

Lake Ann Brewing Company 6535 First Street 49650 (231) 640-2327 http://www.lakeannbrewing.com/index.html

Next is a must-visit brewery in Beulah another half-hour south:

Five Shores Brewing 163 S Benzie Blvd 49617 (231) 383-4400 https://www.fiveshoresbrewing.com/

The award-winning beers here are a complement to anything. Come try an old favorite or something new in a relaxing atmosphere. Just ten minutes south is another must-visit brewery in Frankfort:

Stormcloud Brewing Company 303 Main Street 49635 (231) 352-0118 https://www.stormcloudbrewing.com/

Specialized in brewing Belgian inspired ales. Take a scenic drive to this brewery and enjoy your beer tasting in a beautiful setting. Prepare for an hour and a half drive to the next must-visit brewery at Ludington:

Jamesport Brewing Company Inc. 410 S James Street 49431 (231) 845-2522 http://jamesportbrewingcompany.com/

Offering award-winning beers in a relaxing atmosphere. Offering 14 unique craft beers on tap at any given time. Another twenty-five minutes brings you to Hart and a must-visit brewery:

Big Hart Brewing Company 4086 W Polk Road 49420 (231) 301-8226 https://bighartbrewing.com/

Offering an eclectic mix of New and Old World styles using mostly European malts. You can sample a range of strong, session, and hoppy beers. Spring Lake has a must-visit brewery and is the next stop about an hour south:

Old Boys Brew House 971 West Savidge 49456 (616) 850-9950 https://www.oldboysbrewhouse.com/

Producing fine, handcrafted ales from the freshest ingredients. Also offering a wide variety of foods to pair with your beers. About forty minutes brings you to Saugatuck and another must-visit brewery:

Guardian Brewing Company 3657 63rd Street 49453 (269) 543-2238 https://guardianbrewingco.com/

There are 10 year-round taps and 12 seasonal and barrel-aged taps offering a wide variety of styles. Try their Pegacorn Porter and Gator Bait Golden Ale. Just four minutes away is another brewery at Douglas:

Saugatuck Brewing Company 2948 Blue Star Highway 49406 (269) 857-7222 https://saugatuckbrewing.com/

Another sixteen minutes brings you to South Haven:

Three Blondes Brewing Company 1875 Phoenix Street Suite B 49090 (269) 872-3911 https://www.threeblondesbrewing.com/

Bangor is the next stop fifteen minutes away:

Cognito Brewing Company 143 W Monroe Street 49013 (971) 808-8863 https://www.cognitobrewingcompany.com/

About twenty-minutes away is another brewer at Watervliet:

Arclight Brewing Company 544 N Main Street 49098 (269) 332-0718
https://www.arclightbrewing.com/

The next must-visit brewery is thirteen minutes south in Benton Harbor:

The Livery 190 Fifth Street 49022 (269) 925-8760 http://liverybrew.com/

Offering 18 taps of hand-forged beers. Offering two ales and two dedicated nitro taps. The beer garden is pet friendly and a great place to relax. St. Joseph has the next brewery and is only two minutes away:

Silver Harbor Brewing Company 721 Pleasant Street 49085 (269) 281-7100 https://www.silverharborbrewing.com/

Twelve minutes brings you to the next brewery at Stevensville:

Watermark Brewing Company 5781 Saint Joseph Avenue 49127 (269) 281-0872 https://www.watermarkbrewing.com/

Eight minutes brings you to a must-visit brewery in Bridgman:

Tapistry Brewing 4236 Lake Street 49106 (269) 266-7349
http://www.tapistrybrewing.com/

Come here to try a wide range, including a classic English robust porter and an experimental dark smoked imperial. Next is Sawyer nine minutes south:

Greenbush Brewing Company 5885 Sawyer Road 49125 (269) 405-1076 https://www.greenbushbrewing.com/

End your trip thirteen minutes south near the border at New Buffalo with two breweries:

Beer Church Brewing Company 24 S Whittaker Street 49117 (219) 771-0635 https://www.beerchurchbrewing.com/

Ghost Isle Brewery 17684 US-12 49117 (269) 469-9069
https://www.ghostislebrewery.com/

Upper Peninsula

The UP, as it is known by the locals, has a few great brewery options. You can visit these within a day or two, depending on your trip plans. Start in the north at Copper Harbor:

Brickside Brewery 64 Gratiot Street 49918 (906) 289-4772
https://bricksidebrewery.com/

Head about a half-hour south to Houghton with a must-visit brewery:

Keweenaw Brewing Company 408 Shelden Avenue 49931 (906) 482-5596 https://www.kbc.beer/

Offering seven or eight brews throughout the year. Featuring the Widowmaker Black, Pickaxe Blonde, and Redjacket Amber Ales. Then take about a two-hour drive south to another must-visit brewery in Kingsford:

51st State Brewing Company 115 Harding Avenue 49802 (906) 828-2167 https://www.51ststatebrewingco.com/

Creating ales and lagers that are well balanced and true to style. There are also some wild and crazy "fringe" beers offered on occasion. About an hour east takes you to the next brewery at Escanaba:

Upper Hand Brewery 3525 Airport Road 49829 (906) 233-5005
http://www.upperhandbrewery.com/

An hour north brings you to Marquette with a few breweries including two must-visits:

Blackrocks Brewery 424 N Third Street 49855 (906) 273-1333
https://www.blackrocksbrewery.com/

Marquette Harbor Brewery No. 119 South Front 49855 (906) 228-3533
http://thevierling.com/wp1/

Ore Dock Brewing Company 114 Spring Street 49855 (906) 228-8888
https://ore-dock.com/

Traditional processes and premium ingredients go into the beers made here. The focus is on ales that emphasize balance and drinkability.

Barrel and Beam 260 Northwoods Road 49855 (906) 273-2559
http://barrelandbeam.com/

Offering bottled-conditioned farmhouse ales. The beers have a fine Champagne-like carbonation and a soft foam when poured. End your trip about fifty minutes east in Munising:

East Channel Brewing Company 209 Maple Street 49862 (906) 387-3007 http://eastchannelbrewery.com/

Lake Huron Shore

Not as long as the Lake Michigan shore, there are still some great breweries to visit. You can complete the trip in a day or two, depending on how you plan. Start your trip in Cheboygan to the north at:

Cheboygan Brewing Company 101 North Main Street 49721 (231) 818-2697 https://www.cheboyganbrewing.com/

Head an hour and a half south to Alpena:

Austin Brothers Beer Company 821 W Miller Street 49707 (989) 340-2300 http://www.austinbrosbeerco.com/

About an hour south is the first must-visit brewery at Oscoda:

Wiltse's Brew Pub and Family Restaurant 5606 F-41 48750 (989) 739-2231 http://wiltsesbrewpub.com/

Holding the third brewery license in Michigan. Offering true to style beer that is fresh and clean in taste. Also offering a pub-style menu. A two-hour drive brings you to Bay City and two more breweries:

Tri-City Brewing Company 3020 N Water Street 48708 (989) 894-4950
https://tricitybrewing.com/

Lumber Barons Brewery 804 E Midland Street 48706 (989) 891-0100
https://lumberbaronsbrewery.com/

End your trip with about an hour drive to a must-visit brewery in Caseville:

Thumb Brewery 6758 Pine Street 48725 (989) 856-1228
http://www.thumbbrewery.com/

Currently offering eleven in-house brews that are constantly changing and expanding. Try the West Coast IPA, Oatmeal Stout, and Pilsner.

Northern Michigan

This one or two day trip can take you to most of the main cities in Northern Michigan. Start your trip in Sandusky at:

Elk Street Brewery and Tap Room 3 South Elk Street 48471 (810) 648-1600 https://elkstreetbrewery.com/

Then head west an hour and a half to a must-visit brewery in Midland:

Midland Brewing Company 5011 Saginaw Street 48642 (989) 259-7210
https://midlandbrewing.com/

Developing new selections along with signature brews like Copper Harbor Ale. Stop in to see why this is quickly becoming the regional destination for beer drinkers. Head forty minutes northwest to Clare with another must-visit brewery:

Four Leaf Brewing 412 N McEwan Street 48617 (989) 424-6114
https://www.fourleafcraftbeer.com/

Step into this casual atmosphere to try a beer from their developing style selection or a creative seasonal brew. Then head south about twenty-minutes to a brewery at Mount Pleasant:

Mountain Town Brewing Company 614 W Pickard Street 48858 (989) 400-4666 https://www.mountaintownbrew.com/

Continue south to Alma another twenty-minutes:

Alma Brewing Company 208 E Superior Street 48801 (989) 462-0208 https://www.almabrewing.com/

Head southwest an hour and a half to Rockford:

Rockford Brewing Company 12 E Bridge Street 49341 (616) 951-4677 https://www.rockfordbrewing.com/

Circle northwest fourteen minutes to Sparta and another must-visit brewery:

Cellar Brewing Company 500 E Division Street 49345 (616) 883-0777 https://www.cellarbrewingco.com/

Featuring 24 taps, there are beer, wine, and spirit options. Easy to find and offering a relaxing atmosphere for beer tasting. Continue north about a half-hour to another must-visit brewery at Newaygo:

Newaygo Brewing Company 19 State Road 49337 (231) 452-6551 http://newaygobrewing.com/

Offering refreshing ales that are perfect after a day of exploring the surrounding area. Stop in to try traditional beers with a twist from their tap selection. Big Rapids is about forty minutes north and offers another brewery option:

Cranker's Brewery 213 S State Street 49307 (231) 796-1919 https://www.crankersbrewery.com/

Another fourteen minutes north brings you to Reed City and another must-visit brewery:

Reed City Brewing Company 141 W Upton Avenue 49677 (231) 465-4222 https://reedcitybeer.com/

The first brewery in Reed City. Offering eleven rotating taps with a variety of beer styles to appeal to any palate. The next brewery is in Cadillac about a half-hour north:

Clam Lake Beer Company 106 S Mitchell Street 49601 (231) 775-6150 https://clamlakebeerco.com/

End your trip about an hour east and north in Grayling with two breweries:

Paddle Hard Brewing 227 E Michigan Avenue 49738 (989) 745-6388 http://www.paddlehardbrewing.com/

Dead Bear Brewing Company 2552 S I-75 Business Loop 49738 (989) 745-6289 https://www.deadbearbrewing.net/

Greater Detroit Area

Drive time, you can achieve this route within a day. However, there are so many breweries packed into this small area that you'll need several days if you are going to visit all the breweries. Start out in Wyandotte at:

Sports Brew Pub 166 Maple Street 48192 (734) 285-5060 https://www.sportsbar-grill.com/

Head north about twenty-minutes to Dearborn with a must-visit brewery:

Dearborn Brewing 21930 Michigan Avenue 48124 (313) 914-4187 http://dearbornbrewing.com/

The first microbrewery in Dearborn. Also, offering wine and seltzer options for those who don't want beer. Head east to the main city of Detroit with several options including two must-visit breweries:

Detroit Beer Company 1529 Broadway 48226 (313) 962-1529
https://www.detroitbeerco.com/

Eastern Market Brewing Company 2515 Riopelle 48207 (313) 502-5165
https://easternmarket.beer/

Traffic Jam and Snug Restaurant 511 West Canfield 48201 (313) 831-9470 http://www.trafficjamdetroit.com/

A hidden treasure offering more than just beers; there are also a number of made-from-scratch dishes you can enjoy.

Lake Brothers Beer Company 1401 Abbott Street 48216
http://lakebrothersbeer.com/

Offering a refreshing, flavorful, and drinkable lager. A subtle hop character with a clean finish, be sure to try some today. Then head west to Livonia about twenty-minutes:

Supernatural Brewing and Spirits 36685 Plymouth Road 48150 (734) 469-2251 https://www.supernaturalbrewing.com/

Canton is about twenty-minutes south and has a single brewery:

Canton Brew Works 8521 N Lilley Road 48187 (734) 927-7081
http://www.cantonbrewworks.com/

Head north about twenty-minutes to two breweries in Northville:

Northville Winery and Brewing Company 714 Baseline Road 48167
(248) 349-3181 https://www.thenorthvillewinery.com/

North Center Brewing Company 410 North Center Street 48167 (248) 470-5700 https://www.northcenterbrewing.com/

A short four minutes away is another brewery at Novi:

Ascension Brewing Company 42000 Grand River Avenue 38475 (248) 308-2093 http://ascension.beer/

Head west to South Lyon twelve minutes away with two breweries including a must-visit:

Third Monk Brewing Company 228 S Lafayette Street 48178 (248) 278-6366 http://www.thirdmonkbrewingco.com/

Witch's Hat Brewing Company 22235 Pontiac Trail 48178 (248) 486-2595 https://www.witchshatbrewing.com/

Focused on quality, freshly brewed beers. Offering year-round and specialty beers in addition to wine, mead, and ciders. Wixom is fourteen minutes northeast and has a must-visit brewery:

Drafting Table Brewing Company 49438 Pontiac Trail 48393 (248) 956-7279 https://draftingtablebeer.com/home/

Flagship beers like Rezolute IPA and seasonal beers such as Hefeweizen are just two of the many beers you'll find on tap here. Ten minutes north is Commerce with another two breweries including a must-visit:

Kickstand Brewing Company 3050 Union Lake Road Unit 4A 48382 (248) 301-5941 https://www.kickstandbrewingco.com/

C.J.'s Brewing Company 8115 Richardson Road 48390 (248) 366-7979 https://cjsbrewery.com/

The first brewery in Commerce Township. With nine to ten beers on tap every day, there is always something for everyone. Nine minutes west is another must-visit brewery in Milford:

River's Edge Brewing Company 125 S Main Street Suite 400 48381 (248) 685-1625 http://riversedgebrew.com/

Offering delicious craft beers on tap along with cask-conditioned ales. For those who don't want beer, there is also a selection of house-made wine. About twenty-minutes north in Holly is another brewery:

Northern Oak Brewery 806 N Saginaw 48442 (248) 892-2661 http://www.northernoakbrewery.com/

The next brewery is fifteen minutes southeast in Clarkston:

Parker's Hilltop Brewery 6110 Dixie Highway 48346 (248) 383-8444
https://hilltopbrew.com/

Continue twelve minutes south to Waterford:

Rustic Leaf Brewing Company 7200 Highland Road 48327 (248) 599-9933 http://rusticleafbrewingcompany.com/

Pontiac is the next brewery just eight minutes south:

Fillmore 13 Brewery 7 N Saginaw Street 48342 (248) 977-3972
https://fillmore13brewery.com/

The next brewery is in Birmingham thirteen minutes south:

Griffin Claw Brewing Company 575 S Eton Street 48009 (248) 712-4050 https://griffinclawbrewingcompany.com/

Thirteen minutes south is another brewery at Ferndale:

Urbanrest Brewing Company 2615 Wolcott Street 48026 (586) 945-5121 https://www.urbanrest.com/

Five minutes north is Royal Oak with several options including a must-visit:

Lily's Seafood and B.C. 410 Washington Avenue 48067 (248) 591-5459
http://www.lilysseafood.com/

River Rouge Brewing Company 406 E 4th Street 48067 (310) 498-7809
http://riverrougebrew.com/

Roak Brewing Company 330 E Lincoln Avenue 48067 (248) 268-8780
https://roakbrewing.com/

Royal Oak Brewery 215 E Fourth Street 48067 (248) 544-1141
https://www.royaloakbrewery.com/

Offering seven to nine beers on tap daily. Also offering fresh food and a wine list. Enjoy it all in a comfortable atmosphere. Madison Heights is five minutes away with another brewery:

Cadillac Straits Brewing Company 27651 John R Road 48071 (248) 850-7673 https://cadillacstraits.com/

About twenty-minutes north is another must-visit brewery at Rochester:

Rochester Mills Beer Company 400 Water Street 48307 (248) 650-5080 http://www.rochestermillsbeerco.com/

Brewing handcrafted ales and lagers. Focusing on true-to-style beers, but also offering a unique take on some of these beers as well. End your trip at another must-visit brewery twenty-minutes north in Oxford:

Homegrown Brewing Company 28 N Washington Street 48371 (248) 800-4244 https://www.homegrownbrewco.com/

Small batch brewing from locally sourced ingredients ensures you have the freshest beer possible. Offering everything from a traditional Belgian Wit to a rich Chocolate Stout.

Eastern Michigan

This small area sandwiched between the Greater Detroit area, and the border is home to quite a few great breweries. Timed right, you can visit all the breweries in a day, but if you want to pace yourself and have a more relaxed time, then take at least two days. Start out at the must-visit brewery in Lapeer:

Tilted Axis Brewing Company 303 W Nepessing Street 48446 (810) 969-4477 http://tiltedaxis.beer/

Producing handcrafted ales, lagers, ciders, and meads. Focused on American styles, using local ingredients whenever possible. Head east and then south about an hour to Saint Clair with a few options including a must-visit:

Jamex Brewing Company 21721 Harper Avenue 48080 (586) 944-2030
https://jamexbrewing.com/

War Water Brewery 201 N Riverside Avenue 48079 (810) 289-3921
http://www.warwaterbrewery.com/

Baffin Brewing Company 25113 Jefferson Avenue 48081 (586) 218-7990 https://www.baffinbrewing.com/

Brewing beers of all types, including IPAs, fruit sours, fruit seltzer, and traditional beers. The menu is constantly changing, so there is always something different. Circle south about a half-hour to Clinton Township with another brewery:

Great Baraboo Brewing Company 35905 Utica Road 48035 (586) 792-7397 https://www.greatbaraboo.com/

Warren is eleven minutes southwest and has two must-visit breweries:

Dragonmead Microbrewery 14600 East 11 Mile 48089 (586) 776-9428
http://www.dragonmead.com/index.php?p=home

Founded well before the craft brewery revolution in Michigan. In 20 years, they have offered over 40 styles of beer as the nature of craft brewing changed. Today, they continue to offer you something new all the time.

Kuhnhenn Brewing Company 5919 Chicago Road 48092 (586) 979-8361 https://kbrewery.com/

Handcrafted beer with distinct ingredients. They also use unique brewing techniques to give you a great beer tasting experience. End with a twenty-minute drive north to Washington and a must-visit brewery:

Brown Iron Brewhouse 57695 Van Dyke Road 48094 (586) 697-3300
https://www.browniron.com/

They have brewed 82 unique beers in a variety of styles. You can taste these on a rotating basis while also trying new experimental brews.

Southcentral Michigan

This tour can be done in a day or two with planning and depending on how many breweries you plan to visit. Start at a must-visit brewery in Adrian:

Cotton Brewing Company 343 Lawrence Avenue 49221 (517) 902-6608 http://www.cottonbrewing.com/

Focusing on small-batch craft ales in a wide variety of styles ranging from traditional to experimental. There are plenty of other drink options as well. Head about twenty-minutes north to another must-visit brewery in Tecumseh:

Tecumseh Brewing Company 128 W Chicago Blvd 49286 (517) 815-1726 http://www.tecumsehbrewingco.com/

The brews range from hearty stouts to zesty Belgians. There are also a variety of IPAs and high-gravity ales. The beers here also have a variety of unique ingredients like peanut butter, cucumbers, and berries. Continue to Milan about a half-hour northeast:

Original Gravity Brewing Company 440 County Street 48160 (734) 439-7490 http://www.ogbrewing.com/

From classic styles to experimental brews, you'll always have fantastic beers here. Pair them with their excellent deli sandwiches. Saline is twelve more minutes north with two breweries, including a must-visit:

Salt Springs Brewery 117 S Ann Arbor Street 48176 (734) 295-9191 http://www.saltspringsbrewery.com/

Stony Lake Brewing Company 447 East Michigan 48176 (734) 316-7919 http://www.stonylakebrewing.com/

Producing many styles of big beers with a focus on American ales with a fresh, clean flavor. Fourteen minutes northeast is two breweries in Ypsilanti:

734 Brewing Company 15 East Cross Street 48198 (734) 340-3468
https://www.734brewing.com/

Ypsi Alehouse 124 Pearl Street Suite 100 48197 (734) 477-1555
https://www.ypsialehouse.com/

The city of Ann Arbor is fifteen minutes northwest and has several breweries:

HOMES Brewery 2321 Jackson Avenue 48103 (734) 954-6637
https://www.homesbrewery.com/

Biercamp 1643 S State Street 48104 (734) 995-2437 https://www.bier-camp.com/

Edelbrau Brewing Company 719 W Ellsworth Road Suite 2 48108 (734) 926-5351 https://www.edelbraubrewingcompany.com/

Blue Tractor BBQ and Brewery 207 East Washington Street 48104 (734) 222-4095 http://www.bluetractor.net/bt-a2-temp.html

Arbor Brewing Company 114 E Washington 48104 (734) 213-1393
https://arborbrewing.com/

Grizzly Peak Brewing Company 120 West Washington 48104 (734) 741-PEAK

A one-of-a-kind brewery that has won many awards, including the best brewery in Ann Arbor. Stop by to try one of their beers today.

Wolverine State Brewing Company 2019 West Stadium 48103 (734) 369-2990 https://www.wolverinebeer.com/

Enjoy award-winning lagers along with the best nachos in Michigan and excellent BBQ. They are the only lager brewery in Michigan and know what they are doing. The next brewery is in Chelsea about twenty-minutes west:

Chelsea Alehouse 420 N Main Street #100 48118 (734) 433-5500
https://www.chelseaalehouse.com/

Twelve minutes north brings you to your next brewery at Dexter:

Jolly Pumpkin Artisan Ales 2319 Bishop Circle East 48130 (734) 426-4962 https://www.jollypumpkin.com/jp/landing-page.html

Another half-hour north brings you to two breweries in Howell:

Eternity Brewing Company 4060 E Grand River Avenue 48843 (517) 295-4904 https://www.eternitybrewing.com/

Aberrant Ales 219 W Grand River Avenue 48843 (517) 518-8699
https://www.aberrantales.com/home

Brighton has a must-visit brewery and is a twelve-minute drive south:

Brewery Becker 500 W Main Street 48126 (810) 844-0225
https://brewerybecker.com/

Creating fine artisan, historic ales, and lagers. Offering a full range of styles so you'll find something you enjoy no matter what your taste. Another must-visit brewery is in Fenton about a half-hour north:

Fenton Winery and Brewery 1545 North Leroy Street Suite B 48430 (810) 373-4194 https://fentonbrewery.com/

Producing over 40 recipes for craft beer a year. There are often fourteen beers on tap at a time, and the rotation is constantly changing. End your trip with about a twenty-minute drive north to two breweries in Flint:

Redwood Lodge 5304 Gateway Center 48507 (810) 233-8000
https://www.redwoodsteakhouseandbrewery.com/

Tenacity Brewing 119 N Grand Traverse Street 48503 (810) 339-6676
https://www.tenacitybrewing.com/

Southwest Michigan

There are some great breweries in this area. You can visit them all in a couple days or more based on what you plan to see and do. Start your trip out in Hillsdale at:

Hillsdale Brewing Company 25 Hillsdale Street 49242 (517) 212-8182 https://hillsdale-brewing-company.business.site/

Head north about forty minutes to your next brewery at Jackson:

Grand River Brewery 117 W Louis Glick Highway 49201 (517) 962-2427 https://www.grandriverbrewery.com/

Albion is about twenty-minutes west and has a must-visit brewery:

Albion Malleable Brewing Company 420 S Superior Street 49224 (517) 343-2202 https://www.albionmalleable.com/

Inspired by the Belgian beer tradition, they offer a range of Ambers, IPAs, and Stouts. There is also made-from-scratch food to pair with your beers. Another fifteen minutes west is Marshall:

Dark Horse Brewing Company 511 S Kalamazoo Street 49068 (269) 781-9940 http://www.darkhorsebrewery.com/

Then circle north about an hour to Hastings with a must-visit brewery:

Walldorff Brewpub and Bistro 105 East State Street 49058 (269) 945-4400 https://walldorffbrewpub.com/

Enjoy your craft beer in what has constantly been voted one of the top 100 small towns in America. Pair your wonderful beers with cheap and great pub fare. Head northeast forty minutes to the next brewery in Portland:

ConfluxCity Brewing Company 110 N Water Street 48875 (517) 526-9091 https://confluxcitybrew.com/

Grand Ledge is another fourteen minutes east:

Sanctuary Spirits 902 E Saginaw Highway 48837 (517) 925-1530
https://www.sanctuaryspirits.com/

Slightly north sixteen minutes is your next brewery at DeWitt:

Looking Glass Brewing Company 115 N Bridge Street 48820 (517) 668-6004 https://www.lookingglassbrewingcompany.com/home.html

South eleven minutes brings you to East Lansing with two breweries including a must-visit:

Ellison Brewery and Spirits 4903 Dawn Avenue 48823 (517) 203-5498 http://ellisonbrewing.com/

Harper's Restaurant and Brewpub 131 Albert Avenue 48823 (517) 333-4040 https://www.harpersbrewpub.com/

Voted the best restaurant in East Lansing three years in a row. Organically made beers that have reduced gluten content. Continue south another twelve minutes to Lansing with several options:

Lansing Brewing Company 518 E Shiawassee Street 48912 (517) 371-2600 https://www.lansingbrewingcompany.com/

EagleMonk Pub and Brewery 4906 W Mt Hope Highway 48917 (517) 708-7350 https://www.eaglemonkbrewing.com/

Making English style beers with the occasional wine, cider, and mead. There are always 12 beers on tap along with barrel-aged specialty beers.

Ozone's Brewhouse 305 Beaver Street 48906 (517) 999-2739 https://www.ozonesbrewhouse.com/home.html

Here you can choose true-to-style beers like the house porter and other more experimental session beers such as the sage cream ale. Be sure to try their barrel-aged beers like the Amarillo Black IPA. Dimondale is fourteen more minutes south:

Dimes Brewhouse 145 N Bridge Street 48821 (517) 303-2067
https://www.dimesbrewhouse.com/

About twenty-minutes east brings you to a brewery in Mason:

BAD Brewing Company 440 S Jefferson Street 48854 (517) 676-7664
https://www.badbrewing.com/

A must-visit brewery is about twenty-minutes north to Williamston:

Old Nation Brewing Company 1500 Grand River Avenue 48895 (517)
655-1301 https://oldnationbrewing.com/

Mixing techniques as well as ingredients. Unfiltered, true, plain, and
simple is what you get from the beers here. End your trip with about an
hour drive north to Frankenmuth and a must-visit brewery:

Frankenmuth Brewery 425 S Main Street 48734 (989) 262-8300
https://frankenmuthbrewery.com/

The oldest microbrewery in the United States and the original craft
brewery in Michigan. Come try award-winning ales and lagers. Fifteen
beers are on tap at all times; six core beers and nine rotating seasonal
and special beers.

Decatur

Final Gravity Brewing Company 103 N Phelps Street 49045 (269) 436-
8052 https://www.finalgravitybrew.com/

Dowagiac

Sister Lakes Brewing 92500 CR-690 49047 (269) 332-5135
https://www.sisterlakesbrewing.com/

Minnesota

Southern Minnesota

This circular trip takes you to many great breweries and covers the entire southern area of Minnesota. You'll definitely need several days to see and visit all of the stops along this route. Start in Rochester with several options including a must-visit:

Forager Brewing Company 1005 6th Street NW 55901 (507) 273-6881 https://foragerbrewery.com/

LTS Brewing Company 2001 32nd Avenue NW 55901 (507) 254-8300 https://www.ltsbrewing.com/

Thesis Beer Project 1929 2nd Street SW 55902 (507) 206-3283 https://thesis.beer/

Little Thistle Brewing Company 2031 14th Street NW 55901 (507) 226-8014 https://littlethistlebeer.com/

An emphasis on high-quality beer, whether it be approachable, easy-drinking beer, or unique and experimental styles. Head south about a half-hour to your next brewery at Fountain:

Karst Brewing 315 1st Street 55935 (612) 747-6367 https://www.karstbrewed.com/

Head west to Austin about fifty minutes with two options including a must-visit:

Gravity Storm Brewery Cooperative 309 Main Street N 55912 (507) 396-8808 https://www.gravitystormbrewery.com/

Angry Hog Brewery and Taproom 500 23rd Avenue NW 55912 (507) 402-6718 https://www.angryhogbrewery.com/

Handcrafting a number of brews in ales, porters, and stouts. Currently offering six beers on tap, so you can easily try them all. Continue west another hour to a must-visit brewery in Blue Earth:

Oswald Brewing Company 110 S Main Street 56013 (507) 526-3101 https://www.oswaldbrewingcompany.com/

Offering the finest in Nordic brewing. Choose from a selection of seven craft beers. Try all of their unique handcrafted ales. Luverne is the next brewery almost two hours west:

Take 16 Brewing Company 509 E Main Street 56156 (866) 663-9986 https://www.take16beer.com/agever/

Then about an hour north is the next brewery at Marshall:

Brau Brothers Brewing Company 910 E Main Street 56258 (507) 747-2337 http://braubeer.com/

Circle back southeast about two hours to Madelia:

Lost Sanity Brewing 12 W Main Street 56062 (507) 642-2337 https://www.lostsanitybrewing.com/

Continue a half-hour east to Mankato with two must-visit breweries:

Mankato Brewery 1119 Center Street 56003 (507) 386-2337
http://mankatobrewery.com/

Focused on creating authentic beers that reflect the heritage of the region and the people. They are the first production brewery in the community since the 60s.

LocAle Brewing Company 228 Poplar Street 56001 (507) 779-7082
https://www.localebrew.com/

They aim to serve a wide range of approachable beer styles, including crisp lagers, roasty porters and stouts, juicy pale ales and barrel-aged sours, and strong ales. Another half-hour east brings you to two breweries in Waseca:

Ward House Brewery 111 Elm Avenue W 56093
https://www.wardhousebrewing.com/

Half Pint Brewing Company 40099 150th Street 56093 (507) 461-9235
https://halfpintbrew.com/

New Prague is about forty minutes north and has another must-visit brewery:

Giesenbrau Bier Company 1306 1st Street NE 56071 (952) 758-4226
https://www.giesenbraubierco.com/

A family-owned and operated brewery that makes fresh, locally crafted lagers and ales with an emphasis on the German tradition. Another forty minutes north is a must-visit brewery in Waconia:

Waconia Brewing Company 255 Main Street W 55387 (612) 888-2739
https://www.waconiabrewing.com/

The beers made here have won national and international awards. Offering year-round selections as well as a rotation of seasonal brews.

Head back southeast an hour to Northfield with two breweries including a must-visit:

Imminent Brewing 519 Division Street South Unit 2 55057 (507) 646-2327 https://www.imminentbrewing.com/

Tanzenwald Brewing Company 103 Water Street N 55057 (507) 366-2337 https://www.tanzenwald.com/

Serving an eclectic list of beer styles. Featuring bold, hop-forward IPAs; clean, easy-drinking pale ales and pilsners; and unique barrel-aged and sour beers. Just nine minutes away is another must-visit brewery in Dundas:

Chapel Brewing 15 Hester Street 55019 (763) 213-3369 http://chapelbrewing.com/home

Specializing in American-style ales with inspiration from around the world. The beers here are flavorful, balanced, and bold while still being drinkable. Red Wing has the next must-visit brewery about fifty minutes to the east:

Red Wing Brewery 1411 Old West Main Street 55066 (651) 327-2200 http://redwingbrewing.com/

The first brewery in the area since the 50s. The beers made here are the same as the historic beers made in the 1800s. A half-hour southeast brings you to Reads Landing:

Reads Landing Brewing Company 70555 202nd Street 55968 (651) 560-4777 https://www.rlbrewingco.com/

Just five minutes away is Wabasha with another brewery:

Turning Waters Back Alley Brewing Company 136 Bridge Avenue 55981 (651) 564-1568 https://www.turningwatersbrewing.com/

Another half-hour south is a must-visit brewery at Rollingstone:

Olvalde Farm and Brewing Company 16557 County Road 25 55969
(507) 205-4969 http://www.olvalde.com/

A small, traditional brewery located on a family farm. Making fine ales using ancient brewing techniques. End your trip another fifteen minutes south in Winona at:

Island City Brewing Company 65 E Front Street 55987 (507) 961-5015
http://islandcitybrew.com/

Northern Minnesota

This circular route will take you to the main town and breweries in Northern Minnesota. It will take you at least two to three days to complete. Start your trip out in the waterfront town of Grand Marais at:

Voyageur Brewing Company 233 West Highway 61 55604 (218) 387-3163 http://www.voyageurbrewing.com/

Follow the waterfront an hour and a half to a must-visit brewery in Two Harbors:

Castle Danger Brewery 17 7th Street 55616 (218) 834-5800
https://www.castledangerbrewery.com/

The beers are clean, balanced, and approachable. The beers are designed with a flavor profile in mind rather than a specific style. Head north another hour and a half to Ely with another must-visit brewery:

Boathouse Brewpub and Restaurant 47 E Sheridan Street 55731 (218) 365-4301 https://www.boathousebrewpub.com/

The only brewery in the area that makes everything on-site. As a small brewery with high-quality batches, the options are always changing. Then head northwest about two hours to the border town of Ranier:

Loony's Brew 3481 Main Street 56668 (218) 540-1001
http://www.loonysbrew.com/

From here take a three and a half-hour west to another must-visit brewery at Hallock:

Revelation Ale Works 146 S Atlantic Avenue 56728 (218) 510-0001
https://www.revales.com/

Brewing bright, American style ales with local ingredients. Known for their Blood Orange Wheat and Peanut Butter Stout. Next head south about two hours along the border to the town of Moorhead with a must-visit brewery:

Junkyard Brewing Company 1320 1st Avenue N 56560 (701) 261-8403
https://www.junkyardbeer.com/

A small craft brewery specializing in new and experimental beers. The taproom is family-friendly with several non-alcoholic beverage options. Head back east about two hours to Walker and another must-visit brewery:

Portage Brewing Company 107 South 5th Street 56484 (218) 547-6217
https://portagebeer.com/

Focused on an experimental rotation of small-batch and wood-aged fermented beers. You'll always have something new to try here. Take a forty-minute drive north to a brewery at Bemidji:

Bemidji Brewing Company 211 America Avenue NW 56601 (218) 444-7011 https://bemidjibeer.com/

Head back east again about an hour to Grand Rapids and two brewery options:

Rapids Brewing Company 214 N Pokegama Avenue 55744 (218) 999-9712 https://rapidsbrewingco.com/

Klockow Brewing Company 36 SE 10th Street 55744 (218) 999-7229
https://klockowbrewing.com/

End your trip with an hour and a half drive east back to the waterfront city of Duluth with several brewery options including a couple of must-visits:

340

Dubh Linn Irish Brew Pub 109 W Superior Street 55802 (218) 727-1559 https://dubhlinnpub.com/

Blacklist Brewing Company 120 East Superior Street 55802 (218) 606-1610 https://www.blacklistbeer.com/

Bent Paddle Brewing Company 1912 West Michigan Street 55806 (218) 279-2722 http://www.bentpaddlebrewing.com/

Fitger's Brewhouse 600 E Superior Street 55802 (218) 726-1392 https://fitgersbrewhouse.com/

The original brewpub in Duluth. Offering award-winning ales and lagers produced in small batches. You'll definitely taste the difference.

Hoops Brewing Company 325 S Lake Avenue 55802 (218) 606-1666 https://hoopsbrewing.com/

Brewing 80-100 unique beers a year including pales, IPAs, barrel-aged specials, sours, American and German-style light beers, wheat beers, and unique selections like the No 42 infused with peppers and fruit.

Twin Cities - Greater St. Paul Area

The Twin Cities area of Minnesota is home to two of the largest gatherings of craft beer: St. Paul and Minneapolis. You'll need to divide these two areas, and you'll still need to spend several days to visit all the breweries. Take a look at the list and choose your breweries; otherwise, you'll be taking a long vacation. Start your trip in Anoka at:

10K Brewing 2005 2nd Avenue 55303 (763) 392-4753 https://10kbrew.com/

Seven minutes southeast is the next brewery at Coon Rapids:

Alloy Brewing Company 2700 Coon Rapids Blvd 55433 (763) 432-0939 https://www.alloybrewingcompany.com/

The first must-visit brewery is seven minutes away in Blaine:

Invictus Brewing Company 2025 105th Avenue NE 55449 (763) 208-3063 http://invictusbrewingco.com/

Offering a variety of well-balanced beers. The variety of beers here will appear to all types of beer drinkers. Another ten minutes south is Fridley with another must-visit brewery:

Forgotten Star Brewing Company 38 Northern Stacks Drive 55421 (763) 657-7231 https://www.forgottenstarbrewing.com/

Producing a variety of unique ales and lagers. The beers are fresh and hearty, you won't soon forget your tasting experience here. New Brighton is next, six minutes away, with another must-visit brewery:

Barley John's Brew Pub 781 Old Highway 8 SW 55112 (651) 636-4670 https://www.barleyjohns.com/

One of the original craft breweries in Minnesota. Be sure to try their signature Wild Brunette Wild Rice Brown Ale. Another eight minutes southeast is a brewery at Roseville:

Bent Brewstillery 1744 Terrace Drive 55113 (844) 879-2368 https://www.bentbrewstillery.com/

Eleven minutes brings you to the main city of St. Paul with multiple brewery options:

Stacked Deck Brewing 421 Cedar Street 55101 (651) 353-7118 https://stackeddeckbrewing.com/

Waldmann Brewery 445 Smith Avenue 55102 (651) 222-1857 http://waldmannbrewery.com/

Bad Weather Brewing Company 414 7th Street W 55102 (651) 207-6627 http://www.badweatherbrewery.com/

BlackStack Brewing 755 Prior Avenue N Suite 110 55104 (612) 369-2934 https://www.blackstackbrewing.com/

Summit Brewing Company 910 Montreal Circle 55102 (651) 265-7800
https://www.summitbrewing.com/

Bang Brewing Company 2320 Capp Road 55114 (651) 243-2264
https://www.bangbrewing.com/

Urban Growler 2325 Endicott Street 55114 (612) 501-1128
https://www.urbangrowlerbrewing.com/

The Lab 767 N Eustis Street 55114 (651) 313-6888 https://thelabmn.com/

Vine Park Brewing Company 1254 West 7th Street 55102 (651) 228-1355 http://www.vinepark.com/

St. Paul Brewing 688 Minehaha Avenue E 55116 (651) 698-1945
https://www.stpaulbrewing.com/

Tin Whiskers Brewing Company 125 E 9th Street 55101 (651) 330-4734
https://twbrewing.com/

Burning Brothers Brewing 1750 Thomas Avenue 55104 (651) 444-8882
https://www.burnbrosbrew.com/

Clutch Brewing Company 928 7th Street W 55102 (651) 340-2523
https://www.clutchbeer.com/

Barrel Theory Beer Company 248 E 7th Street 55101 (651) 600-3422
https://barreltheory.com/

Dual Citizen Brewing Company 725 Raymond Avenue 55114 (651) 330-4750 https://dcbc.com/

Offering a modern take on classic style beers. On tap, you'll find a mix of favorites and one-off specialties.

Yoerg Brewing Company 378 Maria Avenue 55106 (651) 330-2076
https://www.yoergbeer.com/

A visit here is like stepping back in time to the 40s and 50s. The beers are also bringing back the recipes made during the original days of the 1800s.

Lake Monster Brewing 550 Vandalia Street #160 55114 (612) 964-6288
http://www.lakemonsterbrewing.com/

Making unique versions of classic beer styles by putting a subtle twist on the flavor. The beers range from esoteric to approachable. When you're ready, head fifteen minutes south to Eagan with two breweries including a must-visit:

Bald Man Brewing 2020 Silver Bell Road Suite 28 55122 (651) 600-3164
https://www.baldmanbrewing.com/

Union 32 Craft House 2864 Highway 55 55121 (952) 807-9777
https://www.union32crafthouse.com/

Featuring 32 homegrown beers, lagers, and ales. With this many choices, you're sure to find something you'll enjoy. About twenty-minutes away is the farthest south you'll travel to Lakeville with two breweries including a must-visit:

Lakeville Brewing Company 8790 208th Street W 55044 (952) 469-2739
https://lakevillebrewing.com/

Angry Inch Brewing 20841 Holyoke Avenue 55044
https://www.angryinchbrewing.com/

Making Belgian-inspired brews with a twist. Balancing flavor, tradition, and craft to give you a taste you won't find anywhere else. The next brewery is about a half-hour east in Hastings at:

Spiral Brewery 111 East 2nd Street 55033 (651) 212-7160
http://spiralbrewery.com/

About twenty-minutes north is a brewery at Woodbury:

3rd Act Craft Brewery 4120 Radio Drive 55129 (651) 998-2337
https://3rdactbrew.com/

Continue north another twenty-minutes to Stillwater with two breweries including a must-visit:

Maple Island Brewing 225 Main Street N 55082 (612) 741-9640
http://mapleislandbrewing.com/

Lift Bridge Brewery 1900 Tower Drive 55082 (888) 430-2337
http://liftbridgebrewery.com/

The sixth-largest craft brewery in Minnesota. Well known for their flagship beers: Farm Girl Saison and Hop Dish IPA. Head back west about twenty-minutes to White Bear Lake:

Big Wood Brewery 2222 4th Street 55110 (612) 360-2986
https://bigwoodbrewery.com/

End your trip about twenty-minutes northwest at a must-visit brewery in Lino Lakes:

HammerHeart Brewing Company 7785 Lake Drive 55014 (651) 964-2160 https://www.hammerheartbrewing.com/

Focused on honoring the old Nordic and Celtic cultures. Brewing 180 recipes of beer not often found outside of Scandinavia and Finland.

Twin Cities - Greater Minneapolis Area

The other half to the craft brewery scene in the Twin Cities area is the Greater Minneapolis area. Minneapolis is home to so many breweries you can easily spend days there alone. So you'll want to go through the list and plan which breweries you want to visit. Start out in Brooklyn Park at:

Blue Wolf Brewing Company 8515 Edinburgh Centre Drive 55443 (763) 390-6700 https://bluewolfbrew.com/

Head west nine minutes to the next brewery at Maple Grove:

OMNI Brewing Company 9462 Deerwood Lane N 55369 (763) 424-6664
https://www.omnibrewing.com/

Robbinsdale has two breweries and is twelve minutes southeast:

Wicked Wort Brewing Company 4165 W Broadway Avenue 55422 (763) 504-9977 https://www.wickedwortbrewingco.com/

Pig Ate My Pizza Kitchen and Brewery 4124 W Broadway Avenue 55422 (763) 537-7267 https://www.pigatemypizza.com/

Another twelve minutes southwest is the main city of Minneapolis with many brewery options:

Northbound Brewpub 2716 East 38th Street 55406 (612) 208-1450 http://northboundbrewpub.com/

Finnegans Brew Company 817 5th Avenue S 55404 (612) 454-0615 https://finnegans.org/

Insight Brewing 2821 East Hennepin Avenue 55413 (612) 722-7222 https://www.insightbrewing.com/

The Freehouse 701 North Washington Avenue 55401 (612) 339-7011 https://www.freehousempls.com/

Day Block Brewing Company 1105 Washington Avenue S 55415 (612) 617-7793 https://www.dayblockbrewing.com/

Wild Mind Artisan Ales 6031 Pillsbury Avenue South 55419 (612) 345-4498 https://www.wildmindales.com/

Boom Island Brewing Company 2014 Washington Avenue North 55411 (612) 227-9635 http://www.boomislandbrewing.com/

HeadFlyer Brewing 861 E Hennepin Avenue 55414 (612) 567-6345 https://www.headflyerbrewing.com/

Bauhaus Brew Labs 1315 Tyler Street NE 55413 (612) 387-1407 http://bauhausbrewlabs.com/

La Dona Cerveceria 241 Fremont Avenue North Unit B 55405 (612) 315-4613 https://dameladona.com/

Falling Knife Brewing Company 783 Harding Street NE #100 55413 (612) 354-7101 https://fallingknife.beer/

Utepils Brewing Company 225 Thomas Avenue North 55405 (612) 249-7800 https://utepilsbrewing.com/

ONE Fermentary and Taproom 618 N 5th Street 55401 (612) 605-7573 https://fermentary.one/

Sisyphus Brewing 712 Ontario West 55403 (612) 444-8674 https://www.sisyphusbrewing.com/

56 Brewing 3055 Columbia Avenue NE 55418 (612) 404-0056 https://56brewing.com/

Modist Brewing Company 505 N 3rd Street 55401 (612) 454-0258 https://modistbrewing.com/

Surly Brewing Company Beer Hall 520 Malcolm Avenue SE 55414 (763) 535-3330 https://surlybrewing.com/

Dangerous Man Brewing 1300 2nd Street NE 55413 (612) 236-4087 https://www.dangerousmanbrewing.com/

Fulton Beer 414 6th Avenue N 55401 (612) 333-3208 https://www.fultonbeer.com/

Minneapolis Town Hall Brewery 1430 Washington Avenue S 55454 (612) 339-8696 https://townhallbrewery.com/

Fair State Brewing Cooperative 2506A Central Avenue NE 55418 (612) 444-3209 https://fairstate.coop/

LynLake Brewery 2934 Lyndale Avenue S 55408 (612) 326-1999 https://www.lynlakebrewery.com/

Eastlake Craft Brewery 920 E Lake Street Suite 123 55407 (612) 217-4668 https://www.eastlakemgm.com/

Broken Clock Brewing Cooperative 3134 California Street NE 55418 (612) 440-4570 https://www.brokenclockbrew.com/

Herkimer Pub and Brewery 2922 Lyndale Avenue S 55408 (612) 812-0101 http://www.theherkimer.com/index.html

Able Seedhouse + Brewery 1121 Quincy Street NE 55413 (612) 405-4642 https://ablebeer.com/

Pryes Brewing Company 1401 West River Road N 55411 (612) 787-7937 https://www.pryesbrewing.com/

612 Brew 945 Broadway Street NE 55413 (612) 217-0437 https://612brew.com/

Producing interesting and balanced beers in a relaxing environment. Stop in to find a new favorite beer today.

Indeed Brewing Company 711 15th Avenue 55413 (612) 843-5090 https://www.indeedbrewing.com/

The diverse offerings include their flagship Day Tripper Pale Ale, innovative brews like the Mexican Honey Light, and set apart by their Wooden Soul series of barrel-aged beers.

Venn Brewing Company 3550 E 46th Street Suite 140 55406 https://www.vennbrewing.com/

Offering a rotating cast of beers including ales and sours, malty and hoppy, common and esoteric.

Clockwerks Brewing 25 4th Street N 55401 (612) 339-9375 http://www.clockwerksbrewing.com/

Focused on carefully crafted, well balanced, session-style beers in a steampunk style setting. When you're ready, head ten minutes west to Golden Valley and a must-visit brewery:

Under Pressure Brewing 8806 7th Avenue N 55427 (763) 269-2978
https://www.underpressurebrewing.com/

So far, the beers brewed here have won over 41 awards. Currently offering 23 beers on tap so you can easily find something you'll enjoy. Eight minutes south is another must-visit brewery at Hopkins:

LTD Brewing Company 725 Mainstreet 55343 (952) 938-2415
http://www.ltdbrewing.com/

Offering a constantly rotating selection of beers and root beer. No matter what you like to drink, you'll find it here. Seven minutes away is St. Louis Park with the next brewery:

Steel Toe Brewing 4848 35th Street W 55416 (952) 955-9965
http://www.steeltoebrewing.com/

Drive five minutes to Edina for the next brewery:

Wooden Hill Brewing Company 7421 Bush Lake Road 55439 (952) 960-9663 https://woodenhillbrewing.com/

Eden Prairie is ten minutes southwest and has two breweries:

Fat Pants Brewing Company 8335 Crystal View Road 55344 (952) 658-6987 https://www.fatpantsbrewing.com/

Lions Tap 16180 Flying Cloud Drive 55379 (952) 934-5299
http://www.lionstap.com/craft_beers.html

Head north about twenty-minutes to a must-visit brewery in Spring Park:

Back Channel Brewing Company 4787 Shoreline Drive 55384 (952) 855-9315 https://www.backchannelbrewing.com/

Serving high-quality, small-batch beers. There is a special emphasis on lagers, IPAs, and imperial stouts. Next is Victoria about twenty-minutes south:

Enki Brewing 1495 Stieger Lake Lane 55386 (952) 300-8408
https://www.enkibrewing.com/

Another ten minutes south is Chaska:

Schram Haus Brewery 3700 Chaska Blvd 55318 (952) 846-9458
http://schramhausbrewery.com/

Seven minutes east is two breweries at Shakopee:

Badger Hill Brewing Company 4571 Valley Industrial Blvd S 55379
(952) 230-2739 https://badgerhillbrewing.com/

Shakopee Brewhall 126 East 1st Avenue 55379 (952) 873-9747
https://www.shakopeebrewhall.com/

Continue southeast about fourteen minutes to Prior Lake:

Boathouse Brothers Brewing Company 16211 Main Avenue SE 55372
(952) 381-9307 https://www.boathousebrothersbrewing.com/

End with about a twenty-minute drive southwest to Belle Plaine and two
breweries:

Oldenburg Brewing Company 116 W Main Street 56011 (952) 818-0504
https://oldenburgbrewing.com/

U4ic Brewing 23436 Union Trail Suite 1 56011 (952) 873-3303
http://u4icbrewing.com/

West Central Minnesota

This is a short trip that can be done in a day or two and allows you to
enjoy some great breweries on a circular trip. Start your trip in Alexandria
with two breweries including a must-visit:

Copper Trail Brewing Company 410 30th Avenue E #103 56308 (320)
219-6688 https://www.coppertrailbrewing.com/

22 Northmen Brewing Company 6693 County Road 34 NW 56308 (320) 846-5443 https://www.22northmen.com/

Offering crafted lagers, adventurous ales, and original blends. Using unique and premium ingredients to make you the perfect beer. Take an hour and a half drive south to your next brewery at Montevideo:

Talking Waters Brewing 205 S 1st Street 56265 (320) 226-5715 https://www.talkingwatersbrewing.com/

Hendricks is about an hour more south and is the next stop:

Bank Brewing Company 200 S Main Street 56136 (612) 309-2513 https://www.bankbrewing.com/

Then head back north with an almost three-hour drive to Fergus Falls with three brewery options:

Union Pizza and Brewing Company 114 S Union Avenue 56537 (218) 988-8888 http://unionpizzaandbrewing.com/

Outstate Brewing Company 309 South Vine Street 56537 (970) 217-5026 https://www.outstatebrewing.com/

Fergus Brewing Company 1683 Ottertail Drive 56537 (218) 770-3547 https://www.fergusbrewing.com/

Head about an hour northeast to Perham with a must-visit brewery:

Disgruntled Brewing 735 2nd Street NE 56573 (218) 346-4677 https://www.disgruntledbeer.com/

Brewing great world-class beer in one of the most beautiful parts of the state. The drive to this brewery is well worth it. End your trip with a half-hour drive southeast to Wadena:

Drastic Measures Brewing Company 101 Jefferson Street S 56482 (218) 632-2900 https://www.drasticmeasuresbrew.com/

Central Minnesota

This is a long trail. You could easily drive it in two days. However, it takes you to a lot of towns and breweries so you'll need to take several days to complete it. Start your trip in New London at:

Goat Ridge Brewing Company 17 Central Avenue West 56273 (320) 354-2383 https://www.goatridgebrewing.com/

Willmar is sixteen minutes south with another brewery:

Foxhole Brewhouse 313 4th Street SW 56201 (320) 441-2071 https://www.foxholebrewhouse.com/

Take about an hour to drive south and then east to Hutchinson to a must-visit brewery:

Bobbing Bobber Brewing Company 900 Highway 15 S 55350 (320) 455-4999 https://www.bobbingbobber.com/

Offering seventeen taps of craft beers and soda in a fishing-themed taproom. The perfect place to experience true Minnesota. Continue east about fifty minutes to Delano:

Lupine Brewing Company 248 River Street 56328 (763) 333-1033 https://lupinebrewing.com/

Long Lake is about twenty-minutes southeast and has two breweries:

Birch's on the Lake Brewhouse and Supperclub 1310 W Wayzata Blvd 55356 (952) 473-7373 https://birchsonthelake.com/

Founding Fathers Brewing Company 1607 W Wayzata Blvd 55356 (952) 767-6403 https://www.foundingfathersbrewingco.com/

Just six minutes away is a brewery in Wayzata:

Wayzata Brew Works 294 Grove Lane E Suite 150 55391 (952) 737-1023 http://www.wayzatabrewworks.com/

Circle about an hour northeast to Chisago City for your next brewery:

Uncommon Loon Brewing Company 10825 Lake Blvd 55013 (651) 321-4468 http://uncommonloonbrewing.com/

Then head forty minutes north to Pine City:

Three Twenty Brewing Company 135 5th Street SE 55063 (612) 819-2892 https://www.threetwentybrewing.com/

Head back west about a half-hour to Mora and a must-visit brewery:

BeerClub Brewing 854 Forest Avenue East 55051 (320) 679-6633 http://www.beerclubbrewing.com/

Specializing in brewing small-batch classic European lagers and ales. Offering Czech Pilsners, Imperial IPA, Belgian Tripel, and other experimental varieties. Circle about an hour southwest to your next brewery at Elk River:

AEGIR Brewing Company 707 Main Street NW 55330 (763) 777-9015 http://aegirbrewco.com/

Big Lake is just nine minutes west:

Lupulin Brewing 570 Humboldt Drive 55309 (763) 263-9549 https://www.lupulinbrewing.com/

A short trip four minutes south to Monticello offers two breweries:

Rustech Brewing 105 W 3rd Street 55362 (763) 272-1593 https://rustechbrewing.com/

The Nordic Brewing Company 530 Cedar Street 55362 (763) 271-2739 https://thenordicbrewing.com/

Another thirteen minutes south is Buffalo with a must-visit brewery:

Hayes' Public House Brewery and Taproom 112 First Street S 55313 (763) 746-6389 http://hayespublichouse.com/

Brewing mostly traditional British ales with an added twist. Stop in the first brewery in the county since Prohibition. Start back northwest nineteen minutes to Annandale:

Spilled Grain Brewhouse 300 Elm Street E 55302 (320) 223-1372 https://www.spilledgrainbrewhouse.com/

Continue a half-hour northwest to a must-visit brewery in Cold Spring:

Third Street Brewhouse 219 Red River Avenue 56320 (320) 685-3690 https://www.thirdstreetbrewhouse.com/

Offering a wide range of beer types, including IPAs, lagers, shandys, and more. There is definitely something for everyone here. A short thirteen minutes northeast is St. Joseph:

Bad Habit Brewing Company 15 E Minnesota Street #108 56374 (320) 980-7711 http://www.badhabitbeer.com/

About twenty-minutes east is St. Cloud with two breweries including a must-visit:

Beaver Island Brewing Company 216 6th Avenue S 56301 (320) 492-7744 https://www.beaverislandbrew.com/

The Pantown Brewing Company 408 37th Avenue N 56303 (320) 428-0007 https://www.pantownbrewing.com/

The newest brewery in St. Cloud with 10 beers currently on tap. Stop in today to try their beers and find a new favorite. Little Falls is about a half-hour north to the next brewery:

Starry Eyed Brewing Company 16757 11th Street NE 56345 (320) 232-0382 https://www.starryeyedbrewing.com/

The next brewery is in Nisswa, about another forty minutes north:

Big Axe Brewing Company 25435 Main Street 56468 (218) 961-2337 http://www.bigaxebrewing.com/

Head back south fifteen minutes to Baxter and a must-visit brewery:

Jack Pine Brewery 7942 College Road #115 56425 (218) 829-3086
https://www.jackpinebrewery.com/

Bringing quality brews across a wide spectrum of flavors. Be sure to try their award-winning pepper beer. Just seven minutes east is Brainerd:

Roundhouse Brewery 1551 Northern Pacific Road 56401 (218) 454-2739 http://roundhousebrew.com/

Continue northeast twenty-minutes to the next brewery at Crosby:

Cuyuna Brewing Company 1 E Main Street 56441 (320) 894-4362
http://www.cuyunabrewing.com/

End your trip seventeen minutes away in Aitkin at:

Block North Brew Pub 302 Minnesota Avenue N 56431 (218) 928-8090
https://www.mncraftbrew.org/2019/11/07/block-north/

Moose Lake

Moose Lake Brewing Company 244 Lakeshore Drive 55767 (218) 485-4585 http://www.mooselakebrewing.com/

There aren't many breweries in Mississippi. You can take a couple days and drive from either north or south to cover the entire state and try all the breweries it has to offer. Start your trip on the waterfront in Gulfport at a must-visit brewery:

Chandeleur Island Brewing Company 2711 14th Street 39501 (228) 701-9985 https://chandeleurbrew.com/

Their Gulf Sour Series is a unique take on sour beers; they have an over the top fruit flavor, a hint of tart and sweet to balance it all. Head a half-hour west to your next brewery at Kiln:

Lazy Magnolia Brewing Company 7030 Roscoe Turner Road 39556 (228) 467-2727 https://www.lazymagnolia.com/

Hattiesburg is about an hour north:

Southern Prohibition Brewing 301 Mobile Street 39401 (601) 582-7148 https://www.soprobrewing.com/

Head west about two and a half hours to Natchez on the border:

Natchez Brewing Company 413 Franklin Street 39120 (828) 713-5311
http://www.natchezbrew.com/

Head north about an hour and a half to a must-visit brewery at Vicksburg:

Key City Brewing Company 1309 Washington Street 39180 (601) 501-7712 https://www.keycitybeer.com/

Brewing classic and experimental styles. Try a range of light beers, hop-bomb IPAs, robust stouts, and excellent sours. Circle northeast about three hours to Starkville and another must-visit brewery:

Mayhew Junction Brewing Company 106 Eckford Drive 39759 (662) 546-0510 http://mayhewjunction.com/

Focused on making highly drinkable beers rather than anything fancy or focusing on a specific style. Currently offering four beers. End your trip by continuing about two hours north to Water Valley:

Yalobusha Brewing Company 102 S Main Street 38965 (855) 925-6273
https://www.yalobrew.com/

Greater St. Louis Area

St. Louis and the surrounding area is home to some great craft breweries. You can easily drive between them in a day or two, but if you plan to visit all the breweries, then you'll want to spend several days. Start in Columbia with three breweries:

Logboat Brewing Company 504 Fay Street 65201 (573) 397-6786
http://www.logboatbrewing.com/

Bur Oak Brewing Company 8250 East Trade Center Drive 65201 (573) 814-2178 https://buroakbeer.com/

Flat Branch Pub and Brewery 115 S Fifth Street 65201 (573) 499-0400
http://www.flatbranch.com/beer/

Head south a half-hour to your next brewery in Jefferson City:

Prison Brews 305 Ash Street 65101 (573) 635-0678
http://www.prisonbrews.com/

Then head east about an hour to Berger with your next brewery:

Gruhlke's Microbrewery 3166 Highway B 63014 (573) 834-5475
http://www.biaswinery.com/micro.html

Continue east another hour to Wentzville:

Friendship Brewing Company 100 East Pitman Avenue 63385 (636) 856-9300 https://www.friendshipbrewco.com/

Eleven minutes away is two breweries at O'Fallon:

Petrichor Brewing 7434 Village Center Drive 63368 (636) 265-4004 https://www.petrichorbeer.com/

Good News Brewing Company 330 Sonderen Street 63366 (636) 294-6593 https://www.goodnewsbrewing.com/

Next is Cottleville another eleven minutes away:

Exit 6 Brewery 5055 Highway N 63385 (636) 244-4343 https://www.exit6brewery.com/

The first nano-brewery in St. Charles County. Offering over 70 different craft brews rotated on 23 taps. Just nine minutes brings you to St. Peters and another must-visit brewery:

Third Wheel Brewing 4008 North Service Road 63376 (636) 323-9810 https://www.thirdwheelbrewing.com/

Offering a wide range of craft beer styles from pilsners to crazy big stouts. With so many to choose from, the staff here will help you select the right beer for you. St. Charles is ten minutes away and has another brewery:

Two Plumbers Brewery 2236 1st Capitol Drive 63301 (636) 224-8626 https://twoplumbers.com/

Ten minutes south is Maryland Heights with two breweries including a must-visit:

Six Mile Bridge Beer 11841 Dorsett Road 63043 (314) 942-2211
http://sixmilebridgebeer.com/

O'Fallon Brewery 45 Progress Parkway 63043 (636) 474-2337
http://ofallonbrewery.com/

The goal is to brew balanced craft beers with a focus on unique ingredients and local collaborations. Come visit and choose between their extensive line. Fifteen minutes northeast is another brewery in Florissant:

Narrow Gauge Brewing Company 1595 N US Highway 67 63031 (314) 831-3222 https://www.narrowgaugestl.com/

Just five minutes away is another brewery in Ferguson:

Ferguson Brewing Company 418 S Florissant Road 63135 (314) 521-BEER https://fergusonbrewing.com/

Continue twenty-minutes south to the main city of St. Louis with multiple brewery options:

Modern Brewery 5231 Manchester Avenue Ste E 63110
https://modernbrewery.supportlocalstl.com/

Center Ice Brewery 3126 Olive Street 63103 (314) 339-5733
https://www.centericebrewery.com/

Wellspent Brewing Company 2917 Olive Street 63103 (314) 328-0505
https://www.wellspentbeer.com/

Rockwell Beer Company 1320 S Vandeventer Avenue 63110 (314) 256-1657 https://www.rockwellbeer.com/

The Civil Life Brewing Company 3714 Holt Avenue 63116
https://www.thecivillife.com/

Alpha Brewing Company 4310 Fyler Avenue 63116 (314) 621-2337
https://www.alphabrewingcompany.com/

4 Hands Brewing Company 1220 South 8th Street 63104 (314) 436-1555 https://4handsbrewery.com/

Cathedral Square Brewery 3914 Lindell Blvd 63108 (314) 803-3605 http://www.cathedralsquarebrewery.com/

Square One Brewery and Distillery 1727 Park Avenue 63104 (314) 231-2537 http://squareonebrewery.com/

Urban Chestnut Brewing Company 3229 Washington Avenue 63103 (314) 222-0143 https://www.urbanchestnut.com/

Earthbound Brewing 2724 Cherokee Street 63118 (314) 769-9576 http://www.earthboundbeer.com/

Perennial Artisan Ales 8125 Michigan Avenue 63111 (314) 631-7300 http://www.perennialbeer.com/

Beers are mostly influenced by Belgian and American craft styles. Made unique with the addition of premium ingredients such as fruits, spices, and wild yeast strains.

Heavy Riff Brewing Company 6413 Clayton Avenue 63139 (314) 971-6179 https://www.heavyriffbrewing.com/#/

Housemade brews of unmatched quality. Featuring 25 taps of beer from both their brewery and other local breweries. They also offer wine and spirits.

Griesedieck Brothers Brewery 1240 Switzer Avenue 63147 (314) 309-3210 http://www.gb-beer.com/

Styles focusing on pre-Prohibition recipes once brewed by the original Griesedieck brothers in the 50s. Using local ingredients to brew hop-centric ales.

Morgan Street Brewery 721 N Second Street 63102 (314) 231-9970 http://www.morganstreetbrewery.com/

One of the oldest craft breweries. Home to a wonderful selection of specialty beers. Here you'll also be within walking distance of some great sites. When you're ready, head eleven minutes southwest to Maplewood and another must-visit brewery:

Side Project Brewing 7458 Manchester Road 63143 (314) 276-4250 https://www.sideprojectbrewing.com/

A 100% barrel-aged brewery. Creating rustic Saisons, Wild Ales, and Spirit Barrel-Aged Ales. Stop in to try these wonderful beers today. Continue another fourteen minutes southwest to another must-visit brewery in Valley Park:

Mackenzie Brewing Company 932 Meramec Station Road 63088 (636) 226-4148 https://www.mknzbrewing.com/

A small-batch brewery focused on Belgian and High Gravity beers. There are eight different beer styles on tap along with three rotating seasonal taps. High Ridge is twelve minutes south with another must-visit brewery:

Bastard Brothers Brewing Company 2114 Penta Drive 63049 (636) 671-7844 https://bastardbrothersbrewery.com/

Delivering a classic line of all-natural crafted lagers and ales. The beers here are clean and smooth tasting. Head west a half-hour to a brewery in Labadie:

Point Labaddie Brewery 1029 Thiebes Road 63055 (314) 566-9346 https://pointlabaddiebrewery.com/

Take about an hour drive southwest to Rolla and a must-visit brewery:

Public House Brewing Company 600 North Rolla Street Suite B 65401 (573) 426-2337 http://www.publichousebrewery.com/

Making balanced and consistent beers through innovative techniques. You won't regret giving these beers a try. End your trip with about an hour drive south to a must-visit brewery in Bucyrus:

Piney River Brewing Company 15198 Walnut Grove Drive 65444 (417) 967-6876 https://pineyriverbrewing.com/

Award-winning beer, brewed on a small local farm. Offering a few year-round selections as well as some truly limited release beers.

Southwest Missouri

This short trip makes a great day trip if you want to enjoy some great breweries and spend a day enjoying the Missouri scenery. Start your trip in Phillipsburg at a must-visit brewery:

Boat Town Brewing 18146 Campground Road 65722 (844) 394-8123 https://boattownbrewing.com/

Offering a variety of beer styles ranging from unfiltered German hefeweizen to barrel-aged barley wines. Their flagship beer is the Perficle and always sells out. Head forty minutes southwest to Springfield with several brewery options including two must-visits:

Show-Me Brewing 1925 E. Bennett 65804 (417) 315-8617 https://showmebrewing.com/

Great Escape Beer Works 4022 S Lone Pine Avenue Ste 200 65804 (417) 840-2150 https://www.greatescapebeerworks.com/

Mother's Brewing Company 215 S Grant 65806 (417) 862-0423 https://www.mothersbrewing.com/

Lost Signal Brewing Company 610 W College Street 65806 (417) 869-4755 https://www.lostsignalbrewing.com/

Offering handcrafted beers and slow-smoked BBQ. So stop in for a drink, enjoy a great meal, and stay awhile.

Springfield Brewing Company 305 South Market 65806 (417) 832-8277 https://www.springfieldbrewingco.com/

Focusing on true to tradition English, German, and American ales and lagers. Their Mayhem Marzen has recently won World Beer Cup Gold. Continue about an hour southwest to another brewery at Cassville:

Hungry Hollow Brewing Company 14396 Farm Road 2140 65625 (417) 342-2072 https://www.hungryhollowbrewing.com/home

End your trip with about an hour drive west to Neosho and their brewery:

Indian Springs Brewing Company 109 E Main Street 64850 (417) 454-9498 https://indianspringsbrewing.com/

Southeast Missouri

This is another great day trip you can take in Missouri. Enjoy some beautiful areas and taste some excellent brews. Start your trip in Cape Girardeau at:

Minglewood Brewery 121 Broadway 63703 (573) 803-0524 https://www.minglewoodbrewery.com/

Head north about a half-hour to Perryville and a must-visit brewery:

Jackson Street BrewCo 106 N Jackson Street 63775 http://www.jstreetbrewco.com/

Focused on providing well-rounded beers. In addition to their award-winning flagship beers, they also offer a number of seasonal, small-batch, and experimental beers. Another half-hour north is Ste. Genevieve with two options including a must-visit:

Crown Valley Brewing and Distilling Company 13326 State Route F 63670 (573) 756-9700 https://www.crownvalleybrewery.com/

Cave Vineyard 21124 Cave Road 63670 (573) 543-5284 https://cavevineyard.com/beer/

Currently brewing an IPA and a Wheat beer. They plan to expand into offering a Chambourcin barrel-aged stout. End your trip with a three and a half-hour drive southwest to West Plains and a must-visit brewery:

Wages Brewing Company 1382 Bill Virdon Blvd 65775 (417) 293-3119
https://www.wagesbrewco.com/

Offering three year-round selections and a rotation of six other beers. Also occasionally offering guest beers from other local breweries.

Western Missouri

This brewery tour can be accomplished in a day or two, depending on how many breweries you visit. The majority of the breweries are in Kansas City and depending on how many you choose to go to, you'll want a few extra days. Start your trip out in Versailles at a must-visit brewery:

Bee's Knees Brewing Company 106 W Jasper Street 65084 (573) 539-2525 https://beeskneesalehouse.wordpress.com/

A microbrewery offering a delicious selection of beers. Choose from a fresh and fun beer menu in an inviting atmosphere. Just eleven minutes west is another brewery at Stover:

Welpman Springs Brewing 517 Hatchery Road 65078 (573) 377-2343
https://welpmanspringsbrewing.weebly.com/

Take about a two-hour drive north and west to Blue Springs:

East Forty Brewing 1201 W Main Street 64015 (816) 988-8217
https://eastfortybrewing.com/

Seventeen minutes south is two breweries at Lee's Summit:

Fringe Beerworks 224 South East Douglas Street 64063 (816) 600-2552
http://fringebeerworks.com/

Diametric Brewing Company 949 NE Columbus Street 64086
http://newaxiombrewco.com/s?height=722&width=1536

Then head north eleven minutes to Raytown and a must-visit brewery:

Crane Brewing 6515 Railroad Street 64133 (816) 352-6782
http://cranebrewing.com/

Brewing dry and rustic ales in the style of the old country. Focused primarily on three styles: Saison, Berliner Weiss, and Lambic. Continue north fifteen minutes to Kansas City with several breweries to choose from along with several must-visits:

Double Shift Brewing Company 412 E 18th Street 64108 (816) 304-7028 https://doubleshiftbrewing.com/

Brewery Emperial 1829 Oak Street 64108 (816) 945-9625
https://www.breweryemperial.com/

Martin City Brewing Company 410 E 135 Street 64145 (816) 214-6637
https://martincitybrewingcompany.com/

Stockyards Brewing Company 1600 Genessee Street Suite #100 64102 (816) 895-8880 http://www.stockyardsbrewing.com/

Rochester Brewing and Roasting Company 2129 Washington Street 64108 (816) 216-7181 https://rochesterkc.com/

Torn Label Brewing Company 1708 Campbell Street 64108 (816) 656-5459 https://tornlabelbrewingco.square.site/

BKS Artisan Ales 633 E 63rd Street Suite 120 64110 (816) 673-3027
https://www.bksartisanales.com/

Using traditional and experimental styles in order to produce hop-forward, barrel-aged, sour, and farmhouse ales.

Alma Mader Brewing 2635 Southwest Blvd 64108
https://www.almamaderbrewing.com/

Specializing in hop-forward ales and lagers that span the gap between tradition and innovation. Try their fresh and approachable beers today.

Casual Animal Brewing Company 1725 McGee Street 64108 (816) 214-5388 https://www.casualanimalbrewing.com/

Small-batch, quality, and fresh beers with a local approach. Stop in to try their unique brews today.

Border Brewing Company 406 E 18 Street 64108 (816) 315-6807 http://www.borderbrewco.com/

Producing a wide variety of beer styles that are approachable and complex in flavor. You'll find a new favorite here, whether it is a high-octane beer or more session-able choices. Just five minutes away is North Kansas City with a few more options including a must-visit:

Cinder Block Brewery 110 E 18th Avenue 64116 (816) 298-6555 https://cinderblockbrewery.com/

Callsign Brewing 1447 Gentry Street 64116 http://callsignbrewing.com/

Colony Handcrafted Ales 312 Armour Road 64116 (816) 800-4699 https://www.colonykc.com/

Calibration Brewing 119 Armour Road 64116 (816) 994-8277 https://www.calibrationbrewery.com/

Offering handcrafted ales and lagers. Stop in for a relaxed, refined, and satisfying tasting experience. Then head northeast about a half-hour to a brewery at Excelsior Springs:

Dubious Claims Brewing Company 451 S Thompson Avenue 64024 (816) 900-1882 https://www.dubiousclaimsbrewingco.com/

Head back west about fifty minutes to another brewery at Weston:

Weston Brewing Company 500 Welt Street 64098 (816) 640-5235 https://westonirish.com/

St. Joseph is a half-hour north to the next brewery:

Liberty Cap Brewing 402 N 13th Street 64501
https://www.libertycapbrewing.com/

End your trip with a fifty-minute drive east to Hamilton:

Levi Garrison and Sons Brewing Company 105 West Bird Street 64644
(417) 294-7564 https://lgsbrewingco.com/

Hannibal

Mark Twain Brewing Company 422 N Main Street 63401 (573) 406-
1300 http://marktwainbrewery.com/

Montana

Bitterroot Valley

There are only three cities on this trip, but there are a lot of breweries in
the area. You can visit the must-visit breweries in a day; otherwise, you
may need at least two days to comfortably visit them all. Start out in the
main city of Missoula with multiple options, including a few must-visits:

Missoula Brewing Company 200 International Drive 59808 (406) 549-8193 https://www.highlanderbeer.com/

Conflux Brewing Company 200 East Main Street 59802 (406) 926-3589 https://confluxbrewing.com/

Big Sky Brewing Company 5417 Trumpeter Way 59808 (406) 549-2777 https://bigskybrew.com/

Gild Brewing 515 S Higgins Avenue 59801 (406) 926-3258 https://www.gildbrewing.com/

Imagine Nation Brewing Company 1151 W Broadway 59802 (406) 926-1251 https://imaginenationbrewing.com/

Great Burn Brewing 2230 McDonald Avenue 59801 (406) 317-1557 https://www.greatburnbrewing.com/

Handcrafted ales with a West Coast flare. The beers here are bold and aggressive with lots of flavors that are considered a hop-forward beer.

Bayern Brewing, Inc. 1507 Montana Street 59801 (406) 721-1482 https://www.bayernbrewery.com/

Offering fully matured, Bavarian tradition beers. The beers take four times longer to make than conventional ales and twice as long as a lager. Come taste the difference.

Draught Works 915 Toole Avenue 59802 (406) 241-2423 https://www.draughtworksbrewery.com/

Brewing a variety of clean beers including traditional ales and lagers, unique American sours, and a wide range of experimental styles. Take a drive a half-hour south to Stevensville with a couple breweries including a must-visit:

Wildwood Brewery 4018 US Highway 93 N 59870 (406) 777-2855 https://www.wildwoodbrewing.com/

Blacksmith Brewing 114 W Main Street 59870 (406) 777-0680
https://blacksmithbrewing.com/

Serving award-winning flagship and seasonal beers. Everything is made from locally grown crops. Another half-hour south is Hamilton with two must-visit breweries:

Higherground Brewing Company 518 North First Street 59840 (406) 375-5204 https://highergroundbrewing.com/

Offering seven flagship beers that are all ales. There are also four to five seasonal beers that vary as to what is available.

Bitter Root Brewing 101 Marcus Street 59840 (406) 363-7468
https://bitterrootbrewing.com/

Producing over 40 different styles of beer a year with 11 on tap at a time. You can also enjoy local, organic food made from scratch.

Glacier Country

Located in northwest Montana, this is some of the most beautiful countryside in the United States. Take a couple days to enjoy the views and visit the wonderful breweries in this area. Start your trip in Libby at a must-visit brewery:

Cabinet Mountain Brewing Company 206 Mineral Avenue 59923 (406) 293-2739 http://cabinetmountainbrewing.com/

Offering six flagship handcrafted ales along with sodas. Pair them with delicious food in a cozy setting. Head east about an hour and a half to Kalispell with several options including two must-visits:

Sacred Waters Brewing Company 3250 US Highway 2 East 59901 (406) 253-0746 https://www.sacredwatersbrewing.com/

SunRift Beer Company 55 1st Avenue West North 59901 (406) 314-6355 http://sunriftbeer.com/

Kalispell Brewing Company 412 Main Street 59901 (406) 756-2739
https://www.kalispellbrewing.com/

Offering traditional German-style lagers and northwest inspired ales. Come try their award-winning flagship beers or one of their rotating seasonal offerings.

Bias Brewing 409 1st Avenue East 59901 (406) 730-3020
https://www.biasbrewing.com/

Exploring new beer styles while honoring traditional classic brews. Currently at 41 unique beers released. Head south seventeen minutes to Lakeside:

Tamarack Brewing Company 105 Blacktail Road #1 59922 (406) 824-0244 https://www.tamarackbrewing.com/

Continue to circle the lake for about a half-hour to your next brewery at Polson:

Glacier Brewing Company 6 10th Avenue East 59860 (406) 883-2595
http://www.glacierbrewing.com/

Circle and head north about forty minutes to Bigfork and a must-visit brewery:

Flathead Lake Brewing Company 116 Holt Drive 59911 (406) 837-2004
https://flatheadlakebrewing.com/

All-natural, unfiltered beer made from the finest ingredients. Come try their award-winning beers, including their new sour beer. Continue north to the foothills of the mountains and Columbia Falls with a must-visit brewery:

Backslope Brewing 1107 9th Street W 59912 (406) 897-2850
https://backslopebrewing.com/

Enjoy handcrafted beer in the shadows of Glacier National Park. Try one of their flagship beers, including ales, a porter and a stout. Then head east over the mountains to end your trip at Cut Bank:

Cut Bank Creek Brewery 315 East Railroad 59427 (406) 229-0298
https://www.cutbankcreekbrewery.com/

Billings/Bozeman Area

This trip will take you to some of the larger cities in Montana. Take a few days to enjoy all the breweries in the area while taking in the beautiful scenery. Start your trip out in Billings with a few options, including two must-visits:

Angry Hank's 20 N 30th Street 59101 (406) 252-3370
http://angryhanks.com/

Thirsty Street Brewing Company 3008 1st Avenue N 59101 (406) 969-3200 https://www.thirstystreet.com/

Montana Brewing Company 113 North Broadway 59101 (406) 252-9200
https://montana-brewing-co.business.site/

The first brewpub and brewery in Montana opened in 1994. Pair your beer with wonderful food offerings.

By All Means Brew Lab 1400 S 24th Street W #3 59102 (406) 534-3075
http://www.byallmeans.beer/

Whether it be smooth and malty to bright and fruity, the beers here offer a rich tasting experience. Each variety is brewed to offer full body flavor. Red Lodge is about an hour away and has another brewery:

Red Lodge Ales 1445 North Broadway 59068 (406) 446-4607
https://www.redlodgeales.com/

It is about a two-hour drive to Livingston and a must-visit brewery:

Neptune's Brewery 119 N L Street 59047 (406) 222-7837
https://neptunesbrewery.com/

A quaint, sea-themed oasis in a small mountain setting. Enjoy a variety of handcrafted brews. Come try an old favorite and discover something new.

Continue west about a half-hour to Bozeman with several brewery options including a must-visit:

Bozeman Brewing 504 N Broadway Avenue 59715 (406) 585-9142
https://bozemanbrewing.com/

Julius Lehrkind Brewing 1717 N Rouse Avenue 59715 (406) 551-0199
https://juliusbrewing.com/

Nordic Brew Works 730 Boardwalk Avenue Suite 1B 59718 (406) 414-0730 https://www.nordicbrewworks.com/

Union Hall Brewery 121 West Main Street Suite B 59715 (406) 219-2533
https://www.unionhallbrewery.com/

MAP Brewing Company 510 Manley Road 59715 (406) 587-4070
https://www.mapbrewing.com/

Mountains Walking Brewery 808 Avocado Street 59715 (406) 219-3480
https://www.mountainswalking.com/

Bridger Brewing 1609 S 11th Avenue 59715 (406) 587-2124
https://www.bridgerbrewing.com/

406 Brewing Company 101 East Oak Suite D 59715 (406) 585-3745
http://www.406brewing.com/

The best of their experimental style has been developed into flagship beers that will appeal to all palates. Stop in today and try a few. There are two breweries about forty minutes away in Big Sky:

Beehive Basin Brewery 245 Town Center Drive 59716 (406) 995-7444
http://www.beehivebasinbrewery.com/

Lone Peak Brewery 48 Market Place 59716 (406) 995-3939
http://www.lonepeakbrewery.com/

Head north about forty minutes to another brewery in Belgrade:

Madison River Brewing Company 20900 Frontage Road 59714 (406) 388-0322 http://www.madisonriverbrewing.com/

Then continue west about an hour to Butte with a couple options including a must-visit:

Quarry Brewing Company 124 W Broadway 59701 (406) 723-0245 http://www.quarrybrewing.net/

Butte Brewing Company 465 East Galena Street 59701 (406) 494-7710 https://www.buttebrewing.com/

Offering a great collection of beers on tap. Whether it be a well-known favorite or a new creation, you'll find something enjoyable. End your trip with about an hour drive south to Dillon:

Beaverhead Brewing Company 218 South Montana Street 59725 (406) 988-0011 http://www.beaverheadbeer.com/

Eastern Montana

This circular trip will take you to several cities and some wonderful breweries. Easily complete in a day or two. Start out in Miles City at:

Tilt Wurks Brewhouse and Casino 420 Pacific Avenue 59301 (406) 874-8458 https://tiltwurks.com/

Take a three-hour drive north to your next brewery at Glasgow:

Busted Knuckle Brewery 303 1st Avenue South 59230 (406) 228-2277 https://www.bustedknucklebrew.com/

Then head east about fifty minutes to Wolf Point:

Missouri Breaks Brewing 326 Main Street 59201 (406) 653-1467 http://www.missouribreaksbrewing.com/

Continue east an hour and a half to Sidney and the first must-visit brewery:

Meadowlark Brewing 117 S Central Avenue 59270 (406) 433-2337
https://meadowlarkbrewing.com/

Handcrafted ales with a focus on quality. Offering a range of unique and one-of-a-kind beers that you won't find anywhere else. Then head south about fifty minutes to the next brewery in Glendive:

Cross Country Brewing 320 E Allard 59330 (406) 377-6912
https://www.crosscountrybrewing.com/

About twenty-minutes east ends your trip in Wibaux near the border with a must-visit:

Beaver Creek Brewing 104 Orgain Avenue 59353 (406) 795-2337
https://www.beavercreekbrewery.com/

Using locally grown barley to create award-winning beers that fit every taste profile. Be sure to stop here on your way through the area.

North Central Montana

This circular trip will take you a couple days at least to complete. There is a lot of nature to explore and beers to enjoy. Start your trip in Philipsburg at a must-visit brewery:

Philipsburg Brewing Company 101 West Broadway 59858 (406) 859-2739 https://www.philipsburgbrew.com/

Creating unique, crisp, and award-winning lagers and ales. Enjoy a fun environment while tasting the wonderful beers they have to offer. Take an hour drive to your next brewery at Deer Lodge:

Elk Ridge Brewing Company 320 Main Street 59722 (406) 846-1866
http://www.elkridgebrewingcompany.com/

Head east about an hour to Helena with a few options including two must-visits:

Ten Mile Creek Brewing 46 N Last Chance Gulch 59601 (406) 231-0575 https://tenmilecreekbrewing.com/

Copper Furrow Brewing 2801 N Roberts Avenue 59601 (406) 422-5975 https://copperfurrow.com/

Lewis and Clark Brewing Company 1517 Dodge Avenue 59601 (406) 442-5960 https://www.lewisandclarkbrewing.com/

Producing the finest ales and lagers while serving them at the peak of freshness. The beers are handcrafted and unpasteurized.

Blackfoot River Brewing Company 54 South Park Avenue 59601 (406) 449-3005 https://blackfootriverbrewing.com/

Producing the finest, handcrafted, traditional beers. Offering a variety of beers on tap, so no matter what your taste, you'll find it here. Great Falls a little more than an hour north has two breweries including a must-visit:

Mighty Mo Brew Company 412 Central Avenue 59401 (406) 952-0342 https://mightymobrewpub.com/

Jeremiah Johnson Brewing Company 215 3rd Street NW 59404 (406) 868-0506 https://jeremiahjohnsonbrewing.com/

Offering seven flagship beers along with many specialized beers that are rotated throughout the year. Stop in to try them and find out the difference. Continue almost two hours further north to Havre with three breweries including a must-visit:

Old Station Brewing Company 140 First Street 59501 (406) 265-3329 https://oldstationbrewing.com/

Vizsla Brewing 1753 US Highway 2 Space 17 59501 (406) 879-8867 https://vizslabrewing.com/

Triple Dog Brewing Company 675 1st Street W 59501 (406) 879-8103 https://tripledogbrew.com/

A small brewery with a relaxing and inviting environment. The award-winning beers are made in house and served fresh. Then circle south with about a three-hour drive to Lewistown and a must-visit brewery:

Big Spring Brewing 220 East Main Street 59457 (406) 535-2337
https://www.bigspringbrewingmt.com/

Producing craft beer with locally grown ingredients. Be sure to try the three most popular beers: Mayfly Rye Pale Ale, Command Bomber IPA, and Highwoods American Wheat. Finish your trip with about a two-hour drive southwest to a brewery in White Sulphur Springs:

2 Basset Brewery 202 E Main Street 59645 (406) 547-2337
http://2bassetbrewery.com/Home.html

Nebraska

Sandhills Region

This short day trip in northern Nebraska takes you to a handful of great breweries in a handful of great small towns. The perfect place to have it all. Start your trip out in Ord at:

Scratchtown Brewing Company 141 South 16th Street 68862 (308) 728-5050 http://scratchtown.beer/

The first brewery in the Sandhill area. Making complex and delicious beer. Stop in to enjoy a beer in a small-town atmosphere. Head northwest a half-hour to Taylor:

Bootleg Brewers 45145 829th Road 68879 (308) 942-3400 https://bootlegbrewers.com/

Then head to Broken Bow forty minutes southwest:

Kinkaider Brewing Company 43860 Paulsen Road 68822 (308) 872-8348 https://www.kinkaider.com/

End your trip with a two-hour drive north to Valentine:

Bolo Beer Company 112 N Main Street 11217 (402) 259-5180 https://www.bolobeer.com/

Southcentral Nebraska

This circular trip can take you a day or two, depending on how much time you want to spend exploring other things in the area. Start out in Grand Island at:

Prairie Pride Brewing Company 115 E South Front Street Suite 1 68801 (308) 850-5375 https://www.prairiepridebrewery.com/

Head west about fifty minutes to Kearney with a must-visit:

Thunderhead Brewing Company 18 E 21st Street 68847 (308) 237-1558 https://www.thunderheadbrewing.com/

A small brewmaster owned brewery that is focused on producing high-quality ales and lagers. Continue west another hour and a half to another must-visit brewery at North Platte:

Pals Brewing Company 4520 S Buffalo Bill Avenue 69101 (308) 221-6715 https://www.palsbrewingcompany.com/

A fun and inviting area to enjoy a beer. There are plenty of activities for the whole family to enjoy a trip here. Now head south about an hour to McCook at:

Loop Brewing Company 404 West A Street 69001 (308) 345-5198 https://loopbrewingcompany.com/

Head back east about an hour to another brewery at Holdrege:

Lost Way Brewery 614 3rd Avenue 68949 (308) 995-0503 http://lostwaybrewery.com/

Continue east another hour to Hastings with two breweries including a must-visit:

Steeple Brewing Company 717 West 1st Street 68901 (402) 519-4205 http://steeplebrewing.com/#welcome

First Street Brewing Company 119 N Saint Joseph Avenue 68901 (402) 834-2400 https://www.firststreetbrewing.com/

Making quality beers from local ingredients that express the region such as herbs and honey. Here you'll be able to enjoy a true local taste. End your trip about another hour east in Ohiowa with a must-visit brewery:

Lazy Horse Brewing 211 Road 20 68416 (402) 295-2550 https://www.lazyhorsevineyard.com/

Serving handcrafted beers along with wines and wood-fired pizza. All while overlooking horses grazing in pastures.

Eastern Nebraska

This tour takes you to two of the biggest cities in Nebraska and has quite a few breweries in a small area. You can easily drive the distances within a day, but you'll probably want a couple of days or more if you plan to go to all the breweries. Start your trip at a must-visit brewery in Elkhorn:

Jukes Ale Works 20560 Elkhorn Drive 68022 (402) 779-8496 https://www.jukesaleworks.com/

Offering nineteen beers on tap, including six year-round beers. The rest are seasonal and specialty brews. Pair them with excellent pub-style food. A half-hour southeast brings you to the first main city of Omaha with several brewery options including two must-visits:

Brickway Brewery and Distillery 1116 Jackson Street 68102 (402) 933-2613 https://www.drinkbrickway.com/

Upstream Brewing Company 514 S 11th Street 68102 (402) 344-0200 https://www.upstreambrewing.com/

Benson Brewery 6059 Maple Street 68104 (402) 934-8668 https://www.bensonbrewery.com/

Scriptown Brewing Company 3922 Farnam Street 68131 (402) 991-0506 http://www.scriptownbrewing.com/

Vis Major Brewing Company 3501 Center Street 68105 (402) 884-4082 https://www.vismajorbrewing.com/

Offering inventive craft beer recipes that deliver new and unique flavors. Stop in to try one of their unique brews today.

Farnam House Brewing Company 3558 Farnam Street 68131 (402) 401-6086 http://www.farnamhousebrewing.com/site/

Specializing in well-traveled styles from the premier beer-producing regions of Europe, including Belgium, France, and Germany. La Vista is fifteen minutes south with two breweries including a must-visit:

Kros Strain Brewing 10411 Portal Road Suite 102 (402) 779-7990 https://krosstrainbrewing.com/

Lucky Bucket Brewing Company 11941 Centennial Road Suite 1 68128 (402) 763-8868 https://www.luckybucket.beer/

Started with a handcrafted, session beer known as Lucky Bucket Pre-Prohibition Lager. Also offer barrel-aged ales, bold stouts, and sour beers. Just five minutes away is Papillion with two must-visit breweries:

Pint Nine Brewing Company 10411 Portal Road Suite 104 68131 (402) 359-1418 https://pintninebrewing.com/

Brewing aroma driven American ales and complex Belgian beers. Also doing one-off batches and barrel-aging.

Nebraska Brewing Company 7474 Towne Center Parkway Ste 101 68046 (402) 934-7100 https://nebraskabrewingco.com/

Brewing quality craft beers and artisanal barrel-aged products. Offering a broad and amazing lineup of beers to choose from. Another fourteen minutes south brings you to Springfield and another must-visit brewery:

Soaring Wings Vineyard 17111 S 138th Street 68059 (402) 253-2479 https://www.soaringwingswine.com/

Enjoy great ales and lagers along with other amazing beers. From velvety smooth stouts to German-style pilsners and everything in between, you're sure to find your favorite beer here. An hour and a half drive towards the southern border brings you to a must-visit brewery at Pawnee City:

SchillingBridge Winery and Microbrewery 62193 710th Road 68420 (402) 852-2400 https://schillingbridgewinery.com/

Brewing for every palate: from the Chocolate Stout to the Blonde Ale. There are also plenty of non-beer options for those who want something different. Then head back northwest to the next main city of Lincoln with several options including two must-visits:

White Elm Brewing Company 2717 South 8th Street 68502 (402) 261-6078 http://whiteelmbrewing.com/

Backswing Brewing Company 500 W South Street #8 68522 (402) 515-4263 https://www.backswingbrewing.com/

Empyrean Brewing Company 729 Q Street 68508 (402) 434-5960 https://empyreanbrewingco.com/

Code Beer Company 200 S Antelope Valley Parkway 68510 (402) 318-5888 http://www.codebeer.co/

Cosmic Eye Brewing 6800 P Street #300 68505 (531) 500-2739 https://www.cosmiceye.beer/

Misty's Steakhouse and Brewery 200 N 11th Street 68508 (402) 476-7766 https://www.mistyslincoln.com/Home

Zipline Brewing Company 2100 Magnum Circle Suite 1 68522 (402) 475-1001 https://ziplinebrewing.com/

Crafting artisan ales and lagers with high-quality precision. Their clean and simple approach allows you to focus on enjoying your beer.

Boiler Brewing Company 129 N 10th Street Suite B 68508 (402) 805-4136 http://www.boilerbrewingcompany.com/

Brewing small-batch beers that are rich in flavor. Also, offering nitro beers, mead, and ciders. Pair them with some great food offerings. Head west about a half-hour to Seward:

Bottle Rocket Brewing Company 230 S 5th Street 68434 (402) 641-4314 https://www.bottlerocketbrewing.com/main.sc

End your trip with about a two-hour trip north to Wayne:

Johnnie Byrd Brewing Company 121 Pearl Street 68787 (402) 833-1522 http://www.johnniebyrd.beer/

Scottsbluff

Flyover Brewing Company 1824 Broadway Street 69361 (308) 575-0335
https://www.flyoverbrewingcompany.com/

Nevada

Take a day or two to drive from the southern point of Nevada up to the Lake Tahoe area. This is where all the great breweries are, and there are plenty of other things to see and do along the way. Start out in the southern town of Henderson with a few options including a must-visit:

Crafthaus Brewery 7350 Eastgate Road Ste 110 89011 (702) 415-9184
https://www.crafthausbrewery.com/

Astronomy Aleworks 7350 Eastgate Road #170 89011
https://astronomyaleworks.com/

Lovelady Brewing 20 S Water Street 89015 (702) 857-8469
https://www.loveladybrewing.com/

Bad Beat Brewing 7380 Eastgate Road Ste 110 89011 (702) 463-4199
https://badbeatbrewing.com/

Offering four tasty year-round beers and eight rotating specialties. Currently starting a barrel-aging program to bring you even more offerings. Seventeen minutes away is the main city of Las Vegas with multiple options including several must-visits:

Chicago Brewing Company 2201 S Fort Apache Road 89117 (702) 254-3333 https://chicagobrewinglv.com/

Ellis Island Casino and Brewery 4178 Koval Lane 89109 (702) 734-8638 https://www.ellisislandcasino.com/ellis-island-brewery.html

Tenaya Creek Brewery 831 W Bonanza Road 89128 (702) 362-7335 https://www.tenayacreek.com/

Triple 7 Restaurant and Brewery 200 N Main Street 89101 (702) 387-1896 https://www.mainstreetcasino.com/dine/triple-7-restaurant-and-microbrewery

Big Dog's Draft House 4543 N Rancho Drive 89130 (702) 645-1404 https://www.bigdogsbrews.com/

Offering seven signature brews year-round along with four to ten seasonal brews at a time. Everything is brewed in small batches for exceptional quality.

Sin City Brewing Company 7935 W Sahara Avenue Ste #201 89107 (702) 809-4939 https://www.sincitybeer.com/

A focus on traditional domestic-style brews. Offering five signature beers year-round along with a variety of seasonal selections.

Able Baker Brewing Company 5990 Long Bay Street 89148 (775) 813-2349 https://ablebakerbrewing.com/

Creating unique, finely-crafted, premium quality beer. Emphasis is on fresh ingredients for bold flavor profiles. When you're ready, take a seven-hour drive north to Carson City with a couple options including a must-visit:

Shoe Tree Brewing Company 1496 Old Hot Springs Road 89706 (775) 222-0108 https://shoetreebrewing.com/

The Union 302 N Carson Street 89701 (775) 885-7307 https://www.theunioncarson.com/

The beers here are cool, crisp, and refreshing. All beers are made fresh in house with a variety of seasonal and local flavors. Another half-hour north is two breweries at Sparks:

Revision Brewing Company 380 S Rock Blvd 89431 (775) 331-2739 https://revisionbrewing.com/

Great Basin Brewing Company 846 Victorian Avenue 89431 (775) 355-7711 https://www.greatbasinbrewingco.com/

End your trip just seven minutes away at another main city, Reno:

IMBIB Custom Brews 785 East 2nd Street 89502 (775) 470-5996 https://imbibreno.com/

The Brewer's Cabinet 475 S Arlington Avenue Ste 1C 89501 (775) 348-7481 https://thebrewerscabinet.com/

Brasserie Saint James 901 S Center Street 89501 (775) 348-8889 https://www.brasseriesaintjames.com/

Lead Dog Brewing 415 East 4th Street 89512 (775) 391-5110 https://www.leaddogbrewing.com/

Silver Peak Restaurant and Brewery 124 Wonder Street 89502 (775) 324-1864 http://www.silverpeakbrewery.com/

Pigeon Head Brewery 840 East 5th Street 89512 (775) 276-6766 https://pigeonheadbrewery.com/

Offering fine lagers and unique ales. Their rotating seasonal beers continue to push the limits. You'll always have something new and unique to try here.

10 Torr Distilling and Brewing 490 Mill Street 89502 (775) 499-5271
https://10torr.com/

Producing precision-crafted beers, vacuum distilled spirits, and all-natural canned cocktails. Come relax and enjoy your favorite drink.

The Depot Craft Brewery Distillery 325 East 4th Street 89503 (775) 737-4330 https://thedepotreno.com/

Replicating classics and creating new beers. Offering a full range of beers, so you're sure to find something to enjoy.

New Hampshire

Seacoast Trail

This wonderful day trip allows you to enjoy beautiful coastlines and sip some wonderful brews. Start your trip in Hampton with two breweries including a must-visit:

Tilton Brothers Brewing 845 Lafayette Road 03842 (603) 926-0119
https://www.tiltonbrothersbrewing.com/

Smuttynose Brewing Company 105 Towle Farm Road 03842 (603) 436-4026 https://smuttynose.com/

No beer style is off-limits here. They are constantly experimenting and evolving, so you'll have something great to taste, no matter what your preference. Four minutes away is another must-visit brewery in North Hampton:

Throwback Brewery 7 Hobbs Road 03862 (603) 379-2317 https://www.throwbackbrewery.com/

A small, inspired brewery focused on crafting delicious, farm-fresh beer. Pair it with food made from local ingredients. Then head north about twenty-minutes to the main town of Portsmouth with a few options including a must-visit:

Loaded Question Brewing Company 909 Islington Street Suite #12 03801 (603) 852-1396 https://www.loadedquestionbrewing.com/

Great Rhythm Brewing Company 229 Miller Avenue Apt 3 03801 (603) 300-8588 https://www.greatrhythmbrewing.com/

Liars' Bench Beer Company 459 Islington Street Number 4 03801 (603) 294-9156 http://www.liarsbenchbeer.com/

Portsmouth Brewery 56 Market Street 03801 (603) 431-1115 https://portsmouthbrewery.com/

The original brewpub of New Hampshire. Offering a wide range of fine, handcrafted beer made to suit any taste. Head west about nine minutes to end your trip at the must-visit brewery in Newington:

Stoneface Brewing Company 436 Shattuck Way 03805 (603) 427-9801 https://stonefacebrewing.com/

Featuring hop-forward IPAs and pales, interesting lagers, delicious dark ales, and an increasing sour beer program. Offering twelve beers on tap.

Northern New Hampshire

This trip takes you into the beautiful White Mountains of New Hampshire. You can choose to visit the breweries in one day or more, depending on the pace. Start your trip in Ashland at:

White Mountain Brewing Company 50 Winter Street 03217 (603) 381-1781 https://whitemountainbrewingco.wordpress.com/

Head north to another brewery at Lincoln 25 minutes away:

One Love Brewery 25 S Mountain Drive Unit 4 03251 (603) 745-7290 https://www.onelovebrewery.com/

Take a detour to the east for fifty minutes to Conway:

Tuckerman Brewing Company 64 Hobbs Street 03818 (603) 447-5400 http://www.tuckermanbrewing.com/

Just ten minutes north is a must-visit brewery in North Conway:

Moat Mountain Smoke House and Brewing Company 3378 White Mountain Highway 03860 (603) 356-6381 https://www.moatmountain.com/

Focusing on specialty ales and lagers, brewed on-site to be enjoyed on-site. Also, offering local food dishes are pair great with the beers. Head back west about an hour to Bethlehem and another brewery:

Rek-lis Brewing Company 44 Pinewood Avenue 03574 (603) 370-1932 https://www.reklisbrewing.com/

Just ten minutes away in Franconia is a must-visit brewery:

Iron Furnace Brewing 115 Main Street 03580 (781) 760-9561 https://www.ironfurnacebrewing.com/

Tending towards hop forward beers, but also offering a wide variety of beers. They are always changing and experimenting with offering you new and better beers. Another must-visit brewery is in Littleton just seven minutes away:

Schilling Beer Company 18 Mill Street 03561 (603) 444-4800
https://schillingbeer.com/

Crafting world-class European-inspired beers. They also have a wild/spontaneous beer program that produces some excellent one-off beers only available in their taproom. About a half-hour north is another brewery at Lancaster:

Copper Pig Brewery 1 Middle Street 03582 (603) 631-2273
https://www.copperpigbrewery.com/

Another fifty minutes north ends your trip in Colebrook near the border at a must-visit:

Coos Brewing Company 13 Merrill Street 03576
https://www.coosbeer.com/

A small brewery focused on making beers by hand. Come try their full line of world-class beers today.

Southern New Hampshire

The cities on this trip are close together and can easily be driven in a day. However, there are so many breweries packed into the southern portion of New Hampshire, you'll probably want two to three days or maybe even more to explore everything. Start your trip out in Meredith at:

Twin Barns Brewing Company 194 Daniel Webster Highway 03253 (603) 279-0876 https://www.twinbarnsbrewing.com/

Head about a half-hour south to a must-visit brewery at Tilton:

Kettlehead Brewing Company 407 W Main Street 03276 (603) 325-8266
https://kettleheadbrewing.com/

A small craft brewery focused on offering better beers. Offering an excellent selection of exceptional ales to choose from. Canterbury is another twelve minutes south and has a must-visit:

Canterbury AleWorks 305 Baptist Hill Road 03224 (603) 491-4539 https://www.canterburyaleworks.com/

Step back in time and place at this unique British inspired wood-fired tasting room. You have a one-of-a-kind craft beer experience here. The next must-visit brewery is twelve minutes south at Concord along with a second option:

Litherman's Limited Brewing Company 126B Hall Street 03301 (603) 818-9102 https://lithermans.beer/

Concord Craft Brewery 117 Storrs Street 03229 (603) 856-7625 http://www.concordcraftbrewing.com/home.html

Brewing a range of beer styles, but all aim to deliver a full, well-balanced, clean, and fresh flavor. Stop in to enjoy a fresh beer today. Circle west about twenty-minutes to a brewery at Henniker:

Henniker Brewing Company 129 Centervale Road 03242 (603) 428-3579 https://hennikerbrewing.com/

Head a half-hour northwest to the brewery in New London:

Flying Goose Brew Pub and Grille Jct. Rtes 11 and 114 03257 (603) 526-6899 https://www.flyinggoose.com/

The next brewery is in Croydon another twenty-minutes northwest:

Polyculture Brewing Company 3 Camel Hump Road 03773 (603) 276-8367 https://www.polyculturebrewing.com/

Then head south about an hour to another brewery in Langdon:

Monadnock Brewing Company 78 Cheshire Turnpike 03602 (603) 313-6318 https://www.monadnockbrewing.com/

Continue south another half-hour to Keene with two breweries including a must-visit:

Branch and Blade Brewing 17 Bradco Street 03431 (603) 354-3478
https://www.babbrewing.com/

Elm City Brewing Company 222 West Street 03431 (603) 355-3335
https://www.elmcitybrewing.com/

Since their opening, they have brewed countless styles of beer. They are always trying new techniques and experimenting with new ingredients. Be sure to try their award-winning Abbey Dubbel. Winchester is twenty-minutes south with the next brewery:

The Outlaw Brewing Company 215 Scotland Road 03470
https://www.theoutlawbrewingcompany.com/

Head back northeast to Swanzey seventeen minutes away:

West LA Beer Company 647 West Swanzey Road 03446 (603) 903-0724 https://westlabeercompany.com/

Just eleven minutes brings you to a brewery at Marlborough:

Frogg Brewing 108 Main Street 03455 https://www.froggbrewing.com/

Twelve minutes southeast is a must-visit brewery at Troy:

Granite Roots Brewing 244 N Main Street 03465 (603) 242-3435
http://graniterootsbrewing.com/

A nano-brewery featuring traditional brews and craft beers with a hint of fruit from the family farm, Monadnock Berries. Peterborough is next and is twenty-five minutes east:

Post and Beam Brewing 40 Grove Street 03458 (603) 784-5361
http://www.postandbeambrewery.com/

Another forty-five minutes east is a brewery at Merrimack:

The Able Ebenezer Brewing Company 31 Columbia Circle 03054 (844) 223-2253 https://www.ableebenezer.com/

Take a fifteen-minute drive south to Nashua with several options including two must-visits:

Odd Fellows Brewing Company 124 Main Street 03060 (603) 521-8129 https://www.oddfellowsbrewery.com/

Martha's Exchange 185 Main Street 03060 (603) 883-8781 https://www.marthas-exchange.com/

Liquid Therapy 14 Court Street Unit B 03060 (603) 402-9391 http://www.liquidtherapynh.com/

Millyard Brewery 25 E Otterson Street 03060 (603) 505-5079 http://millyardbrewery.com/

The original brewery in Nashua. Offering a wide selection of craft beers made from the finest ingredients.

Spyglass Brewing Company 2 Townsend West Unit 8 03063 (603) 546-2965 https://www.spyglassbrewing.com/

Brewing innovative artisan beers. Come try the most amazing, enjoyable, and unique beers you won't find anywhere else. Then head northeast for seventeen minutes to your next brewery at Londonderry:

603 Brewery 12 Liberty Drive Unit 7 03053 (603) 630-7745 https://www.603brewery.com/

Derry is just six minutes away with a couple options including a must-visit:

Rockingham Brewing Company One Corporate Park Drive #1 03038 (603) 216-2324 https://www.rockinghambrewing.com/

Kelsen Brewing Company 80 N High Street Unit 3 03038 (603) 965-3708 http://kelsenbrewing.com/

Award-winning craft beers that push the limits of traditional styles. Full-flavored and strong aroma beers are what you'll find here. Eighteen minutes north brings you to the main city of Manchester with a few options, including two must-visits:

To Share Brewing Company 720 Union Street 03104
https://www.tosharebrewing.com/

Aigean Ales 250 Commercial Street Unit 2001 03101 (603) 518-8550
http://www.aigeanales.com/

Backyard Brewery + Kitchen 1211 South Mammoth Road 03109 (603) 623-3545 https://backyardbrewerynh.com/

Great North Aleworks 1050 Holt Avenue Unit 14 03109 (603) 858-5789
http://www.greatnorthaleworks.com/

Offering three year-round beers: dry-hopped pale ale, robust vanilla porter, and an IPA. There are also seasonal and special brews throughout the year.

Swift Current Brewing Company 500 N Commercial Street 03101
https://swiftcurrentbrewing.com/

Brewing everything from big, bold flavors to classic styles and everything in between. Offering four year-round beers as well as a number of seasonal and specialty beers. Epsom is thirty minutes north and has another brewery:

Blasty Bough Brewing Company 3 Griffin Road 03234 (603) 724-3636
https://www.blastybough.com/

Head east to the next largest city about a half-hour away, Dover, with three options including a must-visit:

Chapel + Main 83 Main 03820 (603) 842-5170
https://www.chapelandmain.com/

Empty Pint Brewing Company 17 Second Street 03820
https://www.emptypintbrewing.com/

Garrison City Beerworks 455 Central Avenue 03820
https://www.garrisoncitybeerworks.com/

Brewing high quality, inventive craft beer. The main focus is the New England IPA, but there is also a constant rotation of fruited sours, Saisons, Stouts, and Lagers. Just eleven minutes north is Somersworth:

Bad Lab Beer Company 460 High Street 03878 (603) 842-5822
https://www.badlabbeer.com/

End your trip with a fifty-minute drive north to a brewery in Wolfeboro:

The Lone Wolfe Brewing Company 36 Mill Street 03894 (603) 515-1273
https://www.thelonewolfe.com/

New Jersey

Southern Shore

There are only a handful of towns and breweries to visit on this trip, but you can easily enjoy it in a day while viewing the beautiful waterfront regions of New Jersey. Start your trip in Cape May at:

Cape May Brewing Company 1288 Hornet Road 08204 (609) 849-9933
https://www.capemaybrewery.com/

Just eight minutes away is another brewery at North Cape May:

Gusto Brewing Company 3860 Bayshore Road 08204 (609) 849-8260
https://www.gustobrewco.com/

Head north up the cape to Rio Grande just nine minutes away:

7 Mile Brewery 3156 Route 9 South 08242 (609) 365-7777
https://7milebrew.com/

Seven minutes southeast is a must-visit brewery at Wildwood:

MudHen Brewing Company 127 W Rio Grande Avenue 08260 (609) 522-8383 https://www.mudhenbrew.com/

They always have something fun in the fermenter waiting for you to sample. Come try some of their award-winning beers today. Continue another thirteen minutes up the cape to Cape May Court House with a must-visit:

Bucket Brigade Brewery 205 North Main Street 08210 (609) 778-2641
https://bucketbrigadebrewery.com/

Offering a variety of ales, pilsners, and lagers. Things are always updated with new seasonal brews. End your trip eleven minutes away in Ocean View at:

Ludlam Island Brewery 9 Stoney Court Unit 3 08230
http://www.ludlamisland.com/

Eastern Shore

There are a lot of breweries crammed into this short trip. You can go to the must-visit breweries and complete it within a day, or you can take several days to travel the coast and visit all the breweries. Start your trip out in the north at a must-visit brewery in Belford:

Belford Brewing Company 84 Leonardville Road 07748 (732) 769-7168 https://www.belfordbrewing.com/

Offering fresh on-tap beers that are very smooth. Also offering a Belgian Tripel and Rye Ales that have been aged in bourbon barrels. Six minutes away is a brewery at Atlantic Highlands:

Carton Brewing Company 6 East Washington Avenue 07716 (732) 654-2337 http://cartonbrewing.com/

The next stop is twelve minutes south in Red Bank with another must-visit brewery:

Red Tank Brewing 77 Monmouth Street 07701 (732) 865-9500 https://www.redtankbrewing.com/

Focusing on brewing the timeless classics, but using the highest quality ingredients from around the world. Eight minutes bring you to Tinton Falls and another brewery:

Jughandle Brewing 4057 Asbury Avenue 07753 (732) 898-2220 http://www.jughandlebrewing.com/

Thirteen minutes away are two breweries in Ashbury Park:

Ashbury Park Brewery 810 Sewall Avenue 07712 (732) 455-5571 https://www.asburyparkbrewery.com/

Dark City Brewing Company 802 2nd Avenue 07712 (732) 455-3792 http://darkcitybrewingcompany.com/

Just three minutes away is another brewery at Bradley Beach:

Bradley Brew Project 714 Main Street 07720 (732) 455-8047
https://www.bradleybrew.com/

Another three minutes brings you to Belmar:

Beach Haus Brewery 801 Main Street 07719 (732) 202-7782
https://beachhausbeer.com/

Drive about twenty-minutes to Point Pleasant with two breweries including a must-visit:

Frye Brewing Company 2257 Bridge Avenue 08742 (732) 604-4263
http://www.fryebrewingcompany.com/

Last Wave Brewing Company 601 Bay Avenue 08742 (732) 903-5278
https://www.lastwavebrewing.com/

Unique, handcrafted ales that please the palate. Come try a few of their brews on tap and see what makes them so different. Another twenty-minutes brings you to Toms River and another must-visit:

Toms River Brewing 1540 Route 37 W 08755 (732) 608-1004
https://tomsriverbrewing.com/

Combining traditional beer styles with an expanded natural flavor palate. This offers you everything from their flagship St. Johns Irish Red to lagers, stouts, Belgians and IPAs. Forked River has another brewery and is twelve minutes away:

Backward Flag Brewing Company 699 Challenger Way 08731 (609) 994-0422 https://www.backwardflagbrewing.com/

Seven minutes away is Waretown:

Oyster Creek Brewing Company 529 US 9 #5 08758 (609) 622-2944
https://www.oystercreekbrewing.com/

A short three minutes away is another brewery at Ocean:

Kane Brewing Company 1750 Bloomsbury Avenue 07712 (732) 922-8600 https://www.kanebrewing.com/

Then about forty minutes brings you to a must-visit brewery at Beach Haven:

Ship Bottom Brewery 830 North Bay Avenue Store 23 08008 (610) 368-5660 https://shipbottombrewery.com/

Handcrafting each batch from the freshest ingredients. The ale and lager recipes used here were created to maximize the complex flavors of malts and hops. About an hour south is another must-visit brewery in Galloway:

Garden State Beer Company 247 E White Horse Pike 08205 (609) 232-2337 https://gardenstatebeerco.com/

Out of 16 taps, there are enough styles available that you'll find a beer you like no matter what your taste. Fourteen minutes away is Atlantic City with one option:

Tun Tavern Two Miss America Way 08401 (609) 347-7800 https://www.tuntavern.com/

About twenty-minutes brings you to Egg Harbor Township and another brewery:

Hidden Sands Brewing Company 6754 Washington Avenue Unit B 08234 (609) 910-2009 https://hiddensands.com/

End your trip ten minutes away at a must-visit brewery in Somers Point:

Somers Point Brewing Company 705 W New York Avenue 08224 (609) 788-0767 https://somerspointbrewing.com/

An independent craft brewery focusing on small-batch beers with an emphasis on premium ingredients, quality, and flavor.

Central New Jersey

The central part of New Jersey is home to some excellent breweries. This circular trip can take you a day or two, depending on how many breweries you choose to visit. Start your trip at a must-visit brewery in Colts Neck Township:

Source Farmhouse Brewery 300 New Jersey 34 07722 (732) 431-2337 https://sourcebrewing.com/

Brewing handcrafted, farm-to-glass ales and lagers. Come here for a memorable beer tasting experience you won't soon forget. Head about a half-hour northwest to another must-visit brewery at New Brunswick:

Harvest Moon Brewery and Café 392 George Street 08901 (732) 249-6666 https://www.harvestmoonbrewery.com/

High quality, handcrafted beers with diverse flavors, textures, and aromas. Pair them with unique American cuisine. Just seven minutes away is another brewery at Edison:

Cypress Brewing Company 30 Nixon Lane Unit E 08837 (732) 243-9565 http://cypressbrewing.com/

Head west to Somerville about twenty-minutes:

Village Brewing Company 34 West Main Street 08876 (908) 333-2990 https://www.villagebrewing.com/

Southwest twenty-minutes brings you to Flemington with two breweries:

Lone Eagle Brewing 44 Stangl Road 08822 (908) 237-2255 http://www.loneeaglebrewing.com/

Conclave Brewing 15 Minneakoning Road Suite 202 08822 (908) 456-0494 https://www.conclavebrewing.com/

Pennington is about twenty-minutes south and has a must-visit brewery:

The Referend Bier Blendery 1595 Reed Road Unit 2 08534 (609) 474-0443 https://www.thereferend.com/home

Specializing in the production of spontaneously fermented beers, this is the way it was done in ancient times. This means you get a beer of depth and character. Another must-visit brewery is ten minutes south in Ewing:

River Horse Brewing Company 2 Graphics Drive 08628 (609) 883-0890 http://www.riverhorse.com/agegate.php

Brewing full-bodied, full-flavored beers that are balanced and appeal to all types of beer drinkers. Come try the best beer you'll ever taste. Another seventeen minutes south is a brewery at Bordentown:

Tindall Road Brewery 102 Farnsworth Avenue Suite 110 08505 https://tindallroadbrewery.wixsite.com/beer

Burlington has a must-visit brewery and is twelve minutes southwest:

Third State Brewing 352 High Street 08016 (609) 387-1620 http://www.thirdstatebrewing.com/

Brewing a wide variety of high-quality craft beers, including a number of award-winning recipes. Stop in to try one of their many on tap beers today. Just nine minutes away is Mt. Holly with two breweries:

Village Idiot Brewing Company 42 High Street 08060 (609) 975-9270 http://villageidiotbrewing.com/

Spellbound Brewing 10 Lippincott Lane Unit 12 08060 (609) 744-0665 http://www.spellboundbrewing.com/

A short four minutes away is Clermont with a must-visit brewery:

Slack Tide Brewing Company 1072 Route 83 08210 (609) 478-2324 https://www.slacktidebrewingco.com/

Offering a diverse, high-quality line of beers using all-natural ingredients. They have recently expanded into a barrel-aging program. End your trip by circling northeast to Cream Ridge and a must-visit brewery:

Screamin' Hill Brewery 83 Emleys Hill Road 08514 (609) 758-8726 http://screaminhill.com/

Enjoy high-quality American ales while overlooking preserved farmland. Whenever possible, the ales here are made with ingredients grown right on the farm.

Northern New Jersey

This winding route through the northern part of New Jersey takes you to a lot of cities and many breweries. You'll want at least two to three days to experience it all, perhaps more depending on what else you want to see and do. Start your trip at a must-visit brewery in Blairstown:

Buck Hill Brewery and Restaurant 45 State Route 94 07825 (908) 854-5300 https://buckhillbrewery.com/

A true farm-to-table experience with everything grown on-site. Brewing a full range from light to bold, including ales, lagers, porters, pilsners, IPAs, and seasonal specialty beers. Head south about forty minutes to another must-visit brewery in Phillipsburg:

Invertase Brewing Company 51 N Broad Street 08865 (908) 349-0067 https://invertasebrewing.com/

While the on-tap offerings will change, they always offer well-hopped IPAs, light low hop options, and dark beers in order to showcase a variety and appeal to a range of tastes. Continue to the next must-visit brewery in Milford about another twenty-minutes south:

The Ship Inn 61 Bridge Street 08848 (908) 995-0188 https://www.shipinn.com/

The first craft brewery in New Jersey. When you stop here, you'll enjoy craft-brewed ales, ciders, and homemade British-inspired foods. Head back northeast to a brewery in Long Valley about forty minutes away:

Long Valley Pub and Brewery One Fairmont Road 07853 (908) 876-1122 https://restaurantvillageatlongvalley.com/long-valley-pub-and-brewery/

Just seven minutes away is Hackettstown with three breweries including a must-visit:

Jersey Girl Brewing Company 426 Sand Shore Road 07840 (908) 591-4186 http://www.jerseygirlbrewing.com/

Man Skirt Brewing 144 Main Street 07840 (908) 989-0286 https://manskirtbrewing.com/

Czig Meister Brewing Company 106 Valentine Street 07840 (908) 651-5492 http://www.czigmeisterbrewing.com/

Making four year-round beers and seasonal offerings; served in an old-world style setting. Stop in today to try all that they have to offer. Another half-hour north is Lafayette with a must-visit brewery:

Angry Erik Brewing 10 Millpond Drive 07848 (862) 432-9003 http://www.angryerik.com/

Offering an ever-changing variety of artfully crafted ales, including both American and Belgian styles. However, they are also exploring the unknown. The next brewery is in Sparta a short eight minutes south:

Krogh's Restaurant and Brewpub 23 White Deer Plaza 07871 (973) 729-8428 https://www.kroghs.com/

Twenty-minutes southeast is a must-visit brewery at Denville:

Fort Nonsense Brewing Company 3118 Route 10 West 07834 https://www.fortnonsensebrewing.com/#

Offering a variety of classic ales and lagers with unique twists and some nonsensical beers for those who want to be more adventurous with their beer. Back northeast about twenty-minutes brings you to Butler and a must-visit brewery:

High Point Brewing Company 22 Park Place 07405 (973) 838-7400 https://ramsteinbeer.com/

The premier brewer of German-style lagers and wheat beers. The head brewer learned and practiced for years in Germany before coming to the United States. Back south, about twenty-minutes is Fairfield with two breweries:

Cricket Hill Brewing Company 24 Kulick Road 07204 (973) 276-9415 https://www.crickethillbrewery.com/

Magnify Brewing Company 1275 Bloomfield Avenue Building 7 Unit 40C 07004 https://www.magnifybrewing.com/

Another sixteen minutes southeast brings you to Montclair:

Montclair Brewery 101 Walnut Street 07042 (973) 850-0541 https://www.montclairbrewery.com/

Back north, about ten minutes is Clifton and another brewery:

Ghost Hawk Brewing Company 321 River Road Unit 6 07014 (973) 259-6037 https://www.ghosthawkbrewing.com/

Next is Carlstadt about ten minutes southeast:

Bolero Snort Brewery 316 20th Street 07072 (201) 464-0639 https://bolerosnort.com/

Head back north ten minutes to two breweries in Hackensack:

The Alementary Brewing Company 58 Voorhis Lane 07601 (201) 968-1290 https://www.alementary.com/

Hackensack Brewing Company 78 Johnson Avenue 07601 (201) 880-1768 https://www.hackensackbrewing.com/

Just five minutes south is a must-visit brewery at Little Ferry:

Brix City Brewing 4 Alsan Way 07643 (201) 440-0865 https://www.brixcitybrewing.com/

Known for their New England style IPAs, but also producing a wide variety of beers, including sours, pilsners, and stouts. About twenty-minutes south is Hoboken with the next brewery:

Hoboken Brewing Company 66 Harrison Street 07030 https://hobokenbrewing.beer/

Just six minutes away is a must-visit brewery at Jersey City:

Departed Soles Brewing Company 150 Bay Street Suite 2A 07302 (201) 479-8578 https://www.departedsoles.com/

The first and only brewery in New Jersey to offer gluten-free beer. It is also a dog-friendly brewery for you to visit with your four-legged family members. About twenty-minutes back west is a brewery at Orange:

Four City Brewing Company 55 South Essex Avenue 07050 (973) 630-1411 http://www.fourcitybrewing.com/

Just five minutes away is another brewery at South Orange:

Gaslight Brewery and Restaurant 15 S Orange Avenue 07079 (973) 762-7077 http://www.gaslightbrewery.net/

Head west about ten minutes to Chatham with a must-visit brewery:

Twin Elephant Brewing Company 13 Watching Avenue 07928 (973) 507-9862 https://www.twinelephant.com/

Not restricted by style and flavor, but does have a decided focus on classic beers that have been enjoyed for years. Just six minutes south is the next brewery at New Providence:

Untied Brewing Company 140 Spring Street Unit C 07974
https://www.untiedbrewingco.com/

Kenilworth is about twenty-minutes back east:

Two Ton Brewing 730 Federal Avenue 07033 (908) 241-1614
http://www.twotonbrewing.com/

Just five minutes away is Roselle Park with a must-visit brewery:

Climax Brewing Company 112 Valley Road 07204 (908) 620-9585
http://www.climaxbrewing.com/index.html

The oldest microbrewery in New Jersey. Each recipe focuses on balanced and flavorful beers that are easy for all people to enjoy. Another must-visit brewery is five minutes away in Cranford:

Yale Terrace Brewery 26 Eastman Street 07016 (973) 996-8601
https://www.ytbrewery.com/

Creating unique quality beers. Producing many varieties and ensuring they are all fresh and flavorful. Ten minutes south is Rahway with the next brewery:

Wet Ticket Brewing 1435 Main Street 07065 (848) 666-7141
https://www.wetticketbrewing.com/

End your trip eight minutes away in Woodbridge:

J.J. Bitting Brewing Company 33 Main Street 07095 (732) 634-2929
http://www.njbrewpubs.com/

Southern New Jersey

This circular route takes you to quite a few towns and breweries. You can complete it in a day or two, depending on how many breweries you choose to visit. Start your trip in Atco at:

Atco Brewing Company 302 White Horse Pike 08004 (856) 292-9041
https://www.craftbeercurbside.com/

Six minutes away is another brewery at West Berlin:

Berlin Brewing Company 220 S White Horse Pike 08091 (856) 336-2038
https://www.berlinbrewco.com/

Another ten minutes northwest is Somerdale:

Flying Fish Brewing Company 900 Kennedy Blvd 08083 (856) 504-3442
https://www.flyingfish.com/

Another brewery at Haddon Heights is just six minutes away:

Lunacy Brewing Company 1500 Kings Highway 08035 (609) 379-5862
https://lunacybrewingcompany.com/

Just three minutes to Oaklyn and another brewery:

Tonewood Brewing 215 W Clinton Avenue 08107 (856) 833-1500
https://www.tonewoodbrewing.com/

Haddonfield is seven minutes away with another brewery:

King's Road Brewing Company 127 Kings Highway East 08033 (856)
577-3196 http://kingsroadbrewing.com/

Five minutes brings you to the next brewery at Cherry Hill:

Forgotten Boardwalk Brewing 1940 Olney Avenue Suite 100 08003
(856) 437-0709 https://potato-polygon-gb88.squarespace.com/

Head about ten minutes east to Marlton:

Zed's Beer/Bado Brewing 19 N Maple Avenue Unit B 08053 (856) 872-
7632 https://www.drinkzeds.com/

Continue east another ten minutes to Medford:

Lower Forge Brewery 14 S Main Street 08055 (609) 975-9532
https://www.lowerforge.shop/

Head southeast about ten minutes to Shamong and a must-visit brewery:

Brotherton Brewing Company 340 Forked Neck Road 08088 (609) 801-2686 https://www.brothertonbrewing.com/bbWP2bk/

Using local botanicals, herbs, and fruits to create various barrel aging projects and seasonal offerings. Circle southwest about twenty-minutes to another must-visit brewery at Hammonton:

Vinyl Brewing Company 300 B 12th Street 08037 (609) 666-5460
https://www.vinylbrewingnj.com/

Three 3's Brewing Company 50 13th Street 08037 (732) 814-1396
https://www.three3sbrewing.com/

The focus is on brewing IPAs and Saison style beers. Offering a number of year-round beers on tap while dedicating one to experiment with new styles. Head a half-hour south to Millville:

Glasstown Brewing Company 10 Peterson Street 08332 (856) 327-7770
http://www.glasstownbrewery.com/

Head back north about a half-hour to a must-visit brewery at Williamstown:

Cross Keys Brewing Company 1038 N Main Street 08094 (856) 371-8018 https://ckbcbeer.com/

Providing a unique, comfortable, and friendly environment to enjoy fresh and delicious beers. Another must-visit brewery is about twenty-minutes northwest at Pitman:

Human Village Brewing Company 148 S Broadway 08071 (856) 556-0639 https://www.humanvillagebrewingco.com/

Taking raw materials found in mother nature to combine them into a natural brewing process that explores beers in a creative way. Continue northwest twelve minutes to Clarksboro:

Death of the Fox Brewing Company 119 Berkley Road 08020 (856) 566-1655 https://www.deathofthefoxbrewing.com/

The first craft brewery and coffeehouse in New Jersey. There are sixteen taps of fresh-brewed craft beer to choose from. End your trip just eight minutes away in Woodbury at a must-visit brewery:

Eight and Sand Beer Company 1003 N Evergreen Avenue 08096 (856) 537-1339 https://www.eightandsandbeer.com/

The styles incorporate the old (European styles) with the new (American ingredients). The majority of the beers are session-able or lower in alcohol content to stay closer to classic styles.

New Mexico

Northern New Mexico

This trip will only take a day or two, depending on how much you choose to see and do around your brewery visits. Start your trip at a must-visit brewery in Farmington:

Three Rivers Eatery and Brewhouse 101 East Main Street 87401 (505) 324-2187 https://www.threeriversbrewery.com/

Come sample many distinctive styles of beer, such as Papa Bear's Golden Honey Ale or Arroyo Amber. There are also a number of specialty beers available at different times. The next brewery is about two and a half hours south in Rio Rancho:

Turtle Mountain Brewing Company 3755 Southern Blvd SE 87124 (505) 994-9497 https://turtlemountainbrewing.com/

Bernalillo is just thirteen minutes east with another brewery:

Kaktus Brewing Company 471 S Hill Road 87004 (505) 379-5072 http://www.kaktusbrewery.com/

Circle north and then south about a half-hour to Cedar Crest:

Ale Republic 28 Arroyo Seco 87008 (505) 281-2828 http://www.alerepublic.com/

Head back north about an hour to Santa Fe with several options including three must-visits:

Santa Fe Brewing Company 35 Fire Place 87508 (505) 424-3333 https://santafebrewing.com/

Second Street Brewery 1814 Second Street 87505 (505) 982-3030 https://www.secondstreetbrewery.com/

Chili Line Brewing Company 204 N Guadalupe Street 87501 (505) 500-7903 https://chililinebrewery.com/

Specializing in a wide range of smoked beers. Offering everything from lagers to Viking ales and everything in between.

Tumbleroot Brewery and Distillery 2791 Agua Fria Street 87507 (505) 303-3808 https://tumblerootbreweryanddistillery.com/

Offering a rotating list of at least eight draft beers. Limited release bottlings include cask-aged sours and strong ales aged in spirit barrels.

Rowley Farmhouse Ales 1405 Maclovia Street 87505 (504) 428-0719 https://www.rowleyfarmhouse.com/

Focused on rustic farmhouse and sour ales. Independently owned and operated, you can also find some other beer options here from around the world. Head northwest to Los Alamos about forty minutes away:

Bathtub Row Brewing Co-op 163 Central Park Square 87544 (505) 500-8381 https://www.bathtubrowbrewing.coop/

Head north another fifty minutes to a must-visit brewery at Embudo:

Blue Heron Brewing Company 2214 Highway 68 87531 (505) 579-9188 https://blueheronbrews.com/

New Mexico's oldest female-owned and operated brewery. Handcrafted beers brewed right along the Rio Grande. Head northeast about an hour to Eagles Nest and another must-visit brewery:

Comanche Creek Brewing Company 225 Comanche Creek Road 87718 (575) 377-2337 http://comanchecreekbrewingco.com/

Due to the small size of the brewery, they are able to rotate the ten taps throughout the year to offer you a wide variety. They also offer seasonal specialty beers. End your trip with about an hour and a half trip northeast to the border town of Raton:

Colfax Ale Cellar 215 S 2nd Street 87740 (575) 445-9727 https://colfaxalecellar.com/

Southern New Mexico

This is a smaller trail in New Mexico but still has some great breweries. It is best to take two days to complete this trip since there is a lot of driving between breweries. Start out in Carlsbad at:

Milton's Brewing 108 E Mermod Street 88220 (575) 689-1026
https://www.miltonsbrewing.com/

Head north almost three hours to your next brewery at Portales:

Roosevelt Brewing Company and Public House 201 South Main Avenue 88130 (575) 226-2739 http://rooseveltbrewing.com/

Then take a three-hour drive west to Moriarty and a must-visit brewery:

Sierra Blanca Brewing Company 1016 Industrial Road 87035 (505) 832-BEER https://www.sierrablancabrewery.com/

One of New Mexico's oldest breweries that has won multiple awards for their beers. Offering seventeen beers and two sodas, there's something for everyone. The next brewery is in Lincoln about three hours south:

Bonito Valley Brewing Company 692 Calle la Placita 88338 (575) 653-4810 https://www.bonitovalleybrewing.com/

Another brewery is about an hour away at Ruidoso Downs:

Lost Hiker Brewing Company 26394 Highway 70 East #6 88346 (512) 825-7521 https://losthikerbrewing.com/

Continue about two hours southwest to Las Cruces with two breweries:

Icebox Brewing Company 2825 W Picacho Avenue 88007 (575) 526-7129 https://iceboxbrewing.com/

High Desert Brewing Company 1201 W Hadley Avenue 88005 (505) 525-6752 http://www.highdesertbrewingco.com/

Just seven minutes away is a must-visit brewery as Mesilla:

Spotted Dog Brewery 2920 Avenida de Mesilla 88005 (575) 650-2729
http://www.spotteddogbrewery.com/

Brewing unfiltered craft beers. The on-tap beers vary each week. For non-alcoholic options, there are sodas available. End your trip about an hour north in Truth or Consequences at:

Truth or Consequences Brewing Company 410 N Broadway 87901 (575) 297-0289 https://torcbrewingco.square.site/

Albuquerque

Albuquerque has a great number of breweries. Enough so that you would need to spend two or three days in the city just to visit all the breweries.

Broken Trail Brewery and Distillery 2921 Stanford Drive NE 87107 (505) 221-6281 https://brokentrailspirits.com/

Starr Brothers Brewing Company 5700 San Antonio Drive NE Ste B 87109 (505) 492-2752 https://www.starrbrothersbrewing.com/

Sidetrack Brewing Company 413 2nd Street SW 87102 (505) 288-6468 http://sidetrackbrewing.net/

Boxing Bear Brewing Company 10200 Corrales Road NW 87114 (505) 897-2327 http://www.boxingbearbrewing.com/

Bombs Away Beer Company 9801 Acoma Road SE 87123 (505) 554-3204 https://bombsawaybeer.com/

Hops Brewery 3507 Central Avenue NE 87106 (505) 369-1378 https://www.hopsbrewery.com/

Nexus Brewery 4730 Pan American Freeway East NE Suite D 87109 (505) 242-4100 https://nexusbrewery.com/

Cantero Brewing Company 3351 Columbia Drive NE 87107 (505) 312-8247 https://www.canterobrewing.com/

High and Dry Brewing 529 Adams Street NE 87108 (505) 433-5591
http://highanddrybrewing.com/

Dialogue Brewing 1501 1st Street NW 87102 (505) 585-1501
https://www.dialoguebrewing.com/

Marble Brewery 111 Marble NW 87102 (505) 243-2739
https://marblebrewery.com/

Differential Brewing Company 500 Yale Blvd SE 87106
https://differentialbrewing.com/

Tractor Brewing Company 1800 4th Street NW 87102 (505) 243-6752
https://getplowed.com/

Bosque Brewing Company 8900 San Mateo Blvd NE 87113 (505) 750-
7596 https://www.bosquebrewing.com/

Toltec Brewing Company 10250 Cottonwood Park 87114 (505) 890-
1455 https://www.toltecbrewing.com/

B2B Bistronomy 3118 Central SE 87106 (505) 262-2222
http://bistronomyb2b.com/

Steel Bender Brewyard 8305 2nd Street NW 87114 (505) 433-3537
https://steelbenderbrewyard.com/

La Cumbre Brewing Company 3313 Girard Blvd NE 87107 (505) 872-
0225 https://www.lacumbrebrewing.com/

Rio Bravo Brewing 1912 Second Street NW 87102 (505) 900-3909
http://www.riobravobrewing.com/

Thirsty Eye Brewing 206 Broadway Blvd SE 87102 (505) 639-5831
https://thirstyeyebrew.com/

Quarter Celtic Brewpub 1100 San Mateo Blvd NE Ste 50 87110 (505)
503-1387 https://quartercelticbrewpub.com/

Ponderosa Brewing Company 1761 Bellamah NW 87104 (505) 639-5941 https://www.ponderosabrewing.net/

Red Door Brewing 1001 Candelaria Road NE 87107 (505) 633-6675 http://reddoorbrewing.com/

Offering solid variety with epic quality. Including hoppy pales, rich stouts, and malty reds. There is surely something for everyone here.

Canteen Brewhouse 2381 Aztec Road NE 87107 (505) 830-4629 http://canteenbrewhouse.com/

The oldest brewery in Albuquerque opened in 1994. The beers here have won over 150 national and international awards.

Alien Brew Pub 6601 Uptown Blvd 87110 (505) 884-1116 http://www.abqbrewpub.com/

Offering quality brews in small batches to showcase a variety of styles. The food is also made with the same fresh creativity for a great pairing.

New York

East Hudson Valley

The Hudson Valley is a very beautiful part of New York State. It is also home to many breweries. In order to see them all, it is best to break the area down into two parts. The east section will take you about a day or two, depending on how many breweries you plan to visit. Start your trip in Troy with two breweries including a must-visit:

Brown's Brewing Company 50 Factory Hill Road 12090 (518) 273-2337 https://brownsbrewing.com/

Rare Form Brewing Company 90 Congress Street 12180 (518) 326-4303 https://www.rareformbrewing.com/

Approaching classic beer styles with tradition and experimentation. Offering a wide-ranging and rotating beer menu. Twelve minutes south is another brewery at Rensselaer:

Emporium Farm Brewery 472 North Greenbush Road 12144 (518) 326-5391 https://emporiumfarmbrewery.com/

Head east about forty minutes to your next brewery in Cherryplain:

The Beer Diviner 241 Bly Hollow Road 12040 (518) 210-6196 https://www.thebeerdiviner.com/

Head south about a half-hour to Chatham and their brewery:

Chatham Brewing 30 Main Street 12037 (518) 697-0202 http://www.chathambrewing.com/

Continue another half-hour to a must-visit in Hudson:

Hudson Brewing Company 60 S Front Street 12534 (518) 828-0438 https://www.hudsonbrew.com/

Twelve rotating taps have a constantly changing selection of seasonal beers. There is also a selection of New York wines and craft cocktails. Next is a must-visit in Red Hook twenty-five minutes south:

From the Ground Brewery 245 Guski Road 12571 (845) 309-8100
https://fromthegroundbrewery.com/

Offering three year-round styles of beer. Each style is an American version of styles from the Old World. Twenty-minutes brings you to Hyde Park and another must-visit brewery:

Hyde Park Brewing Company 4076 Albany Post Road 12538 (845) 229-8277 https://hydeparkbrewing.com/

Each beer here has its own unique character and flavor profile. Yet they are all fresh, clean, and delicious. Order a flight, so you don't have to choose just one. Poughkeepsie is twelve minutes south and has several options, including two must-visits:

Plan Bee Farm Brewery 115 Underhill Road 12603 (765) 307-8589
https://www.planbeefarmbrewery.com/

King's Court Brewing Company 40 Cannon Street 12601 (917) 697-3030 https://www.kingscourtbrewingcompany.com/homw-page

Blue Collar Brewery Inc. 40 Cottage Street 12601 (845) 454-2739
https://www.thebluecollarbrewery.com/

Brewing true American craft beer using true-to-style recipes. A quality pub menu is available to complement the rotating selection of beer styles.

Zeus Brewing Company 178 Main Street 12601 (845) 320-4560
https://www.zeusbrewingco.com/

Offering a rotating selection of world-class craft beer. You can pair it with food from their full-service restaurant. About a half-hour south is two breweries at Beacon:

Hudson Valley Brewery 7 East Main Street 12508 (845) 218-9156
https://hudsonvalleybrewery.com/

2 Way Brewing Company 18 West Main Street 12508 (845) 202-7334
http://www.2waybrewingcompany.com/

Another half-hour is Peekskill and a must-visit brewery:

River Outpost Brewing 5 John Walsh Blvd 10566 (914) 788-4555
https://riveroutpostbrewing.com/

The newest brewery in Westchester. Featuring a wide range of original beers from IPAs to pilsners and stouts. All are brewed on location. Ossining has the next brewery fifteen minutes away:

Sing Sing Kill Brewery 75-77 Spring Street 10562 (914) 502-0578
https://www.singsingkillbrewery.com/

Another fifteen minutes takes you to the next brewery in Elmsford:

Captain Lawrence Brewing Company 444 Saw Mill River Road 10523 (914) 741-2337 https://www.captainlawrencebrewing.com/

Just seven minutes brings you to a must-visit brewery in White Plains:

Wolf and Warrior Brewing Company 195A East Post Road 10605 (914) 368-8617 https://wolfandwarrior.com/

Making a wide range of beer styles including IPAs, Kolsch-style ales, blonde ales, German lagers, fest biers, stouts, porters, saisons, and hefeweizens. Mamaroneck is thirteen minutes south:

Decadent Ales 607A East Boston Post Road 10530 (800) 598-1085

End your trip about twenty-minutes south in Yonkers at:

Yonkers Brewing Company 92 Main Street 10701 (914) 226-8327
https://www.yonkersbrewing.com/

West Hudson Valley

The other half of the Hudson Valley takes you on a winding trip through beautiful wilderness and towns. The trail doesn't take long to drive, but it will take you a while if you plan to visit all the breweries. Give it at least three days. Start your trip out in Pearl River with two breweries:

The Defiant Brewing Company 6 East Dexter Plaza 10965 (845) 920-8602 http://www.defiantbrewing.com/

Gentle Giant Brewing Company 7 North Main Street 10965 (845) 201-8295 https://www.gentlegiantbrewing.com/

Head north ten minutes to the next brewery at New City:

District 96 Beer Factory 391 South Main Street 10956 (845) 499-2409 http://www.district96beer.com/

Another ten minutes brings you to a must-visit brewery in Garnerville:

Industrial Arts Brewing Company 55 W Railroad Avenue Building 25 W 10923 (845) 942-8776 https://www.industrialartsbrewing.com/

Producing fresh, expressive American beers. The beers find the balance between tradition and innovation. Chester is a half-hour northwest with two breweries including a must-visit:

Rushing Duck Brewing Company 1 Battiato Lane 10918 (845) 610-5440 http://www.rushingduck.com/

Long Lot Farm Brewery 153 Johnson Road 10918 (845) 214-7033 https://www.longlotfarmbrewery.com/

The ten beers on tap here, as well as the specialty beers, come from hops grown right on the farm lot, keeping things local. Just eight minutes away is Florida with another brewery:

Glenmere Brewing Company 55 Maple Avenue 10921 (845) 651-1939 http://glenmerebrewingco.com/welcome

Twelve minutes west is another brewery at Pine Island:

Pine Island Brewing Company 682 County Road 1 Suite B 10969 (845) 288-2646 http://pineislandbeer.com/

Westtown is just nine minutes away:

Westtown Brew Works 236 Schefflers Road 10998 (845) 304-4152
https://www.westtownbrewworks.com/

Fifteen minutes northwest is Port Jervis:

Fox N Hare Brewing Company 46 Front Street 12771 (845) 672-0100
https://www.foxnhare-brewing.com/

About twenty-minutes back east brings you to Middletown with two breweries including a must-visit:

Clemson Brothers Brewery 22 Cottage Street 10940 (845) 775-4638
http://www.clemsonbrewing.com/

Equilibrium Brewery 22 Henry Street 10940 https://www.eqbrew.com/

Offering a combination of drinkability with full flavor. Each beer has unique elements that have been optimized to give a unique flavor profile. Continue east another half-hour to Newburgh:

Newburgh Brewing Company 88 South Colden Street 12550 (845) 569-2337 https://newburghbrewing.com/

Highland is about twenty-minutes north with the next brewery:

Hudson Ale Works 17 Milton Avenue 12528 (845) 384-2531
http://www.hudsonaleworks.com/

Twelve minutes to the west is New Paltz with two breweries including a must-visit:

Foreign Objects Beer Company 25 N Ohioville Road Ste 2 12561
https://www.foreignobjectsbeer.com/

Bacchus and the Brewery at Bacchus 4 South Chestnut Street 12561 (845) 255-8636 https://bacchusnewpaltz.com/

The original craft beer bar in Hudson Valley. Crafting American, English, and Belgian beers. The focus is on wild fermentation and oak aging. Just eight minutes away is Gardiner with another must-visit brewery:

Gardiner Brewing Company 699 NY-208 12525 (845) 255-5300

https://www.gardinerbrewingcompany.com/

Using local ingredients to make excellent, seasonal beers. A true small farm operation, stop in to try their beer today. About twenty-minutes northwest is another brewery at Kerhonkson:

Rough Cut Brewing Company 5945 Rte 44/55 12446 (845) 626-9838

http://www.roughcutbrewing.com/

Circle northwest about an hour to Roscoe:

Roscoe Beer Company 145 Rockland Road 12776 (607) 290-5002

https://roscoebeercompany.com/

Circle back northeast about an hour to West Kill with a must-visit:

West Kill Brewing 2191 Spruceton Road 12492 (518) 989-6462

https://www.westkillbrewing.com/

Offering foraged funky ales, crisp, balanced lagers, and heavily hopped IPAs. The brewery reflects the beauty of the nature around it. Fifteen minutes south is a brewery at Phoenicia:

Woodstock Brewing 5581 State Route 28 12464 (845) 688-0054

https://www.drinkwoodstock.com/

Continue a half-hour southeast to Kingston:

Keegan Ales 20 St. James Street 12401 (845) 331-2739

https://www.keeganales.com/

Saugerties is about twenty-minutes north:

The Dutch Ale House 253 Main Street 12477 (845) 247-2337

https://www.dutchalehouse.com/

About another twenty-minutes north is Catskill:

Subversive Malting and Brewing 44 Main Street 12414 (518) 303-1270
https://drinksubversive.com/

Earlton is about another twenty-minutes north:

Honey Hollow Brewing Company 376 E Honey Hollow Road 12058
(518) 966-5560 http://www.honeyhollowbrewery.com/

Next is East Berne about a half-hour north:

Helderberg Mountain Brewing Company 141 Warners Lake Road
12059 (518) 872-9433
https://www.helderbergmountainbrewingcompany.com/

Altamont is fifteen minutes away:

Indian Ladder Farmstead Cidery and Brewery 342 Altamont Road
12009 (518) 768-7793 https://www.ilfcb.com/

Head east about twenty-minutes to Colonie:

Fidens Brewing Company 10 Walker Way 12205 (518) 418-9072
https://www.fidensbrewing.com/

End your trip thirteen minutes southeast in Albany with two breweries:

C.H. Evans Brewing Company 19 Quackenbush Square 12207 (518)
447-9000 https://www.evansale.com/

Fort Orange Brewing 450 North Pearl Street 12204 (518) 992-3103
https://www.fortorangebrewing.com/

Catskills Region

This short day trip takes you to a wonderfully beautiful region of New York
State. All the breweries on this trip are must-visits. Start your trip out in
Accord at:

Arrowood Farms 236 Lower Whitfield Road 12404 (845) 253-0389
https://arrowoodfarms.com/

A unique brewery focused on cultivating, sourcing, and brewing with local ingredients in New York State. All ingredients are sourced within a 100-mile radius. Head west about an hour to Eldred:

Shrewd Fox Brewery 552 NY State Route 55 12732 (845) 557-8255 http://shrewdfoxbrewery.com/

Brewing craft ales and lager beers. Mentioned in multiple newspapers and articles as one of the top breweries in the area. A half-hour northwest is Callicoon:

Callicoon Brewing Company 15 Upper Main Street 12723 (845) 887-5500 http://callicoonbrewing.com/

Offering local ales, lagers, and ciders. Pair it with a pub-style menu and beautiful nature scenes in a quaint small town. Livingston Manor is a half-hour northeast:

Catskill Brewery 672 Old Route 17 12758 (845) 439-1232 http://catskillbrewery.com/

Making fresh ales and lagers from natural ingredients. Made from ingredients found right within the Catskills Region of New York State. Head north about fifty minutes to Andes:

Weaver Hollow Brewery 294 Depot Street 13731 http://www.weaverhollow.com/

Making slow and naturally fermented ales. They utilize the native mineral profile of well-water along with a house-mixed culture to avoid the use of commercial yeast. End your trip in Margaretville fourteen minutes southeast:

Faith American Brewing Company 344 Ruff Road 12455 https://www.faithamerican.com/

Creating and selling beers of all varieties. Their ale offers a hoppy flavor and character that doesn't overwhelm.

I-86 Corridor

Follow along the I-86 Route to check out these breweries. You'll need at least two or three days if you expect to stop at them all. Start your trip in Port Crane at:

Beer Tree Brew Company 197 Route 369 13833 (607) 204-0712
https://beertreebrew.com/

Ten minutes west is Binghamton with a must-visit brewery:

Galaxy Brewing Company 41 Court Street 13901 (607) 217-4815
https://www.galaxybrewingco.com/

Offering a variety of beers brewed on-site. Plus, they offer the only cask-conditioned ale in the region. Just six minutes away is another brewery at Johnson City:

Binghamton Brewing Company 15 Avenue B 13790 (607) 765-2248
https://www.bingbrew.com/

Endicott is eleven minutes west:

The North Brewery 110 Washington Avenue 13760 (607) 785-0524
https://www.northbrewery.com/

Next is Owego with a must-visit brewery about twenty-minutes west:

The FarmHouse Brewery 14 George Street 13827 (607) 227-0638
https://www.thefarmhousebrewery.com/

Using an artisanal process that uses supplies from the local small farms in the area and through a careful small-batch system. About another twenty-minutes west is Chemung:

Diversion Brewing Company 729 Wyncoop Creek Road 14825 (607) 542-9168 https://www.diversionbrewing.com/

Fourteen minutes northwest is another must-visit brewery at Elmira:

Upstate Brewing Company 3028 Lake Road 14903 (607) 742-2750
https://www.upstatebrewing.com/

An award-winning craft brewery focused on locally brewed beer that appeals to a broad audience. About another twenty-minutes northwest is Corning with three breweries:

Liquid Shoes Brewing 26 East Market Street 14830 (607) 463-9726
https://liquidshoesbrewing.com/

Iron Flamingo Brewery 196 Baker Street 14830 (607) 936-4766
http://www.ironflamingobrewery.com/

Market Street Brewing Company 63-65 West Market Street 14830 (607) 936-2337 http://www.936-beer.com/

Head back northeast about an hour to two breweries at Ithaca:

Ithaca Beer Company 122 Ithaca Beer Drive 14850 (607) 273-0766
https://www.ithacabeer.com/

Liquid State Brewing Company 620 West Green Street 14850
https://www.liquidstatebeer.com/

Freeville is another fifteen minutes northeast with a must-visit brewery:

Hopshire Farm and Brewery 1771 Dryden Road 13068 (607) 279-1243
http://hopshire.com/

Growing hops and brewing beer. Using their own grown hops to brew craft ales in a variety of beer styles. Go back west to Trumansburg about a half-hour away:

Garrett's Brewing Company 1 W Main Street 14886 (607) 209-4011
https://garrettsbrewing.com/

Next is Hector about twenty-minutes west with a few breweries including a must-visit:

Scale House Brewery 5930 State Route 414 14841 (607) 546-2030
http://scalehousebrewpub.com/

Lucky Hare Brewing Company 6085 Beckhorn Road 14841 (610) 613-8424 http://www.luckyharebrewing.com/

Pantomime Mixtures 3839 Ball DIamond Road 14841 (607) 378-9601
https://www.pantomimemixtures.com/

Not just unique in style, but unique in character to their location. Focusing on spontaneously fermented ales. Just nine minutes away is another must-visit brewery at Burdett:

Grist Iron Brewing Company 4880 State Route 414 14818 (607) 882-2739 http://gristironbrewing.com/

Making a unique variety of brews primarily in the traditional American style, but with a unique twist thrown into the mix. Another short five minutes takes you to Watkins Glen with two breweries including a must-visit:

Seneca Lodge Craft Brewing Walnut Road and Route 329 14891 (607) 535-2014 http://senecalodge.com/

Rooster Fish Brewing Company 223-301 N Franklin Street 14891 (607) 535-9797 https://roosterfishpub.com/

Brewing unique, world-class craft ale from locally sourced ingredients. Offering a rotation of five craft-style small-batch beers and up to four special and seasonal brews. Almost a half-hour west is Hammondsport with three breweries including a must-visit:

Finger Lakes Beer Company 8462 State Route 54 14840 (607) 569-3311 https://fingerlakesbeercompany.com/

Keuka Brewing Company 8572 Briglin Road 14840 (607) 868-4648
https://www.keukabrewingcompany.com/Home.html

Steuben Brewing Company 10286 Judson Road 14840 (607) 332-3000
https://steubenbrewingcompany.com/

Brewing ales, lagers, and the occasional mixed fermentation beers. A family-owned and operated brewery focused on supporting small, local farms. Hornell is about forty minutes further west:

Railhead Brewing Company 40 Park Drive 14843
https://www.railheadbrewing.com/

Next is Olean about an hour west:

Four Mile Brewing 202 East Green Street 14760 (716) 373-2337
http://4milebrewing.com/

A half-hour northwest is Ellicottville with two breweries:

Steelbound Brewery and Distillery 6600 US-219 14731 (716) 699-2042
https://www.steelboundevl.com/

Ellicottville Brewing Company 28A Monroe Street 14731 (716) 699-2537 https://ellicottvillebrewing.com/

About another hour west is Lakewood:

Southern Tier Brewing Company 2072 Stoneman Circle 14750 (716) 763-5479 https://stbcbeer.com/

About another forty minutes northwest brings you to a brewery at Ripley:

7 Sins Brewery 10593 W Main Road 14775 (716) 736-2444
https://7sinsbrewery.com/

End your trip just ten minutes away at a must-visit brewery in Westfield:

Five and 20 Spirits and Brewing 8398 West Route 20 14787 (716) 793-9463 https://fiveand20.com/

The beers here range from light and refreshing to bold and complex. The small-batch approach allows them to be varied in the beer lineup they offer.

Finger Lakes Region

This is one of the most beautiful regions in New York State and is a popular brewery destination. There are a lot of breweries in this compact area. You'll need at least several days to visit all the breweries here. Start your trip out at a must-visit brewery in Perry:

Silver Lake Brewing Project 14 Borden Avenue 14530 (585) 969-4238 https://silverlakebrewingproject.com/

Beer with character ranging from rustic farmhouse styles to bold but clean American flavor profiles. And they are always experimenting with new styles. Head northeast a half-hour to the next brewery at Avon:

Rising Storm Brewing Company 5750 S Lima Road 14414 (585) 572-3009 https://www.risingstormbrewing.com/

Fourteen minutes west is Linwood and your next brewery:

Dublin Corners Farm Brewery 1906 Main Street 14486 (585) 538-4796 https://www.dublincornersfarm.com/

Twenty-minutes northwest is Batavia:

Eli Fish Brewing Company 111 Main Street 14020 (585) 815-0401 https://elifishbrewing.com/

Brockport is a half-hour east and north with two breweries including a must-visit:

RG Brewery 1360 West Sweden Road 14420 (585) 637-5575 https://www.rgbrewery.com/

Stoneyard Brewing Company 1 Main Street 14420 (585) 637-3390 https://stoneyardbrewingcompany.com/

Come here to try a different kind of beer. They don't do anything ordinary because they want to give your taste buds something they won't find anywhere else. Fifteen minutes is the waterfront town of Hilton and a must-visit brewery:

Wood Kettle Brewing 1192 Manitou Road 14468 (585) 615-4180
http://www.woodkettlebrewing.com/

No matter what you choose, you'll get a flavorful beer. Whether it is their award-winning Local 20 Intro IPA to the dark, roasted Storm Chaser Stout, you'll find something to enjoy. Head back south ten minutes to two breweries in Spencerport:

Griffs Brewery 5324 W Ridge Road 14559 (585) 617-3843
http://www.griffsbrewery.com/

Brindle Haus Brewing Company 377 South Union Street 14559 (585) 488-2034 https://www.brindlehausbrewing.com/

Fourteen minutes east is the main city of Rochester with many brewery options:

Three Heads Brewing 186 Atlantic Avenue 14607 (585) 797-5445
https://threeheadsbrewing.com/

Genesee Brewing Company 445 St. Paul Street 14605 (585) 263-9446
https://www.geneseebeer.com/

Iron Tug Brewing 360 West Ridge Road 14615 (585) 865-0032
https://www.irontugbrewing.com/

Irondequoit Beer Company 765 Titus Avenue 14617 (585) 544-3670
https://irondequoitbeercompany.com/

Swiftwater Brewing Company 378 Mt. Hope Avenue 14620 (585) 747-8478 http://swiftwaterbrewing.com/

Fifth Frame Brewing Company 155 St. Paul Street 14604 (716) 812-8897 http://fifthframe.co/

K2 Brothers Brewing 1221 Empire Blvd 14609 (585) 413-1997
https://www.k2brewing.com/

Rohrbach Brewing Company 3859 Buffalo Road 14624 (585) 594-9800
https://www.rohrbachs.com/

Roc Brewing Company 56 S Union Street 14618 (585) 734-2567
http://rocbrewingco.com/

Nine Maidens Brewing Company 1344 University Avenue Suite 140
14607 https://ninemaidensbrewing.com/

North and east about twenty-minutes is the waterfront town of Webster:

WhichCraft Brews 1900 Empire Blvd 14580 (585) 222-2739
https://www.whichcraftbrews.com/

South eleven minutes is Fairport with two breweries including a must-visit:

Triphammer Bierwerks 111 Parce Avenue Ste 3a-1 14450
http://www.triphammerbierwerks.com/

Fairport Brewing Company 99 S Main Street 14450 (585) 678-6728
https://www.fairportbrewing.com/

Taking an artisan, handcrafted approach to use the best ingredients for
the highest quality beer. The six rotating beers on tap, as well as others,
have won many awards. Just eight minutes away is two breweries in
Pittsford:

Seven Story Brewing 604 Pittsford Victor Road 14534 (585) 330-5027
https://sevenstorybrewing.com/location

Lock 32 Brewing Company 10 Schoen Place 14534 (585) 506-7738
https://lock32brew.com/

An additional two breweries are twelve minutes southeast in Victor:

Stumblin' Monkey Brewing Company 61 School Street 14564 (585)
398-8189 https://www.stumblinmonkeybeer.com/

Twin Elder Brewery 160 School Street #4 14564 (585) 902-8166
https://twinelderbrewery.com/

Nine minutes away is another brewery in Bloomfield:

The Irish Mafia Brewing Company 2971 Whalen Road 14469 (585) 257-5172 https://www.irishmafiabrewing.com/

Ten minutes east is Canandaigua with three breweries including two must-visits:

Naked Dove Brewing Company 4048 State Route 5 and 20 14424 (585) 396-2537 http://www.nakeddovebrewing.com/

Peacemaker Brewing Company 20 Pleasant Street 14424 (585) 396-3561 https://www.peacemakerbrewing.com/

Offering a great collection of beers on tap, including well-known favorites, seasonal selections, and new creations.

Young Lion Brewing Company 24 Lake Shore Drive 14424 (585) 412-6065 https://younglionbrewing.com/

Women-owned and managed, this brewery is award-winning and focused on the community where they are based. Eleven minutes north is the next brewery in Manchester:

Reinvention Brewing 9 N Main Street 14504 (585) 289-7309
http://www.reinventionbrewing.com/

Twelve minutes southeast is Phelps:

Crafty Ales and Lagers 2 Exchange Street 14532 (315) 332-1606
https://www.drinkcraftyales.com/

About twenty more minutes southeast is Seneca Falls:

Fleur De Lis Brew Works 3630 State Route 414 13148 (315) 665-2337
https://fleurdelisbrewworks.com/

Ovid is twenty-minutes south:

Lost Kingdom Brewery and Firehouse Distillery 7160 Main Street 14521 (607) 474-5002 https://www.firehousedistillery.net/

Just five minutes away is Lodi with a must-visit brewery:

Wagner Valley Brewing Company 9322 Rt. 414 14860 (607) 582-6450 https://wagnerbrewing.com/

One of the oldest craft breweries in the Finger Lakes Region and was the first brewery on Seneca Lake. Currently offering 12 styles of beer ranging from light to dark and bitter to sweet. Head back north around the lake a half-hour to Geneva with multiple breweries including two must-visits:

Glass Factory Brew House 4200 Rte 14 14456 (315) 781-9463 https://whitespringswinery.com/

Lake Drum Brewing 16 E Castle Street 14456 (315) 789-1200 http://lakedrumbrewing.com/

WeBe Brewing Company 796 Pre Emption Road 14456 https://www.webebrewing.com/

Bottomless Brewing 3543 East Lake Road 14456 (315) 325-4380 http://bottomlessbrewing.com/

The most awarded craft brewery in the Finger Lakes region. A farm brewery offering excellent small-batch beers.

War Horse Brewing Company 623 Lerch Road 14456 (315) 585-4432 https://www.warhorsebrewing.com/

From custom ales, lagers, and seasonal beers along with house-made ciders and sodas. You're bound to find something you like here. About twenty-minutes south down the other side of the lake is Penn Yan with three breweries:

Abandon Brewing Company 2994 Merritt Hill Road 14527 (585) 209-3276 https://abandonbrewing.com/

LyonSmith Brewing Company 138 Water Street 14527 (315) 536-5603 https://lyonsmithbrewing.com/

Climbing Bines Hop Farm 511 Hansen Point 14527 (607) 745-0221 https://www.climbingbineshopfarm.com/

End your trip about another twenty-minutes south at the must-visit brewery in Rock Stream:

Seneca Lake Brewing Company 4520 State Route 14 14878 (607) 216-8369 https://www.senecalakebrewing.com/

A traditional cask ale brewery located on the edge of Seneca Lake. Enjoy unique beers along with British pub-style food and beautiful views.

Great Lake Region

This short day trip takes you to some excellent breweries in the Great Lakes area. However, if you want to see all the breweries, you may need a second day. Start your trip in Wilson at:

Woodcock Brothers Brewing Company 638 Lake Street 14172 (716) 333-4000 http://woodcockbrothersbrewery.com/

Head twenty-minutes east along the waterfront to the next brewery at Barker:

In the Mix Brewery and Creamery 1693 East Avenue 14012 (716) 795-5009 https://www.inthemixbrewing.com/

Head south thirteen minutes to Gasport and your next brewery:

Becker Brewing Company 3760 Quaker Road 14067 (716) 772-2211 https://www.beckerfarms.com/

Lockport is ten minutes west:

New York Beer Project 6933 South Transit Road 14094 (716) 743-6927
http://www.nybeerproject.com/

About a half-hour west is Lewiston on the border:

Brickyard Brewing Company 436 Center Street 14092 (716) 754-7227
http://brickyardbrewingcompany.com/

Head south along the border to the main city of Buffalo a half-hour away:

Riverworks Brewing 359 Ganson Street 14203 (716) 342-2292
https://buffaloriverworks.com/brewery/

Resurgence Brewing Company 1250 Niagara Street 14213 (716) 381-9868 https://resurgencebrewing.com/

Big Ditch Brewing Company 55 E Huron Street 14203 (716) 854-5050
http://www.bigditchbrewing.com/

Pearl Street Grill and Brewery 72-76 Pearl Street 14202 (716) 856-2337
https://pearlstreetgrill.com/

Community Beer Works 15 Lafayette Avenue 14213 (716) 759-4677
https://www.communitybeerworks.com/

Thin Man Brewery 492 Elmwood Avenue 14222 (716) 923-4100
https://thinmanbrewery.com/

Lafayette Brewing Company 391 Washington Street 14203 (716) 856-0062 https://lafbrewco.com/

Froth Brewing Company 700 Military Road 14216 (716) 783-8060
https://www.frothbrewing.com/

Flying Bison Brewing Company 840 Seneca Street 14210 (716) 873-1557 http://www.flyingbisonbrewing.com/

Old First Ward Brewing 73 Hamburg Street 14204 (716) 855-8948
https://www.genemccarthys.com/

Pouring the freshest beers in Buffalo. In addition to the regular beers on tap, they are constantly experimenting with new styles and flavors. Continue south to Hamburg about twenty-minutes away:

Hamburg Brewing Company 6553 Boston State Road 14075 (716) 649-3249 https://www.hamburgbrewing.com/

Head east about a half-hour to East Aurora with a must-visit brewery:

42 North Brewing Company 25 Pine Street 14052 (716) 805-7500 https://www.42northbrewing.com/

Offering a variety of delicious signature, seasonal, and limited release brews to appeal to everyone. This includes citrusy hops, spicy seasonal drinks, and dark chocolate malts. Circle northwest fourteen minutes to West Seneca and a must-visit brewery:

Rusty Nickel Brewing Company 4350 Seneca Street 14120 (585) 305-5199 http://rustynickelbrewing.com/

As a farm brewery, they produce fresh and local beer. The list of available beers changes based on season and availability of local crops. Williamsville is fourteen minutes north with two must-visit breweries:

Buffalo Brewpub 6861 Main Street 14221 (716) 632-0552 https://www.buffalobrewpub.com/Home

The original brewpub of New York State. With plenty of beers to choose from, you'll want a flight in order to try a few.

12 Gates Brewing Company 80 Earhart Drive 14221 (716) 906-6600 https://12gatesbrewing.com/

The flagship beer is the well-known West Coast Style IPA, but they offer a range of styles from pilsners to double stouts. End your trip thirteen minutes east in Clarence at:

West Shore Brewing Company 10995 Main Street 14031 http://www.westshorebrewing.com/

Central New York

This shorter trip will take you a day or two, depending on how many breweries you choose to visit. Start your trip in Cortland at:

Cortland Beer Company 16 Court Street 13045 (607) 662-4389
https://www.cortlandbeer.com/

Then head north about twenty-minutes to Tully and a must-visit brewery:

ONCO Fermentations 397 NY-281 13159 (315) 652-9304
http://www.oncoferment.com/

Brewing classic, wild and mixed fermentation beers. Stop in at their open tasting room and sample some wonderful beers. About a half-hour west is another brewery at Skaneateles:

Skaneateles Brewery 4022 Mill Road 13152 (315) 975-1747
https://www.skanbrewery.com/

Another eleven minutes west is Auburn:

Prison City Pub and Brewery 28 State Street 13021 (315) 604-1277
https://www.prisoncitybrewing.com/

Weedsport has a must-visit brewery and is eleven minutes north:

Lunkenheimer Craft Brewing Company 8920 N Seneca Street 13166 (315) 834-7027 http://lunkenheimercraftbrewing.com/

A small-batch, handcrafted brewery that is constantly experimenting with offering you a variety of creative and unusual ales. Head east to Baldwinsville about twenty-minutes:

WT Brews 3 West Genesee Street 13027 (315) 430-2390
http://wtbrews.com/index.html

Another eleven minutes brings you to Clay:

Freight Yard Brewing 4975 State Route 31 13041 (315) 834-2529
http://www.freightyardbrewing.com/

Head east and then south about twenty-minutes to the main city of Syracuse with several options:

Willow Rock Brewing Company 115 Game Road 13210 (315) 928-6948
http://willowrockbrew.com/

Stout Beard Brewing 1153 W Fayette Street Ste 102 13204 (315) 399-3016 https://www.stoutbeardbrewery.com/

Talking Cursive Brewing Company 301 Erie Blvd W 13204 (315) 907-6060 https://talkingcursive.com/

IBU Brewery 3703 Brewerton Road 13212 (315) 289-3440
https://www.beermeibu.com/

Syracuse Suds Factory 320 S Clinton Street 13202 (315) 471-AALE
http://s502965190.onlinehome.us/

The first brewery in Syracuse. Give all four of their brews a try: Black Cherry Weizen, Pale Ale, Honey Light Ale, and Sweet Stout.

Middle Ages Brewing Company 120 Wilkinson Street 13204 (315) 476-4250 https://www.middleagesbrewing.com/

Producing modern American and classic British ales since 1995. This makes them the oldest brewery in Syracuse.

Buried Acorn Brewing Company 881 Van Rensselaer 13204 (315) 552-1499 https://www.buriedacorn.com/

Specializing in barrel-aged sour and farmhouse beer. The technique is a mixed-fermentation Wild Ale process.

Red Hawk Brewing 4504 Bussey Road 13215 (315) 491-5158
http://www.redhawkbrewing.com/

Making old world and Belgian style ales made with the finest quality ingredients. The beers here will please the most discerning palate. Twenty-minutes south and then east is another must-visit brewery at Pompey:

Heritage Hill Brewhouse and Kitchen 3149 Sweet Road 13138 (315) 766-7885 https://heritagehillbrewery.com/

Try a wide range of true-to-style beers, including lagers, wheat beers, amber ales, IPAs, Belgian ales, stouts, and barrel-aged beer. Cazenovia is eleven minutes east:

Critz Farms Brewing and Cider Company 3232 Rippleton Road 13035 (315) 662-3355 http://www.critzfarms.com/

Head about twenty-minutes north and then east to Canastota:

Erie Canal Brewing Company 135 James Street 13032 (315) 510-5001 https://eriecanalbrewingcompany.com/

End your trip with a half-hour drive south to Hamilton and a must-visit brewery:

Good Nature Farm Brewery and Tap Room 1727 State Route 12B 13346 (315) 824-2337 http://www.goodnaturebrewing.com/

Making all-natural, unfiltered ales. Everything is farm-to-glass, so you get the most natural form of beer.

North Country New York

In the upper part of the state, there are some great breweries in the beautiful wilderness. Take a day or two for this trip, depending on how many breweries you plan to visit. Start your trip out in Plattsburg with two breweries:

Plattsburgh Brewing Company 411 Route 3 12901 (518) 324-6680 http://www.plattsburghbrewingco.com/

Oval Craft Brewing 111 Ohio Avenue 12903 (518) 324-2739
https://www.ovalcraftbrewing.com/

Head south to Peru fifteen minutes away:

Livingoods Restaurant and Brewery 697 Bear Swamp Road 12972
(518) 643-2020 https://www.livingoodsrestaurant.com/

Just seven minutes away is Keeseville:

Ausable Brewing Company 765 Mace Chasm Road 12944 (518) 900-2739 https://ausablebrewing.tumblr.com/

Take about a half-hour drive south to your next brewery at Westport:

Ledge Hill Brewing Company 6700 Main Street 12993 (518) 837-7637
https://www.ledgehillbrewing.com/

Lake Placid is about forty minutes northwest and has two must-visit breweries:

Big Slide Brewery and Public House 5686 Cascade Road 12946 (518) 523-7844 https://www.bigslidebrewery.com/

Offering ten interesting and world-class beers on tap at a time. From light ales to dark stouts and everything in between, you'll find something you won't find at other breweries.

Great Adirondack Brewing Company 34 Main Street 12946 (518) 523-1629 https://adirondackbrewing.com/

Producing a wide range of ales and lagers, including their well-known Whiteface Stout and John Brown Ale. Just nine minutes away is another brewery at Ray Brook:

Ray Brook Brewhouse 1153 NY-86 12977 (518) 354-8044
https://www.raybrookbrewhouse.com/

The next brewery is just five minutes away at Saranac Lake:

Blue Line Brewery 555 Lake Flower Avenue 12983 (518) 354-8114
http://bluelinebrew.com/

Another nine minutes is Bloomingdale:

Hex and Hop 1719 State Route 3 12913 (518) 323-6116
https://hexandhop.com/

Dickinson Center is about fifty minutes northwest and has a must-visit
brewery:

Township 7 Brewing Company 303 State Rt 11B 12930 (518) 651-9532
http://www.township7brewing.com/

Brewing premium, unfiltered and unpasteurized craft beers. Non-alcoholic
drink options are available as well. Another almost fifty-minute drive brings
you to Chase Mills near the border:

In-Law Brewing Company 5868 County Route 14 13621 (315) 250-3601
https://www.in-lawbrewingcompany.com/

Take about an hour and a half drive southwest to two breweries in
Watertown:

Skewed Brewing 21182 Salmon Run Mall Loop W 13601 (315) 788-2337
https://www.skewedbrewing.com/

Boots Brewing Company 89 Public Square 13601 (914) 906-9057
https://www.bootsbrew.com/

The next brewery in Tupper Lake is almost two hours northeast:

Raquette River Brewing 11 Balsam Street #2 12986 (518) 420-8461
http://www.raquetteriverbrewing.com/

End your trip with about an hour and a half drive southeast to a brewery at
Lake George:

Adirondack Pub and Brewery 33 Canada Street 12845 (518) 668-0002
https://adkbrewery.com/pub/

Mohawk River Valley

This short day trip is a great place to enjoy the wilderness and great beers. Start your trip in Cooperstown with two breweries:

Council Rock Brewery 4861 State Highway 28 13326 (607) 643-3016
https://www.councilrockbrewery.com/

Red Shed Brewery 709 County Highway 33 13326 (607) 282-4380
https://www.redshedbrewing.com/cooperstown-taproom/

Head west about twenty-minutes to a must-visit brewery in Garrattsville:

Butternuts Beer and Ale 4021 State Highway 51 13342 (607) 263-5070
https://butternutsbeerandale.com/

Using a brick-clad and copper-topped kettle, this brewery combines old-world brewing with modern processes in order to give you a beer distinctly unique. Circle south about a half-hour to Oneonta and another must-visit brewery:

Roots Brewing Company 175 Main Street 13820 (607) 433-2925
http://www.rootsbeeroneonta.com/

Offering a rotating selection of handcrafted ales made on-site. The beers are well-balanced and reflect traditional brewing methods. Head northeast about fifty minutes to Middleburg and another must-visit brewery:

Green Wolf Brewing Company 315 Main Street 12122 (518) 872-2503
https://www.greenwolfales.com/

Brewing a variety of styles: robust porters and stouts, pale ales and IPAs, Belgian inspired ales, and 18th-century style wheat beers. Then head northwest about an hour to another must-visit brewery in Utica:

Nail Creek Pub and Brewery 720 Varick Street 13502 (315) 793-7593
https://nailcreekpub.com/

Offering the largest selection of craft beer in Mohawk Valley. Come try various flavors and styles of beer. Another twenty-minutes northwest is Rome and a must-visit brewery:

Copper City Brewing Company 1111 Oneida Street 13440 (315) 225-9958 https://coppercitybrewing.com/

Enjoy a laid back atmosphere while tasting from their 11 beers on taps. You can also choose from ciders and wines. End with an hour drive northeast to Old Forge:

Fulton Chain Craft Brewery 127 North Street 13420 (315) 525-0222 https://www.fccbrewery.com/

Eastern New York

This short day trip is a great way to get out of the city for a little bit. Start your trip in Queensbury at a must-visit brewery:

Northway Brewing Company 1043 US Rt 9 12804 (518) 223-0372 https://northwaybrewingco.com/

Offering three core beers: Perfect Day Pilsner, Sunrise Session IPA, and Avenue of the Pine. In addition, there are always experimental options like the Mango Milkshake. Head south ten minutes to Glens Falls with two breweries:

Cooper's Cave Ale Company 2 Sagamore Street 12801 (518) 792-0007 https://www.cooperscaveale.com/Home

Davidson Brothers Restaurant and Brewery 184 Glen Street 12801 (518) 743-9026 http://www.davidsonbrothers.com/

Just a minute away is another brewery at South Glens Falls:

Common Roots Brewing Company 58 Saratoga Avenue 12803 (518) 409-8248 http://www.commonrootsbrewing.com/

Another half-hour south is Greenwich:

Argyle Brewing Company One Main Street 12834 (518) 692-2585
https://argylebrewing.com/

Saratoga Springs is about twenty-minutes west and has three breweries:

Druthers Brewing Company 381 Broadway 12866 (518) 306-5275
http://www.druthersbrewing.com/

Racing City Brewing Company 250 Excelsior Avenue 12866 (518) 886-1271 http://racingcitybrewing.com/

Artisanal Brew Works 41 Geyser Road 12866 (518) 260-0361
https://artisanalbrewworks.com/

About a half-hour southwest is Glenville with a must-visit brewery:

Wolf Hollow Brewing Company 2305 West Glenville Road 12010 (518) 214-4093 https://www.wolfhollowbrewing.com/

Creating local craft beer with a focus on quality and freshness. Taste their beers in a relaxing and fun environment. End your trip about a half-hour south in Schenectady with two breweries:

Great Flats 151 Lafayette Street 12305 (518) 280-0232
https://www.greatflatsbrewing.com/

Frog Alley Brewing Company 108 State Street 12305 (518) 505-2080
https://www.frogalleybrewing.com/

New York City

Within the state of New York is one of the biggest cities with five boroughs. There are plenty of breweries to visit when you're staying in the city. Consider the following:

Gun Hill Brewing Company 3227 Laconia Avenue 10469 (718) 881-0010 https://www.gunhillbrewing.com/

The Bronx Brewery 856 East 136th Street 10454 (718) 402-1000
https://thebronxbrewery.com/

Interboro Spirits and Ales 942 Grand Street 11211 (877) 843-6545
http://interboro.nyc/

Kings County Brewers Collective 381 Troutman Street 11237
https://www.kcbcbeer.com/

Lineup Brewing 33 35th Street #6A 11232
http://www.lineupbrewing.com/

War Flag Ales and Lagers 649 Morgan Avenue 11222
http://www.warflag.nyc/

Brooklyn Brewery 79 North 11th Street 11211 (718) 486-7422
https://brooklynbrewery.com/

Greenpoint Beer and Ale Company 1150 Manhattan Avenue 11222
(347) 725-3061 https://www.greenpointbeer.com/

Circa Brewing Company 141 Lawrence Street 11201 (718) 858-0055
https://www.circabrewing.co/

Threes Brewing 333 Douglass Street 11217 (718) 522-2110
https://threesbrewing.com/

18th Ward Brewing 300 Richardson Street 11222 (718) 387-4025
https://www.18thwardbrewing.com/

Island to Island Brewery 642 Rogers Avenue 11226 (347) 974-1985
http://islandtoislandbrewery.com/

Sixpoint Brewery 40 Van Dyke Street 11231 (718) 346-8050
https://sixpoint.com/

Five Boroughs Brewing Company 215 47th Street 11220 (718) 355-
8575 https://www.fiveboroughs.com/

Strong Rope Brewery 574A President Street 11215 (929) 337-8699
http://strongropebrewery.com/

Randolph Beer DUMBO 82 Prospect Street 11221 (646) 383-3623
https://www.randolphbeer.com/

Other Half Brewing Company 195 Centre Street 11231 (347) 987-3527
https://otherhalfbrewing.com/

Coney Island Brewing Company 1904 Surf Avenue 11224 (800) 482-9197 https://coneyislandbeer.com/

Keg and Lantern Brewing Company 97 Nassau Avenue 11222 (718) 389-5050 https://www.kegandlanternbrooklyn.com/

Braven Brewing Company 52 Harrison Place 11237 (929) 295-6673
https://www.bravenbrewing.com/

Transmitter Brewing 141 Flushing Avenue Building 77 11205 (646) 378-8529 https://www.transmitterbrewing.com/

Brewing beer with a focus on traditional and farmhouse ales. They maintain a brewhouse library that includes Belgian, French, English, and American yeast.

Grimm Artisanal Ales 990 Metropolitan Avenue 11211 (718) 564-9767
https://grimmales.com/

Specializing in concise and elegant ales that epitomize the creative and experimental spirit of craft beer making. Each limited edition release pushes the boundaries of flavor and style.

Wild East Brewing Company 623 Sackett Street 11217 (718) 797-5135
https://www.wildeastbrewing.com/

Mixing classic European brewing techniques with modern American craft beer innovations to offer you farmhouse style ales and mixed fermentation ales. Focusing on unfiltered hazy IPAs, pilsners, barrel-aged sours, and other wild creations.

Radiant Pig Craft Beers 122 West 27th Street Suite 1022 10001
https://www.radiantpigbeers.com/

Torch and Crown Brewing Company 12 Vandam Street 10013 (201)
452-4196 https://www.torchandcrown.com/

Harlem Blue Beer 2214 Frederick Douglass Blvd 10026 (646) 284-1010
https://www.harlemblue.com/

Ruckus Brewing 253 West 35th Street 6th Floor 10001 (646) 710-5098
http://www.ruckusbrewing.com/

Alphabet City Brewing Company 7th Street and Avenue A 10009 (646)
331- 4183 https://acbcnyc.com/

Offering two year-round beers: an IPA and a blonde ale. There are also a
series of limited releases throughout the year.

Bridge and Tunnel Brewery 15-35 Decatur Street 11385 (347) 392-8593
https://bridgeandtunnelbrewery.square.site/

Iconyc Brewing Company 37-18 Northern Blvd 11101 (347) 342-1360
http://www.iconycbrewing.com/

Evil Twin Brewing 1616 George Street 11385 (718) 366-1850
https://eviltwin.nyc/

Finback Brewery 78-01 77th Avenue 11385 (718) 628-8600
http://www.finbackbrewery.com/

Making great beer with a focus on flavor and complexity. Using quality
ingredients in small-batch brewing. Try their fun and unique beers today.

Kills Boro Brewing Company 62 Van Duzer Street 10301 (347) 277-
8680 https://shop.killsboro.com/

The Flagship Brewing Company 40 Minthorne Street 10301 (718) 448-
5284 http://www.flagshipbrewery.nyc/age_verification.php

Long Island

For a smaller area, Long Island is home to some wonderful breweries. Plus, you get to enjoy them while enjoying scenic water views.

Small Craft Brewing Company 66 Merrick Road 11701 (631) 464-0186 https://www.smallcraftbrewing.com/

Destination Unknown Beer Company 1 South Chicago Avenue 11706 (631) 485-2232 https://www.destinationunknownbeercompany.com/

The Brewers Collective 1460 North Clinton Avenue 11706 (631) 665-9000 https://thebrewerscollective.com/

Hopwins Brewery 1460 N Clinton Avenue Unit L 11706 (631) 708-5639 https://hopwinsbrewery.wixsite.com/hopwins

Great South Bay Brewery 25 Drexel Drive 11706 (631) 392-8472 https://www.greatsouthbaybrewery.com/

Ghost Brewing Company 25 Drexel Avenue 11706 (631) 357-3819 https://www.ghostbrewco.com/

Combining flavor profiles not typically found at a local brewery. Come taste the difference today.

Old Tappan Brew Company 37 Ludlam Avenue 11709 (516) 802-0174 https://www.oldtappanbrewingcompany.com/

The Blind Bat Brewery 420 Harrison Drive 11721 (631) 891-7909 https://www.blindbatbrewery.com/

Lithology Brewing Company 211A Main Street 11735 (516) 962-0585 https://www.lithologybrewing.com/#/

A farm brewery using mostly local New York grown ingredients. Try their award-winning Red Ale and Brown Ale.

Garvies Point Craft Brewery 1 Garvies Point Road 11542 (516) 815-1999 https://garviespointbrewing.com/

1940's Brewing Company 1337 Lincoln Avenue Unit #1 11741 (631) 533-4838 https://www.1940sbrewingcompany.com/

Spider Bite Beer Company 920 Lincoln Avenue Unit #5 11741 (631) 942-3255 https://www.spiderbitebeer.com/

SquareHead Brewing Company 405 High Street 11741 (631) 921-3060 http://squareheadbrewing.com/

Six Harbors Brewing Company 243 New York Avenue 11743 (631) 470-1560 https://sixharborsbrewingcompany.com/

Offering ten plus beers on tap at a time. While some never leave the taproom, they are known for their variety, so it is possible you'll find more than one you enjoy.

Montauk Brewing Company 62 South Erie Avenue 11954 (631) 668-8471 https://montaukbrewingco.com/

Sand City Brewing Company 60 Main Street 11768 (631) 651-2766 http://www.sandcitybeer.com/

Harbor Head Brewing Company 81 Fort Salonga Road 11768 (631) 815-5588 https://www.harborheadbrew.com/

Producing beers in small batches, so the flavors are constantly changing and always giving your palate something different to try.

Barrier Brewing Company 3002 New Street #2 11572 (516) 316-4429 http://barrierbrewing.com/

South Shore Craft Brewery 3505 Hampton Road 11572 (516) 388-6685 https://www.southshorecraftbrewery.com/

Choose from a wide array of traditional beer styles complemented by some unique one-barrel batches. They also produce their own cider.

Oyster Bay Brewing Company 76 South Street 11771 (518) 802-5546 https://oysterbaybrewing.com/

BrickHouse Brewery 6771 West Main Street 11172 (631) 447-2337 http://www.brickhousebrewery.com/

Blue Point Brewing Company 161 River Avenue 11772 (631) 475-6944 https://www.bluepointbrewing.com/

Port Jeff Brewing Company 22 Mill Creek Road 11777 (877) 475-2739 https://www.portjeffbrewing.com/

Po'Boy Brewery 200 Wilson Street Building E3 11776 (631) 828-1131 http://www.poboybrewery.com/

Producing high quality traditional and nontraditional beer styles. Come appreciate the taste of fine artisanal beers.

Long Ireland Beer Company 817 Pulaski Street 11901 (631) 403-4303 https://longirelandbeer.com/

Moustache Brewing Company 400 Hallett Avenue Suite A 11901 (631) 591-3250 http://www.moustachebrewing.com/

Jamesport Farm Brewery 5873 Sound Avenue 11901 (844) 532-2337 https://www.jfbrewery.com/

A pet and family-friendly brewery located on a small farm in Long Island. Enjoy artisan beer while feeling like family.

Shelter Island Craft Brewery 55 North Ferry Road 11964 (631) 749-5977 https://shelterislandcraftbrewery.com/

Specializing in small batches made with local ingredients. Their staple selection of beers is supplemented with an ever-changing selection of seasonal beers.

Southampton Publick House 62 Jobs Lane 11968 (631) 283-2800 https://www.publick.com/

Raleigh Area

Within this small area, there are a lot of great breweries. Most are focused within the main city of Raleigh, but the surrounding area has a number of must-visit breweries as well. Take a single day or more, depending on how many breweries you want to include. Start in Smithfield at a must-visit brewery:

Double Barley Brewing 3174 US Highway 70W 27577 (919) 934-3433 https://doublebarleybrewing.com/

Crafting beer from the finest ingredients. The focus is on big, bold beers. A lot of grains go into their beers. Seventeen minutes north is another brewery at Clayton:

Deep River Brewing Company 700 W Main Street 27520 (919) 368-3424 https://deepriverbrewing.com/

Next is Knightdale twenty-minutes north with a must-visit brewery:

Oak City Brewing Company 616 N First Avenue 27545 (919) 373-8487 https://www.oakcitybrewingcompany.com/

Offering a rotating tap selection of 20 with plenty of options to choose from. They always have everything from a cider to sours on tap and at least three to four of each style and ABV. Fifteen minutes west is the main city of Raleigh:

Funguys Brewing 2408 Paula Street 27608 https://funguysbrewing.com/

Mordecai Beverage Company 2425 Crabtree Blvd 27604 (919) 831-9125 https://mordecaibev.co/

Tobacco Road Sports Cafe - Raleigh Brewery 505 W Jones Street 27603 (919) 301-8793 http://www.tobaccoroadsportscafe.com/

Compass Rose Brewery 3201 Northside Drive Suite 101 27615 (919) 875-5683 https://www.compassrosebrewery.com/

Raleigh Brewing Company 3709 Neil Street 27607 (919) 400-9086 http://raleighbrewingcompany.com/

Clouds Brewing 126 N West Street 27603 (919) 307-8335 https://www.cloudsbrewing.com/

Lonerider Brewing Company 8816 Gulf Court Suite 100 27617 (919) 423-5203 https://loneriderbeer.com/

Brewery Bhavana 218 S Blount Street 27601 (919) 829-9998 https://brewerybhavana.com/

Gizmo Brew Works 5907 Triangle Drive 27617 (919) 782-2099 https://gizmobrewworks.com/

Trophy Brewing 827 West Morgan Street 27601 (919) 803-4849 https://www.trophybrewing.com/

Little City Brewing + Provisions Company 400 West North Street 27603 (919) 502-7155 https://thelocalicon.com/little-city/

Crank Arm Brewing 319 W Davie Street 27601 (919) 291-0643
https://www.crankarmbrewing.com/#/

Big Boss Brewing 1249 Wicker Drive 27604 (919) 834-0045
http://www.bigbossbrewing.com/

Nickelpoint Brewing Company 506 Pershing Road 27608 (919) 916-5961 https://www.nickelpointbrewing.com/

Dedicated to craft and quality with a reverence for the historical beer styles. Come try their inventive beers and find a new favorite.

Neuse River Brewing Company 518 Pershing Road 27608 (984) 232-8479 https://www.neuseriverbrewing.com/

Focusing on Belgian ales and IPAs while also experimenting with contemporary and experimental styles. Offering a wide selection, so there is something for everyone. When you're ready the next must-visit brewery is about twenty-minutes north in Wake Forest:

White Street Brewing Company 218 South White Street 27587 (919) 647-9439 https://www.whitestreetbrewing.com/

Producing high-quality, well-balanced ales and lagers. From the classic styles down to the taproom details, here you'll be stepping back in time to an era that focused on craftsmanship. The next largest city is Durham about a half-hour west:

Bull City Burger and Brewery 107 East Parrish Street 27701 (919) 680-2333 https://www.bullcityburgerandbrewery.com/

The Glass Jug Beer Lab 5410 NC Highway 55 Suite AF 27713 (919) 813-0135 https://www.glass-jug.com/the-beer-lab/

Ponysaurus Brewing Company 219 Hood Street 27701 (978) 482-7701
https://www.ponysaurusbrewing.com/

Bull Durham Beer Company 409 Blackwell Street 27701 (877) 417-4551
https://www.bulldurhambeer.com/

Durty Bull Brewing Company 206 Broadway Street Suite 104 27701 (919) 688-2337 http://www.durtybull.com/

Using old-world brewing techniques along with passion and creativity to create barrel-aged and sour beers along with a full line of unconventional beers.

Fullsteam Brewery 726 Rigsbee Avenue 27701 (919) 682-2337 https://www.fullsteam.ag/

Specializing in true-to-style classics, hazy IPAs, fruited kettle sours, mixed-culture foraged beer, and other limited releases. Head south about twenty-minutes to Cary with three breweries including a must-visit:

Jordan Lake Brewing Company 320 East Durham Road 27513 (919) 694-5096 http://jordanlakebrewing.com/#

Bond Brothers Beer Company 202 E Cedar Street 27511 (919) 459-2670 https://www.bondbrothersbeer.com/

Fortnight Brewing Company 1006 SW Maynard Road 27511 (919) 342-6604 https://www.fortnightbrewing.com/

Using traditional methods to create old school core styles along with modern methods to offer a full range of new styles and flavors. Continue south another twelve minutes to a must-visit brewery in Apex:

Southern Peak Brewery 950 Windy Road 27502 (919) 623-0827 http://www.southernpeakbrewery.com/

Brueprint Brewing Company 1229 Perry Road Suite 101 27502 (919) 387-8075 http://www.brueprint.com/

The first craft brewery in Apex. The taproom features fourteen unique brews with wonderful food options. A family and pet friendly environment. Another eight minutes away is two breweries in Holly Springs:

Carolina Brewing Company 140 Thomas Mill Road 27540 (919) 557-2337 https://www.carolinabrew.com/

Bombshell Beer Company 120 Quantum Drive 27540 (919) 823-1933 https://www.bombshellbeer.com/

Fuquay-Varina is ten minutes away and has a few options including a must-visit:

Aviator Brewing Company 209 Technology Park Lane 27526 (919) 567-2337 https://www.aviatorbrew.com/

Oaklyn Springs Brewery 2912 N Main Street #100 27526 (919) 762-0049 https://www.oaklynsprings.com/

Mason Jar Lager Company 341 Broad Street 27526 (919) 557-5303 https://masonjarlagerco.com/

Fainting Goat Brewing Company 330 S Main Street 27526 (919) 346-7915 http://www.faintinggoatbeer.com/

A small woman and veteran-owned brewery offering high-quality handcrafted beer in small batches. Look for limited release beers as well as flagship and seasonal offerings. Fourteen minutes south is Angier with a must-visit brewery:

Vicious Fishes Brewery 219 Fish Drive 27501 (919) 639-3369 https://www.viciousfishes.com/

Focused on juicy, balanced IPAs, fruited sours, and clean German lagers. Come try their full range of interesting and delicious beers. End your trip about forty minutes away in Sanford with two breweries including a must-visit:

Hugger Mugger Brewing Company 229 Wicker Street 27330 https://www.huggermuggerbrewing.com/

Camelback Brewing Company 804 Spring Lane 27330 (919) 292-2244 https://camelbackbrewingco.com/

Always crafting something new and different. Brewing the most flavorful combinations of specialty grains and unique hop varieties.

Asheville Area

Another main brewery area in North Carolina is around the Asheville area. Aside from the main city, there are plenty of outlying breweries to choose from. Depending on how many breweries you visit, you can complete this trip in one to two days. Start your trip out in Waynesville with two brewery options:

Boojum Brewing Company 50 North Main Street 28786 (828) 246-0350 https://www.boojumbrewing.com/

Frog Level Brewing Company 56 Commerce Street 28786 (828) 454-5664 https://www.froglevelbrewing.com/

Head east about twenty-minutes to another brewery at Canton:

BearWaters Brewing Company 101 Park Street 28716 (828) 237-4200 https://www.bearwatersbrewing.com/

Continue east about twenty-minutes to the main city of Asheville:

Bhramari Brewing Company 101 South Lexington Avenue 28801 (828) 214-7981 https://www.bhramaribrewing.com/

One World Brewing 10 Patton Avenue 28801 (508) 982-3757 https://oneworldbrewing.com/

Burial Beer Company 40 Collier Avenue 28801 (828) 475-2739 https://burialbeer.com/

Hi-Wire Brewing 197 Hilliard Avenue 28801 (828) 738-2448 https://hiwirebrewing.com/

Wicked Weed Brewing 91 Biltmore Street 28801 (828) 575-2890 https://www.wickedweedbrewing.com/

Collaboratory 39 N Lexington Avenue 28801 (828) 348-1622 https://www.collaboratoryavl.com/

Wedge Brewing Company 125 B Roberts Street 28801 (828) 505-2792
https://www.wedgebrewing.com/

Sweeten Creek Brewing 1127 Sweeten Creek Road 28803 (828) 575-2785 https://sweetencreekbrewing.com/

Twin Leaf Brewery 144 Coxe Avenue 28801 (828) 774-5000
http://www.twinleafbrewery.com/

Archetype Brewing 265 Haywood Road 28806 (828) 505-4177
https://archetypebrewing.com/

Ginger's Revenge 829 Riverside Drive 28801 (828) 505-2462
http://www.gingersrevenge.com/

Asheville Brewing Company 675 Merrimon Avenue 28804 (828) 254-1281 https://www.ashevillebrewing.com/

DSSOLVR 63 N Lexington Avenue 28801 https://dssolvr.com/

UpCountry Brewing Company 1042 Haywood Road 28806 (828) 575-2400 https://www.upcountrybrewing.com/

OysterHouse Brewing Company 35 Patton Avenue 28801 (828) 350-0505 https://oysterhousebeers.com/

Highland Brewing 12 Old Charlotte Highway Suite 200 28803 (828) 299-3370 https://highlandbrewing.com/

Hillman Beer 25 Sweeten Creek Road 28803 (828) 505-1312
https://www.hillmanbeer.com/

Serving eighteen beers made in-house. Offering a blend of classic styles ranging from Belgians to English to American styles.

Eurisko Beer Company 255 Short Coxe Avenue 28801 (828) 774-5055
https://euriskobeer.com/

They try to cover as many bases as possible with their offerings. Enjoy West Coast IPAs, dry Belgian Saisons, and traditional German styles.

All Sevens Brewing 777 Haywood Road 28806 (828) 225-9782
http://allsevensavl.com/

Ale-forward focus with a variety of flagship beer styles and plenty of seasonal and limited release beers. The smallest brewery in Asheville ensures you get the freshest beers. Just six minutes away is another brewery in Woodfin:

Zillicoah Beer Company 870 Riverside Drive 28804 (828) 484-6502
https://www.zillicoahbeer.com/

Another seven minutes away is Weaverville with three breweries including a must-visit:

Eluvium Brewing Company 11 Florida Avenue 28787 (828) 484-1799
http://eluviumbrewing.com/

Blue Mountain Pizza and Brew Pub 55 N Main Street 28787 (828) 658-8777 https://www.bluemountainpizza.com/

Zebulon Artisan Ales 8 Merchants Alley 28787
http://www.zebulonbrewing.com/

Focusing on Belgian and French farmhouse ale styles. You can also try a historical, forgotten, and mythological beer style when you visit here. About a half-hour away is Burnsville with a must-visit brewery:

Homeplace Beer Company 6 South Main Street Area C 28714 (828) 536-5147 https://homeplacebeer.com/

Here you'll find lagers, table beers, hoppy American and malty English beers. Everything is made using local ingredients from the nearby area. Marion is about forty minutes away with another brewery:

Mica Town Brewing 25 Brown Drive 28752 (828) 559-3800
https://www.micatownbrewing.com/

Head west about twenty-minutes to Black Mountain and three breweries:

Black Mountain Brewing 131 Broadway Avenue 28711 (828) 357-5010 http://blackmountainbrewing.com/

Pisgah Brewing Company 150 Eastside Business Park 28711 (828) 582-2175 https://www.pisgahbrewing.com/

Lookout Brewing Company 103 South Ridgeway Avenue 28711 (828) 357-5169 http://www.lookoutbrewing.com/

The next brewery is about another twenty-minutes away in Arden:

Mills River Brewery 330 Rockwood Road 28704 (828) 989-3747 http://millsriverbrewingco.com/

Just three minutes away is Fletcher and another brewery:

Blue Ghost Brewing Company 125 Underwood Road 28732 (828) 376-0159 https://www.blueghostbrewing.com/

About twenty-minutes south brings you to Etowah and another brewery:

Sideways Farm and Brewery 62 Eade Road 28729 (828) 595-4001 https://www.sidewaysfarm.com/

Fourteen minutes east is two breweries at Hendersonville:

Dry Falls Brewing Company 425 Kanuga Road 28739 (828) 696-0660 https://dryfallsbrewing.com/

Southern Appalachian Brewery 822 Locust Street Ste 100 28792 (828) 684-1235 http://www.sabrewery.com/

End your trip about a half-hour away at Chimney Rock and a must-visit brewery:

Hickory Nut Gorge Brewery 461 Main Street 28720 (828) 436-7047 https://hickorynutbrewery.com/

Specializing in English Cask style ales. This means beers with more body and a smooth taste. It is often served warmer than traditional beers.

Charlotte Area

Another part of North Carolina that is home to some great breweries is around the Charlotte area. The trip can take you a day or two, depending on how many breweries you choose to visit. Start your trip in Waxhaw at:

The DreamChaser's Brewery 115 E North Main Street 28173 (704) 843-7326 https://www.dreamchasersbrewery.com/

The next brewery is about a half-hour north in Monroe:

Southern Range Brewing Company 151 S Stewart Street 28112 (704) 289-4049 https://getsrb.com/

Fifteen minutes west is another brewery in Indian Trail:

Sweet Union Brewing 13717 E Independence Blvd 28079 (704) 628-5211 https://www.sweetunionbrewing.com/

Just seven minutes away is Matthews with another brewery:

Seaboard Brewing, Taproom, and Wine Bar 213 North Trade Street 28105 (704) 246-8323 https://www.seaboardbrewing.com/#home-section

Another sixteen minutes west is Pineville:

Middle James Brewing Company 400 North Polk Street 28134 (704) 889-6522 https://www.middlejamesbrewing.com/

About twenty-minutes north is the main city of Charlotte:

Wooden Robot Brewery 1440 S Tryon Street Suite 110 28203 (980) 819-7875 https://woodenrobotbrewery.com/

Birdsong Brewing 1016 N Davidson Street 28206 (704) 332-1810 https://www.birdsongbrewing.com/

The Unknown Brewing Company 1327 S Mint Street 28203 (980) 237-2628 https://www.unknownbrewing.com/

Lenny Boy Brewing Company 2224 Hawkins Street 28203
http://www.discoverlennyboy.com/

Suffolk Punch Brewing 2911 Griffith Street 28203 (704) 319-8650
https://thesuffolkpunch.com/

Free Range Brewing 2320 N Davidson Street 28205 (704) 898-4247
https://www.freerangebrewing.com/

Blue Blaze Brewing Company 528 South Turner Avenue 28208 (704) 717-8527 http://www.blueblazebrewing.com/login-screen

Triple C Brewing Company 2900 Griffith Street 28203 (704) 372-3212
https://www.triplecbrewing.com/

Salud Cerveceria 3306 N Davidson Street 28205 (704) 900-7767
https://saludcerveceria.com/

Town Brewing Company 800 Grandin Road 28208 (980) 237-8628
http://townbrewing.com/

Divine Barrel Brewing 3701 N Davidson Street 28205 (980) 237-1803
http://divinebarrel.com/

Protagonist Clubhouse 3123 N Davidson Street 28205 (980) 938-0671
https://protagonistbeer.com/

Armored Cow Brewing Company 8821 JW Clay Blvd #1 28262 (704) 277-6641 https://www.armoredcowbrewing.com/

Heist Brewery and Barrel Arts 2909 North Davidson Street Suite 200 28205 (704) 375-8260 https://www.heistbrewery.com/

Legion Brewing 1906 Commonwealth Avenue 28205 (844) 467-5683
https://www.legionbrewing.com/

The Olde Mecklenburg Brewery 215 Southside Drive 28217 (704) 525-5644 https://www.oldemeckbrew.com/

Resident Culture Brewing Company 2101 Central Avenue 28205 (704) 333-1862 https://residentculturebrewing.com/

Sycamore Brewing 2161 Hawkins Street 28203 (704) 910-3821 https://www.sycamorebrew.com/

Pilot Brewing Company 1331 Central Avenue 28205 (704) 802-9260 https://www.pilotbrewing.us/

NoDa Brewing Company 2229 N Davidson Street 28205 (704) 900-6851 https://nodabrewing.com/

Home to more award-winning beers than any other brewery in the Charlotte area. Come try their extensive line of dependable and delicious beers.

Lower Left Brewing Company 4528 Nations Crossing Road 28217 (704) 469-9861 https://www.llbrewco.com/

The focus is on all styles of IPAs, sour ales, mixed-fermentation styles, farmhouse, and Belgian inspired beers. There is plenty for everyone here.

Sugar Creek Brewing Company 215 Southside Drive 28217 (704) 521-3333 https://sugarcreekbrewing.com/

The focus is on Belgian-inspired ales. The beers are fresh, full-flavored, so they are drinkable and satisfying. The next brewery is in Huntersville about another twenty-minutes north:

Primal Brewing 16432 Old Statesville Road 28078 (704) 947-2920 http://primalbrewery.com/

Just nine minutes away is Cornelius with two breweries including a must-visit:

Eleven Lakes Brewing 10228 Bailey Road 28031 (704) 998-9017 https://www.elevenlakesbrewing.com/

Ass Clown Brewing 10620 Bailey Road Suite E 28031 (704) 995-7767 http://assclownbrewing.com/

With over two hundred beers, they have one of the largest selections of most breweries. They experiment with new and unique ingredients such as boysenberries and ghost chili peppers. East about a half-hour brings you to Concord the second biggest city of the trip:

Commoners Brewing Company 1048 Copperfield Blvd Suite 101 28025 (704) 886-6002 https://commonersbrewingcompany.com/

Red Hill Brewing Company 21 Union Street S 28025 (704) 784-2337 https://www.redhillbrewing.com/

Cabarrus Brewing Company 329 McGill Avenue 28027 (704) 490-4487 http://www.cabarrusbrewing.com/

Twenty-Six Acres Brewing Company 7285 Westwinds Blvd NW 28027 (980) 277-2337 http://www.26acres.com/

Southern Strain Brewing Company 165 Brunley Avenue Ste 3001 28025 (704) 218-9106 https://www.southernstrainbrewing.com/

High Branch Brewing Company 325 McGill Avenue NW Ste 148 28027 (704) 706-3807 http://www.highbranchbrewing.com/

A family-run artisanal brewery focused on Belgian inspired and hop-forward ales with an emphasis on the fermentation profiles. The next must-visit brewery is about a half-hour north in Salisbury:

New Sarum Brewing Company 109 N Lee Street 28144 (704) 310-5048 http://newsarumbrewing.com/

Offering bold flavors with a classic touch. Mixing old-world brewing styles with modern ingredients to give you a beer-drinking experience like no other. Head back west about a half-hour to Mooresville with two breweries including a must-visit:

King Canary Brewing Company 562 Williamson Road 28117 (561) 512-6408 https://www.kingcanarybrewing.com/

Ghostface Brewing 427 E Statesville Avenue 28115 (704) 799-7433 https://www.ghostfacebrewing.com/

Specializing in high-end, big and bold, high caliber, rich and strong flavored, high gravity beers. If you like your beers strong, you'll enjoy what they have to offer. Statesville is twenty-minutes north with two breweries:

Red Buffalo Brewing 108 N Center Street 28677 (704) 380-2219 https://redbuffalobrewing.com/

Fourth Creek Brewing Company 226 W Broad Street 28677 (980) 223-2044 https://www.fourthcreekbrewco.com/

A half-hour west is Hickory:

Olde Hickory Brewery 222 Union Square 28601 (828) 322-1965 https://www.oldehickorybrewery.com/

Gastonia is about forty minutes south:

Cavendish Brewing Company 207 North Chester Street 28052 (704) 830-0435 http://www.cavendishbrewing.com/

End your trip about a half-hour west in Shelby at:

Newgrass Brewing Company 213 S Lafayette Street 28150 (704) 937-1280 https://newgrassbrewing.com/

Coastal North Carolina

This trip will take you two to three days, but as you view the beautiful coastline, you may decide to stay a little longer. Start your trip in Beaufort at:

Fishtowne Brew House 133-B Turner Street 28516 (252) 838-1102 https://fishtownebrewhouse.com/

Head northwest about twenty-minutes to Newport and a must-visit brewery:

Shortway Brewing Company 230 Chatham Street 28570 (252) 777-3065 https://www.shortwaybrewing.com/

Specializing in American ales ranging from blondes to stouts and everything in between. The beers are fresh, easy-drinking, and great tasting. Your next brewery is in New Bern about a half-hour north:

Brewery 99 417F Broad Street 28560 (252) 259-6393 https://brewery99.com/

Take about a two and a half-hour drive to the coastal town of Manteo and a must-visit brewery:

The Lost Colony Brewery and Café 208 Queen Elizabeth Street 27954 (252) 473-6666 http://lostcolonybrewery.com/

Winner of 8 World Beer Championship Medals. Specializing in British and Irish style ales. Known for one of the best porters ever tasted based on reviews. North about twenty-minutes is the next brewery at Kill Devil Hills:

Outer Banks Brewing Station Milepost 8.5 Route 158 27948 (252) 449-BREW https://www.obbrewing.com/

About forty minutes up the coast is the town of Corolla:

Northern Outer Banks Brewing Company 520 Old Stoney Road J 27927 (252) 207-1890 http://www.northernobxbrewing.com/

About an hour away is Grandy with a must-visit brewery:

Weeping Radish Eco Farm and Brewery 6810 Caratoke Highway 27939 (252) 491-5205 https://www.weepingradish.com/

Offering seven draft choices along with seasonal favorites, including their famous Christmas Beer and Oktoberfest style beer. Their best seasonal is the Bitter Bee infused with local honey. A half-hour inland is another brewery at Elizabeth City:

Ghost Harbor Brewing Company 606B E Colonial Avenue 27909 (252) 599-1030 http://www.ghostharborbrewing.com/

Head south about two hours to Greenville and two breweries:

Pitt Street Brewing Company 630 S Pitt Street 27834 (252) 227-4151 https://pittstreetbrewing.com/

Uptown Brewing Company 418 Evans Street 27858 (252) 689-6487 http://www.uptownbrewingcompany.com/

Another two hours south is the coastal city of Surf City:

Salty Turtle Beer Company 103 Triton Lane 28445 (910) 803-2019 https://saltyturtlebeer.com/

About an hour down the coast is Carolina Beach:

Good Hops Brewing 811 Harper Avenue 28428 (706) 713-1594 https://www.goodhopsbrewing.com/

About twenty minutes away is the main city of Wilmington with many brewery options:

Waterman's Brewing Company 1610 Pavilion Place 28403 (910) 839-3103 https://www.watermansbrewing.com/

Wilmington Brewing Company 824 S Kerr Avenue 28403 (910) 392-3315 https://wilmingtonbrewingcompany.com/

Skytown Beer Company 4712 New Centre Drive #100 28405 (910) 660-8721 https://www.skytownbeer.com/

Wrightsville Beach Brewery 6201 Oleander Drive 28403 (910) 256-4938 https://www.wbbeer.com/home

Bill's Front Porch Pub and Brewery 4238 Market Street 28403 (910) 762-6333 https://www.seeyouatbills.com/bills-brewing/

Mad Mole Brewing 6309 Boathouse Road Unit C 28403 (910) 859-8115 http://madmolebrewing.com/

New Anthem Beer Project 116 Dock Street 28401 (910) 399-4683 https://newanthembeer.com/

Broomtail Craft Brewery 6404 Amsterdam Way 28405 (910) 264-1369 http://broomtailcraftbrewery.com/

Ironclad Brewery 115 N 2nd Street 28401 (910) 769-0290 https://www.ironcladbrewery.com/

Edward Teach Brewing 604 N 4th Street 28401 (910) 523-5401 https://edwardteachbrewery.com/

Flytrap Brewing 319 Walnut Street 28401 (910) 769-2881 https://www.flytrapbrewing.com/

Waterline Brewing Company 721 Surry Street 28401 (910) 557-2739 https://www.waterlinebrewing.com/

Currently brewing six flagship ales: Waterline Kolsch, Pale, Red, Classic IPA, Oatmeal Stout, and Triple.

Flying Machine Brewing Company 3130 Randall Parkway 28403 (910) 769-8173 https://www.flyingmachine.beer/

Blending old-world brewing and new innovations, techniques, and traditions. Creating the best ales, lagers, and mixed culture fermentation beers. End your trip with an hour drive down the coast to the border town of Ocean Isle Beach and a must-visit brewery:

Makai Brewing Company 5850 Ocean Highway W 28469 (910) 579-2739 https://www.makaibrewing.com/

Stop in for unique beers such as their popular Carolina Tropical IPA made with pineapple and mango or the Nightingale Coffee Porter with real Kona coffee.

Northern North Carolina

Travel the beautiful countryside while tasting some wonderful beers. This trip will take you a day or two, depending on how many breweries you choose to visit. Start your trip in Oxford at:

Tobacco Wood Brewing Company 117 Wall Street 27565 (919) 725-9402 http://tobaccowoodbrewing.co/

Head southwest about fifty minutes to Chapel Hill with three breweries including a must-visit:

Carolina Brewery 460 W Franklin Street 27516 (919) 942-1800 https://www.carolinabrewery.com/

Top of the Hill Restaurant and Brewery 100 East Franklin Street Third Floor 27514 (919) 929-8676 https://www.thetopofthehill.com/

Starpoint Brewing 901 Clarence Drive 27516 http://www.starpointbrewing.com/

Known for their three small-batch IPAs: an IPA, double IPA, and Pale Ale. They also occasionally offer special limited edition beers. Just five minutes away is two more breweries in Carrboro:

Vecino Brewing Company 300E Main Street C 27510 (919) 537-9591 https://vecinobrewing.com/

Steel String Brewery 106A South Greensboro Street 27510 (919) 370-6971 https://steelstringbrewery.com/

Saxapahaw is about twenty-minutes west and has a must-visit brewery:

Haw River Farmhouse Ales 1713 Sax-Beth Church Road 27340 (336) 525-9270 http://hawriverales.com/

Brewing beer with unique local ingredients such as pine needles, balsamic vinegar, and freshly roasted sunchokes. Another twenty-five minutes west is a must-visit brewery at Whitsett:

Red Oak Brewery 6901 Konica Drive 27377 (336) 477-2055 https://www.redoakbrewery.com/

Using true slow, old-world style brewing of traditional Bavarian brewing. It is the largest lager only brewery in the United States. Continue west seventeen minutes to the main city of Greensboro with multiple options:

Leveneleven Brewing 1111 Coliseum Blvd 27403 (336) 265-8600 https://leveneleven.com/

SouthEnd Brewing Company 117 W Lewis Street 27406 (336) 285-6406 http://www.southendbrewing.com/

Joymongers Brewing Company 576 North Eugene Street 27401 (336) 763-5255 https://joymongers.com/

Natty Greene's Pub and Brewing Company 345 S Elm Street 27401 (336) 274-1373 https://www.nattygreenes.com/

Oden Brewing Company 804 W Gate City Blvd 27403 (910) 515-0889 https://odenbrewing.com/

Little Brother Brewing 348 S Elm Street 27401 (336) 510-9678 https://www.littlebrotherbrew.com/

Pig Pounder Brewery 1107 Grecade Street 27408 (336) 553-1290 https://www.pigpounder.com/

Specializing in English ales like their Gold Medal Winner Boar Brown. They also offer other options, including a cask beer release once a week.

Gibb's Hundred Brewing Company 504 State Street 27406 (336) 763-7087 https://gibbshundred.com/

Craft beer with a focus on ingredients and craftsmanship. The Guilty Party ESB is a gold medal-winning beer. High Point is about twenty-minutes southwest:

Goofy Foot Taproom and Brewery 2762 NC-68 27265 (336) 307-2567
https://goofyfoottaproom.com/

Brown Truck Brewery 1234 N Main Street 27262 (336) 442-7519
https://www.browntruckbrewery.com/

A nationally recognized award-winning brewery offering big flavor beers. Try their award-winning light lager. Head north about forty minutes to the next brewery at Madison:

Hell on Horsecreek Brewing 107 E Murphy Street 27025 (336) 949-9438
https://www.hellonhorsecreek.com/

Head back south a half-hour to Kernersville with two breweries:

Gypsy Road Brewing Company 105 E Mountain Street 27284 (336) 515-3687 https://www.gypsyroadbrewing.com/

Kernersville Brewing Company 210 N Main Street Suite 150 27284 (336) 816-7283 http://kernersvillebrewing.com/

Twelve minutes west is the second largest city of Winston-Salem:

Foothills Brewing Company 638 West Fourth Street 27120 (336) 777-3348 https://www.foothillsbrewing.com/

Fiddlin' Fish Brewing Company 772 N Trade Street 27101 (336) 999-8945 http://www.fiddlinfish.com/#modal

Wise Man Brewing 826 Angelo Bros Avenue 27101 (336) 725-0008
https://www.wisemanbrewing.com/

Incendiary Brewing Company 486 N Patterson Avenue 27101 (336) 893-6714 https://incendiarybrewing.com/

Hoots Roller Bar and Beer Company 840 Manly Street 27101 (336) 608-6026 https://www.hootspublic.com/

Radar Brewing Company 216 E 9th Street 27101 (336) 999-8090 https://www.radarbrewingcompany.com/

The next brewery is fifteen minutes west at Lewisville:

Westbend Winery and Brewery 5394 Williams Road 27023 (336) 945-5032 https://www.westbendwineryandbrewery.com/

End your trip with about a forty-minute drive north towards the border and Mount Airy:

Old North State Winery and Brewery 308 N Main Street 27030 (336) 789-9463 https://oldnorthstatewinery.com/

White Elephant Beer Company 225 Market Street 27030 (336) 648-8277 http://whiteelephantbeer.com/

Western North Carolina

Take a beautiful trip through the hills of Western North Carolina while enjoying some great brews. Start your trip in Murphy at:

Valley River Brewery and Eatery 71 Tennessee Street 28906 (828) 837-2337 https://www.valleyriverbreweries.com/

About twenty-minutes east is Andrews with two breweries:

Hoppy Trout Brewing Company 911 Main Street 28901 (828) 835-2111 https://hoppytroutbrewing.com/

Andrews Brewing Company 565 Aquone Road 28901 (828) 321-2006 https://andrewsbrewing.com/

Bryson City is the next town about forty minutes northeast:

Mountain Layers Brewing Company 90 Everett Street 28713 (828) 538-0115 https://www.mountainlayersbrewingcompany.com/

About twenty-minutes east is Sylva:

Innovation Brewing 414 West Main Street 28779 (828) 586-9678
http://www.innovation-brewing.com/

Twenty-five minutes south is Franklin with two breweries:

Currahee Brewing Company 100 Lakeside Drive 28734 (828) 634-0078
https://curraheebrew.com/

Lazy Hiker Brewing Company 188 W Main Street 28734 (828) 349-2337
https://lazyhikerbrewing.com/

Southeast fifty minutes is Cashiers:

Whiteside Brewing Company 128 NC-107 28717 (828) 743-6000
https://whitesidebrewing.com/

Just thirteen minutes away is Sapphire:

Sapphire Mountain Brewing Company 50 Slicers Avenue 28774 (828) 743-0220 https://www.sapphiremountainbrewingcompany.com/

Northeast about a half-hour is Brevard with a must-visit brewery:

Brevard Brewing Company 63 East Main Street 28712 (828) 885-2101
http://www.brevard-brewing.com/

German-inspired lagers are the specialty, but to keep things diverse, they also offer a few American ale options. Your next brewery is in Marshall about an hour north:

Madison County Brewing (Mad Co Brewing) 45 N Main Street 28753 (828) 649-8600 https://www.madisoncountybrewing.com/

Northeast about an hour is Morganton with three breweries including a must-visit:

Catawba Brewing Company 212 South Green Street 28655 (828) 674-2004 https://catawbabrewing.com/

Fonta Flora Brewery 317 N Green Street 28655 (828) 475-0153
https://fontaflora.com/

Sidetracked Brewery and Taproom 609 S Green Street 28655 (828)
544-5840 https://www.sidetrackedbrew.com/home/

Crafting an expanding variety of beers. All beers are made with local and
sustainable malt from the Carolina Malt House. Fourteen minutes away is
another must-visit brewery in Valdese:

The Levee Brewery and Pub 118 Main Street W 28690
https://www.theleveepub.com/welcome

The only place in the area serving real cask-conditioned ales. Here you'll
have a unique experience not often found outside of the British Isles.
Granite Falls is about twenty minutes away and has another must-visit
brewery:

Granite Falls Brewing Company 47 Duke Street 28630 (828) 212-1222
https://www.granitefallsbrewing.com/

Offering every style of beer for the traditional drinker and some more
adventurous options such as a Saison infused with white pepper and a
Finnish Sahti with juniper berries. About fifty minutes north is Boone with
three breweries:

Booneshine Brewing Company 246 Wilson Drive 28607 (828) 386-4066
https://www.booneshine.beer/

Lost Province Brewing Company 130 N Depot Street 28607 (828) 265-
3506 https://lostprovince.com/

Appalachian Mountain Brewery 163 Boone Creek Drive 28607 (828)
263-1111 http://www.appalachianmountainbrewery.com/

The next brewery is about a half-hour southwest in Banner Elk:

Kettell Beerworks 567 Main Street E 28604 (828) 898-8677
https://kettellbeerworks.com/

About twenty-minutes north is Beech Mountain:

Beech Mountain Brewing Company 1007 Beech Mountain Parkway 28604 (800) 438-2093 https://www.beechmountainbrewingco.com/

About an hour north near the border is Lansing:

New River Brewing 9211-A NC Highway 194N 28643 (919) 452-8367 https://www.newriverbrewing.beer/

End your trip with an hour and a half drive east to Elkin:

Angry Troll Brewing 222 E Main Street Suite U6 28621 (336) 258-2251 https://www.angrytrollbrewing.com/

Northeast North Carolina

This is a great short day trip if you want to try some great breweries. Start your trip at a must-visit brewery in Farmville:

The Duck-Rabbit Craft Brewery 4519 W Pine Street 27828 (252) 753-7745 https://duckrabbitbrewery.com/

Specializing in full-flavored dark beers. Be sure to try their milk stout along with any other beer that you prefer. Head north about a half-hour to the next brewery at Tarboro:

Tarboro Brewing Company 526 N Main Street 27886 (252) 563-6522 http://www.tarborobrewingcompany.com/

Head twenty-minutes northwest to Rocky Mount with three breweries including a must-visit:

HopFly Brewing Company 1147 Falls Road Suite 121 27804 https://www.hopflybrewing.com/

Koi Pond Brewing Company 1107 Falls Road 27804 (252) 231-1660 https://koipondbrewingcompany.com/

BDD Brewing Company 1147 Falls Road Site 107 27804 (919) 632-7551
https://www.rockymountmills.com/brewers/bdd-brewing-company/

Try some unique flavor combinations when you stop here. Consider the French Vanilla Mocha Stout or the Peach Cobbler Wheat Dessert Beer. The next brewery is in Wilson about twenty-minutes south:

217 Brew Works 217 South Street South 27893 (252) 991-6969
http://217brewworks.com/

End your trip with about a fifty-minute drive south to Mount Olive at:

R & R Brewing 541 NW Center Street 28365 (919) 299-4322
https://www.randrbrew.com/

Central North Carolina

This is another great day trip. It is a circular route that will allow you to experience some great breweries. Start out in Aberdeen at:

Railhouse Brewery 105 East South Street 28315 (910) 783-5280
https://www.railhousebrewery.com/

Head about fifty minutes southeast to the next brewery at Hope Mills:

Dirtbag Ales 4427 Pensacola Road 28348 (910) 426-2537
https://www.dirtbagales.com/

Just fifteen minutes away is Fayetteville with two breweries including a must-visit:

Mash House Restaurant and Brewery 4150 Sycamore Dairy Road 28303 (910) 867-9223 https://www.themashhouse.com/

Huske Hardware House Brewing Company 405 Hay Street 28301 (910) 437-9905 https://www.huskehardware.com/

The oldest brewery in Fayetteville. Brewing beers that balance drinkability with a strong flavor. Circle northwest about an hour and a half to the next brewery in Asheboro:

Four Saints Brewing Company 218 S Fayetteville Street 27203 (336) 560-7687 https://www.foursaintsbrewing.com/

Head to Pinehurst about fifty minutes southeast:

Pinehurst Brewing Company 300 Magnolia Road 28374 (910) 235-8218 https://www.pinehurstbrewing.com/

End your trip ten minutes away in Southern Pines:

Southern Pines Brewing Company 565 Air Tool Drive Suite E 28387 (910) 365-9925 https://www.southernpinesbrewing.com/

Fairview

Whistle Hop Brewing Company 1288 Charlotte Highway 28730 (828) 338-9447 https://whistlehop.com/

Turgua Brewing Company 27 Firefly Hollow Drive 28730 (828) 222-0643 https://shop.turguabrewing.com/

There aren't many breweries in North Dakota, so you can visit them all in one trip. The trip can take you a day or two. Start your trip at a must-visit brewery is Bismarck:

Laughing Sun Brewing Company 107 N 5th Street 58501 (701) 400-9750 https://laughingsunbrewing.com/

Come see why people love this destination. Enjoy craft beers along with non-alcoholic options like soda and sparkling water. Pair it with the best BBQ, according to voters. Just ten minutes away is Mandan with two breweries:

Bird Dog Brewing 2608 8th Avenue SE 58554 (701) 751-0691 https://birddogbrewing.beer/

Dialectic Brewing Company 416 West Main Street 58554 (701) 318-1328 https://www.dialecticbrewingcompany.com/

Head west about an hour and a half to the next brewery at Dickinson:

Phat Fish Brewing Company 1031 West Villard 58601 (701) 761-0170 https://www.phatfishbrewing.com/

Watford City is about another hour and a half north:

Stonehome Brewing Company 313 Fox Hill Parkway 58854 (701) 444-2337 https://www.stonehomebrewing.com/

Head east about two hours to your next brewery in Minot:

Souris River Brewing 32 Third Street NE 58701 (701) 837-1884 https://sourisriverbrewing.com/

Continue about three hours east to Grand Forks:

Half Brothers Brewing Company 17 N Third Street 58203 (701) 757-0805 https://halfbrothersbrewing.com/

Head south about an hour to Fargo with three breweries including a must-visit:

JL Beers 518 1st Avenue North 58102 (701) 492-3377 https://jlbeers.com/

Drekker Brewing Company 630 1st Avenue North 58102 (701) 540-6808 https://drekkerbrewing.com/

Fargo Brewing Company 610 North University Drive 58104 (701) 478-2337 https://www.fargobrewing.com/

Offering a variety of traditional, seasonal, and limited release beers. Choose from their selection and find something you'll enjoy. End your trip eleven minutes away at a must-visit brewery in West Fargo:

Flatland Brewery 3140 Bluestem Drive Ste 105 58078 (701) 353-1178 https://www.flatlandbrewery.com/

Offering a unique line-up of craft beers and made-from-scratch sodas. Be sure to try their dark stout made with espresso beans.

Greater Cleveland Area

This short trip takes you to a few areas around the Cleveland area before ending in the city. You can complete the trip in a day if you only visit the must-visit breweries in Cleveland. If you want to visit every brewery in Cleveland, you'll need a couple more days. Start your trip out in Strongsville at:

The Brew Kettle Taproom and Smokehouse/Production Works 8377 Pearl Road 44136 (440) 239-8788 https://thebrewkettle.com/

Ten minutes north is another brewery at Berea:

Cornerstone Brewing Company 58 Front Street 44017 (440) 239-9820 http://www.cornerstonebrewing.com/

Middleburg Heights is five minutes east:

Fat Head's Brewery and Tap House 17450 Engle Lake Drive 44130 (216) 898-0242 http://fatheads.com/

A half-hour drive northeast is a brewery in Chagrin Falls:

Crooked Pecker Brewing Company 8284 E Washington Street 44023 (440) 476-7824 https://crookedpeckerbrewing.com/

Head back northwest to Cleveland Heights about another half-hour:

Boss Dog Brewing Company 2179 Lee Road 44118 (216) 321-2337 https://bossdogbrewing.com/

End your trip sixteen minutes west in Cleveland:

Nano Brew Cleveland 1859 West 25th Street 44113 (216) 621-4000 http://nanobrewcleveland.com/

Platform Beer Company 4125 Lorain Avenue 44113 (216) 202-1386 https://platformbeer.co/

The Cleveland Brewery 777 E 185th Street 44119 (216) 534-6992 https://theclevelandbrewery.com/

Masthead Brewing Company 1261 Superior Avenue 44114 (216) 206-6176 https://mastheadbrewingco.com/

Noble Beast Brewing Company 1470 Lakeside Avenue E 44114 (216) 417-8588 https://www.noblebeastbeer.com/

Saucy Brew Works 2885 Detroit Avenue 44113 (216) 574-9211 https://www.saucybrewworks.com/

Hansa Brewery 2717 Lorain Avenue 44113 (216) 631-6585 https://www.hansabrewery.com/

Forest City Brewery 2135 Columbus Road 44113 (216) 228-9116 http://www.forestcitybrewery.com/

Collision Bend Brewing Company 1250 Old River Road 44113 (216) 273-7879 https://www.collisionbendbrewery.com/

Working Class Brewery 17448 Lorain Avenue 441113 (216) 417-5112 https://www.workingclassbrewery.com/

Goldhorn Brewery 1361 East 55th Street 44103 (216) 465-1352 https://goldhornbrewery.com/

Bookhouse Brewing 1526 W 25th Street Ste C&D 44113 (216) 862-4048 https://bookhouse.beer/

The Jolly Scholar 11111 Euclid Avenue 44106 (216) 368-0090 https://www.thejollyscholar.com/

Brick and Barrel Brewing 1844 Columbus Road 44113 (216) 331-3308 https://www.brickandbarrelbrewing.com/

Making classic brews popular such as cask ales and barrel-aged beers while also rotating small batches of their unique recipes so you'll always have something great to try.

Market Garden Brewery 1947 West 25th Street 44113 (216) 621-4000 http://www.marketgardenbrewery.com/

Stop in to try their award-winning beers. There is the Progress Pilsner, Citramax IPA, and Prosperity, a Bavarian-style Hefeweizen.

Lake Erie Ohio

This simple day trip can take you to some great breweries along the Lake Erie waterfront area of Ohio. Start your trip in Geneva at:

GOTL Brewing Company 5243 Lake Road 44041 (440) 361-4864 http://www.gotlbrewing.com/

Willoughby is about a half-hour west:

Willoughby Brewing 4057 Erie Street 44094 (440) 975-0202
https://www.willoughbybrewing.com/

BRIM Kitchen + Brewery 3941 Erie Street 44094 (440) 306-8183
http://brimbrewery.com/

About forty more minutes west is Avon with two more breweries:

Avon Brewing Company 37040 Detroit Road 44011 (440) 937-1816
https://avonbrewingcompany.com/

Railroad Brewing Company 1010 Center Road 44011 (440) 723-8234
http://railroadbrewingcompany.com/

Just thirteen minutes away is another brewery in Lorain:

Bascule Brewery and Public House 1397 Colorado Avenue 44052 (440) 317-0944 https://www.basculebrewpub.com/

Forty minutes west is the waterfront town of Sandusky:

Bait House Brewery 223 Meigs Street 44870 (419) 271-5094
https://baithousebrewery.com/

End your trip by visiting two islands. The first is an hour away at Kelleys Island:

Kelleys Island Brewery Restaurant and Bar 504 W Lakeshore Drive 43438 (419) 656-4335 https://kelleysislandbrewpub.com/

The second island is Put-in-Bay:

Put-In-Bay Brewing Company 441 Catawba Avenue 43456 (419) 285-HOPS https://putinbaybrewery.com/

Northeast Ohio

There are lots of great breweries in the Northeast corner of Ohio. Take a few days to explore this area and try something new. Start your trip in Chesterland at a must-visit brewery:

Chagrin Beer Company 8706 Cedar Road 44026 (216) 645-1739
http://www.chagrinbeer.com/

Best known for their India Pale Ale. This handcrafted beer has balance and is good for those who enjoy craft beer. You next brewery is about forty minutes south in Hudson:

Hop Tree Brewing 1297 Hudson Gate Drive 44236 (330) 342-0060
https://www.hoptreebrewing.com/

Another fourteen minutes south is Cuyahoga Falls with three breweries including a must-visit:

Missing Mountain Brewing Company 2811 Front Street 44221 (330) 338-5000 https://www.missingmountain.com/

HiHO Brewing Company 1707 Front Street 44221 (234) 334-7564
https://hihobrewingco.com/

Ohio Brewing Company 2250 Front Street 44221 (234) 208-6797
https://www.ohiobrewing.com/

An award-winning microbrewery that produces a wide range of styles from German ales to Irish Red ales and stouts to Oktoberfest lagers. Just six minutes away is the main city of Akron with multiple options:

Missing Falls Brewery 540 S Main Street Suite 112 44311 (234) 231-1000 https://www.missingfalls.com/

Akronym Brewing 58 E Market Street 44308 (717) 348-0789
https://akronymbrewing.com/

Eighty-Three Brewery 1201 E Market Street Ste 110 44305 (234) 571-1067 http://www.eighty-threebrewery.com/

Two Monks Brewing 352 Massillon Road 44312 (234) 678-0088
http://2monksbru.com/

Lock 15 Brewing Company 21 W North Street 44304 (234) 900-8277
https://www.lock15brewing.com/

BrickOven BrewPub 604 Canton Road 44312 (330) 475-7005
https://www.thebrickovenbrewpub.com/

Mucky Duck Brewing Company 3950 South Main Street 44319 (330)
644-5444 https://www.nautivinewine.com/mucky-duck

Hoppin' Frog Brewery 1680 W Waterloo Road Rte 224 Suite F 44306
(330) 352-4578 http://www.hoppinfrog.com/

Thirsty Dog Brewing Company 529 Grant Street Suite B 44311 (330)
252-BREW https://thirstydog.com/

Crafting beers with unique flavor profiles, you won't find in mass-produced
beers today. The brews here have a diverse range of flavor and character.
Try their award-winning beers. About twenty-minutes southwest is a must-
visit brewery in Wadsworth:

Wadsworth Brewing Company 126 Main Street 44281 (330) 475-4935
https://www.wadsworthbrewingcompany.com/

Offering unique craft beers made from ingredients that offer a fun twist like
fruits, spices, and coffees. However, they also offer classic beers if that's
more your thing. Sixteen minutes north is Medina with two breweries:

Lager Heads Smokehouse and Brewing Company 325 W Smith Road
44256 (330) 721-2337 https://lagerheads.us/

Blue Heron Brewery 3227 Blue Heron Trace 44256 (330) 520-8511
https://blueheronmedina.com/

Ashland is about forty minutes southwest:

Uniontown Brewing Company 105 West Main Street 44805 (419) 908-
8542 https://uniontownbrewing.com/

Another twenty-minutes southwest is Mansfield:

The Phoenix Brewing Company 131 N Diamond Street 44902 (419) 522-2552 https://www.phoenixbrewing.com/

Millersburg is about fifty minutes southeast:

Millersburg Brewing Company 60 East Jackson Street 44654 (330) 674-4728 https://www.millersburgbrewing.com/

Visit this award-winning brewery with over 20 beers on taps. Ranging from Double IPAs to Porters and Blondes. About a half-hour south is Fresno:

Wooly Pig Farm Brewery 23631 Township Road 167 43824 (740) 545-8255 https://www.woolypigfarmbrewery.com/

Circle back north about a half-hour to your next brewery in Dover:

Hoodletown Brewing Company 424 West 3rd Street 44622 (330) 447-9354 https://hoodletown.com/

Another fourteen minutes north is Bolivar with a must-visit brewery:

Lockport Brewery 10748 Wilkshire Blvd NE 44612 (330) 874-6037 https://www.lockportbeer.com/

Providing high-quality, locally made beers. Be sure to try their award-winning Gateway beer, an American-style cream ale. Massillon is about another twenty-minutes north with another must-visit brewery:

Paradigm Shift 128 North Avenue NE 44646 (330) 880-0088 http://paradigmshiftbrew.com/

Twelve craft beers on tap along with seasonal offerings. Be sure to try the Neighbor Girl, a Belgian Triple, and a Bronze medal winner. Fifteen minutes east is Canton with two breweries including a must-visit:

Royal Docks Brewing Company 7162 Fulton Drive NW 44718 (330) 353-9103 https://docks.beer//

Shale Brewing Company 7253 Whipple Avenue NW 44720 (330) 776-8812 https://shalebrewing.com/

Offering four flagship beers: Roughneck Red, Cold Rolled Pale Ale, Deep Driller Porter, and Shale Coffee Cream Stout. All beers are fresh and flavorful. Twenty-minutes north is the next brewery at Hartville:

Maize Valley Winery and Craft Brewery 6193 Edison Street NE 44632 (330) 877-8344 https://www.maizevalley.com/beer/

Head south about a half-hour to a must-visit brewery in Minerva:

Sandy Springs Brewing 232 N Market Street 44657 (330) 451-6926 https://www.sandyspringsbrewery.com/

If visiting in the Spring, be sure to try the Happy Sappy beer. Made with maple sap and no water, this is a truly unique beer. Another hour south is Bloomingdale:

Dungeon Hollow Brewing Company 572 County Road 22A 43910 (740) 337-1510 https://www.dungeonhollow.com/

Lisbon is about an hour back north:

Numbers Brewing Company 127 N Beaver Street 44432 (330) 870-5305 https://www.numbersbrewco.com/

Columbiana has two breweries and is thirteen minutes north:

Birdfish Brewing Company 140 E Park Avenue 44408 (330) 397-4010 https://www.birdfishbrew.com/

BrewLounge Beer Company 115 Town Center Avenue 44808 (330) 892-0080 https://www.brewloungebeercompany.com/?utm_source=gmb&utm_medium=referral

About twenty-minutes north is Austintown:

Paladin Brewing 6520 Mahoning Avenue 44515 (330) 550-6338 https://www.paladinbrewing.com/

Lake Milton is about twenty-minutes west:

Lil Paws Winery 17574 Mahoning Avenue 44429 (330) 970-9463
http://lilpawswinery.com/beer/

North about a half-hour brings you to Warren:

Modern Methods Brewing Company 125 David Grohl Alley 44481 (330) 333-1594 https://modernmethodsbrew.com/

End your trip about twenty-minutes away in Garrettsville at:

Garrett's Mill Brewing Company 8148 Main Street 44231 (330) 527-8080 https://www.garrettsmillbrewing.com/

Northwest Ohio

There are some great breweries in this area, and it can take you two to three days, depending on your itinerary. Start your trip in Coldwater at:

Tailspin Brewing Company 626 S 2nd Street 45828 (419) 763-4222 https://tailspinbrewing.co/

The next brewery is fourteen minutes east at Maria Stein:

Moeller Brew Barn 8016 Marion Drive 45860 (419) 925-3005 https://www.moellerbrewbarn.com/

Another ten minutes east is New Bremen:

Gongoozlers Brewery 629 West Monroe Street 45869 https://www.gongoozlersbrewery.com/

Findlay is about an hour north with the next brewery:

Findlay Brewing Company 213 E Crawford Street 45840 (419) 419-2739 https://www.findlaybrewing.com/

About forty minutes back south is a brewery in Nevada:

White Shutter Winery and Brewery 3794 County Highway 56 44849 (419) 310-7533 http://www.whiteshutterwinery.com/index.html

Another fifty minutes south is Marengo:

Hoof Hearted Brewing 300 County Road 26 43334 (567) 233-3115
http://www.hoofheartedbrewing.com/

Head north about two hours to the waterfront town of Port Clinton with two breweries including a must-visit:

Catawba Island Brewing Company 2330 East Harbor Road 43452 (419) 960-7764 https://www.catawbaislandbrewing.com/

Twin Oast Brewing 3630 NE Catawba Road 43452 (419) 573-6126
https://www.twinoast.com/

Mixing traditional German offerings with modern American twists. With finesse and attention to detail, you should try their Apricot Blonde, Cherry Vanilla IPA, or Peppercorn Saison. The main city of Toledo is about fifty minutes northwest:

Patron Saints Brewery 4730 W Bancroft Street #8 43615 (419) 720-2337
https://www.patronsaintsbrewery.com/

Earnest Brew Works 4342 South Detroit Avenue 43614 (419) 340-2589
https://www.earnestbrewworks.com/

Great Black Swamp Brewing Company 3323 Monroe Street 43606 (419) 973-1256 https://greatblackswampbrewing.com/

The first microbrewery in Toledo. Offering six year-round beers for the perfect flight, and you can also ask about seasonal beers.

Maumee Bay Brewing Company 27 Broadway Street 43602 (419) 241-1253 https://mbaybrew.com/

Opened in 1995, the original brewery in Toledo housed in a 19th-century hotel. Featuring an IPA, a double IPA, and a stout along with cider and seasonal options. Sixteen minutes away is the border town of Sylvania:

Inside the Five 5703 N Main Street 43560 (567) 408-7212
https://insidethefivebrewing.com/

Holland is twelve minutes south:

Black Frog Brewery 831 S McCord Road 43528 (419) 389-7136
https://blackfrogbrewery.com/

Grand Rapids is about another twenty-minutes south:

Wild Side Brewing Company 24194 Front Street 43422 (419) 389-2776
https://wildsidebrewing.com/

West a half-hour is Wauseon:

Ramblin' Red's Brewing Company 1493 North Shoop Avenue Ste C
43567 (419) 335-2000 https://redrambler.com/

End your trip a half-hour southwest in Defiance:

4KD Crick Brewing 211 Carpenter Road 43512 (419) 576-5822
https://www.4kdcrickbrewery.com/

Central Ohio

There are a lot of breweries in this small area. Take at least two to three
days to explore everything, depending on your itinerary. Start your trip out
in Buckeye Lake at:

Buckeye Lake Brewery 5176-A Walnut Road 43008 (740) 535-6225
https://www.buckeyelakebrewery.com/

The next brewery is in Heath, eleven minutes north:

Homestead Beer Company 811 Irving Wick Drive West 43056 (740) 358-
0360 http://www.homesteadbeerco.com/

Just six minutes away is Newark with two breweries:

DankHouse Brewing Company 161 Forry Street 43055 (740) 915-6413
https://dankhousebrewing.com/

Trek Brewing Company 1486 Granville Road 43055 (425) 457-9610
https://trekbeer.com/

Another nine minutes brings you to a brewery at Granville:

Granville Brewing Company 5371 Columbus Road 43023
https://www.granvillebrewing.com/

Head north about a half-hour to Mount Vernon:

Stein Brewing Company 10 West Vine Street 43050 (740) 830-6760
https://www.steinbrewco.com/

Delaware is about forty minutes west with three breweries:

Staas Brewing Company 31 W Winter Street 43015 (740) 417-4690
https://www.staasbrewing.com/

Old Dog Alehouse and Brewery 13 West William Street 43015 (740)
990-4506 https://www.olddogalehouse.com/

Restoration Brew Worx 25 North Sandusky Street 43015 (740) 990-7120
http://restorationbrewworx.com/

Next is Lewis Center twelve minutes south:

Olentangy River Brewing 303 Green Meadows Drive S 43035 (740) 803-
1561 https://www.olentangyriverbrewingcompany.com/

Another eleven minutes away is two breweries in Powell:

Ill Mannered Brewing Company 38 Grace Drive 43065 (614) 859-6819
http://www.illmanneredbeer.com/

Nocterra Brewing Company 41 Depot Street 43065 (614) 468-1890
https://www.nocterrabrewing.com/

Northwest about a half-hour is Marysville:

Dalton Union Winery and Brewery 21100 Shirk Road 43040 (937) 645-5889 https://daltonunion.com/

Springfield is about forty minutes southwest:

Mother Stewart's Brewing Company 109 W North Street 45504 (937) 717-0618 https://motherstewartsbrewing.com/

Medway is fourteen minutes west:

Pinups and Pints 10963 Lower Valley Pike 45341 (937) 849-1400 http://www.pinupsandpints.com/

Head back east about an hour to Grove City:

Grove City Brewing Company 3946 Broadway 43123 (614) 991-0422 https://www.grovecitybrewery.com/

Fourteen minutes north is the main city of Columbus with multiple options:

North High Brewing Company 1288 N High Street 43201 (614) 407-5278 http://www.northhighbrewing.com/

Parsons North Brewing 685 Parsons Avenue 43206 (614) 824-4208 https://parsonsnorth.com/

Smokehouse Brewing Company 1130 Dublin Road 43215 (614) 485-0227 https://www.smokehousebrewing.com/

Wolf's Ridge Brewing 215 North 4th Street 43215 (614) 429-3936 https://www.wolfsridgebrewing.com/

Random Precision Brewing 2365 West Dublin Granville Road 43235 (614) 389-3864 https://www.randomprecisionbrewing.com/

Lineage Brewing 2971 N High Street 43202 (614) 461-3622 https://www.lineagebrew.com/

Knotty Pine Brewing 1765 West Third Avenue 43212 (614) 817-1515
https://www.knottypinebrewing.net/

Wild Ohio Brewing Company 930 Freeway Drive N 43214 (614) 262-0000 https://wildohiobrewing.com/

Zaftig Brewing Company 7020-A Huntley Road 43229 (614) 636-2537
https://www.drinkzaftig.com/

Gemut Biergarten 734 Oak Street 43205 (614) 725-1725
https://www.gemutbiergarten.com/

Antiques on High 714 S High 43235 (614) 725-2080
https://www.antiquesonhigh.com/

Somewhere in Particular Brewing 5053 Dierker Road 43220 (614) 826-3723 https://sipbrew.com/

Sideswipe Brewing 2419 Scioto Harper Drive 43204 (614) 719-9654
http://www.sideswipebrewing.com/

Seventh Son Brewing Company 1101 N 4th Street 43201 (614) 421-2337 https://www.seventhsonbrewing.com/

Land-Grant Brewing Company 424 W Town Street 43215 (614) 427-3946 https://www.landgrantbrewing.com/

Barley's Brewing Company 467 North High Street 43215 (614) 228-2537 https://www.barleysbrewing.com/

Commonhouse Ales 535 Short Street 43215
http://commonhouseales.com/

Columbus Brewing Company 2555 Harrison Road 43204 (614) 224-3626 https://www.columbusbrewing.com/

Exploring the flavors of American hops in their two flagship beers:
Columbus IPA and Bodhi. Also experimenting with German-style lagers
and intense barrel-aged beers.

Pretentious Barrel House 745 Taylor Avenue 43219 (614) 887-7687
https://www.pretentiousbarrelhouse.com/

Exclusively focused on barrel-aged sour beers. Offering an award-winning range of sour beers to try, they will change your perspective on this beer style. Eleven minutes away is two more breweries in Gahanna:

Nostalgia Brewing 81 Mill Street 43230 (614) 934-7039
https://www.nostalgiabrewing.com/

Kindred Beer 505 Morrison Road 43230 (614) 528-1227
https://www.kindredbeer.com/

Nine minutes away in Whitehall is another must-visit brewery:

2 Tones Brewing Company 145 N Hamilton Road 43213 (614) 762-6281
https://www.2tonesbrewingco.com/

Try their two flagship beers: Irish Red Ale and Indian Pale Ale. They also have other options such as Kolsch, Double IPA, Coffee Stout, and Bourbon Barrel Barleywine. Another must-visit brewery is sixteen minutes southeast in Pickerington:

Combustion Brewery and Taproom 80 West Church Street 43147 (614) 362-8450 https://www.combustionbrewing.com/index

Stop in to try their many award-winning beers. The Imperial IPA, Scotch Ale, Imperial Breakfast Stout and Coffee Beer have all won multiple awards. The next brewery is eleven minutes south in Canal Winchester:

Loose Rail Brewing 37 W Waterloo Street 43110 (614) 321-6633
https://looserailbrewing.com/

Six minutes away is Lithopolis:

Eldridge and Fiske Brewing 9 E Columbus Street 43136 (614) 829-3186
https://www.eldridgefiske.com/

Carroll is fourteen minutes east:

Outerbelt Brewing 3560 Dolson Court Suite A 43112 (740) 993-0448 https://www.outerbeltbrewing.com/

South sixteen minutes brings you to Lancaster:

Double Edge Brewing Company 158 West Chesnut Street 43130 (740) 277-7465 http://www.double-edge.beer/

Logan is about twenty more minutes south:

Brewery 33 12684 College Prospect Drive 43138 (740) 385-6033 http://www.brewery33.com/

End your trip with about an hour drive northeast to Zanesville at:

Weasel Boy Brewing Company 126 Muskingum Avenue Suite E 43701 (740) 555-7468 http://www.weaselboybrewing.com/wb/

You'll find something for your taste here. The Ornery Otter Blonde Ale is light and refreshing. The Brown Stoat Stout is big and bold.

Southeast Ohio

There isn't much in the way of breweries in Southeast Ohio, but it does make for a great day trip. Start in Athens with two breweries:

Devil's Kettle Brewing 97 Columbus Road 45701 (740) 541-4349 https://www.devilskettlebrew.com/

Little Fish Brewing Company 8675 Armitage Road 45701 (740) 447-5011 https://littlefishbrewing.com/

Drive an hour and a half to Cambridge:

Southside Brewing Company 62920 Georgetown Road 43725 (740) 435-3222 https://www.georgetowntavern.com/

End your trip in Marietta about fifty minutes to the south:

Marietta Brewing Company 167 Front Street 45750 (740) 373-2739
http://mbcpub.com/

Southwest Ohio

There are a lot of breweries in this area, including quite a few in Cincinnati. You'll need at least three days if you plan to visit them all. Start your trip in Mt Orab at:

Sons of Toil Brewing 14090 Klein Road 45154 (513) 431-5078
https://www.sonsoftoilbrewing.com/

Head a half-hour northwest to a must-visit brewery in Milford:

Little Miami Brewing Company 208 Mill Street 45150 (513) 713-1121
https://www.littlemiamibrewing.com/

Offering four series of beers. The classic series is clean, session beer. The Lupulin Series focuses on hop-forward beers. The Experimental Series pushes the boundaries of flavor. The Seasonal Series focuses on using fresh local fruit that is in season. Twelve minutes north is Loveland:

Narrow Path Brewing 106 Karl Brown Way 45140 (513) 312-3414
http://www.narrowpathbrewing.com/

Another sixteen minutes north is Morrow:

Cellar Dweller Craft Beers 2276 E US 22 & 3 Montgomery Road 45152 (513) 899-2485 https://www.valleyvineyards.com/#

Mason is about twenty-minutes west with three breweries:

16 Lots Brewing Company 753 Reading Road 45040 (513) 486-3672
https://16lots.com/

Sonder Brewing 8584 Duke Blvd 45040 (513) 779-2739
http://sonderbrewing.com/

The Common Beer Company 126 East Main Street 45040 (513) 204-0023 https://commonbeercompany.com/

Twelve minutes southwest is West Chester:

Grainworks Brewing Company 7790 Service Center Drive Unit B 45069 (513) 480-2337 https://grainworks.beer/

Eight minutes away is Sharonville:

Third Eye Brewing Company 11276 Chester Road 45246 (513) 771-2739 https://thirdeyebrewingco.com/

Another nine minutes to Blue Ash:

Fretboard Brewing Company 5800 Creek Road 45242 (513) 914-4677 https://fretboardbrewing.com/

The main city of Cincinnati is about twenty-minutes southwest:

3 Points Urban Brewery 331 East 13th Street 45202 (513) 559-5810 https://3pointsbeer.com/

Brink Brewing Company 5905 Hamilton Avenue 45224 (513) 882-3334 https://www.brinkbrewing.com/

Highgrain Brewing Company 6860 Plainfield Road 45236 (513) 791-7000 https://highgrainbrewing.com/

Big Ash Brewing 5230 Beechmont Avenue 45230 (503) 401-6868 https://www.bigashbrewing.com/

Mt. Carmel Brewing Company 4362 Mt Carmel Tobasco Road 45244 (513) 240-2739 https://www.mtcarmelbrewing.com/

Northern Row Brewery and Distillery 111 West McMicken Avenue 45202 (513) 436-7000 https://www.northernrow.com/

Streetside Brewery 4003 Eastern Avenue 45226 (513) 615-5877 https://streetsidebrewery.com/

Urban Artifact 1660 Blue Rock Street 45223 (513) 620-4729
https://www.artifactbeer.com/

MadTree Brewing 3301 Madison Road 45209 (513) 836-8733
https://www.madtreebrewing.com/

Nine Giant Brewing 6095 Montgomery Road 45213 (513) 366-4550
http://www.ninegiant.com/

March First Brewing 7885 E Kemper Road 45249 (513) 718-9173
https://www.marchfirstbrewing.com/

West Side Brewing 3044 Harrison Avenue 45211 (513) 661-2337
https://www.westsidebrewing.com/

Off Track Brewing Company 227 Stark Street 45214 (513) 604-4527
https://www.offtrackbrewingcompany.com/

Listermann Brewing Company 1621 Dana Avenue 45207 (513) 731-1130 https://listermannbrewing.com/

Fifty West Brewing Company 7668 Wooster Pike 45227 (513) 834-8789
https://fiftywestbrew.com/

Taft's Ale House 1429 Race Street 45202 (513) 334-1393
https://taftsbeer.com/

13 Below Brewery 7391 Forbes Road 45233 (513) 975-0613
https://www.13belowbrewery.com/

Bad Tom Smith Brewing 5900 Madison Road 45227 (513) 871-4677
https://www.badtomsmithbrewing.com/

Rhinegeist Brewery 1910 Elm Street 45202 (513) 381-1367
https://rhinegeist.com/

Head back north a half-hour to Fairfield:

Swine City Brewing 4614 Industry Drive 45014 (513) 201-7070
https://www.swinecitybrewing.com/

Hamilton is nine minutes away:

Municipal Brew Works 20 High Street 45011 (513) 642-2424
http://www.municipal.beer/

Twenty-minutes northeast is a must-visit brewery in Middletown:

FigLeaf Brewing 3387 Cincinnati-Dayton Road 45044 (513) 693-5706
https://www.figleafbrewing.com/

Using less common techniques and processes in order to get unique flavors. They strive to give a variety of styles to satisfy all beer drinkers. Another sixteen minutes northeast is Springboro:

Crooked Handle Brewing Company 760 N Main Street 45066 (937) 790-3450 https://crookedhandle.com/

Centerville is twelve minutes north:

Lock 27 Brewing 1035 South Main Street 45458 (937) 433-2739
https://lock27brewing.com/

Eleven minutes away is Miamisburg with two breweries:

Star City Brewing Company 319 S 2nd Street 45342 (937) 701-7827
http://starcitybrewing.com/

Lucky Star Brewery 219 S 2nd Street 45342 (937) 344-9239
http://www.luckystarbrewery.com/

Fourteen minutes north is the second largest city of Dayton:

Carillon Brewing Company 1000 Carillon Blvd 45409 (937) 293-2841
https://www.carillonbrewingco.org/

Branch and Bone Artisan Ales 905 Wayne Avenue 45410 (937) 723-7608 https://www.branchandboneales.com/

The Dayton Beer Company 912 East Dorothy Lane 45419 (937) 640-3107 https://thedaytonbeerco.com/

Warped Wing Brewing Company 26 Wyandot Street 45402 (937) 222-7003 https://warpedwing.com/

Nowhere in Particular Brewing 6826 Loop Road 45459 https://www.nipbrewco.com/

Another twelve minutes is Vandalia:

Hairless Hare Brewery 738 West National Road 45377 (937) 387-6476 https://www.hairlessharebrewery.com/

Huber Heights is ten minutes east:

Alematic Artisan Ales 6182 Chambersburg Road 45424 (937) 612-2337 https://www.alematicbrewing.com/

Southeast about a half-hour is Beavercreek:

The Wandering Griffin Brewery and Pub 3725 Presidential Drive 45324 (937) 607-9807 http://wanderinggriffin.com/

Another twelve minutes is Xenia:

Devil Wind Brewing 130 S Detroit Street 45385 (937) 919-6417 https://www.devilwindbrewing.com/

End your trip twelve minutes north in Yellow Springs at:

Yellow Springs Brewery 305 N Walnut Street 45387 (937) 767-0222 https://yellowspringsbrewery.com/

Oklahoma

Oklahoma doesn't have many breweries, so you can take a single trip in the course of about three days to travel the state and visit all the breweries. Start your trip in Broken Bow at:

Mountain Fork Brewery 85 N Lukfata Trail Road 74728 (580) 494-3233
https://www.mtforkbrewery.com/

About two hours north is the next brewery at Krebs:

Choc Beer Company 120 SW Eighth Street 74554 (918) 423-2042
http://www.chocbeer.com/

Another two hours northwest is Norman with two breweries:

405 Brewing Company 1716 Topeka Street 73069 (405) 801-4053
http://www.405brewing.com/

Lazy Circles Brewing 422 E Main Street 73071 (405) 310-5364
http://lazycirclesbrewing.com/

About a half-hour north is the main city of Oklahoma City with multiple options:

Royal Bavaria Restaurant and Brewery 3401 South Sooner Road 73165 (405) 799-7666 https://www.royal-bavaria.com/

COOP Ale Works 4745 Council Heights Road 73179 (405) 842-2667 https://coopaleworks.com/

Twisted Spike Brewing Company 1 NW 10th Street 73103 (405) 301-3467 https://www.twistedspike.com/

Lively Beerworks 815 SW 2nd Street 73109 (405) 594-8100 https://www.livelybeerworks.com/

Stonecloud Brewing 1012 NW 1st Street 73106 (405) 602-3966 https://stonecloudbrewing.com/

Black Mesa Brewing Company 1354 W Sheridan Avenue 73106 (405) 857-7622 https://www.blackmesabrewing.com/

Vanessa House Beer Company 516 NW 21st Street 73103 (405) 816-4870 http://www.vanessahousebeerco.com/

American Beverage 914 SW 5th Street 73109 (405) 232-3022 http://olglorybeer.com/

Roughtail Brewing Company 1279 N Air Depot Blvd 73110 (405) 771-6517 https://roughtailbeer.com/

Bricktown Brewery 1 N Oklahoma Avenue 73104 (405) 232-2739 https://bricktownbrewery.com/

Angry Scotsman Brewing 520 N Meridian Avenue 73107 (405) 334-7208 http://angryscotbrew.com/

Anthem Brewing Company 908 SW 4th Street 73109 (405) 604-0446 https://www.anthembrewing.com/

One of the original craft breweries in Oklahoma. Blending and using a variety of techniques to ensure there is a wide selection of beers for all tastes.

Elk Valley Brewing Company 1210 N Hudson 73103 (405) 600-6438 https://www.elkvalleybrew.com/

Sample all four core beers: Firefly Crew Witbier, Magic Juice Double IPA, Straight Razor Pale Ale, and Tenkiller Pilsner. In addition, there are seasonal, barrel-aged, and sour beers.

Edmond is about twenty more minutes north:

Battered Boar Brewing Company 14801 Metro Plaza Blvd 73013 (405) 254-5000 http://www.batteredboar.com/

Drive fifty minutes northeast to Stillwater:

Iron Monk Brewing Company and Tap Room 519 S Husband Street 74074 (405) 714-2585 https://www.ironmonkbeer.com/

End your trip about an hour east in the second largest city of Tulsa:

Welltown Brewing 114 W Archer Street 74103 (918) 221-8893 https://www.welltownbrewing.com/

Dead Armadillo Craft Brewing 5866 S Louisville Avenue 74135 (918) 232-8627 https://www.dabrewery.com/

Prairie Artisan Ales 1803B S 49th W Avenue 74107 (918) 302-3002 https://prairieales.com/

Marshall Brewing Company 618 South Wheeling 74104 (918) 292-8781 https://www.marshallbrewing.com/

Stop in to try their most popular beers such as the Atlas IPA, This Land Lager, and Sundown Wheat. Or let the bartenders help find a different beer that works for you.

Central Oregon

There are only four towns to visit, but there are plenty of breweries. The majority of your time is going to be spent in Bend, but then you can take side trips to some other breweries in the area.

Boneyard Beer Company 37 Lake Street Suite B 97701 (541) 323-2325 http://boneyardbeer.com/

Worthy Brewing Company 495 NE Bellevue Drive 97701 (541) 639-4776 https://worthy.beer/

Silver Moon Brewing 24 NW Greenwood Avenue 97701 (541) 388-8331 https://www.silvermoonbrewing.com/

Immersion Brewing 550 SW Industrial Way Suite 185 97702 (541) 633-7821 https://imbrewing.com/

Deschutes Brewery 901 SW Simpson Avenue 97702 (541) 385-8606 https://www.deschutesbrewery.com/

Bevel Craft Brewing 911 SE Armour Road 97702 (541) 972-3835
https://www.bevelbeer.com/

Craft Kitchen and Brewery 803 SW Industrial Way #202 97702 (541) 647-2772 https://craftoregon.com/

GoodLife Brewing Company 70 SW Century Avenue 100-464 97702 (541) 728-0749 https://www.goodlifebrewing.com/

Spider City Brewing 1177 SE 9th Street 97702 (512) 555-1212 https://spidercitybrewing.com/

The Ale Apothecary 61517 River Road 97701 (541) 318-9143 https://thealeapothecary.com/

Riverbend Brewing Company 2650 NE Division Street 97701 (541) 550-7550 http://riverbendbrewing.com/

Crux Fermentation Project 50 SW Division Street 97702 (541) 385-3333 https://www.cruxfermentation.com/

10 Barrel Brewing Company 20750 High Desert Lane #107 97701 (541) 585-1007 https://10barrel.com/

Monkless Belgian Ales 20750 NE High Desert Lane #107 97701 (541) 203-0009 https://www.monkless.com/

Bend Brewing Company 1019 NW Brooks Street 97701 (541) 383-1599 https://www.bendbrewingco.com/

The second oldest brewpub in Bend. They have a long list of award-winning craft beers. Be sure to try their Mocha Porter.

Boss Rambler Beer Club 1009 NW Galveston Avenue 97703 https://bossrambler.com/

An ever-progressing brewery offering some unique beers along with the classic styles. Be sure to taste a sample of their tropical hazy IPA, cocktail-inspired lager, and domestic light beer. Your next stop is in Redmond.

Wild Ride Brewing Company 332 SW 5th Street 97756 (541) 516-8544 https://www.wildridebrew.com/

Cascade Lakes Brewing Company 2141 SW 1st Street 97756 (541) 923-3110 http://www.cascadelakes.com/

In addition to rotating seasonal beers, be sure to sample their five year-round beers: Blonde Bombshell, 20" Brown, Pineapple Kush, Hopsmack IPA, and Salted Caramel Porter. Finally, head on over to Sisters and Sunriver.

Three Creeks Brewing Company 721 Desperado Court 97759 (541) 549-1963 https://www.threecreeksbrewing.com/

Sunriver Brewing Company 57100 Beaver Drive Building 4 Sunriver Village 97707 (541) 593-3007 https://www.sunriverbrewingcompany.com/

Eastern Oregon

There aren't a lot of breweries in this area and what there is can be a bit of a drive. So you'll want at least two to three days if you plan to visit them all while enjoying your drive time. Start your trip in Ontario at:

Beer Valley Brewing Company 937 SE 12th Avenue 97914 (541) 881-9088 http://www.beervalleybrewing.com/index.shtml

The next brewery is at John Day about two-hour northwest:

1188 Brewing Company 141 E Main Street 97845 (541) 575-1188 https://1188brewing.com/

Baker City is an hour and a half northeast:

Barley Brown's Beer 2190 Main Street 97814 (541) 523-4266 http://www.barleybrownsbeer.com/

About forty minutes north is the next brewery at La Grande:

Side A Brewing 1219 Washington Avenue 97850 (541) 605-0163
http://sideabeer.com/

East about an hour and a half is Enterprise:

Terminal Gravity Brewing Company 803 SE School Street 97828 (541) 426-0158 https://terminalgravitybrewing.com/

Northwest about two hours is Milton-Freewater with a must-visit brewery:

Dragon's Gate Brewery 52288 Sunquist Road 97862 (541) 215-2622
https://www.dragonsgatebrewery.com/

Brewing Belgian and Farmhouse style ales with passion and tradition. All of the ales are brewed on a seasonal basis, so what you get will depend on the time you visit. About a half-hour away to the west is Pendleton:

The Prodigal Son Brewery 230 SE Court Avenue 97801 (541) 276-6090
http://prodigalsonbrewery.com/

Another half-hour west is Hermiston:

Hermiston Brewing Company 125 N 1st Street 97838 (541) 289-7414
http://hermistonbrewingcompany.com/

End your trip about a half-hour away in Boardman at a must-visit brewery:

Ordnance Brewing 405 N Olson Road 97818 (541) 481-2231
https://www.ordnancebrewing.com/

Brewing distinct and honest beers. Try their award-winning Blackfisky barrel-aged stout and EOD American-style Indian Pale Ale.

Mt. Hood and Columbia River Area

There are only four cities and a handful of breweries in this area that cover some of the most scenic views in the Pacific Northwest. Take a day to enjoy this wonderful area and try some great beers. Start your trip in Cascade Locks at:

Thunder Island Brewing 515 Portage Road 97014 (971) 231-4599 http://thunderislandbrewing.com/

Nineteen minutes east is Hood River with four options including two must-visits:

Ferment Brewing Company 403 Portway Avenue 97031 (541) 436-3499 https://www.fermentbrewing.com/

pFriem Family Brewers 707 Portway Avenue #101 97031 (541) 321-0490 https://www.pfriembeer.com/

Full Sail Brewing Company 506 Columbia Street 97031 (888) 244-BEER https://fullsailbrewing.com/

Their best selling beer is the Full Sail Amber, a gold medal-winning beer in 1989. Since then, they have continued to produce wonderful beers of all styles.

Double Mountain Brewery and Taproom 8 4th Street 97031 (541) 387-0042 https://www.doublemountainbrewery.com/

Offering four year-round beers along with wide and ever-changing seasonal brews and one-offs. All beers feature a Pilsner malt as the base ingredient. About twenty-minutes south is another must-visit brewery at Parkdale:

Solera Brewery 4945 Baseline Drive 97041 (541) 352-5500 http://www.solerabrewery.com/

Specializing in unique, one-of-a-kind beers. A local favorite is the Hedonist IPA and the only one you'll find year-round. The other offerings will change regularly. Take about a three-hour drive through the mountains and end your trip in Mitchell at:

Tiger Town Brewing Company 108 Main Street 97750 (541) 462-3663
https://www.tigertownbrewing.com/

Oregon Coast

Take a ride down the stunningly beautiful Oregon Coast while sampling some wonderful beers. Take a day or two to fully enjoy your trip. Start your trip out in Astoria at two breweries:

Buoy Beer Company 1 Eighth Street 97103 (503) 325-4540
https://www.buoybeer.com/

Fort George Brewery + Public House 1483 Duane Street 97103 (503) 325-7468 https://fortgeorgebrewery.com/

About twenty-minutes south is the next brewery at Seaside:

Sisu Beer 133 Broadway Street 97138 (503) 739-7188
http://sisubeer.com/

Eleven minutes away is a must-visit brewery at Cannon Beach:

Public Coast Brewing Company 264 Third Street 97110 (503) 436-0285
https://publiccoastbrewing.com/

Making delicious and approachable beers. Be sure to try their award-winning '67 Blonde Ale while you view the beautiful Oregon coastline. About an hour south is Tillamook:

De Garde Brewing 6000 Blimp Blvd 97141 (503) 815-1635
http://www.degardebrewing.com/

Lincoln City is another hour south:

Rusty Truck Brewing Company 4649 SW Highway 101 97367 (541) 994-7729 https://rustytruckbrewing.com/

About forty minutes south is Newport with two breweries including a must-visit:

Rogue Ales 2320 OSU Drive 97365 (541) 867-3660
https://www.rogue.com/

Newport Brewing Company 1118 SW Canyon Way 97365 (541) 272-5033 https://www.newportbrewingcompany.com/

Specializing in IPAs, lagers, stouts, and other popular ales. Try their Flagship Dungeness IPA and Hazy Crazy DIPA. Another half-hour brings you to Yachats:

Yachats Brewing 348 Highway 101 N 97498 (541) 547-3884
https://yachatsbrewing.com/

Just seventeen minutes away is Seal Rock:

Wolf Tree Brewery 199 N Wolkau Road 97376 (541) 961-2030
https://www.wolftreebrewery.com/

A three and a half-hour drive down the coast brings you to Gold Beach and a must-visit brewery:

Arch Rock Brewing Company 28779 Hunter Creek Loop 97444 (541) 247-0555

Currently offering three beers. Gold Beach Lager is a light and crisp German-style lager. Pistol River Pale is an old school IPA. State of Jefferson Porter is a robust beer. End your trip a half-hour south in Brookings at a must-visit brewery:

Chetco Brewing Company 927 Chetco Avenue 97415 (541) 661-5347
https://www.chetcobrew.com/

A vegan brewery that doesn't use any additives or extracts. The beers are clarified using Irish moss. All fruits and herbs used in the beer are free of pesticides and herbicides.

Portland Area

Portland is one of the largest brewing areas in the United States. You could easily spend days just in the city alone. So take the time to look through the Portland listings and choose the breweries you want to visit then plan the outlying trip to determine how many days you'll need. Start your trip in St. Helens at:

Captured by Porches Brewing Company 40 Cowlitz Street 97051 (503) 238-8899 https://www.capturedbyporches.com/

Head south about forty minutes to Hillsboro with several options including a must-visit:

Deep Space Brewing 6255 NW Century Blvd 97124 (503) 629-8700 https://www.deepspacebrewing.com/

Three Mugs Brewing 2020 NW Aloclek Drive Suite 108 97124 (971) 322-0232 https://www.threemugsbrewingco.com/

Ambacht Brewing 1060 NE 25th Avenue Suite B 97124 (503) 828-1400 http://www.ambacht.us/

Vertigo Brewing 21420 NW Nicholas Court Suite D7 97124 (503) 645-6644 https://vertigobrew.com/

Offering award-winning fruit beers and NW style IPAs along with seasonal Barrel-aged beers. Be sure to try their Madagascar Vanilla Porter. Just twelve minutes away is another brewery in Forest Grove:

Kaiser Brewing Company 1607 Hawthorne Street 97116 (503) 412-9628 https://kaiserbrewingco.com/

McMinnville is about a half-hour south and offers several more breweries:

Evasion Brewing 4230 NE Riverside Drive Unit B 97128 (503) 835-5322 https://evasionbrewing.com/

Grain Station Brew Works 755 NE Alpine Avenue Suite 200 97128 (503) 687-2739 http://grainstation.com/

Golden Valley Brewery and Pub 980 NE 4th Street 97128 (503) 472-2739 https://goldenvalleybrewery.com/

Heater Allen Brewing 907 NE 10th Avenue 97128 (503) 472-4898 http://heaterallen.com/

Twenty-minutes northeast is Newberg with two breweries including a must-visit:

Wolves and People Farmhouse Brewery 30203 NE Benjamin Road 97132 (917) 586-2357 https://www.wolvesandpeople.com/

Long Brewing 29380 Owls Lane 97132 (503) 349-8341 http://www.longbrewing.com/

Making handcrafted ales and lagers that are expressive in aroma and flavor. Sample their four year-round beers: Pils, Kolsch style lager, India Pale Ale, and Paul's Porter. Twenty-minutes east is another brewery at Wilsonville:

Vanguard Brewing Company 27501 SW 95th Avenue Suite 945 97070 (503) 929-3774 https://www.vanguardbrewing.com/

Nine minutes away is Tualatin and a must-visit brewery:

Ancestry Brewing 20585 SW Tualatin-Sherwood Road 97062 (503) 454-0821 http://www.ancestrybrewing.com/

Brewing finely crafted ales with a focus on detail and quality. Try their flagship Best Coast IPA and Irish Red. Just thirteen minutes northeast is Lake Oswego:

Stickmen Brewing Company 40 N State Street 97034 (503) 344-4449 https://stickmenbeer.com/

Fourteen minutes north is the main city of Portland:

Occidental Brewing Company 6635 N Baltimore 97203 (503) 719-7102
https://www.occidentalbrewing.com/index.html

Grixsen Brewing Company 1001 SE Division Street #1 97202 (971) 347-3100 http://www.grixsen.com/

West Coast Grocery Co. 1403 SE Stark Street 97214 (503) 850-8425
https://www.westcoastgrocerycompany.com/

Tuebor Beer Company 111 SE Belmont Street 97214 (971) 266-4083
https://tuebor.beer/

13 Virtues Brewing Company 6410 SE Milwaukie Avenue 97202 (503) 239-8544 http://www.13virtuesbrewing.com/

Bethany Public House 4840 NW Bethany Blvd 97229 (971) 371-2954
https://www.bethanypublichouse.com/

Sasquatch Brewing Company 6440 SW Capitol Highway 97239 (503) 402-1999 https://sasquatchbrewery.com/

Von Ebert Brewing 131 NW 13th Avenue 97209 (360) 433-1856
https://www.vonebertbrewing.com/

StormBreaker Brewing 832 N Beech Street 97227 (971) 703-4516
https://www.stormbreakerbrewing.com/home.html

Binary Brewing 6620 SW Scholls Ferry Road 97223 (503) 336-4783
http://www.binarybrewing.co/index.html

Rosenstadt Brewery 4110 SE Hawthorne #735 97214
http://www.rosenstadtbrewery.com/

Assembly Brewing 6112 SE Foster Road 97206
https://assemblybrewingco.com/

Hopworks Urban Brewery 2944 SE Powell Blvd 97202 (503) 232-4677
https://www.hopworksbeer.com/

Culmination Brewing 2117 NE Oregon Avenue 97232 (503) 353-6368
https://culminationbrewingshop.com/

Wayfinder Beer 304 SE 2nd Avenue 97214 (503) 718-2337
https://www.wayfinder.beer/

Upright Brewing Company 240 N Broadway 97227 (503) 735-5337
http://www.uprightbrewing.com/

Laurelwood Public House and Brewery 5115 NE Sandy 97212 (503)
282-0622 https://www.laurelwoodbrewpub.com/

Back Pedal Brewing Company 1425 NW Flanders 97209 (971) 400-
5950 http://backpedalbrewing.com/

The Labrewatory 670 N Russell Street 97227 (971) 271-8151
https://www.labrewatory.com/

Migration Brewing Company 2828 NE Glisan Street 97232 (503) 206-
5221 https://migrationbrewing.com/

Hair of the Dog Brewing Company 61 SE Yamhill Street 97214 (503)
232-6585 https://www.hairofthedog.com/

Base Camp Brewing Company 930 SE Oak Street 97214 (503) 764-
9152 https://www.basecampbrewingco.com/

Kells Brew Pub 210 NW 21st Avenue 97209 (503) 719-7175
http://www.kellsbrewpub.com/

Threshold Brewing and Blending 403 SE 79th Avenue 97215 (503)
477-8789 https://www.threshold.beer/

Fire on the Mountain Brewery 3443 NE 57th Avenue 97213 (503) 894-
8973 https://www.portlandwings.com/_brewery.php

Ascendent Beer Company 412 NW 5th Avenue 97209 (503) 564-2739
https://www.ascendantbeer.com/

Away Days Brewing Company 1516 SE 10th Avenue 97214 (503) 206-4735 https://www.awaydaysbrewing.com/

Ruse Brewing 4784 SE 17th Avenue 97202 (503) 662-8325 https://www.rusebrewing.com/

Portland Brewing Company 2730 NW 31st Avenue 97210 (503) 228-5269 https://www.portlandbrewing.com/

Old Town Brewing Company 5201 NE Martin Luther King Jr. Blvd 97211 (503) 200-5988 https://www.otbrewing.com/

Great Notion Brewing 2204 NE Alberta #101 97211 (503) 548-4491 https://greatnotion.com/

Zoiglhaus Brewing Company 5716 SE 92nd Avenue 97236 (971) 339-2374 http://www.zoiglhaus.com/

Level Beer 5211 NE 148th Avenue 97230 (503) 714-1222 https://levelbeer.com/

Gigantic Brewing Company 5224 SE 26th Avenue 97202 (503) 208-3416 https://www.giganticbrewing.com/

MadCow Brewing Company 4202 SE 166th Avenue 97233 (503) 209-0927 https://madcowbrewing.com/

Old Market Pub and Brewery 6959 SW Multnomah Blvd Suite 101 97223 (503) 244-2337 http://www.drinkbeerhere.com/

Ground Breaker Brewing 715 SE Lincoln Street 97214 (503) 928-4195 https://www.groundbreakerbrewing.com/

Natian Brewery 1321 NE Couch Street 97232 (971) 678-7116 https://natianbrewery.com/

Ex Novo Brewing 2326 N Flint Avenue 97227 (503) 894-8251 http://www.exnovobrew.com/

Second Profession Brewing Company 5846 NE Sandy Blvd 97213
(503) 288-5882 https://www.secondprofessionbrewing.com/

Lucky Labrador Brewing Company 7675 SW Capitol Highway 97219
(503) 244-2537 https://luckylab.com/

Baerlic Brewing Company 2235 SE 11th Avenue 97214 (503) 477-9418
http://baerlicbrewing.com/

Offering two year-round selections: a pre-prohibition lager and IPA. There
are also seasonal and experimental beers to try.

Ecliptic Brewing 825 N Cook Street 97221 (503) 265-8002
http://eclipticbrewing.com/

Enjoy a new beer tasting experience here. Flagship beers to try include
the Starburst IPA, Carina Peach Sour Ale, and Capella Porter.

Cascade Brewing 7424 SW Beaverton-Hillsdale Highway 97225 (503)
296-0110 https://www.cascadebrewing.com/

The originator of the Northwest Sour Ale. Offering distinctive sour beer
blends featuring fruit-forward, barrel-aged ales with a complex range of
flavors.

Montavilla Brew Works 7805 SE Stark Street 97215 (503) 954-3440
https://montavillabrew.com/

Brewing balanced, drinkable ales along with seasonal lagers and Pacific
NW-style beers. Stop in to try them today. When you're ready to head out,
go about twenty-minutes east to your next brewery in Wood Village:

Super Brewing Company 24023 Shea Lane Unit 104 94060 (503) 512-
7492 https://superbrewing.co/

Clackamas is twenty-minutes southwest:

Drinking Horse Brewing Company 11517 SE Highway 212 97015 (503)
564-8165 http://www.drinkinghorsebeer.com/

Just nine minutes away is Oregon City with two breweries including a must-visit:

Oregon City Brewing Company 1401 Washington Street 97045 (503) 908-1948 https://www.ocbeerco.com/

Coin Toss Brewing 14214 Fir Street Suite H 97045 (971) 224-9487 https://www.cointossbrewing.com/

Serving a traditional line of handcrafted beers along with their Heritage Series that comes from historical recipes. East about twenty-minutes is another must-visit brewery in Estacada:

Fearless Brewing Company 326 N Broadway Street 97023 (503) 630-2337 https://fearless.beer/

Escape to the country for some unique beers. Try their award-winning Scottish Ale, Porter, and Loki Red Ale. Fourteen minutes north is Sandy:

Bunsenbrewer 16506 SE 362nd 97055 (503) 308-3150 http://www.bunsenbrewer.com/

End your trip about a half-hour east in Government Camp at:

Mt. Hood Brewing Company 87304 E Government Camp Loop 97028 (503) 272-3172 https://mthoodbrewing.com/

Southern Oregon

This trip is a great trip through a few towns in Southern Oregon with great breweries. Start your trip in Klamath Falls at a must-visit brewery:

Klamath Basin Brewing Company 1320 Main Street 97601 (541) 273-5222 https://www.kbbrewing.com/

The first geothermal brewery in the United States. Stop in to try their award-winning IPAs and ales, along with a Vanilla Porter. Head west an hour and a half to two breweries in Ashland:

Caldera Brewing Company 540 Clover Lane 97520 (541) 482-HOPS
http://www.calderabrewing.com/

Standing Stone Brewing Company 101 Oak Street 97520 (541) 482-2448 https://www.standingstonebrewing.com/

Twenty-minutes northwest is Medford with four breweries:

Common Block Brewing Company 315 E 5th Street 97501 (541) 326-2277 https://www.commonblockbrewing.com/

Portal Brewing Company 100 East Sixth Street 97504 (541) 499-0804
http://portalbrewingco.com/

Bricktowne Brewing Company 3612 Calle Vista Drive 97504 (541) 941-0752 https://bricktownebrewing.com/

Opposition Brewing Company 545 Rossanley Drive Suite 106 97501 (541) 210-8550 http://www.oppositionbrewing.com/

Continue another half-hour west to Grants Pass with four breweries including two must-visits:

Weekend Beer Company 550 SW 6th Street Suite G 97526 (541) 507-1919 https://www.weekendbeercompany.com/

Wild River Brewery and Pizza Company 595 NE F Street 97526 (541) 471-7487 https://www.wildriverbrewing.com/

Climate City Brewing Company 509 SW G Street 97526 (541) 479-3725 https://www.climatecitybrewing.com/home

Serving wonderful beers and upscale pub food. Try their flagship beers: Nookie IPA, Yellow Belly Blonde, Rainie Falls Red, and Hyperion Porter.

Conner Fields Brewing 1494 Kubli Road 97527 (541) 508-2337 https://www.connerfields.com/

Creating a variety of beers from a simple and refreshing lager to a rustic farmhouse ale. Be sure to try their Cream Lager. End your trip about an hour north in Roseburg at two breweries:

Two Shy Brewing 1308 NW Park Street 97470 (541) 236-2055
https://www.twoshybrewing.com/

Old 99 Brewing Company 3750 Hooker Road Suite A 97470 (541) 670-9260 http://old99brewing.com/

Willamette Valley

This area of Oregon is well known for its wineries, and they also feature some great breweries. Visit a few cities and some great breweries in a day or two. Start your trip in Silverton with two breweries including a must-visit:

Silver Falls Brewery 207 Jersey Street 97381 (503) 873-3022
http://www.silverfallsbrewery.com/

Belgian Underground Beers 315 W Center Street 97381 (503) 779-7523
https://www.belgianundergroundbeers.com/

Focusing on Belgian style beers: strong golden ales, farmhouse ales, lagers, fruit beers, and sour beers. Head southwest about twenty-minutes to Salem with a few options:

Vagabond Brewing 2195 Hyacinth Street NE 97301 (503) 512-9007
https://www.vagabondbrewing.com/

Salem Ale Works 2315 25th Street SE 97302 (503) 990-8486
https://salemaleworks.com/

Xicha Brewing 576 Patterson Street NW Suite 140 97304 (503) 990-8292
https://www.xichabrewing.com/

Santiam Brewing Company 2544 19th Street SE 97302 (503) 689-1260
https://www.santiambrewing.com/

Gilgamesh Brewing 2065 Madrona Avenue SE 97302 (503) 584-1789
https://www.gilgameshbrewing.com/

Albany is a half-hour south and has two breweries including a must-visit:

Calapooia Brewing Company 140 Hill Street NE 97321 (541) 928-1931
https://www.calapooiabrewing.com/

Deluxe Brewing Company 635 NE Water Avenue Suite B 97321 (541)
639-4257 https://www.sinisterdeluxe.com/

Specializing in easy-drinking ales and lagers. The three year-round beers
are a Pre-Prohibition Pilsner, Amber Lager, and Schwarzbier, along with
seasonal options. About twenty-minutes to the west are three breweries in
Corvallis:

Mazama Brewing Company 33930A Eastgate Circle 97330 (541) 230-
1810 https://mazamabrewing.com/

Block 15 Brewery and Restaurant 300 SW Jefferson Avenue 97333
(541) 758-2077 http://block15.com/

Sky High Brewing 160 NW Jackson Avenue 97330 (541) 207-3277
https://skyhighbrewing.com/

Head back east about a half-hour to a brewery in Lebanon:

Conversion Brewing 833 S Main Street 97355 (541) 259-2337
https://www.conversionbrewingcompany.com/

The largest city of Eugene is about fifty minutes south:

Ninkasi Brewing Company 272 Van Buren Street 97402 (541) 344-2739
https://ninkasibrewing.com/

Oakshire Brewing 1055 Madera Street 97402 (541) 654-5520
https://oakbrew.com/

Hop Valley Tasting Room 990 W 1st Avenue 97402 (541) 485-2337
https://www.hopvalleybrewing.com/

Claim 52 Brewing 1030 Tyinn Street Suite 1 97402 (541) 554-6786
https://www.claim52brewing.com/

ColdFire Brewing 263 Mill Street 97401 (541) 636-3889
https://www.coldfirebrewing.com/

Falling Sky Brewing 1334 Oak Alley 97401 (541) 484-3322
https://fallingskybrewing.com/

McKenzie Brewing Company 199 East 5th Street 97401 (541) 341-1330
https://mckenziebrewing.com/

Brewing since 1991 with over 40 awards and counting. Try four of their excellent beers: Keller Kolsch, St. Bernard Brown, Steelhead Root Beer, and Hopasaurus Rex Imperial IPA. End your trip just seven minutes away in Springfield at:

Plank Town Brewing Company 346 Main Street 97477 (541) 746-1890
https://planktownbrewing.com/

Pennsylvania

Cumberland Valley

This short day trip will take you to a few towns in the beautiful Cumberland Valley. Start your trip in Chambersburg with two breweries including a must-visit:

GearHouse Brewing Company 253 Grant Street 17201 (717) 552-2427
https://gearhousebrewingco.com/contact/

Roy Pitz Brewing Company 140 North Third Street 17257 (717) 496-8753 http://www.roypitz.com/

Since opening, the brewery has won over twenty awards. Stop in today to try a seasonal beer in addition to their three year-round beers: Best Blonde, a German-style Golden Lager, Daddy Fat Sacks, an American

IPA, and Sour Hound, an American Sour Ale. Drive about a half-hour southeast to Carlisle with four breweries:

Burd's Nest Brewing Company 19 N Hanover Street 17013 (717) 385-7152 https://www.burdsnestbrewingco.com/

Market Cross Pub and Brewery 113 N Hanover Street 17013 (717) 258-1234 http://marketcrosspub.com/

Desperate Times Brewery 1201 Carlisle Springs Road 17013 (717) 706-3192 http://desperatetimesbrewery.com/

Molly Pitcher Brewing Company 10 E South Street 17013 (717) 609-0969 https://mollypitcher.com/

Continue another twenty-minutes to Enola with a must-visit brewery:

Pizza Boy Brewing 2240 Millennium Way 17025 (717) 728-3840 https://www.pizzaboybrewing.com/

Brewing a diverse range of beers, so there is something for everyone. Try a super-hopped IPA or a coffee-infused stout. Eight minutes away is two breweries in Camp Hill:

Ever Grain Brewing Company 4444 Carlisle Pike Suite C 17011 (717) 525-8222 https://evergrainbrewing.com/

Highway Manor Brewing 2238 Gettysburg Road 17011 (717) 743-0613 https://highwaymanorbrewing.com/

End your trip another eight minutes away in Mechanicsburg at:

Mellow Mink Brewing Company 4830 Carlisle Pike 17050 (717) 693-7687 https://mellowmink.com/

Pittsburgh Area

Pittsburgh is home to multiple breweries, but the surrounding area is also dotted with a number of breweries. Depending on how many breweries you want to visit, you'll need two to three days or potentially more. Start your trip in Beaver Falls at:

Beaver Brewing Company 1820 7th Avenue 15010 (412) 555-7112
https://www.beaverbrewingcompany.com/

Just five minutes away is the next brewery in New Brighton at:

Petrucci Brothers Brewing 911 5th Avenue 15066 (724) 987-2579
https://www.petruccibrothers.com/

Head south about a half-hour to Coraopolis:

Cobblehaus Brewing Company 1021 Fifth Avenue 15108 (412) 264-7000 https://www.cobblehaus.com/

Emsworth is just nine minutes away:

Aurochs Brewing Company 8321 Ohio River Blvd 15202 (724) 260-8737 https://www.aurochsbrewing.com/

Twenty-minutes south brings you to another brewery at Heidelberg:

Insurrection AleWorks 1635 E Railroad Street 15106 (412) 276-2030
https://www.insurrectionaleworks.com/

Oakdale is thirteen minutes west and has a must-visit brewery:

Helicon Brewing 102 Union Avenue 15071 (724) 693-4204
http://heliconbrewing.com/

Making beers approachable and appealing to a wide variety of people. With 8 to 12 beers on tap, you'll easily find something to enjoy. Continue west another twenty-minutes to Burgettstown:

Coal Tipple Brewing 1905 Steubenville Pike 15021 (724) 899-3344
http://www.coaltipplebrewery.com/

Half-hour south is Washington:

The Washington Brewing Company 28 East Maiden Street 15301 (724) 222-5050 https://www.thewashingtonbrewingcompany.com/

Charleroi is a half-hour southeast:

Four Points Brewing 400 Washington Avenue 15022 (724) 565-5456 https://fourpointsbrewing.com/

About forty minutes north is the main city of Pittsburgh with multiple options:

Roundabout Brewery 4901 Butler Street 15201 https://roundaboutbeer.com/

Couch Brewery 1351 Washington Blvd 15206 (412) 441-1724 https://www.couchbrewery.com/

Grist House Craft Brewery 10 Sherman Street 15209 (412) 447-1442 https://gristhouse.com/

Allegheny City Brewing 407 Foreland Street 15212 (412) 904-3732 https://www.alleghenycitybrewing.com/

Spring Hill Brewing 1958 Varley Street 15212 https://www.springhillbrewing.com/

East End Brewing Company 147 Julius Street 15206 (412) 537-2337 https://www.eastendbrewing.com/

Hitchhiker Brewing Company 190 Castle Shannon Blvd 15228 (412) 343-1950 https://hitchhiker.beer/

Hop Farm Brewing Company 5601 Butler Street 15201 (412) 726-7912 http://www.hopfarmbrewingco.com/index.htm

Bier's Pub/War Streets Brewery 1416 Arch Street 15212 (412) 224-2163 https://bierspub.com/

Eleventh Hour Brewing Company 3711 Charlotte Street 15201 (412) 699-4074 https://www.11thhourbrews.com/#home-1-section

Mindful Brewing Company 3759 Library Road 15234 (412) 668-3857
https://mindfulbrewing.com/

Church Brew Works 3525 Liberty Avenue 15201 (412) 688-8200
https://churchbrew.com/

Burgh'ers Brewery 3601 Butler Street 15201 (412) 904-2622
http://burgherspgh.com/

Cinderlands Beer Company 3705 Butler Street 15201 (412) 251-0656
https://www.cinderlands.com/

Dancing Gnome 925 Main Street 15215 (412) 408-2083
http://www.dancinggnomebeer.com/

Duquesne Bottling Company 2581 Washington Road Suite 221 15241
(412) 831-2779 http://duquesnebeer.com/

The Duquesne Pilsner is crisp with a smooth finish and a hint of
sweetness. There is also a light beer that is full-flavored and refreshing.

Pennsylvania Brewing Company 800 Vinial Street 15212 (412) 237-
9402 https://www.pennbrew.com/

The oldest and largest brewery in Pittsburgh. Specializing in authentic,
award-winning German-style beers since 1986. Just six minutes away is
another brewery at Millvale:

Strange Roots Experimental Ales 501 E Ohio Street 15209 (412) 407-
2506 http://www.strangerootsbeer.com/

Springdale is twenty-minutes northeast:

The Leaning Cask Brewing Company 850 Pittsburgh Street 15144 (724)
715-7539 https://www.leaningcaskbrewing.com/

About twenty-minutes north is Sarver with another brewery:

Cellar Works Brewing 110 S Pike Road 16055 (724) 524-2120
https://cellarworksbrewing.com/

West about twenty-minutes is Renfrew:

Missing Links Brewery 891 Evans City Road 16053 (724) 486-3777
https://missinglinksbrewery.com/

Mars is sixteen minutes south:

Stick City Brewing 109 Irvine Street 16046 (724) 687-7849
https://stickcitybeer.com/

Fifteen minutes northwest is Harmony:

Big Rail Brewing 230 Mercer Street 16037 https://bigrailbrewing.com/

End your trip just next door in Zelienople at:

ShuBrew 210 S Main Street 16063 (724) 766-4426
https://www.shubrew.com/

Eastern Piedmont

The Piedmont area is home to beautiful sceneries and a lot of breweries. You'll need to take the area in two pieces to enjoying everything. The Eastern portion can be traveled in a day or two. Start your trip in Allentown at:

Hijinx Brewing Company 905 Harrison Street Suite 111 18103 (484) 714-0080 http://hijinxbrewing.com/

Catasauqua is nine minutes away:

Taylor House Brewing 76 Lehigh Street 18032
http://www.taylorhousebrewing.com/

Eleven minutes east is Bethlehem with three breweries including a must-visit:

Fegley's Bethlehem Brew Works 569 Main Street 18018 (610) 882-1300
https://thebrewworks.com/

Bonn Place Brewing Company 310 Taylor Street 18015 (610) 419-6660
https://bonnbrewing.com/

Hop Hill Brewing Company 1988 Blair Avenue 18015 (484) 893-0767
https://www.hophillbeer.com/

Offering twelve taps with a full range of styles: IPAs, a blonde ale, stout, lager, ESB, cream ale, porter, and amber.

Next head north about twenty-minutes to Nazareth:

Birthright Brewing Company 57 South Main Street 18064 (610) 365-2225 http://birthrightbrewingco.com/

Easton is twelve minutes south with three breweries including two must-visits:

Two Rivers Brewing Company 542 Northampton Street 18042 (610) 823-3123 https://www.tworiversbrewing.com/

Weyerbacher Brewing Company 905 Line Street 18042 (610) 559-5561
https://www.weyerbacher.com/

Offering big and bold craft beers. Try their Merry Monks Belgian Tripel, Blithering Idiot Barleywine Ale, and Tiny Imperial Stout.

Separatist Beer Project 1247 Simon Blvd Suite N108 18042
https://www.separatistbeer.com/

Focusing on hops and spontaneous fermentation. Try the always-available easy-drinking Cream Ale, and if you're traveling in the holiday season, try the All the Feels holiday beer. Continue about another twenty-minutes southwest to Hellertown:

Lost Tavern Brewing 782 Main Street 18055 (484) 851-3980
https://www.losttavernbrewing.com/

Coopersburg is another eleven minutes away:

Sage Alley Brewery and Grill 213 North Main Street 18036 (610) 421-6029 https://www.sagealleybrewery.com/

Fifteen minutes west is two breweries at Emmaus:

Yergey Brewing S 5th and Railroad Streets 18049 (484) 232-7055 https://www.yergeybrewing.com/

Funk Brewing Company 19 S Sixth Street 18049 (610) 421-8270 http://www.funkbrewing.com/

Continue another twenty-five minutes to Kutztown:

Saucony Creek Brewing Company + Gastropub 15032 Kutztown Road 19530 (610) 683-3128 http://sauconybeer.com/

Boyertown is about a half-hour south:

The Other Farm Brewing Company 128 E Philadelphia Avenue 19512 (610) 367-1788 http://www.theotherfarmbrewingcompany.com/

Continue another thirteen minutes to Douglassville:

Hidden River Brewing Company 1808 W Schuylkill Road 19518 (484) 273-2266 https://hiddenriverbrewing.com/

End your trip about twenty-minutes northwest in West Reading with two breweries:

Chatty Monks Brewing 610 Penn Avenue 19611 (484) 818-0176 https://www.chattymonks.com/

Broken Chair Brewery 424 East Penn Avenue 19611 https://www.brokenchairbrewery.com/

Western Piedmont

The second has even more breweries in a small area. Depending on your itinerary, you may need two to three days to see all the breweries. Start your trip in Adamstown at:

Stoudts Brewing Company Rt 272 2800 North Reading Road 19501 (717) 484-4386 https://stoudts.com/

Fourteen minutes southwest is two breweries in Ephrata:

Black Forest Brewery 301 West Main Street 17522 (717) 721-9268 https://blackforestbrewery.net/

St. Boniface Craft Brewing Company 1701 W Main Street 17522 (717) 466-6900 https://stbonifacebrewing.com/

Another twenty-minutes is Lancaster with three breweries:

Fetish Brewing Company 325 Ice Avenue 17602 https://fetishbrewing.tumblr.com/

Wacker Brewing Company 417 West Grant Street 17603 (717) 617-2711 https://wackerbrewing.com/

Lancaster Brewing Company 302 North Plum Street 17602 (717) 391-6258 https://www.lancasterbrewing.com/

East Petersburg is twelve minutes north:

Mad Chef Craft Brewing 2023 Miller Road 17520 (717) 690-2655 https://www.madchefcraftbrewing.com/

Just eight minutes away is Manheim:

Swashbuckler Brewing Company 83 Mansion Road 17545 (717) 664-3930 http://www.swashbucklerbrewing.com/

A must-visit brewery is twenty minutes north in Lebanon:

Snitz Creek Brewery 7 North 9th Street 17046 (717) 450-4467 https://www.snitzcreekbrewery.com/

Featuring beers that celebrate the outdoors. Be sure to try flagship beers such as Opening Day, Woolly Bugger, Linebreaker, and Explorer. Ten minutes away is Annville with another brewery:

Rotunda Brewing Company 239 West Main Street 17003 (717) 867-2337 https://www.batdorfrestaurant.com/rbc

Another thirteen minutes is Hershey:

Troegs Brewing Company 200 East Hersheypark Drive 17033 (717) 534-1297 https://troegs.com/

Eighteen minutes west is Harrisburg with multiple options:

Appalachian Brewing Company 50 N Cameron Street 17101 (717) 221-1080 https://www.abcbrew.com/

The Vegetable Hunter 614 N 2nd Street 17101 (717) 695-6229 http://thevegetablehunter.com/boutique-brewery/

Spring Gate Brewery 5790 Devonshire Road 17112 (717) 480-0066 http://www.springgatebrewery.com/

Newfangled Brew Works 8001 Union Station Blvd 17111 (717) 982-6662 https://newfangledbrew.com/

The Millworks 340 Verbeke Street 17102 (717) 695-4888 https://millworksharrisburg.com/

Boneshire Brew Works 7462 Derry Street 17111 (717) 469-5007 http://www.boneshire.com/

Zeroday Brewing Company 250 Reily Street Suite 103 17102 (717) 745-6218 https://www.zerodaytogo.com/

Southeast about twenty-minutes is Middletown:

Tattered Flag Brewery and Still Works 1 S Union Street 17057 (717) 829-8584 https://www.tatteredflagbsw.com/

Elizabethtown is twelve minutes away with two breweries including a must-visit:

Moo-Duck Brewery 79 South Wilson Avenue 17022
https://mooduckbrewery.com/

Cox Brewing Company 276 Heisey Quarry Road 17022 (717) 449-9926
https://www.coxbrewingcompany.com/

Offering twelve varieties on tap. Choose from options like an American Lager, American Ale, Amber Ale, and Baltic Coffee Porter. Eleven minutes away is Mount Joy with two breweries:

Bube's Brewery 102 N Market Street 17552 (717) 653-2056
http://bubesbrewery.com/

Twisted Bine Beer Company 93 E Main Street 17552 (717) 928-4214
http://www.twistedbinebeerco.com/

Marietta is nine minutes away:

Pig Iron Brewing Company 40 E Front Street 17547 (717) 604-1161
http://www.pigironbrewingco.com/

Another seven minutes is Columbia:

Columbia Kettle Works 40 N 3rd Street 17512 (717) 342-2374
http://www.columbiakettleworks.com/

About twenty-minutes south is Dallastown:

Wyndridge Farm Brewing 885 South Pleasant Avenue 17313 (717) 244-9900 http://wyndridge.com/

Continue a half-hour south to Fawn Grove:

South County Brewing Company 104 Mill Street 17321 (717) 382-4016
https://southcountybrewing.com/

West about a half-hour is New Freedom:

Gunpowder Falls Brewing 15556 Elm Drive 17349 (717) 759-0330
http://www.gunpowderfallsbrewing.com/

Hanover is about a half-hour northwest and has four breweries including a must-visit:

Sign of the Horse Brewery 979 York Street 17331 (717) 969-8435
http://www.signofthehorsebrewery.com/

Miscreation Brewing Company 6 Center Square 17331 (717) 698-3666
https://www.miscreationbrewing.com/

Something Wicked Brewing Company 34 Broadway 17331 (717) 316-5488 https://www.somethingwickedbrewing.com/

Aldus Brewing Company 555 Centennial Avenue 17331 (717) 634-2407
https://aldusbrewing.com/

Making approachable and highly drinkable beers. The original beer is the American Blonde Ale. There are a number of other styles to choose from as well. End your trip a half-hour northeast in York with five breweries:

Liquid Hero Brewery 50 East North Street 17401 (717) 814-9250
https://liquidhero.com/

Mudhook Brewing Company 34 N Cherry Lane 17401 (717) 747-3605
http://www.mudhookbrewing.com/

Stony Run Brew House 3605 E Market Street 17402 (717) 755-7599
https://stonyrunbrewhouse.com/

Collusion Tap Works 105 S Howard Street 17401 (717) 848-8400
https://collusiontapworks.com/

Mexitaly 2440 East Market Street 17402 (717) 600-8226
https://mexitaly.com/

Pocono Area

This rugged and beautiful area of wilderness is a great day trip you can take. There are only a handful of breweries in the area, but it is a great chance to get away from it all for a day. Start your trip in Honesdale at two breweries:

Here and Now Brewing Company 645 Main Street 18431 (570) 253-0700 http://www.hereandnowbrewing.com/

Irving Cliff Brewery 2 Chapel Street 18431 (570) 647-0644 http://www.irvingcliffbrewery.com/

Seventeen minutes south is your next brewery at Hawley:

Wallenpaupack Brewing Company 73 Welwood Avenue 18428 (570) 390-7933 http://wallenpaupackbrewingco.com/

About an hour drive south brings you to another brewery at Shawnee on Delaware:

ShawneeCraft Brewing Company 1 River Road 18356 (570) 424-4050 https://www.shawneeinn.com/shawneecraft-brewery/

End your trip about a half-hour northwest in Swiftwater at a must-visit brewery:

Pocono Brewing Company 2092 Route 611 18370 (570) 839-3230 https://poconobrewery.com/

The flagship beer here is the Wally Wilson IPA, offering hints of tropical notes. It is a bold and bitter beer that you won't soon forget.

Coal Country

This is another one day trip you can take through the beautiful mountains of Pennsylvania while enjoying excellent brews. Start your trip in Bangor at a must-visit brewery:

Bangor Trust Kitchen and Brewery 50 Broadway 18013 (610) 452-3232 https://bangortrustbrewing.com/

The flagship beer here is the Pig Earth, a dark copper-colored easy-drinking beer. Another great beer to try is Badunkadunk Porter brewed with chocolate malts. Head west about an hour to Tamaqua:

Stoker's Brewing Company 36 Mauch Chunk Street 18252
http://stokersbrewingcompany.com/

Next head to Conyngham about twenty-minutes north:

Conyngham Brewing Company 309 Main Street 18219 (570) 710-5752
https://www.conynghambrewingcompany.com/verify.html

Head west a half-hour to Bloomsburg with two breweries including a must-visit:

Turkey Hill Brewing Company 991 Central Road 17815 (570) 387-8422
https://www.innatturkeyhill.com/

Marley's Brewery and Grille 18 W Main Street 17815 (570) 784-9600
https://marleysbrewery.com/

Offering a rotating selection of 10-14 award-winning beers. On your first visit, be sure to try the Pack Dog Peanut Butter Ale, winner of two bronze medals. Berwick is about twenty-minutes east with the next brewery:

Berwick Brewing Company 328 W Front Street 18603 (570) 752-4313
https://www.berwickbrewing.com/

Northeast about fifty minutes is Dallas:

North Slope Brewing Company 33 Tunkhannock Highway 18612 (579) 255-4012 https://www.northslopebrewing.com/

End your trip about twenty-minutes east in Pittston:

Susquehanna Brewing Company 635 South Main Street 18640
https://www.sbcbeer.com/

Laurel Highlands

Just outside of Pittsburg, this great day trip allows you to get out of the city for a while. Start your trip in Berlin at:

Whitehorse Brewing 824 Diamond Street 15530 (814) 233-3043
http://www.whbrewing.com/

Head northwest about an hour to Latrobe:

Four Seasons Brewing Company 745 Lloyd Avenue Ext 15650 (724) 520-4111 https://www.fsbrewing.com/

Greensburg is about twenty-minutes west:

All Saints Brewing Company 1602 Route 119 15601 (724) 289-1202
http://allsaintscraftbrewing.com/

Another twenty-minutes south is Mount Pleasant:

Helltown Brewing 13 Henry C Frick Street 15666 (724) 542-4339
https://www.helltownbrewing.com/

End your trip in West Newton about twenty-minutes northwest:

Bloom Brew 100 Riverside Drive Suite A 15089 (724) 322-4494
https://bloombrew.weebly.com/about.html

Bucks and Montgomery Counties

This trip takes you through two counties and quite a few towns and breweries. You'll want to spend at least a few days to comfortably visit everything. Start your trip in Bryn Mawr at:

Tin Lizard Brewing Company 1000 W Lancaster Avenue 19010 (610) 525-1100 https://www.tinlizardbrewingco.com/

Ten minutes north is Conshohocken:

Conshohocken Brewing Company 739 East Elm Street Suite B 19428 (610) 897-8962 http://www.conshohockenbrewing.com/

Nine minutes away is another brewery at King of Prussia:

Workhorse Brewing Company 250 King Manor Drive 19406 (215) 539-3472 https://www.workhorsebrewing.com/

Another eight minutes brings you to Audubon:

Bald Birds Brewing Company 970 Rittenhouse Road Suite 400 19403 (484) 392-7068 https://baldbirdsbrewing.com/

Royersford is eleven minutes away:

Stickman Brews 326 N Lewis Road #240 19468 (484) 938-5900 https://www.stickmanbrews.com/

Another fourteen minutes is Pottstown:

Pottstown United Brewing Company 251 East High Street 19464 (484) 752-4943 https://www.pottstownunitedbrewing.com/

Head about twenty-minutes northeast to Green Lane:

Perkiomen Valley Brewery 101 Walnut Street 18054 (215) 872-6424 https://perkiomenvalleybrewery.com/

Quakertown is another twenty-minutes away:

The Proper Brewing Company 117 W Broad Street 18951 (267) 490-5168 http://www.theproperbrewing.com/

Perkasie is twelve minutes south:

Free Will Brewing Company 410 E Walnut Street Unit 10 18944 (267) 354-0813 https://www.freewillbrewing.com/

Eighteen minutes northeast is Pipersville with a must-visit brewery:

Bucks County Brewery 31 Appletree Lane 18947 (609) 439-2468
https://buckscountybrewery.com/

Offering six beers on tap: a New England IPA, an American pale ale, two Witbiers, a pale German lager, and a German sour wheat beer. Thirteen minutes south is Doylestown with two breweries:

Doylestown Brewing Company 52 E State Street 18901 (267) 454-7240
https://www.doylestownbrewingcompany.com/

Geronimo Brewing 1 W Court Street Ste B 18901 (215) 348-7838
https://www.geronimobrewing.com/home.html

Eight minutes away in Chalfont is the next brewery:

Towerhill Brewery 237 W Butler Avenue 18914 (215) 822-8788
http://www.towerhillbrewery.com/

Eleven more minutes brings you to a must-visit brewery in Hatfield:

Imprint Beer Company 1500 Industry Road Suite O 19440 (215) 285-8254 https://imprintbeer.com/

Stop by the tasting room for everything from hazy IPAs to thick stouts and kettle sours to fruity mixes. There are even hard coffees to try. Next is Lansdale six minutes away with another must-visit brewery:

Round Guys Brewing Company 324 W Main Street 19446 (215) 368-2640 https://roundguysbrewery.com/

Most known for their Berliner, their award-winning Berliner Weisse. For something different, try the Spaceman Wit made with blood oranges and lime. Five minutes away is North Wales with two breweries including a must-visit:

Ten7 Brewing Company 510 Beaver Street 19454 (717) 710-2739
https://ten7brewing.com/

McAllister Brewing Company 810 Dickerson Road 19454 (267) 655-4198 https://www.mcallisterbrewing.com/

The drink to try here is Pete's Boilo. It is based on a historic recipe dating back to the original strong drink given to coal miners. Another ten minutes south is three breweries in Ambler:

Ambler Beer Company 300 Brookside Avenue Building 19 Suite E 19002 https://amblerbeerco.com/

Forest and Main Brewing Company 61 N Main Street 19002 (215) 542-1776 https://www.forestandmain.com/

Tannery Run Brew Works 131 E Butler Avenue 19002 (215) 613-1113 https://tanneryrun.com/

Five minutes away is another brewery in Dresher:

Track 3 Microbrewery and Coffee House 1650 Limekiln Pike Store B-26 19025 (267) 419-8654 https://www.track3brewing.com/

Glenside is five minutes away and has two breweries:

Bill's Best Brewery 57 S Keswick Avenue 19038 (215) 517-6970 https://www.billsbestbrewery.com/

The Ways Brewery and Restaurant 11 S Easton Road 19038 (215) 887-1029 https://thewaysrestaurantandbrewery.com/

Twelve minutes east is two breweries in Huntingdon Valley:

Naked Brewing Company 51 Buck Road 19006 (267) 575-0166 https://naked-brewing.square.site/

Moss Mill Brewing Company 109 Pike Circle 19006 https://www.mossmillbrewing.com/

Ten minutes north is Hatboro with two more breweries:

Crooked Eye Brewery 13 E Montgomery Avenue Suite 3 19040 (267) 246-5046 https://crookedeyebrewery.com/

Artifact Brewery 2 S York Road 19040 https://www.artifactales.com/

Eight minutes away is Jamison with a must-visit brewery:

Warwick Farm Brewing 800 Almshouse Road 18929 (215) 792-7599 https://warwickfarmbrewing.com/

Focusing on growing four different types of hops that are turned into true farm beer in their historic barn. Come visit the brewery that sits on the tallest hill in the area. New Hope is about twenty-minutes northeast:

Great Barn Brewery 12 W Mechanic Street 18938 (215) 803-1592 http://www.greatbarnbrewery.com/

Fourteen minutes south is Newton:

Newtown Brewing Company 103 Penns Trail 18940 (215) 944-8609 https://www.newtownbrewingco.com/

Croydon is about another twenty-minutes south:

Neshaminy Creek Brewing Company 909 Ray Avenue 19021 (215) 458-7081 https://neshaminycreekbrewing.com/

End your trip twenty-minutes north in Yardley at:

Vault Brewing Company 10 S Main Street 19067 (267) 573-4291 https://vaultbrewing.com/

Greater Philadelphia Area

The area around Philadelphia and the city itself are home to a number of great breweries. Take a trip and end in the city. Start in Honey Brook at:

Suburban Brewing Company 2536 Conestoga Avenue 19344 (610) 273-3106 https://suburbanbrewingco.com/

About twenty-minutes southeast is Downingtown with two breweries:

East Branch Brewing Company 202 E Lancaster Avenue 19335 (484) 593-0815 https://eastbranchbrewing.com/

Victory Brewing Company 420 Acorn Lane 19335 (610) 873-0881 https://victorybeer.com/

Eight minutes away is another brewery at Exton:

Stolen Sun Craft Brewing and Roasting Company 342 Pottstown Pike Suite B 19341 (484) 879-4161 https://www.stolensun.com/

Phoenixville is about twenty-minutes northeast with four breweries:

Stable 12 Brewing Company 368 Bridge Street 19460 (610) 715-2665 https://www.stable12.com/

Crowded Castle Brewing Company 242 Bridge Street 19460 (844) 722-7853 http://crowdedcastle.com/

Root Down Brewing Company 1 N Main Street 19460 (484) 393-2337 http://www.rootdownbrewing.com/

Rebel Hill Brewing Company 420 Schuylkill Road 19460 (484) 924-8044 https://www.rebelhillbrewing.com/

Fifteen minutes south is the next brewery at Malvern:

Locust Lane Craft Brewery 50 Three Tunnel Road Steve 4 19355 (484) 324-4141 https://www.locustlanecraftbrewery.com/

West Chester is fourteen minutes southwest:

Levante Brewing Company 208 Carter Drive Suite 2 19383 (484) 999-8761 https://www.levantebrewing.com/

Continue about twenty-minutes to Kennett Square:

Braeloch Brewing 225 Birch Street 19348 (610) 612-9242
https://braelochbrewing.beer/

Glen Mills is about twenty-minutes east:

McKenzie Brew House 451 Wilmington-West Chester Pike 19342 (610) 361-9800 https://www.mckenziebrewhouse.com/

Ten minutes south is Aston:

2SP Brewing Company 120 Concord Road 19014 (484) 483-7860
https://www.2spbrewing.com/

Media is ten minutes northeast:

Sterling Pig Brewery 609 West State Street 19063 (484) 444-2526
https://sterlingpig.com/

Another sixteen minutes brings you to Ardmore:

Tired Hands Brewing Company 16 Ardmore Avenue 19003 (610) 896-7621 https://www.tiredhands.com/

End your trip sixteen minutes away in the city of Philadelphia with multiple brewery options:

Attic Brewing Company 137 Berkeley Street 19144 (267) 748-2495
https://www.atticbrewing.com/

Love City Brewing Company 1023 Hamilton Street 19123 (215) 398-1900 https://lovecitybrewing.com/

Fishtown Brewpub 1101 Frankford Avenue 19125 (215) 990-1396
http://fishtownbrewpub.com/

Brewery ARS 1927-29 West Passyunk Avenue 19145 (215) 960-5173
https://breweryars.com/

Urban Village Brewing Company 1001 N 2nd Street 19123 (267) 687-1961 http://urbanvillagebrewing.com/

Mainstay Independent 901 N Delaware Avenue 19123 (215) 422-3562
https://www.mainstaybrewing.com/

Manayunk Brewery and Restaurant 4120 Main Street 19127 (215) 482-8220 https://www.manayunkbrewery.com/

Yards Brewing Company 901 N Delaware Avenue 19123 (215) 634-2600 https://yardsbrewing.com/

Crime and Punishment Brewing Company 2711 W Girard Avenue 19130 (215) 235-2739 http://crimeandpunishmentbrewingco.com/

Second District Brewing Company 1939 S Bancroft Street 19145 (215) 575-5900 http://seconddistrictbrewing.com/

Triple Bottom Brewing 915 Spring Garden Street 19123 (267) 764-1994 https://triplebottombrewing.com/

Philadelphia Brewing Company 2439 Amber Street 19125 (215) 427-2739 http://philadelphiabrewing.com/

2nd Story Brewing Company 117 Chestnut Street 19106 (267) 314-5770 https://www.2ndstorybrewing.com/

Earth Bread + Brewery 7136 Germantown Avenue 19119 (215) 242-MOON http://earthbreadbrewery.com/

Crafting small batch alchemic beers in unusual styles like Kolsch, Gruit, Biere de Garde, Sticke Alt, Baltic Porter, Rauchbier, ESB, Mild Ale, Saison and Gotlandsdricka.

Dock Street Beer 701 S 50th Street 19143 (215) 726-2337
http://www.dockstreetbeer.com/

The first microbrewery in Philadelphia. Offering an array of award-winning beers in a variety of styles so you'll find something you like.

Northern Pennsylvania

You'll want at least two days here. While there aren't a lot of breweries, they are pretty far apart, so you'll need to give yourself some driving time. Start your trip in Montrose at:

Endless Brewing 20610 SR 29 18801 (570) 967-0985
https://www.endlessbrewing.com/

Drive south about a half-hour to Tunkhannock:

Nimble Hill Brewing Company 3971 SR 6 18657 (570) 836-9463
http://www.nimblehillbrewing.com/

Montoursville is an hour and a half drive to the west:

Therapy Brewing 3978 Quaker Church Road 17754 (570) 560-0987
https://therapybrewing.com/

Eleven minutes west is two more breweries in Williamsport:

Bullfrog Brewery 229 West Fourth Street 17701 (570) 326-4700
http://www.bullfrogbrewery.com/

New Trail Brewing Company 240 Arch Street Building 18 17701 (570) 337-3228 https://www.newtrailbrewing.com/

About forty minutes north is Mansfield with a must-visit brewery:

Yorkholo Brewing Company 19 North Main Street 16933 (570) 662-0241 https://www.yorkholobrewing.com/

Brewing a PA Wild Ale series made with yeast native to the PA Wilds region. Spontaneous fermentation is then used to make these completely local beers. End with about a two-hour drive to St. Marys:

Straub Brewery 303 Sorg Street 15857 (814) 834-2875
https://straubbeer.com/

South Central Pennsylvania

Take a couple of days to drive through this beautiful area and visit all the breweries it has to offer. Start your trip in Bedford at a must-visit brewery:

Olde Bedford Brewing Company 109 Railroad Street 15522 (907) 229-7942 https://oldebbc.com/

Be sure to try their Olde World Porter based on the original recipe from George Washington. All the beers here are based on history.

A half-hour north is the next brewery at Duncansville:

Marzoni's Brick Oven and Brewing Company 165 Patchway Road 16635 (814) 695-1300 http://marzonis.com/

Fifteen minutes further is the next brewery at Altoona:

Railroad City Brewing Company 810 S 12th Street 16602 (866) 902-2337 https://railroadcitybrewing.com/

About forty minutes southeast is State College with two breweries:

Otto's Pub and Brewery 2235 N Atherton Street 16803 (814) 867-6886 https://www.ottos-barrel.com/

Happy Valley Brewing Company 137 Elmwood Street 16801 (814) 234-4406 http://happyvalleybeer.com/

Lewiston is about another forty minutes east:

Shy Bear Brewing 35 Meadowbrook Lane 17044 (717) 242-2663 https://www.shybearbrewing.com/

About another hour east brings you to Selinsgrove and two breweries:

Selin's Grove Brewing Company 119 N Market Street 17870 (570) 374-7308 https://www.selinsgrovebrewing.com/

Isle of Que Brewing Company 6 University Avenue 17870 (570) 809-9350 https://www.quebrew.com/

Lewisburg is about twenty-minutes north:

West Branch Craft Brewing 17 South 6th Street 17837 (570) 939-5692 https://westbranchcraftbrewing.wordpress.com/

About forty minutes west is Millheim:

Elk Creek Cafe + Aleworks 100 W Main 16854 (814) 349-8850 https://elkcreekcafe.com/

Another half-hour is Howard and a must-visit brewery:

MAD-K Brewery 298 Mountain Top Road 16841 (570) 295-1842 https://www.mad-kbrews.com/

All beers are brewed with whole grains, real hops, and homegrown jalapeno peppers. Be sure to stop in a try their unique beers today. About another fifty minutes is Clearfield:

Race Street Brew Works 511 Spruce Street Suite 2 16830 (814) 303-9269 https://www.racestreetbrew.com/

End your trip about an hour northwest in Indiana with two breweries including a must-visit:

Noble Stein Brewing Company 1170 Wayne Avenue 15701 (724) 801-8087 https://www.noblesteinbrewingcompany.com/

Levity Brewing Company 1380 Wayne Avenue Suite A 15701 (724) 840-7611 https://www.levitybrewing.com/

The first brewery in Indiana since 1939. Enjoy a wide variety of craft beers that have been honed to excellence over the years.

Northwest Pennsylvania

This trip will take you to some great breweries in the upper northwest corner of the state. Start your trip in Clarion at:

Clarion River Brewing Company 600 Main Street 16214 (814) 297-8399 https://www.clarionriverbrew.com/

About forty minutes west is another brewery in Grove City:

Koehler Brewing Company 231 Park Street 16127 (833) 563-4537 http://koehlerbrewingcompany.com/

Slippery Rock is ten minutes south:

North Country Brewing 141 South Main Street 16057 (724) 794-2337 https://northcountrybrewing.com/

Butler is about another twenty-minutes south with three breweries:

Butler Brew Works 101 S Main Street 16001 (724) 264-5347 https://www.butlerbrewworks.com/

Recon Brewing 1747 N Main Street Ext 16001 (724) 256-8747 https://www.reconbrewing.com/

Reclamation Brewing 221 S Main Street 16001 (724) 790-4370 http://www.reclamationbrewing.com/

Head northwest about forty minutes to Edinburg:

Crooked Tongue Brewing 2516 Benjamin Franklin Highway 16116 (724) 856-3765 http://crookedtonguebrewing.com/

Greenville is another forty minutes north:

Depot Saloon 9 South Race Street 16125 (724) 588-4201 http://www.depotsaloon.com/

Just nine minutes away is a must-visit brewery at Jamestown:

Mortals Key Brewing Company 4224 East Lake Road 16134
https://www.mortalskey.com/

Using Old World recipes with the freshest ingredients. Be sure to try one of their famous foundation brews: MK Kolsch, MK IPA, and MK Baltic Porter. Head back east about a half-hour to Meadville with two breweries:

Voodoo Brewery 215 ⅓ Arch Street 16335 (814) 337-3676
https://www.voodoobrewery.com/

Timber Creek Tap and Table 11191 Highline Drive 16335 (814) 807-1005 http://www.timbercreektapandtable.com/

About another forty minutes is Titusville:

Blue Canoe Brewery 113 S Franklin Street 16354 (814) 827-7181
https://thebluecanoebrewery.com/

About an hour north is North East:

Arundel Cellars and Brewing Company 11727 East Main Road 16428 (814) 725-1079 http://arundelcellars.com/index.html

Follow the waterfront about twenty-minutes southwest to Erie:

The Brewerie at Union Station 123 W 14th Street 16501
https://www.brewerie.com/

Lavery Brewing Company 128 W 12th Street Unit 101 16501 (814) 454-0405 https://www.laverybrewing.com/

Erie Ale Works 416 W 12th Street 16501 (814) 881-0615
https://www.eriealeworks.com/

Erie Brewing Company 1213 Veshecco Drive 16501 (814) 459-7741
https://www.eriebrewingco.com/

End your trip about forty minutes south in Venango at:

Sprague Farm and Brew Works 22113 US Highway 6 and 19 16440 (814) 398-2885 http://www.sleepingchainsaw.com/brew_works.htm

Rhode Island

There aren't that many breweries in Rhode Island, so you can visit them all in a single trip. However, you'll probably want to take several days. Start your trip in Bristol at:

Twelve Guns Brewing Company 549 Metacom Avenue 02809 (401) 396-9009 https://www.twelvegunsbrewing.com/

Ten minutes south is Portsmouth:

Ragged Island Brewing Company 200 Highpoint Avenue Unit 6B 02871 https://raggedislandbrewing.com/

Twelve minutes further is Middletown with two breweries:

Coddington Brewing Company 210 Coddington Highway 02842 (401) 837-6690 https://coddbrew.com/

Taproot Brewing Company 909 E Main Road 02842 (401) 848-5161 https://www.taprootbeer.com/

Just five minutes away is another brewery at Newport:

Newport Craft Brewing and Distilling Company 293 JT Connell Road 02840 (401) 849-5232 https://newportcraft.com/

Exeter is about twenty-minutes northwest and has a must-visit brewery:

Tilted Barn Brewery 1 Hemsley Place 02822 (401) 500-6765 https://www.tiltedbarnbrewery.com/

The first farm brewery in Rhode Island. Sample from their core series or try one of their experimental beers. Thirteen minutes south is West Kingston:

Shaidzon Beer Company 141 Fairgrounds Road 02892 (401) 829-3147 https://www.shaidzonbeer.com/

Wakefield is another twelve minutes south:

Whalers Brewing Company 1174 Kingstown Road 02879 (401) 552-0002 https://whalers.com/

A half-hour west at the border is Westerly:

Grey Sail Brewing of Rhode Island 63 Canal Street 02891 (401) 212-7592 https://greysailbrewing.com/

About forty minutes back northeast is East Greenwich:

LineSider Brewing Company 1485 South County Trail 02818 (401) 398-7700 https://www.linesiderbrewing.com/

Just five minutes away is Warwick with two breweries:

Apponaug Brewing Company 334 Knight Street 02886 (401) 681-4321 https://www.apponaugbrewing.com/

Proclamation Ale Company 298 Kilvert Street 02886 (401) 787-6450 https://www.proclamationaleco.com/

Another thirteen minutes north is Cranston:

Buttonwoods Brewery 530 Wellington Avenue #22 02910 (401) 461-2337 http://www.buttonwoodsbrewery.com/

Eight minutes away is Providence with two breweries:

Long Live Beerworks 425 W Fountain Street #104 02903 https://www.longlivebeerworks.com/

Trinity Brewhouse 186 Fountain Street 02903 (401) 453-2337 http://www.trinitybrewhouse.com/

Another seven minutes away is Pawtucket with three breweries:

Foolproof Brewing Company 241 Grotto Avenue 02860 (401) 721-5970 https://www.foolproofbrewing.com/

Crooked Current Brewery 560 Mineral Spring Avenue 02860 (401) 473-8312 http://www.crookedcurrentbrewery.com/

Smug Brewing 100 Carver Street 02860 (401) 642-5701 https://smugbrewing.com/

Woonsocket is about twenty-minutes north on the border:

Lops Brewing Company 122 North Main Street 02895 (774) 219-0538 https://www.lopsbrewing.com/

End your trip about twenty-minutes west in Pascoag at:

Bravo Brewing Company 75 Pascoag Main Street 02859 (401) 710-4242 https://bravobrewingcompany.com/home

Mountain Region

This short day trip takes you through some of the most beautiful mountains in South Carolina while enjoying great breweries. Start in Anderson at:

Carolina Bauernhaus 115 W Federal Street 29625 (864) 401-8167 https://carolinabauernhaus.com/

Head north about an hour to Salem:

Jocassee Valley Brewing Company 13412 N Highway 11 29676 (864) 723-5357 https://jocasseevalleybrewing.com/

About another hour southeast is Piedmont:

Golden Grove Farm and Brew 115 Krim Road 29669 (864) 356-1097 https://farmandbrew.com/

About twenty-minutes away is the town of Greenville with multiple options:

The Eighth State Brewing Company 400 Augusta Street 29601 (864) 205-5000 https://www.eighthstatebrewing.com/

Birds Fly South Ale Project 1320 Hampton Avenue Ext 29601 (864) 412-8825 https://bfsbeer.com/

Liability Brewing Company 109 W Stone Avenue 29609 (864) 920-1599 https://liabilitybrewing.co/

Fireforge Crafted Beer 311 E Washington Street 29601 (864) 735-0885 https://www.fireforge.beer/

Quest Brewing Company 55 Airview Drive 29607 (864) 272-6232 http://questbrewing.com/

Thomas Creek Brewery 2054 Piedmont Highway 29605 (864) 605-1166 https://www.thomascreekbeer.com/

Brewery 85 6 Whitlee Court 29607 (864) 558-0104 http://brewery85.com/

Spartanburg is about forty minutes east:

RJ Rockers Brewing Company 226-A West Main Street 29306 (864) 585-2337 https://rjrockers.com/

End your trip thirteen minutes north in Boiling Springs at:

New Groove Artisan Brewery 4078 Highway 9 29316 (864) 586-3900 http://newgroovebrew.com/

Midlands Region

This trip will take you two to three days and gives you a chance to visit some great breweries in the midland area of South Carolina. Start your trip in Aiken at:

Aiken Brewing Company 104 Laurens Street SW 29801 (803) 502-0707 http://www.aikenbrewingcompany.com/

About an hour northwest is your next brewery in Greenwood:

Good Times Brewing 237 Maxwell Avenue 29646 (864) 323-0321
https://millhousepizza.com/

Head east about an hour and a half to Lexington:

Old Mill Brewpub 711 E Main Street 29071 (803) 785-2337
https://www.oldmillbrewpub.net/

Cayce is about twenty more minutes east:

Steel Hands Brewing 2350 Foreman Street 29033 (803) 708-9864
https://www.steelhandsbrewing.com/

Nine minutes away is Columbia with several options including three must-visit breweries:

Columbia Craft Brewing Company 520 Green Street 29201 (803) 799-6027 https://www.columbiacraft.com/

Cottontown Brew Lab 1223 Franklin Street 29201 (844) 427-3952
https://www.cottontownbrewlab.com/

Twisted Spur Brewing 705 Gervais Street 29201 (803) 764-0203
http://www.twistedspurbrewing.com/

Hunter-Gatherer Brewery and Ale House 900 Main Street 29201 (803) 748-0540 https://huntergathererbrewery.com/

Swamp Cabbage Brewing Company 921 Brookwood Drive 29201 (803) 252-0250 https://www.swampcabbagebrewing.com/

No matter what style of beer pleases you, there is a glass for you here. If you simply want to try something, then try their two award-winning beers: Dunkelweizen and Ruby Red IPA.

River Rat Brewery 1231 Shop Road 29201 (803) 724-5712
https://riverratbrewery.com/

When you try the beers here, you'll see why people say they are the best in the world. Be sure to try their award-winning Bohemian Pilsner.

Bierkeller 921 Brookwood Drive 29201 (803) 338-1599
http://bierkellercolumbia.com/

Offering German-style beers made from only four ingredients. Try their Kolumbianer, a top-fermenting lager in the Kolsch style, the Fastenbier, a dark Franconian lager and Rauchbier, a smoked lager in the Bamberg style. An hour north is Rock Hill with two breweries:

Slow Play Brewing 274 Columbia Avenue 29730
https://www.slowplaybrewing.com/

Legal Remedy Brewing 129 Oakland Avenue 29730 (803) 324-2337
https://legalremedybrewing.com/

Twelve minutes to the border is Fort Mill:

Amor Artis Brewing 204 Main Street #101 29715 (803) 547-6464
https://amorartisbrewing.com/

About a half-hour south is Lancaster:

Benford Brewing Company 2271 Boxcar Road 29720 (803) 416-8422
https://benfordbrewing.com/

End your trip about an hour and a half southeast in Florence with two breweries including a must-visit:

Seminar Brewing 1945 W Palmetto Street Suite 348 29501 (843) 665-9200 http://www.seminarbrewing.com/

Southern Hops Brewing Company 911 Sunset Acres Lane 29501 (843) 667-1900 http://southernhops.com/

Try a flight of their five beers, and you'll get an excellent selection of what they make, including a red ale, an IPA, a golden ale, a brown ale, and a porter.

Coastal Region and Islands

This two to three day trip will take you along the beautiful oceanfront coast of South Carolina. Start your trip in Hilton Head at:

Hilton Head Brewing Company 7 Greenwood Drive 29928 (843) 785-3900 https://www.hhbrewingco.com/

Eleven minutes west is a must-visit brewery at Bluffton:

Southern Barrel Brewing Company 375 Buckwalter Place Blvd 29910 (843) 837-2337 http://southernbarrelbrewingco.com/

Offering four year-round beers that you can try in a single flight: a New England style IPA, a lager, a sour ale, and an imperial milk stout. Circle about two hours north to Summerville:

Wide Awake Brewing 1907 Varner Street Ste B5 29486 (843) 608-8597 https://www.wideawakebrewing.com/

North Charleston is twenty-minutes southeast:

Snafu Brewing Company 3280 Industry Drive 29418 (843) 767-4121 http://www.snafubrewingcompany.com/

Holy City Brewing 4155 Dorchester Road Ste C 29405 (843) 637-1161 https://holycitybrewing.com/

Rusty Bull Brewing Company 3005 W Montague Street 29418 (843) 225-8600 https://rustybullbrewing.com/index.php

Pawleys Island Brewing Company 2668 Industrial Avenue 29405 (843) 225-8292 https://www.pawleysislandbrewing.com/

Commonhouse Aleworks 4831 O'Hear Avenue 29405 (843) 471-1400 https://www.commonhousealeworks.com/

Frothy Beard Brewing Company 7358 Peppermill Parkway Ste B 29418 (843) 793-2970 https://frothybeard.com/

Lo-Fi Brewing 2038 Meeting Street 29405 (828) 582-2175
http://lofibrewing.com/

South about a half-hour is Johns Island with two breweries:

Fat Pig Brewing Company 3690 Old Charleston Road 29455 (843) 640-3256 http://fatpigbrewing.com/

Low Tide Brewing 2863 Maybank Highway 29455 (843) 501-7570
https://lowtidebrewing.com/

About twenty minutes up the coast is Charleston:

Cooper River Brewing Company 2201 Mechanic Street 29403 (843) 830-3681 https://cooperriverbrewing.com/

Edmund's Oast Brewing Company 1081 Morrison Drive 29403 (843) 727-1145 http://edmundsoast.com/

Freehouse Brewery 2895 Pringle Street Ste B 29405
https://www.freehousebeer.com/

Revelry Brewing Company 10 Conroy Street 29403 (843) 870-0010
https://revelrybrewingco.com/

Charles Towne Fermentory 809 Savannah Highway 29408 (843) 641-0431 https://www.chsfermentory.com/

Tradesman Brewing Company 1639 Tatum Street 29412 (843) 410-1315 https://www.tradesmanbrewing.com/

Fatty's Beer Works 1436 Meeting Street 29405 (843) 974-5330
https://www.fattysbeerworks.com/

Nine minutes away is Mount Pleasant with two more breweries:

Westbrook Brewing Company 510 Ridge Road 29464 (843) 654-9112
https://westbrookbrewing.com/

Ghost Monkey Brewery 522 Wando Lane 29464 (843) 352-3462
http://www.ghostmonkeybrewery.com/

About an hour up the coast is Pawleys Island:

Quigley's Pint and Plate 257 Willbrook Blvd 28585 (843) 237-7010
https://pintandplate.com/

End your trip about forty minutes up the coast in Myrtle Beach at a must-visit brewery:

New South Brewing Company 1109 Campbell Street 29576 (843) 916-2337 https://newsouthbrewing.com/

The flagship beers here are White Ale and Nut Brown Ale. There is plenty of other core and seasonal beer options to sample with these two.

South Dakota

There aren't many breweries in South Dakota, so you can visit them in one trip. However, they are far apart, so you'll need two to three days to see them all. Start your trip in Spearfish with two breweries including a must-visit:

Spearfish Brewing Company 741 N Main Street #130 57783 (605) 717-6999 https://www.spearfishbrewing.com/

Crow Peak Brewing 125 West Highway 14 57783 (605) 717-0006 https://crowpeakbrewing.com/

Three year-round beers are produced for you to sample: an American style IPA, a blonde ale, and a robust porter. Head south about an hour to two more breweries in Hill City:

Sick N Twisted Brewing Company 23851 Highway 385 57745 (605) 574-2454 https://www.sickntwistedbrewery.com/

Miner Brewing Company 23845 Highway 385 57745 (605) 574-2886 https://www.minerbrewing.com/

Seventeen minutes further south is Custer with a must-visit brewery:

Mt. Rushmore Brewing Company 140 Mt Rushmore Road 57730 (605) 673-5900 http://rushmore.beer/

Try a flight of their four flagship beers: Long Tom, an American IPA; Trust Buster, a Scottish Export; Rail Splitter, a London-style Porter and American Fabius, a blonde ale. Rapid City is fifty minutes east with four breweries:

Hay Camp Brewing Company 201 Main Street Suite 109 57701 (970) 412-5286 http://www.haycampbrewing.com/

Dakota Point Brewing 405 Canal Street Suite 1200 57701 (605) 791-2739 https://www.dakotapointbrewing.com/

Zymurcracy Beer Company 4624 Creek Drive Suite 6 57701 (605) 791-0411 https://zymurcracybeer.com/

Lost Cabin Beer Company 1401 W Omaha Street 57702 (605) 718-5678 https://lostcabin.beer/

When you're ready, drive east across the state about four and a half-hours to Valley Springs:

A Homestead Brew 26685 486th Avenue 57068 (605) 212-4395
http://ahomesteadbrew.com/

About twenty-minutes southwest is Sioux Falls with five breweries:

Fernson Brewing Company 1400 E Robur Drive 57104 (605) 789-3822
https://www.fernson.com/

WoodGrain Brewing Company 101 S Philips Avenue Suite 100 57104
(605) 310-5316 http://www.woodgrainbrew.com/

Severance Brewing 701 N Phillips Avenue Suite 110 57104 (605) 271-5480 https://severancebeer.com/

Gandy Dancer Brew Works 420 E 8th Street 57103 (605) 351-9268
http://monkshouseofalerepute.com/brewery/4578982718/

Covert Artisan Ales 605 S Watson Avenue Suite 130 57106 (605) 681-6139 https://www.covertartisanales.com/

Head north an hour to Brookings with two breweries:

Wooden Legs Brewing Company 309 5th Street Suite 100 57006 (605)
692-2337 https://woodenlegsbrewing.com/

Eponymous Brewing Company 126 Main Avenue South 57006 (605)
692-1880 https://www.eponymousbrewing.com/

Continue about another forty minutes and end your trip in Watertown with two breweries:

Dempsey's Brewery, Restaurant and Pub 127 N Broadway 57201 (605)
882-9760 https://www.dempseybrewpub.com/

Watertown Brewing Company 113 E Kemp 57201 (605) 878-2739
https://www.watertownbrewing.com/

East Tennessee

This two day trip will take you to a handful of towns with several brewery options. Start your trip in Chattanooga with several brewery options:

Chattanooga Brewing Company 1804 Chestnut Street 37408 (423) 702-9958 https://www.chattabrew.com/

Naked River Brewing Company 1791 Reggie White Blvd 37408 (423) 541-1131 https://www.nakedriverbrewing.com/

OddStory Brewing 336 E Martin Luther King Blvd 37403 (256) 309-7208 https://www.oddstorybrewing.co/

Wanderlinger Brewing Company 1208 King Street 37403 (423) 269-7979 https://www.wanderlinger.com/

Heaven and Ale Brewing Company 300 Cherokee Blvd Suite 101 37405 (423) 521-4222 https://www.heavenandalebrewing.com/

Hutton and Smith Brewing Company 431 E Martin Luther King Blvd Ste 120 37403 (423) 760-3600 http://huttonandsmithbrewing.com/

Terminal Brewhouse 6 East 14th Street 37408 (423) 752-8090 https://terminalbrewhouse.com/

About forty minutes north is another brewery in Dayton:

Monkey Town Brewing Company 287 First Avenue 37321 (423) 775-1800 http://monkeytownbrewing.com/index.html

Norris is about two-hour northeast:

Clinch River Brewing 2045 Norris Freeway 37828 (859) 421-3851 https://www.clinchriverbrewing.com/

The city of Knoxville is about twenty-minutes south and offers several options along with a must-visit:

Balter Beerworks 100 S Broadway Street 37902 (865) 999-5015
https://www.balterbeerworks.com/

Alliance Brewing Company 1130 Sevier Avenue 37920 (865) 247-5355
https://alliancebrewing.com/

Elkmont Exchange 745 North Broadway 37917 (865) 249-7904
https://www.elkmontexchange.com/

Pretentious Beer Company 131 S Central Street 37902 (865) 851-7693
https://www.pretentiousbeerco.com/

Hexagon Brewing Company 1002 Dutch Valley Drive Ste 101 37918
(865) 888-5138 https://hexagonbrewing.com/

Last Days of Autumn Brewing 808 East Magnolia Avenue 37917 (865)
202-4298 http://www.lastdaysofautumn.com/

Schulz Brau Brewing Company 126 Bernard Avenue 37917 (800) 245-
9764 http://www.schulzbraubrewing.com/

Crafty Bastard Brewery 6 Emory Place 37917 (865) 755-2358
https://craftybastardbrewery.com/

Downtown Grill and Brewery 424 South Gay Street 37902 (865) 633-
8111 http://www.downtownbrewery.com/

Albright Grove Brewing Company 2924 Sutherland Avenue 37919
(865) 599-0634 https://www.albrightgrovebrewing.com/

Fanatic Brewing Company 2727 North Central Street 37917 (865) 242-
9063 http://www.fanaticbrewing.com/

Elst Brewing Company 2419 N Central Street 37917 (865) 498-3306
https://elst.beer/

Abridged Beer Company 100 Lockett Road 37919 (865) 755-2358
https://www.abridgedbeer.com/

Offering twelve rotating taps that feature 8 barrel-aged sours, 2 kettle sours, an IPA and a lager, so there is always something for everyone. About an hour southeast is another must-visit brewery in Gatlinburg:

Smoky Mountain Brewery and Restaurant 1004 Parkway #501 37862 (865) 436-4200 https://smoky-mtn-brewery.com/

Offering six flagship beers all-year along with four seasonal brews that rotate throughout the year. Be sure to try the Tuckaleechee, a dark ale. End your trip with a two-hour drive northeast to Johnson City with several options:

Great Oak Brewery 601 Spring Street 37604 (423) 232-8845
https://greatoakbrewing.com/

Johnson City Brewing Company 300 E Main Street 37601 (423) 930-4186 http://johnsoncitybrewing.com/

Yee-Haw Brewing Company 126 Buffalo Street 37604 (423) 328-9192
https://yeehawbrewing.com/

JRH Brewing 458 W Walnut Street 37604 (423) 722-3410
http://jrhbrewing.com/

Middle Tennessee

This two to three day trip takes you to some main towns in Middle Tennessee with quite a few brewery options. Start your trip in Clarksville with two breweries:

Blackhorse Brewery 132 Franklin Street 37040 (931) 552-3726
https://www.blackhorsebrews.com/

Strawberry Alley Ale Works 103 Strawberry Alley 37040 (931) 919-4777
https://www.saaleworks.com/

Head southeast about an hour to Hendersonville:

Half Batch Brewing 393 E Main Street Suite 6A 37075
http://halfbatchbrewing.com/

Southwest about twenty-minutes is the main city of Nashville with multiple options including a must-visit:

Southern Grist Brewing Company 1201 Porter Road 37206 (615) 727-1201 https://www.southerngristbrewing.com/

The Black Abbey Brewing Company 2952 Sidco Drive 37204 (615) 755-0070 https://blackabbeybrewing.com/

Harding House Brewing Company 904 51st Avenue N 37209 (615) 678-1047 http://www.hardinghousebrew.com/

Various Artists Brewing 1011 Elm Hill Pike 37210 (615) 445-5422 https://www.variousartistsbrewing.com/

Fat Bottom Brewing 900 Main Street 37206 (615) 678-5895 https://fatbottombrewing.com/

Bearded Iris Brewing 101 Van Buren Street 37208 (615) 928-7988 https://beardedirisbrewing.com/

Jackalope Brewing Company 701 Eighth Avenue S 37203 (615) 837-4313 https://jackalopebrew.com/

Little Harpeth Brewing 30 Oldham Street 37213 (615) 571-7451 https://littleharpethbrewing.com/

Tennessee Brew Works 809 Ewing Avenue 37203 (615) 200-8786 https://www.tnbrew.com/

TailGate Beer 7300 Charlotte Pike 37209 (615) 861-9842 https://www.tailgatebeer.com/

New Heights Brewery 928 5th Avenue S 37210 (615) 669-3944 https://www.newheightsbrewing.com/

Smith and Lentz Brewing Company 903 Main Street 37206
http://www.smithandlentz.com/

East Nashville Beer Works 320 E Trinity Lane 37207 (615) 891-3108
http://www.eastnashbeerworks.com/

Blackstone Brewing Company 2312 Clifton Avenue 37209 (615) 320-9002 https://blackstonebeer.com/

An award-winning Nashville brewery. Try their flagship Chaser Pale and Nut Brown Ale. However, no visit is complete without trying the St. Charles Porter, winner of eight awards. When you're ready, head east about an hour to another brewery at Cookeville:

Red Silo Brewing Company 118 W 1st Street 38501 (931) 252-1862
http://www.redsilobrewing.com/

Sparta is twenty-minutes south:

Calfkiller Brewing Company 1839 Blue Springs Road 38583 (931) 739-2337 http://www.calfkillerbeer.com/

Circle southwest to Tullahoma about an hour away:

Ole Shed Brewing Company 516 East Carroll Street 37388 (931) 212-4277 https://www.oleshedbrewing.com/

About fifty minutes northwest is Murfreesboro:

Mayday Brewery 702 Old Salem Highway 37129 (615) 479-9722
https://www.maydaybrewery.com/

About forty minutes west is Franklin:

Cool Springs Brewery 600-A Frazier Drive 37067 (615) 503-9626
https://www.coolspringsbrewery.com/

End your trip about a half-hour south in Columbia with two breweries:

Bad Idea Brewing Company 307 W 11 Street 38401 (931) 922-2478
https://www.badideabrewing.com/

Asgard Brewing 104 East 5th Street 38401 (615) 828-2218
http://asgardbrewery.com/

Memphis

Ghost River Brewing 827 S Main Street 38106 (901) 278-0087
https://www.ghostriverbrewing.com/

Wiseacre Brewing 2783 Broad Avenue 38112 (901) 888-7000
https://wiseacrebrew.com/

Crosstown Brewing Company 1264 Concourse Avenue 38104 (910)
529-7611 https://crosstownbeer.com/

Memphis Made Brewing Company 768 S Cooper Street 38104 (901)
207-5343 https://www.memphismadebrewing.com/

Currently brewing three year-round options to sample: Cat Nap, an IPA,
Fireside, an amber ale, and Junt, a cream ale.

Goldcrest Brewing Company 1051 N 2nd Street 38103 (501) 712-3548
http://goldcrest51.com/

Brewing the original Goldcrest 51 recipe that was brewed by the
Tennessee Brewing Company in Memphis until they closed in 1954.

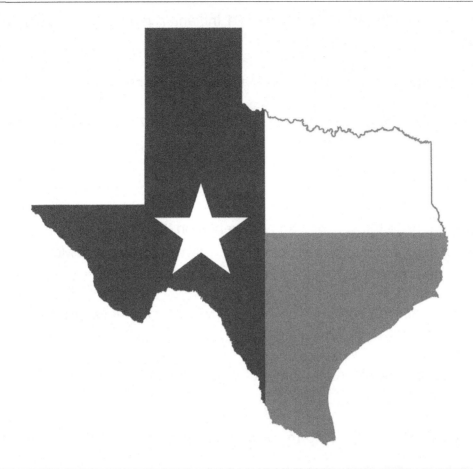

North Texas

This single-day trip takes you to a handful of great breweries in the northern part of Texas. Start your trip in Amarillo at two breweries:

Six Car Pub and Brewery 625 S Polk 79101 (806) 576-3396
https://www.sixcarpub.com/

Big Texan Brewery 7701 I-40 East 79118 (806) 372-6000
https://www.bigtexan.com/big-texan-brewery-amarillo-texas/

Head south about two hours to the next brewery in Lubbock:

The Brewery LBK 1204 Broadway #104 79401 (806) 993-9378
https://www.thebrewerylbk.com/

From here it is about three hours east to Wichita Falls:

Wichita Falls Brewing Company 701 Indiana Avenue 76301 (940) 264-4677 https://www.wichitafallsbrewing.com/

End your trip about forty minutes further east in Nocona:

Nocona Beer and Brewing 915 E Highway 82 76255 (940) 825-7238 https://noconabeer.com/

North Central Texas

There are quite a few towns and breweries on this trip, so you'll need several days if you plan to visit them all. Start your trip out in McKinney with three breweries:

Michael Waltrip Brewing Company 7951 Collin McKinney Parkway 75070 (833) 896-8463 https://michaelwaltripbrewing.com/

Tupps Brewery 721 Anderson 75069 (214) 856-7996 https://tuppsbrewery.com/

Franconia Brewing Company 495 McKinney Parkway 75071 (972) 542-0705 https://franconiabrewing.com/

Eleven minutes south is another brewery at Allen:

Nine-Band Brewing Company 9 Prestige Circle 75002 https://www.ninebandbrewing.com/

Nine minutes away is Plano with a must-visit brewery:

Unlawful Assembly Brewing Company 7800 Windrose Avenue 75024 (469) 210-2337 https://www.unlawfulassembly.com/

An award-winning brewery that focuses on beers that pair well with food and other beers. Be sure to try their Double Justice Imperial IPA and Black Sheep Oatmeal Stout. Richardson is seven months away with another brewery:

Four Bullets Brewery 640 N Interurban Street 75081 (469) 351-0511
https://www.fourbulletsbrewery.com/

Fourteen minutes east is Garland with two breweries:

Lakewood Brewing Company 2302 Executive Drive 75041 (972) 864-2337 https://lakewoodbrewing.com/

Intrinsic Brewing 509 W State Street 75040 (972) 272-2400
http://intrinsicbrewing.com/

Just seven minutes away is Rowlett:

Bankhead Brewing Company 3840 Main Street 75088 (214) 440-2080
https://www.bankheadbrewing.com/

Another nine minutes east is Rockwall:

Woodcreek Brewing Company 1400 E Interstate 30 75087 (972) 589-0048 https://www.woodcreekbrewing.com/

Royse City is twelve minutes northeast:

Thirsty Bro Brewing Company 141 E Main Street 75189 (281) 841-7246
https://www.thirstybrobrewingco.com/

The main city of Dallas is a half-hour southwest with multiple brewery options:

Deep Ellum Brewing Company 2821 Saint Louis Street 75226 (214) 888-3322 https://www.deepellumbrewing.com/

On Rotation 7328 Gaston Avenue Suite 110 75214 (972) 807-2588
https://on-rotation.com/

Oak Highlands Brewery 10484 Brockwood Road 75238 (214) 450-1659
http://www.oakhighlandsbrewery.com/

Texas Ale Project 1001 N Riverfront Blvd 75207 (214) 965-0606
https://www.texasaleproject.com/

Pegasus City Brewery 2222 Vantage Street 75207 (972) 366-7722 https://www.pegasuscitybrewery.com/

Peticolas Brewing Company 2026 Farrington Street 75207 (214) 234-7600 https://www.peticolasbrewing.com/

Four Corners Brewing Company 423 Singleton Avenue 75212 https://fcbrewing.com/

Steam Theory Brewing 340 Singleton Blvd #100 75212 (972) 803-4334 https://steamtheorybrewing.com/

Celestial Beerworks 2530 Butler Street 75235 (832) 493-3110 https://www.celestialbeerworks.com/

Community Beer Company 1530 Inspiration Drive Suite 200 (214) 751-7921 https://communitybeer.com/

White Rock Alehouse and Brewery 7331 Gaston Avenue Suite #100 75214 (214) 989-7570 https://www.whiterockalehouse.com/

An award-winning brewery focused on providing you with fine ales. Be sure to try their silver award-winning IPO IPA. Circle north to Irving sixteen minutes away with a must-visit brewery:

Twin Peaks Brewing Company 1500 Market Place Blvd 75063 (469) 420-9216 https://twinpeaksrestaurant.com/

What sets them apart from others is the signature 29-degree draft beer served in frosted glasses. Try their award-winning blonde ale. Continue north another sixteen minutes to Farmers Branch:

Hop and Sting Brewing Company 2405 Squire Place #200 75234 (817) 488-2337 https://hopandsting.com/

Addison is just eight minutes away:

Bitter Sisters Brewing Company 15103 Surveyor Blvd 75001 (972) 479-0949 http://www.bittersistersbrewery.com/

A half-hour more north is Denton:

Armadillo Ale Works 221 S Bell Avenue 76201 (940) 580-4446
https://www.armadilloaleworks.com/

Keller is a half-hour south with a must-visit brewery:

Shannon Brewing Company 818 N Main Street 76248 (817) 400-1985
https://shannonbrewing.com/

Offering four year-round all-natural fire-brewed beers. Try them all: Shannon Irish Red, Shannon Tejas Light, Shannon Mor IPA, and Shannon Hazelnut Chocolate Stout. Another sixteen minutes south is North Richland Hills with two breweries including a must-visit:

Brutal Beerworks 8447 Blvd 26 76180 (817) 666-2728
https://www.brutalbeerworks.com/

False Idol Brewing 7924 Maplewood Avenue 76180 (817) 631-9875
https://falseidolbrew.com/

Come try their great variety of unique beers such as Trustfund Baby Strawberry Milkshake IPA and Return of the Stack French Toast Imperial Stout. Another sixteen minutes brings you to two breweries in Arlington:

Legal Draft Beer Company 500 E Division Street 76011 (817) 962-2210
http://www.legaldraftbeer.com/

Division Brewing Company 506 E Main Street 76010 (214) 697-8350
https://divisionbrewing.com/

About twenty-minutes away is Mansfield with two breweries:

By the Horns Brewing 109 S Main Street 76063 (682) 341-0051
https://bythehornsbrewing.com/

Dirty Job Brewing 117 N Main Street 76063 (682) 518-1791
https://www.dirtyjobbrewing.com/

The second-largest city of Fort Worth is about twenty-minutes northwest with several options:

Martin House Brewing Company 220 S Sylvania Avenue Suite 209 76111 (817) 222-0177 https://martinhousebrewing.com/

Wild Acre Brewing Company 1734 East El Paso Street 76102 (817) 882-9453 https://www.wildacrebrewing.com/

Panther Island Brewing 501 North Main Street 76164 (817) 882-8121 https://pantherislandbrewing.com/

Funky Picnic Brewery and Café 401 Bryan Avenue Suite 117 76104 (817) 708-2739 https://www.funkypicnicbrewery.com/

HopFusion Ale Works 200 East Broadway 76104 (682) 841-1721 https://hopfusionaleworks.com/

Fort Brewery and Pizza 1001 W Magnolia Avenue 76104 (817) 923-8000 https://www.fortbrewery.com/

Cowtown Brewing Company 1301 East Belknap Street 76102 (817) 489-5800 https://www.cowtownbrewco.com/

Granbury is about forty minutes southwest:

Revolver Brewing 5650 Matlock Road 76049 (817) 736-8034 https://revolverbrewing.com/

End your trip forty minutes north in Willow Park at:

Parker County Brewing 225 Shops Blvd #105 76087 (817) 757-7777 https://www.parkercountybrewing.com/

East Texas

This circular day trip will take you to a handful of towns and great breweries for a little getaway. Start your trip in Sulphur Springs at:

BackStory Brewery 211 Magnolia 75482 (903) 438-2337
https://www.backstorybrewery.com/

Head east an hour and a half to the border town of Texarkana:

Pecan Point Brewing Company 213 Main Street 75501 (903) 306-0661
https://www.pecanpointbrewing.com/

An hour and a half south is Longview with a must-visit brewery:

Oil Horse Brewing Company 101 W Tyler Street 75601 (903) 241-4686
http://www.oilhorsebrewing.com/

Come sample all of their excellent year-round beers - 1877, an Irish Red, Big Inch, a chocolate-flavored beer, Nodding Donkey, a pale ale, and Ossamus, a Saison. About forty minutes west is another must-visit brewery in Tyler:

True Vine Brewing Company 2453 Earl Campbell Parkway 75701 (903) 600-0124 https://www.truevinebrewing.com/

Brewing artistic beers. Best known for their Mermaids and Unicorns Blonde Ale and Rose City IPA. End your trip an hour north in Winnsboro at:

Cypress Creek Southern Ales 200 E Carnegie Street 75494 (208) 841-4159 https://www.cypresscreeksouthernales.com/

West Central Texas

With some planning, you can visit all of the breweries in this area in a day, or you can split it into two days to give you some extra time to explore the area. Start your trip in Cisco at:

Red Gap Brewing 712 Conrad Hilton Blvd 76437 (254) 433-4993
https://redgapbrewing.com/

Head west about forty minutes to your next brewery at Abilene:

Pappy Slokum Brewing Company 409 S Treadaway Blvd 79602 (325) 201-4112 http://www.pappyslokum.com/

Rowena is about an hour south:

Horny Toad Brewing Company 313 Edward Street 76875 (325) 212-1177 http://hornytoadbrewery.com/

About a half-hour southwest is San Angelo:

SoCo Taphouse and Brew Company 113 E Concho Avenue #210 76903 (325) 703-6218 https://www.socotaphouse.com/

When you're ready, take a five and a half-hour drive to the border city of El Paso with four options including a must-visit:

Ode Brewing 3233 N Mesa Street 79902 (915) 351-4377 http://www.odebrewingco.com/

DeadBeach Brewery 408 Durango Street 79901 (855) 915-2337 https://www.deadbeach.com/

El Paso Brewing Company 810 Texas Avenue Suite B 79901 (915) 262-0687 https://elpasobrewing.com/

Blazing Tree Brewery 11426 Rojas Space A-13 79936 (915) 307-3627 http://blazingtreebreweryelpaso.com/

Offering six full-bodied beers that you can sample in a flight: a peanut butter brown ale, pecan porter, honey hefeweizen, mandarin IPA, blonde ale, and medusa hazy IPA. End your trip just seventeen minutes away in Canutillo at a must-visit brewery:

Sun Brewing Company 101 La Union Avenue 79835 (915) 433-3048 https://sunbrewingco.com/

Focusing on indigenous and spontaneous ales. Be sure to try their award-winning Saison de Membrillo and the Tepache Tamarindo Indigenous Beer.

Capital Area

This relatively small area doesn't take long to drive, but there are a lot of breweries crammed into the area. Take at least two days to explore everything or more if needed. Start your trip in San Marcos with three breweries:

AquaBrew 150 South LBJ Drive 78666 (512) 353-2739 https://aqua-brew.com/

Middleton Brewing 101 Oakwood Loop 78666 (512) 847-3435 http://www.middletonbrewingtx.com/

Roughhouse Brewing 680 Oakwood Loop 78666 (512) 667-7000 https://roughhousebrewing.com/

North about twenty-minutes is another brewery at Buda:

Two Wheel Brewing Company 535 S Loop 4 78610 (512) 361-3401 https://www.twowheelbrewing.com/

Sixteen minutes northwest is your next brewery at Driftwood:

Vista Brewing 13551 Ranch to Market Road 150 78619 (512) 766-1842 https://vistabrewingtx.com/

Dripping Springs is just eight minutes away with four more options:

Twisted X Brewing Company 23455 W RR 150 78620 (512) 850-6722 http://twistedxbrewing.com/

Family Business Beer Company 19510 Hamilton Pool Road 78620 (512) 829-4202 https://familybusinessbeerco.com/

Treaty Oak Brewing and Distilling 16604 Fitzhugh Road 78620 (512) 599-0335 https://www.treatyoakdistilling.com/

Acopon Brewing Company 211 Mercer 78620 (512) 829-4723 http://www.acoponbrewing.com/

Head back east about a half-hour to West Lake Hills:

Strange Land Brewery 5902 Bee Caves Road 78746 (512) 276-2295
http://strangelandbrewery.com/

Just seven minutes away is the main city of Austin with lots of breweries including two must-visits:

Infamous Brewing Company 4602 Weletka Drive 78734 (512) 487-8786
http://infamousbrewing.com/

Lazarus Brewing Company 1902 E 6th Street 78702 (512) 394-7620
https://www.lazarusbrewing.com/

Celis Brewery 10001 Metric Blvd 78758 (512) 524-2377
https://www.celisbeers.com/

St. Elmo Brewing Company 440 E St. Elmo Road Suite G-2 78745 (737) 300-1965 https://www.stelmobrewing.com/

The Brewtorium 6015 Dillard Cir A 78752 (512) 524-0323
https://www.thebrewtorium.com/

(512) Brewing Company 407 Radam F200 78745 (512) 707-2337
https://512brewing.com/

Oasis Texas Brewing Company 6550 Comanche Trail Suite 301 Unit B 78732 (512) 266-0111 https://otxbc.com/

Jester King Brewery 13187 Fitzhugh Road Bldg B 78736 (512) 537-5100
https://jesterkingbrewery.com/

Oddwood Ales 2314 Rutland Drive Suite #100 78758 (512) 662-1462
https://www.oddwoodales.com/

Central District Brewing 417 Red River Street 78710 (512) 993-4511
https://centraldistrictbrewing.com/

Nomadic Beerworks 3804 Woodbury Drive Suite A 78704 (512) 587-9669 https://www.nomadicbeerworks.com/

Circle Brewing Company 2340 West Braker Lane Suite B 78758 (512) 814-7599 https://www.circlebrewing.com/

Draught House Pub and Brewery 4112 Medical Parkway 78756 (512) 452-6258 https://www.draughthouse.com/

Austin Beerworks 3009 Industrial Terrace 78758 (512) 821-2494 https://www.austinbeerworks.com/

Austin Beer Garden Brewing Company 1305 West Oltorf 78704 (512) 298-2242 https://theabgb.com/

Frontyard Brewing 1607 Cuernavaca Drive N Suite 202 78733 (512) 772-2600 https://www.frontyardbrewing.com/

Last Stand Brewing Company 12345 Paul's Valley Road Bldg I 78737 (512) 827-9909 https://www.laststandbrewing.com/

4th Tap Brewing Co-Op 10615 Metric Blvd 78758 (512) 904-9817 https://www.4thtap.coop/

Skull Mechanix Brewing 1005 E St. Elmo Road Bldg 2 78745 (737) 300-1002 https://www.skullmechanix.com/

Uncultured Ales 12307 Roxie Drive Suite 206 78729 http://unculturedales.com/

Friends and Allies Brewing 979 Springdale Road 78702 (512) 765-5240 https://friendsandallies.beer/

Zilker Brewing Company 1701 E 6th Street 78702 (512) 765-4946 https://zilkerbeer.com/

Hi Sign Brewing 1201 Old Bastrop Highway 78742 (512) 382-5264 http://www.hisignbrewing.com/

Adelbert's Brewing 2314 Rutland Drive Suite #100 78758 (512) 662-1462 https://www.adelbertsbeer.com/

Hops and Grain Brewing 507 Calles Street Suite 101 78702 (512) 914-2467 https://www.hopsandgrain.com/

Thirsty Planet Brewing Company 8201 South Congress 78745 (512) 826-0948 https://thirstyplanet.beer/

Southern Heights Brewing Company 6014 Techni Center Drive 78721 (512) 358-4350 http://www.southernheightsbrewing.com/

Black Star Co-Op Pub and Brewery 7020 Easy Wind Drive Suite 100 78752 (512) 452-2337 https://blackstar.coop/

Focusing on beers that people want to drink, ranging from classic to unique. For classic beer, be sure to try their award-winning Recalcitrant Dockhand, a robust porter with coffee and chocolate notes.

Blue Owl Brewing 2400 E Cesar Chavez Street #300 78702 (512) 593-1262 https://blueowlbrewing.com/

An all sour brewery focusing on approachable and unique beers. Offering three year-round beers - a session wheat, a pale ale, and a red ale. Your next brewery is about a half-hour southeast in Bastrop:

Iron Bridge Icehouse 601 Chestnut Street #E 78602 (512) 431-0200 https://ironbridgeicehouse.com/

Taylor is about forty minutes north:

Texas Beer Company 201 N Main Street 76574 (512) 466-6939 https://www.texasbeerco.com/

Head west about twenty-minutes to Round Rock:

Bluebonnet Beer Company 1700 Bryant Drive #107 78664 (512) 774-4258 https://bluebonnetbeerco.com/

Another fourteen minutes west is Cedar Park with two breweries:

Hedgehog Brewing 3200 Woodall C1 78613 (512) 944-0501 https://www.hedgehogatx.com/

Whitestone Brewery 601 E Whitestone Blvd Ste 500 Bldg 5 78613 (512) 765-4828 http://www.whitestonebrewery.com/

Seventeen minutes northwest is Liberty Hill:

Bull Creek Brewing 7100 FM 3405 76842 (512) 940-5441 http://www.bullcreekbrewing.com/

Marble Falls is about forty minutes west with two more breweries:

Double Horn Brewing Company 208 Avenue H 78654 (830) 693-5165 https://www.doublehornbrewing.com/

Save the World Brewing Company 1510 Resource Parkway 78654 (830) 637-7654 https://savetheworldbrewing.com/

South about twenty-minutes is Johnson City:

Pecan Street Brewing 106 East Pecan Drive 78636 (830) 868-2500 https://www.pecanstreetbrewing.com/

End your trip another fifteen minutes south in Blanco at:

Real Ale Brewing Company 231 San Saba Court 78606 (830) 833-2534 https://realalebrewing.com/

Brazos Valley

This is a short day trip that takes you to a handful of towns and breweries. Start your trip in Brenham at:

Brazos Valley Brewing Company 201 W First Street 77833 (979) 987-1133 https://brazosvalleybrewery.com/

Twelve minutes east is another brewery at Chappell Hill:

Coalfox Brewing 2855 FM 1155 S 77426 (713) 899-5100 https://coalfox.com/

College Station is about fifty minutes north:

New Republic Brewing Company 11405 N Dowling Road Unit H 77845 (713) 489-4667 https://www.newrepublicbrewing.com/

Head northeast an hour and a half to Lovelady:

Stesti Brewing Company 1328 FM 2915 75851 (936) 204-6858 http://www.stestibrewingcompany.com/

Another hour east is Lufkin:

Angelina Brewing Company 118 S First Street 75901 (936) 301-2739 https://www.angelinabeer.com/

End your trip about twenty-minutes north in Nacogdoches at:

Fredonia Brewery 138 N Mound Street 75961 (936) 305-5125 https://fredoniabrewery.com/

Houston-Galveston Area

Circle around this area of Texas, and you'll have a lot of breweries to visit. The majority are in Houston, but there are also plenty in the surrounding area. Start your trip in Alvin at two breweries:

Fetching Lab Brewery 1578 County Road 423 Ste B 77511 (281) 414-7355 http://www.fetchinglabbrewery.com/

Gordon Street Tavern 114 N Gordon Street 77511 (281) 968-7402 https://www.gordonstreettavern.com/home

Head north fifteen minutes to Pearland with two breweries including a must-visit:

Bakfish Brewing 1231 Broadway Street 77581 (281) 993-8658 https://www.bakfishbrewing.com/

Vallenson's Brewing Company 4081 Rice Drier Road 77581 (281) 705-4063 http://www.vallensons.com/

Try a flight of their three flagship brews named for the historic area: The Settler's Oatmeal Stout, The Depot Pale Ale, and The Advocate Amber Ale. Head west about twenty-minutes to Missouri City:

Texas Leaguer Brewing Company 13503 Pike Road 77489 (832) 895-9000 https://www.txleaguer.com/

Katy is about a half-hour northwest and offers two breweries:

No Label Brewing Company 5373 First Street 77493 (281) 693-7545 https://www.nolabelbrew.com/

Battlehops Brewing 6801 Highway Blvd 77494 http://battlehopsbrewing.com/

Another twelve minutes west brings you to Brookshire:

Baa Baa Brewhouse 539 FM 359 Road S 77423 (562) 552-1481 https://www.baabaabrewhouse.com/

Head northwest about a half-hour to Bellville:

Huff Brewing Company 9807 Koehn Road 77418 (979) 270-1365 http://huffbrewing.com/

Head back east about forty minutes to Cypress:

Wicked Boxer Brewing 16326 Mueschke Road Suite E-10 77433 (832) 653-2580 http://wickedboxer.com/

Tomball is nineteen minutes north with two brewery options:

Bearded Fox Brewing 11729 Springs Cypress Road Suite R 77377 (832) 761-7928 http://www.beardedfoxbrewing.com/

Fire Ant Brewing Company 308 Market Street 77375 (832) 720-7491 https://tomballbrewery.com/

Another fifteen minutes brings you to Magnolia:

The Lone Pint Brewery 507 Commerce Street 77355 (281) 731-5466
https://lonepint.com/

Montgomery is twenty-minutes north:

Cycler's Brewing 12684 FM 149 Road 77356 (713) 569-2485
https://cyclersbrewing.com/

Head southeast to Conroe about twenty-minutes away with three breweries:

Southern Star Brewing Company 1207 N FM 3083 E 77303 (936) 441-2739 https://www.southernstarbrewing.com/

Copperhead Brewery 822 N Frazier Street 77301 (281) 919-6134
https://www.copperheadbrewery.com/

B-52 Brewing Company 12470 Milroy Lane 77304 (936) 447-4677
http://b52brewing.com/

Twenty-minutes south is Spring:

Fortress Beerworks 2606 Spring Cypress Road 77388 (713) 557-2340
https://www.fortressbeerworks.com/

Seventeen minutes east is Porter:

Back Pew Brewing Company 26452 Sorters McClellan Road 77365
(281) 608-7526 http://www.backpewbrewing.com/

Seven minutes away is Kingwood:

Megaton Brewery 808 Russell Palmer Road 77339
https://megatonbeer.com/

Another six minutes away is Humble:

Ingenious Brewing Company 1986 S Houston Avenue 77396 (832) 412-2142 https://ingeniousbeer.com/

About twenty-minutes south is the main city of Houston with many options:

Walking Stick Brewing Company 956 Judiway Street 77018
https://walkingstickbrewing.com/

Klaus Brewing Company 10142 Jones Road 77065 (346) 284-1473
http://www.klausbrewing.com/

Astral Brewing 4816 N Shepherd Drive 77018 (713) 534-1067
https://www.astralbrewing.com/

True Anomaly Brewing Company 2012 Dallas Street 77003 (346) 704-5701 https://trueanomalybrewing.com/

Under the Radar Brewery 1506 Truxillo Street 77004 (832) 512-0237
https://www.undertheradarbrewery.com/

Holler Brewing Company 2206 Edwards Street Suite A 77007 (832) 781-0555 https://hollerbeer.com/

Saint Arnold Brewing Company 2000 Lyons Avenue 77020 (713) 686-9494 https://www.saintarnold.com/

Buffalo Bayou Brewing Company 5301 Nolda Street 77007 (713) 750-9795 https://www.buffbrew.com/

Sigma Brewing Company 3118 Harrisburg Blvd 77003 (346) 352-3190
http://www.sigmabrewingcompany.com/

8th Wonder Brewery 2202 Dallas Street 77003 (713) 229-0868
https://8thwonder.com/

Eureka Heights Brewing Company 941 W 18th Street 77008 (832) 953-4677 https://www.eurekaheights.com/

Karbach Brewing Company 2032 Karbach Street 77092 (713) 680-2739
https://www.karbachbrewing.com/

Southern Yankee Beer Company 930 FM 1960 Ste G 77073 (832) 563-9681 https://www.southernyankeebeer.com/

City Acre Brewing 3421 Folger Street 77093 (832) 377-0237
https://www.cityacrebrewing.com/

4J Brewing Company 1348 Cedar Post Lane 77055 (713) 678-0776
https://www.4jbrewingcompany.com/#/

Brewing fun and simple beers that are easy to drink and higher in alcohol content. Sample all four of their year-round beers: amber ale, blonde ale, IPA, and an American stout. About a half-hour southeast is Webster:

Saloon Door Brewing 105A Magellan Circle 77598 (409) 939-3992
https://saloondoorbrewing.com/

Eleven minutes further is Dickinson:

Galveston Bay Beer Company 12900 FM 3436 Road 77539 (281) 339-3210 https://www.galvestonbaybeer.com/

End your trip a half-hour southeast at the waterfront town of Galveston and a must-visit brewery:

Galveston Island Brewing Company 8423 Stewart Road 77554 (409) 740-7000 http://www.galvestonislandbrewing.com/

Stop in here to try their flagship TIKI Wheat along with their Citra Mellow IPA. The rotating tap also features seasonal releases to try.

Alamo Area

There are only a handful of towns along this route, but if you want to visit all the breweries, then you'll need to take a couple days. Start your trip in Adkins at:

Cactus Land Brewing Company 368 County Road 325 78101 (210) 414-2776 https://cactuslandbrewing.com/

Head northeast about twenty-minutes to Seguin with two breweries:

Seguin Brewing Company 320 Beicker Road 78155 (830) 463-5097
http://www.seguinbrewing.com/

BS Brewing 1408 Old Lehmann Road 78155 (830) 660-8124
https://www.bsbrewingtx.com/

Twenty-minutes northwest is New Braunfels and three breweries:

Guadalupe Brewing Company 1580 Wald Road Suite 1 78132 (512) 878-9214 http://www.guadalupebrew.com/

Faust Brewing Company 240 Sequin Avenue 78130 (830) 625-7791
https://www.faustbrewing.com/

New Braunfels Brewing Company 180 West Mill Street 78130 (830) 626-2739 http://www.nbbrewing.com/

Southwest about a half-hour brings you to the main city of San Antonio with multiple options:

Busted Sandal Brewing Company 7114 Oaklawn Drive 78229 (210) 872-1486 http://www.bustedsandalbrewing.com/index.html

Mad Pecker Brewing Company 6025 Tezel Road #122 78250 (210) 562-3059 https://www.madpeckerbrewing.com/

Blue Star Brewing Company 1414 South Alamo 78210 (210) 212-5506
https://bluestarbrewing.com/

Roadmap Brewing 723 N Alamo 78215 (210) 254-9962
https://www.roadmapbrewing.com/

Back Unturned Brewing Company 516 Brooklyn Avenue 78215 (210) 257-0011 https://www.backunturned.com/home

Ranger Creek Brewing and Distilling 4834 Whirlwind Drive 78217 (210) 775-2099 https://drinkrangercreek.com/

Freetail Brewing Company 4035 N Loop 1604 W Suite 105 78257 (210) 395-4975 https://www.freetailbrewing.com/

Alamo Beer Company 202 Lamar Street 78202 (210) 872-5589
https://www.alamobeer.com/

Kunstler Brewing 302 East LaChapelle 78204 (210) 688-4519
https://www.kuenstlerbrewing.com/

HighWheel Beerworks 1902 S Flores Street 78204 (210) 229-0607
http://dorcolspirits.com/beer-1/

Boerne is a half-hour northwest and has three breweries including a must-visit:

Cibolo Creek Brewing Company 448 S Main Street 78006 (830) 816-5275 https://www.cibolocreekbrewing.com/

The Dodging Duck Brewhaus 402 River Road 78006 (830) 248-3825
https://www.dodgingduck.com/

Boerne Brewery 9 Hill View Lane 78006 (830) 331-8798
http://boernebrewery.com/

Brewing ales that reflect the landscape. Be sure to try a flight of all four year-round beers: a wheat ale, an English ESB, an IPA, and an English old ale.

The next brewery is a half-hour west in Bandera:

Bandera Ale Project (Bandera Brewery) 3540 State Highway 16 South Suite 2A 78003 (830) 522-4226 https://www.banderabrewery.com/

Circle north about an hour to Fredericksburg and two breweries:

Fredericksburg Brewing Company 245 East Main Street 78624 (830) 997-1646 http://www.yourbrewery.com/

Altstadt Brewery 6120 US Highway 290 East 78624 (830) 304-2337
https://www.altstadtbeer.com/

End your trip another hour southeast to Spring Branch and a must-visit brewery:

Rough Diamond Brewery 101 Kendalia Circle 78070 (830) 885-6616
http://www.roughdiamondbrewery.com/new/

Different from other beers you've tried. The aromas are distinct and hit specific palette notes. Try their two flagships brews, the IPA and Sunset Lager.

Southern Coastal Texas

This short day trip is a great way to visit a few towns and enjoy some great brews. Start your trip in Corpus Christi with a few options including a must-visit:

Rebel Toad Brewing Company 425 William Street 78404 (512) 221-1267 http://www.rebeltoadbrewing.com/

Lorelei Brewing Company 520 Nas Drive 78418 (361) 445-1084
https://loreleibrewing.beer/

Nueces Brewing Company 401 S Water Street 78401 (361) 356-6404
https://www.nuecesbrewing.com/

Railroad Seafood Station Brewing Company 1214 N Chaparral Street 78401 (361) 883-6200 https://www.railroadseafoodstation.com/

Lazy Beach Brewing 7522 Bichon #100 78414 (361) 215-9107
http://lazybeachbrewing.com/

Come try everything from the classics like their Texas Bock to their unusual, like the Imperial Mint Chocolate Stout. A two and a half-hour drive south brings you to Mission:

5x5 Brewing Company 801 N Bryan Road Ste 174 78572 (956) 445-5421 https://5x5brewing.com/

Pharr is thirteen minutes east:

Big River Brewery 505 West Nolana Loop 78577 (956) 961-4979
https://bigriverbrewery.net/

Continue east about an hour and a half to the coast at South Padre Island:

Padre Island Brewing Company 3400 Padre Blvd 78597 (956) 761-9585 http://www.pibrewingcompany.com/

Waco

Brotherwell Brewing 400 E Bridge Street 76704 (254) 301-7152 https://www.brotherwell.com/

Port Lavaca

O'Neil and Sons Brewing Company 502 Half League Road 77979 (361) 676-6023 http://www.oneilandsons.com/

Gainesville

Krootz Brewing Company 315 W Elm Street 76240 (940) 668-0307 http://www.krootzbrewingcompany.com/

Sherman

903 Brewers 1718 S Elm Street 75090 (214) 243-8090 http://903brewers.com/

Salado

Barrow Brewing Company 108 Royal Street 78765 (254) 947-3544 https://barrowbrewing.com/

Utah offers several towns and brewery options. You can travel from the southwest corner of the sate to the Salt Lake City area and visit all of the breweries. You'll need at least several days to do this. Start your trip in Saint George at:

Silver Reef Brewing Company 4391 S Enterprise Drive 84790
https://www.stgeorgebev.com/

Head east about fifty minutes to Springdale:

Zion Canyon Brew Pub 95 Zion Park Blvd #2 84767 (435) 772-0336
https://zionbrewery.com/

Cedar City is about an hour north:

Policy Kings Brewery 223 N 100 W 84721
http://policykingsbrewery.com/

When you're ready, make an almost four-hour drive northeast to Moab and a must-visit brewery:

Moab Brewery 686 South Main Street 84532 (435) 259-6333
https://themoabbrewery.com/

When you stop in here, be sure to try the Dead Horse Ale that is popular with locals and tourists alike. Also, try the Red Rye IPA and Raven Stout. Take another almost four-hour drive north to Vernal:

Vernal Brewing Company 55 South 500 East 84078 (435) 781-2337
http://www.vernalbrewing.com/

The last long drive is to head west about two and a half hours to Park City with a couple options including a must-visit:

Park City Brewery 2720 Rasmussen Road Suite A1 84098 (435) 200-8906 https://www.parkcitybrewery.com/

Wasatch Brew Pub 250 Main Street 84060 (435) 649-0900
https://wasatchbeers.com/

Brewing award-winning beers since 1986. Be sure to try their Polygamy Porter and Island Hop IPA. Nineteen minutes south is Heber:

Heber Valley Brewing Company 501 N Main Street 84032 (435) 315-3815 https://www.hebervalleybrewing.com/

Springville is about forty minutes south:

Strap Tank Brewing Company 1715 W 500 N 84663 (801) 490-9091
https://straptankbrewery.com/

Head back north about forty minutes to Midvale with three breweries including a must-visit:

2 Row Brewing 6856 South 300 West 84047 (801) 987-8663
https://2rowbrewing.com/

Hoppers Grill and Brewing Company 890 Fort Union Blvd 84047 (801) 566-0424 https://www.hoppersbrewpub.com/

Bohemian Brewery 94 E 7200 S Fort Union Blvd 84047 (801) 566-5474 http://www.bohemianbrewery.com/

Focusing on traditional lagers, be sure to try their flagship beers: 1842 Pilsner Lager, 1841 Viennese Lager, and Cherny Bock Schwarzbier.

Eleven minutes north is South Salt Lake:

Saltfire Brewing 2199 S West Temple 84115 (385) 955-0504 https://www.saltfirebrewing.com/

Six minutes away is the main city of Salt Lake City:

Hopkins Brewing Company 1048 E 2100 S 84106 (385) 528-3275 http://hopkinsbrewingcompany.com/

Salt Flats Brewing 2020 Industrial Circle 84104 (801) 828-3469 https://saltflatsbeer.com/

Fisher Brewing Company 320 West 800 South 84101 (801) 487-2337 https://www.fisherbeer.com/

Level Crossing Brewing Company 2496 South West Temple 84115 (385) 270-5752 https://levelcrossingbrewing.com/

Shades Brewing 154 W Utopia 84115 (435) 200-3009 https://www.shadesbrewing.beer/

Red Rock Brewing Company 254 South 200 West 84101 (801) 521-7446 https://redrockbrewing.com/

Desert Edge Brewery 273 Trolley Square 84102 (801) 521-8917 https://desertedgebrewery.com/

Uinta Brewing Company 1722 S Fremont Drive 84104 (801) 467-0909 http://www.uintabrewing.com/

Toasted Barrel Brewery 412 West 600 North 84103 (801) 657-6942
https://www.toastedbarrelbrewery.com/

Templin Family Brewing 936 South 300 West 84101 (801) 232-0936
https://www.tfbrewing.com/

Squatters Pub Brewery 147 W Broadway 84101 (801) 363-2739
https://www.squatters.com/default.aspx

RoHa Brewing Project 30 E Kensington Avenue 84115 (385) 227-8982
https://rohabrewing.com/

Kiitos Brewing 608 West 700 South 84104 (801) 423-4243
https://kiitosbrewing.com/

Bewilder Brewing 445 S 400 W 84101 (385) 528-3840
https://bewilderbrewing.com/

Head west about a half-hour to Tooele:

Bonneville Brewery 1641 N Main Street 84074 (435) 248-0652
https://bonnevillebrewery.com/

End your trip an hour north in Ogden with three breweries:

UTOG Brewing Company 2331 Grant Avenue 84401 (801) 689-3476
https://utogbrewing.com/

Cerveza Zolupez Beer Company 205 W 29th Street Unit #2 84401 (801) 917-2319 https://zolupez.com/

Talisman Brewing Company 1258 S Gibson Avenue 84404 (801) 791-3322 https://www.talismanbrewingco.com/

Northern Vermont

You'll want to take at least a couple days to enjoy this area and visit the breweries. Start your trip in Newport at:

Kingdom Brewing 1876 VT Rt 105 05855 (802) 334-7096
https://kingdombrewingvt.com/

Head south about fifty minutes to St. Johnsbury and a must-visit brewery:

Saint J Brewery 2002 Memorial Drive 05819 (802) 424-1700
https://saintjbrewery.com/

Try their wide variety of full-flavored ales and lagers. Be sure to try their popular Smokin' J IPA and Brown Chaga. Head northwest about a half-hour to Greensboro:

Hill Farmstead Brewery 403 Hill Road 05842 (802) 533-7450
https://hillfarmstead.com/

Another half-hour brings you to Hyde Park:

Ten Bends Beer 590 E Main Street 05655 (801) 521-7139
https://www.tenbendsbeer.com/

Two more breweries are just five minutes away in Morrisville:

Rock Art Brewery 632 Laporte Road 05661 (802) 888-9400
http://www.rockartbrewery.com/

Lost Nation Brewing 254 Wilkins Street 05661 (802) 851-8041
http://lostnationbrewing.com/

Thirteen minutes south is Stowe with three breweries including a must-visit:

The Alchemist 100 Cottage Club Road 05672 (802) 882-8165
https://alchemistbeer.com/

Von Trapp Brewing 1333 Luce Hill Road 05672 (802) 253-0900
https://www.vontrappbrewing.com/

Idletyme Brewing Company 1859 Mountain Road 05672 (802) 253-4765
https://idletymebrewing.com/

You won't be disappointed with the beers here, no matter what your interests. Consider the Helles Lager and Idletyme Double IPA. Richmond is a half-hour southwest:

Stone Corral Brewery 83 Huntington Road 05477 (802) 434-6318
https://stonecorral.com/

Seven minutes away is Williston with the next brewery:

Burlington Beer Company 25 Omega Drive Suite 150 05495 (802) 863-2337 http://burlingtonbeercompany.com/

Ten minutes northwest is Essex Junction:

1st Republic Brewing Company 39 River Road 05452 (802) 857-5318
https://www.1strepublicbrewingco.com/

Another brewery is five minutes away in Colchester:

Green Empire Brewing 478 Hegeman Avenue 05446
https://www.gebrew.com/

St. Albans is about twenty-minutes north:

14th Star Brewing Company 133 North Main Street #7 05478 (802) 528-5988 https://www.14thstarbrewing.com/

A half-hour back south is Winooski:

Four Quarters Brewing Company 150 West Canal Street Suite 1 05404 (802) 391-9120 http://www.fourquartersbrewing.com/

Five minutes brings you to South Burlington and two breweries:

Magic Hat Brewing Company 5 Bartlett Bay Road 05403 (802) 658-BREW https://www.magichat.net/

Halyard Brewing Company 80 Ethan Allen Drive Suite 2 05403 (802) 497-1858 https://halyardbrewing.us/

Another five minutes takes you to the main city of Burlington and several options:

Zero Gravity Craft Brewery 716 Pine Street 05401 (802) 861-2999 https://www.zerogravitybeer.com/

Switchback Brewing Company 160 Flynn Avenue 05401 (802) 651-4114 https://www.switchbackvt.com/

The Vermont Pub and Brewery 144 College Street 05401 (802) 865-0500 https://www.vermontbrewery.com/

Queen City Brewery 703B Pine Street 05401 (802) 540-0280 http://queencitybrewery.com/

Freak Folk Bier 703 Pine Street 05401 https://www.freakfolkbier.com/

Foam Brewers 112 Lake Street 05401 (802) 399-2511 https://www.foambrewers.com/

House of Fermentology 777 Pine Street 05401 (802) 999-3020 http://www.houseoffermentology.com/

When you're ready there is a must-visit brewery thirteen minutes south in Shelburne:

Fiddlehead Brewing Company 6305 Shelburne Road 05483 (802) 399-2994 https://fiddleheadbrewing.com/

Enjoy a sampling of their flagship Fiddlehead IPA. There are also a number of other ales and IPAs on tap that you can try. Thirteen minutes east is Hinesburg:

Frost Beer Works 171 Commerce Street 05461 (949) 945-4064
https://www.frostbeerworks.com/

End your trip with about an hour drive south to Rutland:

Hop'n Moose Brewing Company 41 Center Street 05701 (802) 775-7063 https://rutlandbeerworks.wixsite.com/hopnmoose

Central Vermont

This is a great day trip you can make to several great towns and breweries. Start your trip in Vergennes at:

Hired Hand Brewing Company 33 Green Street 05491 (802) 870-7191
http://www.hiredhandbrewing.com/

Head about fifty minutes east to Waitsfield:

Lawson's Finest Liquids 155 Carroll Road 05673 (802) 496-4677
https://www.lawsonsfinest.com/

Waterbury is seventeen minutes north with two breweries:

Big Tree Brewing Company 1 South Main Street 05676 (802) 244-7827
https://www.waterburyreservoir.com/

Prohibition Pig 2 Elm Street 05676 (802) 244-4120
https://www.prohibitionpig.com/

Half-hour south is Northfield:

Good Measure Brewing Company 17 East Street 05663 (802) 485-4600
https://www.goodmeasurebrewing.com/

Another seventeen minutes south is Braintree:

Bent Hill Brewery 1972 Bent Hill Road 05060 (802) 249-1125
https://www.benthillbrewery.com/

End your trip with about an hour drive southwest to Middlebury with two breweries including a must-visit:

Otter Creek Brewing 793 Exchange Street 05753 (800) 473-0727
http://ottercreekbrewing.com/home

Drop-In Brewing Company 610 Rt 7 South 05753 (802) 989-7414
https://dropinbrewing.com/

Three flagship beers reflect the passion and experience of the head brewer: Sunshine & Happiness, a golden ale, Heart of Lothian, a Scottish ale, and Red Dwarf, an American amber ale.

South Vermont

A great day trip to enjoy some great brews and quaint towns. Start your trip in Bennington at:

Madison Brewing Company 428 Main Street 05201 (802) 442-7397
http://madisonbrewingco.com/

Head east about a half-hour to Jacksonville:

J'ville Craft Brewery 201 VT Route 112 05342 (802) 368-2233
http://www.jvillebrewery.com/

Another half-hour brings you to Brattleboro:

Hermit Thrush Brewery 29 High Street Suite 101C 05301 (802) 257-2337 https://www.hermitthrushbrewery.com/

Take a forty-minute drive north to Springfield and a must-visit brewery:

Trout River Brewing Company 100 River Street 05156 (802) 345-2756
https://www.troutriverbrewing.com/

Come here to try some of the best craft beers in the state of Vermont, including Rainbow Red Ale, Chocolate Oatmeal Stout, and Knight Slayer Imperial Stout. Proctorsville is nineteen minutes northwest:

Outer Limits Brewing 60 Village Green 05153 (802) 287-6100
https://www.outerlimitsbrewing.com/

Another hour northwest is Brandon:

Red Clover Ale Company 43 Center Street 05733 (802) 465-8412
https://www.redcloverale.com/

End your trip with about an hour drive east to White River Junction at:

River Roost Brewery 230 S Main Street 05001
http://www.riverroostbrewery.com/

Virginia

Shenandoah Valley

This beautiful area can be visited in a single day for a chance to sample some great beers and enjoy beautiful countryside views. Start out in Natural Bridge at:

Great Valley Farm Brewery 60 Great Valley Lane 24578 (540) 521-6163
http://greatvalleyfarmbrewery.com/

Head about an hour north to McGaheysville:

Cave Hill Farms Brewery 1001 Jacob Burner Drive Building 11 22840 (540) 246-1185 https://cavehillfarmsbrewery.com/

Another ten minutes north is Elkton:

Elkton Brewing Company 100 N Fifth Street 22827
https://www.elktonbrewing.com/

Luray is another half-hour away:

Hawksbill Brewing Company 22 Zerkel Street 22835 (540) 860-5608
https://www.hawksbillbrewing.com/

Another fifty minutes north is Middletown with a must-visit brewery:

Backroom Brewery150 Ridgemont Road 22645 (540) 869-8482
https://www.backroombreweryva.com/

A small boutique farm brewery with many award-winning beers. Be sure to try: Backroom Blonde Ale, Festival Wheat Beer, Lemon Basil Wheat Beer, Oatmeal Stout and the Ferminator. End your trip twenty-minutes south in Woodstock at:

Woodstock Brewhouse 123 E Court Street 22664 (540) 459-2739
http://www.woodstockbrewhouse.com/

Blue Ridge Highlands

Take a beautiful day trip into the mountains and enjoy some great beers. Start your trip in Blacksburg with three breweries:

Eastern Divide Brewing Company 3175 Commerce Street 24060 (540) 577-6877 https://easterndivide.com/

Right Mind Brewing 1410 S Main Street 24060 (540) 552-7000
http://www.leftysgrille.com/brewery/

Rising Silo Brewery 2351 Glade Road 24060 (410) 596-1200
https://www.risingsilobrewery.com/

Head south eleven minutes to Christiansburg:

Sinkland Farms Brewery 3060 Riner Road 24073 (540) 835-3395
https://sinklandfarms.com/

Floyd is another half-hour south:

Buffalo Mountain Brewery 332 Webbs Mill Road 24091 (540) 745-2491
https://www.buffalomountainbrewery.com/

About an hour southwest is another brewery at Wytheville:

7 Dogs Brew Pub 360 W Spring Street 23482 (276) 228-0994
https://7dogsbrewpubva.com/

End your trip about fifty minutes southwest at Abingdon:

Wolf Hills Brewing Company 350 Park Street 24210 (276) 451-5470
http://wolfhillsbrewing.com/

Central Virginia

There are a lot of breweries to visit in the central region of Virginia, many of them in quaint small towns where you'll have lots of sites to see. So take at least a few days to explore everything. Start your trip in Crozet with two breweries:

Starr Hill Brewery 5391 Three Notched Road 22932 (434) 823-5671
https://starrhill.com/

Pro Re Nata Brewery 6135 Rockfish Gap Turnpike 22932 (434) 823-4878 https://prnbrewery.com/

Fourteen minutes southwest is Afton with two breweries including a must-visit:

WildManDan Brewery 279 Avon Road 22920 (434) 270-0404
https://www.wmdb3.com/wildmandan-brewery

Blue Mountain Brewery 9519 Critzers Shop Road 22920 (540) 456-8020
https://bluemountainbrewery.com/

Stop by to try a flight of all five flagship beers - a Pre-Prohibition Lager, a German Ale, an Orange Infused IPA, a DIPA, and a Pale Ale. Nellysford is fifteen minutes south:

Wild Wolf Brewing Company 2461 Rockfish Valley Highway 22958 (434) 361-0088 https://www.wildwolfbeer.com/

Another seventeen minutes brings you to a must-visit brewery in Roseland:

Devils Backbone Brewing Company 200 Mosby's Run 22967 (434) 361-1001 https://www.dbbrewingcompany.com/

Brewing true-to-style beers with their own unique recipes. If you want something strong, try the 12% ABV Barleywine or for something milder try the 4.5% Gold Leaf Lager. Amherst is about another twenty-minutes south:

Loose Shoe Brewing Company 198 Ambriar Plz 24521 (434) 946-2337 https://www.looseshoebrewing.com/

Head back north about twenty-minutes to Lovingston:

Wood Ridge Farm Brewery 165 Old Ridge Road 22949 (434) 422-6225 https://woodridgefarmbreweryva.com/home

Now head east about a half-hour to Scottsville:

James River Brewery 561 Valley Street 24590 (434) 286-7837 https://jrbrewery.com/

Farmville is fifty minutes south:

Three Roads Brewing Company 312 W Third Street 23901 (434) 430-5360 https://www.thirdstbrewing.com/

About forty minutes northeast is Powhatan:

Fine Creek Brewing Company 2425 Robert E Lee Road 23139 (804) 372-9786 https://finecreekbrewing.com/

Continue east to two breweries in Midlothian, eighteen minutes away:

Extra Billy's Smokehouse and Brewery 1110 Alverser Drive 23113 (804) 379-8727 http://www.extrabillys.com/

Steam Bell Beer Works 717 East Oak Lake Blvd 23112 (804) 728-1875 http://www.steambell.beer/

About twenty-minutes northeast is Glen Allen:

Intermission Beer Company 10089 Brook Road 23059 (804) 585-0405 https://www.intermissionbeer.com/

Thirteen minutes north is Ashland with two breweries:

Center of the Universe Brewing Company 11293 Air Park Road 23005 (804) 368-0299 https://cotubrewing.com/

Origin Beer Lab 106 S Railroad Avenue 23005 (804) 299-2389 http://www.originbeerlab.com/

Head back west about twenty-minutes to Rockville:

Midnight Brewery 2410 Granite Ridge Road 23146 (804) 356-9379 https://www.midnightbrewery.com/

Continue about twenty-minutes to Goochland and two more breweries:

Kindred Spirit Brewing 12830 W Creek Parkway Ste J 23238 (804) 708-0309 http://kindredspiritbrewing.com/

Lickinghole Creek Craft Brewery 4100 Knolls Point Drive 23063 https://www.lickingholecreek.com/

Ruckersville is about an hour northwest:

Octonia Stone Brew Works 14902 Spotswood Trail 22968 (434) 939-9678 http://octonia.beer/

Fourteen minutes northeast is Madison:

Bald Top Brewing Company 1830 Thrift Road 22727 (540) 999-1830 http://www.baldtopbrewing.com/

Just nine minutes away in Leon is a must-visit brewery:

Tap 29 Brewery 154 Winery Lane 22725 (540) 547-3707 https://www.tap29brew.com/

Brewing beers for everyone, no matter what their tastes. Be sure to try their three flagship brews - Pit Stop Pilsner, Big Wheels Wheat, and Amber Waves. About twenty-minutes south is Orange and two more breweries:

Willow Spring Brewery/The Light Well 110 E Main Street 22960 (540) 661-0004 https://www.thelightwell.com/brewery/

Iron Pipe Alewerks 319 N Madison Road Suite A 22960 (540) 212-8773 https://ironpipealewerks.com/

End your trip eleven minutes east in Unionville at:

Unionville Brewing Company 24333 Narrow Gauge Road 22567 http://unionvillebrewingco.com/

Coastal Virginia

Whether on the cape or along the bay, there is a lot of waterfront in Virginia. Take a couple days to drive this coastal route and visit some great breweries. Start your trip in Montross at:

Montross Brewery 15381 Kings Highway 22520 (804) 452-7394 https://www.montrossbrewery.com/

Travel about an hour south down the coast to a must-visit brewery in Gloucester:

Gloucester Brewing Company 6778 Main Street 23061 (804) 210-1407 https://www.globrewco.com/

This hometown brewery focuses on the science behind the beer making. Be sure to try their three perfected flagship beers - Brown Ale, IPA, and Stout. Another thirteen minutes brings you to Hayes:

That Damn Mary Brewing Company 5036 George Washington Memorial Highway 23072 (804) 761-1085 http://thatdamnmarybrewing.com/

Smithfield is about fifty minutes south and has a must-visit brewery:

Wharf Hill Brewing Company 25 Main Street 23430 (757) 357-7100 https://www.wharfhillbrewing.com/

Enjoy local beers and food in a historic building. You must try the following: Isle of Wheat, Outage IPA, and Holy Brale. Circle north to the cape town of Cape Charles about an hour and a half away:

Cape Charles Brewing Company 2198 Stone Road 23310 (757) 695-3909 https://www.capecharlesbrewing.com/

End your trip about an hour and a half north in Chincoteague at:

Black Narrows Brewing Company 4522 Chicken City Road 23336 (757) 336-7001 https://blacknarrowsbrewing.com/

Virginia Mountains

This short day trips takes you into the beautiful mountains of Virginia to taste some wonderful beers. Start your trip in Bedford at:

Beale's Brewery and BBQ 510 Grove Street 24523 (540) 583-5113 https://www.bealesbeer.com/

Head east about twenty-minutes to Forest:

Apocalypse Ale Works 1257 Burnbridge Road 24551 (434) 258-8761 https://www.endofbadbeer.com/

When you're ready take a two hour drive north to Hot Springs:

Bacova Beer Company 2814 Main Street 24445 (540) 505-4411 https://www.bacovabeer.com/

Clifton Forge is about a half-hour south:

Jack Mason's Tavern and Brewery 400 East Ridgeway Street 24422 (540) 862-5624 https://www.jackmasonstavern.com/

Continue about an hour south to Vinton:

Twin Creeks Brewing 111 Pollard Street 24179 (540) 265-8062
http://www.twincreeksbrewing.com/

About twenty-minutes further south is Boones Mill:

Hammer and Forge Brewing Company 70 Main Street 24065 (540) 909-3200 https://www.hammerandforgebrewing.com/

End your trip just eighteen minutes south in Callaway at:

Chaos Mountain Brewing 3135 Dillons Mill Road 24067 (540) 334-1600
http://chaosmountainbrewing.com/

Northeast Virginia

With good scheduling and timing you may be able to visit all the breweries here in a single day. But if you want to relax and enjoy your trip, you should plan at least two days. Start your trip in Spotsylvania at:

1781 Brewing Company 11109 Plank Road 22553 (540) 841-2598
https://www.1781brewing.com/home

Head north about a half-hour to Stafford:

Barley Naked Brewing Company 15 Tech Pkwy 22556 (540) 623-4475
https://barleynaked.com/

Lake Ridge is about another twenty-minutes north:

Water's End Brewery 12425 Dillingham Sq 22192 (571) 285-1997
https://www.watersendbrewery.com/

Just four minutes away is Woodbridge:

Brew Republic Bierwerks 15201 Potomac Town Place 22191 (703) 594-7950 https://brewrepublic.beer/

Another four minutes is Lorton:

Fair Winds Brewing Company 7000 Newington Road Suites K&L 22043 (202) 413-6176 https://fairwindsbrewing.com/

Vienna is about a half-hour north:

Caboose Brewing Company 520 Mill Street NE 22180 (703) 865-8580 https://www.caboosebrewing.com/

Fourteen minutes northwest is Reston with two breweries:

Bike Lane Brewing 11150 Sunset Hills 20190 (703) 689-2671 https://www.thebikelane.com/articles/bike-lane-brewing-and-cafe-pg2176.htm

Lake Anne Brew House 11424 Washington Plaza W 20190 (571) 758-2739 http://lakeannebrewhouse.com/

Eleven minutes south is three breweries at Chantilly:

Ono Brewing Company 4520 Daly Drive Suite 102 20151 (571) 409-6662 https://www.onobrewco.com/

Mustang Sally Brewing Company 14140 Parke Long Court Suite A 20151 (703) 378-7450 https://msbrewing.com/

Honor Brewing Company 14151 Newbrook Drive #200 20151 (866) 920-9463 http://www.honorbrewing.com/

Yorkshire is another thirteen minutes south:

Eavesdrop Brewery 7223 Centreville Road 20111 (703) 420-8955 https://eavesdropbrewery.com/

Head west eighteen minutes to Gainesville and a must-visit brewery:

Tin Cannon Brewing Company 7679 Limestone Drive #130 20155 (571) 210-5671 https://www.tincannonbrewing.com/

Offering a rotating selection of seasonal and experimental beers, but there are two exceptional year-round beers to try, Virginia Blonde Ale and

Revenge of the Zyth IPA. End your trip twelve minutes south in Nokesville at:

Cedar Run Brewery 12801 Hazelwood Drive 20181 (703) 594-0420 http://www.cedarrunbrewery.com/

Northwest Virginia

The breweries in this area are close together, so driving to all of them doesn't take that long. However, there are a lot to choose from. So if you want to visit all of the breweries you'll need two or three days at least. Start your trip in Sperryville at two breweries:

Hopkins Ordinary Bed and Breakfast + Ale Works 47 Main Street 22740 (540) 987-3383 http://www.hopkinsordinary.com/ale-works

Pen Druid Brewing 7 River Lane East Annex 22740 (540) 987-5064 https://www.pendruid.com/

Head southeast about twenty-minutes to Culpeper with two more breweries:

Far Gohn Brewing Company 301 South East Street 22701 (540) 321-4578 https://www.fargohnbrewing.com/

Old House Brewing 18351 Corkys Lane 22701 (540) 423-1032 https://oldhousetoday.com/

Another brewery is twelve minutes northeast in Brandy Station:

Old Trade Brewery 13270 Alanthus Road 22714 (774) 218-8645 https://oldtradebrewery.com/

Continue fifteen minutes to Midland:

Powers Farm and Brewery 9269 Redemption Way 22728 (540) 272-5060 https://www.powersfarmbrewery.com/

Fifteen minutes northwest will bring you to Warrenton and four brewery choices:

Old Bust Head Brewing Company 7134 Lineweaver Road 20187 (540) 347-4777 https://www.oldbusthead.com/

Barking Rose Brewing Company 9057 Old Culpeper Road 20186 (540) 935-6206 https://www.barkingrose.com/

Altered Suds Beer Company 36A Main Street 20186 (540) 216-3490 https://alteredsudsbeer.com/

Wort Hog Brewing Company 50A S 3rd Street 20186 (540) 300-2739 http://www.worthogbreweryllc.com/

Another fourteen minutes north is Broad Run:

The Farm Brewery at Broad Run 16015 John Marshall Highway 20137 (703) 753-3548 https://www.thefarmbreweryatbroadrun.com/

Aldie is twenty-minutes north:

Quattro Goomba's Brewery 22860 James Monroe Highway 20105 (703) 327-6052 http://www.goombabrewery.com/

Twelve minutes southeast is another brewery at Dulles:

Solace Brewing 42615 Trade West Drive #100 20166 (703) 345-5630 https://solacebrewing.com/

Sixteen minutes northeast is three breweries at Sterling:

Rocket Frog Brewing Company 22560 Glenn Drive Suite #103 20164 (571) 375-7920 https://rocketfrogbeer.com/

Beltway Brewing Company 22620 Davis Drive Ste 110 20164 (571) 989-2739 https://www.beltwaybrewco.com/

Twinpanzee Brewing Company 101-D Executive Drive 20166 (703) 791-9363 https://twinpanzee.square.site/

Eleven minutes back northwest is Ashburn with multiple options including a must-visit:

The Craft of Brewing 21140 Ashburn Crossing Drive Suite 170 20147 (703) 687-3932 https://www.thecraftob.com/

House 6 Brewing 44427 Atwater Drive #160 20147 (585) 520-5710 https://www.house6brewing.com/

Dynasty Brewing 21140 Ashburn Crossing Drive Suite #130-135 20147 (571) 246-5991 http://www.dynastybrewing.com/home.html

Old Ox Brewery 44652 Guilford Drive Suite 114 20147 (703) 729-8375 https://www.oldoxbrewery.com/

Lost Rhino Brewing Company 21730 Red Rum Drive 20147 (571) 291-2083 https://www.lostrhino.com/

Offering classic styles with local flavor. Be sure to try all of their most popular options -New River Pale Ale, Rhino Chasers Pilsner, and Face Plant IPAs. Leesburg is only ten minutes away with several more options:

Barnhouse Brewery 43271 Spinks Ferry Road 20176 (703) 675-8480 https://www.barnhousebrewery.com/

Black Hoof Brewing Company 11 South King Street 20175 (571) 707-8014 https://blackhoofbrewing.com/

Phase 2 Brewing 19382 Diamond Lake Drive 20176 (540) 987-0219 https://www.phase2brewing.com/

Crooked Run Brewing 205 Harrison Street SE 20175 (703) 609-9241 https://www.crookedrunbrewing.com/

Dog Money Restaurant and Brewery 50 Catoctin Circle NE 20176 (703) 687-3852 https://www.dogmoneyllc.com/

Loudoun Brewing Company 310 East Market Street 20176 (703) 350-8553 https://loudounbrewing.com/

MacDowell Brew Kitchen 202 Harrison Street SE 20175 (703) 777-2739
http://macdowellsbrewkitchen.com/

Vanish Beer 42264 Leelynn Farm Lane 20176 (703) 779-7407
https://vanishbeer.com/

Another twelve minutes is Waterford:

Wheatland Spring Farm Brewery 38506 John Wolford Road 20197
(540) 746-6080 https://www.wheatlandspring.com/

Twelve minutes to the west is Hillsboro:

Hillsborough Winery and Brewery 36716 Charles Town Pike 20132
(540) 668-6216 https://www.hillsboroughwine.com/

Nine minutes south is Purcellville with three breweries:

Notaviva Craft Fermentations 13274 Sagle Road 20132 (540) 668-6756
http://www.notavivavineyards.com/beer

Belly Love Brewing Company 725 E Main Street 20132 (540) 441-3159
https://www.bellylovebrewing.com/

Adroit Theory Brewing Company 404 Browning Court Unit C 20132
(703) 722-3139 https://www.adroit-theory.com/

Ten minutes west is Bluemont with two breweries:

Dirt Farm Brewing 18701 Foggy Bottom Road 20135 (540) 554-2337
https://dirtfarmbrewing.com/

Bear Chase Brewing Company 18294 Blue Ridge Mountain Road 20135
(540) 554-8210 https://bearchasebrew.com/

End your trip a half-hour west in Round Hill at:

B Chord Brewing Company 34266 Williams Gap Road 20141
https://www.bchordbrewing.com/

The state of Virginia is also home to multiple Independent Cities. Many of these have several great breweries. If you find yourself in the area or staying in one of these cities, then stop in to check out what breweries they have to offer.

Alexandria

Port City Brewing 3950 Wheeler Avenue 22304 (703) 797-2739 https://www.portcitybrewing.com/

Bristol

State Street Brewing 801 State Street 24201 http://www.statestreetbrewing.com/home

Bristol Station Brews and Taproom 41 Piedmont Avenue 24201 (276) 608-1220 https://www.bristolbrew.com/

Charlottesville

Three Notch'd Brewing Company 520 2nd Street Southeast 22902 (434) 961-0959 https://threenotchdbrewing.com/

Rockfish Brewing Company 900 Preston Avenue 22903 (434) 566-9783 https://www.rockfishbrewcompany.com/

South Street Brewery 106 South Street 22902 (434) 293-6550 https://www.southstreetbrewery.com/

Reason Beer 1180 Seminole Trail Suite 290 22901 (434) 260-0145 https://www.reasonbeer.com/

Champion Brewing Company 324 6th Street SE 22902 (434) 295-2739 http://championbrewingcompany.com/

Random Row Brewing Company 608 Preston Avenue 22903 (434) 284-8466 http://www.randomrow.com/

Offering a rotating tap selection for all interests and tastes. Ranging from the light Helles Lager to the Mosaic Pale Ale and everything in between.

Chesapeake

Big Ugly Brewing Company 845 S Battlefield Blvd 23322 (757) 609-2739 https://biguglybrewing.com/

Danville

Ballad Brewing 600 Craghead Street 24541 (434) 799-4677 http://www.balladbrewing.com/

2 Witches Winery and Brewing Company 209 Trade Street 24541 (434) 549-2739 https://www.2witcheswinebrew.com/

Fairfax

Ornery Beer Company 3950 University Drive Suite 209 22030 (571) 459-2143 http://www.ornerybeer.com/

Chubby Squirrel Brewing Company 10382 Willard Way 22030 (571) 989-1082 http://www.chubbysquirrelbrewing.com/

Falls Church

Audacious Aleworks 100 E Fairfax Street Ste 112 22046 (571) 303-0177 https://audaciousaleworks.com/

Settle Down Easy Brewing Company 2822 Fallfax Drive 22042 (703) 269-5090 https://settledowneasybrewing.com/

Hampton

Bull Island Brewing Company 758 Settlers Landing Road 23669 (757) 788-9489 https://www.bullislandbrewing.com/

Capstan Bar Brewing Company 2036 Exploration Way 23666 (757) 788-7276 https://www.capstanbarbrewing.com/

Fredericksburg

Highmark Brewery 390 Kings Highway Ste 107 22405 (540) 207-1725
https://highmarkbrewery.com/

6 Bears and a Goat Brewing 1140 International Parkway 22406 (540) 356-9056 https://www.6bgbrewingco.com/

Maltese Brewing 11047 Pierson Drive Unit B 22408 (540) 385-9360
https://www.maltesebrewing.com/

Spencer Devon Brewing 106 George Street 22401 (540) 999-6253
https://spencerdevonbrewing.com/

Galax

Creek Bottom Brews 307 North Meadow Street 24333 (276) 236-2337
http://www.cbbrews.com/lil-bottom/

Harrisonburg

Restless Moons Brewing 120 W Wolfe Street 22802 (540) 217-2726
https://www.restlessmoons.com/

The Friendly Fermenter 20 S Mason Street Suite B10 22801 (540) 217-2614 https://www.friendlyfermenter.com/

Pale Fire Brewing Company 217 S Liberty Street 22801 (540) 217-5452
https://www.palefirebrewing.com/

Brothers Craft Brewing 800 N Main Street 28802 (540) 421-6599
https://www.brotherscraftbrewing.com/

Manassas

2 Silos Brewing Company 9925 Discovery Blvd 20109
https://2silosbrewing.com/

Tucked Away Brewing 8420 Kao Circle 20110 (703) 420-2890
https://www.tuckedawaybrew.com/

BadWolf Brewing Company 9776 Center Street 20110 (571) 358-9774
https://badwolfbrewingcompany.com/

Negus Brewing Company 8485 Euclid Avenue 20111 (703) 649-1161
https://www.negusbeer.com/

Sinistral Brewing Company 9419 Main Street 20110 (703) 686-4575
https://sinistralbrewingcompany.com/

Newport News

Tradition Brewing 700 Thimble Shoals Blvd 23606 (757) 592-9393
https://traditionbrewing.com/

Twisted Knot Brewing 11838 Canon Blvd Suite 400 23606 (757) 782-5941 https://www.twistedknotbrewing.com/

Norfolk

Smartmouth Brewing Company 1309 Raleigh Avenue 23507 (757) 624-3939 https://smartmouthbrewing.com/

Makers Craft Brewery 735 E 23rd Street 23504 (757) 226-8506
https://www.makers.beer/

Elation Brewing 5104 Colley Avenue 23508 (757) 550-4827
https://www.elation.beer/

The Bold Mariner Brewing Company 1901 E Ocean Avenue 23508
(757) 952-6533 https://boldmariner.com/

Rip Rap Brewing Company 116 E 25th Street 23517 (757) 632-0159
https://www.riprapbrewing.com/

O'Connor Brewing Company 211 W 24th Street 23517 (757) 623-2337
https://oconnorbrewing.com/

Benchtop Brewing Company 1129 Boissevain Avenue 23507 (757) 321-9482 https://benchtopbrewing.com/

Offering bold creations with some of the most unique sounding ingredients. For example, the Oyster Gose with local oysters, lemon zest, and Indian coriander.

Petersburg

Trapezium Brewing Company 423 3rd Street 23803 (804) 477-8703 http://www.trapeziumbrewing.com/

Portsmouth

MoMac Brewing 3228 Academy Avenue 23703 (757) 383-9572 https://momacbrewing.com/

Radford

River Company Restaurant and Brewery 6633 Viscoe Road 24141 (540) 633-3940 http://therivercompanyrestaurant.com/

Richmond

Castleburg Brewery and Taproom 1626 Ownby Lane 23220 (804) 353-1256 https://castleburgbrewery.com/

The Answer Brewpub 6008 W Broad Street 23230 (804) 282-1248 http://theanswerbrewpub.com/

Strangeways Brewing 2277A Dabney Road 23230 (804) 303-4336 https://strangewaysbrewing.com/

The Veil Brewing Company 1301 Roseneath Road 23230 https://www.theveilbrewing.com/

Garden Grove Brewing Company 3445 W Cary Street 23221 (804) 918-6158 https://www.gardengrovebrewing.com/

Dogtown Brewing 1209 Hull Street 23224 (804) 724-2337
https://www.dogtownbrewingco.com/

Triple Crossing Brewing 113 South Foushee Street 23220 (804) 495-1955 https://triplecrossing.com/

Bingo Beer Company 2900 West Broad Street 23232 (804) 386-0290
https://www.bingorva.com/

Hardywood Park Craft Brewery 2408 Ownby Lane 23220 (804) 420-2420 https://hardywood.com/

Vasen Brewing Company 3331 W Moore Street 23230 (804) 588-5678
http://www.vasenbrewing.com/

Richbrau Brewing 5 South 20th Street 23223 (804) 621-4100
https://www.richbraubrewing.com/

Canon and Draw Brewing Company 1527 West Main Street 23220
(804) 353-0536 https://www.canonanddraw.beer/

Ardent Craft Ales 3200 West Leigh Street 23230 (804) 359-1605
https://ardentcraftales.com/

Tabol Brewing 704 Dawn Street 23222 (804) 303-5528
http://tabolbrewing.com/

Legend Brewing Company 321 W 7th Street 23224 (804) 232-3446
https://www.legendbrewing.com/index.asp

Isley Brewing Company 1715 Summit Avenue 23230 (804) 499-0721
https://www.isleybrewingcompany.com/

One of the top three breweries in Richmond and one of the top 50 in the US, thanks to the Choosy Mother, voted best IPA.

Roanoke

Big Lick Brewing Company 409 Salem Avenue SW 24016 (540) 562-8383 https://biglickbrewingco.com/

Salem

Parkway Brewing Company 739 Kessler Mill Road 24153 (540) 314-8234 https://parkwaybrewing.com/

Olde Salem Brewing Company 21 E Main Street 24153 (540) 404-4399 https://www.oldesalembrewing.com/

Staunton

Skipping Rock Beer Company 414 Parkersburg Turnpike 24401 (540) 446-5692 https://skippingrockbeer.com/

Queen City Brewing Limited 834 Springhill Road 24401 (540) 213-8014 http://www.qcbrewing.com/

Redbeard Brewing Company 120 S Lewis Street 24401 (540) 430-3532 https://www.redbeardbrews.com/

Virginia Beach

Commonwealth Brewing Company 2444 Pleasure House Road 23455 (757) 305-9652 https://www.commonwealthbrewingcompany.com/

Wasserhund Brewing Company 1805 Laskin Road 23454 (757) 351-1326 https://wasserhundbrewing.com/

Reaver Beach Brewing Company 1505 Taylor Farm Road 23453 (757) 563-2337 https://www.reaverbeach.com/

Back Bay Brewing Company 614 Norfolk Avenue 23451 (757) 531-7750 http://www.backbaybrewingco.com/

Home Republic 328 Laskin Road 23451 (757) 226-9593
http://www.homerepublicvabeach.com/

Pleasure House Brewing 3025 Shore Drive 23451 (757) 647-8597
http://www.pleasurehousebrewing.com/

There is always something for everyone on tap here. Try their award-winning beers: Glo Belgian Blond, Rudee Inlet DIPA, and OB's Wattleseed Stout.

Waynesboro

Seven Arrows Brewing Company 2508 Jefferson Highway Suite 1 22980 (540) 221-6968 https://www.sevenarrowsbrewing.com/

Basic City Beer Company 1010 E Main Street 22980 (540) 943-1010
https://www.basiccitybeer.com/

Stable Craft Brewing 375 Madrid Road 22980 (540) 490-2609
https://www.stablecraftbrewing.com/

Williamsburg

Alewerks Brewing Company 189-B Ewell Road 23188 (757) 220-3670
https://www.alewerks.com/

The Virginia Beer Company 401 Second Street 23185 (757) 378-2903
https://www.virginiabeerco.com/

Brass Cannon Brewing 5476 Mooretown Road 23188 (757) 566-0001
https://brasscannonbrewing.com/

Billsburg Brewery 2054 Jamestown Road 23185 (757) 926-0981
https://billsburg.com/

Try one of their limited beers or enjoy a flight of their regular options: Fly Away IPA, Betty the Hefe, Planet 4 Red Ale, Tourist Trap IPA, Ghost Wind Stout, and James City Export Lager.

Winchester

Escutcheon Brewing 142 Commercial Street 22601 (540) 773-3042
https://www.escutcheonbrewing.com/

Winchester Brew Works 320 N Cameron Street 22601 (540) 692-9242
https://www.winchesterbrewworks.com/

Alesatian Brewing Company 23 North Loudoun 22601 (540) 667-2743
https://alesatianbrewing.com/

St. Paul

Sugar Hill Brewing Company 16622 Broad Street 24283 (276) 738-1088
https://www.sugarhillbrewing.com/

Axton

Mountain Valley Brewing 4220 Mountain Valley Road 24054 (276) 833-2171 https://www.mountainvalleybrewing.com/

Clarksville

Buggs Island Brewing Company 110 College Street 23927 (434) 470-4070 https://buggsislandbrewing.com/

Arlington

New District Brewing Company 2709 South Oakland Street 22206 (703) 994-3586 http://www.newdistrictbrewing.com/

Washington

The Islands

Go island hopping in Washington harbor. There are several great breweries that you can visit within a day with some planning. Start your trip in Langley at:

Double Bluff Brewing Company 112 Anthes Avenue 98260 (360) 333-9113 https://www.dblfbrewing.com/

Just seven minutes south is Clinton:

Ogres Brewing 7693 Cultus Bay Road 98236 (425) 418-9005 https://ogresbrewing.com/

Oak Harbor is about fifty minutes north:

Flyers Restaurant and Brewery 32295 Route 20 98277 (360) 675-5858 https://www.eatatflyers.com/

Another hour and a half northwest is Lopez Island:

Lopez Island Brewing Company 4817 Center Road 98261 (360) 468-2646 http://www.lopezislandbrewingco.rocks/

Friday Harbor is about fifty minutes west with a must-visit brewery:

San Juan Island Brewing Company 410 A Street 98250 (360) 378-2017 https://www.sanjuanbrew.com/

Award-winning beer made entirely on the island. Try all three of their award-winning simple beers: Quarry No. 9 Pale Ale, Bull Kelp ESB, and Black Boar Porter.

End your trip an hour north in Eastsound at:

Island Hoppin' Brewery 33 Hope Lane 98245 (360) 376-6079 http://www.islandhoppinbrewery.com/

Peninsulas and Coast

Start out with a drive up the coast and then cross over to the peninsula. You'll have excellent views while enjoying some great brews. You'll need at least two days to visit them all, but you'll want to take longer to enjoy the views. Start out in Seaview at:

North Jetty Brewing 4202 Pacific Way 98644 (360) 642-4234
https://northjettybrew.com/

Head north about an hour and a half to Westport:

Blackbeard's Brewing Company 700 W Ocean Avenue 98595 (360)
268-7662 https://blackbeardsbrewing.com/

Head about a half-hour east to Aberdeen with two breweries:

Mount Olympus Brewing 105 W Heron Street 98520 (360) 637-9972
http://mountolympusbrewing.com/

Steam Donkey Brewery 101 E Wishkah Street 98520 (360) 637-9431
https://www.steamdonkeybrewing.com/

Just eight minutes away is another brewery at Hoquiam:

Hoquiam Brewing Company 526 8th Street 98550 (360) 637-8252
https://www.hoquiambrews.com/

Cross over to the peninsula with about a two-hour drive to Port Orchard at:

Slaughter County Brewing 1307 Bay Street 98366 (360) 329-2340
https://www.slaughtercountybrewing.com/

Just fifteen minutes north is Bremerton:

Silver City Brewery and Taproom 206 Katy Penman Avenue 98312
(360) 813-1487 https://www.silvercitybrewery.com/

Poulsbo is about twenty-minutes north with several options:

Slippery Pig Brewing 18801 Front Street NE 98370 (360) 394-1686
https://slipperypigbrewing.com/

Rainy Daze Brewing 650 NW Bovela Lane Suite 3 98370 (360) 692-1858
http://rainydazebrewing.com/

Western Red Brewing 19168 Jenson Way NE 98370 (360) 626-1280 https://westernredbrewing.com/

Valholl Brewing Company 18970 3rd Avenue NE 98370 (360) 930-0172 https://valhollbrewing.com/

Another eighteen minutes is Kingston with two breweries:

Downpour Brewing 10991 NE State Highway 104 98346 (360) 881-0452 https://www.downpourbrewing.com/

Hood Canal Brewing 26449 Bond Road NE 98370 (360) 297-8316 https://www.hoodcanalbrewery.com/

About a half-hour west is Quilcene:

101 Brewery at Twana Roadhouse 294793 US 101 98376 (360) 765-6485 https://101brewery.com/

Port Townsend is about a half-hour north with two breweries including a must-visit:

Propolis Brewing 2457 Jefferson Street 98368 (360) 531-2493 https://propolisbrewing.com/

Port Townsend Brewing Company 330 10th Street 98368 (360) 385-9967 http://www.porttownsendbrewing.com/

There are over ten ales to choose from, but you'll want to try the two beers that started it all: Port Townsend Pale Ale and The Port Townsend Brown Porter. End your trip about an hour further west in Port Angeles at a must-visit brewery:

Barhop Brewing and Taproom 2358 Highway 101 West 98363 (360) 460-5155 http://www.barhopbrewing.com/

Enjoy craft beer and artisan pizzas. Try rotating seasonal beers and one-offs or enjoy a flight of their most popular beers - Citrasonic IPA, Judge Porter, and Redneck Lager.

North Cascades

With some planning, you can accomplish this trip in a day. However, once you relax to take in the beautiful scenery, you'll probably want to take a few extra days. Start your trip in Anacortes at:

Anacortes Brewery and Rockfish Grill 320 Commercial Avenue 98221 (360) 588-1720 http://www.anacortesrockfish.com/index.cfm

Head east twenty-minutes to the next brewery at La Conner:

La Conner Brewing Company 117 South 1st Street 98257 (360) 466-1415 https://www.laconnerbrewery.com/

Continue east thirteen minutes to Mount Vernon with three breweries:

Farmstrong Brewing Company 110 Steward Road 98273 (425) 301-8833 https://www.farmstrongbrewing.com/

North Sound Brewing Company 17406 State Route 536 98273 (360) 982-2057 http://www.northsoundbrewing.com/

Skagit River Brewery 404 South Third Street 98273 (360) 336-2884 https://www.skagitbrew.com/

Seven minutes north is another option in Burlington:

Garden Path Fermentation 11653 Higgins Airport Way 98233 (360) 503-8956 https://gardenpathwa.com/

Head north about forty minutes to Deming:

North Fork Brewing 6186 Mt Baker Highway 98244 (360) 599-2337 https://northforkbrewery.com/

Head west about twenty-minutes to Bellingham with several options:

Gruff Brewing 104 E Maple Street 98225 https://www.gruff-brewing.com/

Stemma Brewing 2039 Moore Street 98229 (360) 746-8385
https://www.stemmabrewing.com/

Structures Brewing 1420 N State Street 98225 (360) 582-7475
https://www.structuresbrewing.com/

Wander Brewing 1807 Dean Avenue 98225 (360) 647-6152
https://wanderbrewing.com/

Kulshan Brewing Company 2238 James Street 98225 (360) 389-5348
https://kulshanbrewing.com/

Stones Throw Brewing Company 1009 Larrabee Avenue 98225 (360) 362-5058 https://www.stonesthrowbrewco.com/

Aslan Brewing Company 1330 N Forest Street 98225 (360) 902-1805
https://aslanbrewing.com/

Boundary Bay Brewery and Bistro 1107 Railroad Avenue 98227 (360) 647-5593 https://www.bbaybrewery.com/

Chuckanut Brewery and Kitchen 601 W Holly Street 98225 (360) 752-3377 http://chuckanutbreweryandkitchen.com/

End your trip fourteen minutes northwest in Ferndale at:

FrinGe Brewing 5640 3rd Avenue 98248 (360) 398-6071
https://fringebrewing.com/

Seattle-Everett Area

There are a lot of breweries and towns to visit in such a small area. So if you plan to visit them all, you'll want to give yourself up to a week of time. Otherwise, research the breweries first and choose how many you can fit into your trip. Start your trip in Darrington at:

River Time Brewing 25909 Clear Creek Road 98241 (267) 483-7411
https://rivertimebrewing.com/

Head west about a half-hour to Arlington:

Skookum Brewery 17925A 59th Avenue NE 98223 (360) 652-4917
https://skookumbrewery.com/

Sixteen minutes south is Marysville and a must-visit brewery:

Whitewall Brewing Company 14524 Smokey Point Blvd Suite 1 98271
(425) 308-7992 https://www.whitewallbrewing.com/

There are plenty of beers to choose from here, but if you want to try the top two flagship beers, then be sure to consider - Oxymoron Black IPA and Dirt Track Brown Ale.

Another eight minutes is Everett with four options:

Scuttlebutt Brewing Company 1524 W Marine View Drive 98201 (425) 257-9316 https://scuttlebuttbrewing.com/

At Large Brewing Company 2730 W Marine View Drive 98201 (425) 324-0039 https://atlargebrewing.com/

Crucible Brewing 909 SE Everett Mall Way Unit D440 98208 (425) 374-7293 https://www.cruciblebrewing.com/

Lazy Boy Brewing 715 100th Street SE / Ste A-1 98208 (425) 423-7700
http://www.lazyboybrewing.com/

Twelve minutes southwest is another brewery at Mukilteo:

Diamond Knot Brewery 621 Front Street 98275 (425) 355-4488
https://diamondknot.com/

Another eleven minutes brings you to Lynnwood:

Ellersick Brewing Company 5030 208th Street SW Ste A 98036 (425) 672-7051 https://www.bigeales.com/

Edmonds is ten minutes west with a couple options:

Salish Sea Brewing Company 518 Dayton Street Suite 104 98020 (425) 582-8474 http://salishbrewing.com/

American Brewing Company 180 West Dayton Street 98020 (425) 774-1717 https://americanbrewing.com/

Southeast sixteen minutes is Kenmore with two more options:

Cairn Brewing 7204 NE 175 Street 98028 (425) 949-5295 https://www.cairnbrewing.com/

192 Brewing Company and Lake Trail Taproom 7324 NE 175 Street 98028 (425) 424-2337 http://192brewing.com/

Five minutes away is Bothell with three breweries including a must-visit:

Beardslee Public House 19116 Beardslee Blvd 98011 (425) 286-1001 https://beardsleeph.com/

Decibel Brewing Company 18204 Bothell-Everett Highway 98012 (425) 408-1946 http://www.decibelbrewing.com/

Foggy Noggin Brewing 22329 53rd Avenue SE 98021 (206) 553-9223 http://www.foggynogginbrewing.com/

There are over ten different beers to choose from here. But if you want to go back to where it all started, then try their two flagship beers: Bit O' Beaver, an English Bitter, and Christmas Duck, a robust Porter. Several more options are in Woodinville just four minutes away:

Sumerian Brewing Company 15510 Woodinville-Redmond Road NE #E110 98072 (425) 486-5330 https://sumerianbrewingco.com/

Metier Brewing Company 14125 NE 189th Street 98072 (425) 415-8466 https://metierbrewing.com/

Triplehorn Brewing Company 19510 144th Avenue NE #E6 98072 (425) 242-7979 https://triplehornbrewing.com/

Vessel Ales 19405 144th Avenue NE Bldg D 98072 (206) 629-5024
https://vesselwines.com/vessel-ales/

20 Corners Brewing 14148 NE 190th Street 98072 (425) 375-5223
https://www.20cornersbrewing.com/

Locust Cider and Brewing 19151 144th Avenue NE Unit B/C 98072
(206) 494-5968 https://www.locustcider.com/

Snohomish is seventeen minutes north with several options including a
must-visit:

Three Bull Brewing 809 19th Street 98290 (206) 550-5244
https://threebullbrewing.com/

Sound to Summit Brewing 1830 Bickford Avenue Suite 111 98290 (360)
294-8127 http://www.soundtosummitbrewing.com/

Spada Farmhouse Brewery 106 Union Avenue 98290 (425) 330-6938
http://www.spadafarmhousebrewery.com/

Scrappy Punk Brewing 9029A 112th Drive SE 98290 (503) 810-1655
http://scrappypunk.com/

Try their two unique beers that are on tap at all time, with other options
rotating based on when you stop by; there is the Mango Champagne IPA
and Coconut Blonde Ale. Twelve minutes southeast is two breweries in
Monroe:

Dreadnought Brewing 16726 146th Street SE Suite 153 98272 (360)
453-7267 https://www.dreadnoughtbrewing.com/

Circle 7 Brew Works 20290 Corbridge Road SE 98272 (206) 747-0269
http://circle7brewing.com/

Duvall is another thirteen minutes south:

Valley House Brewing 16111 Main Street NE 98019 (425) 318-6363
https://valleyhousebrewing.com/

About a half-hour southeast is Snoqualmie with three breweries:

Snoqualmie Falls Brewing Company and Taproom 8032 Falls Avenue SE 98065 (425) 831-BEER https://www.fallsbrew.com/

No Boat Brewing Company 35214 SE Center Street #2 98065 (425) 292-0702 http://noboatbrewing.com/

Dru Bru 10 Pass Life Way #3 98068 (425) 434-0700 https://www.drubru.com/

About a half-hour northwest is a must-visit brewery at Sammamish:

Big Block Brewing 3310 E Lake Sammamish Parkway SE 98074 (425) 457-0515 http://big-block.squarespace.com/

With 20 taps available, you'll be able to sample all of their award-winning beers: "The Boss" Honey Pale, Raspberry Blonde, "Berry Cuda" Blackberry Wheat, Cherry Sour, Brown Ale, and Flathead Irish Red. Continue twelve minutes to Redmond with two breweries:

Mac and Jack's Brewery 17825 NE 65th Street 98052 (425) 558-9697 https://www.macandjacks.com/

Postdoc Brewing 17625 NE 65th Street 98052 (425) 658-4963 http://postdocbrewing.com/

Seven minutes west is Kirkland with two breweries:

Flycaster Brewing Company 12815 NE 124th Suite I 98034 (206) 963-6626 https://flycasterbrewing.com/

Chainline Brewing Company 503 6th Street S 98033 (425) 242-0923 http://www.chainlinebrewing.com/Chainline_Brewing/Home.html

Seven minutes south is two more breweries at Bellevue:

Bellevue Brewing Company 1820 130th Avenue NE Suite 2 98005 (425) 497-8686 http://www.bellevuebrewing.com/

Resonate Brewery + Pizzeria 5606 119th Avenue SE 98006 (425) 644-3164 http://resonatebrewery.com/

Twelve minutes west is the main city of Seattle with many options:

West Seattle Brewing Company 4415 Fauntleroy Way SW 98126 (206) 405-0972 https://westseattlebrewing.com//

Georgetown Brewing Company 5840 Airport Way S Unit #201 98108 (206) 766-8055 https://www.georgetownbeer.com/

Elysian Brewing 1221 E Pike Street 98122 (206) 860-1920 https://www.elysianbrewing.com/age-gate

Urban Family Brewing Company 1103 NW 52nd Street 98107 (206) 861-6769 https://www.urbanfamilybrewing.com/

Seapine Brewing Company 2959 Utah Avenue South 98134 (206) 682-7985 http://www.seapinebrewing.com/

Elliott Bay Brewing Company 4720 California Avenue SW 98116 (206) 932-8695 https://www.elliottbaybrewing.com/

Lucky Envelope Brewing 907 NW 50th Street 98107 (206) 659-4075 https://www.luckyenvelopebrewing.com/

Lantern Brewing 938 N 95th Street 98103 (206) 729-5350 https://www.lanternbrewing.com/

Pint Size Brewing 7410B Greenwood Avenue N 98103 https://www.pintsizebrewing.com/

Lowercase Brewing 8103 8th Avenue South 98108 (206) 258-4987 http://www.lowercasebrewing.com/

Peddler Brewing Company 1514 NW Leary Way 98107 (360) 362-0002 https://www.peddlerbrewing.com/

Populuxe Brewing 826 NW 49th Street Suite B 98107 (206) 706-3400 https://www.populuxebrewing.com/

Machine House Brewery 5840 Airport Way S 98108 (206) 402-6025
https://www.machinehousebrewery.com/

Floating Bridge Brewing 722 NE 45th Street 98105 (206) 466-4784
http://www.floatingbridgebrewing.com/

Flying Lion Brewing 5041 Rainier Avenue S #106 98118 (206) 659-9912
https://flyinglionbrewing.com/

Holy Mountain Brewing Company 1421 Elliott Avenue W 98119
https://holymountainbrewing.com/

Figurehead Brewing Company 4001 21st Avenue W Unit B 98199 (206)
492-7981 https://www.figureheadbrewingcompany.com/

Hellbent Brewing Company 13035 Lake City Way NE 98125 (206) 361-
3707 http://www.hellbentbrewingcompany.com/

Jellyfish Brewing 917 South Nebraska Street 98108 (206) 397-4999
http://jellyfishbrewing.com/

Outlander Brewery and Pub 225 N 36th Street 98103 (206) 486-4088
https://outlanderbrewing.com/

Rooftop Brewing Company 1220 W Nickerson Street 98119 (206) 276-
4091 https://rooftopbrewco.com/

Best of Hands Barrelhouse 7500 35th Avenue SW 98126 (206) 708-
1166 https://www.bestofhandsbarrelhouse.com/

Maritime Pacific Brewing Company 1111 NW Ballard Way 98107 (206)
782-6181 https://www.maritimebrewery.com/

Pike Brewing Company 1415 1st Avenue 98101 (206) 622-6044
https://www.pikebrewing.com/

Two Beers Brewing Company 4700 Ohio Avenue S Unit A 98134 (206)
274-9353 https://www.twobeersbrewery.com/landing/

Obec Brewing 1144 NW 52nd Street 98107 (206) 659-0082
https://www.obecbrewing.com/

Optimism Brewing Company 1158 Broadway 98122 (206) 651-5429
https://optimismbrewing.com/

Cloudburst Brewing 2116 Western Avenue 98121 (206) 602-6061
https://cloudburstbrew.com/

Flying Bike Cooperative Brewery 8570 Greenwood Avenue N 98103
(206) 428-7709 https://flyingbike.coop/

NW Peaks Brewery 5718 Rainier Avenue S 98118 (206) 981-0887
https://nwpeaksbrewery.com/

Ravenna Brewing Company 5408 26th Avenue NE 98105 (206) 251-1332 http://www.ravennabrewing.com/

Ghostfish Brewing Company 2942 1st Avenue S 98134 (206) 397-3898
https://ghostfishbrewing.com/

Hale's Ale Brewery and Pub 4301 Leary Way NW 98107 (206) 782-0737
https://halesbrewery.com/

Fair Isle Brewing 936 NW 49th Street 98107
https://www.fairislebrewing.com/

Snapshot Brewing 8005 Greenwood Avenue N 98103 (206) 607-9277
https://www.snapshotbrewing.com/

Perihelion Brewery 2800 16th Avenue S 98144 (206) 200-3935
http://www.perihelion.beer/

Outer Planet Craft Brewing 1812 12th Avenue Suite 100 98122 (206)
763-7000 https://www.outerplanetbrewing.com/

Fremont Brewing Company 3409 Woodland Park Avenue N 98103
(206) 420-2407 https://www.fremontbrewing.com/

Counterbalance Brewing Company 503B S Michigan Street 98108 (206) 453-3615 http://counterbalancebeer.com/

Burke-Gilman Brewing Company 3626 NE 45th Street 98105 (206) 612-1439 http://www.burkegilmanbrewing.com/

Olympic Range Brewing Company 2506 Lorentz Place N 98109 http://www.olympicrangebrew.com/

Future Primitive Brewing Company 9832 14th Avenue SW 98106 https://www.futureprimitivebeer.com/

Stoup Brewing 1108 NW 52nd Street 98107 (206) 457-5524 https://www.stoupbrewing.com/

Reuben's Brews 5010 14th Avenue NW 98107 (206) 784-2859 https://reubensbrews.com/

Big Time Brewery and Alehouse 4133 University Way NE 98105 (206) 545-4509 http://bigtimebrewery.com/index.html

Offering twelve beers on tap and a cask-conditioned ale. Try a flight of their flagships: Scarlet Fire IPA, Atlas Amber Ale, and Coal Creek Porter.

Tin Dog Brewing 309 S Cloverdale Street Unit A2 98108 (206) 438-4257 https://tindogbrewing.com/

The focus is on blended sours. Try their award-winning sour beers including: Errant Whispers, CatWalk, Melange Deux, and Mandala. Southwest about fifty minutes is Vashon:

Camp Colvos Brewing 17636 Vashon Highway SW 98070 (206) 369-5952 https://campcolvos.com/

About forty minutes back east is Tukwila:

Odin Brewing Company 402 Baker Blvd 98188 (206) 241-1013 https://odinbrewing.com/

Just six minutes away is Renton with another brewery:

Four Generals Brewing 229 Wells Avenue S 98057 (425) 282-4360
http://www.fourgenerals.com/

Ten minutes south is Kent with two breweries:

Airways Brewing Company 6644 S 196th Street #T-100 98032 (253) 200-1707 http://airwaysbrewing.com/

Four Horsemen Brewery 30221 148th Avenue SE 98042 (253) 981-4258 https://fourhorsemen.beer/

Another ten minutes is Auburn:

Geaux Brewing 425 E Main Street 98002 (253) 397-3939 https://www.geauxbrewing.com/

Rail Hop'n Brewing Company 122 W Main Street #101B 98001 (253) 217-6800 https://railhopn.com/

Thirteen minutes northeast is Maple Valley:

Lumber House Brewing 21830 284th Avenue SE 98038 (425) 432-0121 https://lumberhousebrew.com/

End your trip twenty-minutes south in Enumclaw at:

Cole Street Brewery 2551 Cole Street Suite R 98022 (425) 275-7396 http://www.colestreetbrew.com/

Tacoma-Olympia Area

Take a day or two to travel to the towns and breweries in this area. Start your trip in Gig Harbor with three breweries:

Wet Coast Brewing Company 6820 Kimball Drive Suite C 98335 (253) 948-7772 http://www.wetcoastbrewing.com/

7 Seas Brewery and Taproom 3207 57th Street CT NW 98335 (253) 686-3703 https://www.7seasbrewing.com/

Fox Island Brewing 2416 14th Avenue NW 98335 (253) 882-7752
http://foxislandbrewing.com/

Head southeast seventeen minutes to the main city of Tacoma with several options:

Black Fleet Brewing 2302 Fawcett Avenue 98402 (253) 327-1641
https://www.blackfleetbrewing.com/

E9 Brewing Company 2506 Fawcett Avenue 98402 (253) 383-7707
https://e9brewingco.com/

Narrows Brewing Company 9007 S 19th Street Suite 200 98466 (253) 327-1400 https://narrowsbrewing.com/

Pacific Brewing and Malting Company 610 Pacific Avenue 98402 (253) 272-2739 https://pacificbrewingandmalting.com/

Odd Otter Brewing Company 716 Pacific Avenue 98402 (360) 430-4312
https://www.oddotterbrewing.com/

Dystopian State Brewing Company 611 South Baker Street 98402 (253) 302-3466 https://www.dystopianstate.com/

Dunagan Brewing Company 1126 Commerce S 98402 (253) 226-9829
https://www.dunaganbrewing.com/

Gig Harbor Brewing Company 3120 S Tacoma Way Ste A 98409 (253) 474-0672 http://www.gigharborbrewing.com/

North 47 Brewing Company 1000 Town Center NE Ste 160 98422 (253) 517-9865 https://www.north47brewery.com/

Sluggo Brewing 409 E 26th Street 98421 (253) 327-1894
https://www.sluggobrewingtapandkitchen.com/

Wingman Brewers 509 ½ Puyallup Avenue 98421 (253) 256-5240
https://wingmanbrewers.com/

Continue east another eighteen minutes to Sumner:

Half Lion Brewing Company 1723 W Valley Highway E 98390 (253) 750-4479 https://www.halflion.com/

DuPont is about a half-hour southwest:

Forward Operating Base Brewing Company 2750 Williamson Place Suite 100 98327 (254) 507-4667 https://www.fobbrewingcompany.com/

Continue to Lacey thirteen minutes away:

Top Rung Brewing Company 8343 Hogum Bay Lane NE Suite E 98516 (360) 915-8766 https://www.toprungbrewing.com/

Just six minutes away is Olympia with two breweries:

Three Magnets Brewing 600 Franklin Street SE Suite 102 98501 (360) 972-2481 http://www.threemagnetsbrewing.com/

Fish Brewing Company 515 Jefferson Street SE 98501 (360) 943-6480 https://www.fishbrewing.com/

End your trip seven minutes south at Tumwater with two breweries:

Hoh River Brewing Company 2442 Mottman Road 98512 (360) 705-4000 http://www.hohriverbrewery.com/

Matchless Brewing 8108 River Drive SE Suite #207 98501 (503) 317-3284 http://www.matchlessbrewing.com/

The Gorge

Follow the southern border of Washington and enjoy some brews in this rugged wilderness. You'll only need a day or two. Start your trip in Battle Ground at:

Northwood Public House/Little Dipper Brewing 1401 Rasmussen Blvd 98604 (360) 723-0937 http://northwoodpublichouse.com/

About twenty-minutes south is the main city of Vancouver with several options including a must-visit brewery:

Fortside Brewing 2200 NE Andresen Road #B 98661 (360) 524-4692
http://www.fortsidebrewing.com/

Loowit Brewing Company 507 Columbia Street 98660 (360) 566-2323
https://loowitbrewing.com/

Ghost Runners Brewery 4216 NE Minnehaha Street #108 98661 (360) 989-3912 http://www.ghostrunnersbrewery.com/

The Heavy Metal Pizza and Brewing Company 809 MacArthur Blvd 98661 (360) 258-1691 http://www.theheavymetalbrewingco.com/

Trusty Brewing Company 114 E Evergreen Blvd 98660 (360) 258-0413
https://www.trustybrewing.com/

Mt Tabor Brewing 113 West 9th Street 98660 (502) 312-8964
http://mttaborbrewing.com/

Brother Ass Brewing 11700 NE 54th Court 98686 (360) 607-3275
https://brotherassbrewing.com/

Heathen Brewing 5612 NE 119th Street 98686 (360) 601-7454
https://heathenbrewing.com/

Brothers Cascadia Brewing 9811 NE 15th Avenue 98665 (360) 718-8927 https://www.brotherscascadiabrewing.com/

Victor 23 Craft Brewing 2905 St Johns Blvd 98661 (503) 310-9250
https://victor23.com/

A brewery focused on the DB Cooper case. Reflect on the case while sampling beers like Skyjacker IPA, Flight 305 Amber, Jet Fuel Imperial IPA and Schaffner Pilsner. Seventeen minutes east is Camas:

Grains of Wrath 230 NE 5th Avenue 98607 (360) 210-5717
https://gowbeer.com/

Washougal is just five minutes away:

Doomsday Brewing Company 421 C Street Unit 1B 98671 (360) 335-9909 https://www.doomsdaybrewing.com/

A half-hour further east is Stevenson:

Walking Man Brewing Company 240 1st Street 98648 (509) 427-5520 https://www.walkingmanbeer.com/

Just six minutes away is another brewery in Carson:

Backwoods Brewing Company 1162 B Wind River Road 98610 (509) 427-3412 https://www.backwoodsbrewingcompany.com/

Next is White Salmon about twenty-minutes east:

Everybody's Brewing 151 East Jewett Blvd 98672 (509) 637-2774 https://everybodysbrewing.com/

End your trip with about an hour drive east to Goldendale at:

Dwinell Country Ales 206 W Broadway Street 98620 (509) 773-3138 https://www.countryales.com/

Yakima Valley

The Yakima region of Washington is well known as one of the top winery regions in the world. It is also home to several excellent breweries. Be sure to take at least a day to enjoy what this area has to offer. Start your trip in Cowiche at:

Cowiche Creek Brewing Company 514 Thompson Road Building #2 98923 (509) 678-0324 http://www.cowichecreekbrewing.com/

Just eight minutes north is another brewery in Naches:

Bron Yr Aur Brewing Company 12160 US Highway 12 98937 (503) 653-1109 https://www.bronyraurbrewing.com/

Yakima is sixteen minutes southeast with four options:

Wandering Hop 508 N 20th Avenue 98902 (509) 426-2739
https://wanderinghop.com/

Hop Nation Brewing Company 31 North First Avenue 98902 (509) 367-6552 https://hopnationbrew.com/

Single Hill Brewing 102 N Naches Avenue 98901 (509) 367-6756
https://singlehillbrewing.com/

Bale Breaker Brewing Company 1801 Birchfield Road 98901 (509) 424-4000 https://www.balebreaker.com/

About a half-hour brings you to Sunnyside:

Snipes Mountain Microbrewery and Restaurant 905 Yakima Valley Highway 98944 (509) 837-BREW http://snipesmountain.com/

About forty minutes east is Richland with three breweries:

Atomic Ale Brewpub and Eatery 1015 Lee Blvd 99352 (509) 946-5465
http://www.atomicalebrewpub.com/

Bombing Range Brewing 2000 Logston Blvd Ste 126 99354 (509) 572-9140 https://bombingrangebrewing.com/

White Bluffs Brewing Company 2034 Logston Blvd 99354 (509) 521-1589 https://whitebluffsbrewing.com/

Another fourteen minutes away is Kennewick:

Ice Harbor Brewing Company 206 N Benton Street 99336 (509) 582-5340 http://iceharbor.com/

End your trip with about an hour drive east to Walla Walla with two breweries:

Burwood Brewing Company 1120 E Street 99362 (509) 876-6220
http://www.burwoodbrewing.com/

Quirk Brewing 425 B Street 99362 (509) 301-6325
http://www.quirkbrewing.com/

Southeast Washington

This is a great little short day trip if you want to get away from the city and sample a few great beers while taking in the scenery for a day. Start your trip in Clarkston at:

Riverport Brewing Company 150 9th Street Suite B 99403 (509) 758-8889 http://www.riverportbrewing.com/content.php?page_id=1

Head north about forty minutes to a must-visit brewery in Pullman:

Paradise Creek Brewery 245 SE Paradise 99163 (509) 338-9463
https://paradisecreekbrewery.com/

The variety of beers here will ensure everyone finds something they like, whether it is the Pokerface Blonde, Over the Hop IPA, or the MooJoe Coffee Milk Stout. End your trip with an hour and a half drive southwest to Dayton at:

Chief Spring's Fire and Irons Brew Pub 148 E Main Street 99328 (509) 382-4677 https://www.fireandironsbrewpub.com/

Northeast Washington

This circular route will take a bit of driving between breweries so you'll need maybe two days to leisurely visit them all. Start your trip in Mead at:

Bodacious Berries, Fruits and Brews/Big Barn Brewery 16004 N Applewood Lane 99021 (509) 238-2489 http://www.bigbarnbrewing.com/

Head northwest about two hours to Republic:

Republic Brewing Company 26 North Clarke Avenue 99166 (509) 775-2700 https://www.republicbrew.com/

Odessa is about two and a half-hours south:

Rocky Coulee Brewing Company 205 N 1st Street 99159 (509) 279-9870 http://www.rockycouleebrewingco.com/

Head east about an hour to the main city of Spokane with multiple options including a must-visit:

Little Spokane Brewing Company 154 S Madison Street Suite 101 99201 http://www.littlespokanebrewingco.com/

Perry Street Brewing Company 1025 S Perry Street #2 99202 (509) 279-2820 https://www.perrystreetbrewing.com/

Iron Goat Brewing Company 1302 W 2nd Avenue 99201 (509) 701-8245 https://www.irongoatbrewing.com/

No-Li Brewhouse 1003 East Trent Avenue 99202 (509) 242-2739 https://www.nolibrewhouse.com/

Mountain Lakes Brewing Company 201 W Riverside Avenue 99201 (509) 596-0943 https://mountainlakesbrewco.com/

Square Wheel Brewing Company 4705 N Fruit Hill Road 99217 (509) 994-2600 http://www.squarewheelbrewing.com/

Black Label Brewing Company W 19 Main 99201 (509) 822-7436 https://www.blacklabelbrewing.com/

Whistle Punk Brewing Company 112 S Monroe 99201 (509) 315-4465 https://www.whistlepunkbrewing.com/

Bellwether Brewing Company 2019 N Monroe 99205 (509) 280-8345 http://www.bellwetherbrewing.net/

Young Buck Brewing Company 154 S Madison Street 99201 (509) 270-3306 https://www.youngbuckbrewing.com/

Creating crazy and experimental brews. The Gose, Sour German Wheat Beer is always on tap and the rest are rotating seasonal beers. End your trip twelve minutes east in Spokane Valley at:

Bardic Brewing 14719 E 15th Avenue 99037 (509) 723-6105
https://bardicbrewing.wordpress.com/

North Central Washington

This nearly circular route takes you through the rugged central mountain area of Washington. Take at least a couple days to drive to all the breweries on this list. Start your trip in Oroville at:

Alpine Brewing Company 821 Fourteenth Street 98844 (509) 476-9662
http://www.alpine-brewing.com/

Head south almost three hours to Moses Lake:

Ten Pin Brewing Company 1165 N Stratford Road 98837 (509) 765-1248 https://tenpinbrewing.com/

Ellensburg is about an hour west and has two options:

Iron Horse Brewery 1000 Prospect Avenue #4 98926 (509) 933-3134
https://www.ironhorsebrewery.com/

Whipsaw Brewing 704 N Wenas Street 98926 (360) 463-0436
https://www.whipsawbrewing.com/

A half-hour northwest is Roslyn:

Roslyn Brewing 208 Pennsylvania Avenue 98941 (509) 649-2232
http://roslynbrewery.com/

Just eight minutes away is Cle Elum and another brewery:

Mule and Elk Brewing Company 811 Highway 970 Suite 7 98922 (206) 321-1911 http://www.muleandelk.com/

Head northeast about an hour to Leavenworth and three breweries:

Blewett Brewing Company 911 Commercial Street 98826 (509) 888-8809 https://www.blewettbrew.com/

Icicle Brewing Company 935 Front Street 98826 (509) 548-2739
https://iciclebrewing.com/

Doghaus Brewery 321 9th Street 98826 (509) 548-5250
https://www.doghausbrewery.com/

Wenatchee is about a half-hour south:

Wenatchee Valley Brewing 7 Worthen Street 98801 (509) 888-8088
https://www.wenatcheevalleybrewing.com/

About an hour away is Chelan:

Stormy Mountain Brewing 133 E Woodin Avenue 98816 (509) 888-5665
http://stormymountainbrewing.com/

End your trip about an hour further north at Winthrop at:

Old Schoolhouse Brewery 155 Riverside Avenue 98862 (509) 996-3183
https://oldschoolhousebrewery.com/

Centralia

Dick's Brewing Company 3516 Galvin Road 98531 (360) 736-1603
http://dicksbeer.com/

West Virginia

West Virginia has several excellent breweries and you can visit them all by taking a winding four to five day trip through the state while stopping at these great tasting rooms. Start your trip in Maxwelton at:

Greenbrier Valley Brewing Company 862 Industrial Park Road Suite A 24957 (304) 520-4669 https://www.gvbc.beer/

Head west about an hour to Beckley:

Dobra Zupas 600 S Oakwood Avenue 25801 (304) 253-9872
https://dobrazupas.com/

About twenty-minutes north is Fayetteville and two breweries:

Bridge Brew Works 335 Nick Rahall Greenway 25840 (304) 574-1998
https://bridgebrewworks.com/

The Freefolk Brewery 1690 Court Street 25840 (304) 900-5238
https://freefolkbrew.com/

Charleston is about an hour north:

Bad Shepherd Beer Company/Black Sheep Burrito and Brews 702
Quarrier Street 25301 (304) 343-2739 https://blacksheepwv.com/

Continue another hour north to Parkersburg with two options including a
must-visit:

Parkersburg Brewing Company 707 Market Street 26106 (304) 916-
1502 https://parkersburgbrewing.com/

North End Tavern and Brewery 3500 Emerson Avenue 25321 (304)
428-5854 https://www.netbrewery.com/

Stop in for both award-winning food and plenty of beer choices. Try their
award-winning Roedy's Red, amber ale. Next head about two hours east
to Elkins:

Big Timber Brewing 1210 South Davis Avenue 26241 (304) 614-6288
https://www.bigtimberbrewing.com/

Northeast about fifty minutes is Thomas:

Mountain State Brewing Company 1 Nelson Blvd 26292 (304) 463-4500
http://mountainstatebrewing.com/

Just four minutes away is Davis:

Stumptown Ales 390 William Avenue 26260 (304) 259-5570
https://www.stumptownales.com/

Charles Town is about a two hour drive east:

Abolitionist Ale Works 129 W Washington Street 25414 (681) 252-1548
http://abolitionistaleworks.com/

Eighteen minutes north is Shepherdstown:

Bavarian Brothers Brewing 164 Shepherd Grade Road 25443 (304) 876-2551 http://www.bavarianinnwv.com/bavarian-brothers-brewing.php

About fifty minutes northwest is Berkeley Springs:

Berkeley Springs Brewing 91 Sugar Hollow Road 25411 (304) 258-3369
https://www.berkeleyspringsbrewingcompany.com/

About a two hour drive west brings you to Terra Alta:

High Ground Brewing 102 Railroad Avenue 26764 (304) 789-1216
https://www.highgroundbrewing.co/

A half-hour north is Bruceton Mills:

Screech Owl Brewing 2323 Ralph Livengood Road 26525 (304) 379-4777 https://www.screechowlbrewing.com/

Morgantown is about twenty-minutes west with two breweries:

Chestnut Brew Works 444 Broadway Avenue 36501 (304) 212-5079
http://www.chestnutbrewworks.com/

Morgantown Brewing Company 1291 University Avenue 26505 (304) 292-6959 https://www.morgantownbrewing.com/

A half-hour south is Rivesville:

Short Story Brewing 5904 Fairmont Road 26588 (304) 933-2165
https://www.shortstorybrewing.com/

End your trip about an hour and a half north in Wheeling at:

Wheeling Brewing Company 2247 Market Street 26003 (304) 905-8757
http://www.wheelingbrewing.com/

Northern Wisconsin

Travel around and enjoy the northern portion of the state with this two to three day trip. Start your trip in Ashland at a must-visit brewery:

South Shore Brewery 808 Main Street W 54806 (715) 682-9199
https://www.southshorebrewery.com/

Sit back and relax while enjoying a flight of their five flagship beers: Nut Brown Ale, Northern Lights Cream Ale, Rhoades' Scholar Stout, Inland Sea Pilsner, and Wisconsin Pale Ale.

About an hour and a half west is Superior on the border with two breweries:

Earth Rider Brewery 1617 N 3rd Street 54880 (715) 394-7391
https://earthrider.beer/

Thirsty Pagan Brewing 1623 Broadway Street 54880 (715) 394-2500
https://www.thirstypaganbrewing.com/

Circle south about two hours to Grantsburg:

Brickfield Brewing 130 W Olson Drive 54840 (715) 463-1900
https://brickfieldbrewing.com/

A half-hour south is another brewery at Saint Croix Falls:

Trap Rock Brewing Company 520 N Blanding Woods Road 54024 (651) 269-6013 http://traprockbrewing.com/

Spooner is about an hour northeast:

Round Man Brewing Company 234 Walnut Street 54801 (715) 939-1800
https://roundmanbrewing.com/

Another half-hour brings you to a must-visit brewery in Hayward:

Angry Minnow Brewpub 10440 Florida Avenue 54843 (715) 934-3055
https://angryminnow.com/

Brewing flavorful beers in small batches. Some great options to try include River Pig Pale Ale, Honey Wheat, and Oakys Oatmeal Stout. Another must-visit brewery is at Manitowish Waters about two hours east:

Some Nerve Brewing Company 5586 US Highway 51 54545 (608) 576-6040 https://www.somenervebrewing.com/

Offering four flagship beers year-round: a Cream Ale, an Oatmeal Stout, an IPA, and an Irish Red. Southeast about a half-hour brings you to Minocqua and a must-visit brewery:

Minocqua Brewing Company 238 Lake Shore Drive 54548 (715) 356-2600 https://minocquabrewingcompany.com/

Offering unique off-beat recipes that are viewed as some of the best in the industry. Be sure to try their five flagship beers: Largemouth Blonde, Minocqua Pale Ale, Road Kill Red, Bear Naked Brown, and Pudgy Possum Porter. Just five minutes away is Woodruff:

Rocky Reef Brewing Company 1101 1st Avenue 54568
http://www.rockyreefbrewing.com/

A half-hour east is Eagle River:

Tribute Brewing Company 1106 Bluebird Road 54521 (715) 480-2337
https://tributebrewing.com/

Another half-hour south is Rhinelander:

Rhinelander Brewing Company 43 S Brown Street 54501 (715) 550-2337 https://www.rhinelanderbrewery.com/

About fifty minutes further south is the last stop on the trip in Merrill:

Sawmill Brewing Company 1110 E 10th Street 54452 (715) 722-0230
http://www.sawmillbrewing.net/

Northeast Wisconsin

Take this two to three day trip around the Northeastern area of Wisconsin. You'll be able to enjoy a number of great breweries. Start out in Marinette at:

Rail House Restaurant and Brewpub 2029 Old Peshtigo Road 54143 (715) 732-4646 https://www.railhousebrewpub.com/

Head an hour south to Green Bay with several options:

Hinterland Brewery Restaurant 1001 Lombardi Avenue 54304 (920) 438-8050 https://hinterlandbeer.com/

Stillmank Brewing Company 215 N Henry Street 54302 (920) 785-2337 https://stillmankbrewing.com/

Copper State Brewing Company 313 Dousman Street 54303 (920) 489-8575 https://www.copperstate.beer/

Noble Roots Brewing Company 2790 University Avenue 54311 (920) 328-3746 https://www.noblerootsbrewing.com/

Titletown Brewing Company 320 Dousman Street 54303 (920) 437-2337 https://www.titletownbrewing.com/

Head north about fifty minutes to Sturgeon Bay:

Starboard Brewing Company 151 N 3rd Avenue 54235 (920) 818-1062 https://starboardbrewing.com/

Baileys Harbor is another half-hour north and has two breweries:

Hacienda Beer Company 8099 Highway 57 54202 (920) 839-1515 https://www.haciendabeerco.com/

Door County Brewing Company 2434 County Road F 54202 (920) 839-1515 https://www.doorcountybrewingco.com/

Fifteen minutes west is Egg Harbor:

Shipwrecked Brew Pub, Restaurant 7791 Egg Harbor Road 54209 (920) 868-2767 https://www.shipwreckedmicrobrew.com/

About fifty minutes south is Algoma:

Ahnapee Brewery 105 Navarino Street 54201 (920) 785-0822 https://www.ahnapeebrewery.com/

Eighteen minutes southwest is Luxemburg:

Thumb Knuckle Brewing Company E0208 State Highway 54217 https://www.thumbknuckle.beer/

Another fifty minutes south is Manitowoc:

PetSkull Brewing Company 220 North 9th 54220 http://www.petskullbrewing.com/

West about a half-hour is Chilton:

Rowland's Calumet Brewery 25 North Madison 53014 (920) 849-2534 https://www.rowlandsbrewery.com/

Appleton is about a half-hour northwest and has a few options:

McFleshman's Brewing Company 115 S State Street 54911 (920) 903-8002 https://www.mcfleshmans.com/

Appleton Beer Factory 603 W College Avenue 54914 (920) 364-9931 https://www.appletonbeerfactory.com/

Stone Arch Brew House 1004 S Olde Oneida Street 54915 (920) 731-3322 https://stonearchbrewpub.com/

Thirteen minutes south is Neenah with two options:

Barrel 41 Brewing Company 1132 S Commercial Street 54956 (920) 558-4021 https://barrel41.com/

Lion's Tail Brewing Company 116 S Commercial Street 54956 (920) 843-3020 http://lionstailbrewing.com/

Another seventeen minutes south is Oshkosh with two breweries, including a must-visit:

Bare Bones Brewery 4362 County Road S 54904 (920) 744-8045 http://barebonesbrewery.us/

Fox River Brewing Company 1501 Arboretum Drive 54901 (920) 232-2337 https://www.foxriverbrewing.com/

Handcrafted beers with seasonal specials as well as flagship offerings: Blu Bobber, Red Bobber, Reel it in IPA, Marble Eye Scottish Ale, and Two Dams Blonde Ale. About a half-hour southwest is Ripon:

Knuth Brewing Company 221 Watson Street 54971 (920) 748-5188 http://www.knuthbrewingcompany.com/

Coloma is about an hour northwest:

Mecan River Brewing Company 113 E Main Street 54930 (715) 281-3506 https://mecanriverbrewing.com/

An hour and a half northeast brings you to Marion:

Pigeon River Brewing Company 1103 N Main Street 54950 (715) 256-7721 https://www.pigeonriverbrewing.com/

End your trip about forty minutes south in Waupaca at:

H.H. Hinder Brewing 804 Churchill Street 54981 (715) 942-8018 https://hinderbrewingco.com/

South Central

This three-day trip will take you on an almost circular route through the southern central area of Wisconsin. There are plenty of great breweries to visit in this area. Start your trip in Arena at:

Lake Louie Brewing Company 7556 Pine Road 53503 (608) 753-2675 http://www.lakelouie.com/

West about forty minutes is Richland Center:

Mel's Micro 21733 US Highway 14 53581 (608) 647-1116 https://melsmicro.com/

Westport is about a half-hour southwest:

Parched Eagle Brewpub 5440 Willow Road Suite 112 53597 (608) 204-9192 http://parchedeaglebrewpub.com/

Head south about fifty minutes to Potosi:

Potosi Brewing Company 209 South Main Street 53820 (608) 763-4002 https://www.potosibrewery.com/

Now head east about fifty minutes to Darlington:

City Service Brewing 404 Main Street 53530 (608) 482-1930 https://cityservicebrewing.wixsite.com/cityservicebrewing

Gratiot is another seventeen minutes:

Pecatonica Beer Company 5875 Main Street Suite A 53541 (608) 558-5257 http://pecatonicabeer.com/

Continue about a half-hour to Monroe with two breweries:

Cheese City Beer Company N1671 Honey Creek Road 53566 (608) 558-8393 https://cheesecitybeer.com/

Minhas Craft Brewery 1208 14th Avenue 53566 (608) 325-3191 http://minhasbrewery.com/

About forty minutes brings you to the southern border town of Beloit:

G5 Brewing Company 1895 Gateway Blvd 53511 (608) 368-7492 https://www.g5brewing.net/

Head north about an hour to Lake Mills with two breweries:

Tyranena Brewing Company 1025 Owen Street 53551 (920) 648-8699
http://tyranena.com/

Sunshine Brewing Company 121 S Main Street 53551 (920) 320-9735
https://www.sunshinebrewco.com/

Continue north another forty minutes to Beaver Dam:

Ooga Brewing Company 301 South Spring Street 53916 (920) 306-5100
https://oogabrewing.com/

Sun Prairie is a half-hour southwest:

Right Bauer Brewing 239 E Main Street 53590 (608) 318-5002
https://rightbauerbrewing.com/

Full Mile Beer Company and Kitchen 132 Market Street Ste 100 53590
(608) 318-2074 https://www.fullmilebeercompany.com/

Another twenty-minutes brings you to the largest city of Madison with
several options:

Ale Asylum 2002 Pankratz Street 53704 (608) 663-3926
http://www.aleasylum.com/

Union Corners Brewery 2438 Winnebago Street 53704 (608) 709-1406
https://www.unioncornersbrewery.com/

Delta Beer Lab 167 E Badger Road 53713 (608) 640-4500
https://www.delta.beer/

Lucky's 1313 Brew Pub 1313 Regent Street 53715 (608) 250-8989
https://luckys1313.com/

Dead Bird Brewing Company 4539 Helgesen Drive 53718 (608) 514-
2721 https://www.deadbirdbrewing.com/

Next Door Brewing Company 2439 Atwood Avenue 53704 (608) 729-3683 http://www.nextdoorbrewing.com/

Great Dane Pub and Brewing Company 123 E Doty Street 53703 (608) 284-0000 https://www.greatdanepub.com/

Working Draft Beer Company 1129 East Wilson Street 53703 (608) 709-5600 https://www.workingdraftbeer.com/

Karben4 Brewing 3698 Kinsman Blvd 53704 (608) 241-4811 https://www.karben4.com/

Rockhound Brewing 444 S Park Street 53715 (608) 285-9023 http://rockhoundbrewing.com/

Alt Brew 1808 Wright Street 53704 (608) 352-3373 http://www.altbrew.com/

Vintage Brewing Company 674 S Whitney Way 53719 (608) 204-2739 https://vintagebrewingcompany.com/

One Barrel Brewing Company 2001 Atwood Avenue 53704 (608) 630-9286 https://www.onebarrelbrewing.com/

Seventeen minutes away is Verona with three breweries:

Boulder Brewpub 950 Kimball Lane 53593 (608) 845-3323 https://www.boulderbrewpub.com/

Wisconsin Brewing Company 1079 American Way 53593 (608) 848-1079 https://www.wisconsinbrewingcompany.com/

Hop Haus Brewing Company 231 S Main Street 53593 (608) 497-3165 https://www.hophausbrewing.com/

About twenty-minutes further south is New Glarus:

New Glarus Brewing Company 2400 State Highway 69 53574 (608) 527-5850 https://newglarusbrewing.com/

Head back northwest about twenty-minutes to Mount Horeb:

The Grumpy Troll Restaurant and Brewery 105 South Second Street 53572 (608) 437-2739 https://thegrumpytroll.com/

Cross Plains is thirteen minutes north:

Cross Plains Beer Company 2109 Hickory Street 53528 (608) 798-3911 http://www.essersbest.com/

Eleven minutes east is a must-visit brewery at Middleton:

Capital Brewery 7734 Terrace Avenue 53562 (608) 836-7100 https://www.capitalbrewery.com/

Founded in 1984, the flagship beer here is the Capital Amber. Stop in today to try this beer, along with plenty of other options. Waunakee is fifteen minutes northeast:

The Lone Girl Brewing Company 114 E Main Street #101 53597 (608) 850-7175 https://thelonegirl.com/

Octopi Brewing 1131 Uniek Drive 53597 (608) 620-4705 https://drinkoctopi.com/

End your trip about an hour north in Wisconsin Dells with two breweries:

Port Huron Brewing Company 805 Business Park Road 53965 (608) 253-0340 http://www.porthuronbeer.com/

Wisconsin Dells Brewing Company 110 Wisconsin Dells Parkway So 53965 (608) 254-1122 https://www.dellsbrewing.com/

South East

The breweries in this area are close together, but there are many to try. So you'll want at least three to four days or more to visit them all. Start your trip in West Bend at:

Riverside Brewery and Restaurant 255 South Main Street 53095 (262) 334-2739 https://riversidebreweryandrestaurant.com/

Head north about a half-hour to Plymouth:

Plymouth Brewing Company 222 E Mill Street 53073 (920) 400-1722 https://www.plymouthbrewingcompany.com/

Nine minutes away is Elkhart Lake:

SwitchGear Brewing Company 44D Gottfried Street 53020 (920) 781-5120 https://www.switchgearbrewing.com/

Head east about twenty-minutes to Sheboygan on the waterfront with two breweries:

3 Sheeps Brewing 1837 North Avenue 53083 (920) 395-3583 https://www.3sheepsbrewing.com/

8th Street Ale Haus 1122 N 8th Street 53081 (920) 208-7540 http://sheboyganalehaus.com/

Follow the waterfront about a half-hour to Port Washington:

Inventors Brewpub 435 N Lake Street 53074 (262) 284-4690 https://www.inventorsbrewpub.com/

Eleven minutes inland is Grafton:

Sahale Ale Works 1505 Wisconsin Avenue Suite 170 53024 https://www.sahalebeer.com/

Cedarburg is just seven minutes away:

The Fermentorium 7481 WI-60 53012 (262) 421-8593 https://thefermentorium.com/

Twelve minutes south is Mequon:

Foxtown Brewing 6411 W Mequon Road 53092 (262) 292-5700
https://foxtownbrewing.com/

Another fourteen minutes is Glendale with two breweries:

Sprecher Brewing Company 701 West Glendale Avenue 53209 (414) 964-2739 https://www.sprecherbrewery.com/

Bavarian Bierhaus 700 W Lexington Blvd 53217 (414) 236-7000
https://www.thebavarianbierhaus.com/

Fourteen minutes brings you to the main city of Milwaukee with multiple options, including three must-visits:

Eagle Park Brewing 823 E Hamilton Street 53202 (414) 585-0123
https://www.eagleparkbrewing.com/

Lakefront Brewery 1872 N Commerce Street 53212 (414) 372-8800
https://lakefrontbrewery.com/

Component Brewing Company 2018 S 1st Street #207 53207 (414) 979-1088 https://componentbrewing.com/

Good City Brewing 2108 N Farwell Avenue 53202 (414) 539-4343
https://www.goodcitybrewing.com/

Urban Harvest Brewing Company 1024 S 5th Street 53204 (414) 249-4074 https://www.urbanharvestbrewing.com/

1840 Brewing Company 342 E Ward Street 53207 (414) 236-4056
https://www.1840brewing.com/

MobCraft Beer 505 S 5th Street 53204 (608) 535-4553
https://www.mobcraftbeer.com/

Milwaukee Brewing Company 613 S 2nd Street 53202 (414) 226-2336
https://mkebrewing.com/

Enlightened Brewing Company 2018 S 1st Street Suite 207 53207 (414) 704-4085 http://enlightenedbeer.com/

Gathering Place Brewing Company 811 E Vienna Avenue 53212 (414) 364-6328 https://www.gatheringplacebrewing.com/

Third Space Brewing 1505 W St. Paul Avenue 53233 (414) 909-2337 https://thirdspacebrewing.com/

You'll find quality and consistency in everything here, as is seen in the number of award-winning beers. Be sure to try these brews: Unite the Clans Scottish Ale and Unbridled Enthusiasm Juicy Double IPA.

Broken Bat Brewery 231 E Buffalo Street 53202 (414) 316-9197 https://brokenbatbrewery.com/

There is a wide range of beers to enjoy here from traditional to unique. Some that you need to try are Ugly Finger, a Hazy NE IPA, Corre Corre, a Mexican lager, and Straight Chedd, an Apricot Pale Ale.

Buffalo Water Beer Company 309 N Water Street Suite 315 55202 (414) 273-4680 http://buffalowaterhome.blogspot.com/

Try their signature Bison Blonde Lager, brewed according to the Bavarian purity law. There are no fillers and only four ingredients, making it a traditional craft beer. Head west ten minutes to West Allis.

Westallion Brewing Company 1825 S 72nd Street 53214 (414) 578-7998 https://www.westallionbrewing.com/

Just eight minutes away is Wauwatosa:

Stock House Brewing Company 7208 W North Avenue 53213 (414) 739-9876 https://stockhousebrewing.com/

Brookfield is twelve minutes west:

Biloba Brewing Company 2970 N Brookfield Road 53045 (262) 309-5820 https://www.bilobabrewing.com/

Another fifteen minutes is Waukesha and a must-visit brewery:

Raised Grain Brewing Company 1725 Dolphin Drive 53186 (262) 505-5942 https://www.raisedgrainbrewing.com/

Here you'll taste boldly brewed beers. Be sure to try their award-winning Paradocs Red Double IPA and Guitar City Gold Lager. Another fifteen minutes is Delafield with two must-visit breweries:

Delafield Brewhaus 3832 Hillside Drive 53018 (262) 646-7821 https://www.delafieldbrewhaus.com/

There are plenty of options here, including a range of seasonal and specialty beers. Be sure to try their two award-winning beers, Delafield Amber and Naga-Wicked Pale Ale.

Water Street Brewery 3191 Golf Road 53018 (262) 646-7878 https://waterstreetbrewery.com/

One of the oldest breweries in Wisconsin, offering a wide range of beers, with many of them award-winning. Be sure to try Raspberry Weiss, Oktoberfest, and Bavarian Weiss. Just ten minutes away is Hartland with another brewery:

Melms Brewing Company 418 Merton Avenue - Lower 53029 (262) 993-2566 http://www.melmsbrewing.com/

Oconomowoc is twelve minutes west with two breweries:

SteelTank Brewing Company 1225 Robruck Drive 53066 (414) 581-4406 https://steeltankbrewing.com/

Brewfinity Brewing Company N58W39800 Industrial Road Suite D 53066 (262) 456-2843 https://www.brewfinitybrewing.com/

About forty minutes south is Whitewater:

841 Brewhouse 841 East Milwaukee Street 53190 (262) 473-8000 https://www.841brewhouse.com/home

Second Salem Brewing Company 111 W Whitewater Street 53190 (262) 473-0335 http://secondsalem.com/

Continue to Elkhorn about a half-hour south:

Duesterbeck's Brewing Company N5543 County Road O 53121 (262) 729-9771 https://www.dbcbrewery.com/

Fifteen minutes north is East Troy:

East Troy Brewery 2905 Main Street 53120 (262) 642-2670 https://etbrew.com/

About a half-hour back towards the waterfront is Greendale:

The Explorium Brewpub 5300 S 76th Street Ste 1450A 53129 (414) 553-7702 https://exploriumbrew.com/

South about forty minutes is Racine on the waterfront:

Racine Brewing Company 303 Main Street 53403 (262) 631-0670 https://www.racinebrewingcompany.com/

Eighteen minutes south along the waterfront is Kenosha at the end of your trip with four breweries:

Kenosha Brewing Company 4017 80th Street 53142 (262) 694-9494 https://www.kenoshabrewingcompany.com/

R' Noggin Brewing Company 6521 120th Avenue 53142 (262) 960-1298 https://rnoggin.com/

Public Craft Brewing Company 716 58th Street 53140 (262) 818-4460 http://www.publiccraftbrewing.com/

Rustic Road Brewing Company 5706 Sixth Avenue 53140 (262) 320-7623 https://www.rusticbrewing.com/

West Central

There are a lot of breweries to see in this slightly spread out area. You'll want to spend at least four days or more to be able to sample everything in the area. Start your trip in Amherst at:

Central Waters Brewing Company 351 Allen Street 54406 (715) 824-2739 https://centralwaters.com/

West nineteen minutes is Plover:

O'so Brewing Company and Tap House 3034 Village Park Drive 54467 (715) 254-2163 https://www.osobrewing.com/

Stevens Point is eleven minutes north:

Stevens Point Brewery 2617 Water Street 54481 (800) 369-4911 https://www.pointbeer.com/

About another twenty-minutes is Mosinee:

Mosinee Brewing Company 401 4th Street 54455 (715) 693-2739 https://www.mosineebrewing.com/

Eighteen minutes north is Wausau with two breweries:

Red Eye Brewing Company 612 Washington Street 54403 (715) 843-7334 http://www.redeyebrewing.com/

Bull Falls Brewery 901 East Thomas Street 54403 (715) 842-2337 https://bullfallsbrewery.com/

When you're ready, head west about two hours to Bloomer:

Bloomer Brewing Company 1526 Martin Road 54724 (715) 271-3967 http://bloomerbrewingco.com/

New Richmond is a further hour west:

Barley John's Brewing Company 1280 Madison Avenue 54017 (715) 246-4677 https://www.barleyjohnsbrewery.com/

Ten minutes more is Somerset:

Oliphant Brewing 350 Main Street Suite 2 54025 (651) 705-6070 https://www.oliphantbrewing.com/

Eighteen minutes south is Hudson with two breweries including a must-visit:

Pitchfork Brewing 709 Rodeo Circle 54016 (715) 245-3675 https://www.pitchforkbrewing.com/

Hop and Barrel Brewing Company 310 2nd Street 54016 (715) 808-8390 https://hopandbarrelbrewing.com/

A modern approach to classic beer styles. Try all four flagship beers: Crooked Grin IPA, Minnesconsin Helles Lager, Space Force Double IPA, and Hudson Haze. River Falls is fifteen minutes away with two more breweries:

Rush River Brewing Company 990 Antler Court 54022 (715) 426-2054 http://rushriverbeer.com/

Swinging Bridge Brewing Company 122 S Main Street 54022 (715) 629-1464 https://swingingbridgebrewing.com/

Head back east about fifty minutes to Menomonie with four breweries:

Zymurgy Brewing Company 624 Main Street East 54751 (715) 578-9026 https://www.zymurgybrew.com/

Brewery Nonic 621 4th Street 54751 (715) 578-9078 https://www.brewerynonic.com/

The Raw Deal/Real Deal Brewing 603 S Broadway 54751 (715) 231-3255 http://www.rawdeal-wi.com/

Lucette Brewing Company 910 Hudson Road 54751 (715) 233-2055
https://www.lucettebrewing.com/

Curve slightly south a half-hour to Eau Claire with two breweries including a must-visit:

The Brewing Projekt 2000 N Oxford Avenue Building 3 54703 (715) 214-3728 https://www.thebrewingprojekt.com/

Lazy Monk Brewing 320 Putnam Street 54703 (715) 271-5887
https://www.lazymonkbrewing.com/

There are 12 rotating seasonal beers to sample, but you can always try their two flagship beers, a Pilsner and Dark Lager from the finest imported ingredients. Just nine minutes away is Altoona:

Modicum Brewing Company 3732 Spooner Avenue 54720 (715) 895-8585 https://www.modicumbrewing.com/

Osseo is about twenty-minutes south:

Northwoods Brewpub and Grill 50819 West Street 54758 (715) 597-1828 https://northwoodsbrewpub.com/

Another half-hour is Black River Falls with a must-visit brewery:

Sand Creek Brewing Company 320 Pierce Street 54615 (715) 284-7553
http://www.sandcreekbrewing.com/

One of the largest microbreweries in Wisconsin. Offering both beers and hard lemonades. Be sure to try the Badger Porter, Bugler Brown Ale, and Oscar's Chocolate Oatmeal Stout. Take a drive an hour and a half south to Soldiers Grove:

Driftless Brewing Company 102 W Sunbeam Blvd 54655 (608) 624-5577 https://www.driftlessbrewing.com/

Head back north an hour to La Crosse and three breweries:

Turtle Stack Brewery 125 2nd Street South 54601 (608) 519-2284
https://turtlestackbrewery.com/

Pearl Street Brewery 1401 Saint Andrew Street 54603 (608) 784-4832
https://pearlstreetbrewery.com/

608 Brewing Company 83 Copeland Avenue 54603 (608) 519-9686
https://www.608brewingcompany.com/

Just eleven minutes away is Onalaska:

Skeleton Crew Brew 570 Theater Road Suite 100 54650 (715) 570-9463
https://www.skeletoncrewbrew.com/

Follow the border forty minutes northwest to Fountain City:

Fountain City Brewing Company 19 North Main Street 54629 (608) 687-
4231 https://www.monarchtavern.com/

End your trip about forty minutes northeast in Whitehall at:

FFats Brewing 18517 Blair Street 54773 (715) 538-3162
https://www.ffatsbrewingco.com/

Wyoming

You can take a four to five day trip around the state of Wyoming to visit all
of the great breweries they have to offer. Start your trip in Gillette at:

Gillette Brewing Company 301 S Gillette Avenue 82716 (307) 670-8948
http://gillettebrewing.com/

Head northeast an hour a half to Sheridan with two breweries including a
must-visit:

Luminous Brewhouse 504 Broadway Street 82801 (307) 655-5658
https://luminousbrewhouse.com/

Black Tooth Brewing Company 312 Broadway Street 82801 (307) 675-2337 https://www.blacktoothbrewingcompany.com/

One of the leading craft breweries in the Rocky Mountains. In addition to seasonal offerings, you can try their flagship beers: Saddle Bronc Brown Ale, Bomber Mountain Amber Ale, and Hot Streak IPA. Ten Sleep is another hour and a half southwest:

Ten Sleep Brewing Company 2549 E US Highway 16 82442 (307) 366-2074 http://tensleepbrewingco.com/

Continue west about two hours to Powell:

WYOld West Brewing Company 221 North Bent Street 82435 (307) 764-6200 http://wyoldwest.com/

About twenty-minutes further is Cody:

Millstone Pizza Company and Brewery 1057 Sheridan Avenue 82414 (307) 586-4131 http://www.millstonepizzacompany.com/

Take a long four and a half-hour drive circling west and then south to Jackson with three breweries:

Roadhouse Brewing Company 1225 Gregory Lane 83001 (307) 264-1900 https://roadhousebrewery.com/

StillWest Brewery and Grill 45 East Snow King Avenue 83001 (307) 201-5955 https://www.stillwestbreweryandgrill.com/

Snake River Brewing Company and Brewpub 265 S Millward 83001 (307) 739-2337 https://snakeriverbrewing.com/

Alpine is about fifty minutes further south:

Melvin Brewing 624 County Road 101 83128 (307) 733-0005 https://melvinbrewing.com/

An hour and a half southeast is Pinedale:

Wind River Brewing Company 402 W Pine Street 82941 (307) 367-2337 https://windriverbrewingco.com/

Another long drive takes you to Evanston, two and a half hours south:

Suds Brothers Brewery 1012 Main Street 82930 (307) 444-6274 https://www.sudsbrothersbrewery.com/

Rock Springs is about an hour and a half east:

Bitter Creek Brewing Company 604 Broadway Street 82901 (307) 362-4782 http://www.bittercreekbrewing.com/

About two hours north is Lander with a must-visit brewery:

Lander Brewing Company 148 West Main Street 82520 (307) 699-1369 https://www.landerbrewing.com/

Brewing fresh, high-quality, to-style beers. Be sure to sample the Atlantic City Gold, Jack Mormon Pale Ale, Rockchuck Rye, and On Belay IPA. A little over two hours east is Casper with two breweries:

Frontier Brewing Company and Taproom 117 E 2nd Street 82601 (307) 337-1000 https://frontier-brewing.square.site/

Gruner Brothers Brewing 1301 Wilkins Circle 82601 (307) 439-2222 https://grunerbrewing.com/

Continue another two hours to the border town of Torrington:

The Open Barrel Brewing Company 1930 Main Street 82240 (307) 401-0107 https://openbarrelbrewing.com/

A little over an hour south brings you to the southern border town of Cheyenne and three breweries:

Danielmark's Brewing Company 209 E 18th Street 82001 (307) 514-0411 https://www.danielmarksbrewing.com/

Accomplice Beer Company 115 W 15th Street 82001 (307) 632-2337
https://accomplicebeer.com/

Freedom's Edge Brewing Company 301 West 16th Street 82001 (307) 514-2623 https://www.freedomsedgebrewing.com/

Head west about fifty minutes to Laramie with two breweries including a must-visit:

Coal Creek TAP 108 E Grand Avenue 82070 (307) 460-9555
https://www.coalcreektap.com/

Bond's Brewing Company 411 S 2nd Street 82070 (307) 460-3385
http://bondsbrewing.com/

Using fresh, natural ingredients, they make beers that overflow with flavor. Depending on when you come, try the seasonal Hatch Chili Ale or Pumpkin Ale. If not, you can also try the American style stout and Citra-Hop-A-Dopolis. End your trip about an hour and a half west in Saratoga with two breweries:

Brush Creek Brewery 66 Bruch Creek Ranch Road 83331 (307) 327-5284 https://www.brushcreekranch.com/thefarm/brush-creek-brewery

Snowy Mountain Brewery 601 East Pic Pike Road 82331 (307) 326-5153 http://snowymountainbrewery.com/

Conclusion

Now we've given you everything you need to tour breweries wherever you go. You'll be a beer expert in no time. So plan your next brewery tour and get to sampling your favorite beers or experiment with something new.

If this book has helped you In any way, would you kindly consider leaving a review online where you purchased this book? Reviews really help me reach a wider audience. Thanks in advance!

Glossary

AHA - The American Homebrewers Association, founded in 1978, is an advocate for homebrewers' rights.

Acetaldehyde - A bi-product and chemical from fermentation that has the aroma and flavor of green apples.

Acid Rest - A step early in the mash about 95 degrees Fahrenheit that helps to lower the pH of the mash.

Acrospire - The shoot that grows when a barley grain is germinated.

Adjunct - Any unmalted grain or fermentable ingredient in the brewing process. Commonly found in mass-produced light American lager-style beers.

Aeration - The action of introducing oxygen or air to the wort at various stages during brewing. Proper aeration before the primary fermentation helps with the health and vigorous fermentation of yeast. After fermentation, aeration can lead to off-flavors such as cardboard or paper aromas as a result of oxidation.

Alcohol - Can either be ethyl alcohol or ethanol. For beer, the alcohol content can range from less than 3.2% to greater than 14%. Most craft beers range around 5.9%.

Alcohol By Volume (ABV) - This is the measurement of alcohol content. This is higher than Alcohol by Weight.

Alcohol By Weight (ABW) - A measurement of the alcohol content in terms of the percentage weight of alcohol per volume of beer.

Ale Yeast - The scientific name is Saccharomyces Cerevisiae. It is a top-fermenting yeast that ferments at temperatures of 60 to 70 degrees Fahrenheit and often produces more flavor compounds.

All Extract Beer - Beers made with malt extract instead of those made from barley malt or a combination of malt extract and barley malt.

All Malt Beer - Beer made entirely from mashed barley malt without any adjuncts like sugars or additional fermentable ingredients.

Alpha Acid - One of two mostly naturally occurring soft resins found in hops. During wort boiling, they are converted to iso-alpha acids that cause the majority of bitterness in beer. Alpha acids can oxidize as they age and lessen the bitterness of beer.

Alpha and Beta Amylase - These enzymes come from sugars derived from starch. The activity of these enzymes is optimized at different temperatures to result in different mixtures of fermentable and unfermentable sugars.

Apparent Attenuation - A simple measure for the extent of fermentation that wort has undergone as it becomes beer.

Aromatic Hops - Hop additions later in the boiling process. Shorter boil times will provide more aromatic characteristics over bittering characteristics.

Astringency - A beer taste characteristic that is caused by tannins, oxidization, and various aldehydes. It causes the mouth to pucker and is often described as dryness.

Attenuation - The reduction in wort specific gravity that results when yeast consumes wort sugars and converts them to alcohol and carbon dioxide gas in the fermentation process.

Autolysis - The process of excess yeast cells feeding on each other. Resulting in a rubbery or vegetable aroma.

Barley - A cereal grain used as a base malt in the production of beer.

Barrel - Both a wooden vessel used to age/condition/ferment beer and a standard measure in the US that equals 31 gallons.

Beta Acids - One of two primary naturally occurring soft resins found in hops. Contributes little to the bitterness of beer and some of the preservative quality.

Bitterness - This is caused by tannins and iso-humulones of hops. It is perceived in the taste of beer and is one of the defining characteristics of a beer style.

Bittering Hops - Refers to hop additions early in the boiling stage of the brewing process. The longer hops are boiled, the more bittering characteristics will come.

Blending - Mixing different batches of beer to create a final brew.

Body - The consistency, thickness, and mouth-filling property of beer. Can range from thin- to full-bodied.

Boiling - A critical part of the brewing process when the wort is boiled inside the brew kettle. During boiling, one or more additions can occur to achieve bittering, hop flavor and hop aroma in a final product. Boiling also removes volatile compounds and sterilizes a beer.

Bomber - A 22-ounce beer bottle.

Bottle Conditioning - A process of naturally carbonating beer in the bottle through the fermentation of additional wort or sugar that is added during packaging.

Bottle Fermentation - One of two fermentation methods. Characterized by yeast cells that tend to sink to the bottom of the fermentation vessel. Beers brewed in this way are commonly called lagers or bottom-fermented beers.

Brettanomyces - A type of yeast that can cause acidity and other sensory notes of leather or barnyard, which can be desirable or undesirable. Typically it is found in styles like Lambic, Oud Bruin, and other acidic American-derived styles or barrel-aged styles.

Brewpub - A restaurant-brewery that sells 25 percent or more of their beer on-site. The beer is often dispensed directly from storage tanks. If allowed by law, they will often sell beer "to-go" and/or distribute to other accounts off-site.

Brew Kettle - A vessel used in the brewing process to boil the wort.

Bung - A sealing stopper made of wood or plastic that is fitted into the mouth of a cask or older style kegs.

Bung Hole - The round hole in the side of a cask or older style keg used to fill beer.

Burton Snatch - The aroma of Sulphur that indicates the presence of sulfate ions.

Byproducts - Both desirable and undesirable compounds that result from fermentation, mashing, or boiling.

Calcium Carbonate (CaCO3) - A mineral found in water from different origins. Also known as chalk. Can be added to the brewing process to increase calcium and carbonate content.

Calcium Sulfate (CaSO4) - A mineral found in water from different origins. Also known as gypsum. Can be added to the brewing process to increase calcium and sulfate content.

Carbohydrates - Organic compounds such as sugars and starches that serve as food for yeast and bacteria.

Carbon Dioxide (CO2) - A gaseous byproduct of yeast that provides the carbonation or bubbles in beer.

Carbonation - The introduction of carbon dioxide into a liquid through one of four methods:

1. Pressurizing a fermentation vessel in order to capture carbon dioxide that is naturally produced.

2. Injecting carbon dioxide into the finished beer.

3. Adding young fermenting beer into a finished beer to provide renewed fermentation.

4. Priming fermented wort by adding sugar prior to packaging, creating a secondary fermentation in the bottle.

Cask - A barrel-shaped container that holds beer. Originally iron-hooped wooden staves, but now mostly stainless steel and aluminum.

Cask Conditioning - The process of storing unpasteurized, unfiltered beer in cool cellars for several days to complete conditioning and allow carbonation to build.

Cellaring - The storing or aging of beer at a controlled temperature to allow it to mature.

Chill Haze - A hazy or cloudy appearance that results when proteins and tannins naturally found in finished beer combine upon chilling, forming particles large enough to reflect light or become visible.

Closed Fermentation - Fermentation that occurs under closed, anaerobic conditions in order to reduce oxidation and contamination.

Cold Break - The flocculation of tannins and proteins when wort cools.

Color - The hue or shade of a beer that often comes from grains; but can also come from fruit or other ingredients.

Conditioning - A part of the brewing process during which beer is matured or aged after the initial fermentation to prevent unwanted compounds and flavors.

Contract Brewing Company - A business that hires another brewery to produce some or all of its beer.

Craft Brewery - A small (annual production of 6 million barrels or less) and independent (less than 25 percent is owned or controlled by a beverage alcohol industry member) brewer.

Decoction Mash - A method of mashing that increases the mash temperature by removing a portion, boiling it, and returning it to the mash tun. Can be done several times in some mash programs.

Degrees Plato - An empirical hydrometer scale used to measure the density of beer wort in terms of percentage of extract by weight.

Dextrin - A group of carbohydrates that are complex, tasteless, and unfermentable. They are produced by the partial hydrolysis of starch and contribute to the gravity and body of the beer. They are responsible for a malty sweetness if undissolved in the finished beer.

Diacetyl - This volatile compound is produced by some yeasts and adds a caramel, nutty, or butterscotch flavor. It is acceptable at low levels in some traditional beers such as English and Scottish Ales, Czech Pilsners, and German Oktoberfest. Otherwise, it is often an unwanted or accidental flavor.

Diastatic - The enzymes that are created when a grain sprouts. They convert starch to sugars, which are eaten by the yeast.

Dimethyl Sulfide (DMS) - In low levels, it adds a favorable sweet aroma to beer. At high levels, it can have the aroma and taste of cooked vegetables. Low levels are acceptable and found in some lager beer styles.

Draught Beer - Beer that comes directly from kegs, casks, or serving tanks rather than cans, bottles, or other packages.

Dry Hopping - Adding hops late in the brewing process in order to increase the hop aroma without affecting the bitterness.

Dual Purpose Hops - Hops added to provide both bittering and aromatic properties.

Endosperm - The starch-containing sac of a barley grain.

Essential Hop Oils - They are isomerized in wort and provide the aromatic and flavor compounds from hop additions.

Esters - Volatile flavor compounds formed through the interaction of organic acids with alcohols during fermentation and lead to a fruity aroma and flavor. Commonly found in ales.

Ethanol - Also known as ethyl alcohol. The primarily colorless alcohol found in beer.

Fermentable Sugars - Sugars consumed by yeast cells that result in the production of ethanol alcohol and CO_2.

Fermentation - The chemical conversion of fermentable sugars into equal parts ethyl alcohol and carbon dioxide gas through the action of yeast. Beer brewing relies on two basic forms of fermentation: top fermentation for ales and bottom fermentation for lagers.

Fermentation Lock - A one-way valve made from plastic or glass and placed in a fermenter to allow carbon dioxide gas to escape while excluding ambient wild yeasts, bacteria, and contaminants.

Filtration - Passing liquid through a permeable or porous substance in order to remove solid matter, often yeast.

Final Gravity - The specific gravity of beer that is measured after fermentation.

Fining - The addition of clarifying agents like isinglass, gelatin, or silica gel to beer during a secondary fermentation in order to speed up the precipitation of suspended matter like proteins, tannins, or yeast.

Flocculation - Suspended particles in wort or beer that clump together in a large mass and settle out. When brewing, protein, and tannin particles will flocculate out of the kettle, coolship, or fermenter during a hot or cold break. At the end of fermentation, yeast cells flocculate depending on their strain.

Forced Carbonation - Beer that is placed in a sealed container with rapidly added carbonation. Under this high pressure, the CO_2 is absorbed into the beer.

Fresh Hopping - Adding freshly harvested hops that haven't been dried to different stages of the brewing process. This will add unique flavors and aromas to beer that aren't typically found.

Fusel Alcohol - High molecular weight alcohols that come from excessively high fermentation temperatures. They impart a harsh or solvent-like characteristic similar to lacquer or paint thinner and are responsible for hangovers.

Germination - The growth phase of a barley grain when it produces a rootlet and acrospire.

Grainy - The taste or smell of cereal or raw grains.

Grist - Ground malt and grains that are ready for mashing.

Growler - A jug- or pail- like container used to carry draught beer. Often ½ gallon or 2 liters in volume and typically made of glass. To-go growlers aren't legal in all US states.

Gruit - An old-fashioned herb mixture that was used to bitter and flavor beer before the use of hops. Beverages made with this are referred to as gruit or grut ale.

Head Retention - The foam stability of a bear. Measured in seconds it takes for a 1-inch foam collar to collapse.

Heat Exchangers - Used to cool the wort before fermentation.

Hops - A perennial climbing vine. The female plant yields flowers, and once ripe, they are used to flavor beer.

Hopping - The process of adding hops to unfermented wort or fermented beer.

Hot Break - The flocculation of tannins and proteins during wort boiling.

Husk - The dry outer layer of some cereal seeds.

Hydrometer - A glass instrument that is used to measure the specific gravity of liquids compared to water.

Immersion Chiller - Often, a copper wort chiller used to submerge hot wort before fermentation as a cooling method.

Infusion Mash - A method of mashing that uses the addition of heated water at specific temperatures to achieve target mashing temperatures.

Inoculate - Introduce a microbe such as yeast into surroundings capable of supporting its growth.

International Bitterness Units (IBU) - The measurement of the bittering substances in beer. Often depends on the style of beer. Light lagers typically have a rating between 5-10, while bitter IPAs can have a rating between 50-70.

Isinglass - A gelatinous substance that is made from the swim bladder of fish that can be added to beer in order to clarify and stabilize the final product.

Keg - Usually, steel and sometimes aluminum container used to store, transport, and serve beer under pressure.

Kilning - The process of heat-drying malted barley in a kiln. This stops germination and produces a dry, easily milled malt. It also removes the raw flavor so new aromas, flavors, and colors can develop based on the intensity and duration of the kilning process.

Kraeusen - During fermentation, this is the rocky head of foam that appears on the surface of the wort. It can also refer to the method of conditioning where a small amount of unfermented wort is added to fully fermented beer in order to start a secondary fermentation and natural carbonation.

Lace - The foam that forms a lacelike pattern on the sides of the glass after it is partially or totally emptied.

Lager Yeast - The scientific name is Saccharomyces pastorianus. It is a bottom-fermenting yeast that often lends to sulfuric compounds and ferments in cooler temperatures.

Lagering - The action of storing bottom-fermented beers in cold cellars at near-freezing temperatures for a few weeks to years so that the yeast and proteins can settle out and improve the taste of the beer.

Lauter Tun - A large vessel with a false slotted bottom and a drain spigot. This allows the mash to settle so the sweet wort can be removed through a straining process. The mash tun can be used for both mashing and lautering.

Lautering - The process of separating the sweet wort from the spent grains either in a straining apparatus or a lauter tun.

Lightstruck - Also referred to as Skunked. This is a flavor and aroma in beer that is caused by exposure in light-colored bottles or ultra-violet or fluorescent light.

Liquor - The name for water that is used in mashing and brewing. Often this is natural or treated water that has high levels of calcium and magnesium salts.

Lovibond - This is a scale that measures color in grains and sometimes beer.

Malt - Processed barley that has been steeped in water, germinated, and later dried in kilns. This is done to stop the germination and convert the insoluble starch to soluble substances and sugars.

Malt Extract - A thick syrup or dry powder that comes from malt and is sometimes used in the brewing process.

Maltose - The most common fermentable sugar found in beer.

Mash - A mixture of ground malt and hot water to form sweet wort after straining.

Mash Tun - The vessel used to soak the grist in water and heat it to convert the starch to sugar and to remove the sugars, colors, flavors, and other solubles from the grist.

Mashing - The process of mixing crushed malt with hot water to convert grain starches to fermentable sugars and non-fermentable carbohydrates that add body, head retention, and other characteristics to the final beer. Mashing also extracts flavors and colors that carry through to the final product and provide a way to degrade the haze-forming proteins. The process takes several hours and produces the sugar-rich liquid known as wort.

Mashing Out - The process of raising the mash temperature to 170 degrees Fahrenheit. This will stop the enzymatic activity and prevent the starches from convert to sugars.

Milling - The grinding of malt into grist to extract sugars and other soluble substances. The endosperm needs to be crushed to medium-sized grits rather than flour consistency. The husks must remain intact to help act as a filter later during lautering.

Modification - The physical and chemical changes in barley as a result of malting. Also refers to the degrees to which these changes occur based on the growth of the acrospire.

Modified Malts - Refers to the length of the germination process and how much the internal malt structures and compounds have been broken down.

Mouthfeel - The textures you feel in a beer. This can include carbonation, fullness, and aftertaste.

Musty - A moldy, mildewy character that often results from cork or bacterial infection in a beer. It can be in the form of both taste and aroma.

Natural Carbonation - When sugar is added to beer in its container and then sealed. The fermentation process starts again, releasing CO_2 that is absorbed into the liquid.

Nitrogen - When used to carbonize beer, it contributes a thick creamy mouthfeel that is different from CO_2.

Noble Hops - Traditional European hop varieties known for their flavor and aroma. Only found in four small areas of Europe.

Oasthouse - A farm-based facility where hops are dried and baled.

Original Gravity (OG) - The specific gravity of wort before fermentation.

Oxidation - A chemical reaction in which beer undergoes the addition of or reaction with oxygen or another oxidizing agent.

Oxidized - A stale, winy aroma or flavor, often similar to wet cardboard or paper.

pH - The abbreviation for potential Hydrogen. It expresses the degree of acidity and alkalinity in an aqueous solution, usually ranging from 1-14. 7 is neutral, 1 is the most acidic and 14 is the most alkaline.

Phenols - A class of chemical compounds that impact taste and aroma.

Pitching - The addition of yeast to the wort after it has cooled down to the desired temperature.

Primary Fermentation - This is the first stage of fermentation that is often done in open or closed containers and lasts from two to twenty days. During this time, the majority of fermentable sugars are converted to ethyl alcohol and CO_2.

Priming - Adding small amounts of fermentable sugars to fermented beer before bottling to renew fermentation to carbonate the beer.

Punt - The hollow found at the bottom of some bottles.

Quaff - Drink deeply.

Racking - The process of transferring beer between vessels, especially into the final package.

Reinheitsgebot - A German purity law passed in 1516 that states beer can only contain water, barley, and hops. Yeast was added later once its role in fermentation was discovered.

Residual Alkalinity - The measurement of a mashs' ability to buffer or resist attempts to lower the pH.

Residual Sugar - Any sugar leftover that the yeast doesn't consume during the fermentation process.

Resin - An organic gummy substance that is produced by some trees and plants. Humulone and lupulone are bitter resins found in the hop flower.

Saccharification - The conversation of malt starch into fermentable sugars, mostly maltose.

Secondary Fermentation - This is the second, slower stage of fermentation when it comes to top-fermenting beers. It can take from a few weeks to many months, depending on the type of beer being made. It can also refer to a renewed fermentation in a bottle or cask through the priming or addition of fresh yeast.

Sediment - The refuse of solid matter that will settle to the bottom of fermenters, conditioning vessels, and bottles of conditioned beer.

Solvent-like - An aromatic character or flavor similar to acetone or lacquer thinner. It is often the result of high fermentation temperatures.

Sorghum - A cereal grain that comes from grasses. It is also an option for those who are gluten intolerant.

Sour - A taste that is acidic and tart. Sometimes can be an intended bacterial influence.

Sparging - In lautering, it is the operation of spraying spent mash grains with hot water to get the liquid malt sugar and extract that remains in the grain husks.

Specific Gravity - The ratio of the density of a substance to the density of water. It is used to determine how much dissolved sugars exist in wort or beer.

Standard Reference Method (SRM) - An analytical method and scale used to quantify and measure the color of a beer. The higher the SRM, the darker the beer.

Steeping - Soaking a solid in a liquid in order to extract flavors.

Step Infusion - A mashing method where the temperature of the mash is increased by adding very hot water and then stabilizing and stirring the mash at the target step temperature.

Sulfur - An aroma of rotten eggs or burnt matches. It is the by-product of some yeasts or when a beer is light struck.

Tannins - Organic compounds found in some cereal grains and other plants. They are found in the hop cone and also referred to as "hop tannin."

Temperature Rests - During the brewing process, these allow the brewer to adjust fermentable sugar profiles to determine the characteristics of the final beer.

Top Fermentation - One of two main fermentation methods. Ale yeast is top-fermenting and tends to rise to the surface of the fermentation vessel.

Trub - Wort particles that come from the precipitation of proteins, hop oils, and tannins through the boiling and cooling stages of the brewing process.

Turbidity - Suspension of sediment such as hazy or murky.

Volatile Compounds - Chemicals at a high vapor pressure in ordinary room temperature will evaporate large numbers of molecules. These enter the surrounding air.

Volumes of CO2 - The measurement of CO_2 in a beer and indicates the carbonation level.

Vorlauf - At the start of lautering and right before collecting wort in the brew kettle, it is the process of recirculating the wort from the lauter tun outlet back onto the top of the grain bed in order to help clarify the wort.

Wet Hopping - Adding freshly harvested hops that haven't dried during different stages of the brewing process. This adds unique flavors and aromas that aren't typically found when using hops dried and processed as normal.

Whirlpool - The method of collecting hot break material from the center of the kettle by stirring until a vortex is formed. It can also refer to a specific brewhouse vessel that separates the hot break trub particles from boiled wort.

Wort - This is the bittersweet sugar solution that results from mashing the malt and boiling in the hops, which later becomes beer through fermentation.

Yeast - Yeast converts natural malt sugars into alcohol and CO_2 during the fermentation process.

Yeast Cake - Living yeast cells that are compressed with starch into a cake for use in the brewing process.

Yeast Pitching - The period in the brewing process when yeast is added to cool wort before fermentation.

Zymurgy - The branch of chemistry that focuses on fermentation processes such as brewing.

Made in the USA
Las Vegas, NV
10 December 2023

82518626R10372